CORNERSTONE
BIBLICAL
COMMENTARY

CORNERSTONE
BIBLICAL
COMMENTARY

Ephesians
Harold W. Hoehner

Philippians, 1 & 2 Thessalonians
Philip W. Comfort

Colossians, Philemon
Peter H. Davids

GENERAL EDITOR
Philip W. Comfort

featuring the text of the
NEW LIVING TRANSLATION

TYNDALE HOUSE PUBLISHERS, INC. CAROL STREAM, ILLINOIS

Cornerstone Biblical Commentary, Volume 16

Visit Tyndale's exciting Web site at www.tyndale.com

Ephesians copyright © 2008 by Harold W. Hoehner. All rights reserved.

Philippians and *1 & 2 Thessalonians* copyright © 2008 by Philip W. Comfort. All rights reserved.

Colossians and *Philemon* copyright © 2008 by Peter H. Davids. All rights reserved.

Designed by Luke Daab and Timothy R. Botts.

Library of Congress Cataloging-in-Publication Data

Cornerstone biblical commentary.
    p. cm.
    Includes bibliographical references and index.
    ISBN-13: 978-0-8423-8344-8 (hc : alk. paper)
    ISBN-10: 0-8423-8344-1 (hc : alk. paper)
    1. Bible—Commentaries. I. Comfort, Philip W. II. Davids, Peter.
III. Hoehner, Harold W.
BS491.3.C67 2006
220.7'7—dc22   2005026928

Printed in the United States of America

14   13   12   11   10   09   08
7   6   5   4   3   2   1

CONTENTS

CONTRIBUTORS TO VOLUME 16

Ephesians: Harold W. Hoehner
BA, Barrington College;
ThM, Dallas Theological Seminary;
ThD, Dallas Theological Seminary;
PhD, Cambridge University;
Postdoctoral study at Tubingen University and Cambridge University;
Distinguished Professor of New Testament Studies at Dallas Theological Seminary.

Philippians, 1 & 2 Thessalonians: Philip W. Comfort
BA, Cleveland State University;
MA, The Ohio State University;
D. Litt. et Phil., University of South Africa;
Tyndale House Publishers;
Coastal Carolina University

Colossians, Philemon: Peter H. Davids
BA, Wheaton College;
MDiv, Trinity Evangelical Divinity School;
PhD, Manchester University;
Professor of Biblical Theology, St. Stephen's University

GENERAL EDITOR'S PREFACE

The *Cornerstone Biblical Commentary* is based on the second edition of the New Living Translation (2004). Nearly 100 scholars from various church backgrounds and from several countries (United States, Canada, England, and Australia) participated in the creation of the NLT. Many of these same scholars are contributors to this commentary series. All the commentators, whether participants in the NLT or not, believe that the Bible is God's inspired word and have a desire to make God's word clear and accessible to his people.

This Bible commentary is the natural extension of our vision for the New Living Translation, which we believe is both exegetically accurate and idiomatically powerful. The NLT attempts to communicate God's inspired word in a lucid English translation of the original languages so that English readers can understand and appreciate the thought of the original writers. In the same way, the *Cornerstone Biblical Commentary* aims at helping teachers, pastors, students, and laypeople understand every thought contained in the Bible. As such, the commentary focuses first on the words of Scripture, then on the theological truths of Scripture—inasmuch as the words express the truths.

The commentary itself has been structured in such a way as to help readers get at the meaning of Scripture, passage by passage, through the entire Bible. Each Bible book is prefaced by a substantial book introduction that gives general historical background important for understanding. Then the reader is taken through the Bible text, passage by passage, starting with the New Living Translation text printed in full. This is followed by a section called "Notes," wherein the commentator helps the reader understand the Hebrew or Greek behind the English of the NLT, interacts with other scholars on important interpretive issues, and points the reader to significant textual and contextual matters. The "Notes" are followed by the "Commentary," wherein each scholar presents a lucid interpretation of the passage, giving special attention to context and major theological themes.

The commentators represent a wide spectrum of theological positions within the evangelical community. We believe this is good because it reflects the rich variety in Christ's church. All the commentators uphold the authority of God's word and believe it is essential to heed the old adage: "Wholly apply yourself to the Scriptures and apply them wholly to you." May this commentary help you know the truths of Scripture, and may this knowledge help you "grow in your knowledge of God and Jesus our Lord" (2 Pet 1:2, NLT).

PHILIP W. COMFORT
GENERAL EDITOR

ABBREVIATIONS

GENERAL ABBREVIATIONS

b.	Babylonian Gemara	Heb.	Hebrew	NT	New Testament
		ibid.	*ibidem,* in the same place	OL	Old Latin
bar.	baraita			OS	Old Syriac
c.	*circa,* around, approximately	i.e.	*id est,* the same	OT	Old Testament
		in loc.	*in loco,* in the place cited	p., pp.	page, pages
cf.	*confer,* compare			pl.	plural
ch, chs	chapter, chapters	lit.	literally	Q	Quelle ("Sayings" as Gospel source)
contra	in contrast to	LXX	Septuagint		
DSS	Dead Sea Scrolls	𝔐	Majority Text	rev.	revision
ed.	edition, editor	*m.*	Mishnah	sg.	singular
e.g.	*exempli gratia,* for example	masc.	masculine	*t.*	Tosefta
		mg	margin	TR	Textus Receptus
et al.	*et alli,* and others	ms	manuscript	v., vv.	verse, verses
fem.	feminine	mss	manuscripts	vid.	*videur,* it seems
ff	following (verses, pages)	MT	Masoretic Text	viz.	*videlicet,* namely
		n.d.	no date	vol.	volume
fl.	flourished	neut.	neuter	*y.*	Jerusalem Gemara
Gr.	Greek	no.	number		

ABBREVIATIONS FOR BIBLE TRANSLATIONS

ASV	American Standard Version	NCV	New Century Version	NKJV	New King James Version
CEV	Contemporary English Version	NEB	New English Bible	NRSV	New Revised Standard Version
		NET	The NET Bible		
ESV	English Standard Version	NIV	New International Version	NLT	New Living Translation
GW	God's Word	NIrV	New International Reader's Version	REB	Revised English Bible
HCSB	Holman Christian Standard Bible				
		NJB	New Jerusalem Bible	RSV	Revised Standard Version
JB	Jerusalem Bible				
KJV	King James Version	NJPS	The New Jewish Publication Society Translation (*Tanakh*)	TEV	Today's English Version
NAB	New American Bible				
NASB	New American Standard Bible			TLB	The Living Bible

ABBREVIATIONS FOR DICTIONARIES, LEXICONS, COLLECTIONS OF TEXTS, ORIGINAL LANGUAGE EDITIONS

ABD *Anchor Bible Dictionary* (6 vols., Freedman) [1992]

ANEP *The Ancient Near East in Pictures* (Pritchard) [1965]

ANET *Ancient Near Eastern Texts Relating to the Old Testament* (Pritchard) [1969]

BAGD *Greek-English Lexicon of the New Testament and Other Early Christian Literature,* 2nd ed. (Bauer, Arndt, Gingrich, Danker) [1979]

BDAG *Greek-English Lexicon of the New Testament and Other Early Christian Literature,* 3rd ed. (Bauer, Danker, Arndt, Gingrich) [2000]

BDB *A Hebrew and English Lexicon of the Old Testament* (Brown, Driver, Briggs) [1907]

BDF *A Greek Grammar of the New Testament and Other Early Christian Literature* (Blass, Debrunner, Funk) [1961]

BHS *Biblia Hebraica Stuttgartensia* (Elliger and Rudolph) [1983]

CAD *Assyrian Dictionary of the Oriental Institute of the University of Chicago* [1956]

COS *The Context of Scripture* (3 vols., Hallo and Younger) [1997–2002]

DBI *Dictionary of Biblical Imagery* (Ryken, Wilhoit, Longman) [1998]

DBT *Dictionary of Biblical Theology* (2nd ed., Leon-Dufour) [1972]

DCH *Dictionary of Classical Hebrew* (5 vols., D. Clines) [2000]

DJD *Discoveries in the Judean Desert* [1955–]

DJG *Dictionary of Jesus and the Gospels* (Green, McKnight, Marshall) [1992]

DOTP *Dictionary of the Old Testament: Pentateuch* (T. Alexander, D.W. Baker) [2003]

DPL *Dictionary of Paul and His Letters* (Hawthorne, Martin, Reid) [1993]

EDNT *Exegetical Dictionary of the New Testament* (3 vols., H. Balz, G. Schneider. ET) [1990–1993]

HALOT *The Hebrew and Aramaic Lexicon of the Old Testament* (L. Koehler, W. Baumgartner, J. Stamm; trans. M. Richardson) [1994–1999]

IBD *Illustrated Bible Dictionary* (3 vols., Douglas, Wiseman) [1980]

IDB *The Interpreter's Dictionary of the Bible* (4 vols., Buttrick) [1962]

ISBE *International Standard Bible Encyclopedia* (4 vols., Bromiley) [1979–1988]

KBL *Lexicon in Veteris Testamenti libros* (Koehler, Baumgartner) [1958]

LCL Loeb Classical Library

L&N *Greek-English Lexicon of the New Testament: Based on Semantic Domains* (Louw and Nida) [1989]

LSJ *A Greek-English Lexicon* (9th ed., Liddell, Scott, Jones) [1996]

MM *The Vocabulary of the Greek New Testament* (Moulton and Milligan) [1930; 1997]

NA^{26} *Novum Testamentum Graece* (26th ed., Nestle-Aland) [1979]

NA^{27} *Novum Testamentum Graece* (27th ed., Nestle-Aland) [1993]

NBD *New Bible Dictionary* (2nd ed., Douglas, Hillyer) [1982]

NIDB *New International Dictionary of the Bible* (Douglas, Tenney) [1987]

NIDBA *New International Dictionary of Biblical Archaeology* (Blaiklock and Harrison) [1983]

NIDNTT *New International Dictionary of New Testament Theology* (4 vols., C. Brown) [1975–1985]

NIDOTTE *New International Dictionary of Old Testament Theology and Exegesis* (5 vols., W. A. VanGemeren) [1997]

PGM *Papyri graecae magicae: Die griechischen Zauberpapyri.* (Preisendanz) [1928]

PG *Patrologia Graecae* (J. P. Migne) [1857–1886]

TBD *Tyndale Bible Dictionary* (Elwell, Comfort) [2001]

TDNT *Theological Dictionary of the New Testament* (10 vols., Kittel, Friedrich; trans. Bromiley) [1964–1976]

TDOT *Theological Dictionary of the Old Testament* (8 vols., Botterweck, Ringgren; trans. Willis, Bromiley, Green) [1974–]

TLNT *Theological Lexicon of the New Testament* (3 vols., C. Spicq) [1994]

TLOT *Theological Lexicon of the Old Testament* (3 vols., E. Jenni) [1997]

TWOT *Theological Wordbook of the Old Testament* (2 vols., Harris, Archer) [1980]

UBS^3 *United Bible Societies' Greek New Testament* (3rd ed., Metzger et al.) [1975]

UBS^4 *United Bible Societies' Greek New Testament* (4th corrected ed., Metzger et al.) [1993]

WH *The New Testament in the Original Greek* (Westcott and Hort) [1882]

ABBREVIATIONS FOR BOOKS OF THE BIBLE

Old Testament

Gen	Genesis	1 Sam	1 Samuel	Esth	Esther
Exod	Exodus	2 Sam	2 Samuel	Job	Job
Lev	Leviticus	1 Kgs	1 Kings	Ps, Pss	Psalm, Psalms
Num	Numbers	2 Kgs	2 Kings	Prov	Proverbs
Deut	Deuteronomy	1 Chr	1 Chronicles	Eccl	Ecclesiastes
Josh	Joshua	2 Chr	2 Chronicles	Song	Song of Songs
Judg	Judges	Ezra	Ezra	Isa	Isaiah
Ruth	Ruth	Neh	Nehemiah	Jer	Jeremiah

Lam	Lamentations	Amos	Amos	Hab	Habakkuk
Ezek	Ezekiel	Obad	Obadiah	Zeph	Zephaniah
Dan	Daniel	Jonah	Jonah	Hag	Haggai
Hos	Hosea	Mic	Micah	Zech	Zechariah
Joel	Joel	Nah	Nahum	Mal	Malachi

New Testament

Matt	Matthew	Eph	Ephesians	Heb	Hebrews
Mark	Mark	Phil	Philippians	Jas	James
Luke	Luke	Col	Colossians	1 Pet	1 Peter
John	John	1 Thess	1 Thessalonians	2 Pet	2 Peter
Acts	Acts	2 Thess	2 Thessalonians	1 John	1 John
Rom	Romans	1 Tim	1 Timothy	2 John	2 John
1 Cor	1 Corinthians	2 Tim	2 Timothy	3 John	3 John
2 Cor	2 Corinthians	Titus	Titus	Jude	Jude
Gal	Galatians	Phlm	Philemon	Rev	Revelation

Deuterocanonical

Bar	Baruch	1–2 Esdr	1–2 Esdras	Pr Man	Prayer of Manasseh
Add Dan	Additions to Daniel	Add Esth	Additions to Esther	Ps 151	Psalm 151
Pr Azar	Prayer of Azariah	Ep Jer	Epistle of Jeremiah	Sir	Sirach
Bel	Bel and the Dragon	Jdt	Judith	Tob	Tobit
Sg Three	Song of the Three	1–2 Macc	1–2 Maccabees	Wis	Wisdom of Solomon
	Children	3–4 Macc	3–4 Maccabees		
Sus	Susanna				

MANUSCRIPTS AND LITERATURE FROM QUMRAN

Initial numerals followed by "Q" indicate particular caves at Qumran. For example, the notation 4Q267 indicates text 267 from cave 4 at Qumran. Further, 1QS 4:9-10 indicates column 4, lines 9-10 of the *Rule of the Community*; and 4Q166 1 ii 2 indicates fragment 1, column ii, line 2 of text 166 from cave 4. More examples of common abbreviations are listed below.

CD	Cairo Geniza copy of the *Damascus Document*	1QIsa^b	Isaiah copy ^{b}	4QLam^a	Lamentations
		1QM	*War Scroll*	11QPs^a	Psalms
1QH	*Thanksgiving Hymns*	1QpHab	*Pesher Habakkuk*	11QTemple^{a,b}	*Temple Scroll*
1QIsa^a	Isaiah copy ^{a}	1QS	*Rule of the Community*	11QtgJob	*Targum of Job*

IMPORTANT NEW TESTAMENT MANUSCRIPTS

(all dates given are AD; ordinal numbers refer to centuries)

Significant Papyri ($\mathfrak{P}$ = Papyrus)

$\mathfrak{P}$1 Matt 1; early 3rd
$\mathfrak{P}$4+$\mathfrak{P}$64+$\mathfrak{P}$67 Matt 3, 5, 26; Luke 1-6; late 2nd
$\mathfrak{P}$5 John 1, 16, 20; early 3rd
$\mathfrak{P}$13 Heb 2-5, 10-12; early 3rd
$\mathfrak{P}$15+$\mathfrak{P}$16 (probably part of same codex) 1 Cor 7-8, Phil 3-4; late 3rd

$\mathfrak{P}$20 James 2-3; 3rd
$\mathfrak{P}$22 John 15-16; mid 3rd
$\mathfrak{P}$23 James 1; c. 200
$\mathfrak{P}$27 Rom 8-9; 3rd
$\mathfrak{P}$30 1 Thess 4-5; 2 Thess 1; early 3rd
$\mathfrak{P}$32 Titus 1-2; late 2nd
$\mathfrak{P}$37 Matt 26; late 3rd

$\mathfrak{P}$39 John 8; first half of 3rd
$\mathfrak{P}$40 Rom 1-4, 6, 9; 3rd
$\mathfrak{P}$45 Gospels and Acts; early 3rd
$\mathfrak{P}$46 Paul's Major Epistles (less Pastorals); late 2nd
$\mathfrak{P}$47 Rev 9-17; 3rd

𝔓49+𝔓65 Eph 4-5; 1 Thess
  1-2; 3rd
𝔓52 John 18; c. 125
𝔓53 Matt 26, Acts 9-10;
  middle 3rd
𝔓66 John; late 2nd
𝔓70 Matt 2-3, 11-12, 24; 3rd
𝔓72 1-2 Peter, Jude; c. 300

𝔓74 Acts, General Epistles; 7th
𝔓75 Luke and John; c. 200
𝔓77+𝔓103 (probably part of
  same codex) Matt 13-14, 23;
  late 2nd
𝔓87 Phlm; late 2nd
𝔓90 John 18-19; late 2nd
𝔓91 Acts 2-3; 3rd

𝔓92 Eph 1, 2 Thess 1; c. 300
𝔓98 Rev 1:13-20; late 2nd
𝔓100 James 3-5; c. 300
𝔓101 Matt 3-4; 3rd
𝔓104 Matt 21; 2nd
𝔓106 John 1; 3rd
𝔓115 Rev 2-3, 5-6, 8-15; 3rd

Significant Uncials

א (Sinaiticus) most of NT; 4th
A (Alexandrinus) most of NT;
  5th
B (Vaticanus) most of NT; 4th
C (Ephraemi Rescriptus) most
  of NT with many lacunae;
  5th
D (Bezae) Gospels, Acts; 5th
D (Claromontanus), Paul's
  Epistles; 6th (different MS
  than Bezae)
E (Laudianus 35) Acts; 6th
F (Augensis) Paul's Epistles; 9th
G (Boernerianus) Paul's
  Epistles; 9th

H (Coislinianus) Paul's
  Epistles; 6th
I (Freerianus or Washington)
  Paul's Epistles; 5th
L (Regius) Gospels; 8th
Q (Guelferbytanus B) Luke,
  John; 5th
P (Porphyrianus) Acts—
  Revelation; 9th
T (Borgianus) Luke, John; 5th
W (Washingtonianus or the
  Freer Gospels) Gospels; 5th
Z (Dublinensis) Matthew; 6th
037 (Δ; Sangallensis) Gospels;
  9th

038 (Θ; Koridethi) Gospels;
  9th
040 (Ξ; Zacynthius) Luke; 6th
043 (Φ; Beratinus) Matt,
  Mark; 6th
044 (Ψ; Athous Laurae)
  Gospels, Acts, Paul's
  Epistles; 9th
048 Acts, Paul's Epistles,
  General Epistles; 5th
0171 Matt 10, Luke 22;
  c. 300
0189 Acts 5; c. 200

Significant Minuscules

1 Gospels, Acts, Paul's Epistles;
  12th
33 All NT except Rev; 9th
81 Acts, Paul's Epistles,
  General Epistles; 1044
565 Gospels; 9th
700 Gospels; 11th

1424 (or Family 1424—a
  group of 29 manuscripts
  sharing nearly the same
  text) most of NT; 9th-10th
1739 Acts, Paul's Epistles; 10th
2053 Rev; 13th
2344 Rev; 11th

f^1 (a family of manuscripts
  including 1, 118, 131, 209)
  Gospels; 12th-14th
f^{13} (a family of manuscripts
  including 13, 69, 124, 174,
  230, 346, 543, 788, 826,
  828, 983, 1689, 1709—
  known as the Ferrar group)
  Gospels; 11th-15th

Significant Ancient Versions

SYRIAC (SYR)
syr^c (Syriac Curetonian)
  Gospels; 5th
syr^s (Syriac Sinaiticus)
  Gospels; 4th
syr^h (Syriac Harklensis) Entire
  NT; 616

OLD LATIN (IT)
it^a (Vercellenis) Gospels; 4th
it^b (Veronensis) Gospels; 5th
it^d (Cantabrigiensis—the Latin
  text of Bezae) Gospels, Acts,
  3 John; 5th
it^e (Palantinus) Gospels; 5th
it^k (Bobiensis) Matthew, Mark;
  c. 400

COPTIC (COP)
cop^bo (Boharic—north Egypt)
cop^fay (Fayyumic—central Egypt)
cop^sa (Sahidic—southern Egypt)

OTHER VERSIONS
arm (Armenian)
eth (Ethiopic)
geo (Georgian)

TRANSLITERATION AND NUMBERING SYSTEM

Note: For words and roots from non-biblical languages (e.g., Arabic, Ugaritic), only approximate transliterations are given.

HEBREW/ARAMAIC

Consonants

א	aleph	= '	מ, ם	mem	= m
בּ, ב	beth	= b	נ, ן	nun	= n
גּ, ג	gimel	= g	ס	samekh	= s
דּ, ד	daleth	= d	ע	ayin	= '
ה	he	= h	פּ, פ, ף	pe	= p
ו	waw	= w	צ, ץ	tsadhe	= ts
ז	zayin	= z	ק	qoph	= q
ח	heth	= kh	ר	resh	= r
ט	teth	= t	שׁ	shin	= sh
י	yodh	= y	שׂ	sin	= s
כּ, כ, ך	kaph	= k	תּ, ת	taw	= t, th (spirant)
ל	lamedh	= l			

Vowels

ַ	patakh	= a	ָ	qamets khatuf	= o
ַה	furtive patakh	= a	ֹ	holem	= o
ָ	qamets	= a	וֹ	full holem	= o
ָה	final qamets he	= ah	ֻ	short qibbuts	= u
ֶ	segol	= e	ֻ	long qibbuts	= u
ֵ	tsere	= e	וּ	shureq	= u
ֵי	tsere yod	= e	ֲ	khatef patakh	= a
ִ	short hireq	= i	ֳ	khatef qamets	= o
ִ	long hireq	= i	ְ	vocalic shewa	= e
ִי	hireq yod	= i	ַי	patakh yodh	= a

Greek

α	alpha	= a	ε	epsilon	= e
β	beta	= b	ζ	zeta	= z
γ	gamma	= g, n (before γ, κ, ξ, χ)	η	eta	= ē
			θ	theta	= th
δ	delta	= d	ι	iota	= i

κ	*kappa*	= *k*	τ	*tau*	= *t*
λ	*lamda*	= *l*	υ	*upsilon*	= *u*
μ	*mu*	= *m*	φ	*phi*	= *ph*
ν	*nu*	= *n*	χ	*chi*	= *ch*
ξ	*ksi*	= *x*	ψ	*psi*	= *ps*
ο	*omicron*	= *o*	ω	*omega*	= *ō*
π	*pi*	= *p*	‘	*rough*	= *h (with*
ρ	*rho*	= *r (ṗ = rh)*		*breathing*	*vowel or*
σ, ς	*sigma*	= *s*		*mark*	*diphthong)*

THE TYNDALE-STRONG'S NUMBERING SYSTEM

The Cornerstone Biblical Commentary series uses a word-study numbering system to give both newer and more advanced Bible students alike quicker, more convenient access to helpful original-language tools (e.g., concordances, lexicons, and theological dictionaries). Those who are unfamiliar with the ancient Hebrew, Aramaic, and Greek alphabets can quickly find information on a given word by looking up the appropriate index number. Advanced students will find the system helpful because it allows them to quickly find the lexical form of obscure conjugations and inflections.

There are two main numbering systems used for biblical words today. The one familiar to most people is the Strong's numbering system (made popular by the *Strong's Exhaustive Concordance to the Bible*). Although the original Strong's system is still quite useful, the most up-to-date research has shed new light on the biblical languages and allows for more precision than is found in the original Strong's system. The Cornerstone Biblical Commentary series, therefore, features a newly revised version of the Strong's system, the Tyndale-Strong's numbering system. The Tyndale-Strong's system brings together the familiarity of the Strong's system and the best of modern scholarship. In most cases, the original Strong's numbers are preserved. In places where new research dictates, new or related numbers have been added.[1]

The second major numbering system today is the Goodrick-Kohlenberger system used in a number of study tools published by Zondervan. In order to give students broad access to a number of helpful tools, the Commentary provides index numbers for the Zondervan system as well.

The different index systems are designated as follows:

TG Tyndale-Strong's Greek number	ZH Zondervan Hebrew number
ZG Zondervan Greek number	TA Tyndale-Strong's Aramaic number
TH Tyndale-Strong's Hebrew number	ZA Zondervan Aramaic number

So in the example, "love" *agapē* [TG26, ZG27], the first number is the one to use with Greek tools keyed to the Tyndale-Strong's system, and the second applies to tools that use the Zondervan system.

1. Generally, one may simply use the original four-digit Strong's number to identify words in tools using Strong's system. If a Tyndale-Strong's number is followed by a capital letter (e.g., TG1692A), it generally indicates an added subdivision of meaning for the given term. Whenever a Tyndale-Strong's number has a number following a decimal point (e.g., TG2013.1), it reflects an instance where new research has yielded a separate, new classification of use for a biblical word. Forthcoming tools from Tyndale House Publishers will include these entries, which were not part of the original Strong's system.

Ephesians

HAROLD W. HOEHNER

INTRODUCTION TO
Ephesians

THE LETTER TO THE EPHESIANS has long been a favorite among Christians over the centuries. It contains the leading themes of Pauline literature, and it expresses Paul's motive for his ministry as an apostle to the Gentiles. The ideas in Ephesians represent the crown of Paulinism (Dodd 1929:1224-1225) or the "quintessence of Paulinism" (Bruce 1967:303). The book of Ephesians, presenting an exalted view of the church and its relationship to the exalted Christ, contributed richly to the first-century believers' understanding of eternal truths. Its message is just as rich and relevant to today's church.

AUTHOR

Prior to the last two centuries, Paul's authorship of this letter was not questioned, but much has been written in the past 200 years that casts doubts on his authorship. An examination of this problem will be divided into two parts: The traditional view of Pauline authorship will be stated, and then various arguments used to suggest that Ephesians was written by someone other than Paul will be introduced.

The Traditional View of Pauline Authorship. The traditional view of Pauline authorship is based on internal and external evidence. Regarding internal evidence, Ephesians clearly claims to have been written by Paul. In typical Pauline fashion, he opened his letter with the identifier: "Paul, chosen by the will of God to be an apostle of Christ Jesus" (1:1; cf. 1 Cor 1:1; 2 Cor 1:1; Gal 1:1; Col 1:1). He again mentioned his name in 3:1, which is consistent with his other letters (2 Cor 10:1; Gal 5:2; Col 1:23; 4:18; 1 Thess 2:18; 2 Thess 3:17; Phlm 1:19). Descriptions mentioned in the first person singular (3:1; 4:1) correspond with depictions of Paul from his other letters (Phil 1:13, 17; Col 4:3; Phlm 1:1, 9) and from Acts (Acts 25:14, 27; 28:17; cf. 16:37; 21:33; 24:27; 26:29). Thus, the internal evidence of Paul's claim of authorship of this letter clearly corresponds with other letters written by him.

Regarding external evidence, Ephesians has the earliest attestation of any New Testament book. As early as the late first century or very early second century, Clement of Rome (fl. 96) mentions "one God and one Christ and one Spirit," which probably alludes to Ephesians 4:4-6. Furthermore, Clement's prayer that God would "open the eyes of our heart that we might know you [God]" is an allusion to Ephesians 1:17-18, the mention of "the senseless and darkened heart" is an allusion to Ephesians 4:18, and his exhortation to "let each be subject to his neighbor" is reminiscent of Ephesians 5:21. Ignatius (AD 35–107/8), bishop of Antioch, seems to allude to Ephesians 5:1-2 when he mentions that the Ephesians were imitators of God by their demonstration of love to him, and he also shows familiarity with the armor of God described in chapter 6. Polycarp (AD 69–135), bishop of Smyrna, quotes Ephesians 4:26 and Psalm 4:5 and calls them both Scripture, making Ephesians the first New Testament epistle to be called "Scripture" by the apostolic fathers. Polycarp also makes reference to Ephesians 2:5, 8-9 and 6:11-17, further indicating his acquaintance with the letter. Furthermore, Irenaeus (AD 130–200), Clement of Alexandria (AD 150–215), the Muratorian Canon (possibly from Rome; ca. AD 170–200), and Tertullian of Carthage (AD 166–220) acknowledge that Ephesians is a letter by Paul. Hence, Ephesians is not only the first New Testament book to have been recognized as Scripture, but its attestation of Pauline authorship is very early and from various geographical areas of the New Testament world.

The Dispute over Pauline Authorship. Despite this early and diverse attestation to Paul as the author of Ephesians, many scholars throughout the past 200 years have posited arguments for rejecting Pauline authorship. Six of the major objections will be discussed here—each followed by an analysis and a rebuttal.

1. *Impersonal nature.* It was not until 1792 that an English clergyman named Evanson (1792:261-262) first doubted Pauline authorship of Ephesians. He posited that it was inconsistent for the writer of Ephesians to claim that he had just heard of the Ephesians' faith (1:15-16), when according to Acts, Paul had spent more than two years at Ephesus. Paul first arrived in Ephesus at the end of his second missionary journey in the autumn of 52, and after a short ministry he left for Jerusalem, leaving Priscilla and Aquila there (Acts 18:18-21). A year later (in autumn of 53), on his third missionary journey, he returned to Ephesus and remained there for two and a half years, leaving in the spring of 56 (Acts 19:1–20:1). A year after that (in spring of 57), he visited the elders of Ephesus at Miletus on his way to Jerusalem from Corinth (Acts 20:16-38). It is argued that since Paul spent considerable time with the Ephesians, it seems remarkable that he speaks of "having heard" of their faith and love (1:15) and further that he closes the letter with a brief impersonal farewell. In addition, Paul questions whether or not they had heard of the administration of the grace of God given him to minister to Gentiles, including those at Ephesus (3:2), and also questions their reception of the instruction they received (4:21). Interestingly, there are no personal greetings to individuals in the Ephesian church. By contrast, in letters such as the one addressed to Rome, a place he had never visited, there are extended greetings from him in the last two chapters of the book.

The impersonal tone of the letter, however, is not extraordinary. First, Paul was not obligated to give personal greetings at the end of each letter; there are none in 2 Corinthians, Galatians, 1 and 2 Thessalonians, or Philippians, for example. In the case of 2 Corinthians, Paul had stayed with them for 18 months, and in that of Galatians, he had been with them only a few months before he wrote his letter.

Even though greetings are absent in these books, very few deny their Pauline authorship. Second, though the letter addresses those in Ephesus, it may have been an encyclical letter intended for other churches in the area. An example of this is the Colossian letter, which was addressed specifically to the Colossians (Col 1:2) but was to be read by the Laodiceans, who in turn were to let the Colossians read the letter addressed to them (Col 4:16). It is not improbable to surmise that a letter addressed to a city like Ephesus may have been intended to go elsewhere as well. It is true that the letter to the Colossians is more personal, but this may be explained by the fact that Colossae and Laodicea were neighboring villages and the people of both communities knew each other. On the other hand, Ephesus was not only a commercial and political center in western Asia Minor but also the center of Paul's ministry from which many other churches were started by him and his disciples during and after his stay there. Hence, it is reasonable to think that this letter would go to many other churches within Ephesus and the surrounding areas, which would explain the lack of the personal element. As already mentioned, Galatians has no personal greetings and was an encyclical letter, since it was addressed to the "churches of Galatia" (Gal 1:2). Third, since Paul had not visited Ephesus for five or six years, it is likely that there were many new believers with whom he had little or no acquaintance. Furthermore, he may not have wished to single out those whom he knew since his emphasis was on the unity of all believers. Fourth, the letter to the Ephesians is not completely impersonal. Paul mentions the fact that he is praying for them (1:16), and he asks for their prayers (6:19-20), which indicate some familiarity with the believers there. Moreover, it seems that the better Paul knew a church, the fewer personal greetings he gave. For example, Romans, where Paul had never been, has the most extensive greetings, while in the letters to the church in Thessalonica, where Paul had been only a few weeks earlier, has no greetings. It may be that one of the reasons for personal greetings was to strengthen his credibility. If this were the case, greetings would be most necessary in the cities where he had never been. Conversely, it would be least necessary in letters to churches where the recipients knew him well. Thus, the impersonal tone of the letter in no way necessitates the denial of Pauline authorship of Ephesians.

   2. Language and style. With regards to language it is suggested that Ephesians has too many unique words to be Pauline. Statistically, Ephesians has 2,425 words with a total vocabulary of 529 words. There are 41 words Paul used only in Ephesians while 84 words in Ephesians are not found elsewhere in Paul's writings but do occur elsewhere in the New Testament. How does this compare with other Pauline literature? Galatians has similar characteristics, namely, 2,220 words with a total vocabulary of 526 words; and virtually no one doubts its Pauline authorship. There are 35 words Paul used only in Galatians and there are 90 words in Galatians that are not found elsewhere in Paul but do occur elsewhere in the New Testament. Hence, the total vocabulary is about the same, Ephesians has slightly more words unique to the NT than Galatians, and Galatians has more words not used elsewhere in Paul but elsewhere in the New Testament—even though Galatians is ten percent shorter than Ephesians! Does this suggest that Paul did not write Galatians? Most would not say so. Even Mitton (1951:29) admits that several undisputed works of Paul have a higher percentage of words not found in other Pauline letters. Hence, the unique use of vocabulary does not demonstrate the non-Pauline authorship of Ephesians.

The same reasoning can be applied to unique phrases used in Ephesians. Lincoln (1990:lxv) lists 15 word combinations or phrases in Ephesians unique within Pauline literature. However, there are more than 15 unique expressions in Galatians compared to the Pauline corpus. Again these unique expressions in Galatians do not prove Paul did not write this letter. Unique expressions are due to the mood and content of the letter, the recipients of the letter, and the flexibility and ingenuity of the author. It is also pointed out that the Greek prepositions *en* [TG1722, ZG1877] (in) and *kata* [TG2596, ZG2848] (down, according to) are used more frequently in Ephesians than in Paul's undisputed letters (the "undisputed" corpus varies from four to seven letters). However, in examining the undisputed letters one notices much greater frequency of the prepositions *dia* [TG1223, ZG1328] (through), *epi* [TG1909, ZG2093] (on), *para* [TG3844, ZG4123] (from, with) in Romans, and *ek* [TG1537, ZG1666] (out of, *para* [TG3844, ZG4123] (from, with) and *hupo* [TG5259, ZG5679] (by, under) in Galatians. Other similar examples could be cited, but none would cause one to conclude that Romans and Galatians were not written by Paul. Although the preposition *kata* [TG2596, ZG2848] (down, according to) is used more frequently in Ephesians than in other Pauline letters, it is used quite often in Galatians; in fact, its use with the genitive case occurs much more frequently in Galatians than in any other Pauline letter, but it does not follow that Galatians is not Pauline. Therefore, on the basis of vocabulary one cannot determine the authorship of a letter.

In addition to language, the style in which Ephesians is written has caused some to question Pauline authorship. For example, Ephesians has eight lengthy sentences. However, van Roon (1974:105-111) has pointed out that Paul uses long sentences in doxologies and prayers (cf. 1:3-14, 15-23; 3:14-19; Rom 8:38-39; 11:33-36; 1 Cor 1:4-8; Phil 1:3-8; 1 Thess 1:2-5; 2 Thess 1:3-10), doctrinal content (cf. 2:1-7; 3:2-13; Rom 3:21-26; 1 Cor 1:26-29; 2:6-9) and parenthetical materials (cf. 4:1-6, 11-16; 6:14-20; 1 Cor 12:8-11; Phil 1:27-2:11). Furthermore, would one argue that since Galatians uses short incisive language and abrupt statements not found in other Pauline letters, it could not be by the hand of Paul? Unlikely. Others have argued that the style of Ephesians is not out of character with the other Pauline literature (Turner 1963:84-85; Neumann 1990:194-199, 206-211, 213-226).

In conclusion it is extremely difficult, if not impossible, to determine authorship on the basis of language and style. This is readily evident in the present day. For example, an engineer uses different vocabulary and style when he writes to his colleague, his senator, his friend, his wife, or his children.

3. Literary relationships. It is proposed that certain remarkable similarities in vocabulary, phraseology, and thematic development between Ephesians and Colossians point to a Pauline imitator as the author of Ephesians. Regarding vocabulary, Mitton (1951:58-59, 97) concludes that Colossians verbally parallels 26.5 percent of Ephesians and Ephesians parallels 34 percent of Colossians. However, these statistics are not as formidable as they might first appear. By using a database to observe the parallels, it becomes apparent that only 246 words are shared between the two epistles out of a total of the 2,429 words in Ephesians and 1,574 words in Colossians. Furthermore, many of the 246 words are used many times since they include conjunctions, pronouns, prepositions, and proper nouns (e.g., God, Christ). The repeated use of these 246 words makes up 2,057 words (out of the 2,429 words) in Ephesians and 1,362 words (out of the 1,574 words) in Colossians. Finally, these similarities are understandable since the two works have similar content.

Conversely, there are 21 words in Ephesians and Colossians not found elsewhere in Paul but found elsewhere in the New Testament and only 11 words in Ephesians and Colossians that are not found elsewhere in the New Testament. It seems that an imitator's letter to the Ephesians would have more closely corresponded to Paul's letter to the Colossians, especially since much of the content is similar.

Beyond individual words, one needs to look at the linkage of words to see if the similarities between Ephesians and Colossians are enough to suggest non-Pauline authorship. In three verses, there is a string of seven consecutive words that correspond exactly in the two letters (Eph 1:1-2 = Col 1:1-2; Eph 3:2 = Col 1:25; Eph 3:9 = Col 1:26). Twice there is exact correspondence of five consecutive words (Eph 1:7 = Col 1:14; Eph 4:16 = Col 2:9). Finally, in the information about Tychicus (6:21-22; Col 4:7-8) there are 29 consecutive words of Colossians repeated in Ephesians, except the words "and fellow servant" are omitted. Because of these literary correspondences, Mitton (1951:58-59, 67) concludes that the author of Ephesians must have known Colossians almost by heart. Why would anyone memorize such spiritually insignificant details regarding Tychicus? It is more likely that Paul wrote both letters at approximately the same time and when he came to the end of the second letter, he referred to the conclusion of the first letter since it was applicable to both. If the author of Ephesians had known Colossians almost by heart, he would likely have memorized the more important portions for the sake of accuracy in order to convince the recipients that it was Paul's work. There is actually very little consecutive verbal agreement between the two letters.

Regarding thematic development, much of the thought and sequence of the themes in Ephesians and Colossians are similar. Lincoln (1990:li-lviii) believes that the author of Ephesians used Colossians in writing his letter. He notes two reasons for this conclusion. First, there is verbal correlation within parallel sections. The greetings are similar, both having "saints" and "faithful in Christ (Jesus)," a combination not found in other Pauline letters. There is verbal correspondence with key words (e.g., redemption, reconciliation, body, flesh, tribulation, ministry, mystery, power) in parallel sections, which, according to Lincoln and others, indicates that the author of Ephesians "clearly" borrowed from Colossians (e.g., 2:11-16; Col 1:15-22). In the last half of the book, the author of Ephesians appears to utilize

Colossians regarding putting off the old humanity and putting on the new (4:25–5:20; Col 3:5-17), the household codes (5:21–6:9; Col 3:18–4:1), and the information about the sending of Tychicus (6:21-22; Col 4:7-8). Second, there are terminological links outside the major parallel sections. Lincoln argues that Ephesians 1:4 is taken from Colossians 1:22 with some alteration, and Ephesians 1:6-7 uses Colossians 1:13-14, 20 with some changes in expressions, such as substituting (literally rendered) "in the beloved" for "in the Son of his love." These expressions demonstrate that the author of Ephesians depended on Colossians "in terms of its overall structure and sequence, its themes, and its wording. Yet what is also absolutely clear is that this is a free and creative dependence, not a slavish imitation or copying" (Lincoln 1990:lv). Thus, some conclude that the writer of Ephesians had seen Colossians but may not have memorized it; many also conclude that Paul could not have been the author because only an imitator would have copied it so closely.

However, there are four things that must be pointed out regarding these proposals. First, one cannot be certain that Colossians was written before Ephesians; in fact, there are a few scholars who think that Ephesians was written before Colossians (e.g., van Roon 1974:413-437). Second, there is no proof that the author of Ephesians had Colossians in front of him. It is easier to postulate that Paul wrote Ephesians and that many of the themes and thoughts are written from memory of what he had said and taught over the years. The variations in vocabulary and expressions may be due to his own development and the varying needs of his audiences. This is true in the present time, for a scholar may read a paper to a scholarly society that is later rewritten to be presented to an audience of lay people. Although there are changes, much of the vocabulary and expressions will remain the same. To make claims that the author of Ephesians "clearly" borrowed from Colossians cannot be demonstrated (Best 1997:72-92). Third, it is more likely that the same author would vary to a greater degree than an imitator. An imitator would feel more bound to use the same vocabulary and expressions than would a genuine author. Fourth, if an imitator wrote Ephesians, it seems odd that there was not more wholesale copying of Colossians in vocabulary, expressions, and content so as not to be detected as an imitator.

In conclusion, the literary relationship between Ephesians and Colossians is quite evident. The similarities and differences between the two letters are best explained by the fact that they are written by the same author. It seems appropriate to accept the internal evidence of Ephesians, which states that Paul wrote it (1:1-2; 3:1), and to accept that what he wrote is consistent with Colossians and with his other letters. It is much easier to understand the differences as the creative variations of an author than to expect them of an imitator. The differences arose due to differences of purpose, content, time, mood, and audience. This also explains similarities and variances in wording of specific content. It is easier to believe that Paul wrote these two letters and that when he penned Ephesians he would have similar vocabulary and content on similar topics and would vary in vocabulary when addressing different issues. One must allow for development of Paul's thought.

4. *Pseudonymity.* The subject of pseudonymity is an outgrowth of the preceding discussion. If Paul did not write Ephesians, then who did? Throughout the years many suggestions have been made, but most conclude that the author of Ephesians was most likely a writer from the Pauline school, a disciple or secretary who was familiar with Paul's thoughts. The idea of the pseudonymity of Ephesians is based on the claim that it was a widely used practice in the Greco-Roman, Jewish, and Christian cultures (Moffatt 1918:40-44; Meade 1986:1-16, 116-118, 153-161, 190-193). It is suggested that the pseudonymous author was not consciously misrepresenting Paul in that he was not deceiving anyone and that the church received the letters with warm appreciation without any misunderstanding (Mitton 1951:222, 259-260; Meade 1986:194-218; Lincoln 1990:lxxii-lxxiii). However, Green cogently argues, "If this assessment were wholly true, and if nobody was taken in by the device, it is hard to see why it was adopted at all" (1961:32). Though pseudepigraphy was widespread among the Greeks and Romans, no writing was ever accepted as genuine if it were known that it was not written by the author it claimed (Donelson 1986:11). Even within Judaism there were many pseudepigraphical works, but they were composed centuries after the lives of those named in their works and were never accepted as canonical by Jews.

Furthermore, most of these pseudepigraphical works are apocalyptic and not epistolary in form. Only two pseudepigraphical writings, the Epistle of Jeremiah and the *Letter of Aristeas,* are epistolary in form, though neither of these are strictly epistles. Both of these works were considered pseudepigraphical by the Jews and were never considered genuine either by the Jewish rabbis or the Christian church in the first century AD. During the time of the early church, many writings bore the names of the apostles, such as *Gospel of Thomas, Gospel of Peter,* and *Apocalypse of Peter.* The church from its earliest times critically examined the writings with apostolic claims and rejected those that were heretical or pseudonymous. In fact, in one of his earliest letters Paul warns his readers not to be troubled or anxious by a letter purported to have come from him (2 Thess 2:2). At the end of this same letter, he affirms it by stating that the greeting is by his own hand (2 Thess 3:17). Clearly, Paul was opposed to pseudonymous writings.

Even after the first century, pseudonymous works were rejected by the church. Two such works come to the forefront. First, *Epistle to the Laodiceans* was a forgery whose title was no doubt inspired by Colossians 4:16, where the Colossian believers were encouraged to read the letter Paul sent to the Laodiceans. Already by the end of the second century, it is stated in the Muratorian Canon (c. AD 170–200) that the letter to the Laodiceans is a letter forged in Paul's name. Jerome (AD 345–419) stated that it was rejected by all. Second, *Acts of Paul and Thecla* was rejected by Tertullian as a spurious work. The author of the work was convicted by church leaders of passing it off under Paul's name and thus using Paul's reputation for his own purpose. Although he protested that he had done it in good faith and out of love for Paul, he was removed from his office as presbyter due to the deception. Hence, not only Paul but also the church (attested as early as the second century) rejected pseudonymous writings.

It is often asserted that pseudonymous origins do not impugn either the inspiration or canonicity of the work (Meade 1986:215-216). This is simply not true. For example, Serapion, bishop of Antioch (c. AD 190–211), at first allowed the *Gospel of Peter* to be read in church, but later when he heard that some used it for the support of Docetism, he examined it, found it unorthodox, and consequently rejected it as a forgery (Eusebius *Ecclesiastical History* 6.12.2-3). A forgery was considered uninspired and thus noncanonical. If the opposite were true, it would seem that there would have been many clear-cut examples of such works in the early church that would have been accepted as canonical.

In conclusion, there is a tendency among those who favor pseudepigraphical authorship to minimize the fraudulence of pseudonymity. The claim that authorship, plagiarism, and copyright are modern concerns and were not concerns in the first century is untenable. As mentioned above, in the Greco-Roman world, no pseudepigraphical writing identified as such was ever considered to have prescriptive or proscriptive authority and was thus rejected. There is uniform testimony in the first four centuries of the church that any pseudepigraphical writing was to be rejected as a forgery. This perspective is not different from the contemporary view of literary proprietorship. Hence, it is more logical that Ephesians was authored by Paul (as stated in 1:1 and 3:1) than that Ephesians was the work of a pseudonymous writer. This, after all, has been the accepted view throughout church history until the nineteenth and twentieth centuries.

5. *Theological distinctives.* Every book of the New Testament has theological distinctions, but it is thought by some, such as Kümmel, that "the theology of Ephesians makes the Pauline composition of the letter completely impossible" (1975:360). Four areas of theology will be considered: Christology, soteriology, ecclesiology, and eschatology.

First, regarding Christology the designations "Jesus Christ," "Christ Jesus," "Jesus," or "Christ" occur very often in this small epistle. Ephesians 1:3 and 1:17 designate God as the Father of our Lord Jesus Christ, indicating that Christ is distinct from the Father and also affirming him as the Son of God (4:13). He is called the "beloved" (1:6, NLT mg), a messianic title (cf. Jesus' baptism, Matt 3:17; Mark 1:11; Luke 3:22; and transfiguration Matt 17:5; Mark 9:7). His eternality is distinctly affirmed, as he is the one who existed before the foundation of the world (1:4-5, 11). Jesus is the Christ (1:5, 17; 4:20-21) and Lord (1:2-3, 15, 17; 3:11; 4:5; 5:20; 6:23-24) who became human (2:14), died on the cross (2:13, 16; 5:2, 25), was raised from the dead by God (1:20), and is now seated at the right hand of God in the heavens (1:20; 4:8). Christ's divinity is affirmed by the declaration that he has provided redemption for believers (1:7; 2:13; 5:2, 23, 25-26), that is, the forgiveness of sins (1:7; 5:25-27), which, as the religious leaders had protested to Jesus, is the prerogative of God only (Mark 2:7, 10; Luke 5:21, 24). Believers are to place their faith in him as their Lord (1:15; 4:5; cf. 3:12). The Father's predestination of believers to adoption as children is through Christ (2:18; 5:20). His sovereignty is demonstrated by the fact that he is the one who has put all creation, animate and inanimate, human and angelic, under God (1:22), and in the future all of creation will be united under him (1:10). Christ is filled with God's fullness (1:23) and fills the church and the cosmos with that fullness (3:19; 4:10). Therefore, Christ, eternal and divine, is not only the cosmic head of all things but also the head of the church. The Christology in Ephesians is similar to that of Colossians and is in agreement with the rest of Pauline literature.

Second, regarding soteriology, it is suggested that, on the one hand, the death of Christ and the theology of the Cross is less prominent in Ephesians than in other Pauline literature. The cross is mentioned only in 2:16 (which parallels Col 1:20), in connection with the reconciliation of Jews and Gentiles into one body, and Christ's death is mentioned only in traditional formulations (1:7; 5:2, 25). By contrast, Christ's resurrection, exaltation, and cosmic lordship are given prominence (Lincoln 1990:lxiii-lxiv; Mitton 1951:20). In response to this, it can be argued that the references to Christ's death do speak to his death as a substitutionary sacrifice for humanity in line with the other Pauline letters. The fact that there are four references to Christ's death in a six-chapter book is noteworthy. Though there is an emphasis on Christ's exaltation, it is in line with the early preaching of the church as seen in the sermons by Peter (Acts 2:24-36; 3:15-16, 21, 26) and by Paul (Acts 13:30-37), both of whom stressed Christ's resurrection and exaltation. Also, in his defense speeches, Paul stressed the hope of the Resurrection (Acts 23:6; 24:14-15; 26:23). In other letters Paul accentuates resurrection and exaltation (1 Cor 15:3-28; Phil 2:5-11).

It is also noted by some that in Ephesians there is an absence of the concept of justification by grace. Granted, this terminology is not used, but certainly that is the essence of Ephesians 2:8-10. Moreover, the noun and verb for justification occur 85 times in Paul's writings, but 61 of these are in Romans and Galatians—the books that specifically address the issue of justification. In fact, the noun occurs only once and the verb only twice in the long letter of 1 Corinthians, and neither the noun nor verb are found in Colossians or 1 and 2 Thessalonians. Clearly, the subject of justification need not be in every Pauline letter, much less these two particular words.

Finally, it is alleged that salvation is viewed as something completed in the past (by the use of the perfect tense for "saved" in 2:8-9) with no future implication. However, there is mention of (1) the enjoyment of salvation in a future consummation (1:10); (2) the placement of a seal upon believers until (literally) the "redemption of the purchased possession" (1:13-14); (3) the "future age(s)" (1:21; 2:7); (4) the "day of redemption" (4:30), and (5) the future presentation of the church as glorious "without a spot or wrinkle" (5:27). Though believers are portrayed as being presently seated with Christ (2:6) to indicate their deliverance from the cosmic powers of the devil, in no way does this imply that salvation is fully realized in the present day without a future consummation. In conclusion, then, Ephesians contains differences from Paul's other writings in his expression of soteriology, but creative differences must be allowed by a thinker like Paul. Though there are differences, they do not contradict anything stated in the undisputed Pauline letters.

Third, regarding ecclesiology, it is surmised that the "church" is viewed exclusively as universal (cf. 1:22; 3:10, 21; 5:23-25, 27, 29, 32) and that this stands in contrast with the undisputed Pauline Epistles, which most frequently refer to local churches. In addition, it is suggested that the emphasis on the church as one body (4:4), universal (1:22-23), built on the apostles and prophets (2:20), and holy and blameless (5:26-27) probably reflects a stage after the ministry of Paul—a kind of emergent Catholicism (Lincoln 1990:lxiv; Mitton 1951:18-20). In answer to these suggestions, it should be noted that the undisputed letters of Paul also speak of a universal church. Paul mentions that he persecuted the church of God (Gal 1:13; Phil 3:6) and gives instruction not to offend the church of God (1 Cor 10:32), referring to the universal church. When he speaks of the body of Christ as composed of individual members out of which God has appointed apostles, prophets, teachers, and other ministries (Rom 12:4-8; 1 Cor 12:27-28), as he did in Ephesians 4:11, he is not limiting his instruction to a local assembly of believers. Paul also mentions that all Christians are baptized into one body (1 Cor 12:13; cf. Gal 3:27), which again must have reference to the universal rather than the local church. Granted, the author of Ephesians makes no mention of the local church in the letter, but this is explainable if this letter is considered to be a circular letter addressed to several churches in Asia Minor. Furthermore, the use of the singular "church" rather than the plural "churches" may be due to his theme of unity throughout the book (Arnold 1989:164-165).

Furthermore, some suggest that the author of Ephesians views the apostles and prophets as the foundation of the church (2:20), which differs from 1 Corinthians 3:11 where Christ is regarded as the foundation. But authors must be allowed to use different imagery as it suits the situation. Moreover, if the foundation is viewed as consisting of apostles and prophets with Christ as the chief cornerstone of that foundation, then it is not a contradiction but an extension of the imagery in 1 Corinthians 3:11, reflecting further development in Paul's thought. Hence, though there may be differences in nuances and emphases, the ecclesiology expressed in Ephesians is in line with other Pauline literature, albeit with possible further reflection and development in thought.

Fourth, with regard to eschatology, some suggest that in Ephesians the expectation of Christ's return evidenced in the early years of Paul's ministry has faded into the background (Mitton 1951:21-22; Lindemann 1975:21-24, 120-125; Lincoln 1990:lxiv). It is true that Ephesians speaks of presently being made alive together with Christ (2:5), but this is not speaking about eschatology per se but about the believer's position as one who is justified, as mentioned in other Pauline literature (Rom 6:5-11; 8:15-17). Moreover, in other places in Ephesians, Paul expresses the return of Christ as the time of the redemption of the purchased possession (1:14; 4:30) and that though we are presently seated with Christ in the heavenly realms (2:6), we will be demonstrated as the wealth of his grace in the future (2:7). In other words, although there is a present realization of our position in Christ, there will be a future consummation. He speaks of the fullness of time (1:10), which has reference to future fulfillment. Still, it is suggested that since Christ had not returned by the time this epistle was written, the emphasis in Ephesians shifted from Christ's future reign to the believers' present relationship to Christ in the heavenly realms (1:3, 20-21; 2:6) and the believers' maturity in the present age (4:15). In response to this, it should be noted that, although there is much on eschatology in the Thessalonian letters, there is very little on the subject in Paul's earliest letter, namely, Galatians, so its lack of emphasis in Ephesians is not out of character for Paul.

In conclusion, it can be seen that although in Ephesians there may be differences from other letters by Paul, the differences, in many cases, may be ones of emphasis, possibly due to differences in the circumstances of the audience. A different emphasis is not indicative of a different author.

6. *Historical considerations.* Regarding historical considerations in assessing the authorship of Ephesians: neither external nor internal evidence count against Paul. As far as external evidence, the authorship of Ephesians was not questioned until the last two centuries, as was noted above. Mitton, who denies Pauline authorship of Ephesians, confirms the long history that attests Pauline authorship and states that "the burden of proof lies with those who seek to maintain a contrary opinion" (1951:15-16, 25). Second, with regard to internal evidence, it is thought that the resolution of the Jewish–Gentile controversy intimated in Ephesians reflects a period after Paul's lifetime (Mitton 1951:16; Lincoln and Wedderburn 1993:84). Though this controversy did exist in the early church, it was not as great as has been suggested by the Tübingen school of the last century. Moreover, it is difficult to assess the state of the debate based on any of the Pauline letters, let alone from the contents of Ephesians. More importantly, the passage in Ephesians 2:11-21 is not discussing the controversy within the church but rather the rift between unconverted Jews and Gentiles prior to the Cross and the reconciliation of believing Jews and Gentiles in the death of Christ. Hence, there is nothing within the letter that reflects a period after Paul's time of ministry.

Conclusion. The Pauline authorship of Ephesians has the earliest attestation of any New Testament book. In addition, though there are differences in Ephesians compared to other Pauline literature, none of them are out of character with Pauline style and theology. These differences are easily explained by the varying content of Paul's letters, as well as the varying needs and character of his recipients. Furthermore, one must allow for differences of expression and thought due to Paul's own development of thought. Content, development of thought, mood, and recipients affect the vocabulary and style of an author, whether in the first or the present century. Let Paul be Paul!

DATE AND OCCASION OF WRITING

Paul makes the explicit statement that he was in prison when he wrote this epistle (3:1; 4:1). Traditionally, it has been thought that Paul wrote four letters (Ephesians, Philippians, Colossians, and Philemon) while he was imprisoned in Rome. This view is a natural inference from Acts 27–28. He had traveled from Caesarea to Rome and was allowed to live by himself in rented private quarters under guard (Acts

28:16) for a period of two years (Acts 28:30). Although he was chained to a soldier (Acts 28:20), he was free to receive visitors (Acts 28:17, 23, 30). This corresponds to the Prison Epistles, which speak of his imprisonment or chains (6:20; Phil 1:7, 13; Col 4:18; Phlm 1:10, 13) and his reception of visitors or friends—namely, Tychicus (6:21; Col 4:7), Timothy (Phil 1:1; 2:19; Col 1:1; Phlm 1:1), Epaphras (Col 1:7; 4:12; Phlm 1:23), Epaphroditus (Phil 2:25; 4:18), Onesimus (Col 4:9; Phlm 1:10), Jesus or Justus (Col 4:11), Mark, Aristarchus, Luke, and Demas (Col 4:10, 14; Phlm 1:24). Thus, the Roman imprisonment of Paul fits well as the background for the Prison Epistles.

However, some question whether the Prison Epistles were written from Rome and suggest two other alternatives. The first suggested alternative is that Paul wrote the Prison Epistles while imprisoned in Caesarea (AD 57–59; Robinson 1976:60-67, 77-85). It is more reasonable to assume that Onesimus traveled to Caesarea rather than to Rome, for in Caesarea it is less likely that he would have been recognized as a runaway slave. However, it could be argued that Onesimus could be more easily found in a smaller city such as Caesarea. So this is not a very strong argument.

It is also suggested that the imprisonment in Rome would pose a distance too great and the time too short for the frequent interchanges between him in Rome and the church in Philippi. However, the problem of time and distance for the interchanges between Rome and Philippi is not insurmountable. Many people who could have conveyed the reports or interchanges traveled between Rome and Philippi, an important Roman city. Hence, the Caesarean imprisonment as the place where Paul wrote the Prison Epistles is not convincing or necessary. The second alternative to the Roman imprisonment is an imprisonment at Ephesus (Duncan 1929). It is suggested that the Prison Epistles were written during his imprisonment at Ephesus shortly after the riot there in May 56. However, there is no indication that Paul was imprisoned there after the riot, and it seems odd that this is not specifically mentioned in Ephesians if that were the case.

In conclusion, then, the traditional Roman imprisonment has the best biblical support (Acts 25:6–28:31) and continues to be the view of most students of the New Testament. This being the case, it means that Ephesians would have been written after his imprisonment in Caesarea (AD 57–59)—hence, sometime in the years 60–62. To further narrow the date of the composition of Ephesians may be helpful but is conjectural. According to Philippians 2:19, 24, Paul anticipated his release and, therefore, that letter was written toward the end of his incarceration, around the spring of AD 62. The Epistle to the Colossians was sent with Tychicus and Onesimus (Col 4:7-9), and it is reasonable to think that the letter to Philemon was also sent at this time (Phlm 1:12). Paul instructed Philemon to prepare a guest room for him (Phlm 1:22), which may indicate an imminent release from prison. As such, these epistles may have been written toward the end of his two-year imprisonment. Nothing is mentioned in Ephesians regarding his release or his hope of visiting them soon. However, Ephesians most likely was sent with Colossians because both mention that Tychicus (6:21; Col 4:7) would report Paul's situation. It is unlikely that

Tychicus was sent two different times. Thus, the occasion for the letter was Tychicus' travel to Colossae and Ephesus. This means that Ephesians may have been written toward the end of his Roman imprisonment, some time in late 61 or early 62.

AUDIENCE

The destination of Ephesus is obvious when one reads most English translations of the first verse of the book (KJV, ASV, NASB, NEB, NIV, NRSV, NLT). However, most scholars have serious doubts that the words "in Ephesus" should be included in the verse. They point out that these words are omitted from some of the earliest and most reliable manuscripts, namely, the renowned fourth-century codices Sinaiticus (א) and Vaticanus (B) and the second-century papyrus 𝔓46. In addition, it is proposed that the impersonal tone of the letter and the omission of any specific problems make it unlikely that Paul was writing to believers in Ephesus, whom he had come to know well in his three-year ministry among them. Thus, consensus of opinion is that the words "in Ephesus" were either written by someone other than Paul (see "Author" above) or that the letter was a circular.

The omission of "in Ephesus" makes for a very difficult reading and there have been several proposals to explain the omission. Some suggest that it should be read with the omission of the city and translated "to the saints and those who are faithful in Christ Jesus" (cf. RSV, JB, NJB). To use the participle *tois ousin* ("those who are"; cf. *eimi* [TG1510, ZG1639]) without naming a city is grammatically awkward, if not impossible. Furthermore, no other Pauline letter uses this construction without naming the city (cf. Rom 1:7; 1 Cor 1:2; 2 Cor 1:1; Phil 1:1). Others suggest that this letter was encyclical and that possibly the city name was omitted so that Tychicus or the recipients of the letter would fill in the city's name. However, there is no blank space in any manuscript in which the city's name might be written, even in those manuscripts that omit "in Ephesus," and no such lacunae exist in examples of letters in the ancient world. Moreover, the manuscripts that omit "in Ephesus" insert no other city in its place. Other suggestions, such as the insertion of the superscription from outside the scroll (Best 1987:325), or that originally two cities, Hierapolis and Laodicea, were mentioned so as to explain the awkward conjunction "and" (or "also") (van Roon 1974:80-85; Lincoln 1990:3-4), have not gained acceptance because they have no manuscript support.

The best solution, in my opinion, is to accept "in Ephesus" as the original reading (see Hoehner 2002:146-148). This is also the opinion of several scholars (Conzelmann 1965:56; Gnilka 1971:6; Barth 1974:67; Arnold 1993:243-245). It has good manuscript support. Within the Alexandrian text-type there are Codex Alexandrinus (A), some important minuscules, and the early versions such as Coptic and Vulgate, all of which give very good Alexandrian support. Furthermore, there is solid Western and Byzantine manuscript tradition for the inclusion of these words. All the manuscripts that do mention a name always have "Ephesus" and no other city. Regarding internal evidence, the omission may have been accidental, which would explain why this phenomenon appears in so few manuscripts within only one text-type. Although the canons of a shorter reading and more difficult reading are preferred, Griesbach (as cited in Metzger 1992:120), who proposed both of these canons, was careful to point out that if the shorter reading utterly lacks sense and is out of keeping with the style of the author, the longer reading is to be preferred. This is certainly true here, for other Pauline letters mention the locale to which they were sent (cf. Rom 1:7; 1 Cor 1:2; 2 Cor 1:1; Phil 1:1).

Although it is best to accept the inclusion of "in Ephesus," the contents of the letter may suggest more than one church in Ephesus. There may well have been many house churches rather than one large church in Ephesus and in western Asia Minor. On his third missionary journey, Paul ministered for two and a half years and may have, with the help of his disciples, founded many churches in the area of Ephesus. The impersonal tone of the letter and the lack of personal greetings, as in some of the other Pauline letters, is understandable if it was to go to many churches in the area. However, congregations in the city of Ephesus would still have been the center of activity and hence the letter was addressed to Ephesus.

The City and the Historical Setting. Today, the remains of ancient Ephesus are located about four miles inland from the Aegean Sea on the west coast of modern-day Turkey. However, the first-century geographer Strabo (64/63 BC—AD 21) describes the city as a seaport located about the middle of the western coast of the Roman province of Asia (Asia Minor) at the mouth of the Cayster River. Over the years the silting of the Cayster River made Ephesus a gulf city. In Paul's day it was difficult for large ships to dock at Ephesus, and perhaps this is one reason why Paul met the Ephesian elders at Miletus in AD 57 (Acts 20:16).

According to legend, the founders of the city were having difficulty in selecting a site for the city. They consulted an oracle, which told them to build a city wherever a fish and wild boar would lead them. Subsequently, some fishermen were cooking a meal when a fish with a live coal jumped out of the fire, fell into some straw, and ignited a thicket where a wild boar happened to be. Frightened, the boar fled but was pursued and killed at the place where the temple of Athena was later built. Outside this legendary account, there are records of Ephesus' existence that go back to around 1100 BC. There was a constant struggle between Greece and Anatolia (modern Turkey) for the possession of the western coast of Asia Minor. Anatolia came under Persian control in 546 BC and then under Greek control with the invasion of Alexander the Great in 334 BC. Finally, in 133 BC Ephesus came under Roman control, and Asia Minor was a Roman province until the fifth or sixth century AD.

Ephesus was a renowned city. Within its confines was the temple of Artemis, which was considered one of the seven wonders of the ancient world. It was rebuilt after its destruction by fire in 356 BC. According to the Roman writer Pliny (AD 23–79) the temple measured 225 by 425 feet with 127 columns 60 feet high and 6 feet in diameter. Some think that he refers to the temple platform and that the temple itself was 180 by 361 feet, an area slightly larger than an American football field (160 by 360 feet including end zones). It was one of the largest buildings known in antiquity.

Although there were many cults and religions in this ancient city, including emperor worship, the cult of Artemis was the most prominent. It was a great honor to be the temple warden of Artemis and of her image that fell from the sky (Acts 19:35). The goddess Artemis has a long history with many transformations due to Anatolian and Greek influences. Many statues of her have been found in the excavations in Ephesus. The lower halves of the statues have bulls, lions, and sphinxes, probably representing the animal world, which the Greek Artemis was supposed to have loved and protected. The upper half has two or three rows of bulbous objects on her chest, portraying among other things multiple female breasts, ostrich eggs, grapes, nuts, or acorns. This reflects Anatolian influence, namely, the life of gods embodying and representing the life of nature. It seems that Artemis was considered the legitimate wife of Ephesus, and she was the protector and nourisher of the city. Little is known about the mystery rites of Artemis, with only Strabo's brief mention of the annual festival commemorating her birth. Ephesus was known as a center for the practice of magic. Arnold (1989:22) notes that though Artemis was not by nature a goddess of magic, she was thought to have direct links with magical practices and to be very powerful in helping the devotees face opposing powers and spirits. The worship of Artemis was extensive. Demetrius, a silversmith in Ephesus, claimed that people throughout Asia Minor and the whole world worshiped Artemis (Acts 19:27). This claim is substantiated by Strabo, who mentions that there were temples of Artemis in Magnesia and Perge of Asia Minor, in Sparta of Greece, in Marseilles of France, and in Hemeroscopeium, Emporium, and Rhodus of Spain. The influence was worldwide with Ephesus as its headquarters.

Ephesus was also influential politically and commercially. Politically, it was the provincial capital of the senatorial province of Asia Minor. Commercially, it was the largest trading center in Asia Minor west of the Taurus Mountains (on the eastern end of Asia Minor). The mouth of the Cayster River provided a harbor for Ephesus (except for the largest ships in Paul's day) connecting shipping routes of the northern Aegean with Syria and Egypt to the east and with Italy via the Corinthian straits on the west. Furthermore, travelers on the main road from the East (Persia) who were heading to the West (Italy) would go through Ephesus. The city was considered the greatest metropolis of Asia Minor, ranking behind only Rome and Athens (and possibly behind Syrian Antioch and Alexandria), with an estimated population between 200,000 and 250,000.

The influence of Ephesus both as a secular and religious center emanated to the other parts of the Roman Empire. Paul seemed to select strategic cities such as this from which the influence of the gospel would spread to surrounding cities. He considered the gospel to be the power of God unto salvation to everyone who believes, whether they be Jews or Gentiles (Rom 1:16).

Paul's first contact with the Ephesians was on his second missionary journey. After his ministry in Corinth, Paul, accompanied by Priscilla and Aquila, arrived at Ephesus, probably in the autumn of 52. He remained there only a short time and then departed for Antioch, leaving Priscilla and Aquila behind (Acts 18:18-21).

Paul's second visit was on his third missionary journey when he remained there for approximately two-and-a-half years, most likely from the autumn of 53 to the spring of 56. Those converted under Paul's ministry gave up their magic practices and burned their magic books worth 50,000 pieces of silver, the yearly income of 137 men (Acts 19:11-20). The impact of his ministry had such an effect in the city that Demetrius, a leader of the local silversmiths' trade union, incited a mob against Christian teaching at the theater (Acts 19:23-41). His motive was less religious than economic. The problem was that, due to Paul's ministry, widespread conversion occurred. This meant that people were not purchasing the cultic paraphernalia of Artemis, and this created a significant income loss for the silversmiths. So Demetrius, in order to sway opinion, persuaded the crowds that Christianity was not only detrimental to their business, but it brought disrepute to the goddess Artemis, whom all Asia and the world worshiped. The message of Christianity was making inroads into Asia Minor. Paul's message reached both Jews and Gentiles (Acts 19:10, 17; 20:21). After leaving Ephesus he ministered in Macedonia and Greece, and on his return he visited the Ephesian elders at Miletus in the spring of 57, where he reminded them of his ministry, warned them about false teachers, and prayed with them before his departure (Acts 20:15-38).

CANONICITY AND TEXTUAL HISTORY

The canonicity of Ephesians is supported by the fact that it was included in the earliest collections of New Testament writings circulating in the early church. Paul's major epistles (this would exclude the Pastoral Epistles) and the four Gospels were two collections that the early church read widely and esteemed as Scripture. Manuscripts evidencing a Pauline collection are as follows: $\mathfrak{P}$46 (second century, all of Paul's major epistles), $\mathfrak{P}$15+$\mathfrak{P}$16 (third century, from the same codex preserving portions of 1 Corinthians and Philippians), $\mathfrak{P}$30 (third century), $\mathfrak{P}$49+$\mathfrak{P}$65 (third century), and $\mathfrak{P}$92 (third century). (For further discussion, see Comfort 2005:34-37.) Paul's Epistle to the Ephesians appears in the oldest extant lists of books of the New Testament canon. It is also included in all the major New Testament canons, such as those indicated by Eusebius in his *Ecclesiastical History*, Athanasius of Alexandria in his *Festal Letters* (AD 367), and the Council of Carthage (AD 397).

As for the text of Ephesians, it is preserved in some early papyrus manuscripts ($\mathfrak{P}$46, $\mathfrak{P}$94, $\mathfrak{P}$92), as well as in the fourth-century codices Sinaiticus ($\aleph$) and Vaticanus (B) and the fifth-century codices Alexandrinus (A), Ephraemi Rescriptus (C), and Washington (I). These are good Alexandrian witnesses, the earliest being $\mathfrak{P}$46. The "Western" text of Paul's epistles, which includes Ephesians, is found in manuscripts such as the Greek-Latin diglots D, F, and G.

LITERARY STYLE

Genre. Since many papyri have been discovered in the last hundred years—many of which preserve ancient letters—there has been much discussion regarding the literary form of Paul's writings. It is thought that the Pauline Epistles follow the normal ancient pattern of Hellenistic letters—namely, opening, body, and closing. Although Ephesians is different in some regards, it is not out of character with other Pauline or Hellenistic letters. Normally, in the opening of the letter there is the greeting, followed by an introductory thanksgiving (e.g., 1 Cor 1:4; Phil 1:3; Col 1:3). In Ephesians there is an extended eulogy between the greeting (1:1-2) and thanksgiving (1:15-23). Though different, it is possible within normal letter writing. The body of a letter has much variation not only within Hellenistic circles but also within the Pauline corpus. Ephesians contains instruction (1:3–3:21), exhortation (paraenesis) (4:1–6:20), and commendation (6:21-22). As mentioned above, there is a eulogy (1:3-14) before thanksgiving (1:15-23), and it could be argued that the body of the letter begins with 2:1. However, since the eulogy contains instructions concerning God's eternal purpose, it seems best to view the body of the letter as beginning with 1:3. Both the second part of the letter body—paraenesis (4:1–6:20)—and the third part—commendation (6:21-22)—are in line with other letters of Paul. Also, the closing part of Ephesians (6:23-24) is similar to other letters of Paul, which leave out the customary well-wishing and farewell found in typical Hellenistic letters.

Because Ephesians does not address specific issues and lacks personal greetings typical of other Pauline letters, some see it more as a theological tractate, a baptismal liturgy in the form of a letter, or a homily, rather than a Hellenistic letter. Counter to this argument, it can be posited that other epistles like Romans do not address specific issues, and other epistles like 2 Corinthians, Galatians, 1 and 2 Thessalonians, and Philippians lack personal greetings. Moreover, the commendation of Tychicus as an emissary to the readers, and presumably the bearer of the letter, is meaningful only if there was a real letter for him to bear to real recipients. In conclusion, although there is a mixture of genre and styles within Ephesians, it can be classified as a letter similar to other Pauline letters and Hellenistic letters.

Structure. Like many other Pauline letters, Ephesians is divided into two parts: doctrine, chapters 1–3, and duties, chapters 4–6. After the prologue (1:1-2) the first part offers extended praise to God for all the spiritual benefits for those who are in Christ (1:3-14). This is followed by a petition for wisdom and revelation (1:15-23). Paul reminds the Ephesian believers of their lives before and after conversion (2:1-10) and of the union of believing Jews and Gentiles as one new man, the church (2:11-22). This new union is further explained in a parenthetical section—namely, the mystery of the union of Jews and Gentiles, of which Paul serves as steward for the Gentiles (3:1-13). Paul concludes this portion of the letter with a prayer that the Ephesian believers would utilize God's power and be strengthened in Christ's love, in order to make the union of believing Jews and Gentiles a reality.

The second portion of the letter deals with the application of these spiritual truths in the everyday lives of the believers in Christ. This portion is divided into six sections, five governed by the imperative "walk" (translated as "live" or "lead a life" in NLT; 4:1, 17; 5:2, 8, 15) and the final section that exhorts believers to be strengthened in the Lord in order to be able to stand against evil powers (6:10). The last four verses conclude the letter (6:21-24).

There are several links between the first and second half of the book. First, the term "walk," which has reference to conduct (or the way one lives life), is prominent throughout the book—both negatively (2:1-2; 4:17) and positively (2:10; 4:1, 17; 5:2, 8, 15). Second, the theme of love is prominent in the book. The noun and verb for "love" are used 20 times: 7 times in the first portion and 13 times in the second. The frequency of this concept in such a small book shows its importance. Love is to be practiced between believing Jews and Gentiles, who are united in one body, based on the love of God. Third, the Spirit is prominent in both portions: The Spirit is mentioned 8 times in the first half and 6 times in the second. The Spirit who seals and indwells the believers (1:13; 2:22) is the one who brings unity among them (4:3-4) and the means by which they are filled with God's moral excellence and power (5:18). Fourth, the concept of the church as the body of Christ is prominent. In the first part, the church is defined as Christ's body (1:22-23; cf. 5:23), composed of believing Jews and Gentiles (2:16). In the second portion, Paul speaks of the unity exhibited in one body (4:4), and gifted people are given to the church for the purpose of building up the body (4:12, 16). Fifth, the concept of mystery is prominent in both portions. The mystery that was hidden in past times is now revealed (3:3-5, 9)—namely, that believing Jews and Gentiles are united in one body. Paul asked for prayer to make known this mystery (6:19). Sixth, the power of the evil one is shown as the one who governed the lives of the Ephesians before conversion (2:2) and the one who was scheming against them once they became believers (6:10-20). Finally, the book begins with spiritual blessings (1:3-14) and ends with spiritual warfare (6:10-20).

MAJOR THEMES
Though there are no particular problems raised in the book, there has been much discussion regarding the purpose of Ephesians. Some scholars have suggested that Ephesians is concerned about baptismal liturgy (Dahl 1951:261-264; Kirby 1968:145-161), but the only reference to baptism (4:5) does not concern the ritual of baptism. Rather, baptism is simply listed as one of the uniting elements in the Christian faith. Barth (1974:47-48, 58-59) sees the Ephesian situation much like the parable of the Prodigal Son, where the son (like the Gentiles) returns not only to the father and the servants but also to the older son (analogous to Israel) who never left home. However, the stress in the book is not on reconciliation of all Jews and Gentiles, but the reconciliation of believing Jews and believing Gentiles. Schnackenburg (1991:34-35) mentions two scenarios: the first regarding the internal unity of the church because of the motif of one church founded by Christ, and the second regarding believers who are called to live a distinctly Christian lifestyle in contrast to the unbelievers' lifestyle. Along similar lines, Bruce (1984:245) suggests that believers are to appreciate their heavenly calling and destiny and to live accordingly. Arnold (1989:123-124, 167-172) sees Ephesians as a pastoral letter

addressing those who had been steeped in the evil spiritual "powers" (2:2; 6:12) of the cult of Artemis. The believers, he proposes, needed to recognize the real power in Christ as protection from those hostile powers, rather than resort to their former magical practices in combination with their Christian faith. This view has some merit, but again there is insufficient evidence from the letter itself to support this as the main purpose of the letter.

Most commentators agree that one dominant theme of Ephesians is unity. Patzia (1984:133-139) has made a good contribution in this area. The term "unity," not used elsewhere in the New Testament, is used twice in this letter (4:3, 13) and "one" (sometimes translated "same" in NLT) is used fourteen times (e.g., 2:14-16, 18; 4:4-7). The phrases "in Christ," "in whom," "in the Lord," or similar expressions occur 38 times in Ephesians, indicating the means by whom or the sphere in whom the unity is achieved. The Greek preposition *sun* [TG4862, ZG5250] (with, together with) is combined with fourteen words to denote union or unity (e.g., 2:5-6, 21-22; 3:6). Unity is depicted in the church, a term used nine times (e.g., 1:22; 3:10, 21), and the church is described by various metaphors: biological (the body of Christ: 1:22, 23; 2:16; 4:4, 12, 16; 5:23, 30), architectural ("a holy temple": 2:20-22; 4:12), and social (the wife: 5:21-33). Furthermore, this body is united under the head, Christ (1:22; 4:15; 5:23).

Although unity is a dominant theme, how is it achieved? Forced unity is unacceptable because it is not genuine; it must originate from within. It must come from love, which is a dominant theme in the book. Nearly a third of Paul's uses of the verb "to love" are found in Ephesians (10 out of 34 uses). The noun form also occurs 10 times in Ephesians out of a total of 75 times in all of Paul's letters; that is, 1 out of every 7½ times Paul uses the noun, he uses it in Ephesians. The frequent use of "love" in such a short book is notable. Out of the 20 occurrences of "love" in Ephesians, 8 refer to God's or Christ's love for humanity (e.g., 2:4; 5:2), 11 refer to the believers' love for one another (e.g., 4:2, 16), and one refers to the believers' love for Christ (6:24). Love in action within the community of believers fosters unity.

The theme of love is further substantiated in light of Paul's contacts with the Ephesians. When he met with the Ephesians elders at Miletus (AD 57) at the end of his third missionary journey, Paul told them that he had labored in love among them—by teaching, preaching, and giving. He warned them that evil teachers from without and within would attempt to disrupt them (Acts 20:18-35). After his Roman imprisonment, Paul reiterated the theme of love when he wrote to Timothy at Ephesus (c. AD 62), stating that the goal of his instruction was "love that comes from a pure heart, a clear conscience, and genuine faith" (1 Tim 1:5). He again warned them of false teachers and their teachings (1:3-20). Paul's ministry to the Ephesians continually emphasized love.

The only other time the Ephesian church is addressed in the New Testament is in Revelation 2:1-7. The messenger compliments the church at Ephesus for their refusal to tolerate false teachers but reprimands them for their failure to maintain the vibrancy of their first love for Christ (Rev 2:2-6). This demonstrates that it is not enough to separate from false teachers without maintaining love for Christ, which, if they had maintained it, would not only have given them wisdom and power to separate themselves from false teachers but also the ability and desire to love one another.

In conclusion, the theme of love has a dominant place within the book of Ephesians and in the other instance where the Ephesian church is addressed. It seems reasonable to conclude that the purpose of Ephesians is to promote love for one another with the love of God and Christ as its basis. Such love provides the basis for unity among believers. Paul, possibly realizing that the Ephesians were starting to forsake their first love, wrote this letter to encourage them to love both God and their fellow believers more deeply.

THEOLOGICAL CONCERNS

Ephesians, rich in theological themes, in large measure summarizes the leading themes in Paul's letters. Some of these are as follows.

The Trinity or Triune God. Ephesians is known as the Trinitarian letter. The activity of the three persons of the Trinity is found in eight passages (1:4-14, 17; 2:18, 22; 3:4-5, 14-17; 4:4-6; 5:18-20). In the opening eulogy (1:3-14), God is praised for the spiritual blessings bestowed on believers. These blessings are based on the work of the three persons of the Trinity: the selection of the Father (1:4-6), the sacrifice of the Son (1:7-12), and the seal of the Holy Spirit (1:13-14). Paul prays that God, who is identified as the Father of Jesus Christ, will give the Ephesians "a spirit of wisdom" (1:17, NRSV), which is best identified with the Holy Spirit himself. In the body of the letter, the believers are said to have access to God the Father through Christ in one Spirit (2:18). Paul speaks of the Father as the one who creates the new humanity into a holy temple. Christ, through his reconciliation, is the cornerstone of this new temple, and God dwells in this new structure by his Spirit (2:22). It is God the Father who reveals the mystery of Christ (believing Jews and Gentiles in one body) by means of the Holy Spirit (3:3-5). Paul himself prays to the Father that Ephesian believers might be strengthened by the Spirit so that Christ may be permanently at home in them through faith (3:14-17). The role of the Trinity is also prominent in the practical portion of the letter (chs 4-6). Paul exhorts believers to walk in the unity provided by the Trinity (4:4-6). Finally, Paul states that one of the results of being filled by the Spirit is that we as believers give thanks to the Father in the name of our Lord Jesus Christ (5:18-20).

Therefore, the work of the Trinity is important in Ephesians. It is the Father who is over all; he plans or initiates all things. It is the Son in whom the believers live; the Son is the one who carries out the Father's plan in redemption, reconciliation, and unification of believers. It is the Holy Spirit who seals, indwells, and empowers the believers.

Salvation. Having already discussed soteriology above (see Theological Distinctions), I need only to treat the subject briefly here. Though the specific terminology of justification is lacking in Ephesians, it is in line with Pauline teaching on salvation. Some consider the teaching in Ephesians 2:8-10 to be an able summary of Paul's doctrine of salvation by grace. This salvation is given on the basis of God's grace by means of faith apart from works (cf. Rom 3:20, 28; 4:2, 6; 9:11, 32; 11:6). Salvation is based on Christ's death on the cross (1:7; 2:13, 16; 5:2, 25), which provides believers access to the Father (2:18; 3:12). This salvation will be consummated in the future when God will redeem those he has already purchased (1:14; 4:30), and Christ will present them to himself without any imperfection (5:27). As elsewhere in Paul's writings, good works or fruit are not a basis *for* salvation but a result *of* it (2:10; Rom 6:22; Gal 5:22-23; Phil 1:11, 22; 4:17).

The Church or Ecclesiology. The term "church" appears nine times in Ephesians (1:22; 3:10, 21; 5:23-25, 27, 29, 32); it is always used in reference to a universal church, never to a local church. This is somewhat unusual, but Paul elsewhere did have the concept of the universal as well as the local church when, for example, he addressed the Corinthian church and also "all people everywhere who call on the name of our Lord Jesus Christ" (1 Cor 1:2). In Ephesians the church is depicted biologically as the body of Christ (1:22; 4:16; 5:23-25, 29); architecturally as the holy temple (2:20-22); psychologically as the new person (2:15; 4:13); sociologically as a wife (5:23-32) a reconciled unity between two hostile groups (2:11-22), yet at war with the evil spiritual powers (6:10-20); topologically as located in the heavenly realms (1:3; 2:6); and cultically as that which Christ sanctifies in order to present it to himself as glorious, blameless, and holy, without any imperfections (5:26-27).

The church's existence and function is based on Christ's work (1:22; 5:2, 23-27, 29; cf. 1 Cor 1:2; 15:3). Its foundation is made up of apostles and prophets, with Christ as the cornerstone (2:20-22). Christ has enriched it with gifted people for ministry so that it might continue to grow (4:11-16; cf. also 2:21; 3:18-19). Christ also strengthens the church so that it can stand against the evil powers in the heavens, who desire to rob the church of her blessings (6:10-20).

Reconciliation. Paul wrote about reconciliation in other letters, but much emphasis is given to it in Ephesians. In the beginning of the first chapter, he outlines the eternal plan of God with its purpose to unite all things in Christ (1:10). Because of sin, there is a great gulf between God and humanity, but God, displaying his rich mercy and great love, reconciled us to himself by saving us completely—even to the extent that we are united to Christ (2:1-10). Beyond this, there is a reconciliation of Jews and Gentiles who put their faith in Christ for the purpose of creating one new humanity, the church—with the further purpose of reconciling both to God, making an end of hostility between God and humanity (2:11-22). Within this passage reconciliation is stressed by the expressions "united Jews and Gentiles into one people" (2:14), "one new people" (2:15), "one body" (2:16), "all of us can come to the Father through the same Holy Spirit" (2:18), "citizens along with all of God's holy people" (2:19), "God's family" (2:19), "joined together" (2:21), and "a holy temple" (2:21). This new entity of the church, according to God's eternal purpose, was not known in previous generations but now has been revealed by the Spirit to the apostles and prophets. Paul was specifically commissioned to proclaim this to the Gentiles (3:1-12). Further, the theme of reconciliation is seen in the expressions "Both are part of the same body, and both enjoy the promise of blessings" (3:6) and "we can now come boldly and confidently into God's presence" (3:12).

Finally, Paul prays that the believers might know the love of Christ, which surpasses knowledge (3:17-19) in the hope that the reconciliation is not just external but a reality of the heart. The evidence of reconciliation is that believers live in unity, which has its basis in the Trinity (4:1-6). In order to accomplish this, Christ gave gifts to the church so that the corporate body of believing Jews and Gentiles might continue to be built up until the unity of faith is realized in practical life (4:7-16). Believers are exhorted not to live as the Gentiles do but to develop an honest and loving relationship with one another (4:17–5:14). They are instructed to be filled by the Spirit, which results in praising, singing, and giving thanks to God the Father through Christ, all of which is evidence of their new spiritual unity due to Christ's reconciliation (5:15-20). Instructions regarding relationships of wives with husbands, children with parents, and slaves with masters are for the purpose of promoting harmony—another evidence of reconciliation (5:21-6:9).

The theology of reconciliation is prominent in this letter, and the heart of reconciliation is love. The basis of reconciliation between God and humanity is God's love (2:4) and Christ's love (3:17-19; 5:2). Likewise, the reconciliation of Jews and Gentiles is to be characterized by love for one another (1:15; 3:17-19; 4:2, 15-16; 5:2, 25, 28, 33; 6:23). Reconciliation with love is genuine reconciliation because it reveals a change of heart and a mutual trust of one another.

OUTLINE
   I. The Calling of the Church (1:1–3:21)
      A. Prologue (1:1-2)
      B. Praise for God's Planned Spiritual Blessings (1:3-14)
         1. The provision of spiritual blessings (1:3)
         2. The basis of spiritual blessings (1:4-14)
            a. God's election (1:4-6)
            b. God's redemption in Christ (1:7-12)
            c. God's seal with the Spirit (1:13-14)
      C. Prayer for Wisdom and Revelation (1:15-23)
      D. New Position Individually (2:1-10)
         1. The old condition: dead to God (2:1-3)
         2. The new position: alive in God (2:4-10)
      E. New Position Corporately (2:11-22)
         1. Statement of the union (2:11-13)
         2. Explanation of the union (2:14-18)
         3. Consequence of the union (2:19-22)

COMMENTARY ON
Ephesians

◆ **I. The Calling of the Church (1:1–3:21)**
  A. Prologue (1:1–2)

This letter is from Paul, chosen by the will of God to be an apostle of Christ Jesus.

I am writing to God's holy people in Ephesus,* who are faithful followers of Christ Jesus.

²May God our Father and the Lord Jesus Christ give you grace and peace.

1:1 The most ancient manuscripts do not include *in Ephesus.*

NOTES

1:1 *This letter is from Paul.* As with other Pauline letters, Ephesians follows the normal pattern of Hellenistic letters with respect to its opening, body, and closing. The opening is similar to openings of other letters by Paul. As discussed in the Introduction, there has been considerable debate in recent centuries as to whether or not Paul is truly the author of this epistle. Although some differences exist when compared to the other Pauline letters, there is no reason to doubt Pauline authorship, which has the earliest attestation among the church fathers concerning any New Testament book (see Introduction).

chosen by the will of God to be an apostle of Christ Jesus. This statement is in keeping with other Pauline literature; it affirms that Paul was not self-appointed.

I am writing to God's holy people in Ephesus. "God's holy people" is rendered "saints" in other translations. It refers to people who have put their trust in Christ Jesus. The word "saints" (*hagiois* [TG40/A, ZG41]) does not imply inherent goodness but rather separateness, that is, people set aside to serve God (L&N 53.46). As indicated in the Introduction (see "Audience"), many scholars have questioned the reading "in Ephesus," because the words are lacking in the three earliest mss (𝔓46 ℵ B) and the tone of the letter is very impersonal, strongly suggesting it was an encyclical (Comfort 2005:345-346). However, the words "in Ephesus" have decent manuscript support with widespread geographical attestation (ℵ² A B² D F G 0278 33 𝔐 it syr cop) and are included in most English versions (KJV, NASB, NEB, NIV, NRSV, NLT). Notably, the letter is not addressed to a church in Ephesus, but to the saints in that city, and this may well mean that there were many congregations within the city and also that it may have been read by many churches started by Paul or his converts in the surrounding area, namely, western Asia Minor.

who are faithful followers of Christ Jesus. This may appear to imply that only faithful believers are being addressed. Actually in the Greek text it is not the relative pronoun "who" that introduces these words but the conjunction *kai* [TG2532, ZG2779] (and), which could be translated "that is," and the word "faithful" could be translated "believers"; the resulting translation would be "that is, believers in Christ Jesus." Hence, "God's holy people in Ephesus" are further defined as "believers in Christ Jesus."

1:2 *May God our Father and the Lord Jesus Christ give you grace and peace.* This is a greeting that is not unlike other Pauline letters (Rom 1:7; 1 Cor 1:3; 2 Cor 1:2; Gal 1:3; Phil 1:2; Col 1:2; 2 Thess 1:2; 1 Tim 1:2; 2 Tim 1:2; Titus 1:4; Phlm 1:3).

COMMENTARY

The writer of this letter immediately identifies himself as Paul, an apostle, belonging to and sent by Christ Jesus. The greeting is typical of letters in Paul's day. In modern Western culture, a letter begins with the address followed by the date of writing, then we greet the recipient: "Dear ____." The body of the letter follows with our name signed at the end. In Paul's day the writer began the letter by identifying himself or herself. Translating the Greek text literally, the letter begins, "Paul, an apostle of Jesus Christ through the will of God, to the saints in Ephesus." Here the sender is identified as Paul the apostle of Christ, and the recipients are identified as the saints who reside in Ephesus. The fact that he presents himself as an apostle of Jesus Christ gives Paul authority. An apostle is one who is sent as a messenger and who represents the full authority of the one who sent him or her. It is similar to a present-day ambassador who represents his or her country with the full authority of that country's government. Paul, as an apostle of Christ Jesus, had the full authority of Christ himself; therefore, he needed to be heard. To further enhance his claim as an apostle of Christ, Paul stated that this appointment was made through the will of God and not by self-appointment. As an ambassador is appointed by the head of state, so Paul was appointed by God to be his representative.

The recipients of the letter are "God's holy people" or literally "the saints." The Greek term for "saint" (*hagios* [TG40/A, ZG41]) can be translated "holy" and is used with reference to things, places, and persons. The term "holy" or "saint" did not indicate inherent goodness but rather that which was set aside for service. In fact, the related Hebrew root *qadash* [TH6942, ZH7727] was even used of foreign cult prostitutes (*qadash* [TH6945, ZH7728]; cf. Deut 23:17; 1 Kgs 14:24; 15:12; 22:46) that were set aside for "service" in temple ritual (TDOT 12.524). Today the term "saint" is used by some to identify those thought to have earned the title by holy living. However, the New Testament teaches that all who become believers in Christ are saints—that is, ones set apart for God's service. It is because of this position as saints that believers should live saintly lives. The fact that saints are not inherently holy is substantiated in Paul's letters, including Ephesians, where he exhorts saints to live holy lives. If saints were inherently holy, there would be no need for the exhortations. Paul further describes the saints as ones "who are faithful followers of Christ Jesus" or better "believers in Christ Jesus." Later (2:1-10) Paul writes that they were at one time unbelievers who were part of the world system, but by God's grace they were saved by faith. While the Ephesian believers were geographically located in Ephesus, they were spiritually positioned "in Christ." Paul used "in Christ Jesus," "in Christ," or "in him/whom" 11 times in 1:1-14. This applies to all Christians whether they live in Ephesus, Paris, Trivandrum, or San Francisco.

The greeting in verse 2 is not normal Greek style, but it accords with Paul's style in other letters (cf. Rom 1:7; 1 Cor 1:3; 2 Cor 1:2; Gal 1:3; Phil 1:2; 2 Thess 1:2;

Phlm 1:3). Instead of the normal Greek greeting "rejoice," Paul uses "grace" and "peace" which had become a distinctively Christian greeting (cf. 1 Pet 1:2; 2 Pet 1:2; 2 John 1:3; Rev 1:4). Grace speaks of God's favor in providing salvation for sinners through Christ's sacrificial death (e.g., 1:7; 2:8; Rom 3:23-24) and his empowering of the believer to lead a holy life (4:7, 29; 1 Cor 15:10). Peace was used as a common greeting in the Semitic world (*shalom* [TH7965, ZH8934]; Gen 43:23; Judg 19:20 [KJV]; 1 Sam 25:6), denoting the idea of "well-being" (Gen 29:6; 43:27; 2 Sam 18:29). In Ephesians it may signify the sinner's peace with God (e.g., 2:14, 17) and the believer's peace with others (e.g., 2:15; 4:3). Thus, grace expresses the motivation behind God's gracious work, and peace, the effect of God's work. Characteristic of Paul, these words of greetings are followed by "God our Father and the Lord Jesus Christ" (cf. Rom 1:7; 1 Cor 1:3; 2 Cor 1:3; Gal 1:3; Phil 1:2; 2 Thess 1:2; Phlm 1:3), indicating the source of grace and peace. God is not only called Father but "our" Father to denote personal relationship. Furthermore, grace and peace come not only from God but also from the Lord Jesus Christ. Since only one preposition is used to denote the source of grace and peace, from both the Father and the Son, it strongly implies that the Father and Son are equal and thus Jesus Christ is divine. In conclusion, then, believers are to appreciate and appropriate the grace that brought salvation and its resulting peace, both of which come from God our Father and the Lord Jesus Christ.

◆ ## B. Praise for God's Planned Spiritual Blessings (1:3-14)
1. The provision of spiritual blessings (1:3)

³All praise to God, the Father of our Lord Jesus Christ, who has blessed us with every spiritual blessing in the heavenly realms because we are united with Christ.

NOTES

1:3 who has blessed us with every spiritual blessing. The term "blessed" (*eulogeō* [TG2127, ZG2328]) is rather vague in English. In OT usage, to be blessed by God meant to receive benefits from God such as possessions, prosperity, or power. The term is used over 40 times in the NT, and though many times it is used when people "praise" God (e.g., Luke 1:64; Jas 3:9) or Jesus (Matt 21:9; Mark 11:9-10; Luke 19:38; John 12:13) and invoke God's enabling power (Luke 2:34; 24:50, 51; Heb 7:1, 6), it is also used, as in the present context, where God is the subject who "provides benefits" to the recipients (Matt 25:34; Acts 3:25, 26; Gal 3:9; Heb 6:14). This is followed with a cognate noun "blessing" (*eulogia* [TG2129, ZG2330]), which conveys the idea of "benefits" both in the OT (Gen 27:35-36, 38, 41; 49:25-26; Isa 44:3) and in the NT (Rom 15:29; Gal 3:14; Heb 6:7; 12:17; 1 Pet 3:9). Such usage is fitting in the present context. The nature of the enrichment or benefit is "spiritual." The sense, therefore, is that God has enriched us with every spiritual benefit necessary for our spiritual well-being.

in the heavenly realms. The heavenly realms (traditionally, "heavenlies") in classical Greek can refer to the place where the gods dwell and from which they come. This word appears in the LXX 5 times but only once in the canonical books (Ps 67:15; numbered 68:14 in English Bible) where it refers to the Almighty or possibly to God's rule. In the NT it occurs 19 times, 5 of which are in Ephesians (1:3, 20; 2:6; 3:10; 6:12). It has a local sense, denoting the place where the exalted Christ is and the place from which believers derive their spiritual blessings. Later Paul mentions evil hosts in the heavenly realms (3:10) and the believer's struggle with them in the present day (6:12). The spiritual benefits for the believers are from the heavenly realms and the unbelievers' opposition to the believers finds its source in wicked spiritual leaders who also reside in the heavenly realms (6:12). In other words, the struggles in the heavenlies are also played out on earth. Hence, the believers reside on earth having been enriched with every spiritual blessing in the heavenly realms necessary for their spiritual well-being.

because we are united with Christ. The phrase "in Christ" (or "in the Lord") occurs 36 times in Ephesians. It may convey the idea of instrumentality ("through Christ"), but surely it can have the local sense of "the place" in whom the believers are. It speaks of a definite union between the believer and Christ. Thus, it has the local sense of the believer being incorporated in Christ. The believer, who is united with Christ who is in heaven, partakes of the spiritual benefits from the heavenly realms.

COMMENTARY

Usually after the greeting Paul would give an introductory thanksgiving for the recipients of the letter. However, in this letter he first offered a paean of praise for God's benefits to the believers (1:3-14), which is then followed by thanksgiving (1:15-23). In the Greek text, verses 3-14 are one long sentence of 202 words, considered by one scholar to be the most monstrous sentence in the Greek language (Norden 1913:253). This is the first of eight lengthy sentences in the book (1:3-14, 15-23; 2:1-7; 3:2-13, 14-19; 4:1-6, 11-16; 6:14-20). Three of these (1:3-14, 15-23; 3:14-19) are praise and prayer, for which it is not unusual to have lengthy sentences. Even in present times, it is not uncommon in extemporaneous praise and prayer to have long, complicated sentences, with many subordinate clauses and phrases.

In the last hundred years there has been much discussion on the form and structure of this passage. In the final analysis, it appears that 1:3-14 is a eulogy (literally, "a well-speaking of," not reserved just for funerals) whose style accords with other Jewish-Hellenistic eulogies, but its content goes beyond them. In the abundance of descriptive words in this long, complicated sentence regarding God's purpose, plan, and action, there is form and development of thought. The form is demonstrated by the refrain "praise and glory to God" (1:12; see also 1:6, 14), which is given after mentioning each person of the Trinity in the order of the Father, Son, and Holy Spirit. The development is demonstrated by the progression from a pronouncement of praise to God (1:3), to a description of God's great plan and action (1:4-12), and finally to its application to the believers (1:13-14). This eulogy is a very fitting introduction to the letter as a whole.

In this eulogy, Paul calls upon the believers to praise "God, the Father of our Lord Jesus Christ." Praise means "to speak well of," and the one to be praised is the eternal God, who is further described as the Father of our Lord Jesus Christ. In the Old Testament, the title "Father" is rarely used to describe God, whereas in the New Testament more than 50 percent of the occurrences of the word "father" refer to God (250 times out of 413 total). Paul says God is the Father of "our Lord Jesus Christ." "Jesus" is his personal name, and the designation "Lord" indicates his status as master and his identity with Yahweh ("Jesus is Lord" was an early confession of the church—Acts 2:36; 8:16; 10:36; 11:17; 19:5; Rom 10:9; 14:9; 1 Cor 12:3; 2 Cor 4:5; Phil 2:11). His designation "Christ" is the Greek rendering of the Hebrew word *messiah;* it denotes that he is the promised, anointed one who would bring salvation.

The reason to praise God is twofold: for who he is—the eternal God—and for what he has done—having blessed us with every spiritual blessing in the heavenly realms. The verb "to bless" is rarely used in Greek literature, but, as stated above, it is frequently used in the Old Testament, where God is said to enrich his people with possessions, prosperity, or power. It is the opposite of a curse, which signifies a pronouncement of destruction. The nature of these God-given benefits is spiritual, having their source in the Spirit of God; they are supernatural, in contrast to that which is natural—originating from an earthly source. These spiritual benefits enable believers to live effectively here on earth by God's empowerment and enrichment. The number of benefits is indicated by the word "every," signifying the complete adequacy of these blessings for the believer's spiritual well-being. Also, the location of the source is significant because these spiritual benefits issue from the believers' union with Christ, with whom they are seated in the heavenly realms (2:6).

The text indicates that this provision of every spiritual benefit has already been made available, although the appropriation of them occurs during the course of the believer's lifetime. An analogy of this is God's promise to Joshua (Josh 1:3) that every place in the Promised Land on which he placed his foot had already been given to him, in accordance with God's promise to Moses. Although it had been given, it was not a reality until he placed his foot on it. It would have been unnecessary for Joshua to pray for land that already had been given to him. He was to place his foot on it by faith. Likewise, it is unnecessary for believers to pray for spiritual blessings already provided for them. The reason why believers do not receive spiritual benefits is not because God is stingy or they have not prayed for them, but because they are not appropriating by faith what God has already given to them. Every spiritual benefit is at our disposal for our spiritual well-being.

◆   ## 2. The basis of spiritual blessings (1:4-14)
a. God's election (1:4-6)

⁴Even before he made the world, God loved us and chose us in Christ to be holy and without fault in his eyes. ⁵God decided in advance to adopt us into his own family by bringing us to himself through Jesus Christ. This is what he wanted to do, and it gave him great pleasure. ⁶So we praise God for the glorious grace he has poured out on us who belong to his dear Son.*

1:6 Greek *to us in the beloved.*

NOTES

1:4 *Even before he made the world, God loved us and chose us in Christ.* The NLT text leaves out the adverb *kathōs* [TG2531, ZG2777], which conjoins verses 4-14 to verse 3. The adverb also indicates that the following verses serve as the basis of the spiritual benefits with which believers are enriched. The adverb could be rendered "even as" (ASV, RSV) or "just as" (NASB, NRSV), to signify that the way God enriches believers is through the work of the Trinity, as described in verses 4-14 (Gaugler 1966:29-30). But the adverb can also have a causal sense and may be rendered "because" or "for" (Eadie 1883:18; Best 1998:119). Such an interpretation would convey that spiritual benefits are "because of" or "on the basis of" the Father's election (1:4-6), the Son's redemption (1:7-12), and the Spirit's seal (1:13-14). Both concepts seem to be included: Spiritual benefits are the work of the Trinity, and the work of the Trinity is the basis of all spiritual benefits (Ellicott 1884:6; Hoehner 2002:175). The NLT uses the words "God loved us and chose us," whereas the Greek text reads simply "God chose us." Granted, "love" is in the text, but it is at the end of the verse in conjunction with being holy and without fault "in love," indicating that holiness is to be combined with love.

1:5 *God decided in advance.* This has reference to predestination, namely, that God has predetermined our destiny of adoption into God's family.

and it gave him great pleasure. This signifies the pleasure God takes in his plan for our adoption.

1:6 *So we praise God.* This refrain of praise is repeated after describing the work of the other two persons of the Trinity (1:12, 14).

C O M M E N T A R Y

Having established that God is to be praised because he has enriched believers with every spiritual benefit for their spiritual well-being, Paul now explains that these spiritual benefits are based on the work of the three persons of the Trinity: the selection of the Father (1:4-6), the sacrifice of the Son (1:7-12), and the seal of the Holy Spirit (1:13-14). The adverb that introduces verse 4 seems to indicate that the selection of the Father, redemption of the Son, and the sealing of the Holy Spirit serve as both the *way* ("just as") we have been enriched with spiritual benefits—and the *basis* ("because") of our enrichment.

In verses 4-6, Paul deals specifically with the work of God the Father. He begins by stating that God "chose us in Christ." Such an affirmation provides great comfort to believers, because if this were not the case, no one would be qualified to be in God's family. It is very clear, according to Romans 3:10-11, that there are none who are righteous and who seek God. This is best illustrated in the story of Adam and Eve. They were born without sin and had perfect fellowship with God. When they sinned and were alienated from God, they knew what they were missing, and yet they did not seek God; rather, God sought them (Gen 3:6-20).

The use of the verb "to choose" in the Bible has several interesting facets. First, in most instances in the Old Testament and New Testament, as it is here, God is the subject. God is also the subject in 1 Corinthians 1:27-28, the only other Pauline passage that uses the word. God chose the foolish, the weak, and the nobodies of this world to shame the wise, the strong, and the somebodies of the world (1 Cor 1:27-28). God chose us in Christ (1:4). God chooses those the world would not choose. Hence, God does not choose people because of some inherent strength or good character. This demonstrates his love without regard for human priorities. Second, the one who chooses does not choose blindly but in the light of all the known options. For example, Lot surveyed all the land before selecting the Jordan valley (Gen 13:11), Jesus selected the twelve disciples out of all the disciples who were following him (Luke 6:13; John 13:18; 15:19), and the church selected seven deacons out from among their number (Acts 6:5). In all these instances the options were known before the choice was made. God's choice of believers is in light of all the known options—namely, the whole of the human race. Third, there is no dislike of those who were not chosen. The choice of the twelve disciples (Luke 6:13) does not indicate that Jesus spurned other disciples. When God chose the tribe of Levi to serve as the priesthood (Deut 18:5), it was not based on his dislike for the other tribes. In fact, neither the Ephesian context nor any other context mentions those not chosen, much less gives indication of dislike toward them. Fourth, the choice is made on the basis of the elector's preference and not because the recipient had some legal claim on the subject. God chose the people of Israel because he loved them, not because he was obligated to them in some way (Deut 7:6-8; 10:15). Briefly, then, the elector is the initiator of the choice, the choice is not made randomly nor engendered by a whim, those who are not chosen are not necessarily disliked, and the choice is not made in payment for an obligation. On the contrary, the act of choosing is one of grace. Fifth, in the present context the choice was made "even before he made the world," in eternity past. In other words, the choice was made before there was any evidence of good or bad works, similar to the choice of Jacob over Esau (Rom 9:10-13). Knowing all the options, God chose each of his children in eternity past. If there were no election, none would be saved—it is an act of grace. God chose us for a purpose, namely, that we might "be holy and without fault in his eyes" (1:4). This was accomplished through Christ's redemption and the outpouring of the Holy Spirit. Although complete holiness will be achieved in eternity, the goal of believers is to live holy and blameless lives while here on earth.

"God decided in advance" (1:5) refers to predestination. The biblical discussion of predestination emphasizes more *what* God's children have been predestined to than *who* has been predestined. God has predestined us *to something*, here, it is namely adoption into God's family. In other words, the believers' predetermined destiny is their adoption as full-fledged sons of God through Jesus Christ, the agent of the adoption. The concept of adoption is also found in Romans 8:15, 23 and Galatians 4:4-7. In Roman culture, adoption normally occurred when a man had no children and would adopt a son, usually a teenager, by means of a minor court procedure. Once the young lad was adopted into the new family, he was no longer accountable to his natural father, only to his newly acquired father. Likewise, believers are now accountable to their new father, the heavenly father, and no longer to the old father, Satan (cf. John 8:38, 44), the ruler of the realm of the air (2:2). When they served Satan they were labeled as (literally) "sons of disobedience" and "children of wrath" (2:2-3). They are now children of God. This whole process of election and adoption as children in God's family was not a grim duty for God; rather, it gave him "great pleasure" (1:5). He was delighted to impart spiritual benefits to his children.

It is no wonder, then, that God is to be praised! Along with Paul all believers should "praise God for the glorious grace he has poured out on us who belong to his dear Son" (1:6). "Grace" refers to "undeserved favor," and the verb translated as "poured out" is the cognate verb of "grace" (*echaritōsen* [TG5487, ZG5923]), which is used only one other time in the New Testament where Mary is said to be "favored" (Luke 1:28). Hence, Paul praises God for the grace with which he "graced" us. The marvel is that he has given this grace because "we belong to his dear Son," or, literally, he graciously bestowed grace on us "in the beloved one." Of course, "the beloved one" is a reference to Christ, the Son God loves (Col 1:13). This reference to Christ furnishes the transition to the second person of the Trinity discussed in verses 7-12.

◆   ## b. God's redemption in Christ (1:7-12)

7He is so rich in kindness and grace that he purchased our freedom with the blood of his Son and forgave our sins. 8He has showered his kindness on us, along with all wisdom and understanding.

9God has now revealed to us his mysterious plan regarding Christ, a plan to fulfill his own good pleasure. 10And this is the plan: At the right time he will bring everything together under the authority of Christ—everything in heaven and on earth. 11Furthermore, because we are united with Christ, we have received an inheritance from God,* for he chose us in advance, and he makes everything work out according to his plan.

12God's purpose was that we Jews who were the first to trust in Christ would bring praise and glory to God.

1:11 Or *we have become God's inheritance.*

NOTES

1:7 *He is so rich in kindness and grace that he purchased our freedom with the blood of his Son and forgave our sins.* The purchase of freedom is a good way to define the word "redemption." Redemption is the payment of a ransom price in order to secure release (Morris 1965:16-18, 40-44). It was used in reference to slaves who were purchased and could be set free by the one who purchased them. The forgiveness of our sins further elaborates on our freedom. The term "forgiveness" means "to release" or "to cancel" and thus denotes a permanent release from the punishment for sins, which have been paid for by Christ's sacrifice. God no longer holds the sins against us. This further defines our freedom from the bondage that enslaved us. The noun *ploutos* [TG4148, ZG4458], "wealth, riches," is used 22 times in the NT, 15 times by Paul, 5 of which are in Ephesians (1:7, 18; 2:7; 3:8, 16) and means to have abundance, riches, or wealth. It took the wealth of God's grace to redeem and forgive the sinner. The cost of sin was the supreme sacrifice of God's Son, Jesus Christ.

1:8 *He has showered his kindness on us.* The verb translated "showered" (also in JB, NJB) has the basic idea of overabundance, hence it is rendered "lavished" in some translations (RSV, NASB, NEB, NIV, NRSV).

1:9 *God has now revealed to us his mysterious plan.* "God's secret plan" might be a better rendering of the Greek, "mystery of his will," because it eliminates the idea of a mystery that cannot be comprehended, or possibly is comprehended by only a certain few. Rather, the phrase signifies that this plan was not known because God had not yet chosen to reveal it. The term *mustērion* [TG3466, ZG3696] occurs 21 times in the LXX, 8 times in canonical books, all of them in Daniel (Dan 2:18, 19, 27, 28, 29, 30, 47 twice) referring to the content and interpretation of Nebuchadnezzar's dream, which no one but God could reveal. Jewish apocalyptic literature speaks of God's being and actions as great mysteries (*1 Enoch* 63:3). The mysteries were initially given only to seers who would selectively pass them on only to the wise (*4 Ezra* 12:36-38; 14:5-6, 45-47). In the Qumran literature mysteries were known only to God and hidden from humankind (1QS 11:5-6) but revealed to the Teacher of Righteousness who is to reveal them to the community (cf. 1QH^a 9:21 [1:21]). Only the fully initiated in the community are to appropriate the truths of the mysteries (1QS 9:18-19) but keep them hidden from the uninitiated (1QS 4:6). In the NT *mustērion* occurs 27 times, 20 times by Paul, 6 times in Ephesians (1:9; 3:3, 4, 9; 5:32; 6:19). According to Paul, a mystery is something known to God and is revealed by God to all believers and not restricted to the few. The content of mystery in Ephesians (except 5:32) is the union of believing Jews and Gentiles in one body, the church. It was hidden for ages in God but now is revealed to his holy apostles and prophets by the Spirit, being made known to all believers.

1:11 *we have received an inheritance from God.* The reading in the NLT mg, "we have become God's inheritance," reflects an alternative interpretation. The reading in the text denotes the believers' possession as a portion or a share of what God has, and it could be rendered "we were made partakers of the inheritance" or "we were appointed an inheritance" (NEB, JB, NJB; Abbott 1897:20; Schnackenburg 1991:62). The alternative reading denotes the believers as God's inheritance; it could be translated "we were made God's heritage" (KJV, ASV; Robinson 1903:146; Barth 1974:93-94; Hoehner 2002:226-227), much like Israel is called God's possession (Deut 4:20; 9:26, 29; 32:9) or treasure (Deut 7:6; 14:2).

for he chose us in advance, and he makes everything work out according to his plan. This does not refer to our election, as in 1:4; rather, it refers to our predestination as in 1:5 and would be better rendered "for his unchanging plan is the working out of all things just as he decided long ago."

1:12 *we Jews who were the first to trust in Christ.* This does not accurately reflect the Greek text. Rather than "trust," it should be rendered "hope." This first hope is a reference to the believers' hope, which is based on their experience of redemption and the revelation of God's secret plan to consummate all things in Christ, already discussed in verses 7-11. There are some who think the "we" in v. 12 refers to Jews and the "you" in v. 13 refers to gentile Christians. Others think that the "we" refers to Paul and those with him and the "you" to the Ephesian believers. A third opinion is that the interchange of "we" and "you" has no significance but is normal epistolary style. The first view is untenable for the following reasons. First, up to v. 12 the "we" in the eulogy stands for all Christians who are in Christ, and there is no indication in v. 12 that the "we" refers particularly to the Jews. Second, the personal pronoun "we" of v. 12 refers to the same people as the "us" in 1:5 and 8. Third, "our inheritance" in 1:14 is not just for Jewish Christians but for all. It would be odd for v. 12 to refer to Jewish Christians, v. 13 to gentile Christians, and v. 14 back to Jewish Christians. Fourth, the "hope" mentioned in v. 12 is no different from the hope that gentile Christians have in the parallel passage of Col 1:5. Fifth, Paul really does not take up the discussion of the Jews and Gentiles until 2:11, and in the discussion in 2:11–3:21 "we" is used of all believers, Jews and Gentiles, not just Jewish Christians.

bring praise and glory to God. This is a refrain of praise that is repeated after describing the work of the other two persons of the Trinity (1:6, 14).

COMMENTARY

Believers have been enriched with every spiritual benefit (1:3), which is first demonstrated in their selection by God the Father, who has, according to his unchanging plan, adopted them into his family (1:4-6). Now the second person of the Trinity, Christ, is introduced as the one through whom God provided both redemption (1:7) and wisdom to understand the mystery of his will (1:8-10) and by whom God obtained his inheritance of the believers (1:11-12). First, "he purchased our freedom with the blood of his Son" (1:7). As mentioned above, the idiom "purchased our freedom" is a rendering of the theological term "redemption," which is repeated in 1:14 and 4:30. Redemption is payment of a ransom price for the purpose of securing release; it was paid to free slaves. The picture in the present context shows our enslavement to sin and release from it. Although, by our own abilities we might overcome certain sins, our abilities are inadequate for our complete release, rendering us unprepared to stand before the judgment of a perfect God. But God in his rich mercy made payment to set us free from that bondage and thus from future judgment. God valued us so highly that the ransom paid to set us free was the blood of his Son shed on the cross. Some want to emphasize only the release and exclude the payment of ransom. Granted, the main import of redemption is release or setting free, but it does not exclude payment of ransom. It is not either–or but both–and. Otherwise, the mention of the payment through the blood of his Son would be pointless. This is bolstered by the next words, "and forgave our sins." The term "forgiveness" means a permanent cancellation of or release from the punishment of sin since it has been paid for by Christ's sacrifice. Redemption is the cause of our release from punishment, and forgiveness is the effect. God is not lenient with sin, as is exhibited in the high cost of redemption, the supreme sacrifice of Christ. As such, Paul spoke of God being rich in kindness.

Second, not only has God's kindness been exhibited in redemption, but he has also enabled us to understand his will (1:8-10) by providing us with "all wisdom and understanding" (1:8). "Wisdom" in the Old Testament refers to a combination of theoretical and practical knowledge, which results in skillful living (Exod 35:31, 35; Prov 4:11); true wisdom is apparent in those who fear the Lord (Job 28:28; Prov 9:10). It is insight into the true nature of things. Here it is insight into the true nature of God's revelation. Understanding conveys the sense of discernment of the relevance of God's revelation in the present time. The declaration that "all" wisdom and understanding has been showered on us does not mean that we have wisdom and understanding in all things but that we are given all wisdom and understanding sufficient to live wisely in the present age and to understand God's plan for the ages. The manner in which he showers us with kindness is by revealing God's secret plan, which is centered in Christ (1:9). God's "secret plan" might be a better rendering of "mystery of his will" because it does not connote an incomprehensible mystery that a few, if any, might understand. Rather, it is hidden truth that no one can discern until God chooses to reveal it. This secret plan was designed by God and centered on Christ long ago according to "his own good pleasure." God takes pleasure in revealing his plan to humanity in this age.

The goal of this secret plan is for everything in heaven and on earth to come under the authority of Christ (1:10). When will this occur? It appears that there are two stages. The initial stage refers to the present time, based on Christ's work on the cross (1:7; 2:16) and his exaltation (1:20-21; 2:6-7), whereby all things are sub-jected to Christ. In his exaltation, God gave Christ to the church as head over every-thing, which would include headship over the church (1:22). The spiritual powers controlling people were broken by Christ's death and resurrection (2:1-6). Believers are given the ability to stand against spiritual foes (6:10-20). However, this verse seems to speak not only of the initial stage of the present age but more particularly to the final stage, which is yet future to us. This ultimate stage is the time when God will unite all creation under Christ's headship in the fullness of time, the age of Christ's rule, to which all creation looks forward (Rom 8:19-23). To be sure, the defeat of Satan's power was accomplished at the Cross, but at the present time God chooses to allow Satan's armies to continue in their opposition to him (2:2; 6:11-13; cf. 1 Pet 5:8). However, in the future age, all creation in heaven and on earth will be subject to Christ (1 Cor 15:24-28; Rev 19–21). There will be no oppo-sition. This will be the messianic age.

Third, believers not only experience God's kindness in redemption and the enablement to understand God's will, but they are also a part of God's inheritance (1:11-12). This inheritance could be taken as the believers' possession of God (the reading of the text) or that the believers are God's possession (the marginal read-ing). In the first option, it would appear that God predestines himself to be pos-sessed by believers. The latter reading seems to be more in keeping with the passive usage of *klēroō* [TG2820, ZG3103], which means "to be assigned"—hence, "to be assigned as God's inheritance." Furthermore, it fits better in the immediate context: "we are God's possession in order that we might praise him." This coincides with Israel, who was God's possession and treasure. Accordingly, believers are possessed by God and in turn possess every spiritual benefit. None of this was an accident but was according to God's plan in the working out of his purpose after careful deliberation in eternity past.

It is no wonder that we are to praise God. As praise marked the end of the first strophe with regard to God the Father (1:4-6), so praise ends this strophe with regard to God the Son (1:7-12). Briefly, God provides redemption in his Son, enables believers to understand his secret plan to head up all things in Christ, and makes believers his inheritance. Because of all this, believers have hope that is great cause to praise God's glory. How different is the outlook of life for those who have not believed, for they have no hope and no knowledge that their sins have been forgiven.

◆   ### c. God's seal with the Spirit (1:13-14)

13And now you Gentiles have also heard the truth, the Good News that God saves you. And when you believed in Christ, he identified you as his own* by giving you the Holy Spirit, whom he promised long ago. 14The Spirit is God's guarantee that he will give us the inheritance he prom-ised and that he has purchased us to be his own people. He did this so we would praise and glorify him.

1:13 Or *he put his seal on you.*

NOTES

1:13 *he identified you as his own by giving you the Holy Spirit.* This refers to the sealing of the Spirit, which identifies believers as God's own and gives them the security that they belong to him (cf. 4:30; 2 Cor 1:22).

1:14 *The Spirit is God's guarantee that he will give us the inheritance he promised.* The seal of the Holy Spirit is an initial installment that will continue until he redeems or sets free his possession that he purchased on the Cross. This alludes to the time when Christ will return and set the believers free from the presence of sin. Furthermore, this is an installment of our inheritance (*klēronomia* [TG2817, ZG3100]). Whereas in verse 8 believers are identified as God's inheritance, the present verse reverses it and speaks of God's Spirit as the believers' inheritance. A better translation might be "who is the initial installment of our inheritance, until the redemption of the purchased possession."

COMMENTARY

Believers have been enriched with every spiritual benefit (1:3), as seen in their selection by God the Father, who has adopted them into his family, redeemed them, and revealed to them his eternal purpose. He has also given them the Holy Spirit of promise, with whom they are sealed until he sets his purchased possession free (1:13-14).

Paul mentioned that the believers had heard the Good News that God saved them in Christ when they believed. At the time of salvation, they were sealed with the promised Holy Spirit. This seal denotes identification of ownership (cf. 4:30; 2 Cor 1:22; Rev 7:3-8; BDAG 980; L&N 33.484). A present-day example would be a rancher who brands his cattle to indicate his ownership. So the sealing ministry of the Holy Spirit identifies those who trust in God's provision of salvation and are now owned by God. This fits well with the previous verses because believers are God's inheritance (1:11). The seal of the Holy Spirit was "promised long ago." The prophets promised that the Spirit would appear when the new covenant was initiated (Ezek 36:26-27; 37:14; cf. also Joel 2:28-29). Christ also told his disciples that he would send the Spirit (Luke 24:49; John 14:16-17; 15:26; Acts 2:33; Gal 3:14; cf. also John 16:13; Acts 1:5; 10:47). Thus, God seals believers in Christ with the promised Holy Spirit when they have not only heard but also believe the gospel of salvation.

The sealing with the Spirit must not be confused with the other ministries of the Spirit. The Spirit resides in every believer (Rom 8:9; 1 John 2:27). The baptizing ministry of the Spirit places believers into the body of Christ (1 Cor 12:13). The filling by the Spirit indicates the Spirit's control over believers' lives (5:18). Finally, the sealing ministry of the Spirit identifies believers as God's own and thus gives them the security that they belong to him (1:13; 4:30; 2 Cor 1:22). Furthermore, it should be noted that the indwelling, baptizing, and sealing ministries of the Spirit are bestowed on every believer at the moment of conversion. There are no injunctions regarding them because they are an integral part of the gift of salvation. This is not to be confused with the exhortation to believers to be continually filled by the Spirit—from the moment of their conversion to the end of their lives here on earth.

This seal of the Holy Spirit also serves as a deposit or down payment, providing a guarantee of more to come. It is the initial installment of the believers' future inheritance. As ones adopted into God's family with all the accompanying privileges, we have an inheritance from God that qualifies us to live eternally in his presence in heaven. The initial installment of the Holy Spirit is a little bit of heaven in the believers' lives—with a guarantee of much more yet to come. This initial deposit continues literally "until the redemption of the purchased possession." God is going to set free what he had already purchased. The purchased possession refers to Christ's redemption, accomplished on the cross to set believers free from sin and its obligation. There is going to be a second phase of redemption in the future, when Christ comes for believers, who will then be set free from the presence of sin. This is analogous to Romans 8:23, where it says that believers who have been adopted into God's family (1:5; Rom 8:15) have the firstfruits of the Spirit and are now eagerly awaiting Christ's return to fully realize their adoption, the redemption of their bodies. In the meantime, we have the initial installment, the Holy Spirit, as our portion.

As praise marked the end of the first strophe with regard to God the Father (1:4-6) and the end of the second strophe with regard to God the Son (1:7-12), so praise ends this strophe with regard to God the Spirit (1:13-14). The knowledge that we are sealed with the Holy Spirit until Christ's coming to free us from sin causes us to praise God.

◆ C. Prayer for Wisdom and Revelation (1:15-23)

15Ever since I first heard of your strong faith in the Lord Jesus and your love for God's people everywhere,* 16I have not stopped thanking God for you. I pray for you constantly, 17asking God, the glorious Father of our Lord Jesus Christ, to give you spiritual wisdom* and insight so that you might grow in your knowledge of God. 18I pray that your hearts will be flooded with light so that you can understand the confident hope he has given to those he called—his holy people who are his rich and glorious inheritance.*

19I also pray that you will understand the incredible greatness of God's power for us who believe him. This is the same mighty power 20that raised Christ from the dead and seated him in the place of honor at God's right hand in the heavenly realms. 21Now he is far above any ruler or authority or power or leader or anything else—not only in this world but also in the world to come. 22God has put all things under the authority of Christ and has made him head over all things for the benefit of the church. 23And the church is his body; it is made full and complete by Christ, who fills all things everywhere with himself.

1:15 Some manuscripts read *your faithfulness to the Lord Jesus and to God's people everywhere.* 1:17 Or *to give you the Spirit of wisdom.* 1:18 Or *called, and the rich and glorious inheritance he has given to his holy people.*

NOTES

1:16 This first half of the verse continues the sentence begun in 1:15. The NLT shows this by its punctuation: A comma is placed at the end of 1:15, and a period is placed at the end of the first half of 1:16.

1:17 *God, the glorious Father of our Lord Jesus Christ.* The Greek reads, "God of our Lord Jesus Christ, the Father of glory." "The Father of glory" (a unique expression in the NT), whom Paul addresses as "God, the glorious Father," is a further description of God. It encompasses the idea that God is the source of Jesus' splendor and also that glory is his characteristic feature.

spiritual wisdom and insight. Lit., "spirit of wisdom and revelation." There are two problems with this translation. First, translating *apokalupsis* [TG602, ZG637] as "insight" rather than "revelation" is misleading because human understanding or ingenuity is not capable of discerning God's way. This can be accomplished only when God unveils it. Second, the word "spirit" may refer to the human spirit or the Holy Spirit. Those who prefer the human spirit think it refers to the attitude or spiritual disposition toward insight and openness to revelation. Others think it refers to the Holy Spirit because the qualities of wisdom and revelation cannot be generated by humans. The latter view is preferred because, though the "spirit of wisdom" may be defined as "a wise disposition," the same cannot be applied to the "spirit of revelation," for revelation (*apokalupsis* [TG602, ZG637]) is not the understanding of hidden things but the disclosing of them (Salmond 1903:273-274). The context of the book supports the idea that revelation comes by God's Spirit and not the human spirit (3:3-6), for as already stated, the human spirit cannot disclose the hidden mysteries of God. Furthermore, even those who think "spirit" refers to human spirit admit that the disposition is not self-generated but generated by the Holy Spirit. So ultimately the source is the Holy Spirit.

1:18 *I pray that your hearts will be flooded with light.* This is translated as a request and means that Paul prayed that God might give them the spirit of wisdom and revelation and also that their hearts would be flooded with light. However, instead of a request, the structure of the original text, though difficult, may better support the idea that this is an ancillary thought to the request. Hence, Paul prays that God would give them the spirit of wisdom and revelation since their hearts were flooded with light (presumably when they first responded to the gospel—see 1:3-14).

who are his rich and glorious inheritance. The verb for inheritance was used in verse 11 and the noun for inheritance (*klēronomia* [TG2817, ZG3100]) is used in verses 14 and 18. The marginal reading in verse 18, "the rich and glorious inheritance he has given to his people," indicates that God has given believers an inheritance. The reading of the text is preferred.

1:19 *I also pray that you will understand the incredible greatness of God's power for us who believe him. This is the same mighty power.* There are four words for power in this verse. First, is the word *dunamis* [TG1411, ZG1539], which means "power, ability, capability of acting"—with the sense of being living and dynamic. This power is further described as "incredible greatness" to indicate that it is God's active power or the ability of God himself. It is also defined by the other three words for power. Second, is the word *energeia* [TG1753, ZG1918], from which we derive the word "energy"; it has the idea of power that is in actual operation—or as here, the active exercise of supernatural power. Third is *kratos* [TG2904, ZG3197], which means "strength, might," and has the sense of dominion or mastery—the ability to overcome resistance. Fourth, is the word *ischus* [TG2479, ZG2709], meaning inherent "strength" or "power." In full force, God's dynamic power consists of his inherent strength that is actively able to overcome resistance.

1:20 *seated him in the place of honor at God's right hand in the heavenly realms.* This phrase refers to Psalm 110:1 ("The LORD said to my Lord: 'Sit in the place of honor at my right hand until I humble your enemies, making them a footstool under your feet")," the OT passage most often quoted in the NT. In the present context it shows that God exercised his power in raising Christ and then seated him at his right hand. This is an exalted position with all authority (cf. Matt 28:18) and this same power is available to believers to appropriate in their lives.

1:22 *God has put all things under the authority of Christ.* This is a good translation of
the literal "put all things under his [Christ's] feet."

has made him head over all things for the benefit of the church. This is a very difficult
text to translate and understand. There has been much discussion as to whether "head"
connotes "authority" (Grudem 1985) or "source" (Bedale 1954:211-215). The word itself
seems to suggest "preeminence" or "prominence" (Cervin 1989), and the context determines its meaning. In this context "authority" is surely correct because earlier in the verse,
Paul stated that God had put all things under Christ's feet, which means he gave him
authority over everything. The text reads literally, "he [God] gave him [Christ] as head over
everything to the church" or it could be read "he gave him (as the one who has authority
over everything) to the church." It can not mean "he gave him authority," as if "authority"
were the direct object; rather, "him" is the direct object, with "the church" as the indirect
object: "he gave him to the church." The verse does not specifically say that God made
Jesus head of the church, but that Christ gave to the church the one who has authority
over everything. However, having authority over everything implies that Christ also has
authority over the church.

1:23 *it is made full and complete by Christ, who fills all things everywhere with himself.*
Lit., "the fullness of him who fills all in all." This is a complex passage to interpret because
in the Greek text "fill" is used twice, once as a verb and once as a noun. Furthermore, the
adjective "all" or "every" is used twice. To further complicate matters, the verb could be
taken as passive or middle, the noun could be rendered in an active or passive sense, and
"all/every" could be interpreted adjectively or adverbially. Of the many interpretations, two
come to the forefront: (1) "the church fills or completes Christ who fills all things" (KJV,
ASV, RSV, NASB, NIV, NRSV; Abbott 1897:35-38; Robinson 1903:42-45, 255-259), and
(2) "the church is filled by Christ who is being filled [by himself or more likely by God]
entirely or in every way" (JB, NEB, NJB; Westcott 1906:28; Best 1998:185, 188; O'Brien
1999:150-151; Hoehner 2002:298-300). The first interpretation is unlikely because it suggests that Christ is incomplete and that the church will make him complete. Such a concept
is unknown in the NT. Furthermore, in the first interpretation it is difficult to know the
import of the adjective "all." The second interpretation, which states that Christ fills the
church, accords with Pauline thought (cf. 3:19; 4:10, 13; Col 2:9-10). Moreover, this view
allows sense to be made of the adjective "all." It may well have the idea that the church is
being filled by Christ, who is being filled wholly, entirely, or in every way by God. This
appears to be the general interpretation taken by the NLT. One must take care not to interpret the NLT's rendering "who fills all things everywhere with himself" as implying panthe-
ism, which views God as existing in everything including inanimate objects. It is better to
view it in terms of the church being filled with God's divine attributes. The church receives
its fullness from Christ, who is receiving complete fullness from God.

COMMENTARY

Having completed the magnificent eulogy, Paul offered a prayer for the believers—
believers who had been given every spiritual benefit, including election, adoption,
grace, redemption, forgiveness, insight, knowledge of God's secret plan, and the
sealing of the Holy Spirit. He prayed that they would deepen their relationship with
God and that they would experience in a deeper way the spiritual benefits with
which they have been enriched. As usual, Paul began the prayer with commendation (1:15-16a), followed by his supplication before God on their behalf (1:16b-
23). This prayer is the second of eight long sentences in this epistle (1:3-14, 15-23;

2:1-7; 3:2-13, 14-19; 4:1-6, 11-16; 6:14-20)—with 169 words. In Scripture it is not unusual to have lengthy sentences in prayers.

According to this prayer, the believers' spiritual progress had developed in two ways (1:15). First, Paul noted their believing relationship with Christ—the personal pronoun "your" indicates a personal and active faith in their Lord Jesus. This is not speaking of initial faith but of continuing faith. Prior to Paul's ministry among these believers, many had placed their trust in the gods—particularly, Artemis, a favorite goddess among the Ephesians and those in the surrounding area. Second, Paul noted their love for Christians everywhere. It is important to recognize that this love was not directed to the world in general but to Christians in particular who are throughout the world. True faith in God should result in love for fellow believers (cf. 1 John 2:9-11; 4:19-20), thus showing to the world that they are disciples of the Lord (John 13:35). It was because of their ongoing faith in the Lord Jesus and their constant love for their fellow believers that Paul continually thanked God for them.

Paul's prayer was directed to "God, the glorious Father of our Lord Jesus Christ." In other words, God is the Father to whom all glory belongs (as stated in the NEB, "the all-glorious Father"). "Glory" speaks of the awesomeness of God, and "Father" signifies approachability. The one request that Paul makes here is stated with great elaboration. His one request is that the believers might be given "spiritual wisdom and insight." He was not praying for them to be given the Holy Spirit, for they already had the Holy Spirit; rather, he was praying for a specific manifestation of the Spirit so that they would have insight and know more of God as a result of the Holy Spirit's revelation. In fact, he stated that the object of the Spirit's insight and revelation is knowledge of God himself. This ministry of the Holy Spirit is necessary because humans lack the ingenuity to know God. Elsewhere, Paul states that the Holy Spirit searches the deep things of God and reveals them to believers (1 Cor 2:10-16). The deep things of God are God's wisdom and power to change individuals through the crucified Christ. Paul prayed that the believers would know him and, as a result, become acquainted with God's actions described in the following verses.

The goal, then, is to know God personally and intimately, not just to acquire facts about him. One can know many facts about the leader of a nation through the news media, but that is quite different from personally knowing that leader in the same way that his or her family does. Likewise, one may know facts about God by reading the Bible, but the only way to really know God personally is by the Holy Spirit's wisdom and revelation. In the end, philosophy exhorts "know yourself," whereas Christianity exhorts "know your God" through the Holy Spirit. This knowledge of God is available to all Christians and not just to the apostles, prophets, or a select group within the community.

Paul's Threefold Prayer Request. Was Paul's request that God would give the Ephesian believers the spirit of wisdom and revelation in the knowledge of God an impossible request? Not at all; their hearts were already flooded with light when they responded to the message of the gospel. What is the purpose of this request?

It is threefold—that they might know (1) the wonderful future promised to those God called (1:18b), (2) the richness of his inheritance in the believers (1:18c), and (3) his mighty power for the believers (1:19-23). Paul was not asking God for these three items, for the Ephesians already possessed them. Rather, he was asking that the believers might grasp these concepts as a result of knowing God more intimately. The following explains each more fully.

The first thing to be grasped is the wonderful hope promised to those God has called (1:18b). Inextricably bound with this future hope is the reason for the hope, namely, God's call on their lives in the past. The promise of eternity future is assured only because of God's plan in eternity past.

The second matter to be comprehended is the wealth of God's glorious inheritance in the believers (1:18c). As mentioned in the notes, the marginal reading suggests that the "glorious inheritance" is God, whom the believers possess, but the reading in the text indicates that the "glorious inheritance" is the sum total of all the believers whom God owns. The two readings indicate the difficulty in interpreting the text. The context better supports the interpretation that the believers are God's inheritance. This corresponds to 1:11, where the believer is assigned as God's inheritance. Because he chose, redeemed, adopted, and sealed us, we are his possession. Not only do we have an inheritance (1:14), but God also has an inheritance (1:11, 18). This demonstrates that believers are valuable to God because he purchased them in order to inherit them. This inheritance will be fully realized in the future.

The third concept to be grasped is the greatness of God's power, which he gives to the believers (1:19-23). Whereas the first and second concepts concern the past and future respectively, the third concerns the power of God for his believers in the present time. Paul first pointed to the magnitude of God's power and then to the manifestation of that power. He states that the extraordinary greatness of God's power is directed toward believers. The word that is used for power is *dunamis* [TG1411, ZG1539], from which the word "dynamite" is derived. However, there is no suggestion in the Bible that God's power is instantaneous or explosive, for dynamite was not invented until at least a millennium after Paul used the term. Rather, *dunamis* [TG1411, ZG1539] expresses a dynamic power or ability. This power is further described by three nouns: *ischus* [TG2479, ZG2709] depicts inherent strength, *kratos* [TG2904, ZG3197] portrays the force of power, and *energeia* [TG1753, ZG1918] delineates power in action. By way of illustration, a bulldozer has the ability, capacity, and potential strength of rooting out trees. One may sense its inherent strength (*ischus*), but when its engine roars and it begins to move, its force of power (*kratos*) becomes active (*energeia*) as it demonstrates its ability to topple trees in its path. Thus, an intimate knowledge of God enables believers to experience the incredible greatness of God's power available to them. This power is needed to survive the satanic and worldly systems that surround us.

The Manifestation of God's Power in Christ. It is one thing to understand the concept of power, but it is quite another to understand how this power operates. In 1:20-23, Paul explains that the power directed toward believers is the same power

(1) God exerted in raising Christ from the dead and seating him at his right hand (1:20-21), (2) by which God subjected all things under Christ's feet (1:22a), and (3) by which God gave Christ to the church as head (1:22b-23).

First, the active exertion of God's power in Christ occurred in the past when God raised Christ from the dead and seated him at his right hand in the heavenly realms (cf. 2:6; Rom 8:34; Col 3:1; Heb 1:3; 8:1; 12:2; 1 Pet 3:22). This same power is available to believers in the present (Phil 3:10) as a source of spiritual vitality and strength for living the Christian life (Col 1:11).

Paul then described the extent and duration of Christ's exaltation (1:21). Regarding the extent, Christ is "above any ruler or authority or power or leader or anything else." The references to ruler, authority, power, and leader are abstract and difficult to pin down. Although they could refer to human authorities, more likely they refer to angelic authorities. Other references to "powers" in this letter clearly affirm that they are angelic, as well as evil (6:11-12, 16). The last description "anything else" is literally "every name that is named." This is a comprehensive statement specifying that regardless of the designation or title a ruling power may have (whether in heaven or on earth), it is inferior to Christ, who is at the right hand of God. Christ's name is above every name (Phil 2:9)—a further indication of his majestic power.

The duration of Christ's exaltation is defined by the words "in this world but also in the world to come." Christ is not only presently above all powers, but he will continue forever in his position at the right hand of God. His position is all-powerful and all-enduring. Therefore, to know God is to realize his power that raised Christ from the dead and placed him permanently in the heavenly realms above all powers. This same power is available to believers in their continuing spiritual warfare.

The second manifestation of God's power in Christ is demonstrated by the fact that he has placed "all things under the authority of Christ" (1:22a). In the previous verse, Paul stated that Christ was placed in the position of authority. This next statement further defines this role—he is allowed to exercise that authority. Adam lost his headship over creation when he sinned. Christ as the "second Adam" is now head over all creation. Some think that the full realization of this authority occurred at the exaltation of Christ. However, as Paul warns in 6:12, there are still evil powers that war against the believers, who must put on the armor of God. So it might be said that presently it is an "already/not-yet" situation.

Presently, the manifestation of Christ's control is not always evident to humanity, for there are many inequities, injustices, disasters, unholy actions, and evidence of outright defiance against Christ and God. However, Christ is exercising control even though it is not obvious to humanity; without his control, things would be much worse. The full realization of this authority will be in the future. This is in keeping with 1 Corinthians 15:24-28, which states that God presently has subjected everything under Christ. In the end times Christ will subjugate all God's enemies and will hand the Kingdom over to God the Father. Hence, Christ has the right to exercise his control but chooses not to do so immediately in every instance of violation against

God's holy character. Nonetheless, his exercise of power is evident each time he rescues a sinner from the most despicable powers of all, Satan and sin. The full exercise of his control will be in the future, and it will be evident to all creation.

The third manifestation of God's power in Christ is demonstrated by the fact that God placed everything under the authority of Christ. Furthermore, God gave him, who has authority over everything, to the church. Although it is not directly stated, this implies that Christ has authority over the church (1:22). This power of God, which placed all creation under Christ's authority, is directed toward the believers. Giving Christ to the church demonstrates God's care for the church. First, he gave Christ as a sacrifice for their sins, and now he gives Christ to the church for her spiritual well-being. We learn from other passages that Christ, as head of the church, is our intercessor to help us in our weakness (Rom 8:34; Heb 7:25), and he is our advocate (1 John 2:1; Rev 12:10).

The Church Body. The word "church" *ekklēsia* [TG1577, ZG1711] (1:22-23) means "assembly," such as any group of citizens who gather for a specific purpose. It is used 114 times in the New Testament, 62 times by Paul, and 9 times in Ephesians. It can refer to a local church (1 Cor 1:2; 1 Thess 1:1), to several churches in a province or country (Acts 15:41; 1 Cor 16:1; Gal 1:2, 22), or to the universal church (1 Cor 12:28; 15:9; Gal 1:13), as it does in all occurrences in Ephesians. The church is composed of believers who transcend cultural, language, ethnic, gender, and geographical domains.

In verse 23, a very difficult verse, Paul further defines the church by calling it Christ's body (see also 5:30; Rom 12:4-5; 1 Cor 12:12-13, 27). Two significant features about the body of Christ are revealed in Ephesians (as well as in parallel passages in Colossians). First, the body of Christ, referring to the whole assembly of believers, is specifically identified as the "church" in the singular (1:22-23; 5:23; Col 1:18, 24). Second, and more importantly, Christ is named as the head of the body (1:22-23; 4:15-16; 5:23; Col 1:18, 24; 2:19).

In regard to the "body" there appears to be a progression of thought in Paul's letters. In 1 Corinthians 12:21 when he refers to "head," it is not identified as Christ but as one of the members of the body. In Romans 12:4-5 and 1 Corinthians 12:12-14, 27 the church is the body, which is Christ. In Ephesians and Colossians, the church is the body and Christ is the head, thus making Christ both the body and the head. Such differences reveal a development of the theology of the church. In Romans 12:4-5 and 1 Corinthians 12:14-27, the church is described as the body of Christ; by analogy of the human body, the utilization of gifts of all the members of the body conveys the sense of organic unity. In Ephesians and Colossians, this organic unity is animated by its head, Christ. Hence, each member is integrally bound and responsible to the head and to each other.

Finally, Paul expanded on the nature of this body. He declared that it is being filled with the fullness of Christ, who in turn is being filled wholly, entirely, or in every way by God—which most likely refers to God's power and moral excellence. Later, in 3:19, Paul prays that all believers might be filled with God's fullness, which comes by knowing the love of Christ. But in the present context, "power" is central. Therefore, believers are to be filled with the moral excellence and power of God by Christ, who in turn is being filled entirely by God with the same moral excellence. Believers are to appropriate this fullness in order to be more like Christ. They are to utilize this fullness at all times. When believers are attacked by those in the world or by satanic forces, the fullness of God's power and moral excellence are needed. Also, in times of blessings and joy, Christians are to exhibit this fullness by reflecting Christlike qualities.

This marks the end of Paul's first prayer. He prayed that the believers might know God more personally and intimately. The purpose of such knowledge was three-fold: that they might know the hope of his calling (which looks at the past), the wealth of God's glorious inheritance in the believers (which looks to the future), and the greatness of his power (which looks at the present time). The greatness of God's power is not only described but also demonstrated in Christ by his resurrection and ascension into the heavens, by subjecting all things under Christ's authority, and by giving him to the church. This prayer is built upon God's enrichment of believers with every spiritual benefit for their spiritual well-being. Paul prayed that they might deepen their relationship with God by knowing him more intimately through being filled with his moral excellence and power. Believers who enjoy intimate fellowship with God will experience a life full of joy and power. They will enjoy the benefits of being God's inheritance.

◆   ## D. New Position Individually (2:1-10)
1. The old condition: dead to God (2:1-3)

Once you were dead because of your disobedience and your many sins. ²You used to live in sin, just like the rest of the world, obeying the devil—the commander of the powers in the unseen world.* He is the spirit at work in the hearts of those who refuse to obey God. ³All of us used to live that way, following the passionate desires and inclinations of our sinful nature. By our very nature we were subject to God's anger, just like everyone else.

2:2 Greek *obeying the commander of the power of the air.*

NOTES

2:1-7 This portion forms a part of the third of the eight long sentences in this epistle (1:3-14, 15-23; 2:1-7; 3:2-13, 14-19; 4:1-6, 11-16; 6:14-20) with 124 words. In the Greek, the subject and the main verbs do not occur until 2:4-6.

2:1 *Once you were dead because of your disobedience and your many sins.* This verse indicates the Ephesian believers had been dead in their sins; verse 2:5 will explain their new life. The Greek is literally "transgressions and sins," which are synonyms denoting conscious and deliberate false steps.

2:2 *You used to live in sin, just like the rest of the world.* This clause may refer to the lifestyle of the world, but more likely it alludes to the temporal values of the world.

obeying the devil—the commander of the powers in the unseen world. The Greek text speaks of the prince of the authority of the air but does not identify him as the devil.

According to the ancients, "air" is not a reference to an impersonal ideology or *Zeitgeist*; instead it was the personal abode of living evil spirits (*1 Enoch* 15:10-11; *2 Enoch* 29:4-5; *Ascension of Isaiah* 7:9-12; 10:29; Philo *Dreams* 1.22.134-135; *Giants* 1.2.6-11; Plutarch *Morals* 274b).

those who refuse to obey. This is a good rendering of the literal "sons of disobedience."

2:3 *following the passionate desires and inclinations of our sinful nature.* A more literal rendering is "living in the desires of our flesh, doing the wishes of the flesh and the reasoning processes." This rendering attests that sinners live according to their flesh, gratifying the cravings and pleasures of the flesh, which are distorted by sin. The flesh dictates their lives. Furthermore, they not only satisfy the wants of the flesh but also rationalize this self-centeredness.

All of us used to live that way . . . By our very nature we were subject to God's anger, just like everyone else. Whereas Paul used the second person plural pronouns ("you") in the first two verses of chapter 2, in this verse he uses the first person plural pronouns ("we/us"). Some scholars (Abbott 1897:43; O'Brien 1999:280) think Paul was making a contrast between Ephesians as Gentiles ("you") and Paul as a Jew ("we/us"), but more likely the contrast is between him as a writer and them as recipients (so Lincoln 1990:88; Best 1998:208). If the first alternative were the case, not only would the "all" in 2:3 refer only to Jews, then also in 2:4-7, 10 the first person plural would imply that only the Jews were the objects of God's love and workmanship, and in 2:5 and 8 the second person plural would imply that only Gentiles need to be saved by grace. In either case, such a concept does not agree with NT teaching. Therefore, it is best not to make the distinction between Jews and Gentiles until 2:11.

COMMENTARY

In chapter 1, Paul spoke of God's eternal plan in choosing those who were predestined to adoption in his family and who were brought together under Christ, the head of the church. Chapters 2–3 explain the execution of this eternal plan by showing how God makes sinners into saints and then creates a new humanity, the church, Christ's body. Paul begins by contrasting the past unregenerate condition of believers and their present regeneration.

In a sense, the first three verses of chapter 2 is a parenthetical section, describing the believers' condition before they experienced God's transforming power. Before expounding on this extraordinary power, Paul described the awful condition of sinners who deserved nothing but God's wrath (2:1). He explained to the believers that they had once been dead. This, of course, does not refer to physical death; it refers to spiritual death. As one who is physically dead cannot communicate with the living, so also those who are spiritually dead cannot communicate with the eternal living God and thus are separated from God. In this context, their spiritual death was a result of their sins. As mentioned above (see note on 2:1), the Greek text includes "trespasses" along with "sins." These are synonyms, depicting humanity's deliberate acts against God and his righteousness—with resultant failure to live holy lives. When people are dead, they have no capability to generate life. Therefore, only the power of God can transform sinners into saints.

Having stated the sinners' shared condition, Paul then gives more details to substantiate his claim. Their spiritual condition is described in three ways. First, he states that they had lived according to the temporal values of the world (2:2a). Literally, "they had been walking previously according to the age of this world." The word "walking" has reference to their conduct of life. The Greek preposition *kata* [ᵀᴳ2596, ᶻᴳ2848] (according to) indicates a standard. Here that standard is conformity with the age of this world. The expression "age of this world" appears to be vague, but it probably indicates a way of life or a lifestyle. This stresses the temporal aspect, which is consistent with Paul's usage elsewhere in Ephesians (1:21; 2:7; 3:9, 11, 21). Hence, it has the nuance of age or a span of time within this world.

To better understand this concept, it is necessary to consider the word "world." Although it can have reference to the created material world (cf. 1:4), here it likely refers to the ethical order of the world, which is a satanically organized system that hates and opposes all that is godly (cf. John 15:18, 23; 18:36; 1 Cor 3:19). Accordingly, "to live like the rest of the world" is to be in step with the world by embracing its temporal values. Those thus described are so involved with the activities and values of the present age that they have no time to be concerned with God, eternal values, or with the judgment to come.

Second, unbelievers follow the prince of the power of the air, who is known as Satan (2:2b). The Bible declares that the whole world is "under the control of the evil one" (1 John 5:19), also called "the god of this world" (2 Cor 4:4). Therefore, not only do unbelievers conform to the temporal values of this world, they also conform to the ruler of this realm. As mentioned in the notes above, people of the first century viewed "air" not as an impersonal ideology, "the spirit of the age," but as the personal abode of evil spirits. Thus, not only do Satan and his emissaries reside in the air and heaven (6:12) but also work in the hearts of those who disobey God. These verses make it clear that unbelievers do not inadvertently sin but actually defy God by deliberate disobedience. In short, unbelievers conform both to the values of the world and to the dictates of Satan and his emissaries.

Third, unbelievers not only conform to the pressures of the world and to Satan but also to sin because they enjoy doing so (2:3). "Sinful nature" is a rendering of the term "flesh" (*sarx* [ᵀᴳ4561, ᶻᴳ4922]). This term may have reference to the material part of human beings, but it can also refer, as here, to the moral dynamics of fallen humanity. It is that which opposes God (Rom 8:5-8; Gal 3:3; 5:16-17). Unbelievers are inclined toward the things of the flesh (Rom 8:5), which produce works that are contrary to the character of God (Gal 5:19-21). Hence, one who lives in the flesh is depicted as one whose existence is apart from God and thus opposed to God and his ways. This is the result of a fallen reasoning process, which corrupts the will. It suggests that sinners consider their actions through a self-centered lens. They also use their minds to rationalize their sinful activity (Rom 2:15). Therefore, sinners are by nature ones who deserve God's wrath. This wrath is depicted as both a present wrath (John 3:36; Rom 1:18) and a future wrath (5:6; Rom 2:5; 5:9). This may not be a very pleasant picture of humanity; nevertheless, it is true. Only God can change the scene, as is depicted next.

◆   ## 2. The new position: alive in God (2:4-10)

⁴But God is so rich in mercy, and he loved us so much, ⁵that even though we were dead because of our sins, he gave us life when he raised Christ from the dead. (It is only by God's grace that you have been saved!) ⁶For he raised us from the dead along with Christ and seated us with him in the heavenly realms because we are united with Christ Jesus. ⁷So God can point to us in all future ages as examples of the incredible wealth of his grace and kindness toward us, as shown in all he has done for us who are united with Christ Jesus.

⁸God saved you by his grace when you believed. And you can't take credit for this; it is a gift from God. ⁹Salvation is not a reward for the good things we have done, so none of us can boast about it. ¹⁰For we are God's masterpiece. He has created us anew in Christ Jesus, so we can do the good things he planned for us long ago.

NOTES

2:4 But God is so rich in mercy, and he loved us so much. The conjunction "but" denotes a strong contrast to what was said before. The contrast is between mankind's sinfulness and God's gracious acts of love. Paul includes so many qualifiers that it makes it difficult to see the main assertions in the English text. God is the subject (2:4) and the main verbs are in the next two verses (2:5-6). Leaving out the qualifying clauses, it would read, "But God made us alive together with Christ and raised us up with him and seated us with him in the heavenly realms in Christ Jesus." This verse deals with the subject and two qualifiers— namely, that God is rich in mercy, which is further qualified by "he loved us so much." The expression "and he loved us so much" is not a secondary concept to "rich in mercy" but, rather, is the cause or motive of God's mercy. It could be rendered, "God is so rich in mercy because he loved us so very much."

2:5 he gave us life when he raised Christ from the dead. These 11 English words are expressed by three words in the Greek text, literally translated "enlivened with Christ." The verb is a compound verb, which denotes that God made us alive together with Christ. Thus, when Christ was made alive physically, we were made alive spiritually.

(It is only by God's grace that you have been saved!) This parenthetical clause has only three words in Greek. It is a perfect periphrastic construction focusing on the present results of salvation. Although it is translated "you have been saved" (as in ASV, RSV, NASB, NIV, NJB, NRSV), it is better to render it "you are saved" (as KJV, NEB) in order to convey the idea of the continuing results of salvation.

2:6 because we are united with Christ Jesus. In place of "because we are united with Christ Jesus" the Greek text has only "in Christ Jesus." The prepositional phrase "in Christ Jesus" is rather difficult to understand, but the NLT rendering clarifies it well.

2:7 God can point to us in all future ages as examples of the incredible wealth of his grace and kindness toward us. The Greek text makes it clear that this verse expresses a purpose that will be accomplished in the future—most likely after Christ's return when believers will be physically resurrected.

2:8 God saved you by his grace when you believed. The better-known rendering of this part of the verse is "for by grace are you saved through faith." The word "believed" is the cognate verb of the noun "faith." Essentially this clause states that the basis of our salvation is God's grace or favor and the means is faith.

it is a gift from God. Much debate revolves around the word "it" here. To what does "it" refer? Some think it refers back to either "favor" or "faith" (Westcott 1906:32), but neither of these suggestions are acceptable because in Greek both of these nouns are feminine, whereas the demonstrative pronoun *touto* [TG3778, ZG4047] (this) is neuter. It is better to view the neuter as collective, in which case "it" would refer to the concept of salvation (2:4-8a), which includes grace and faith (Lincoln 1990:112; Best 1998:226; O'Brien 1999:175).

2:9 *Salvation is not a reward for the good things we have done.* Not only is salvation not a "reward for the good things we have done," it also is not a payment or wage that has been earned "for the good things we have done." In other words, we cannot earn salvation. Since salvation is not obtained by our efforts, we cannot boast.

2:10 *He has created us anew in Christ Jesus, so we can do the good things he planned for us long ago.* The NLT makes it clear that "the good things" are what God has planned for us. The Greek is literally translated, "for good works which he prepared beforehand in order that we might walk in them." The relative pronoun "which" (*hois* [TG3739, ZG4005]) presents a problem. Some view it as a dative of destination and render it "to which God prepared us beforehand" (Luther, cited by Eadie 1883:158-159). However, the absence of the personal pronoun *hēmas* [TG1473, ZG1609] (us) is fatal to this view. Others suggest that *hois* is masculine and translate it, "for whom God prepared us beforehand" (Eadie 1883:158-159; Abbott 1897:54-55). But in this case, who is the antecedent? The antecedent "we" (*hēmeis* [TG1473, ZG1609]) is too remote (2:3, 7), whereas the nearest antecedent, "good works" (*ergois agathois* [TG2041/0018, ZG2240/0019]), as well as the following pronoun "them" (*autois* [TG846, ZG899]) refer to works and not people. Thus, the interpretation that makes the best sense is that the dative plural relative pronoun *hois* has shown up in place of the expected neuter nominative plural "which" (*ha* [TG3739, ZG4005]) under the influence of the dative plural *ergois agathois;* hence, "which [good works] God prepared beforehand."

COMMENTARY

With humanity in a desperate condition of sinfulness, the words "But God" may conjure fear in anticipation of his wrath. However, Paul continues by explaining that God is rich in mercy to a humanity in a deplorable situation. To further define "mercy," Paul continues by stating that God loves humanity so very much. This is a welcome relief. Did he forget their dilemma? Not at all. But before Paul made his main assertions regarding God's mercy based on love (2:5b-6), Paul reminded the believers once again of their sinful past condition (2:5a). This reminder was necessary to establish the need for God's mercy. We should have died, but Christ died in our stead in order that we can have forgiveness and acceptance before God. This is mercy based on love.

Although the subject ("God") and its qualifiers are in 2:4-5a, the main assertions are made in 2:5b-6 with three clauses, each introduced by a verb: "gave us life [with Christ]," "raised us from the dead along with Christ," and "seated us with him in the heavenly realms." These three verbs are compound verbs prefixed with the preposition "with." First, unbelievers are given life by God in association with Christ (2:5b). This refers to spiritual life and not the physical resurrection of believers. Christ died physically; we were dead spiritually. Christ was raised physically (1:20); we were raised together with Christ spiritually. We were dead spiritually, and now he has made us alive spiritually. This new life occurred at the time of our conversion.

Before proceeding to the second verb, Paul parenthetically exclaims, "by grace you are saved," or as the NLT renders it, "it is only by God's grace that you have been saved!" Grace is God's unmerited or undeserved favor toward sinners that provides salvation to them through the sacrificial death of Christ. The word "saved" indicates deliverance. This context states that we were dead in our sins and under God's wrath; the rescue or deliverance from that wrath could not be obtained outside of God's grace. "Saved" is a perfect passive participle, which further amplifies grace. It is often called a divine passive, where God clearly is the subject who saves sinners by his gracious act. The perfect tense expresses a completed action with continuing results. The completed action occurred the moment we were made alive together with Christ at our conversion. In other words, God, by his grace, initially saved us, and by that same grace he keeps us safe or saved from his wrath, as well as from sin's grip of death from which we were delivered. However, one must not think that the use of the perfect tense in itself indicates a future deliverance. It is the God behind the perfect tense that guarantees the future deliverance.

Second, God raised us up with Christ (2:6a). This does not refer to future physical resurrection but spiritual resurrection. Our spiritual resurrection corresponds with Christ's physical resurrection. When Christ was resurrected, all power was given to him (Matt 28:18; Rom 1:4), and now believers are identified with him. Furthermore, he dwells in us and gives us his enabling power in order that we might live the new, resurrected life.

Third, not only were we made alive with Christ and resurrected with him, but God has seated us with him in the heavenly realms (2:6b). As God raised and seated Christ in the heavenly realms physically (1:20), so has God raised and seated us together with Christ in the heavenly realms spiritually. As discussed in 1:3, it is from the heavenly realms that believers derive all their spiritual benefits. Seated in the heavenly realms, believers now have a heavenly status with heavenly power to overcome the powers of sin and death. Paul adds "in Christ Jesus," which is rendered in the NLT as "because we are united with Christ Jesus." In other words, believers are raised with Christ and seated with Christ in the heavenly realms because they are in Christ Jesus. This is evidence of the magnitude of God's grace.

In 2:6, Paul asserts that God has given us life with Christ, raised us from the dead along with Christ, and seated us with him in the heavenly realms. Verse 7 explains that the purpose of these actions is to demonstrate the incredible wealth of his grace in the coming ages. The text not only speaks of God's favor but also points out that this favor is kindness directed toward us. The word "kindness" basically means that which is appropriate or fitting; it refers to God's act of setting us free and seating us with Christ in the heavenly realms. The kindness encompasses the entire work of salvation which is appropriate or fitting to God and was done in connection with or located in Christ Jesus and directed toward us. The mention of the incredible wealth of his favor is reminiscent of 1:7 where the same Greek phrase is used in speaking of Christ's redemption as "so rich in kindness and grace." Redemption means to set us free from sin, and this will happen completely "in all future ages." God is going to display us as his trophies of grace—we who once deserved nothing but wrath. Even the angels in heaven will be awestruck at this incredible display of God's favor and kindness because they will realize what it cost him.

This description of undeserved salvation is further expanded in 2:8-10. In these verses Paul explains that salvation is totally by grace, apart from any person's involvement. He begins by stating that God saved us by his special favor when we believed in what God did for us in the work of redemption in Christ Jesus. Again, salvation is not credited to us as though we had earned it. This is made very clear by the next sentence: Paul states that we cannot take credit for it, because it was not obtained through our efforts. Rather, salvation is a gift from God. This is grace. In 2:9 Paul reinforces this by stating that because we have not earned salvation we cannot boast. It is God's grace, and not human effort, that is the basis of salvation. We receive this gracious gift of salvation through faith, that is, through trusting in the salvation God has offered us.

Furthermore, Paul explains that this great salvation cannot be earned, because the recipients of it are God's masterpiece. The word "masterpiece" refers to the work of a skilled craftsman creating a work of art. In the New Testament, it is used only here and in Romans 1:20. In Romans 1:20, it refers to God's creation (as in Pss 92:4 [91:5, LXX]; 143:5 [142:5, LXX]); in Ephesians it is used of God's new creation. The first reference speaks of the physical Creation of God, and the second, the spiritual re-creation of God. Paul makes it clear that he was speaking about spiritual re-creation: "He has created us anew in Christ Jesus." God's purpose for this new creation is to have a vehicle though whom he might work, as he had planned long ago. The literal translation of the Greek text would be, "for we are his masterpiece, having been created in Christ Jesus unto good works which God prepared beforehand in order that we might walk in them." Hence, we were created by Christ Jesus as his masterpiece with the goal of good works. God's workmanship is not achieved by good works, but it results in good works (Titus 2:14; 3:8). But how are these works accomplished? Are they to be done by our efforts? No! What is portrayed here is just the opposite. God has prepared for each of us a path of good works that cannot be accomplished by our efforts but by his effective working in us. Essentially, Paul was telling the Ephesians that God had prepared a path of good works for the believers and that he would perform these works in and through them as they lived by faith. Thus, we do not do a work for God; instead, God performs his work in and through his children (cf. Phil 2:13). Since these are God's good works, there is no cause for any person to boast.

In conclusion, 2:1-10 explains how, though humanity was spiritually dead and deserved only God's anger, God, in his marvelous grace, has provided salvation through faith. Believers are God's masterpiece in whom and through whom he performs his good works that he had already prepared in advance. This section, presenting the essence of the gospel, provides the best summary concerning salvation in all of Paul's writings.

◆   E. New Position Corporately (2:11-22)
     1. Statement of the union (2:11-13)

¹¹Don't forget that you Gentiles used to be outsiders. You were called "uncircumcised heathens" by the Jews, who were proud of their circumcision, even though it affected only their bodies and not their hearts. ¹²In those days you were living apart from Christ. You were excluded from citizenship among the people of Israel, and you did not know the covenant promises God had made to them. You lived in this world without God and without hope. ¹³But now you have been united with Christ Jesus. Once you were far away from God, but now you have been brought near to him through the blood of Christ.

NOTES

2:11 *Don't forget that you Gentiles used to be outsiders.* The words "used to be" is a translation of the Greek indefinite particle of time "formerly" (*pote* [TG4218, ZG4537]), which is in contrast to the adverb "now" (*nuni* [TG3570, ZG3815]) in 2:13. The words "uncircumcised heathens" are a good rendering of the Greek "Gentiles in the flesh."

who were proud of their circumcision, even though it affected only their bodies and not their hearts. This is a good rendering of the Greek text: "the so-called 'circumcision,' which is performed in the flesh by hands." It shows that its physical affects did not guarantee spiritual results.

2:12 *you did not know the covenant promises God had made to them.* God made many promises in the OT, but there were specific covenants of promise he made to the nation Israel. These included the covenants made to Abraham (Gen 12:1-4; 15:1-6; 17:1-8), and David (2 Sam 7:8-16; Ps 89:1-4), as well as the new covenant (Jer 31:31-34; Ezek 36:22-32). The covenants of promise were unconditional promises regarding land, seed, and blessing. The Mosaic covenant is not included as one of the covenants because it was conditional (i.e., God's promises were dependent on Israel's obedience); elsewhere Paul lists it separately from the covenants of promise (e.g., Rom 4:13-17; 9:4; see discussion in Hoehner 2002:357-359).

You lived in this world without God and without hope. In the Greek text, the words "God" and "hope" are reversed. The phrase "without God" is a translation from the Greek word *atheoi* [TG112, ZG117], from which is derived the English word "atheist."

2:13 *But now you have been united with Christ Jesus.* This phrase indicates two contrasts. First, the conjunction "but" (*de* [TG1161, ZG1254]) marks the contrast between what the Gentiles were before and after conversion. Second, the adverb "now" (*nuni* [TG3570, ZG3815]) reinforces the contrast between what the Gentiles were formerly (*pote* [TG4218, ZG4537], "used to be"—2:11) and what they are "now" (*nuni*), that is, belonging to Christ Jesus.

Once you were far away from God. Lit., "you who were formerly far away." Here the indefinite particle of time, "formerly" (*pote*), is used again in contrast to the adverb "now" (*nuni*) at the beginning of the verse.

now you have been brought near to him through the blood of Christ. Gentiles have been brought near either "through" or "by means of" or "in connection with" the blood of Christ.

COMMENTARY

Although individual sinners have received the gracious gift of salvation on the basis of God's favor by faith, they are not isolated but are brought into union with other believers. In 2:11-22 Paul develops the concept of corporate unity of believing Jews and Gentiles in the church, Christ's body (cf. 1:22-23). This forms the basis for the rest of the epistle.

Before discussing the union of Jewish and Gentile Christians, Paul clearly reminds the Ephesian believers of the great chasm that existed between Jews and Gentiles. The Gentiles were formerly outsiders because they did not undergo circumcision, the seal of the covenant, and consequently had no favor with God. The Jews labeled them "uncircumcised heathens." Without circumcision Gentiles did not have the privileges that God graciously gave to the Jews. The Jews were proud of their circumcision, though often they allowed it to affect them only physically and not spiritually. Thus, though the only difference between Jews and Gentiles was the physical sign in the flesh, the Jews were very proud of this distinction. It gave them the status of insiders and of recipients of the privileges God had promised them. The Gentiles were the outsiders who had no privileges from God.

Paul then itemized the five privileges the Gentiles lacked. First, they were living apart from Christ. It must be carefully noted, however, that unbelieving Jews were also apart from Christ, because Paul also states (in 2:17) that those who were near—namely, Jews—also needed the message of peace. Second, they were also excluded from the citizenship of Israel. This is a political identification—that is, it signifies membership in a commonwealth or state. Third, they were unaware of the covenants of promise made to Israel. These covenants of promise are known as the Abrahamic, Davidic, and New covenants (see note on 2:12 above). The Mosaic covenant is not among those covenants because it is not unconditional; it stands in stark contrast to the covenant of promise made to Abraham (mentioned in Rom 4:13-17 and Gal 3:6–4:31). Fourth, Gentiles lacked the messianic hope enjoyed by Israel, who looked forward to messianic deliverance and blessings from which the Gentiles were excluded. Fifth, though the Gentiles may have worshiped many gods, they did not know the true God revealed in the Scriptures (cf. Rom 1:18-32). Thus, the Gentile believers had previously lived in a world without any hope and trust in God as Creator and Redeemer. Although Israel had all these privileges, it did not necessarily mean that they took full advantage of them, a fact that is seen both in the Old Testament and the Gospels. Nevertheless, the main point of this passage is that the Gentiles were really in a dire situation.

At one time, Gentiles were unconverted outsiders, "living apart from Christ" and "in this world without God" (2:12), but their relationships have changed, for they now are "united with Christ Jesus" or "belong to Christ Jesus" (2:13). There was a change in spheres or realms of life (from "in this world" to "with Christ") indicating a change in relationship. Once they "were far away from God" (2:13), but now they are near because Christ shed his blood for their sins. The repetition of the contrasts emphasizes the stark differences in the status of the Gentiles before and after conversion. These contrasts serve to enhance the magnitude of God's grace. Sinners who were totally apart from God, who deserved nothing but wrath have experienced God's grace.

◆   ## 2. Explanation of the union (2:14-18)

¹⁴For Christ himself has brought peace to us. He united Jews and Gentiles into one people when, in his own body on the cross, he broke down the wall of hostility that separated us. ¹⁵He did this by ending the system of law with its commandments and regulations. He made peace between Jews and Gentiles by creating in himself one new people from the two groups. ¹⁶Together as one body, Christ reconciled both groups to God by means of his death on the cross, and our hostility toward each other was put to death.

¹⁷He brought this Good News of peace to you Gentiles who were far away from him, and peace to the Jews who were near. ¹⁸Now all of us can come to the Father through the same Holy Spirit because of what Christ has done for us.

NOTES

2:14 *For Christ himself has brought peace to us. He united Jews and Gentiles into one people.* Lit., "for he is our peace, the one having made the both one." The text portrays Christ as the center of peace. In Greek, the personal pronoun "he" is placed at the beginning of the verse for emphasis. This is also supported by the grammatical structure. The anarthrous subject ("he") is joined by a copulative verb to an articular predicate ("the peace"); this construction demonstrates that Christ is the personification of peace.

in his own body. This prepositional phrase is difficult to interpret, as is evident in various translations, which present three views: (1) The phrase relates to the previous verse, which signifies that he has broken down the wall of hostility in his flesh (NEB, TEV, NRSV, NLT; Abbott 1897:61-62). Not only did Christ's death destroy the hostility between mankind and God, but also the hostility between Jews and Gentiles. (2) The prepositional phrase relates to "hostility," which is equated with "the law" in verse 15: "he broke down the wall by abolishing in his flesh the hostility, that is, the law (KJV, ASV, NASB, NJB; Barth 1974:298; Lincoln 1990:142). The problem with this viewpoint is that it places the law in apposition to hostility, and nowhere in Scripture is the law presented as hostile. Also, it construes the participle (*katargēsas* [TG2673, ZG2934]) in 2:15 as meaning "to abolish, to put to death," when it only means "to make inoperative, to nullify." The meaning "abolish" is proper for the participle in 2:14 (*lusas* [TG3089, ZG3395], translated "broke down" in NLT), but not for *katargēsas*. (3) The last option is that the prepositional phrase is attached to the beginning of the next verse and is translated "he has broken down the wall of hostility by nullifying in his flesh the law" (RSV; so also NIV; NLT; Eadie 1883:174-175). The last view is the most acceptable because it interprets the hostility in apposition to the dividing wall (hence, "wall of hostility"), and the prepositional phrase relates not to the previous participle "he has broken down/destroyed" but to the succeeding participle; hence, "he has rendered inoperative the law in his flesh" or "he has nullified the law by his death."

he broke down the wall of hostility that separated us. Walls are instruments of division, and this particular wall was one of hostility.

2:15 *ending the system of law.* The rendering of *katargēsas* [TG2673, ZG2934] as "ending" could be construed to mean "destroy," which would be inaccurate. The word actually means "to render inoperative, nullify, invalidate." Thus, it conveys the idea of neutralizing the effect. The nullification of the law applies to both parties—that is, believing Jews and Gentiles. Elsewhere Paul states that Christ is the end of the law to those who believe (Rom 7:1-6; 10:4). The translation "the system of law with its commandments and regulations" is a good rendering of the Greek "the law of commandments in decrees." It is the whole law and not only a part of the law that was rendered inoperative. Some have made a false dichotomy between moral and ceremonial laws, making only the ceremonial laws inoperative. Here, as elsewhere in the Bible, the whole law, not only part of the law, was rendered inoperative for believers.

2:16 *Together as one body, Christ reconciled both groups to God.* This speaks of reconciliation, not between Jews and Gentiles but between humanity (both Jews and Gentiles) and God.

our hostility toward each other was put to death. In light of the previous statement, this is probably another reference to hostility between humanity and God.

2:17 *He brought this Good News of peace to you Gentiles who were far away from him, and peace to the Jews who were near.* Lit., "and coming he preached peace to you who were far off and peace to those who were near."

2:18 *Now all of us can come to the Father through the same Holy Spirit because of what Christ has done for us.* Rather than "can come," the Greek text has "have access," which denotes openness. The NLT translates the preposition *en* [TG1722, ZG1877] as "through" (so KJV, NIV) to indicate means, but "in the same Holy Spirit" is a better rendering because the Greek text introduces this verse with "that through him" (*hoti di autou* [cf. *dia* TG1223, ZG1328]) "we both have access"—referring to Christ. It would be unusual for this to be followed with "through the same Holy Spirit." It is more likely that the preposition *en* [TG1722, ZG1877] (in) indicates sphere.

C O M M E N T A R Y

After portraying the union of Jews and Gentiles in light of their former disunity, Paul further explains how this union was achieved. This is an important section because it gives added insight into the deep rift between Jews and Gentiles prior to Christ's work of bringing the two parties into one entity. This section can be divided into two sections: (1) the proclamation of peace between believing Jews and Gentiles and between humanity and God (2:14-16), and (2) the announcement of peace, explaining both its content and result (2:17-18). Because of Christ's sacrificial death on the cross, there can be peace between believing Jews and believing Gentiles. Much had to be changed for this peace to survive. The law, which was so important to the Jews, could no longer be the operating principle, otherwise the old rift would reemerge.

The centerpiece of this peace is Christ himself, the personification of peace, who makes peace possible between the two hostile parties, namely, Jews and Gentiles. This peace does not just entail the cessation of hostility but also acceptance or friendship between the two parties. The Hebrew word for "peace" (*shalom* [TH7965, ZH8934]) conveys the idea of completeness, safety, and blessings. Paul explained that peace was accomplished by Christ, who broke down the wall of hostility that separated them, thus uniting them. Some have suggested that this wall may refer to the wall in the Jerusalem Temple precincts that separated the court of the Gentiles from the court of the Jews in order to prohibit entrance by any foreigner. But this is unlikely because (1) there is no reference to the Jerusalem wall in the context, (2) the Jerusalem wall was never known as the wall of hostility, (3) it was still standing when Paul wrote this letter, and (4) it would have been unfamiliar to the average Gentile living outside of Judea. Others have proposed that it refers to the curtain in the Jerusalem Temple that separated the holy place from the Holy of Holies.

However, that was a curtain, not a wall, and it separated all people including Jews (except the high priest on the Day of Atonement). Rather than a physical wall, it more likely refers to a metaphorical wall. In fact, some rabbis considered the Mosaic law to be a wall that acted as a "fence" that separated the Jews from the Gentiles (cf. *Letter of Aristeas* 139). And while the protection of the law, not the hostility, is involved in this concept, it is nevertheless true that the same law that protected Jews from the pollution of gentile practices also caused hostility between them. For instance, certain laws prevented Jews from eating with Gentiles or intermarrying with them. It was such that led to the hostility of Jews toward Gentiles, which in turn caused Gentiles to hate the Jews. The hostility, therefore, was not the law itself but attitudes that resulted from its practice. This hostility had been destroyed.

How then has the destruction of hostility between Jews and Gentiles been accomplished? This is explained in 2:15, where Paul declares that it was Christ's death that nullified the whole system of Jewish law. One needs to note that Paul does not say that Christ destroyed the law, since this would contradict Jesus' statement in the Gospels, "I did not come to abolish the law of Moses or the writings of the prophets. No, I came to accomplish their purpose" (Matt 5:17). Rather, he has destroyed the hostility by rendering the law inoperative. Hence, the nullification of the law has great significance for Jews and Gentiles who are in Christ. Since the law has become inoperative, all believers in the present age are not under its jurisdiction. Christ is the end of the law for believers (Rom 10:4), and they are no longer under this pedagogue (Gal 3:25). In fact, they have "died to it" (Rom 7:6). This does not mean that there are no laws within the Mosaic law that present-day believers are obligated to obey. However, they are obligated to obey those laws that have been reiterated in the New Testament. They are under the new covenant; the old covenant has been nullified. It is no longer the *modus operandi*.

Rendering the law inoperative had a twofold purpose: to create a new person (2:15b) and to reconcile both Jews and Gentiles to God (2:16). In the first purpose, Paul clearly states that from the "two" groups (Jews and Gentiles) Christ created in himself "one" new person, thus making peace. In 2:14 Christ was portrayed as the personification of peace, and here is the outworking of that peace. The result is cessation of hostility, which had previously existed between these two entities. It needs to be emphasized that this is a totally "new" entity. Gentiles did not become Jews, as gentile proselytes did in pre-New Testament times, nor did Jews become Gentiles. Rather both became "a new person" or "one new humanity." This new creation does not refer to individual Christians, as in 2 Corinthians 5:17, but to the creation of a new corporate entity. The next verse bears this out by stating that this new entity is called "one body," referring to the church. Hence, believers are no longer Jews or Gentiles but Christians. A whole new race has been formed—a race that is raceless! The result is peace.

The second purpose for nullifying the law was to reconcile the one body of Jewish and gentile believers to God himself (2:16). This moves the argument one step beyond the prior verse, where the two groups were brought together into one entity resulting in reconciliation between them. Continuing on, verse 16 declares that this wholly new body is now reconciled to God through his Son's death on the cross. Both the reconciliation of Jews and Gentiles and their reconciliation to God exacted a heavy price—the death of God's Son. In a way, it would seem that in these two verses the two different reconciliations have been mentioned in a reversed order. Normally, one would expect the reconciliation between God and man to be mentioned first and the resulting reconciliation between Jews and Gentiles second. However, in the context of 2:14-18 the main point is the reconciliation of Jews and Gentiles rather than their reconciliation to God. (Paul has already explained humanity's reconciliation to God in 2:1-13.) Paul stresses this by concluding in 2:16 that the hostility between humanity and God was put to death. Peace now exists between believing Jews and Gentiles and between God and people.

Having established the basis of peace between Jews and Gentiles and between God and humanity, Paul directs his attention to God's proclamation of that peace and its result (2:17-18). At the beginning of 2:17, the Greek text has a coordinating conjunction, *kai* [TG2532, ZG2779] (and), that most likely makes the present statement parallel to "Christ himself has brought peace" (or "he is our peace") in 2:14. Thus, not only is Christ our peace but also he preaches peace. The recipients of this message of peace are the Gentiles who were far away from God and the Jews who were near. The fact that the word "peace" is repeated for both those far away and those near emphasizes that both parties need the message of peace, not just those who were far away. It also reinforces the formation of the new entity. The content of this peace was discussed in the previous verse—namely, peace horizontally between Jews and Gentiles and peace vertically between them and God—all made possible by Christ's work on the cross.

As a result of this newly found peace, both Jewish and gentile believers have access to God the Father (2:18). The fact that "both" have such access further substantiates their reconciliation. The idiom translated "can come" can mean "have introduction" or "have access" to one such as a king. Typically, an introduction makes access possible; the Greek text distinctly states that believers have access to the Father through Christ. This access is "in the sphere of" or "in connection with" the one Spirit, clearly the Holy Spirit, perhaps referring to the power of the Spirit. In this verse, as in 1:4-14, 17, the three persons of the Trinity are involved (cf. 4:4-6). In 1:4-14 all three persons of the Trinity work to redeem humanity. Here the three are involved in the believer's access to God. Not only the initiation, but also the continuation of humanity's relationship to God involves all three persons of the Trinity, thus demonstrating the intensity of God's personal interest.

In conclusion, in 2:14-18 the union of Jews and Gentiles is explained in four different ways: (1) We are made all *one* people (2:14). (2) Christ created in himself *one* new person from *two* groups (2:15). (3) Christ reconciled *both* groups together as *one* body (2:16). (4) Christ gave *both* Jews and Gentiles access to God in *one* Spirit (2:18). This new union replaces the old hostility.

◆   ## 3. Consequence of the union (2:19-22)

¹⁹So now you Gentiles are no longer strangers and foreigners. You are citizens along with all of God's holy people. You are members of God's family. ²⁰Together, we are his house, built on the foundation of the apostles and the prophets. And the cornerstone is Christ Jesus himself. ²¹We are carefully joined together in him, becoming a holy temple for the Lord. ²²Through him you Gentiles are also being made part of this dwelling where God lives by his Spirit.

NOTES

2:19 *So now you Gentiles are no longer strangers and foreigners.* The Greek does not specifically state "you Gentiles" but only "you." Nevertheless, the pronoun most likely refers to the Gentiles.

2:20 *the foundation of the apostles and prophets.* Does this refer to OT or NT prophets? Most likely they are NT prophets for the following reasons. First, here and elsewhere in the NT (3:5; 4:11; 1 Cor 12:28, 29), when mentioned together, apostles are mentioned first and prophets second. If it were a reference to OT prophets, it seems probable that they would have been mentioned before the apostles. Second, in 3:5, Paul reveals the mystery of the church—that is, the union of believing Jews and believing Gentiles. There it states that this mystery had been hidden from former generations but now is revealed "by his Spirit" to "his holy apostles and prophets." This assertion is evidence that the prophets were contemporaries with the apostles, both receiving from the same Spirit the revelation of the former (OT times) hidden mystery. Hence, it is best to see these as NT prophets (Best 1998:282-283; O'Brien 1999:214-215).

And the cornerstone is Christ Jesus himself. Although some have suggested that the Greek word *akrogōniaios* [TG204/A, ZG214] means the "capstone" or "topstone" of a gate or column (Joachim Jeremias, "κεφαλὴ γωνίας—Ἀκρογωνιαῖος," *Zeitschrift für die Neutestamentliche Wissenschaft* 29, no. 3/4 [1930]: 264-280; idem, "Eckstein—Schlußstein," *Zeitschrift für die Neutestamentliche Wissenschaft* 36, no. 1/2 [1937]:154-157; Barth 1974:271, 317-319; Bruce 1984:304-306; Lincoln 1990:154-156; Best 1998:284-286), most scholars think it means the "cornerstone" of the foundation (BDAG 39-40; L&N §7:44; W. Mundle, NIDNTT 3.390; Calvin 1965:155; Eadie 1883:198-199; Abbott 1897:70; Schnackenburg 1991:123-124; O'Brien 1999:216-218; Hoehner 2002:404-407).

2:21 *We are carefully joined together in him.* Lit., "in whom the whole building being fitted together." The prepositional phrase "in whom" refers back to Christ, the cornerstone in 2:20. The concentration is on the building process. There is debate as to whether the adjective *pas* [TG3956, ZG4246] should be translated "every building" or "whole building." In this context it is talking about one building and thus it is best to render it "all, whole, entire" building (Barth 1974:271-272; Lincoln 1990:156).

becoming a holy temple for the Lord. Lit., "growing into a holy temple in the Lord." This emphasizes the living dynamic growth of the building process. As discussed in 1:1, the word "holy" does not mean inherent goodness but that which is set apart for God's use or service. Hence, the building is identified as a "holy temple."

2:22 *Through him.* Rather than "through him," this phrase could be rendered "in him," referring back to "in whom" in 2:21a, which in turn refers back to Christ Jesus in 2:20. Gentiles are joined together in Christ.

this dwelling where God lives by his Spirit. Rather than "by his Spirit," some would render this phrase "in the Spirit"—speaking not so much about the means but the manner in which God dwells in his temple. Either rendering is acceptable.

COMMENTARY

This section can be divided into two parts: the consequence of the union of Jews and Gentiles (2:19) and the result of the union (2:20-22). Paul explained the consequences of the new union in terms of what they are not and in terms of what they are. His opening comment in 2:19, "Gentiles are no longer strangers and foreigners," is good news because over the years they had been excluded from God's covenants to Israel. Rather than strangers and foreigners, they had become a part of a company of "saints" or "holy people." As mentioned earlier (1:1) the word "saints" (or "holy people") does not imply inherent goodness but rather separateness, people set apart to serve God. Hence, Gentiles are fellow citizens with those who are set apart to serve God. Also, they are now members of the household of God or "God's family." The question is, "With whom are they fellow citizens and members of God's family?" There are three interpretations to consider. The first suggests that gentile Christians have become fellow citizens with Jewish Christians (Dibelius 1953:71; Caird 1976:60). But this contradicts the context that has stated that those who become believers are neither Jewish Christians nor gentile Christians, just Christians.

The second interpretation proposes that they are fellow citizens with Israel and, as such, members of God's family (Westcott 1906:40; Barth 1974:269-270). But Paul mentions "one new people" (2:15) and "one body" (2:16), referring to the incorporation of believing Jews and Gentiles into one new race or class, the church, as distinct from a continuation of something old. Also, Paul specifically states that Gentiles are fellow citizens with the saints and members of God's family, not fellow citizens with Israel. Clearly, Gentiles before conversion were alienated from the citizenship of Israel (2:12) and God's family, but Paul states that after conversion they became fellow citizens with the saints, not with Israel. Rather, believing Jews and Gentiles became fellow citizens with the saints of all ages and became a part of God's family, even those who lived before the formation of Israel. Paul also explains that this new entity is "built on the foundation of the apostles and the prophets. And the cornerstone is Christ Jesus himself" (2:20). This new entity began at Pentecost, not in Old Testament times. It is true that believing Gentiles are incorporated with the saints of all ages (2:19), but the incorporation spoken of in the present context speaks of believing Jews and Gentiles united into one new people, which distinctly began when the church came into existence at Pentecost.

The third interpretation proposes that all holy people are fellow citizens with the redeemed of all ages and that these redeemed people are God's family (Abbott 1897:69; Lincoln 1990:150-151). This view makes the most sense. Before Abraham, there were saints who were members of God's family. Subsequently, those who followed in the footsteps of their father Abraham (Rom 4:12) were considered saints or holy people. In our era, believing Jews and Gentiles composing the church are fellow citizens with the saints of past generations. Though some distinctions exist between the generations, all are fellow citizens and belong to God's family. All saints have been redeemed and reconciled, and they have fellowship with and access to God.

The high calling, which is ours as fellow citizens with the saints, is possible because we have become the new humanity portrayed here as a holy temple in which God dwells (2:20-22). Paul moved from the metaphor of a body to the metaphor of a building. The foundation of this new temple is the apostles and prophets with Christ Jesus as the cornerstone. Some suggest that this contradicts 1 Corinthians 3:10-11, where it states that Christ is the foundation, whereas here the apostles and prophets are the foundation. However, it is perfectly legitimate for a writer to use a metaphor in two different ways for different purposes. Also, it is possible that the apostles who laid the foundations (Rom 15:2; 1 Cor 3:10) thought of themselves as foundation stones. Furthermore, this may be a development of Pauline thought. Whereas, previously, Christ was considered the foundation, later he was designated as the cornerstone, the most important stone of the foundation and the building as a whole.

To whom do the foundational "apostles" and "prophets" refer? As discussed previously (1:1), an apostle is one who is sent as a messenger and represents the full authority of the one who sent him or her. There are three kinds of apostles represented by the New Testament in that era. First, there were those who had been with Jesus in his ministry and had witnessed his resurrection (Acts 1:21-22). Second, there are those who received the gift of apostleship mentioned in 4:11. They would include people such as Barnabas (Acts 14:4, 14; 1 Cor 9:5-7), James the Lord's brother (1 Cor 15:7; Gal 1:19), and Apollos (1 Cor 4:6, 9). The first category is to be regarded as an office, while the second is a gift. Third, there is simply Paul, who seems to be an exception because he was "born at the wrong time" (1 Cor 15:8-9). Though he had not been with Jesus in his ministry nor witnessed his resurrection, he appears to have been given the office of an apostle (cf. Rom 1:1; 1 Cor 1:1; 2 Cor 1:1; Col 1:1; 1 Tim 1:1; 2 Tim 1:1; cf. Gal 1:1). In the present context, "apostles" may have reference to all three. Certainly, Paul would have considered himself an apostle and would have been included in the foundation along with those who had been with Jesus in his ministry and those who had the gift of apostleship. The prophets are listed along with other gifts to the church (4:11; 1 Cor 12:28; cf. Rom 12:6). Similar to the Old Testament prophets, the New Testament prophets were involved in receiving and transmitting God's revelation. We are not told much about the role of the prophet in New Testament times, but it is very likely that, while the Canon was still incomplete, prophets may have received and passed on revelation to complete what was needed in order that every person could be presented perfect before God (4:12; Col 1:28). Such a prophetic voice was important in the early formation of the church. Of primary importance to the foundation consisting of apostles and prophets is Christ Jesus, the cornerstone. Today a building's cornerstone is structurally insignificant. Many times it is installed the day a building is dedicated, in other words, after its construction. This was not at all true in the first century. The cornerstone was the first and most important stone of the foundation. It was carefully laid because the builders would line up the rest of the building from that one stone. In fact, in Isaiah 28:16 it is literally called "a stone of testing" by which every other stone in the foundation and the superstructure must be measured. Thus, it was imperative that the church's foundation of apostles and prophets be correctly aligned with Christ. Moreover, all other believers are built on that same foundation and must also align their lives with the cornerstone, Christ Jesus.

Moving from the foundation, Paul discusses the formation of the building. The NLT directs attention to the people who make up the edifice, whereas the Greek text concentrates more on the building process. Paul has established the composition of the foundation and identified the cornerstone. He now explains that the whole building grows by the joining or fitting together of the various pieces. Today the process of fitting stones together is simple because mortar is used. In Paul's day, without the use of mortar, stones had to be cut so that they properly fit with one another in order to be perfectly joined together. The stones represent individual believers (2:16) who, before conversion, were at enmity with one another but now are being joined together into one new humanity, the church. Because each member of this body is aligned to the cornerstone, Christ, all are aligned together as one building. As they are joined, the building grows corporately into a holy temple. The particular term used for "temple" (*naos* [TG3485, ZG3724]) refers to the inner sanctuary within the entire temple area (*hieron* [TG2411, ZG2639]).

In pagan temples the inner sanctuary was where the gods dwelt (cf. Acts 17:24), and in the Jewish tabernacle or temple it was the Holy of Holies where God dwelt (Exod 15:17; 1 Sam 3:3; 2 Sam 22:7; 1 Chr 28:11; Matt 23:16, 21). With the rending of the veil of the temple (*naos* [TG3485, ZG3724]; Matt 27:51; Mark 15:38; Luke 23:45), God no longer dwells in a temple built with stones but in a new temple made up of believers. Its designation as a "holy" temple indicates that this body of believers is set apart for God's use. It is important to notice that the whole temple grows—giving emphasis not to individual growth but to corporate growth. This new structure's place of growth is in the Lord Jesus Christ.

Now that the construction of the building has been described, the function of the building is discussed in 2:22. In the previous verse, the metaphor of the joined building stones was employed, and in this verse those stones are identified as Gentiles who are united together with believing Jews. In 2:21 the building was described as growing into a holy temple in the Lord, and here Paul characterizes the building as the dwelling place of God, which is being formed as believing Jews and believing Gentiles unite together. As the Old Testament Temple was the dwelling place of God by his manifest glory, so now the body of believers is the dwelling place of God by the Spirit. It is true that the Holy Spirit indwells each individual believer (cf. John 14:17; Rom 8:9, 11; Gal 3:2; 4:6; 1 John 3:24; 4:13), thus each is a "temple" (1 Cor 6:19), but the present text is not referring to this. Rather, it is speaking of the Spirit's dwelling in the new temple (*naos* [TG3485, ZG3724]) of the corporate body of believers, the church (1 Cor 3:16; 2 Cor 6:16).

In conclusion, Paul has shown that though the Gentiles were formerly foreigners outside of God's household, they are now one new people together with the Jews who became Christians. This new entity is portrayed as a temple built on the foundation of apostles and prophets, with Christ as the cornerstone. This temple is indwelt by God's Spirit. All three persons of the Trinity are here involved: God the Father, the subject of the passage, is creating the new holy temple, consisting of the corporate body of believing Jews and Gentiles; Christ is the cornerstone of this new temple; and the Holy Spirit resides within. Before Christ came, the Jews thought of God as the one who resided in the man-made Temple from which Gentiles were excluded. The pagan Gentiles in Ephesus thought that the goddess Artemis resided in the renowned temple in their city. These were two diametrically different views of who God was and where he resided. After conversion, both believing Jews and Gentiles were created into one new person portrayed as a temple, the foundation of which consisted of apostles and prophets with Christ as the cornerstone and in which God dwells in the person of the Holy Spirit. Whereas there previously was nothing but hostility between Jews and Gentiles, now there is one body of believers called the church.

◆   F. The Mystery Explained (3:1-13)
     1. The mystery (3:1-6)

When I think of all this, I, Paul, a prisoner of Christ Jesus for the benefit of you Gentiles*... ²assuming, by the way, that you know God gave me the special responsibility of extending his grace to you Gentiles. ³As I briefly wrote earlier, God himself revealed his mysterious plan to me. ⁴As you read what I have written, you will understand my insight into this plan regarding Christ. ⁵God did not reveal it to previous generations, but now by his Spirit he has revealed it to his holy apostles and prophets.

⁶And this is God's plan: Both Gentiles and Jews who believe the Good News share equally in the riches inherited by God's children. Both are part of the same body, and both enjoy the promise of blessings because they belong to Christ Jesus.*

3:1 Paul resumes this thought in verse 14: "When I think of all this, I fall to my knees and pray to the Father."
3:6 Or because they are united with Christ Jesus.

NOTES

3:1 *When I think of all this.* The Greek text begins this verse with the prepositional phrase "for this reason" (*toutou charin* [ᵀᴳ3778/5484, ᶻᴳ4047/5920]; it points the reader back to 2:11-22, which was concerned with Jewish and Gentile believers who had been made into a new humanity in Christ. It appears that Paul was just about to begin a prayer for these believers (3:1; see NLT mg), but he stopped in the middle of his sentence and digressed to the subject of the mystery of Christ, giving an explanation of the mystery and speaking of his responsibility to make it known. This digression forms a part of the fourth long sentence in this epistle (3:2-13; cf. 1:3-14, 15-23; 2:1-7; 3:14-19; 4:1-6, 11-16; 6:14-20) with 189 words. Even today it is not unusual for digressions to involve one long and cumbersome sentence. After the digression, he commences his prayer, beginning with 3:14.

3:2 *that you know.* This is a good rendering of "if indeed you heard," which has reference to Paul's ministry among the Ephesians and his ministry elsewhere. However, the omission of "if" makes it difficult for the reader of this translation to recognize that Paul was introducing a conditional sentence, which will conclude with 3:13.

God gave me the special responsibility of extending his grace to you Gentiles. The words "special responsibility" is actually "administration" (*oikonomia* [TG3622, ZG3873]), which indicates Paul's God-given activity of administering grace. This administration has the sense of stewardship or a trust to be dispensed (in 1 Cor 9:17 *oikonomia* is translated "sacred trust," and in Col 1:25 it is rendered "responsibility").

3:3 *As I briefly wrote earlier.* This could be a reference to Paul's earlier writings, but it seems that he was referring to an earlier portion of this letter, more particularly 2:11-22.

God himself revealed his mysterious plan to me. The word "reveal" means the unveiling of something that was previously hidden. "His mysterious plan" is a good rendering of the Greek word "mystery" (*mustērion* [TG3466, ZG3696]). It is a secret plan hidden in God (3:9), which cannot be unraveled or understood by human ingenuity or study. It is unveiled by God. The word "mystery" is translated in the NLT as "mysterious plan" (1:9; 3:3, 9; 6:19), "plan" (3:4), and "mystery" (5:32).

3:4 *you will understand my insight into this plan regarding Christ.* The word "plan" is the same as the expression "his mysterious plan" in 3:3, a translation of *mustērion* [TG3466, ZG3696].

3:5 *God did not reveal it to previous generations.* This is a good rendering of the literal reading, "which [mystery] in other generations was not made known to the sons of men."

but now . . . he has revealed it. Lit., "as now it was revealed." Some think that there was some revelation of God's secret plan in the OT, albeit not as great as in the NT. However, "as" is not a comparison of degree but a comparison of kind. Moreover, in place of "as," the parallel passage in Col 1:26 uses the adversative conjunction "but" (*de* [TG1161, ZG1254]) to indicate a distinct contrast.

3:6 *And this is God's plan: Both Gentiles and Jews who believe the Good News share equally in the riches inherited by God's children. Both are part of the same body, and both enjoy the promise of blessings because they belong to Christ Jesus.* The NLT's rendering is an expanded paraphrase of this short verse, which literally is, "that the Gentiles are fellow heirs and fellow members of the body and fellow participants of the promise in Christ through the gospel." The expansion contains a restatement of the secret plan mentioned in 3:3. In 3:6 the specifics of the plan are given. Nothing in the Greek text of this verse specifically mentions belief in the Good News. It is, however, because of the Good News that Gentiles are fellow heirs, fellow members of the body, and fellow participants of the promise in Christ. The Good News in the present context does not refer to the salvation of sinners but to the union of believing Jews and Gentiles in Christ.

COMMENTARY

As noted above, Paul was going to pray for the gentile believers but then abruptly digressed. He chose, instead, to discuss further the new humanity that he had mentioned in the previous context (2:11-22). He introduced his remarks by reminding the believers that he was in prison on behalf of the Gentiles to whom he was called to minister (Acts 9:15; 22:21; 26:17-18; Rom 1:5; 11:13; Gal 1:16; 2:7-9; 1 Tim 2:7). The Jews had claimed that he was distorting God's message; consequently, they were instrumental in obtaining his imprisonment in Jerusalem (Acts 21:20-36). Later, he was taken to Caesarea, tried, and granted an appeal to Caesar (Acts 24:23–25:12), which resulted in his imprisonment in Rome (Acts 27–28). Thus, his Roman incarceration was the result of his mission to the Gentiles.

As an apostle to the Gentiles, Paul wanted to share with them three truths. First, he relates that he is responsible to administer God's grace to the Gentiles (3:2). In the succeeding verses, Paul explains that the grace to be administered is the revelation of the mystery of Jews and Gentiles being united into one body. This grace was given to Paul to dispense to the Gentiles (3:2—"to you Gentiles") because he was an apostle to the Gentiles (Rom 1:5; 11:13; Gal 2:7, 9). Second, he discusses the revelation of the mystery, or God's secret plan (3:2-5). This subsection deals with the revelation of the mystery (3:3), the ability to understand it (3:4), and the time of its disclosure in the apostolic age (3:5). Third, he describes the content of God's secret plan (3:6).

Paul had discussed previously (in 2:11-22) the fact that believing Jews and Gentiles are made into one new person, the body of believers. This is now identified as a mystery (*mustērion* [TG3466, ZG3696]) or God's secret plan. As mentioned earlier, this is not something that is mysterious in the common sense of today's usage but rather it is a revealed secret to be understood by all believing people, not just a few elite. Paul tells us that the understanding does not come by human ingenuity but by God's revelation. It is not clear when this secret was revealed to Paul. It may have been at the time of his conversion on the Damascus road when he was told to go to the Gentiles (Acts 9:15-16; 26:17-18; Gal 1:16), when he was in Arabia (Gal 1:17), or perhaps when he first returned to Jerusalem (Acts 9:25-28; 22:21). Or it may have been revealed in stages, for it was not understood fully by the early church when Peter was criticized for baptizing Cornelius (Acts 11:1-3). Nor was it understood by the Jerusalem council in AD 49, which occurred 16 years after the inception of the church (Acts 15). It may have taken years for Paul to completely understand this new concept and many years thereafter for others to understand it.

Paul then declares that this mystery can be understood simply by reading what he had written. In short, they could know what he knew. In saying this, he was not claiming brilliance, for he clearly states that it was made known to him by revelation (3:3) and that it was revealed to him by the Holy Spirit (3:5). The secret plan centers on Christ. This is slightly different from Colossians 1:27, where Paul states that the mystery is "Christ lives in you." In Colossians 1:27 Paul states that Christ is resident in individual gentile believers, whereas in the present context he emphasizes that both Jews and Gentiles are fellow partakers. Colossians emphasizes Christology, and Ephesians focuses more on the church.

Paul affirmed that this secret plan was not known in previous generations as it was presently revealed (3:5). As mentioned previously for this verse, there have been some interpreters who suggest that the Greek conjunction "as" is used in a restrictive way to indicate a comparison of degree—hence, the secret plan was revealed to some degree in the Old Testament but now is revealed to a greater degree (Westcott 1906:45; Hendricksen 1967:145; Caird 1976:64). Others see the conjunction used in a descriptive way to indicate a comparison in kind, thereby meaning that no revelation of this mystery was given in the Old Testament but that it was revealed for the first time in the New Testament (Barth 1974:333-334; Lincoln 1990:177; Best 1998:305-306). The second interpretation is preferred for the following five reasons. First, though use of "as" in the restrictive sense is more common, it is also used in the descriptive sense. For example, Peter said at Pentecost that the disciples were not drunk "as" the Jews thought (Acts 2:15). This does not refer to the degree of drunkenness but rather the lack of it. Second, the context supports this interpretation, for Paul wrote that the "mysterious plan" was hidden in the past (3:9). Third, the verb "reveal" in 3:5 means "to uncover, unveil" something that has been previously completely covered or hidden. Fourth, the parallel passage in Colossians 1:26 does not use the conjunction "as" but uses the adversative conjunction "but" (*de* [TG1161, ZG1254]), which clearly states this "message was kept secret for centuries and generations past, but now it has been revealed to God's people." Fifth, the temporal adverb "now" (*nun* [TG3568, ZG3814]) is used both in the present verse and the parallel passage of Colossians 1:26 to mark the contrast between the past and present ages. This is substantiated by the same temporal adverb in Ephesians 3:10 where it states that God's purpose was that the manifold wisdom (reference to the secret plan or mystery) might "now" be made known to the rulers and authorities in the heavenly places through the church. Since the heavenly hosts learned of the secret plan through the church (which did not exist before Pentecost), certainly the people of the Old Testament did not know of it. Granted, there were Gentiles included within Israel (Lev 19:34; Deut 10:18-19; 1 Kgs 8:41-42), but they had become a part of Israel. This is not the same as Jews and Gentiles forming a new entity as described in this secret plan. Therefore, the secret plan was not revealed until New Testament times.

Paul declared that God revealed the secret plan "by his Spirit . . . to his holy apostles and prophets." This means that it did not come by human ingenuity. Interestingly, although Paul was responsible to disseminate this plan, he said it was revealed to all the apostles and prophets and not to Paul only. Who were the apostles and prophets? They were those gifted individuals given to the church; they formed the foundation mentioned in 2:20 and are later mentioned in 4:11. As discussed earlier (1:1; 2:20), the apostles were sent as Christ's representatives. They had full authority and were commissioned to proclaim authoritatively the message in oral and written form and to establish and build up churches. The prophets were endowed by the Holy Spirit with the gift of prophecy for the purpose of edification, comfort, and encouragement (1 Cor 14:3, 31); they were enabled by the Spirit to understand and communicate the mysteries and revelation of God to the church (1 Cor 12:10; 13:2; 14:22-25, 30-31).

These prophets are New Testament prophets, as also in 2:20. When prophets are listed with apostles (2:20; 4:11; 1 Cor 12:28, 29), the apostles are listed first and prophets second. If they referred to Old Testament prophets, it seems they most likely would have been listed before apostles. Also, when mentioned in 2:20 they are included with the apostles as part of the foundation of the new temple, the church, which is the content of this secret plan not revealed in the Old Testament. Furthermore, the present verse talks about the secret plan, which has been revealed in the New Testament era, as opposed to Old Testament times. Thus, the prophets here must be New Testament prophets. The designation "holy" given to the apostles and prophets signifies that they were set apart to receive God's message from the Holy Spirit and consequently pass it on to all.

The content of the secret plan is that the Gentiles are fellow heirs, fellow members of the body, and fellow participants of the promise in Christ through the Good News. The union of Jews and Gentiles is described by three Greek adjectives. First, Gentiles are fellow heirs. The Greek adjective *sunklēronomos* [TG4789, ZG5169] ("fellow heirs" or "joint heirs" with Christ) is used in Romans 8:17 of all believers who have been united to Christ. In Ephesians the term is used in an ecclesiological context designating believing Gentiles as joint heirs with believing Jews. Gentiles do not become Jews and thus fellow Israelites, rather they are fellow heirs with the Jews in Christ.

Second, Gentiles are "fellow members" (*sussōma* [TG4954, ZG5362]) of the body. This adjective could be literally translated "concorporate," but a smoother rendering is "members of the same body" or "fellow members of the body." Again, Gentiles are not merely fellow members with Jews but fellow members with the Jews in the body of Christ. This concept is discussed in chapter 2, where it states that both believing Jews and believing Gentiles are created into one new people (2:15), both are in one body (2:16), both are growing into a holy temple (2:21), and both are being built together as a place where God's Spirit dwells (2:22).

Third, Gentiles are fellow participants (*summetocha* [TG4830, ZG5212]) of the promise. Although the "promise" is not specified, it probably alludes to the covenants of promise from which the Gentiles were excluded before the New Testament era (2:12). Before the Cross, Gentiles could come under the pale of the covenants of promise by becoming Jews. Now in the New Testament era, Gentiles are fully accepted and are fellow participants of the promise with believing Jews. This promise includes Messiah, salvation, and the promise of the Spirit (Gal 3:14). The sphere of the union described by these three Greek adjectives is "in Christ." Hence, Gentiles (with Jews) are fellow heirs in Christ, fellow members of the body in Christ, and fellow participants of the promise in Christ (not "through Christ"). This concept is important; it counters the notion proposed by some that there is now a union of all Jews and Gentiles, whereas in actual fact, it is only Jews and Gentiles "in Christ." This makes good sense, for unbelieving Jews and unbelieving Gentiles are not united. The gospel proclaims the union of those who believe; it does not refer to the union of all humanity.

In conclusion, the secret plan is not that Gentiles would be saved, because the Old Testament already gives evidence for their salvation, but that believing Jews and believing Gentiles are together in Christ. This is a revolutionary concept for both Jews and Gentiles alike. The only way this union can be obtained is through the Good News. Those who respond, whether Jews or Gentiles, will receive not only salvation but will be united with all other believers in one body in Christ.

◆   ## 2. The ministry (3:7-13)

⁷By God's grace and mighty power, I have been given the privilege of serving him by spreading this Good News.

⁸Though I am the least deserving of all God's people, he graciously gave me the privilege of telling the Gentiles about the endless treasures available to them in Christ. ⁹I was chosen to explain to everyone* this mysterious plan that God, the Creator of all things, had kept secret from the beginning.

¹⁰God's purpose in all this was to use

the church to display his wisdom in its rich variety to all the unseen rulers and authorities in the heavenly places. ¹¹This was his eternal plan, which he carried out through Christ Jesus our Lord.

¹²Because of Christ and our faith in him,* we can now come boldly and confidently into God's presence. ¹³So please don't lose heart because of my trials here. I am suffering for you, so you should feel honored.

3:9 Some manuscripts do not include *to everyone.*   3:12 Or *Because of Christ's faithfulness.*

NOTES

3:7 *I have been given the privilege of serving him by spreading this Good News.* The emphasis is not on spreading the Good News but the fact that Paul has been placed into God's ministry on the basis of God's grace and power. The Greek word for "minister" (*diakonos* [TG1249, ZG1356]) is used for a king's servant (Esth 1:10, LXX) or waiter at a wedding feast (John 2:5). Another word for "servant," *doulos* [TG1401, ZG1528], emphasizes the servile relationship to a master, whereas *diakonos* stresses the activity of the servant.

3:8 *Though I am the least deserving of all God's people.* The term "God's people," from the word *hagios* [TG40/A, ZG41], means one set apart for God's use or God's service.

3:9 *mysterious plan.* The Greek is *mustērion* [TG3466, ZG3696] (so also 3:4; see note).

kept secret from the beginning. The phrase "from the beginning" is a good translation of the literal "from the ages"; it signifies that the mysterious plan was hidden before time. This indicates that the mystery was hidden in God before he created "all things"; according to 3:5, it was not revealed until the time of the apostles and prophets.

3:10 *God's purpose in all this was to use the church.* The Greek text includes the adverb "now" (hence, "to use the church now") to indicate again that God's multifaceted wisdom regarding the revelation of his secret plan is displayed "now" as opposed to in OT times.

3:11 *This was his eternal plan, which he carried out through Christ Jesus our Lord.* The verb in the second clause, *poieo* [TG4160, ZG4472], can mean "to conceive, form" in reference to planning (cf. Mark 3:6; 15:1), which would indicate that God formed his eternal plan in the person of Christ (NASB, NJB; Abbott 1897:90; Best 1998:328). The verb can also mean "to accomplish, achieve" (3:20; 6:6; Matt 21:31; John 6:38); in this context it indicates that God accomplished his eternal plan in Christ's death (RSV, NEB, TEV, NIV, NRSV, NLT; Eadie 1883:236; Lincoln 1990:189; O'Brien 1999:248). The latter interpretation is preferred because (1) it makes better sense of the aorist tense; otherwise, a present or perfect tense would be expected. (2) Its voice is active rather than middle, conveying the idea of achievement or accomplishment, and (3) the context indicates that the union of believing Jews and believing Gentiles into one body was accomplished by Christ's death.

Christ Jesus our Lord. There are three elements in this title: (1) Christ's lordship as our "Lord"; (2) his name, "Jesus"; (3) his title, "Christ," which denotes that he is the promised Messiah who would bring salvation both to the Jews and Gentiles.

3:12 *Because of Christ and our faith in him, we can now come boldly and confidently into God's presence.* Lit., "in whom we have boldness and access in confidence through faith in him." The preposition *en* [TG1722, ZG1877] with the relative pronoun *hō* [TG3739, ZG4005] relates back to Christ as the sphere in whom we have access to the Father.

3:13 *So please don't lose heart because of my trials here.* The NLT translation "so" is a rendering of the strong inferential conjunction *dio* [TG1352, ZG1475] ("therefore" or "for this reason") to introduce the conclusion of a long conditional sentence that began with 3:2 (see notes on 3:2).

COMMENTARY

In this section Paul discusses his ministry: dispensing God's secret plan to the Gentiles. There are three parts to this discussion. First, he relates how God placed him in the ministry and his feeling of unworthiness (3:7-8a). Second, he explains that he carries out this ministry by preaching the unfathomable wealth of Christ (3:8b) and by enlightening all humanity concerning this mysterious plan (3:9). Third, he develops the purpose of his ministry (3:10-12), which is threefold: to make known God's wisdom to angelic rulers through the church (3:10), to show that God accomplished his eternal plan in Christ (3:11), and to explain the free access to God that believers enjoy (3:12).

Paul had already explained his administration of the secret plan, how and when it was revealed, and its content (3:2-6). Now he relates how he was placed into the ministry of imparting the knowledge of the secret plan to the Gentiles (3:7-8a), and then he speaks about his responsibility in that ministry (3:8b-12). He told his readers that he did not earn nor work for this responsibility; rather, it was a gift of God's grace. This gracious gift was accomplished by the working of God's power. So by God's grace, he was made a minister, and by God's enabling power he was able to carry out the ministry. God does not give responsibility without the provision of his enabling power to carry it out. In the end God is to be praised, for people can neither initiate nor accomplish God's work by their own energy or efforts. Further, Paul exclaims that he did not deserve the privilege of this ministry. He considered himself not just the least of all the apostles but the least of all the believers. This was not false modesty but true humility. Elsewhere, Paul called himself the foremost of sinners and not worthy of God's salvation (1 Tim 1:15). He was ever mindful of the past when he had blasphemed and persecuted Christ (Acts 9:4-5; 26:11, 14-15; 1 Tim 1:13) and had persecuted the church (Acts 8:1-3; 9:1-2, 4-5, 7-8; 26:9-11, 14-15; 1 Cor 15:9; Gal 1:13; Phil 3:6). Yet God, in his grace, had chosen Paul as his minister.

By God's appointment, Paul's ministry was among the Gentiles (Acts 9:15; 22:21; Rom 11:13; Gal 2:8-9; 1 Tim 2:7). He was called upon to preach to the Gentiles the "endless treasures available to them in Christ." The word for "endless" does not mean "inexhaustible" but refers to the "inscrutable, incomprehensible, unfathomable" wealth of Christ (3:8b). This unfathomable wealth of Christ refers to the gracious provision of redemption (1:7; 2:8-10). Before Christ came, the covenant nation of Israel was the recipient of God's grace, but now the endless treasures of Christ are available to the Gentiles! Furthermore, not only was Paul to make known the endless treasures of Christ to the Gentiles, but he was also to enlighten all people of the administration of God's mystery or secret plan, which had been hidden in God from the beginning (3:9). This statement indicates that the mystery had not been partially revealed in the Old Testament and then more fully revealed in the New Testament. Rather, it was not known in Old Testament times but is now finally revealed in the New Testament era. Although Gentiles had been included within Israel in Old Testament times by becoming Jewish, the hidden plan had now revealed that believing Jews and believing Gentiles formed a new entity called the church. In conclusion, then, the endless treasures of Christ include the message of redemption and the enlightenment of the mystery or secret plan to all humanity.

Paul has established his placement in the ministry, stating that it was by God's enabling grace (3:7-8a), in order to preach the unfathomable treasures of Christ and to enlighten all people regarding the hidden mystery (3:8b-9). He now states that the purpose of this ministry is, through the church, to make known God's wisdom to the angelic powers (3:10-12). As discussed in 1:8 and 17, wisdom is insight into the true nature of things. Here the adjective *polupoikilos* [TG4182, ZG4497] further describes wisdom as multifaceted. The root of this adjective was used to describe intricate embroidery, such as Joseph's coat of many colors (Gen 37:3, LXX). In the present context, it alludes to the variegated facets of God's wisdom and hence the translation, "his wisdom in its rich variety." Although in the past God had demonstrated a multifaceted wisdom in his various dealings with humanity, in the present context Paul was referring specifically to the unification of believing Jews and believing Gentiles into one new humanity in Christ. By commissioning Paul to preach the unfathomable treasures of Christ and enlighten all humanity of the hidden mystery, God, through the church, is making known his multifaceted wisdom to the rulers and authorities in the heavenly realms. As mentioned in 1:21, the "rulers and authorities" most likely have reference to angelic leaders. They may include both good and evil angels. Throughout time, good angels had desired to decipher God's plan (1 Pet 1:12) but had been unable to do so. It is probable that evil angels would want to know God's plans in advance in order to attempt to frustrate them. It is very possible that animosity between Jews and Gentiles is encouraged by evil angels. However, this animosity is also a very natural one (as seen in 2:11-12). But now with the revelation of God's secret plan, whereby believing Jews and Gentiles compose one body, the church, God's multifaceted wisdom is manifested through the church so that the angelic leaders, both good and evil, can have this knowledge. Both good and evil angels would have considered this inconceivable, even impossible. It should be noted that the members of this union do not preach to the "rulers and authorities" but rather serve as a witness to them.

According to 3:11, the revelation of God's multifaceted wisdom to the rulers and authorities had been planned by God in eternity past but was to be accomplished in Christ. The last part of this verse presents an interpretative problem. It could be interpreted that God's eternal plan was formed or conceived in connection with Christ in eternity past. This view emphasizes the personal element of Christ's involvement in the making of the plan. However, it could be interpreted that the revelation of God's wisdom was God's eternal plan and was carried out or accomplished in Christ's death. The latter interpretation makes better sense in the present context because, as Paul discussed the revelation of the mystery of the union of believing Jews and Gentiles into one body, he specifically stated that it was accomplished on the cross "by" or "in" Christ Jesus our Lord (2:14).

Having established that God's eternal plan was conceived in the past and achieved in the death of Christ Jesus our Lord, Paul explains the wonderful privilege of access that believers have to their Heavenly Father. This access is described by two nouns. The first is *parrēsia* [TG3954, ZG4244], which was used of free speech in Athens and was characterized by a frankness that could be misused when there was a lack of restraint. In the New Testament it conveys openness, speaking freely (Mark 8:32; John 7:4, 13, 26; Col 2:15), boldness or candor (Acts 2:29; 4:13), and confidence (2 Cor 7:4). Basically, it means freedom to speak without restraint. Believers in Christ can speak freely, boldly, or openly with confidence to the Father. In the Old Testament, there are many illustrations of people speaking openly with God. Moses and David are two such examples (see Exod 32:11-13; Pss 6; 13). In the New Testament, Jesus' honest communication with his Father is clearly illustrated in Gethsemane (Matt 26:36-44; Mark 14:32-39; Luke 22:40-44). Whereas the first noun gives the idea of the freedom of address, the second noun *prosagōgē* [TG4318, ZG4643], already used in 2:18, means access and freedom of approach. These two nouns are followed by a prepositional phrase *en pepoithēsei* [TG1722/4006, ZG1877/4301], which means "with confidence." Thus, believers may not only speak freely to the Father and approach him freely, but both may be done with confidence. This confidence must not stem from arrogance or presumptuousness but from faith in Christ. The present tense of the verb indicates a continuous action, showing that we may, with confidence, continually speak freely to God and enter his presence with boldness. For the Gentiles in particular, this was astounding news. Previously they had been far from God, but now they were able to come into God's presence without fear and speak openly and frankly to him, just as Moses and David of old had done.

In the final verse of this section, Paul tells his readers that if they truly had understood the administration of God's grace entrusted to him, they would not be in despair about his present sufferings for them. Rather, they would feel honored that he was in prison for them. Paul was not a masochist. He was simply stating that if he had not been disseminating the message of God's secret plan of the union of believing Jews and Gentiles into one body, then Jews would not have been hostile to him and he would not have been imprisoned. His faithfulness in disseminating the message of God's secret plan had made it possible for many Gentiles to become members of the church, Christ's body.

◆ **G. Prayer for Strengthened Love (3:14-21)**
   1. The approach to prayer (3:14-15)

14When I think of all this, I fall to my knees and pray to the Father,* 15the Creator of everything in heaven and on earth.*

3:14 Some manuscripts read *the Father of our Lord Jesus Christ.* 3:15 Or *from whom every family in heaven and on earth takes its name.*

NOTES
3:14 *When I think of all this.* The Greek text begins this verse with the prepositional phrase "for this reason" (*toutou charin* [TG3778/5484, ZG4047/5920]), which indicates a resumption of the sentence begun in 3:1, a sentence interrupted by the long digression of 3:2-13.

I fall to my knees and pray to the Father. The Greek text does not have "and pray," but it is clearly implied when Paul states, "I fall to my knees." There are three parts to the prayer: the approach to prayer (3:13-14), the appeal in prayer (3:16-19), and the ascription of praise (3:20-21). This prayer is the fifth of the eight long sentences in this epistle (1:3-14, 15-23; 2:1-7; 3:2-13, 14-19; 4:1-6, 11-16; 6:14-20) with 126 words. Generally speaking, it is not unusual to employ lengthy sentences for prayer.

to the Father. After "Father" some texts add the words "of our Lord Jesus Christ." The additional words have wide distribution in the manuscript tradition, while their omission is found primarily in the Alexandrian text-type.

3:15 *the Creator of everything in heaven and on earth.* The Greek text literally states, "from whom every family in heaven and on the earth is named." Although difficult to decipher, it probably refers to God's sovereignty in his creation, stressing his continued activity in history, which is demonstrated by his naming of every family in heaven and on earth.

COMMENTARY

As previously mentioned, in 2:11-22 Paul had discussed the union of believing Jews and Gentiles into one body, the church. At the beginning of chapter 3, it appears that he was intending to offer a prayer on behalf of these believers, but he stopped right in the middle of the sentence (at the end of 3:1) and digressed to the subject of the secret plan of God. He then resumed his prayer by first explaining that he fell to his knees before the Father. This coincides well with 3:12, where he had just mentioned believers' access to God. His action provides a timely example to them.

The Father to whom Paul prayed is described as the one who names every family in heaven and on earth. There is a play on words here because Paul prays to the *patera* [TG3962, ZG4252] (father) from whom every *patria* [TG3965, ZG4255] (family) is named. This last word conveys the sense of a family headed by a father (Exod 12:3; 1 Chr 23:11, LXX) or a nation that is composed of many families, all of which have originated from one father (cf. Acts 3:25). Paul described the Father as the one who names every family in heaven and on earth. As a human father gives names to children born into his family, so the heavenly Father names all those whom he creates. The present tense may well indicate that God continues to name every family, since he is still creating them. He is a God who is alive and acting in the present time, rather than a god who has died and is no longer active in history.

This was Paul's second prayer in Ephesians. His first prayer (1:15-23) for the believers was that they would have a deeper relationship with the God who had enriched them with every spiritual benefit, and that they would experience those benefits in a deeper way (1:3-14). His second prayer sprang out of what he had developed in 2:11–3:13. He had explained that believing Jews and believing Gentiles had become "one new person," the body of Christ—positionally speaking. He now proceeds to pray that they would be united experientially. He desired that they would experience the power of Christ's love in them and through them in their love for one another.

◆   ## 2. The appeal in prayer (3:16-19)

¹⁶I pray that from his glorious, unlimited resources he will empower you with inner strength through his Spirit. ¹⁷Then Christ will make his home in your hearts as you trust in him. Your roots will grow down into God's love and keep you strong. ¹⁸And may you have the power to understand, as all God's people should, how wide, how long, how high, and how deep his love is. ¹⁹May you experience the love of Christ, though it is too great to understand fully. Then you will be made complete with all the fullness of life and power that comes from God.

NOTES

3:16 *I pray that from his glorious, unlimited resources.* This is a good rendering of the literal text, "I pray that he may grant you according to the wealth of his glory." "According to the wealth of his glory" indicates that the wealth is in accordance with the infinite nature of God's glory.

3:17 *Christ will make his home in your hearts as you trust in him.* Rather than another request, this is a continuation of the request in 3:16 for their inner spiritual strength. Continuing, Paul prays that the result of this strength is that Christ would be at home in their hearts. "As you trust in him" is literally "through/by faith."

Your roots will grow down into God's love. This is a participial clause syntactically related to the subject of the following verb—hence the rendering, "that you, being rooted and grounded in love, might have power to understand with all of God's people . . . ." This expression combines two metaphors, *rooting* from agriculture and *grounding* from architecture. Though there is some debate as to whether it might refer to God's love (NLT; Best 1998:343; O'Brien 1999:260) or Christ's love (John Chrysostom, *Ephesians* 3:18-19; PG 62.51), it is best to see this as the believers' love (Eadie 1883:249; Lincoln 1990:207), which is rooted in God's love that he displayed in choosing, redeeming, and sealing them (1:4-14).

3:18 *And may you have the power to understand, as all God's people should.* The "power to understand" refers to the "ability" to understand. "God's people" is a translation of "saints," those who are set apart for God and his service.

3:19 *May you experience the love of Christ.* This verse begins with the postpositive conjunction *te* [TG5037, ZG5445] to indicate an internal logical relationship and can be translated "and so, to know the love of Christ."

though it is too great to understand fully. This comment is intended to intimate the vastness of the love of Christ, which is too great to comprehend fully. Rather than stating it negatively, the Greek text states it positively, "which surpasses knowledge."

Then you will be made complete with all the fullness of life and power that comes from God. The KJV and RSV translations ("that you may be filled with all the fullness of God") wrongly imply that the whole fullness of God can be contained in a believer's life. They ignore the preposition *eis* [TG1519, ZG1650], which indicates movement toward a goal and is more accurately translated in the NIV "to the measure of." So it can be translated "that you might be filled up to all the fullness of God."

COMMENTARY

Paul's request in this prayer can be divided into two parts: his petition (3:16-17a) and its purpose (3:17b-19). His petition is that believers will be strengthened in the inner person. He asks for the power of God that is according to the wealth of his glory. The word "glory" conveys the idea of the reflection of the essence of one's being, the summation of all of one's attributes. The wealth of God's glory is the wealth of his essential being. Hence, the rendering "unlimited resources" accurately portrays his wealth. Continuing, he prays that they would be strengthened with power in the inner person. Paul uses two words for power. The first is *dunamis* [TG1411, ZG1539], already defined in the note on 1:19 as "power, ability, capability to act." It has a living and dynamic sense. The second word is a complementary infinitive, *krataiōthēnai* [TG2901, ZG3194], meaning "to be strengthened with power/ability." The passive voice reinforces the idea that it is God who gives the strength; it is not self-endowed.

The following prepositional phrase "through his Spirit," a reference to the Holy Spirit, underscores that it is God's power. It is the Holy Spirit that enables believers to be strengthened with God's power. This power is to be in the sphere of the inner person, which is described in 2 Corinthians 4:16 as being renewed day by day, in contrast to the "outer" person, who is perishing. Hence, the inner person (or, innermost being) is to be strengthened with God's power through God's Spirit. The words "inner strength" correspond with the "heart" in the following verse. Paul proceeds to explain in 3:17a that this renewal is necessary so that Christ may dwell in their hearts by faith. At first glance, this is a curious request since Christ already dwells in their hearts. However, the word "dwell" is accurately rendered in the NLT as "make his home in your hearts." The infinitive *katoikēsai* [TG2730, ZG2997] is a compound verb that means "to dwell, reside, inhabit, settle down"—a settled dwelling. Hence, there is the objective strengthening through God's Spirit and the subjective means by which believers obtain this. The infinitive "to dwell" expresses the result of this innermost strength, which is the deep indwelling of Christ in peoples' hearts by faith. Thus, the Trinity—Father (3:14), Spirit (3:16), and Son (3:17)—is involved in the spiritual growth of believers. Paul prayed to the Father for the believers to be strengthened by the Spirit with the result that Christ would be deeply rooted in their lives through faith.

Having made the petition (3:16-17a), Paul now states its purpose, namely, that believers would at least partly understand Christ's love and that this would result in a deep love for one another (3:17b-19). The participial clause is difficult to decipher. Rather than expressing a new request, it most likely relates syntactically to the following verb. Two metaphors are used to express the same idea. The first one is agricultural, *firmly rooted*, and the second one is architectural, *firmly founded*. The root and foundation of love is God, who chose believers, predestinated them, graciously bestowed grace on them in the Beloved One, redeemed them, made them a heritage, sealed them with the Holy Spirit, made them alive, raised and seated them in the heavenly realms, and placed them equally in one new person in the body of Christ. Paul's previous request for them to be strengthened in the inner person (3:16), with the result that Christ would be at home in their hearts (3:17), was for the purpose that they, who had been rooted and grounded in love, might be able to comprehend Christ's love (3:18-19). This applies to all of God's people.

Much discussion has been generated concerning the four dimensions: width, length, height, and depth. Although they could have reference to the wisdom or power of God, they probably refer to Christ's love. This suits the context well, since in the preceding verse (3:17) Paul referred to Christ's dwelling deeply in their hearts, and in the next verse (3:19) they are enjoined to know the love of Christ. Also, the spatial dimensions fit well with the agricultural and architectural metaphors used to portray rooting and grounding in love, which has its source in the love of God. The four dimensions delineate not so much the thoroughness of the comprehension as the vastness of the thing to be comprehended. Paul prayed that the believers might be able to comprehend the vast dimensions of Christ's love, with the result that they might know experientially that love that surpasses knowledge. To fully comprehend the sacrificial love of Christ is beyond the capability of any human being. His continued love for believers is equally incomprehensible. In fact, no matter how much knowledge believers have about Christ, his amazing love surpasses that knowledge, and the more we know of that love, the more we should praise him for it. However, mere knowledge of his love is not the end; rather, it issues into a final purpose, namely that we might be filled up toward all the fullness of God.

The fullness of the Godhead dwells in Christ, and only through him is a believer made complete (Col 2:9-10). Though in Christ this divine fullness already belongs to the believer positionally, Paul prayed that it might be experientially appropriated in each one (cf. 4:13). In 1:23 Paul concluded that the church was being filled with the moral excellence and power of God; in the present context the fullness involves the love of Christ. It is important to keep in mind that this vast love cannot be fully experienced by any single individual; it takes all the believers to appreciate the fullness of Christ's love (see also 1:23; Col 2:9-10).

As believing Jews and Gentiles experience God's moral excellence, perfection, and power, a love for each other will result. Positionally, we are one in Christ (2:11–3:13); experientially, we are to love one another as one in him. As a result, Jesus' asserts that "Your love for one another will prove to the world that you are my disciples" (John 13:35). This starkly contrasts with the situation prior to redemption when there was animosity between Jews and Gentiles.

◆   ## 3. The ascription of praise (3:20-21)

20Now all glory to God, who is able, through his mighty power at work within us, to accomplish infinitely more than we might ask or think. 21Glory to him in the church and in Christ Jesus through all generations forever and ever! Amen.

NOTES

3:20 *Now all glory to God, who is able.* Lit, "Now to the one who is able." What God is meant to receive (i.e., "glory") is not stated in the Greek text until the next verse.

3:21 *through all generations forever.* This speaks of the generations of human life that continue into eternity.

COMMENTARY

Paul ended his prayer with a doxology. This doxology provides a very fitting conclusion to his prayer, as well as to the previous section in which the mystery was revealed (2:11–3:13), and finally, to the entire first three chapters.

Before Paul offers this praise to God, he delineates who God is—that is, he is the one who is able to do infinitely beyond all that we might ask or think. Humanly speaking, it might be readily surmised that true reconciliation between Jews and Gentiles could never happen. Paul had prayed that there would be true love between them, achievable only in the power of the Holy Spirit. Paul believed that God is able to do infinitely beyond what we ask or think. Earlier, Paul prayed that believers would be strengthened with power through the Spirit (3:16); now he gives praise to God for that power and then continues by stating that believers can appropriate that power, which is working in them. He again uses *dunamis* [TG1411, ZG1539] to indicate a dynamic, living power that is capable of working in the believers. Paul expresses confidence that true reconciliation between Jewish and Gentile believers is possible through God's infinite and matchless power of love in the life of each believer.

In his concluding remarks in this chapter, Paul gives glory to God. This is the last time "glory" (*doxa* [TG1391, ZG1518]) is used in the letter. It conveys the reflection of the essence of one's being, the summation of all of one's attributes, and here it refers to God's splendor, power, and radiance. God's great work of reconciling Jewish and Gentile believers cannot but prompt an outflow of praise to him who is glorified in the church. Our praise must also go to Christ Jesus, the person in whom the reconciliation was accomplished. It is his creation, the church, into which believing Jews and Gentiles are united. Indeed, the church could not have come into existence without him. The ending to this doxology is unique. Both the terms "generation" and "forever" are used, indicating an apparent mixture of both time on earth and in eternity. All generations, that is, all human life, will give praise eternally. Therefore, God is to be glorified, beginning with the present age and continuing into eternity.

Paul marked the end of his prayer and doxology with "amen," a term he used almost exclusively to end doxologies. Its basic use is to confirm what has just been stated. Here it is a "yes" to the praise just expressed. It does not reflect Paul's pride in his own wording but rather his sense of being overwhelmed by God's grace and glory. He was essentially saying, "Let me repeat that again." This "amen" not only concludes his prayer and doxology but also concludes the doctrinal section of this book. It is a truly fitting response to the powerful message Paul has imparted in these three chapters.

◆ II. The Conduct of the Church (4:1–6:24)
    A. Live in Unity (4:1–16)
        1. The basis of unity (4:1–6)

Therefore I, a prisoner for serving the Lord, beg you to lead a life worthy of your calling, for you have been called by God. ²Always be humble and gentle. Be patient with each other, making allowance for each other's faults because of your love. ³Make every effort to keep yourselves united in the Spirit, binding yourselves together with peace. ⁴For there is one body and one Spirit, just as you have been called to one glorious hope for the future. ⁵There is one Lord, one faith, one baptism, ⁶and one God and Father, who is over all and in all and living through all.

NOTES

4:1 *Therefore I, a prisoner for serving the Lord, beg you.* The first three words in the Greek text are the same as Rom 12:1, *parakalō oun humas*—"therefore, I urge you" (cf. *parakaleō* [TG3870, ZG4151] "urge"). The expression signals the beginning of an appeal.

to lead a life worthy of your calling. "To lead a life" is a good rendering of the Greek word "walk." It does not speak of a literal walk; it is used as a metaphor for one's lifestyle. Believers are first exhorted to have a proper attitude toward unity (4:1-3) and then are shown how the three persons of the Trinity serve as the basis of this unity (4:4-6). This section (4:1-6) is the sixth of eight long sentences in this epistle (cf. 1:3-14, 15-23; 2:1-7; 3:2-13, 14-19; 4:1-6, 11-16; 6:14-20) with 71 words.

4:2 *making allowance for each other's faults because of your love.* The participle "making allowance" or "forbearing" carries an imperatival force and appears to relate back to the enjoinder to lead a life worthy of one's calling, implying that it is accomplished by forbearing one another in love. The word "forbear" is frequently used in classical literature, meaning "to take up, to bear up, to endure." It is used 16 times in the LXX, where it includes the idea of God's endurance of the Israelites' vain offerings (Isa 1:13) and Job's endurance through great trials (Job 6:11, 26). It is used in the NT 15 times. It is used when Jesus asks how long he must put up with the disciples (Matt 17:17; Mark 9:19; Luke 9:41) and when Paul speaks of enduring in persecution (1 Cor 4:12; cf. 2 Thess 1:4). Hence, this word refers to bearing or enduring with respect to things or persons. The word "faults" does not appear in the Greek text, and its use in the NLT is perhaps too restrictive. We are to make allowance not only for faults but also for differences.

4:3 *binding yourselves together with peace.* This is not a new or additional exhortation, but further explains the first part of the verse. Believers are to keep or maintain the unity established by the Holy Spirit in a bond consisting of peace.

COMMENTARY

The first three chapters laid the foundation by revealing that God has chosen, from among Jews and Gentiles, a people for himself who are united into one body, the church. Paul has characterized the unity of believing Jews and Gentiles as "one new people" (2:15), the body of Christ, and has prayed for the perfection of that unity through the mutual experience of Christ's empowering love (3:16-19). He now demonstrates how this is accomplished by God's power through the ministry of gifted people given by Christ to the church so that the body might grow into spiritual maturity.

In the latter three chapters of this epistle, Paul instructs God's people how to conduct themselves in union with Christ and with each other. Paul used only one imperative in chapters 1–3 (2:11), whereas forty imperatives appear in chapters 4–6. In chapters 4 and 5, the inferential conjunction "therefore" (*oun* [TG3767, ZG4036]) is used five times in connection with the imperative "live your lives" (lit., "walk" from *peripateō* [TG4043, ZG4344]; see 4:1, 17; 5:2, 8, 15), and in the conclusion the exhortation "to stand" (*histēmi* [TG2476, ZG2705]) is given to defend against satanic attacks (6:10-20). All of these data emphasize the fact that Paul was exhorting the believers to live out the spiritual realities that had been given to them. In particular, in the first three chapters of Ephesians they were taught that believing Jews and Gentiles were united into one body; on this basis, Paul then exhorts them to walk in unity. He reminds them that his imprisonment had come about because he had declared to believing Gentiles (3:13) that they were fellow heirs in Christ with believing Jews. Thus, he told them to live "worthily" (*axiōs* [TG516, ZG547]) of this new position. The Greek adverb *axiōs* suggests a comparison of two things, like a weighing on a scale. Thus, to live worthily of our calling is to live in a way that matches the stature of that calling. Our conduct is to be "worthy," "comparable," or "suitable" to God's calling.

Paul's exhortation to lead a life worthy of their calling is further qualified by a declaration of the manner in which it is to be accomplished (4:2-3). First, believers are to be humble. Whereas formerly, pride engendered deep divisions between Jews and Gentiles, humility engenders unity among them. The supreme example of humility is Christ (Phil 2:6-8).

Second, along with humility believers are to exhibit gentleness or meekness, the opposite of roughness. This word does not imply that one should become a "doormat." Aristotle categorized the quality Paul is speaking of as a moral virtue that is the mean between one who is angry against everyone on all occasions and the one who is never angry about anything (*Magna Moralia* 1.22.2-3). One can illustrate this with the temperament of dogs. A well-trained dog is always angry at the master's foe and never angry at the master's friends. So a gentle person is angry when a wrong has been done, but accepting and friendly when all is right and good. This quality of gentleness is seen in Jesus, who was gentle and humble in heart (Matt 11:29) and yet displayed anger, for example, toward those who had transformed the Temple into a den of thieves (Matt 21:12-13). Moses is depicted as one who was more gentle than all people on earth (Num 12:3), and yet he displayed anger when he found the people of Israel sinning against God by creating a golden calf (Exod 32).

Third, believers are to display patience. Patience is achieved only by means of a true perspective of hope. For instance, Rome would wait patiently in the midst of defeat with the hope of winning the war (1 Macc 8:4). Farmers wait patiently for the anticipated harvest. The Old Testament prophets waited patiently for God to act (Jas 5:7-11). God patiently holds back his anger against humanity with the hope of repentance (Rom 2:4). In fact, Paul lists patience as among the fruit of the Spirit (Gal 5:22). Most believers want patience—but they want it immediately! Certainly, in the present context Paul enjoins patience as a necessary ingredient for the life of Jewish and Gentile believers who comprise the body of Christ.

The concluding participial clause, "making allowance for each other's faults because of your love" is not a fourth quality after "humbleness, gentleness, and patience" but rather refers back to the exhortation for believers to lead a life worthy of their calling. This participial clause most likely has an imperatival force, calling for the church, which is composed of believing Jews and Gentiles—once hostile to one another—to be united into one body. As noted above, the word "faults" is not in the Greek text. Therefore, it may be construed that we are enjoined not only to forbear one another's faults but also each other's differences—that is, in areas where no wrongdoing is involved. No doubt there remained many such differences between the two groups, even as in today's church with all its diverse elements. Obedience to this exhortation eliminates resentment among members within the body of Christ.

Along with the participial clause "making allowance for each other's faults," Paul introduces a second participial clause: "[making] every effort to keep yourselves united in the Spirit, binding yourselves together with peace." As with the first participial clause, so also this participial clause has an imperative force, as it relates back to the injunction to lead a life worthy of the believers' calling (4:1). It must be observed that believers are not instructed to *make* unity but to *keep* the unity already in existence. It refers to the union of believing Jews and Gentiles brought about by the creation of "one new people," so making "peace" (2:15). In the present context, Paul states that this unity was achieved by the Holy Spirit and is exhibited in a bond that consists of peace, by which believers will lovingly maintain relationships with each other in spite of differences.

In 4:4-6 Paul develops the basis for unity, listing seven elements centered on the three persons of the Trinity. The sevenfold use of "one" gives emphasis to the concept of unity. First, there is one body, referring to the universal church already mentioned (1:23; 2:16; 3:5-6). As previously stated, it is not Gentiles becoming Jews, as in the Old Testament, nor Jews becoming Gentiles, but believing Jews and Gentiles becoming one body of believers. They are no longer two entities but one. Second, there is one Spirit. This refers to the Holy Spirit mentioned in 2:18, 22, where it states that this body of believers has access to God in one Spirit and where the body is portrayed as a temple in which the Spirit dwells. Third, there is one hope, which all believers have in common regarding their future with God, a confidence that began at the time they were "called" (1:18; see also 1:4; 2:7; 4:1). Before conversion, the Gentiles were without hope and without God in the world (2:12). Now having been brought near to God, united into one body in Christ and reconciled to God (2:11–3:13), they have hope. Since both believing Jews and Gentiles have "one" (or "the same") hope, it further supports the concept of unity portrayed in these verses.

The fourth element of unity is "one Lord" (4:5), no doubt a reference to Christ, since Paul has just mentioned the Holy Spirit in 4:4 and will mention the Father in 4:6. Christ is the "one Lord" who provided redemption (1:7), hope (1:12), and headship over the church (1:22-23). It is Christ who brought believing Jews and Gentiles into one body; so he is the "one" Lord. Fifth, there is one faith. The reference to faith here most likely is not the object of faith, that is, the body of truth believed by Christians (as in Acts 6:7; 1 Tim 3:9; 4:1, 6; Jude 1:3, 20) but the act of faith, which is exercised by all Christians in Christ their Lord (cf. Col 2:7). Earlier, Paul had mentioned that the Ephesians had expressed their faith when they heard the message (1:13) and that their faith in the Lord Jesus was widely known (1:15). Thus, it is one faith in one Lord. Sixth, there is one baptism. Most commentators consider this a reference to water baptism (e.g., Abbott 1897:109; Lincoln 1990:240; Best 1998:369). In the early church, faith in Christ was closely tied to water baptism (Acts 2:38; 8:16, 35-39; 19:5; 1 Cor 1:13-15). However, water baptism is an outward manifestation of the inward reality of the believers' union with Christ in his death and resurrection. Hence, the "one baptism" may refer to the believers' identification with Christ (O'Brien 1999:284; Hoehner 2002:517-518). This is similar to the baptism of Israel into Moses as they went through the Red Sea (1 Cor 10:2) and the baptism of the disciples with reference to Christ's death (Mark 10:38). This same concept is seen in other New Testament passages (Rom 6:1-11; Gal 3:27; Col 2:12). Hence, the "one baptism" may refer to our identification with Christ's death and resurrection, which serves as the basis for the ritual of water baptism. It is unlikely that the baptism refers to Spirit baptism because the phrase "one baptism" is in the triad of elements of unity that pertain to the second person of the Trinity ("one Lord") and because nothing in the broader context (4:1-16) refers to the Spirit's baptism.

The seventh and final element of unity is "one God and Father" (4:6). In spite of claims that many gods exist, there is only one true God (cf. 1 Cor 8:5-6), who is also "Father" (cf. Rom 15:6; 1 Cor 15:24; 2 Cor 1:3; 11:31; Gal 1:4). God is further described as "over us all," which refers not to all humanity but to all believers (John 1:12; Gal 3:26). That this is not a reference to all humanity is borne out in the present context, which speaks of the unity of all believers modeled by the Father of all believers. Furthermore, the next words of the verse "and in us all and living through us all" would argue against the universal Father of all humanity. The New Testament does not depict that God is in every human being but that he resides in believers only (Rom 8:9). Believers need to recognize his transcendent sovereignty over them ("over all") and his imminent involvement with them ("in all and living through all"). The indication that God is in all believers ("over all") is the indwelling Spirit (John 14:16-17; Rom 8:9; 1 Cor 2:12; 6:19-20; Gal 3:2; 4:6; 1 John 2:27; 3:24; 4:13) and his intimate presence. Paul had previously prayed (in 3:17) that Christ might be at home in their hearts. Although Christ was already in them, Paul wanted him to be central in their lives. Earlier Paul spoke about God, in the person of the Holy Spirit, dwelling in the corporate body of the church (2:22); he now is talking about the personal dwelling of God in individual believers.

Two observations should be noted about this list of the seven unifying elements (4:4-6). First, the Trinity is an integral part of this treatise on unity. The one body of believers is vitalized by one *Spirit*, so that all believers have hope. That body is united to its one *Lord* (Christ) by each member's one act of faith and identification with him in one baptism. One *God*, the Father, is supreme over all, resides in all, and is operative in all. This is in line with the rest of Ephesians, which is known for its abundant references to the Trinity (cf. 1:4-14, 17; 2:18, 22; 3:4-5, 14-17; 4:4-6; 5:18-20).

Second, the order in the listing of the three persons of the Trinity is worth noting. Rather than God the Father, the Holy Spirit is listed first. Most likely, the reason for this is that in the preceding verses Paul has discussed being "united in the Spirit" (4:3) and in the immediately following verses (4:7-13) he elaborates on the gifts of the Spirit. The same order of the persons of the Trinity is given in 1 Corinthians 12:4-6, where Paul also expatiates on the gifts of the Spirit. From a theological perspective, Paul works back to the ultimate source—the Father, since all proceeds from him.

◆   2. The preservation of unity (4:7-16)

7However, he has given each one of us a special gift* through the generosity of Christ. 8That is why the Scriptures say,

"When he ascended to the heights,
he led a crowd of captives
and gave gifts to his people."*

9Notice that it says "he ascended." This clearly means that Christ also descended to our lowly world.* 10And the same one who descended is the one who ascended higher than all the heavens, so that he might fill the entire universe with himself. 11Now these are the gifts Christ gave to the church: the apostles, the prophets, the evangelists, and the pastors and teachers. 12Their responsibility is to equip God's people to do his work and build up the church, the body of Christ. 13This will continue until we all come to such unity in our faith and knowledge of God's Son that we will be mature in the Lord, measuring up to the full and complete standard of Christ.

14Then we will no longer be immature like children. We won't be tossed and blown about by every wind of new teaching. We will not be influenced when people try to trick us with lies so clever they sound like the truth. 15Instead, we will speak the truth in love, growing in every way more and more like Christ, who is the head of his body, the church. 16He makes the whole body fit together perfectly. As each part does its own special work, it helps the other parts grow, so that the whole body is healthy and growing and full of love.

4:7 Greek *a grace.*   4:8 Ps 68:18.   4:9 Or *to the lowest parts of the earth.*

NOTES

4:7 *However, he has given each one of us a special gift.* "However" marks a contrast with what precedes it. "Special gift" is a translation of the word "grace" (*charis* [TG5485, ZG5921]). This indicates that the spiritual gift is an act of God's grace.

through the generosity of Christ. Lit., "according to the measure of the gift of Christ." The literal sense makes it clear that a certain measure is given to each. This does not imply, however, that God lacked some degree of generosity with certain people.

4:8 *That is why the Scriptures say.* Lit., "therefore, it says." The NLT's use of the plural "Scriptures" might lead to the impression that there are several references, whereas the use of the singular, "Scripture," would allow for reference either to a single verse, several verses, or the whole Bible. Also, the singular is more consistent with the NLT's use of the singular pronoun "it" in 4:9, which refers back to "Scriptures" in the present verse.

he led a crowd of captives. Lit., "he captured the captives." Who were the captives? There are two interpretations. (1) They were the enemies of Christ, namely, Satan, sin, and death, and they were defeated by Christ's death (Eadie 1883:288; Abbott 1897:113); or (2) they were captives of Satan, sin, and death that were taken captive by Christ through his redemption and now are his followers (Hendriksen 1967:191; O'Brien 1999:292-293; Hoehner 2002:529-530). The second view is favored by the NLT by its translation "crowd of captives."

4:9 *Notice that it says "he ascended."* Lit., "Now what is the 'he ascended?'" In other words, what does "he ascended" mean? The NLT is a good rendering, for it draws one's attention to those words.

Christ also descended to our lowly world. There is an ongoing debate about the prepositional phrase *eis ta katōtera merē tēs gēs* (cf. *katōteros* [TG2737, ZG3005] "lower parts") "unto the lower parts of the earth." Some would interpret the genitives as comparative genitives with reference to parts lower than the earth or under the earth, that is, Christ's descent into Hades (Ellicott 1884:85; Robinson 1903:96, 180). Others, including the translators of the NLT, would view the genitives as appositional, signifying "the lower parts, namely, the earth" (Eadie 1883:293-294; Best 1998:386; O'Brien 1999:295-296). Still others would view them as possessive genitives rendering them "the earth's lowest part, the grave" (John Chrysostom, *Ephesians* 4:9-10; PG 62.81-82; O'Brien 1999:295-296). More discussion of this follows in the commentary.

4:10 *the one who ascended higher than all the heavens.* This is a good rendering. Most translations (KJV, ASV, RSV, NASB, NEB, NRSV) render the adverb (used as an improper preposition) "far above," but this is an unusual meaning for the word.

4:11 *the apostles, the prophets, the evangelists, and the pastors and teachers.* In Greek these gifted persons are listed as predicate accusatives; it is best translated "some to be apostles, some to be prophets, some to be evangelists, and some to be pastors and teachers." This brings out the distinction that each gifted person has a particular function among the assembly of believers and is to function in the measure of the gift given (4:7). This verse begins a sentence that does not end until 4:16, making it the seventh of the eight long sentences in this epistle (cf. 1:3-14, 15-23; 2:1-7; 3:2-13, 14-19; 4:1-6, 11-16; 6:14-20) with 125 words.

4:12 *Their responsibility is to equip God's people to do his work and build up the church.* Lit., "for the equipping of the saints to the work of the ministry to the building up of the body of Christ." The task is to determine the relationship between the three prepositional phrases introduced by the prepositions *pros . . . eis . . . eis* [TG4314/1519, ZG4639/1650]. Most likely the first preposition gives the purpose to the main verb in 4:11 ("gave"), the second preposition depends on the first preposition, and the third preposition depends on the second. This signifies that the first preposition expresses the immediate purpose while the second and third prepositions signify the goal. The progression indicates that Christ gave gifted people to the church for the immediate purpose of equipping all believers with the goal of preparing them for the work of the ministry, which in turn has the final goal of building up the body of Christ.

4:13 *until we all come to such unity in our faith and knowledge of God's Son that we will be mature in the Lord, measuring up to the full and complete standard of Christ.* This verse begins with the word *mechri* [TG3360, ZG3588] (until), which is parallel to the first preposition in 4:12. It also relates back to the verb "he gave" in 4:11, denoting that Christ gave gifted individuals to the church, a process that will continue until the full maturity of the church is attained. This is followed with three prepositional phrases, each introduced by the preposition *eis* [TG1519, ZG1650]. Lit., the three prepositional phrases are "we all attain [1] unto the unity of the faith and the knowledge of the Son of God, [2] unto a mature man, [3] unto the measure of Christ's full stature."

4:14 *Then we will no longer be immature like children.* This rendering considers that the conjunction *hina* [TG2443, ZG2671] introduces result rather than its normal usage of introducing purpose. This is certainly possible and so rendered in many recent translations (RSV, NASB, TEV, JB, NIV, NJB).

4:15 *Instead, we will speak the truth in love.* The NLT's use of the adverb "instead" rightly marks the stark contrast with the previous verse. The rendering "speak the truth" is a translation of the participle "truthing." It conveys the idea of truthfulness both in speech and conduct.

4:16 *He makes the whole body fit together.* Lit., "from whom the whole body being joined together." The preposition with the relative pronoun literally means "out of, from." The relative pronoun refers back to Christ, not the head, and means "from whom the whole body is fitted," designating the source of growth.

As each part does its own special work. This refers back to the word *metron* [TG3358, ZG3586] (measure) in 4:13; it indicates that each member is to function in the measure of the gift that has been given to it (4:7).

full of love. Lit., "in love"—that is, building itself up in love. This corresponds to the truthfulness in love mentioned in the preceding verse.

COMMENTARY

After establishing the basis of the unity (4:1-6), Paul now examines the means of preserving the unity of the body—namely, by means of the various gifts given to the church (4:7-16). In this section Paul explains the giving of the gifts (4:7-10) and their distribution among the believers (4:11-16).

First, Paul states that each believer is sovereignly and graciously given a gift or gifts. Such gifts are not, as some think, limited only to church leaders. We know this because Paul begins with the adversative conjunction *de* [TG1161, ZG1254], translated "however"; it marks a contrast with the preceding verses, which refer to the church as a whole. The contrast signals that Paul was shifting from the "all" in 4:6 to the particular "each one of us" in 4:7. This indicates that every individual is included; no one is excluded. The gifts are not only for the leaders of the assembly. The gifts are specific "enablements" or "endowments" given to each believer to empower them for ministry. These gifts are closely connected with *charisma* [TG5486, ZG5922] (gift), which is used in the parallel passage on gifts (1 Cor 12:4, 9, 28, 30, 31). Moreover, in Romans 12:6, Paul places these two terms side by side in the passage on spiritual gifts. The present text clearly indicates that God gives each individual a specific ability that is to be used to minister for his glory.

As indicated in the notes above, the next prepositional phrase is literally translated "according to the measure of the gift of Christ." This denotes that God not only gives each believer a gift; he also determines the amount of the gift. The term "gift," already used in 3:7, means something graciously given by God. The source of this gift is clearly Christ. The "measure" (*metron* [TG3358, ZG3586]) of the gift carries significant import. It is used three times in the present passage (4:7, 13, 16). Compare the similar word *analogia* [TG356, ZG381] (proportion) in the parallel passage on spiritual gifts (Rom 12:6-8), where Paul states that gifts differ according to the grace given and are to be used accordingly, no more and no less. It follows that since the gift is measured out by Christ, there should be no jealousy within the body.

And now, we need to turn our attention to Paul's use of the Old Testament to validate the giving of gifts (4:8). Most scholars think that Paul was quoting from Psalm

68:18, with two major and four minor variations. The two major changes are the changes of both verbs from the second person singular "you ascended" to the third person singular "he ascended" and the change of the action of the last verb from the receiving of gifts from people (the defeated foes) to the giving of gifts to people (the believers). Much has been written in an attempt to reconcile the variations mentioned above. There have been two basic approaches. One view is that Paul altered the text of Psalm 68:18 to bring out its full meaning (Eadie 1883:83). The problem with this view is that instead of giving it a full meaning, it changes the meaning. Others suggest that Paul's replacement of "receive" with "give" resulted from his use of the Old Testament textual tradition found in the Targum (Lincoln 1990:242-243). Since the Targumist perceived that the "gifts" referred to the words of the law, he rendered the difficult expression "you received gifts from among people" in a way that he considered more appropriate to God's majesty, "you gave them as gifts to the sons of men." This was accomplished by a simple transposition of Hebrew consonants from *lqkh* (to receive) to *khlq* (to give). The Midrash (commentary) on Psalm 68 has the same interpretation. The problem with this rendering is that the Targum and Midrash are dated no earlier than fourth or fifth century AD, though some think they represent a pre-Christian interpretation.

However, it is possible that Paul did not cite a particular verse of the psalm; rather, he may have been summarizing the entire psalm using many words similar to those of Psalm 68:18. This approach is analogous to a news reporter who summarizes a thirty-minute speech in just two or three sentences. This psalm of victory portrays God as victor over the enemies of his people; he receives the spoils of victory, which he then disperses to his people Israel. The point is made that the victor has the right to give gifts to those who are joined with him. The proponents of this view assert that Paul applied this to the church in that Christ had victory over his enemies—namely, Satan, sin, and death—and gives gifts of the Spirit to those who have been identified with him. The problem with this view is that Christ does not receive gifts from defeated foes (as is stated in Ps 68), for such would be useless to God and his children. Consequently, those who were held in bondage to Satan, sin, and death have been freed and have obtained the gifts of the Spirit from their victorious Lord and Savior Jesus Christ.

Another way to look at Paul's use of Psalm 68 is that Paul was interpreting it for believers in this age (4:9-10). His interpretation revolves around two verbs from the psalm—namely, "ascended" (expounded in 4:9-10) and "gave" gifts (discussed in 4:11-16). Paul's discussion of the first word, "ascended" in 4:9-10 is somewhat parenthetical because the main theme in the context is the giving of gifts. Nevertheless, these two verses are important in order to establish that after his descent to the earth Christ ascended as victor over the enemy, thus giving him the right to give gifts. There has been some debate over the meaning of "ascent" and "descent" in this verse. The traditional interpretation views the "descent" as a reference to Christ's descent from heaven to earth at the time of his incarnation and the "ascent" as a reference to his ascent from earth to heaven after the Resurrection.

Others suggest, however, that the descent refers not to Christ's descent at the Incarnation but to his descent at Pentecost to give his spiritual gifts to the church (Caird 1976:74-75; Harris 1996:143-159; Lincoln 1990:242-244). This is parallel to the rabbinic tradition that associates Psalm 68 with Moses' ascent of Mount Sinai to "capture" the words of the Torah (in connection with the feast of Pentecost) and his descent from Mount Sinai to distribute to the people the "gifts" of the Torah. This view has not gained wide acceptance for the following reasons: (1) It assumes that the recipients of this letter (most of whom were Gentiles) would have had a necessary acquaintance with rabbinic traditions. Furthermore, though some elements of the rabbinic material may be dated in the first century, much of it is fifth century AD or later. (2) In Acts 2:33 there is mention of Jesus' exaltation, reception of the Holy Spirit from the Father, and the outpouring of the Spirit, but there is no mention of the giving of gifts (*domata* [TG1390, ZG1517]) as noted in the present context and in the psalm (Ps 67:19, LXX). (3) In the present context, the descent occurs before the ascent. The next verse makes this clear. If the ascent preceded the descent, 4:10 is meaningless. (4) In the present context, the same person descended and ascended, whereas this proposed interpretation views Christ's descent as the descent of the Holy Spirit. (5) The climax of Christ's activity is his ascension, since it is at that time that he fills all things (4:10), which includes filling the universe with the message of Christ by means of the messengers on whom he has bestowed the gifts. Thus, the traditional view that Christ's descent was at the incarnation and that he ascended to heaven shortly after his resurrection better fits with this passage.

The place to which Christ descended is delineated by the following prepositional phrase, *eis ta katōtera merē tēs gēs* (cf. *katōteros* [TG2737, ZG3005], "lower parts"). As noted above (see note on 4:9), this phrase is problematic. Below I discuss three views regarding its meaning.

The first view assumes the genitive *tēs gēs* (cf. *gē* [TG1093, ZG1178], "earth") is a comparative genitive denoting the "lower parts" as lower than the earth or beneath the earth; thus, the statement would refer to Christ's descent into Hades. This is the view put forth in the Apostles' Creed. Support for this view is seen in the next verse, where it states that Christ ascended above all the heavens, and in 1 Peter 3:19, where it suggests that between the time of Jesus' death and resurrection he preached to the departed spirits in this region. Most scholars question this interpretation for the following reasons. First, there is no indication that Jesus ascended from Hades, but there are references to his ascension from the earth (John 8:21-23; 16:28). Second, no time is suggested as to when Jesus would have gone to Hades. Third, the place where Jesus gained victory over Satan and sin was not Hades but the Cross (2:16; Col 2:14-15) where he said, "It is finished" (John 19:30). Fourth, in Ephesians the warfare with the satanic forces does not happen in Hades but in the heavenly realms (1:20-21; 2:2; 6:12). Fifth, there is no specific mention of Hades (*hadēs* [TG86, ZG87]) or the abyss (*abussos* [TG12, ZG12]) in this passage, which would serve to verify that it was the intended meaning.

The second view regards the genitive as appositional, signifying "the lower parts, namely, the earth"; therefore, this is a reference to Christ's incarnation. This interpretation is supported first by the fact that Jesus' descent from heaven is always viewed as being to earth and not to Hades (John 3:13; 6:62; 16:28) and second by the fact that there is no indication in the Gospels that after the burial of Jesus he went to Hades, even during the fifty days between his resurrection and ascension.

The third view understands the genitive as possessive; it indicates that Christ descended into "the earth's lower part" [i.e., the grave]. This interpretation includes both Christ's incarnation and his death by which he won the victory over Satan and sin. His burial substantiates his death. In support of this view, it makes good sense of the comparative adjective *katōtera* [TG2737, ZG3005] (lower), signifying the earth's lower part, namely, the ground. Also, it is parallel with 1:20 in that the death of Christ (1:20; 2:16; 5:2, 25) is connected with his resurrection (1:20-23; 2:5) and not with his incarnation nor with a descent into Hades. Finally, it uses the same construction as in Psalm 63:9, where David speaks of the depths of the earth with reference to the grave. In conclusion, of the three views mentioned, it seems that the first view, denoting Hades, is unlikely, and either the second or third view is likely correct, with preference for the last view because it makes good sense and has the fewest problems.

Verse 10 makes it clear that the Christ who descended also ascended. The destination of his ascension was "higher than all the heavens" for the purpose that he might fill all things. What does it mean to fill all things? It is unlikely that this filling is limited to the church; otherwise, Paul would have made the church the sole object of the filling. Also, it is unlikely that it refers to the Lutheran doctrine of the ubiquity or omnipresence of Christ's body. More likely, the object of Christ's ascension was to allow him to enter into a sovereign relationship with the whole world and in that position have the right to bestow gifts on whomever he wills. According to 1:23, Christ is filled with God's fullness, and Christ fills the church with that fullness. According to 1:10, Christ, the head of all of the universe, unites all things under his headship (1:22) and fills the universe with the message of redemption through the messengers on whom he has granted the gifts as he willed (4:7-8, 11). Hence, Christ, as victor over Satan, sin, and death, grants gifts to the redeemed, who then can minister in his power.

The next portion (4:11-16) explains the distribution of the gifts—this is a return to the central point of this section introduced in 4:7. In regards to the distribution of the gifts, Paul indicates the persons involved (4:11), the process (4:12), the product (4:13), and their purpose (4:14-16). The first verse in this section provides a commentary on the second part of the citation of Psalm 68 in Ephesians 4:8—namely, Christ's bestowal of gifts to the church. Whereas 4:7 speaks of gifts given to each believer, 4:11 speaks of the gifted people—that is, the people who have the gifts. But before we take a look at those delineated in this verse, some preliminary items should be noted. First, the order of the list of gifts is similar to 1 Corinthians 12:28. Second, though there is no mention of the Holy Spirit, his involvement can be assumed since this passage in many ways corresponds to the text concerning the gifts of the Spirit in 1 Corinthians 12:4-11, 28. Third, this is a list of gifts and not offices.

Interestingly, the term "office" is never used in the New Testament in connection with the gifts. There are distinctions between the gift and the office. (1) Offices seem to be limited to apostles (Acts 1:21-25), elders (1 Tim 3:1-7; Titus 1:5-11), deacons (Acts 6:1-6; 1 Tim 3:8-13), and possibly deaconesses (depending on one's interpretation of Rom 16:1 and 1 Tim 3:11). (2) Those who obtain any of these offices are either appointed (Acts 14:23; Titus 1:5) or elected (Acts 1:26; 6:3; 1 Tim 3:1-13) based on qualifications, whereas the gifts are sovereignly bestowed by God (4:7; Rom 12:6; 1 Cor 12:11, 18, 28). (3) Everyone has a gift (4:7; 1 Cor 12:7, 11; Rom 12:4), but not every one has an office. (4) Marital status is mentioned for the offices of elders and deacons (1 Tim 3:2, 4-5, 12; Titus 1:6), but no such qualification is mentioned for those gifted. The office of either an elder or deacon appears to require a married person, never divorced, whereas there is no such restriction on those given gifts. Hence, a person who has a change in marital status does not lose his or her gift. (5) Those holding office cannot be novices (1 Tim 3:6, 10; Titus 1:8-9), whereas the gifts are given to each person regardless of age or maturity. (6) Some offices have a gender distinction (e.g., an elder must be the husband of one wife—1 Tim 3:2), whereas those who have gifts may be of either gender (e.g., Acts 21:9; 1 Cor 11:5). Inexplicably, most commentators mix gift and office, yet they are not confused in the New Testament. Clearly there is nothing in the present context about an office.

As previously noted, in 4:7, Paul emphasized the gifts given to believers, but in 4:11 he depicts those given these gifts. There is no contradiction here because the person who receives a gift is a gifted person. This is analogous to 1 Corinthians 12, where he lists the gifts and in the same context talks about the gifted people (cf. 4:4-12). This is again true in the other passage regarding gifts (Rom 12:4-8). In all three passages the verb *didōmi* [TG1325, ZG1443] (give) is used to indicate that it is a gracious gift of God to the church.

In this passage the first gifted persons mentioned are "apostles." An apostle was Jesus Christ's official delegate with the task of authoritatively proclaiming Christ's message in oral and written form and of establishing and building up churches. In the commentary on 2:20 there was mention of three kinds of apostles: those who had been with Jesus in his ministry and had witnessed his resurrection (Acts 1:21-22), Paul, who was born at the wrong time (1 Cor 15:8-9), and those who received the gift of apostleship. The first two categories refer to an office whereas the last, the gift of apostleship, is discussed in the present context.

Some of the apostles who were not a part of the Twelve who had been with Jesus in his ministry or witnessed his resurrection were Barnabas (Acts 14:4, 14; 1 Cor 9:5-7), Apollos (1 Cor 4:6, 9), and probably Epaphroditus (Phil 2:25) and Andronicus and Junia (Rom 16:7). These had the gift of apostleship. The main function of an apostle is to establish churches in areas that have not been reached by others (Rom 15:20). They are God's messengers who open up new territories for Christ.

The second gifted person, the prophet, is also mentioned in 1 Corinthians 12:28 and Romans 12:6. Here, as elsewhere (2:20; 3:5; 1 Cor 12:28-29), the prophets are listed after apostles, indicating that they are New Testament prophets rather than

Old Testament prophets. In studying the term "prophet" in Ephesians 2:20 and 3:5, it was concluded that the prophet was one who was endowed by the Holy Spirit with the gift of prophecy for the purposes of edification, comfort, and encouragement (cf. 1 Cor 14:3, 31); it was the prophet's task also to understand and communicate the mystery and revelation to the church (1 Cor 12:10; 13:2; 14:23, 30-31). The prophetic gift may have, at least initially, included a predictive element (1 Thess 3:4; 4:6, 14-18). In light of the fact that in the time of the early church the Canon was incomplete, the prophet may well have received revelation to complete what was needed so that every person could be presented perfect before God (4:12; Col 1:28). In the present verse, the prophets are listed with the gifted persons who prepare the believers for ministry and build up this new body, the church. Although there may be overlapping functions with other gifts, it seems that the apostles were given a divine commission to a specific task of proclaiming authoritatively the message in oral and written form and of establishing and building up churches, whereas the prophets were primarily communicating divine revelation.

The third gifted person is the evangelist. The term occurs only two other times in the New Testament: as a designation for Philip (Acts 21:8), and as a description for the kind of ministry Paul exhorted Timothy to perform (2 Tim 4:5). Whereas the prophets spoke as the occasion required revelation, evangelists continually spoke the message of Christ's salvation. Their function resembles that of modern missionaries, who bring the message to new territories. In the early days of the church, Philip proclaimed Christ's message on a journey between Jerusalem and Gaza, where he met the Ethiopian eunuch and explained the message of Jesus to him. Philip continued his ministry in various places from Azotus to Caesarea (Acts 8:26-40). In conclusion, the evangelist's ministry was to win converts to the faith, the apostles was to establish churches, and the prophets was to bring revelation as needed for believers. Some of these functions may overlap.

Because only one article is used for "pastors" and "teachers," there has been debate as to whether or not two different gifted persons are intended (Calvin 1965:179; Schnackenburg 1991:181-182) or one person with a combination of two gifts (Eadie 1883:304-306; Barth 1974:438-439). In 2:20, there is only one article used for apostles and prophets, which are clearly different roles; therefore, the article here does not require that pastors and teachers be seen as identical. Rather, one is possibly a subset of the other—namely, all pastors are teachers though not all teachers are pastors. The term "pastor" means "shepherd" and is sometimes used metaphorically as "leader" of people. As a shepherd cares for his flock, so a pastor cares for his people by exhorting, comforting, and leading them in the things of God. Again, it is important to note that this term refers to a gift and does not refer to an office, as is so commonly misunderstood today. The "teacher" is the one who instructs, not only in doctrinal matters and skills, but also in moral evaluation. Jesus, the model teacher, did not teach as the scribes, who tended merely to present various views on a subject, but rather he taught with authority (Matt 7:29; Mark 1:22; Luke 4:32). The teacher differs from a prophet, who speaks under the immediate impulse and influence of the Holy Spirit (1 Cor 14:30). The teacher gives instruction either on what is revealed by the prophet or written in Scripture. Also, the predictive function included in the prophet's role is not a part of the purview of the teacher.

There has been a great deal of controversy about spiritual gifts for the modern church, particularly regarding the gift of prophecy. Although some think there is little distinction between prophecy and teaching, most maintain that a prophet imparts new revelation directly from the Lord (1 Cor 14:30-31), whereas a teacher illumines the hearer about past events and revelations. The prophet was prominent in the early church but became virtually unknown by the end of the second century. One can only speculate the reason for the demise of the prophet. Although some propose that it was due to the institutionalization of the church or the abuse of prophecy in Montanism, it is more likely that with the completion of the New Testament canon, the need for revelation ceased. Hence, the gift of prophecy does not seem to be operative today. By contrast, there are many modern examples of gifted men and women who are evangelists, pastors, and teachers. Some may question the validity of women pastors or pastor-teachers, but one must keep in mind that these are gifts and not offices. There should be no problem with women who pastor or shepherd other women (Titus 2:3-4), for example. It must be noted, however, that Priscilla, along with Aquila, taught Apollos the way of God more accurately (Acts 18:25-26), which indicates that women may not be limited to teaching only women. The gift of apostleship for today may function similarly to the early church in establishing churches in areas not reached by the gospel. Missionaries who are establishing churches may be fulfilling that role in the present time. Once again, one needs to remember that these are gifts and not offices. Christ has sovereignly given gifted people to the church. These gifts are not to be used for self-promotion but for building up believers. Paul now proceeds to elaborate on this.

Having demonstrated that Christ has given gifts to the church, Paul specifies that their immediate purpose is to build up the church (4:12), a process that will continue until the further purpose of the maturation of believers is accomplished (4:13), which is not only to protect them from instability but also to build them up in love (4:14-16). Concentrating on 4:12, the purpose of the giving of gifts is indicated by three prepositional phrases, each building on the previous phrase. The first prepositional phrase asserts that gifts were given in order to prepare or equip God's people. The second prepositional phrase states that the goal of equipping believers is to prepare them for the work of the ministry. Hence, ministry is the responsibility of all believers and not just a few. This fact eliminates the distinction between clergy and laity, a distinction with little, if any, support in the New Testament. The third prepositional phrase indicates the final goal—namely, building up the body of Christ. The gifts are never for self-edification but for the edification of the whole body of believers. The concept that ministry belongs exclusively to clergy is foreign to this context because every believer is given a gift (4:7) and thus every believer must be involved in ministry.

Continuing, Paul states that the function of these gifts will continue until believers mature unto the measure of the fullness of Christ (4:13). As in 4:12, so also in the present verse, the three prepositional phrases indicate not three goals but three aspects of one goal—that is, attaining maturity. The first aspect is the unity of faith and the knowledge of God's Son. The unity of faith corresponds to the "one faith" in 4:5, which was given as the evidence of unity among believers. The following prepositional phrases indicate that this is not organizational unity but the practical unity of the faith. This first aspect contains not only the achievement of unity of the faith but also the unity in the "knowledge of God's Son," without which unity of the faith would be impossible. This is not merely factual knowledge about God's Son but intimate knowledge of him. Such knowledge applies not only to individuals but also to the body of believers, who together come to a unity of the knowledge of Christ.

The second aspect of the goal of attaining maturity is that believers grow into mature personhood. The word "mature" refers to a person who is fully grown and mature, as opposed to a child who is gullible to false teachings, as mentioned in 4:14. This particular reference to the mature person does not refer to individuals but to the church, the body composed of individuals. This is analogous to 2:15-16, where it states that believing Jews and Gentiles were created into one new person and brought into one body. Although the generic term for humanity (*anthrōpos* [TG444, ZG476]) is used in 2:15, in the present context the term *anēr* [TG435, ZG467] (man) is used. It normally distinguishes between male and female, but here it distinguishes between a boy and an adult man. The emphasis is not on gender (males only) but rather on adulthood, because the present context makes reference to "God's people" (4:12-13), each receiving a gift (4:7), all in one body (4:4, 12). Hence, each believer is to utilize his or her gift in order for the body to attain full maturity.

Building on the first two aspects of the goal, the third component is to attain to the measure of Christ's full stature. As the church is filled by Christ, so is the stature of the church filled by him. Again, it is not speaking of any individual believer; rather, "we" are to measure up to this extent. Each member is to use the gift that has been given to him or her in measure (4:7), and as each member fulfills this, then the body will measure (4:13) to Christ's full stature. This does not imply that the church completes Christ.

When will the church reach its full measure—now or in the future? Although no time frame is given, certainly this goal can be accomplished in the present age, otherwise one could conclude that either the gifts or the power of the Holy Spirit are inadequate. Also, since one goal of maturity is that believers will not accept false teachings (4:14), it would necessarily refer to the present age and not the eschatological consummation. Hence, full maturity is the goal of the gifts. This maturity is accomplished as each utilizes the gift(s) given to him or her. As individuals grow, they are to share this growth so that the whole body grows.

Paul then explains the ultimate purpose for Christ's giving gifts (4:14-16). First, there is the negative, a warning of the danger of remaining immature and thus susceptible to false teaching (4:14). Then comes the positive growth to maturity in Christ, which causes the body to grow in love (4:15-16). Negatively, believers are no longer to be children who are inexperienced and unstable and open to false teaching. Often, such teaching is presented by cunning people who by their deceit lead others into error. This is obvious in the machinations of present-day cults. They propagate their erroneous system by trickery and deceit, especially in the use of Scripture. This confuses immature believers who lack a proper understanding of God and his Word. Generally, cults tend to shy away from those who are well-acquainted with Scripture and the God of Scripture. Consequently, it is of utmost importance for believers to understand God's Word.

The positive purpose of the gifts is the maturation of believers. In stark contrast to the false teachers portrayed in 4:14, believers are to be truthful both in conduct and speech (4:15). Being truthful means being transparent, revealing the real state of affairs. The following prepositional phrase "in love" tempers truthfulness. Truth must be presented gently in love. Again, this is in contrast with the previous verse, which indicates that false teachers use deceit for their selfish ends, whereas truth with love considers the interest of others supremely important. This manner of conduct makes it possible for believers to become more like Christ, who is the embodiment of love (3:19; 5:2, 25; Rom 8:35; 2 Cor 5:14) and truth (4:21; John 14:6). Believers are called upon to grow in their love for God and others. Paul described the process of growth using a physiological model (4:16). As each individual member of the body functions properly, the whole body develops. The same is true for the body of Christ. Each believer is to utilize his/her gift(s) in conjunction with other believers. As this occurs, it will cause the whole body to develop. Again the ingredient of love is an important part of the process. As in a physical body, so also in the body of Christ—when members of the body fail the body becomes deformed. Each member is to utilize the gift(s) in measure (4:16) as it was measured to him or her (4:7; cf. Rom 12:3)—no more and no less. Here again it is each member, not just a few members, who is to function so that the body can grow into maturity.

In conclusion, the emphasis of this section is that each believer is given a gift according to the measure of Christ (4:7-10), which enables each believer to minister toward the goal of edifying the body of Christ. All of this growth is done in the context of love. The past animosity between Jews and Gentiles can no longer exist because now, in Christ, both are reconciled to each other, making it possible for them to utilize their gifts to build up one another and, in turn, build up the whole body, the church.

◆   B. Live in Holiness (4:17-32)
     1. Description of the old unregenerated person (4:17-19)

¹⁷With the Lord's authority I say this: Live no longer as the Gentiles do, for they are hopelessly confused. ¹⁸Their minds are full of darkness; they wander far from the life God gives because they have closed their minds and hardened their hearts against him. ¹⁹They have no sense of shame. They live for lustful pleasure and eagerly practice every kind of impurity.

NOTES

4:17 *they are hopelessly confused.* Lit., "they walk in the futility of their minds" or "they live without purpose." Their confusion is the result of a life without purpose.

4:18 *Their minds are full of darkness.* The literal rendering "their minds are being darkened" gives a better sense of process.

because they have closed their minds and hardened their hearts against him. The NLT rendering appears to suggest two parallel causes but more likely the latter cause is built on the former cause. So it could be rendered "because they have shut their minds due to their hardened hearts against him."

4:19 *They have no sense of shame.* The idea is that they have become calloused and thus insensitive to God's will and way.

lustful pleasure. Lit. "licentiousness," meaning "freedom with no boundaries," usually referring to sensual appetites.

COMMENTARY

This is the second of five sections delineated by the use of *peripateō* [TG4043, ZG4344], which is literally "walk," and means "to conduct one's daily life"; at the head of each section, *peripateō* is used in conjunction with the inferential conjunction *oun* [TG3767, ZG4036] (therefore) (4:1, 17; 5:1-2, 7-8, 15). Having discussed unity in the first half of the chapter, Paul now instructs believers on how to walk in holiness. Holiness is not automatically a result of unity; otherwise, there would be no need for instruction. This portion of the chapter is divided into two parts: negatively, how believers should not live (4:17-19), then positively, how believers should live (4:20-32).

Paul began this section by exhorting his readers not to live as unbelievers (4:17-18), continuing the exhortation of 4:1 to live worthy of their calling. The ungodly live in the futility of their minds. The noun *mataiotēs* [TG3153, ZG3470] (futility) occurs only three times in the New Testament (see also Rom 8:20; 2 Pet 2:18) and has the sense of being unable to achieve one's goals. In this case, futility (in connection with the mind) is a moral attitude or disposition whereby the mind cannot achieve its goal of receiving the revelation of God and thus cannot make proper moral decisions necessary for life (Rom 1:18-32). Since the unbelievers' minds cannot receive the revelation of God, their understanding is darkened—referring to spiritual darkness. Further, they are alienated from the life of God due to their ignorance, which is the result of their hardened hearts. This description is parallel to that found in Romans 1:18-32, where Paul describes human degradation in terms of people purposefully rejecting the manifest knowledge of God through creation. Instead of glorifying or thanking God, people allowed their reasoning process to become purposeless, and their senseless hearts became darkened as they exchanged God's incorruptible glory for corruptible idolatry. Such is not innocent but deliberate refusal of God and his will; it is twice pronounced as inexcusable (Rom 1:23; 2:1). As in Romans 1, the present context makes it clear that the hardness of their hearts caused their insensitivity to God and his ways. In these two verses a series of causes and effects becomes clear. In reverse, the hardness of their hearts causes their ignorance. Their ignorance of God and his will causes their alienation from the life of

God, their alienation from God causes their minds to be darkened, and their darkened minds cause them to walk in the futility of the mind. This is in sharp contrast to those who are believers who have been enlightened by God to do his will.

The natural outgrowth of the unbelievers' condition is their conduct (4:19). Their lack of care for what is right and wrong is described as callousness, resulting in moral apathy. Giving themselves over to immoral ways indicates their wanton freedom and usually encompasses sexual desires. The same concept is found Romans 1:24, 26, 28, where it states that God gives people over to their immoral conduct because of their refusal to accept his revelation. As people exercise their perversion of free will and give themselves over to sin, so God responds by giving them over to the sin that enslaves them. Therefore, they practice every kind of impurity, particularly moral impurity. This impurity is closely linked with greed. Normally, greed is used in connection with coveting material things (Luke 12:15; 2 Cor 9:5)—a desire for more of everything (5:3; Col 3:5; 2 Pet 2:14). In secular and biblical literature, it conveys unfavorable or undesirable characteristics, selfishness to the nth degree, the opposite of moderation. That which is coveted becomes the center of one's life; hence it is identified as idolatry (Col 3:5). The powerful combination of moral apathy, impurity, and greediness describe the unregenerate, who are totally consumed with themselves. The selfishness in which the godless are immersed stands in direct contrast to Christ, who was selfless in offering himself as a sacrifice to God for the sins of the world (5:2).

◆   ## 2. Description of the new regenerated person (4:20–32)

20But that isn't what you learned about Christ. 21Since you have heard about Jesus and have learned the truth that comes from him, 22throw off your old sinful nature and your former way of life, which is corrupted by lust and deception. 23Instead, let the Spirit renew your thoughts and attitudes. 24Put on your new nature, created to be like God—truly righteous and holy.

25So stop telling lies. Let us tell our neighbors the truth, for we are all parts of the same body. 26And "don't sin by letting anger control you."* Don't let the sun go down while you are still angry, 27for anger gives a foothold to the devil.

28If you are a thief, quit stealing. Instead, use your hands for good hard work, and then give generously to others in need. 29Don't use foul or abusive language. Let everything you say be good and helpful, so that your words will be an encouragement to those who hear them.

30And do not bring sorrow to God's Holy Spirit by the way you live. Remember, he has identified you as his own,* guaranteeing that you will be saved on the day of redemption.

31Get rid of all bitterness, rage, anger, harsh words, and slander, as well as all types of evil behavior. 32Instead, be kind to each other, tenderhearted, forgiving one another, just as God through Christ has forgiven you.

4:26 Ps 4:4.   4:30 Or *has put his seal on you.*

NOTES
4:20 *But that isn't what you learned about Christ.* What Paul refers to is more than learning "about" Christ. The purpose is to know him personally.

4:21 *Since you have heard about Jesus and have learned the truth that comes from him.* Lit., "inasmuch as you heard about him and were taught in him, just as the truth is in Jesus."

4:22 *throw off.* This is an imperative in the NLT, but the Greek may well have an indicative force. The verb is literally an infinitive ("to throw off"); two more infinitives follow, at the beginning of each of the next verses. They serve as complements of the verb "you were taught" in 4:21. Their function in this context is debated (see commentary).The first ("to put off") and third ("to put on") are aorist middle infinitives, whereas the second ("to be renewed") is a present middle infinitive.

your old sinful nature and your former way of life. The Greek *ton palaion anthrōpon* [cf. TG3820/0444, ZG4094/0476] is better translated "the old person" rather than "sinful nature." Paul was not making a dichotomy between two natures but was referring to the old unregenerate person in contrast to the new redeemed person.

corrupted by lust and deception. More likely this could be rendered "in accordance with deceptive desires" or better "in accordance with the desires coming from deceit."

4:23 *Instead, let the Spirit renew your thoughts and attitudes.* Again, this gives an imperative sense, when it may well be an indicative force. The literal rendering of the Greek text, "but to be renewed by the spirit in your mind" is difficult to unpack; the NLT's rendering makes good sense.

4:24 *Put on your new nature.* Again, "new nature" is not a good rendering of the Greek, which is *ton kainon anthrōpon* [TG2537/0444, ZG2785/0476] (the new person). As in 4:22, Paul was not making a dichotomy between two natures, but making a contrast between the old unregenerate person and the new redeemed person.

truly righteous and holy. A better rendering would be "righteousness and holiness that originates from truth."

4:25 *stop telling lies.* The construction in the Greek text is an aorist middle participle and not an imperative and thus could be rendered "so having put away falsehood." Because the believer has put away the old person and his or her lifestyle, it can be assumed that falsehood has been put away.

4:26 *And "don't sin by letting anger control you."* The Greek text has the positive followed by a negative, namely, "Be angry and do not sin."

4:28 *give generously to others in need.* In other words, share the material goods that have been gained by hard labor.

4:29 *Don't use foul or abusive language.* "Foul or abusive" is an expansion of a single Greek word, *sapros* [TG4550, ZG4911] (rotten, putrid). In context, the word includes the use of unwholesome or unhelpful words that fail to build up one another. This is supported by the contrast in the next clause, *let everything you say be good and helpful.* Unwholesome words destroy, whereas beneficial words build up.

so that your words will be an encouragement to those who hear. The NLT's rendering "encouragement" is a translation of *charis* [TG5485, ZG5921] (grace), which refers to the bestowal of unmerited favor and/or enablement.

4:30 *do not bring sorrow to God's Holy Spirit by the way you live.* The expression "bring sorrow" (*lupeite* [TG3076, ZG3382]) occurs 63 times in the LXX, where, for example, Joseph told his brothers not to be distressed or grieved for what they had done to him (Gen 45:5). It is used 26 times in the NT, 15 times by Paul, and only here in Ephesians. It is used when the disciples were distressed or grieved over Jesus' announcement of his death (Matt 17:23) and when the rich young ruler went from Jesus grieving because he was not willing to sell all his goods (Matt 19:22). In the present context Paul enjoins the believers not to grieve the Holy Spirit. If the Holy Spirit can be grieved, it must follow that he is a person. An inanimate object cannot grieve. In the present context then, unwholesome words are forbidden for two reasons: First, they impede spiritual growth of fellow believers; second, they grieve the Holy Spirit.

by the way you live. In the context it might be better to render it "by the way you speak."

Remember, he has identified you as his own. This is a reference to the sealing of the Spirit, which identifies believers as God's own and gives them the security of belonging to him (cf. 1:13; 2 Cor 1:22).

guaranteeing that you will be saved on the day of redemption. The sealing of the Holy Spirit will continue until he redeems us or sets us free from sin. Redemption has two phases: The first phase frees believers from sin and its obligation; the second phase, alluded to in this verse, sets believers free from the presence of sin in the eschatological future when Christ returns.

4:31 *as well as all types of evil behavior.* The words "as well as" are translated from the preposition *sun* [TG4862, ZG5250] (with), which connotes an inclusive idea. Hence, believers are enjoined to put away the five vices (listed immediately preceding) along with malice.

4:32 *forgiving one another, just as God through Christ has forgiven you.* The verbs "forgiving and forgiven" are the verb forms of "grace"; they are to be gracious to one another, just as God in Christ is gracious to them.

COMMENTARY

In this section, Paul discusses the position (4:20-24) and practice (4:25-32) of the "new person." God not only redeems a person but also demands and enables a new lifestyle to be practiced before the world. Regarding the position of the new person, Paul reminded his readers of what they had been taught previously (4:20-21a). The new person, who stands in contrast to the old person (4:17-19), did not come to know (literally "learn") Christ by the previous lifestyle. The word "learned" does not refer to the factual knowledge about Christ but rather a personal knowledge of him. The new life of believers is not ordered by knowledge of the law but by hearing about Christ and thus "learning" the living Christ so as to live a life pleasing to him. Though the Ephesian believers did not hear Christ personally, they heard him through Paul and other preachers and teachers.

The Ephesian believers not only heard "about" Christ but they were also taught "in" him. The preposition does not express means ("taught by him"), as suggested by the KJV, because the Ephesians never saw Christ. Rather, it is the sphere or locale of the teaching, "in connection with him" or "in communion with him." As such, Christ is the object and the sphere of a believer's learning. By contrast, followers in other religions may continue to study about their chosen religion but never experience an intimate knowledge of the leader and/or founder of their religion. Believers in Christ not only "learn" Christ at the time they hear the gospel but they continue to "learn" him as they study God's Word and as they are ministered to by gifted people in the body. The nature of the instruction is the truth in Jesus (4:21b). This truth is not relative truth, which assumes that what may be existentially true for one person may not be true for another. Truth here denotes reality, in contrast to that which is false or deceptive, as seen in the next verse, where Paul characterizes the unregenerate Gentiles mentioned in 4:17-18. Jesus is the embodiment of truth (John 14:6). The Messiah promised in the Old Testament was the Jesus of history, who died to pay for sins, brought forgiveness (1:7; 2:13-18), and rose to guarantee the truth of his predictions and the validity of redemption. Some conjecture that there is a difference between the Christ of faith and the Jesus of history. Not so, they are one and the same person.

As noted above, scholars have proposed various interpretations of 4:22-24 with respect to the use of the three infinitives: put off, be renewed, put on. Most scholars understand them to have imperatival force (Barth 1974:543-545; Lincoln 1990:283-284; Best 1998:430-431). The support for this rendering is that every other occurrence of an aorist infinitive in indirect discourse in the New Testament relates back to an imperative, but in all these cases the indirect discourse relates back to a verb that implies a command. Another support for this view is that it fits the context well in that believers are first taught in principle to "throw off" and "put on" (4:22, 24) and then they are given specific applications relating to that principle (4:25-32). In addition, it is thought that since this is the practical section of Ephesians, it would be natural for these infinitives to function as imperatives. Others suggest that these infinitives of indirect discourse function analogously to indicatives in direct discourse or as complementary infinitives—yielding the translation: "you were taught that you have put off the old person, you are renewed in spirit, you have put on the new person" (C. F. D. Moule 1959:126; H. C. G. Moule 1886:225-226; Turner 1963:78; Wallace 1996:605). Support for this view comes from the fact that it is common in the New Testament to have infinitives of indirect discourse after verbs of perception, as here: "you were taught." I prefer the position that views the infinitives of indirect discourse functioning analogous to indicatives in direct discourse. Otherwise, if 4:22-24 are viewed as being imperative, then 4:25-32 would seem redundant. Furthermore, the parallel passage in Colossians 3:9-10 supports the second view because the aorist passive participles indicate that the putting off and the putting on has already been accomplished. These participles are used in conjunction with imperatives (Col 3:8,12), namely, they are commanded to put off sins like anger and wrath because they have already put off the old person.

Thus, Paul was not instructing the believers to put off the "old person" because that was accomplished at the time of conversion. The old person is characterized by a lifestyle that is rotten to the core and full of lust—both of which are engendered by deceit. This deceit, which brings people to ruin, is based on the false idea that fulfillment of natural desires is all that is necessary for human life. Self-centered lusts are deceitful because they promise happiness but fail to provide it. This old person was put off at the time of conversion. It is an accomplished fact. In 4:23 Paul states that the Ephesian believers were being renewed by the spirit located in the mind, or in other words, by the spirit that governs the mind. Although this speaks of the human spirit, ultimately only the Spirit of God quickens the human spirit. Such renewal will transform lives in very practical ways. Paul continues in 4:24 by stating that believers have put on the new person, who is created in God's likeness of righteousness and holiness that originates from truth. Righteousness and holiness refer to right actions or conduct before God and people. This verse stands in contrast to 4:22 in three ways. First, it speaks of having put on the new redeemed person as opposed to having put off the old unregenerate person. Second, the new person has been created according to God's likeness in righteousness and holiness that is based on truth, whereas the old person's lifestyle was being corrupted by desires that were based on deceit. Third, conduct based in righteousness and holiness is truth, whereas the basis of lustful conduct is deceit. In conclusion, the Ephesians were taught that they have put off the old person and put on the new person at the time of their conversion. The new person is characterized by righteousness and holiness based on truth, and the resulting attributes will be manifested in many ways, as seen in 4:25-32.

Having instructed the Ephesians to refrain from living as the Gentiles, who have lost all moral sensitivity and given themselves over to impurity (4:17-19), and having taught them that they had thrown off the old person and put on the new person (4:22-24), Paul now gives practical applications as to how the new person in Christ lives day by day (4:25-32). There are five specific exhortations for believers. All but one of these exhortations has three parts: (1) a negative command, (2) a positive command, and (3) the reason for the positive command. In the second exhortation the first two parts are reversed.

The first exhortation warns against participation in falsehood and urges the speaking of truth (4:25). The participial construction in Greek ("having put away falsehood") assumes that falsehood has been put away. Thus, he exhorts them to speak the truth with their neighbors. This should be the natural consequence of the new person's conduct, which is based on righteousness and holiness, and these, in turn, are based on truth (4:24). The present active imperative indicates that, having laid aside falsehood, they are to make a habit of speaking the truth to their neighbor. "Neighbor" refers primarily to fellow believers for two reasons. First, it is a quotation from Zechariah 8:16, where the neighbor refers to someone within the community of the remnant. Second, the next clause in the present context speaks of being members of one another. Now that they are members of this new community, they are to speak the truth to one another. Nevertheless, this does not negate the fact that believers are to speak the truth at all times, even in their contacts with unbelievers. Since believers base their lifestyle on reality, there is no need to bring falsehood into any relationship, within or without the church.

The second exhortation acknowledges that believers may, at times, be legitimately angry, yet they are admonished not to sin (4:26-27). Instead of the usual pattern, Paul here begins with the positive and then states the negative, namely, "be angry and do not sin." Since there are references in the Bible to God's anger, it cannot be said that there is anything intrinsically evil about anger. Paul was quoting Psalm 4:4, which had probably become a proverbial statement. Anger is not to be acted out in a sinful manner, such as when it develops into a prolonged irritation, allowing the devil to gain an inroad into the life of the believer. No one should make a practice of harboring anger overnight. It is essential to keep short accounts of anger. Prolonged anger gives opportunity to the devil to twist and distort truth, causing anger to mount and possibly resulting in dissension and revenge. Again, anger is not intrinsically sinful, for God expresses anger. However, when God is angry, he is always in control of his anger. Unlike God, however, people have a tendency to allow anger to control them. Thus, the second command "do not sin" is necessary. Hence, if someone in the body of believers has been wronged, it is correct for one to be angry but not to be consumed by that anger.

The third exhortation tells the believer to refrain from stealing. Instead, they should work so that they can give to the needy (4:28). Whereas a thief takes from others for his own benefit, a believer is to work with his own hands for the purpose of sharing. Stealing is a characteristic of the old person, who has been put off; working for those in need must characterize the new person. Honest gain is not for self-indulgence but for doing something beneficial for others within the believing community. A believer is to work diligently to gain what is good for the purpose of sharing with those who have need.

The fourth exhortation concerns the use of language (4:29-30). Again the negative command is given first, exhorting believers not to use any unwholesome (*sapros* [TG4550, ZG4911], "rotten, putrid") words but instead to speak that which is good so as to edify others. The preceding verse dealt with the physical needs of believers; this verse speaks of spiritual needs. Unwholesome words destroy; good and wholesome words build up, thereby accomplishing the purpose of giving "encouragement to those who hear." This encouragement enables them to fill the lack or need among them. Clearly, believers need to watch their language to make sure their words build up and do not tear down. Paul then said that unwholesome, destructive language grieves the Holy Spirit by whom believers are sealed until the day of redemption (see discussion of this at 1:13-14). The seal of the Holy Spirit identifies believers as God's possession, and it will remain until the time when Christ brings them to himself. In light of this, the use of worthless words not only hurts the body of Christ but also grieves the Holy Spirit, who seals them.

The fifth exhortation warns believers against maliciousness and enjoins them to edify one another (4:31-32). Again, the negative exhortation is first stated (4:31), followed by a positive exhortation (4:32). Paul now exhorts believers to put away five vices (4:31) on the basis of having thrown away the old person (4:22): bitterness (*pikria* [TG4088, ZG4394], "bitterness, resentment"), rage (*thumos* [TG2372, ZG2596], "outburst of anger"), anger (*orgē* [TG3709, ZG3973], "settled state of anger"), shouting (*kraugē* [TG2906, ZG3199], "shouting, screaming"), and slander (*blasphēmia* [TG988, ZG1060], "defamation, abusive speech"). The first word, "bitterness," deals with attitude, the next two words, "rage" and "anger," deal with disposition, and the last two, "shouting" and "slander," refer to manner of speech. Following the recitation of these five vices, Paul concludes with the inclusive phrase, "with all malice" or as in the NLT, "as well as all types of evil behavior." The word "malice" denotes "badness, vice, evil," which is the opposite of "moral excellence, virtue." In this respect, it is an all-inclusive word for ill will or maliciousness; it casts a pall on any action with which it is connected. This word enhances the meaning of the five vices listed earlier.

Following this there are three positive injunctions (4:32). The first promotes kindness. The word "kindness" has the idea of that which is fitting, pleasant, and good. Its noun form is used in 2:7, where it states that God is going to demonstrate in the heavenly realms his kindness in giving salvation. In 4:32 the adjective has the same connotation where believers are instructed to exhibit kindness toward each other. Such an attitude does not come naturally. According to Galatians 5:22, it is the fruit of the Spirit. Reliance on the Holy Spirit enables one to exhibit kindness. The second positive quality is to be "tenderhearted" or "compassionate." This compound noun (*eusplanchnos* [TG2155, ZG2359]), used in the New Testament only here and 1 Peter 3:8, is based on the noun *splanchnon* [TG4698, ZG5073], which refers to the inner emotions of affection—hence, compassion (cf. 2 Cor 6:12; 7:15; Phil 1:8; 2:1; Col 3:12; Phlm 1:7, 12, 20; 1 John 3:17). It is the opposite of harshness or maliciousness. The final positive quality is stated as "forgiving one another." As mentioned in the notes above, "forgiving" and "forgiven" are verb forms of "grace." Paul enjoins the believers to be gracious, be kind, and show favor. It is very fitting to the context because graciousness is the antithesis of bitterness, anger, wrath, shouting, and slander. Graciousness is broader than forgiveness but includes forgiveness. We are to be gracious to one another just as God in Christ was gracious to us. God directed his graciousness toward us by sending his Son to die on the cross for us. This gracious act serves as an illustration and example for believers in their relationship to each other.

In conclusion, the first part of this chapter concerns the believers living in unity (4:1-16); the second part concerns their living in holiness (4:17-32). In his discussion of the life of holiness, Paul first described the nature and practice of the old person (4:17-20), whom the believers had put off. Then, he followed this with a discussion about the new person each had become (4:20-32). In 4:25-32, he gives specific exhortations regarding the lifestyle of the new person. Since believers have already put off the old person (4:22) and put on the new person (4:24), they are not to continue in the destructive lifestyle of the unbelievers, but rather they are to be characterized by a new lifestyle that honors God and builds up the body of Christ.

◆ ## C. Live in Love (5:1-6)

Imitate God, therefore, in everything you do, because you are his dear children. ²Live a life filled with love, following the example of Christ. He loved us* and offered himself as a sacrifice for us, a pleasing aroma to God.

³Let there be no sexual immorality, impurity, or greed among you. Such sins have no place among God's people. ⁴Obscene stories, foolish talk, and coarse jokes— these are not for you. Instead, let there be thankfulness to God. ⁵You can be sure that no immoral, impure, or greedy person will inherit the Kingdom of Christ and of God. For a greedy person is an idolater, worshiping the things of this world.

⁶Don't be fooled by those who try to excuse these sins, for the anger of God will fall on all who disobey him.

5:2 Some manuscripts read *loved you.*

NOTES

5:1 *Imitate God, therefore, in everything you do.* The conjunction *oun* [TG3767, ZG4036] (therefore) functions as a resumptive inferential conjunction that goes back to 4:1 and 17 and denotes another application stemming from the first three chapters.

5:2 *Live a life filled with love.* Lit., "and walk in love"—that is, "live in love." The NLT's rendering makes this point.

pleasing aroma. Or, "fragrant aroma," words used frequently in the OT with reference to sacrifices that were acceptable to God (e.g., Exod 29:18, 25, 41; Lev 1:9, 13, 17; Num 15:3, 5, LXX).

5:3 *Let there be no sexual immorality, impurity, or greed among you.* The Greek text has "impurity of any kind," which means that the impurity is not limited strictly to sexual impurity but all sorts of impurity.

5:4 *Obscene stories, foolish talk, and coarse jokes.* "Obscene stories" may be better rendered "obscenity" (NIV, NRSV) because it is broader than just speech (the more limited word *aischrologia* [TG148, ZG155] is used in Col 3:8) and also can include conduct. It serves as a good transition from the previous verse.

5:5 *You can be sure that no immoral, impure, or greedy person will inherit the Kingdom of Christ and of God.* The Greek text introduces this verse with the conjunction *gar* [TG1063, ZG1142] (for) to indicate reason. The reason believers should not act like unbelievers is that, unlike unbelievers, they are going to inherit the Kingdom of Christ and God.

For a greedy person is an idolater, worshiping the things of this world. The Greek text simply reads "no immoral, impure, or greedy person, who is an idolater."

5:6 *all who disobey him.* This is a good rendering of "sons of disobedience." This rendering is similar to the translation of the same expression in 2:2.

COMMENTARY

To make application to the doctrines set forth in the first three chapters, Paul, now for the third time, uses *peripateō* [TG4043, ZG4344] ("walk"; 4:1, 17; 5:2). Since the term does not appear until 5:2, a break could be made between 5:1 and 5:2, rather than between 5:2 and 5:3. However, the key to the division of this section of the book is not only the verb but also the conjunction *oun* [TG3767, ZG4036] (therefore), which is found in 5:1. God's children are commanded to walk in unity (4:1-16), in holiness (4:17-32), and in love (5:1-6). This section is divided into two parts: the positive, walk in love (5:1-2), and the negative, abstain from evil (5:3-6).

In his concluding statement in chapter 4, Paul had instructed believers to be gracious in the same way that God had been gracious in Christ. He now enjoins believers to become imitators of God as beloved children. Our status as his beloved or dear children, the objects of his love, is the result of the gracious way he has acted toward us, as described in the first three chapters. Paul exhorted believers, as God's beloved children, to live in the sphere of love. Paul's mention of the sphere of love is reminiscent of Christ's command to the disciples in his farewell discourse, where he told them to love one another as he has loved them (John 13:34; 15:12, 17). Our model is Christ who, out of love, gave himself for us as an offering and sacrifice to God. He willingly died on behalf of sinners, who had no love for him, and many, in fact, despised him. What a model! God was pleased with Christ's sacrifice, which to him was a fragrant aroma. In the Old Testament many animal sacrifices, even when properly prepared, were not received by God as a fragrant aroma because the offerer had a wrong attitude and a heart far from him. In contrast, Christ willingly gave himself to be offered, and he did it to be a pleasant aroma to God. In the same manner, believers are enjoined to exhibit sacrificial love so as to be a sweet perfume not only to God but also to fellow believers (2 Cor 2:14-16). Christ's love cost him his life. Should our love be without cost?

Paul then informed believers that there should be no place in their lives for evil practices. To live like unbelievers runs counter to living in love. The self-serving vices in conduct and speech (5:3-4) are opposite of the self-sacrificing love spoken of in 5:1-2. In light of this, believers are not to participate in sexual immorality. The word *porneia* [TG4202, ZG4518] is translated "fornication" in some versions (KJV, ASV, NEB, NRSV) but more precisely "sexual immorality" in other versions (RSV, NASB, NIV). It is used of aberrant sexual conduct normally thought of as extramarital relationships (Matt 5:32; 19:9; 15:19; Mark 7:21; John 8:41; Acts 15:20, 29; 21:25; 1 Cor 7:2; Rev 2:21; 9:21), including incest (1 Cor 5:1). Furthermore, there should not be impurity of any kind among believers. This refers not only to sexual impurity but any kind of impurity of thought, speech, or deed. Neither should greed be a part of their lifestyle. Greed is the opposite of moderation, for it is selfishness to the nth degree. Due to the context, some think it has reference to sexual greed, which expresses itself in self-gratification at the expense of others. Accordingly, the injunction in the tenth commandment against coveting one's neighbor's wife (Exod 20:17; Deut 5:21) may be in mind here. However, it may simply be greed for material possessions used for self-consumption rather than being shared with the community of believers and dependence on the Lord to supply as the need arises. Paul exhorted believers that no such conduct should even be mentioned among God's people. These negative exhortations against the sins of self-love are in sharp contrast to the love displayed in Christ's sacrificial death noted in 5:1-2.

Paul's instruction regarding the believers' lifestyle includes speech as well as conduct. The first word, "obscenity," can include both speech and conduct. It has the sense of that which is shameful, disgraceful, and base. The second term, *mōrologia* [TG3473, ZG3703], is accurately translated as "foolish talk," with reference to futile talk that detracts from the issues of faith and does not lend to edifying discussion. The term *eutrapelia* [TG2160, ZG2365], translated "coarse jokes," more likely refers to jesting that has gone too far and has become sarcastic ridicule that cuts people down and embarrasses others who are present. It is humor in bad taste—at someone's expense. This runs counter to Paul's injunction to build up one another (4:29). This does not mean that Christians must be humorless, but they must be controlled. These sins of speech are really inappropriate for those who call themselves Christians. In contrast, appropriate speech includes thankfulness to God for deliverance from sin, for gifts he has given to the church, and for each other. Hence, destructive speech should be replaced by edifying speech.

Continuing, Paul elaborated on the reason to refrain from evil deeds, emphasizing that those who are immoral, impure, or greedy will not inherit the Kingdom of

Christ and of God. These are the same three vices mentioned in 5:3. However, in this instance, he further described the greedy person as an idolater. That which is coveted becomes the center of one's life and is worshiped instead of the Creator (Rom 1:23); the greedy person has exchanged the glory of the incorruptible God for a corruptible idol (Rom 1:25). This is idolatry. It is also a flawed perspective. For example, Esau was so covetous of the stew that he sold his birthright—a ten-minute transaction in exchange for a life's inheritance! In Galatians 5:19-21, Paul also stated that those who practice the works of the flesh such as immorality, impurity, and idolatry will not inherit the Kingdom of God. Likewise, 1 Corinthians 6:9-11 also states that the unrighteous—the immoral, idolaters, thieves, and the greedy—will not inherit the Kingdom of God. The Corinthian believers were counted among such before they were washed, sanctified, and justified in the name of the Lord Jesus Christ and by the Spirit of God.

The Kingdom of God has two aspects. In Colossians 1:13 Paul had spoken of the present dimension, where believers have been delivered from the authority of darkness to the Kingdom of God's beloved Son. Second, there is also a future dimension, where in the end times Christ will hand the Kingdom to the Father (1 Cor 15:24), which cannot be inherited by flesh and blood (1 Cor 15:50) but only by belief in the gospel of Christ's death and resurrection (1 Cor 15:1-4). Therefore, the Kingdom of God is not for saints who have never sinned but for sinners who have become saints through redemption made possible by Christ's supreme sacrifice (1:7, 14; 2:4-10; 4:32). Here in Ephesians Paul rightly addresses believers as those who have inherited the Kingdom of God.

Paul reinforced the truth of the believers' inheritance of the Kingdom of God by stating in 5:6 that believers must not be deceived by empty words because the wrath of God comes on the sons of disobedience. The present tense in this verse describes God's wrath as coming on all those who disobey. As there are present and future aspects to the Kingdom, so also for the wrath of God. In Romans, Paul states that the present wrath of God is revealed from heaven (1:18) and that there is a future wrath for those who are hardhearted and who continue to store up wrath for the day of God's judgment (2:5). Consequently, those who practice these vices in the present day are not in the Kingdom of God and the wrath of God is on them. If they continue in unbelief they will never be a part of the Kingdom of God and will face the wrath that is stored up for the day of God's judgment.

◆   D. Live in Light (5:7-14)

7Don't participate in the things these people do. 8For once you were full of darkness, but now you have light from the Lord. So live as people of light! 9For this light within you produces only what is good and right and true.

10Carefully determine what pleases the Lord. 11Take no part in the worthless deeds of evil and darkness; instead, expose them. 12It is shameful even to talk about the things that ungodly people do in secret. 13But their evil intentions will be exposed when the light shines on them, ¹⁴for the light makes everything visible. This is why it is said,

"Awake, O sleeper,
rise up from the dead,
and Christ will give you light."

NOTES

5:7 Don't participate in the things these people do. NLT omits the inferential conjunction *oun* [TG3767, ZG4036] (therefore), which marks a new section.

5:8 For once you were full of darkness, but now you have light from the Lord. Lit., "for you were formerly darkness, but now you are light in the Lord."

5:9 For this light within you produces only what is good and right and true. The Greek text does not state that the light is within us but rather it speaks of the "fruit of light." Since there is no verb in this parenthetical statement, one needs to be supplied. NLT translates it as "produces."

5:11 worthless deeds of evil and darkness. Lit., "unfruitful works of darkness." The rendering "worthless deeds" captures the idea well. It is not literally "deeds of evil and darkness" but rather "evil deeds of darkness," possibly indicating the source of evil deeds.

5:13 But . . . when the light shines on them. This pronoun "them" is a reference to deeds and not to people, as in the previous verse, because the Greek text has "but everything exposed by light becomes visible."

5:14 for the light makes everything visible. Lit., "for everything that becomes visible is light." This is difficult to translate. It means that everything that becomes visible is light and no longer darkness.

This is why it is said. These words serve as an introductory formula that usually points to an OT passage. Or it could refer to a known Christian hymn that includes OT thoughts.

COMMENTARY

This is the fourth of five sections delineated by the use of *peripateō* [TG4043, ZG4344] ("walk"; 4:1, 17; 5:2, 8, 15) in conjunction with the inferential conjunction *oun* [TG3767, ZG4036] (therefore). Here, the inferential conjunction is found in 5:7 and the verb "walk" in 5:8. This section is divided into three parts or mandates: (1) Do not become involved with evildoers (5:7-10). (2) Do not become involved with their works (5:11-13). (3) Gain the approval of Christ's light instead (5:14).

Because the wrath of God is coming upon those who disobey, believers are not to become partakers with them (5:7). The term *summetochos* [TG4830/A, ZG5212] (fellow participants) occurs only here and in 3:6, where, conversely, the believer is a fellow participant of the promise. The word denotes one who is a partner or an accomplice in a plot. In the present context the participation does not refer to the sins but to the sinners mentioned in 5:3-6 who are the objects of God's wrath. Because believers participate in fellowship with the Lord and his saints, they are not to be fellow participants with sinners, who are going in the opposite direction. This does not preclude believers from associating with unbelievers but rather it precludes them from participating in their lifestyle. The conjunction *gar* [TG1063, ZG1142] (for) indicates that the reason for this is that Christians are changed persons who are no longer darkness but now are the light in the Lord (5:8a). The darkness signifies their status under the realm and power of sin before they believed the gospel. The light indicates their status as new persons who are his created work-manship (2:10), hence, "light from the Lord."

Since they are light from the Lord, Paul exhorts them to live as children of light (5:8b-10). Previously they lived in darkness and hated light (5:8a; cf. 2:1-3; John 3:20), but, exposed by the light, they became children of light who appropriately should hate the darkness. The qualities of the children of light are stated next in 5:9, which is parenthetical. It begins with the explanatory conjunction *gar* [TG1063, ZG1142] (for), which introduces the three things by which light is characterized. First is goodness, (*agathōsunē* [TG19, ZG20]), a term that is used three other times in the New Testament: (1) when Paul was convinced that Roman believers were "full of good-ness" (Rom 15:14), (2) when Paul lists it as a fruit of the Spirit (Gal 5:22), and (3) when Paul prays that God would make the Thessalonians worthy of his call that they might fulfill every "good" desire (2 Thess 1:11). It is abstract and difficult to ascertain its meaning, but as the adjective *agathos* [TG18, ZG19] (good) has reference to moral and beneficial good (2:10; 4:28-29), so does this noun. This "goodness" is that which embraces generosity toward others. It is the opposite of the adjective *kakos* [TG2556, ZG2805], meaning "bad, evil, injurious" (Luke 16:25; Rom 12:17, 21; 13:10; 1 Thess 5:15; 1 Pet 3:9). The second term, *dikaiosunē* [TG1343, ZG1466] is nor-mally translated "righteousness" and most likely in this context signifies righteous action or works. The third word, *alētheia* [TG225, ZG237] (truth) means reality or that which is actual as opposed to that which is false (cf. 4:21, 24-25). In this context it depicts the idea of right acting or living as opposed to false living. These last two qualities are identified with the new person mentioned in 4:24. Therefore, the fruit of light consists in goodness with generosity, righteous actions, and real or transpar-ent living. Light characteristically will expose that which is opposite of these quali-ties. It will not tolerate evil or falsity. Those in darkness are characterized by the opposite of the fruit of light: evil, wickedness, and falsehood.

Concluding the parenthesis (5:9), Paul finished his thought begun in 5:8b, that believers are to live as children of light by approving what is pleasing to their Lord. The word *dokimazō* [TG1381, ZG1507] means to test or scrutinize something or someone in order to approve that entity rather than testing with the possibility of failure in mind. This is analogous to Romans 12:1-2, where believers are enjoined not to be conformed to this age but to be transformed by the renewal of their minds in order that they might approve what the will of God is. Approving what is pleasing to the Lord goes beyond the moral will of God because his moral will is revealed in spe-cific commands, which do not need to be tested. Rather, it is to test the will of God in every aspect of life and to approve that which would be pleasing to him. The Word of God is a guide for this purpose. However, where specific situations in life are not directly addressed in the Scriptures, believers need to look for principles from the Scriptures whereby they might be able to make a choice or choices that will please the Lord. Although not mentioned here, as believers examine the Scriptures, they also need the enlightenment and enablement of the Holy Spirit to discern what is pleasing to the Lord. This will result in living as children of light.

Paul then emphasized that believers are not to be fellow participants with evildoers, nor are they to become involved with their works. Further, they are to expose those works (5:11). Believers are not to become involved with such activity because those works are too shameful even to mention (5:12-13).

Not only are believers to refrain from being fellow participants with the evildoers (5:7-10), but they also are not to become involved with their deeds (5:11-13), which have their source in darkness. In 5:8 Paul had reminded them that they were darkness but now they are light in the Lord. When they were darkness, they did the deeds of darkness, but now they are light and should not participate in the sins that come from the place to which they had previously been in bondage. Instead of participating in those evil deeds, believers are to expose them. This exposure refers to the deeds themselves, not the perpetrators. In 5:8 believers were not to participate with evildoers, but in 5:11 they are not to participate in their evil deeds of darkness. This is substantiated in 5:14, where Paul states that "everything," not "everyone," exposed by light becomes visible. Whose evil deeds are to be exposed? Although it is easy to assume that it refers to evil deeds of those in darkness, in this case it more likely refers to believers who are participating in the evil works of darkness. First, the context concerns believers. Second, Paul exhorts believers (not unbelievers) to refrain from participating in the works of darkness and to do the works or fruit of light. It is probable that some believers were participating in the works of darkness, making this injunction necessary. Third, the believers are not encouraged to reprimand those in the world but only those in the church (cf. 1 Cor 5:12-13). In light of this, believers are not only to refrain from participation in the evil deeds of darkness but are also to help fellow believers who are found in such activity. This is done by exposing their works and showing them how their acts are inconsistent with light. In this respect, Paul reprimanded the Corinthians for not exposing the sin of incest that was being practiced by one of the believers in their church. Some commentators who argue that this exposure refers to unbelievers rather than believers participating in evil works of darkness also suggest that Paul was not referring to verbal exposure but rather exposure by example—that is, by maintaining a contrastive lifestyle consisting of deeds of light. It is difficult to imagine Paul instructing the Corinthians to remain silent and just live a good lifestyle, expecting evil to disappear. No, to expose evil deeds includes verbal rebuke.

According to 5:12, these worthless deeds must be exposed because they are done in secret (the Greek word *kruphē* [TG2931, ZG3225] means that which is covered and not open to light) and are shameful even to mention. Doing deeds in secret does not characterize people who are light. Darkness conceals sins that must be exposed. These sins, done in secret and too shameful to mention, must not be allowed to spread and encompass the community of believers. In this respect, Paul explained that these unfruitful works of darkness will become visible when exposed by the light (5:13). In the present context light refers both to believers (5:8) and their fruit (5:9). Continuing, Paul explains (*gar* [TG1063, ZG1142], "for") that everything that becomes visible is light. Though it is difficult to explain Paul's assertion, it seems that once the worthless deeds of darkness are exposed, they become visible, and once they are visible, they are light. To understand this it helps to remember that Paul is addressing believers and not unbelievers. If this had reference to unbelievers, then automatic conversion would be the logical outcome, since darkness confronted with the power of the light of Christian truth would automatically become light. This is not the case, however. He is addressing believers who have been engaged in the evil works of unbelievers. These works are to be exposed in order that the offending believers might produce the fruit of light, namely, goodness, righteousness, and truth (5:9).

Verse 14 serves as a conclusion. Most think it is part of an early Christian hymn, possibly a hymn of repentance and encouragement that was influenced by Isaiah 26:19 and 60:1-2. It portrays as asleep believers who participate in the unfruitful works of darkness and urges that they be awakened from the dead. Since most sleep is done in darkness, it is here used as a metaphor of works of darkness. In 5:5-6 believers were told that those who continually practice the works of darkness will not inherit the Kingdom of Christ and of God but will receive God's wrath. True believers will respond to exposure by allowing the Holy Spirit to lead them back and enable them to live a life consisting of the fruit of light—goodness, righteousness, and truth (5:9). In their spiritual awakening, Christ will shine upon them with approval.

◆   E. Live in Wisdom (5:15–6:9)
     1. Admonition (5:15–21)

¹⁵So be careful how you live. Don't live like fools, but like those who are wise. ¹⁶Make the most of every opportunity in these evil days. ¹⁷Don't act thoughtlessly, but understand what the Lord wants you to do. ¹⁸Don't be drunk with wine, because that will ruin your life. Instead, be filled with the Holy Spirit, ¹⁹singing psalms and hymns and spiritual songs among yourselves, and making music to the Lord in your hearts. ²⁰And give thanks for everything to God the Father in the name of our Lord Jesus Christ.

²¹And further, submit to one another out of reverence for Christ.

NOTES
5:16 *Make the most of every opportunity.* This is a good rendering of "redeeming the time." It means buying up or taking full advantage of any opportunity.

5:19 *making music to the Lord in your hearts.* The NLT combines "singing and psalming" into "making music," which summarizes the sense well.

5:20 *give thanks for everything.* This could be translated either as "give thanks for all humanity" or "give thanks for all things." NLT opted for the latter, which is preferable, because the context implies more than giving thanks for or on behalf of all people. Certainly, the parallel passage in Col 3:17 indicates this.

5:21 *out of reverence for Christ.* This is true to the literal "in the fear of Christ." The word "fear" has a broad range of meaning—from absolute terror to respect. Barth (1974:608-609, 662-668) thinks that "reverence" is not strong enough and suggests that "fear" is more suitable as long as it is exercised in the context of love. Both the noun and verb occur frequently. In the NT there are only five times where "fear" is followed by one of the persons of the Godhead as an objective genitive (5:21; Acts 9:31; Rom 3:18; 2 Cor 5:11; 7:1). In all these examples the softer term "respect" is not adequate. Rather the stronger sense of "awe" and "reverence" is more suitable. Hence, here it has the sense of reverential fear or respect.

COMMENTARY

This is the last of five sections set forth by the use of *peripateō* [TG4043, ZG4344] ("walk"; 4:1, 17; 5:1-2, 7-8, 15) introduced by the inferential conjunction *oun* [TG3767, ZG4036] (therefore). On the basis of the doctrinal foundation laid out in chapters 1–3, Paul exhorted believers to walk in unity (4:1-16), holiness (4:17-32), love (5:1-6), and light (5:7-14), and now finally he exhorts them to walk in wisdom (5:15–6:9). This last section can be broadly subdivided: the admonition (5:15-21) and the application (5:22–6:9).

Believers are exhorted to conduct their lives with great care, not as unwise but as wise. It is easy to become entrenched in habits and patterns and fail to give much thought to one's daily existence and activity. As mentioned in 1:8, wisdom is a combination of theoretical and practical knowledge, which results in skillful living (Exod 35:31, 35; Prov 4:11); true wisdom is apparent in those who fear the Lord (Prov 9:10). True wisdom is insight into the true nature of things, and this can only come from God. The unwise person lives as one who despises or has no insight into God's plan. The evidence of true wisdom is spelled out concretely in 5:16—namely, by making the most of every opportunity because the days are evil, controlled by the god of this age (2:2) who opposes God and his Kingdom and works to prevent opportunities for the declaration of God's gospel and purposes. The redeemed of all ages have experienced this evil (Ps 49). Throughout the relentless warfare between the God of heaven and the god of this age, believers are not to be intimidated but to take advantage of every opportunity to live a life that pleases the Lord.

In addition to the injunction to walk wisely by making the most of every opportunity (5:15-16), Paul encouraged the believers to have a proper perspective that also will enable them to live a life that will please the Lord (5:17-21). Negatively, he exhorted them not to become thoughtless, and positively, he enjoined them to understand the Lord's will (5:17). A person who is "thoughtless" is one who thinks carelessly and as a result lacks understanding or discernment in practical living. The positive exhortation is to understand what the will of the Lord is. The word "Lord" occurs 26 times in Ephesians, and it always has reference to Christ and not to God; thus, believers are to understand the will of their Lord, Christ. This fits well with the context, for 5:10 states that believers are to walk in the manner of approving what is pleasing to the Lord Jesus Christ. By understanding the will of the Lord, they will be wise not foolish, following the will of the flesh (2:3), as they did in their unregenerate days.

In 5:18-21 Paul sheds light on how better to understand the Lord's will. He gives the usual negative command and then the positive one (5:18). In the negative sense, he tells believers not to be drunk with wine because this will ruin their lives, and this accordingly would correspond to unwise or foolish conduct. He does not forbid the drinking of wine but forbids excess, which leads to wastefulness and ruin. Such behavior does not exhibit the necessary wisdom needed to take full advantage of every opportunity (5:15-16). Conversely, Paul's positive command is to be filled by the Spirit. The contrast is not between the wine and the Spirit but between the two resulting behaviors. This is expressed by the two verbs: being drunk with wine, which leads to ruination, and being filled by the Spirit, which leads to joy in fellowship and obedience to the commands of the Lord. Some commentators think that "spirit" refers to the human spirit (Abbott 1897:161-162; Westcott 1906:81), but they have difficulty explaining the nature of the filling. Ultimately, they relate the human spirit with the Holy Spirit. Therefore, it is better to view "spirit" as referring directly to the Holy Spirit, for this is consistent with its usage in Ephesians (Eadie 1883:398; Lincoln 1990:343-345; Best 1998:508; O'Brien 1999:391-393). In its grammatical usage in this passage, the Holy Spirit is the means by which believers are filled. The content of the filling is not specifically mentioned in the present verse but most likely refers to the fullness of the moral excellence and power of God mentioned in 1:23. Similarly, in 3:19 Paul prays that believers would be filled up to all the fullness of God, again pertaining to God's moral excellence and power and experiencing the love of Christ. Also, the preceding verse signifies that we are to understand the will of the Lord, this being a reference to Christ. Hence, the Holy Spirit is the means by which believers are filled with Christ and discover his will. This concept corresponds well with the parallel passage in Colossians 3:16, where Paul states "Let the message about Christ, in all its richness, fill your lives. Teach and counsel each other with all the wisdom he gives. Sing psalms and hymns and spiritual songs to God with thankful hearts."

In comparing "drunk with wine" and "filled by the Spirit," two observations can be made. Persons controlled by wine are no longer in control of their actions, as is demonstrated by their inability, for instance, to walk a straight line. Neither do those who are filled by the Spirit control their actions as they relinquish their will to the Lord. It is interesting to note that, at times, this produces unusual results, as in the case of the believers at Pentecost (Acts 2:4, 13, 15). The present imperative probably indicates the repeated action of filling by the Spirit. The imperative mood places the responsibility on believers, and the passive voice suggests that believers cannot fill themselves. Thus, believers are instructed to be filled repeatedly by the Holy Spirit wherever they are or amid whatever they are doing. This pattern of behavior is not limited to church services, as some suggest. In fact, there are four ministries of the Spirit at the time of and subsequent to conversion. There is the sealing ministry of the Spirit (1:13; 4:30; 2 Cor 1:22), which serves as a mark of identification or ownership indicating that believers belong to God. Then there is the indwelling ministry of the Spirit, which is enjoyed by every believer (Rom 8:9-11; 1 Cor 2:12; 6:19; 2 Cor 5:5; Gal 4:6; cf. John 14:17; 1 John 3:24; 4:13) and is the source of God's presence and power for the believer. Third, in 1 Corinthians 12:13, believers are baptized by the Spirit into the body of Christ (cf. also Acts 1:5; 11:16)—that is, they are identified with one body of believers in Christ. Fourth, as indicated in the present verse, they are to be filled by the Spirit. The injunction to "follow the Spirit" (Rom 8:4; see also Gal 5:16-18) seems to be parallel to being filled by the Spirit, for those who follow the Spirit do not fulfill the desires of the flesh but rather put to death the deeds of the flesh (Rom 8:13-16). Consequently, following the Spirit or being filled by the Spirit allows the Spirit of God to direct and empower believers to live lives pleasing to God and to do his will. These first three ministries of the Spirit—sealing, indwelling, and baptism—are bestowed on every believer at the time of salvation. There are no injunctions in connection with these ministries because all are an integral part of the gift of salvation. The imperative "be filled with" the Spirit, expressed in the present imperative, indicates that this is not an automatic bestowment at the time of salvation but an injunction for every believer to follow continually. The filling with the Spirit includes more than the Spirit's indwelling—it is his activity realized in and through us. With the indwelling, each Christian has all of the Spirit, but the command to be filled with the Spirit enables the Spirit to have all of the believer. Being filled with wisdom is an impersonal concept, whereas being filled with the Spirit adds God's personal presence, influence, and enablement to walk wisely, thus pleasing the Lord. The wise walk, therefore, is one that is characterized by the Holy Spirit's control.

Paul then related four resultant characteristics of those filled with the Spirit (5:19-21). The characteristics are delineated by four participles of result (Lincoln 1990:345; Schnackenburg 1991:237; O'Brien 1999:387-388), all of which are dependent on the imperative "be filled with the Spirit" in 5:18. The first is communication with one another by means of psalms, hymns, and spiritual songs (5:19a). Such psalms were most likely from the Old Testament, and the singing was accompanied by a stringed instrument. The hymns were probably songs of praise to God. The spiritual songs sung by believers resulted from being filled by the Holy Spirit rather than generated by wine. In 1 Corinthians 14:26, when the church assembled, believers were to have, among other things, a psalm. Singing had been important in the worship of Israel, and it continued to be important in the early church and the church throughout history. However, there is nothing in the text to suggest that singing praises to God is limited just to the time when believers are assembled. If one is filled by the Spirit, songs of praise to God will be a natural result anywhere and at anytime.

The second resultant characteristic of being filled with the Spirit is found in "making music to the Lord in your hearts." As mentioned in the notes (see 5:19), "making music" is a good translation of the Greek "singing and psalming." Clearly, singing should not be just verbalization but should involve the heart, where the Holy Spirit resides (Rom 8:9). The following qualifying phrase indicates that making music occurs within the heart directed to the Lord (5:19b). Music is one means by which believers minister to each other and worship the Lord.

The third resultant characteristic is giving thanks for everything to God the Father in the name of our Lord Jesus Christ (5:20). Believers filled with the Spirit will never cease to be thankful for their salvation and the provision of every spiritual blessing. Furthermore, the Spirit-filled believer will give thanks for all that they encounter on life's journey. It should be noted that thanksgiving is directed to God the Father in the name of the Lord Jesus Christ. Once again, this is in keeping with other parts of Ephesians, which mention the three persons of the Trinity (cf. 1:4-14, 17; 2:18, 22; 3:4-5, 14-17; 4:4-6; 5:18-20).

The final resultant characteristic is submission to one another (5:21). The verb *hupotassomai* [TG5293/A, ZG5718] is a part of a word group built on the Greek root *tag-*, signifying order or arrangement (see 1 Cor 15:23), and with the prepositional prefix of *hupo* [TG5259, ZG5679] the word literally means "to order oneself under a leader," hence, "to be subject" or "to submit." With regards to its form, the participle is rendered by some as in the middle voice—"submitting or subjecting yourselves" (KJV, ASV, NIV), while others render it as a passive "be subject" (RSV, NASB, JB, NJB, NRSV). There is not much difference between the middle and passive. The passive could connote that the subject has no control of the action, like a drunken person controlled by wine. The middle expresses the idea of cooperation, where the subject acts as a free agent. The latter is more in keeping with the context, for all four previous participles (communicating, singing, psalming [5:19], thanking [5:20]) are active, indicating that the subject is taking action under the guidance and control of the Holy Spirit. Thus, when believers are filled with the Holy Spirit the result will be mutual submission to one another. Whereas unbelievers prize individualism and independence, which lead to selfishness, believers are to love one another (John 13:34-35), prefer one another by showing honor (Rom 12:10), and count others better than themselves (Phil 2:3). Although mutual submission is accomplished by means of the filling by the Holy Spirit, how is this practiced? And how does one know when or in what areas to submit? Fortunately, the next section (5:22–6:9) sheds a great deal of light on the practice of submission. There are those who submit (wives, children, slaves), and there are those to whom they submit (husbands, fathers, masters). In brief, it will be seen that submission involves the willingness to submit to those who have authority, whether it be in the home, in the church, or in society. One thing is clear. Submission should not be taken lightly, because it is to be done out of fear of Christ. Though the range of meaning for "fear" is anywhere from absolute terror to one of respect, in this context it connotes reverential fear or reverential respect. Thus the NLT's rendering "out of reverence for Christ" captures the idea well. In conclusion, 5:21 serves as a guideline for believers to be filled by the Spirit and to submit to one another out of fear of Christ. In the following verses, Paul becomes more specific regarding the practical outworking of submission.

◆   ## 2. Application (5:22–6:9)
a. Wives and husbands (5:22-33)

22For wives, this means submit to your husbands as to the Lord. 23For a husband is the head of his wife as Christ is the head of the church. He is the Savior of his body, the church. 24As the church submits to Christ, so you wives should submit to your husbands in everything.

25For husbands, this means love your wives, just as Christ loved the church. He gave up his life for her 26to make her holy and clean, washed by the cleansing of God's word.* [27]He did this to present her to himself as a glorious church without a spot or wrinkle or any other blemish. Instead, she will be holy and without fault. [28]In the same way, husbands ought to love their wives as they love their own bodies. For a man who loves his wife actually shows love for himself. [29]No one hates his own body but feeds and cares for it, just as Christ cares for the church. [30]And we are members of his body.

[31]As the Scriptures say, "A man leaves his father and mother and is joined to his wife, and the two are united into one."* [32]This is a great mystery, but it is an illustration of the way Christ and the church are one. [33]So again I say, each man must love his wife as he loves himself, and the wife must respect her husband.

5:26 Greek *washed by water with the word.*   5:31 Gen 2:24.

NOTES

5:22 *submit to your husbands.* The verb "submit" is not present in the best witnesses (𝔓46 B Clement) but must be supplied from the previous verse.

5:25 *this means love your wives, just as Christ loved the church.* Jesus stated that he is the good shepherd and he will lay down his life for the sheep (John 10:11, 15, 17). Also, there is no greater love than when one lays down his life for his friends (John 15:13). Christ laid down his life of his accord and in doing that he willingly did the Father's will. So also the husband should exhibit sacrificial love.

5:26 *to make her holy and clean, washed by the cleansing of God's word.* Lit., "in order that he might sanctify her having cleansed [her] with the washing of the water with the word."

5:28 *In the same way, husbands ought to love their wives as they love their own bodies.* "In the same way" refers to Christ's sacrificial love for the church (5:25). Likewise, husbands ought to love their wives as Christ loves the church.

5:30 *And we are members of his body.* In the Greek text the causal conjunction *hoti* [TG3754, ZG4022] (because) introduces the reason why Christ lovingly cares for the church; that is, because we are members of his body. A textual problem is posed by the additional wording found in some manuscripts, namely, "of his flesh and of his bones." Although most of the Western and Byzantine witnesses (D F G 𝔐 it syr) add these words, it is generally accepted that they are not original but had been added by a scribe who took them from Gen 2:23. NLT has omitted them, per the testimony of 𝔓46 ℵ B 048 33 1739*.

5:31 *As the Scriptures say.* The Greek text has "for this reason" and then quotes Gen 2:24 as follows: "A man leaves his father and mother and is joined to his wife, and the two are united into one." Paul quotes Gen 2:24 with only two minor changes from the text of the LXX: He uses different Greek words for "for this reason" and he excludes the personal pronoun "his" (LXX "a man leaves *his* father and *his* mother").

united into one. Rather than "the two are united into one," Paul (following LXX and MT) has "the two shall be one flesh." This refers back to 5:29, where Paul states that no one hates his own "flesh," though the NLT has rendered it "body."

5:32 *but it is an illustration of the way Christ and the church are one.* This is difficult to translate, and the NLT may have overstated it. The text reads, "but I speak [with reference] to Christ and the church."

5:33 *the wife must respect her husband.* The word "respect" is a translation of the Greek word for "fear." As in 5:21, also here, it is best understood as "reverential fear" or "reverential respect."

COMMENTARY

Overview of 5:22–6:9. In the previous section, Paul indicated that those who are filled by the Spirit should be characterized by (1) communication with one another by means of psalms, hymns, and spiritual songs; (2) singing songs and psalms with their hearts; (3) giving thanks for everything to God the Father in the name of Christ; and (4) submitting to one another out of reverence for Christ (5:19-21). While all of these characteristics relate to a church setting, the last relates to life both inside and outside the church. Believers' submission to one another not only serves as a final characteristic of a life filled by the Spirit but it also serves as an introduction to the next section. Since there is no conjunction introducing the new section, it is possible that it was not intended as a new section but as a continuation of the concept of wise living begun in 5:15. Unfortunately, all too often the next section (5:22–6:9) is viewed as isolated from the previous context. Rather, it adds to and elaborates on what has just been stated. It is relatively easy to exhibit for a few hours in church the characteristics of one who is being filled by the Spirit. However, Paul's injunction to be filled with the Spirit extends beyond a church service to lives at home and at work, where believers will be under scrutiny 24 hours a day. The power of the Spirit is absolutely necessary to live a life pleasing to the Lord in daily life at home or at work.

As previously stated, the submission mentioned in 5:22 serves not only as the last resultant characteristic of a life that is being filled by the Spirit, but also as an introduction to the next section (5:22–6:9). In these next verses Paul discusses three sets of relationships: wife and husband, children and parents, and slaves and masters. In each instance the one who is to submit is discussed first—namely, the wife, the children, and the slaves. Paul then discusses the responsibility of those in position of authority, namely, the husband, the parents, and the masters.

In recent times there has been much discussion on the household codes—that is, the rules for the household as portrayed in Ephesians 5:22–6:9; Col 3:18–4:1; 1 Pet 2:18–3:7; 1 Tim 2:8-15; 6:1-10; Titus 2:1-10. Some have attempted to identify the source of the New Testament household codes. However, even though the New Testament household codes may have similarities to Stoic, Jewish, Hellenistic Jewish, or Roman codes, care must be taken in the attempt to identify any one of these as *the* source. Each society had its own rules for maintaining order. Although there may be similarities to other codes, the New Testament household codes are presented as a new Christian ethic for believers to follow. They serve to instruct believers in their conduct with one another and within the secular society. Believers, as new people in Christ, have a new code of conduct that befits their new position. Its intended function is to enable believers to implement the theme of Ephesians—namely, the unity of the church. The practical outworking of this unity in the present context is for believers to live wisely by being filled by the Spirit (5:15-21), and the household code (5:22–6:9) gives details for enhancing this unity.

The first of the three pairs discussed in the household code concerns wives and husbands. This section is disproportionately large, consisting of twelve verses. The second pair, children and parents, is discussed in four verses (6:1-4), and the final pair, slaves and masters, occupies five verses (6:5-9). As mentioned above, first there are instructions to those who are to submit and then exhortations to those in the position of authority.

Husbands and wives (5:22-33). Paul discussed the responsibility of wives in 5:22-24, followed by the responsibility of husbands in 5:25-32, and finally he reviewed each partner's responsibilities (5:33). Although most commentators do not accept the verb "to submit" as a genuine reading (because it is missing from a few manuscripts, and it is easy to surmise a scribal insertion—see note on 5:22), the same verb is supplied from the previous verse with an imperatival force. Whether one accepts the verb as genuine in 5:22 or not is dependent on the participle in 5:21; both are either middle or passive in form. The middle is preferable, where the subject volitionally submits as the act of a free agent, because it is in keeping with the context. There is no indication that the church's submission to Christ is forced. Also, the duty of the husband is expressed in the active imperative, whereby the subject chooses to love his wife. Finally, in the previous context (5:18-21), four out of the five participles are active, but the fifth is best assessed as middle (rather than passive) where the subject is responsible for the action. In light of this, submission here is best viewed as in the middle voice, with the wife acting freely before God.

How does this instruction correlate with 5:21, where Paul states that all believers are to be submissive to one another? Some suggest that 5:21 contains the controlling thought of mutual submission, and the rest of the passage should be seen as mutual submission between husbands and wives rather than the submission of wives only (Wall 1988:276, 280-284; Beck 1989:61-66; Scholer 1996:43-44, 51). One needs to note, however, that 5:21 refers to all believers, whereas in the household code specific roles of submission and authority are addressed. There is no indication in the household codes that husbands are to submit to their wives, parents to their children, or masters to their slaves. This does not indicate an inherent contradiction between 5:21 and 5:22. Rather, as stated earlier, Paul's statement in 5:21 concludes the section of 5:15-21 regarding the characteristics of believers filled by the Spirit. The last of these is the general resultant characteristic of submission to one another—that is, within the body of believers. Proceeding to the household code, Paul addresses the wives specifically (5:22-24). This is analogous to the broad general command to walk in love (5:2), which is directed to all believers, but in the household code is addressed specifically to husbands (5:25, 28, 33). Others consider that Paul's instruction for wives to submit to their husbands was engendered by the time in which he lived, where women were considered inferior to men and thereby should be subject to their husbands (Scholer 1987:416-417). But Paul clearly states in Galatians 2:28 that men and women are equal before God. Further, he taught that husbands and wives are equal concerning conjugal rights (1 Cor 7:2-4), a concept that was unheard of in that day. There is, however, a distinction between equality and lines of authority. For example, all citizens of a country are equal, but there are also many different ranks in the power structure of the country.

This does not mean that those in authority are better citizens of the country than those whom they rule. There is no qualitative difference between rulers and citizens. By way of example, there is equality and yet lines of authority within the Godhead. All three persons of God are qualitatively equal (4:4-6; Matt 28:19; 2 Cor 13:14; 1 Pet 1:2; cf. also John 13:16; 17:21), but there is also the subordination of the Son to the Father (Matt 10:40; 26:39, 42; John 8:29, 42; 12:49), Holy Spirit to the Father (John 14:26; 15:26; 16:13-15), and the Holy Spirit to the Son (John 16:7; cf. 14:26; 15:26). Thus, lines of authority do not imply qualitative inequity.

Next, Paul gives the motivation for wives to submit to their husband—that is, they are to submit to their husbands as they also submit to Christ. In other words, since the Lord has instructed wives to submit to their husbands, by doing so they are also submissive to the Lord. A wife's submission, then, has to do with the lines of authority. The husband's headship over his wife corresponds to Christ's headship over the church (5:23). As discussed in 1:22, the term "head" connotes the idea of authority over someone. Christ's headship over the church is a model for the husband's headship over the wife. This concept of the wife's submission to her husband and the husband's authority over his wife was at odds with the structure of the Roman family in Paul's day. At that time the father had absolute power over his entire family (*patria potestas*), even the power of life and death, and a married woman was still under her father's authority, and he could even initiate the divorce of his daughter (although during Roman history there were changes). Thus, Paul's injunction for the wife to submit to her husband countered the social structure of that day. The husband's replacement of the father in authority over his wife places him at the head of the new family (cf. 5:31 which quotes Gen 2:24).

The statement "He is the Savior of his body, the church" (5:23) is literally, "he is the savior of the body." Although most commentators think it has sole reference to Christ (Abbott 1897:166; Barth 1974:615-617; Lincoln 1990:370), the absence of "the Church" in the Greek leads some to think that Paul intended both Christ and the husband here (Robinson 1903:124, 205; Hendriksen 1967:248-249), thus making the husband the savior of his wife. However, the context suggests that the former interpretation is correct, for the husband could not be savior of the body in the same sense as Christ, who redeemed sinners from eternal doom. Nonetheless, the term "savior" could apply to the husband in a limited way as the protector of the wife (see 5:29-30) in times of both physical and spiritual danger. For example, under the Mosaic law, the husband could protect his wife from carrying out a rash vow (Num 30:6-14), thus protecting her reputation. Adam failed as a husband in the area of protecting his wife—he did not protect Eve from the serpent's lie. The husband, then, does not save the wife from eternal doom, as Christ does the church, but rather he acts as her protector in a temporal sense. This concept of husband as "savior" in this sense should be viewed as application rather than interpretation.

Paul related that the church's submission to Christ serves as an illustration of the wives' submission (5:24). The words "in everything" are problematic. A similar expression is used for children's obedience to their parents (Col 3:20, NLT:

"always") and slaves to their masters (Col 3:22; Titus 2:9). It is difficult to know the precise meaning of this and is best viewed in the light of other Scripture. Most likely, it denotes full submission of wives to their husbands but certainly would not suggest that a wife should submit to her husband in anything that is contrary to the commands of God, for one needs to obey God over people (Acts 5:29). In other words, the wife is not to submit to her husband in anything sinful. In light of the physical abuse so rampant in today's society, it should also be included as a sin to which a wife should not and must not submit. No Christian is to do something that is contrary to God's commands or God's will. If the husband orders his wife to steal or kill a person, for example, then she is not to submit to the husband's order. In conclusion, two observations should be made. First, there is no indication that a wife's submission is based on the degree to which her husband demonstrates his love. Second, her submission is to be of her own accord in obedience to the Lord (5:22), not by the demand of her husband.

Having discussed the responsibility of the wives to husbands (5:22-24), Paul turned to the responsibility of husbands to wives (5:25-32). Significantly, in addressing their responsibility Paul used 116 words (he uses only 10 words in Col 3:19), as compared with the 41 words used in his exhortation to wives. He again used the analogy of Christ and the church by instructing husbands to love their wives as Christ sacrificially loved the church. The amount of space given to the subject and the analogy of Christ's love signifies the unique importance of a husband's responsibility to his wife. Paul's instruction to wives in 5:22-24 states the measure of their submission, and his teaching in 5:25-32 expresses the measure of the husband's love. Properly fulfilling this responsibility will not only enrich their wives but will also bring harmony to marriages and thus to the believing community.

"For husbands this means love your wives" (5:25a). The verb "to love" (*agapaō* [TG25, ZG26]), a key word in this section, is used six times (5:25 [twice], 28 [three times], 33). It refers to love irrespective of merit, even to the undeserving. In other words, husbands are to love their wives unconditionally. Just as the wife's submission is not dependent on the husband's response, likewise, a husband's love is not dependent on the wife's response. Also, the present imperative reinforces the idea that the husband's love for his wife is to be an ongoing process, not governed by the vagaries of emotion but rather by an act of the will. This is not to say that love is an act of the will that is entirely devoid of any emotion, but if based entirely on emotion, the husband's love would be based only on a good response. This exhortation to husbands to love their wives is unique. It is not found in the Old Testament, rabbinic literature, or in the household codes of the Greco-Roman era. Although the patriarchal model of the home is maintained, it is amended by this revolutionary exhortation that husbands are to love their wives as Christ loved the church.

As submission of wives to husbands is illustrated by the church's submission to Christ, likewise husbands' love toward wives is illustrated by Christ's love for the church (5:25b-27). In the present analogy between husbands and Christ, it should be noted that the emphasis is not on headship but on love—that is, not "be heads over your wives" but "love your wives." Christ's unconditional love serves as the model. Interestingly, this is the only time in the New Testament that there is specific mention of Christ's love for the church. He demonstrated this love by voluntarily offering himself as a sacrifice for our redemption. Paul points out that Christ's supreme sacrifice is the evidence of his love.

Christ's sacrificial love for the church continues to operate by his cleansing of the church (5:26). The conjunction *hina* [TG2443, ZG2671] (in order that) signifies that the purpose of Christ's love for the church is to make her holy—that is, sanctified. To sanctify or to make holy means to set apart or consecrate to God or to God's service. But how does God accomplish this? Verse 26 states that the church is cleansed by the washing of the water with the word. The description given here has engendered much discussion. Essentially, to sanctify or to make holy is the positive aspect of being set apart to God, while the cleansing is the negative aspect of being purified of defilement from sin. The two aspects are two sides of the same coin. Paul continued the sanctification metaphor with the additional words in the Greek text "with the washing of water." Some think the "water" refers to baptism (Abbott 1897:160; Lincoln 1990:375; Schnackenburg 1991:249-250), but this is reading patristic and modern liturgy into the first century. There is no indication from the context that it is speaking about a baptismal rite. The rite of baptism does not cleanse one from sin. Even the Qumran community recognized that the ritual washing did not cleanse them; only God was able to wipe out their transgression and justify them. Nor is this a reference to the baptism of the Spirit (Barth 1974:695-698; Dunn 1970:163-164) because there is nothing in the present context to suggest this. Instead, it is best to view this as a metaphorical expression of redemption using the imagery of the bridal bath practiced in the first century (O'Brien 1999:422-423; Hoehner 2002:753-754). It was a prenuptial bath taken by the bride-to-be so as to prepare herself to be ready for her husband. It was a Jewish marital custom that reflected the imagery of God's marriage to Israel related in Ezekiel 16. Ezekiel declared that at the time of Israel's birth, it was in a pitiable condition; so when she grew up, God entered into a covenant with her and bathed her with water, anointed her with oil, and clothed her with the finest materials, making her exceedingly beautiful, fit to be queen. It is fitting, then, to view the cleansing in the present verse as analogous to this. Only this time, it involves Christ and his church instead of God and Israel.

Similarly, 1 Corinthians 6:9-11 speaks of the believers who were washed, sanctified, and justified in the name of the Lord Jesus Christ and in the Spirit of God. Also in Titus 3:5 there is the mention of washing of regeneration, indicating that cleansing is part of salvation and is necessary to make us acceptable before a holy God. Water is used in the metaphorical expression since water is the most common element used for washing (see Heb 10:22). Further Paul states that this washing of water is in connection with the "word." It should be noted that the term "word" (*rhēma* [TG4487, ZG4839]), referring to the "spoken word," is never used in connection with a ritual such as baptism. It probably refers to the preached word that tells of

Christ's love for the church, which was demonstrated in his giving of himself for her (5:25) in order to sanctify her by cleansing her with the washing of water (5:26). It was a Jewish custom that at the time of betrothal the young man would present his bride-to-be with a gift and say to her, "Behold, you are consecrated unto me, you are betrothed to me; behold, you are a wife unto me" (b. Qiddushin 5a). With this spoken word, they would be betrothed and then married about a year later. As discussed earlier, just before the wedding the bride was bathed to symbolize her being set apart to her husband. It was the spoken word that set her apart to the husband and not the bathing itself. In the same way Christ gave himself for the church to sanctify her on the basis of the fact that he cleansed her with the washing of the water. The cleansing is a metaphor for Christ's sacrificial death, which is proclaimed by use of the spoken word.

The initial purpose of Christ's death is to sanctify the church with the further purpose to present to himself a glorious church (5:27). In the first century, the bride prepared herself for the bridegroom, who then presented her to his father. In the spiritual realm, Christ, the bridegroom, prepares the bride by sanctification and then presents her to himself. Since he has overseen her preparation, it is certain that her appearance will be characterized by gloriousness. This quality of gloriousness is next explained, first negatively and then positively. Negatively, the glorious church will not be tainted in any way—not a stain or wrinkle or anything else that would suggest imperfection. In a positive sense, she will be holy and blameless. The allusion to the church's holiness and blamelessness is important not only in the immediate context but also because it serves as a climax to the argument and theology of the whole book. Paul began in 1:4 by stating that God chose some to be holy and blameless before him in love. This was accomplished by the Father's selection, Christ's redemption, and the Holy Spirit's sealing (1:4-14). New life was given to sinners (2:1-10), who were placed into a new entity, the church (2:11-3:13). This body of believers is to live in unity (4:1-16), holiness (4:17-32), love (5:1-6), light (5:7-14), and wisdom (5:15-6:9). That which was planned in eternity past (1:4) will be accomplished when Christ presents to himself a church that is holy and without blame (5:27). Presently, Christ is sanctifying the church as the body of Christ, but in the future Christ will present the church to himself as his bride. Christ's love, as demonstrated in the redemption, sanctification, and presentation of the church to himself, serves as an illustration of husbands' love for their wives. It is to this subject that Paul now returns.

In developing the argument in 5:28-32, Paul declares again that as Christ sacrificially loved his body, the church, so husbands are responsible to love their wives as their own bodies (5:28). The intent of the comparative phrase "as their own bodies" is debated. Its force may be that husbands are to love in a similar fashion—to love even as they love their own physical bodies—or it may mean that husbands are to love their wives "as being" their own bodies. It could be a combination of these ideas but with emphasis on the second, because Paul states in the latter part of 5:28 that the one who loves his own wife loves himself, and in 5:31 he quotes Genesis

2:24, which states that the husband and wife are one flesh. To love another in the same way as one loves oneself does not present itself as a duty but as something that is consistent with one's nature. This concept is further illustrated by describing how everyone cares for their own bodies (5:29a). A truism of nature is that no one hates one's own body but nurtures and takes tender care of it, even with all its imperfections. By way of application, husbands should care for their wives though they may be imperfect. Once again, Christ's care for the church (5:29b-30) serves as an illustration. He loves the church because its members are "members" of his body. The Greek term *melos* [TG3196, ZG3517] (members) refers to limbs of a body, whether human or animal. It is never used of a member of an organization but always of a member of an organism. This portrayal demonstrates the close-knit relationship of the members with Christ. Paul continues in 5:31 by quoting Genesis 2:24 (also quoted in Matt 19:5; Mark 10:7-8; 1 Cor 6:16). The Genesis passage states only that the man is to leave his parents and to be joined to his wife, but Paul expanded on this by adding that the two become one flesh. Before marriage man and woman are two independent entities; after marriage they become glued or cemented (*proskollaomai* [TG4347, ZG4681]) to each other, each maintaining their distinctive features. It is not the same as an alloy, which is an admixture of metals, because in that case the distinctiveness of each person would be lost. As a result of this union, the husband should nurture and tenderly care for the wife.

The conclusion Paul presents in 5:32 is difficult to understand. He states that he speaks of a great mystery and follows this by stating that he speaks of Christ and the church. As mentioned in 3:3 the word "mystery" (*mustērion* [TG3466, ZG3696]) is a secret plan hidden in God that cannot be unraveled or understood by human ingenuity or study. It is unveiled by God. In Ephesians (3:3, 4, 9) "mystery" refers to believing Jews and Gentiles who are united in one body, the church. But how is this concept of "mystery" used in this context?

Some, mainly Roman Catholics, think the mystery refers to the human marriage mentioned in Genesis 2:24, and due to the Vulgate's translation of *mustērion* [TG3466, ZG3696] as *sacramentum*, they interpret the institution of marriage as a sacrament of the church, which conveys grace (Gnilka 1971:288-289; Schnackenburg 1991:256). Therefore, they think the marriage of a Christian man and woman is a reenactment of the marriage of Christ and the church. Most outside the Roman Catholic Church find this unacceptable because Genesis 2:24 does not suggest a "Christian" marriage as opposed to a secular marriage. Whether secular or religious, marriage is the joining of two into one flesh. Others think the mystery reflects a deeper meaning to the human marriage than in Genesis 2:24—namely, that it points typologically to the union of Christ and the church (Brown 1968:82-84; Bockmuehl 1990:204). However, this use of *mustērion* [TG3466, ZG3696] is without parallel in Ephesians or anywhere in the entire New Testament. Finally, many view this mystery of "two becoming one" as a reference simply to the union of Christ and the church (Lincoln 1990:382-383; Best 1998:557; O'Brien 1999:432-435).

The third view has validity in that the only other time Paul quotes Genesis 2:24 is in 1 Corinthians 6:16, where he declares that when a person and a prostitute are joined, they become one body. He immediately follows with the declaration that the one who is joined to the Lord is one spirit with him. Likewise, here in Ephesians Paul moves from the spiritual (5:30) to the quotation from Genesis 2:24, which speaks of physical union (5:31), and then shifts back to the spiritual by proclaiming that this mystery is great, referring to the spiritual union of Christ and the church (5:32). Thus, in both passages Paul uses the same pattern by going from the spiritual to the physical (Gen 2:24) and returning to the spiritual. Furthermore, the context portrays Christ as the model for the husband and the church as the model for the wife (5:24-27), and thus the union of the husband and wife into one flesh ("the two are united into one") is a model for the union of Christ and the church (5:31-32). Hence, this mystery is not the union of believing Jews and Gentiles nor of human marriage but the union of Christ and the church (which serves as a model for human marriage). This is clarified by the following statement, "It is an illustration of the way Christ and the church are one." Although Genesis 2:24 refers to the union of husband and wife, Paul specifically applied it to the union of Christ and the church. And as there is the union of Christ and the church, so also there is the union of husband and wife.

Having discussed the responsibility of wives (5:22-24) and the responsibility of husbands (5:25-32), Paul concluded with a summary review of each of their responsibilities (5:33). The introductory adverb *plēn* [TG4133, ZG4440] marks a contrast to what has been mentioned and draws one's attention to what is essential. It can be rendered "nevertheless," "in any case," "however," "so again." Having just stated that the mystery is the union of Christ and the church (5:29-32), Paul used this adverb to return to the main subject of his discussion: marriage. This time he mentioned husbands first, since this flows logically from the immediately preceding discussion about their responsibility toward their wives. Also, he addressed each spouse in the singular rather than the plural (not done elsewhere in the NT household codes), possibly to emphasize individual responsibility. He reiterated that the husband is to love his wife as he loves himself. It is interesting to note that while this was repeated, he did not reiterate the submissive role of the wife. Rather, he mentioned, again, her duty to fear her husband. As discussed in 5:21 it seems fitting to view "fear" as reverential fear or respect. In regard to the wife, this fear could be defined as reverence for her husband's position as head of the home. Thus, as believers are to submit themselves to one another in the fear of Christ (5:21), so the wife should submit to her husband with fear (5:33).

In conclusion, the first part of the household code has been concerned with the responsibility of wives and husbands. Wives are to submit to their husbands as the church submits to Christ, and the husbands are to love their wives as Christ loves the church. Much more space is devoted to the husbands' responsibility than to the wives'. Marriage is the union of two individuals into one flesh (Gen 2:24), which should produce a loving harmonious relationship. Believers' marital harmony is not to be dependent on their own ingenuity but rather should be motivated by obedience to God and by the enabling power of the Holy Spirit. The successful development of this relationship requires Spirit-filled partners who are truly concerned for each other and who have a real desire to see God work in their lives. The primary goal of marriage is not to please oneself but to see God's purposes work in and through each partner individually and corporately. Noteworthy is the fact that the illustration of the union of Christ and his church is used only for husband and wife. This indicates that their relationship holds a uniqueness not shared by the relationships discussed next, which follow in chapter 6.

◆   ### b. Children and parents (6:1-4)

Children, obey your parents because you belong to the Lord,* for this is the right thing to do. 2"Honor your father and mother." This is the first commandment with a promise: 3If you honor your father and mother, "things will go well for you, and you will have a long life on the earth."*

4Fathers, do not provoke your children to anger by the way you treat them. Rather, bring them up with the discipline and instruction that comes from the Lord.

6:1 Or *Children, obey your parents who belong to the Lord;* some manuscripts read simply *Children, obey your parents.*   6:2-3 Exod 20:12; Deut 5:16.

NOTES
6:1 *Children, obey your parents because you belong to the Lord.* The NLT's rendering of the literal "obey your parents in the Lord" captures the meaning well.

6:3 *If you honor your father and mother, "things will go well for you, and you will have a long life on the earth."* The Greek text does not repeat the command "honor your father and mother" but has only "that it may be well with you and you may live long on the earth."

6:4 *do not provoke your children to anger by the way you treat them.* The Greek text has simply "do not make your children angry." Paul implicitly acknowledged that there is a place for discipline of children. However, the fathers were to make it a practice not to provoke their children lest they become discouraged (Col 3:21). It is very possible that the irritation caused by nagging and demeaning fathers in everyday life may in turn cause children to become angry, frustrated, and ultimately discouraged because they are unable to please their fathers.

COMMENTARY
The second of the three pairs in the household code is concerned with children and parents. The broader context of these four verses includes the injunction to live wisely by understanding the will of the Lord and by being filled by the Spirit (5:15-18) so that a proper harmony between children and parents can be achieved. There are similarities to other parts of the household code. First, the subordinate partner is addressed first, then the ruling partner. Second, each of those addressed are ultimately answerable to the Lord and not to the other partner. Third, the form is the same for each: The party is addressed, the imperative is stated, amplification is given, and the motivation is presented.

Paul addresses the children in 6:1-3, then the fathers in 6:4. Children are to obey both parents in the Lord (6:1), in spite of the fact that only the father is addressed in

6:4. It is difficult to ascertain from the Greek what the prepositional phrase "in the Lord" modifies. It could modify "parents," giving the sense that children are to obey parents who are "in the Lord," that is, parents who are believers. However, most likely it modifies the verb "to obey" thus emphasizing the children's obedience to the Lord, exhibited here by obedience to their parents. This is substantiated in the parallel passage in Colossians 3:20 where children are enjoined to "obey parents with respect to all things, for this is pleasing in the Lord" (my translation). Therefore, the prepositional phrase does not define the limits of obedience but rather shows the spirit in which the obedience is practiced. As mentioned in the notes above, the NLT's rendering "obey your parents because you belong to the Lord" captures this sense well. The verb "to obey" is active, demonstrating children's responsibility as free moral agents to carry out this instruction before God. Most likely Paul was addressing those who were still home as dependent children, yet old enough to understand the instruction themselves.

To support this injunction for children to obey their parents, Paul cited the Old Testament (6:2-3). The exhortation for children to honor their fathers and mothers is most likely from Exodus 20:12 or possibly Deuteronomy 5:16, the fifth commandment in the Decalogue. The parenthetical clause following this command, which states that this is the first commandment with promise, presents some difficulty. How can this fifth commandment of the Decalogue be the first commandment with promise when the second commandment has a promise attached to it— namely, punishment for those who hate God but steadfast love for those who love God (Exod 20:4-6; Deut 5:8-10)? There are five interpretations that attempt to solve this dilemma: (1) This fifth commandment is the first one of the second table of the Decalogue that deals with human relationships; the first four commandments deal with a person's relationship to God. The problem with this view is that there is no general agreement as to which commandments belong to the first table and which belong to the second table (Schnackenburg 1991:261-262). (2) Since children are addressed, it is the first commandment to be learned by children (Abbott 1897:177). But the text does not say that this is the first commandment for children but the first commandment with a promise. Also, the first, not the fifth, commandment is the more important to learn first. (3) The adjective "first" does not refer to numerical order, rather to degree of difficulty (Dibelius 1953:95). According to rabbinic tradition, two commandments promise prolonged life if obeyed: The "easiest commandment" states that when one comes across a bird's nest, one is to keep the young bird and let the mother go (Deut 22:6-7) and the "most difficult or weighty commandment" is the fifth commandment (Exod 20:12). But this interpretation seems foreign to the present context. (4) The adjective "first" refers to first in importance (Hendriksen 1967:260; Best 1998:567). However, Jesus made it clear that the greatest and "first" commandment is to love God and the second is to love your neighbor (Matt 22:36-40; Mark 12:28-31). Nonetheless, proponents of this view would counter by saying that this is the most important command with a promise. (5) The fifth commandment is the first commandment with a specific promise because the promises with the second commandment (Exod 20:5-6) are of a general nature applicable to all the commandments (Lincoln 1990:404; O'Brien 1999:443). Furthermore, it is suggested that these promises are referring to a "jealous God," who punishes and rewards, rather than relating specifically to the second commandment "you shall not make a graven image." One problem with this view is that it would render the fifth commandment not only the first with a promise but the *only* one with a promise. In conclusion, views 4 and 5 appear to be the most plausible, and of these, view 5 is perhaps the best. The objection against the last view, that it would be the only one with promise, can be countered by the fact that the Ten Commandments serve as an introductory summary of the whole law, which contains many commandments with promises.

The promise for those who honor their fathers and mothers is that "things will go well for you, and you will have a long life on the earth" (6:3). This promise of well-being and longevity of life is not clearly defined, and there are no clear examples in the Old Testament. However, the Old Testament does offer some clues. In that context, children who dishonored parents by striking or cursing them were to be put to death (Exod 21:15, 17), and a son who persistently disobeyed his parents was to be stoned (Deut 21:18-21). Conversely then, when parents were honored, children were not punished by death and could expect physical well-being and longevity of life. "Well-being" or "full of blessing" is vague, but, again from the Old Testament context, could refer to stability and discipline necessary to function well within the family and society. Therefore, as a general rule, honor/obedience fosters self-discipline, which in turn brings stability, longevity, and well-being; dishonor/ disobedience promotes lack of discipline that in turn brings instability, a shortened life, and a lack of well-being. When applying this to New Testament times, one cannot spiritualize this as a reference to eternal life, but the same principle as in Old Testament times applies—namely, that honoring/obeying father and mother will culminate in well-being and a long life on earth.

Keeping to his pattern, Paul secondly addresses those with authority: the fathers (6:4). Fathers represent the governmental head of the family on whom rests the responsibility of child discipline. Paul gave both the negative and positive exhortations. In Paul's day the father, according to Roman law, had absolute control over his family. This power was called *patria potestas* and often was used ruthlessly. However, Paul's instructions to fathers present a new perspective on the treatment of their children. Fathers are warned not to make a practice of provoking their children to anger. Such conduct is not conducive to a friendly and loving atmosphere within the home. In contrast, fathers are to bring them up in the discipline and instruction that comes from the Lord or is prescribed by the Lord. The word *paideia* [TG3809, ZG4082] reflects training or "discipline." The second word *nouthesia* [TG3559, ZG3804] is similar in meaning and is used of admonition and warning. It may well be that the first word refers to education with an emphasis on activity and discipline, and the second word refers to education with an emphasis on verbal communication of either encouragement or reproof. All is to be done "in the Lord," that is, Christ, who is their Lord. In other words, the father's training and admonition is not to be man-centered, as it was in Hellenism, nor centered around the law, as in the rabbinics, but rather Christ-centered training and admonition that is approved by the Lord. When set in the larger context, fathers must be filled by the Spirit (5:18), who enables them to restrain from provoking their children to anger and gives them the wisdom and ability to train and instruct them. The present imperative emphasizes the continuous action of their responsibility.

◆   ### c. Servants and masters (6:5-9)

[5]Slaves, obey your earthly masters with deep respect and fear. Serve them sincerely as you would serve Christ. [6]Try to please them all the time, not just when they are watching you. As slaves of Christ, do the will of God with all your heart. [7]Work with enthusiasm, as though you were working for the Lord rather than for people. [8]Remember that the Lord will reward each one of us for the good we do, whether we are slaves or free.

[9]Masters, treat your slaves in the same way. Don't threaten them; remember, you both have the same Master in heaven, and he has no favorites.

NOTES

6:5 *Slaves, obey your earthly masters with deep respect and fear.* The NLT's translation serves well the literal rendering of the Greek text: "Slaves, obey your earthly masters with fear and trembling."

Serve them sincerely as you would serve Christ. This is a good translation of "in singleness of your heart as to Christ."

6:7 *Work with enthusiasm.* The literal wording is "serving with goodwill." "Goodwill" is a better choice than "enthusiasm" because one can show enthusiasm without actually having goodwill.

6:9 *treat your slaves in the same way.* As slaves are to serve with integrity, dedication, and goodwill, so also masters must treat them in the same way.

COMMENTARY

The third of the three pairs in the household code is concerned with slaves and masters, again keeping in mind the broader context of these verses, that is, believers who are to walk in wisdom by understanding the will of the Lord and who are to be filled by the Holy Spirit (5:15-18). With these principles in mind, a harmonious relationship between slaves and masters could be fostered. Once more, there are similarities with the previous two pairs in the household code. First, the subordinate partner is addressed. Second, each of those addressed are ultimately answerable to the Lord. Finally, the form is the same: The party is addressed, the imperative is stated, amplification is given, and the motivation is presented.

Before examining this portion, it must be pointed out that the slavery practiced in Paul's time had little in common with that which was once practiced in the United States. It was not imposed upon people of one ethnicity. Rather, as regards the Jews, it was practiced in the manner laid out in the Old Testament (cf. Exod 21:2-11;

Lev 25:39-55; Deut 15:12-18). In Paul's day the Romans considered slaves to be human beings, in contrast to the Greeks, who considered them property. In Roman society a free person could sell himself or herself into slavery in order to pay off a debt but later could regain freedom. Slaves not only could regain freedom but could even become Roman citizens—a status held by only the elite of society. Nevertheless, the life of a slave depended on the master. Although there were good masters, there was also much cruel treatment as well.

Though Paul did not advocate the abolition of slavery, neither did he encourage slavery. There were many evils occurring in the secular world during his time; however, his primary mission was not to rail against them but to present the one who had triumphed over them by his act of redemption. Also, speaking speculatively, if he promoted the abolition of slavery, undoubtedly many slaves might have become Christians for the wrong reason. Christianity does not promise a release from the present circumstances but gives one power to endure those circumstances. Though Paul did not promote the abolition of the institution of slavery, he did instruct believers to avoid becoming slaves (1 Cor 7:23) and, in fact, enjoined those slaves who are able to gain freedom to do so (1 Cor 7:21).

Paul's exhortation is directed first toward the slaves (6:5-8). The specific exhortation of obedience to their masters is in 6:5a. How this was to be carried out is explained in 6:5b-7, and the rationale for obedience is mentioned in 6:8. Unlike the Stoics, who usually addressed only their social peers, Paul directly addressed Christian slaves (cf. also Col 3:22-25). Apparently slaves were a part of the church at Ephesus, where they heard the message directly.

Slaves were to obey their earthly masters with reverential fear or respect (6:5b). This fear is further described by *tromos* [TG5156, ZG5571] meaning a "trembling" or "quivering" fear, which seems to denote outward manifestation, fear so great that it cannot be concealed. Furthermore, slaves were to obey wholeheartedly or completely just like they would obey Christ, their heavenly master. Undoubtedly, this was not always easy to carry out. There may have been times when unbelieving masters would not let them fellowship with other Christians. Also, tension between a Christian master and a Christian slave was a possibility, since the slave knew that—in the eyes of God—they were equal. Regardless, slaves were to obey their masters as they would obey their heavenly master, the Lord Jesus Christ. Furthermore, obedience was not to be practiced only when their masters were watching but rather they were to do the will of God wholeheartedly at all times (6:6). As obedient slaves of Christ, then, they were ultimately doing God's will, the emphasis being on wholeheartedly pleasing God rather than people. This is further amplified by "as though you were working for the Lord rather than for people" (6:7). Hence, though ostensibly slaves were carrying out the orders of earthly masters, the attitude of goodwill that was to accompany their service was to please their heavenly Lord and not their faulty earthly masters. This frame of mind helped to prevent resentment toward their masters. Obedience with integrity and a proper attitude would ultimately be rewarded by their heavenly master, even when reward from earthly masters was not forthcoming (6:8). Ultimate reward is to be realized in the future, most likely at the judgment seat of Christ (2 Cor 5:10), where rewards will be given fairly to all, whether slaves or free men, based on righteous standards and not on the whim of an earthly master.

Paul next instructed the masters, using positive and negative arguments (6:9). He exhorted them to "treat your slaves in the same way" meaning exhibit integrity, dedication, and goodwill toward their slaves as they do to the Lord. This is in keeping with Colossians 4:1, where Paul exhorted masters to treat their slaves justly and fairly. Masters were not to intimidate slaves, as was often the custom, with threats of beatings, sexual harassment of female slaves, or threats to sell male slaves (thereby severing them from their families), for example. Christian masters were instructed to treat their slaves differently because they were accountable to their master in heaven, who was also their slaves' master and who is impartial in his judgments. Paul warned them not to use their power wrongly. Instead, he reminded them, as he had the slaves, that they would be judged by the same master with no regard to social status.

Most societies today no longer tolerate or condone slavery (though, deplorably, it does still exist in some places). This altered social context, however, does not render this passage irrelevant to believers today since this passage may be applied in a broader sense to employer–employee relationships in the present time. Primarily, Christian employees should serve their employers (believing or unbelieving) with fear, diligence, integrity, and goodwill. Christian employers should deal with their employees (believing or unbelieving) with integrity and goodwill, and without threats. Both Christian employees and Christian employers need also to realize that they have a heavenly master to whom they are accountable for their attitudes and conduct. Furthermore, the behavior of both parties should be a testimony to the unbelievers with whom they work.

In conclusion, the instructions given in the household code are God's formula for the wise walk of wives, husbands, children, parents, slaves, and masters. Each of these groups of people must be filled by the Spirit in order to consistently carry out the exhortations given. Many of these verses emphasize selflessness, which results in harmony—one evidence of the Spirit's work.

◆ **F. Stand in Warfare (6:10-20)**
   1. Put on the armor (6:10-13)

[10]A final word: Be strong in the Lord and in his mighty power. [11]Put on all of God's armor so that you will be able to stand firm against all strategies of the devil. [12]For we* are not fighting against flesh-and-blood enemies, but against evil rulers and authorities of the unseen world, against mighty powers in this dark world, and against evil spirits in the heavenly places.

[13]Therefore, put on every piece of God's armor so you will be able to resist the enemy in the time of evil. Then after the battle you will still be standing firm.

6:12 Some manuscripts read *you.*

NOTES

6:10 *A final word: Be strong in the Lord and in his mighty power.* Rather than "with," which denotes instrument (and is grammatically defensible), "in," denoting sphere (or source) is probably a better choice, hence, "be strong in the Lord."

6:12 *against evil rulers and authorities of the unseen world.* NLT adds "of the unseen world" in order to clearly delineate that the rulers and authorities are spiritual, not human.

against mighty powers in this dark world. This is a good rendering of the literal "world rulers of this darkness" or "cosmic potentates of this darkness."

against evil spirits in the heavenly places. The Greek text has "against spiritual beings of wickedness in the heavenly realms." The use of "spiritual" is juxtaposed to spiritual benefits (1:3) and spiritual songs (5:19). It shows that the character of the enemy is not human but supernatural.

COMMENTARY

Whereas thus far, every division of 4:1–6:9 was introduced by the Greek inferential conjunction *oun* [TG3767, ZG4036] (therefore) along with the imperative *peripateite* [TG4043, ZG4344] ("walk," "live"; 4:1, 17; 5:1-2, 7-8, 15), this final division is signaled by the articular adjective *tou loipou* [TG3064, ZG3370] (finally) to indicate that these are Paul's final thoughts before he ends the epistle. He encouraged believers to be strengthened in the Lord in order to stand against the spiritual wickedness in the heavenly places (6:10-12), which is engendered by the devil and his spiritual hosts, who desire to rob believers of their spiritual benefits. This section is divided into three parts: (1) putting on the armor (6:10-13); (2) standing with the armor (6:14-16); and (3) taking up the last pieces of armor (6:17-20).

In order to prepare for battle, believers were instructed to "be strong in the Lord" (6:10), followed immediately by the charge to put on the armor of God (6:11a) for the purpose of withstanding the strategies of the devil (6:11b-12). Verse 13 reinforces the preceding verses by declaring that believers must take up God's armor in order to stand in the time of evil.

In this final section of the letter, Paul exhorted believers to be strengthened in the Lord—that is, in the might of his strength. As in 1:19, he used various words for power. He began with the present passive imperative *endunamousthe* [TG1743/A, ZG1904] with the sense, like the noun (*dunamis* [TG1411, ZG1539]), of dynamic power or ability, which in this context means "to be imbued with power, to become able, to be strengthened." Although in form it could be rendered as a middle voice, it is best understood in the passive voice, "to be made strong" or "to be strengthened," as elsewhere in the New Testament (Acts 9:22; Rom 4:20; 2 Tim 2:1). "In the Lord" indicates the sphere from which the believer's strength comes, namely, in the Lord Jesus Christ. Immediately following, the conjunction *kai* [TG2532, ZG2779] (and) most likely is used as epexegetical ("that is"), further explaining the particulars of the preceding words, "be strengthened in the Lord." Believers are to be strengthened in the *kratos* [TG2904, ZG3197], the supernatural "might" of his *ischus* [TG2479, ZG2709], which denotes inherent "strength" or power. Consequently, believers are strengthened not only by the person of the Lord Jesus Christ but also by his resources.

Once the command had been given, "be strong in the Lord," Paul explained how this is to be accomplished (6:11a): "put on all of God's armor." The word *endusasthe* [TG1746/A, ZG1907], meaning "put on clothes" (either in a literal or metaphorical sense), is used with an imperatival force three times in Ephesians (4:24; 6:11, 14), although each is a different form of the word. The middle voice indicates that believers themselves are responsible for putting on the *panoplia* [TG3833, ZG4110] (the suit of armor of the foot soldier), which in this case refers to "the full armor of God." God's provision of this armor indicates that this is not a physical battle but a spiritual one, requiring spiritual armor provided supernaturally.

The purpose for donning God's armor is to enable believers to stand against the strategies of the devil (6:11b-12). The ability "to stand" results in firmly holding one's position. Notably, then, this is not speaking of offensive but defensive warfare, to hold one's ground, against the schemes or strategies of the devil. In 1 John 3:8 he is identified as one who has sinned from the beginning and, according to Jesus, has nothing to do with the truth because there is no truth in him; he is a liar and the father of lies (John 8:44). John identified the devil as Satan, who is the deceiver of the whole world (Rev 12:9; 20:2). Due to this, one must always be cognizant that the strategies or schemes of the devil are based on lies and are designed to deceive believers. Paul exhorted believers to put on the full armor of God in order to stand firmly against the deceptive strategies of the devil. Paul is not calling believers here to attack the devil or advance against him; they are only to "stand"—to hold the territory that Christ and his body, the church, have already conquered. Without the armor of God, it is certain that believers would be deceived and defeated by those "schemes" of the devil, which have been effective for thousands of years. God's spiritual armor is required since it is not physical but spiritual warfare (6:12). In other words, the believers' struggle is not against human beings composed of flesh and blood but is a spiritual battle against spiritual enemies, whom Paul lists as "evil rulers and authorities." These powers already mentioned in 1:21 and 3:10 are most likely angelic leaders in league with the devil, who is portrayed as the one who is "the commander of the powers in the unseen world" (2:2), the evil one who controls this world (1 John 5:19), and "the god of this world" (2 Cor 4:4). Next, in Ephesians 6:12, Paul mentions "mighty powers in this dark world," who are cosmic potentates unknown before New Testament times. Paul describes these as having universal power. Their realm is in darkness, and they are in conflict with the God of light. The final descriptive statement, "evil spirits in the heavenly places," may not depict a new foe but may further describe the hostile rulers mentioned earlier as well as identify the realm of these foes. Clearly, the struggle is not human but supernatural. The words "evil spirits" are descriptive of the essential character of those spiritual beings. Their sphere of activity is in *tois epouraniois* [TG2032B, ZG2230] "the heavenly places"—the fifth occurrence of this phrase, which occurs in this form in the New Testament only in Ephesians 1:3, 20; 2:6; 3:10; 6:12. The idea that evil spiritual leaders are located in the heavenly places is not new. In the Old Testament, God and Satan converse with one another in heaven (Job 1:6-12). Also, good and evil angels struggle with each other in heaven and on earth (Dan 10:13, 20). Earlier in this epistle (3:10), the church is told to demonstrate the manifold wisdom of God toward both good and evil spiritual leaders in the heavenly places. Though the locale of the evil rulers is in the heavenly places, the conflict is both on earth and in the heavenly places. Although believers are blessed with all the spiritual benefits in the heavenly places (1:3) and are seated there together with Christ (2:6), they do live on earth in the present evil age (5:16), where the devil and his followers are active. The present battle, then, is played out in the heavenly realms and on earth between those who align themselves with the devil and his angelic leaders and those who align themselves with Christ and his angels. Although Christ has won the ultimate victory at the Cross, at the present time, it is his plan for the struggles to continue, and hence believers urgently need to put on the full armor of God. This struggle will continue until the defeat of the devil and his angels at the second coming of Christ (1:10, 21; cf. 1 Cor 15:24-28).

In conclusion, believers are urged to put on the armor of God so that they can stand against the onslaughts of the devil and his cohorts (6:13). The active imperative ("put on") indicates it is the responsibility of believers themselves to put on the full armor in order to be able to resist or withstand in the evil day. "The time of evil" refers to the present evil days (5:16), which are compounded with heightened and unexpected satanic assaults against believers and for which they must be prepared. The final clause, which is literally "and having done everything, to stand," is interpreted by some, including NLT, to convey the idea that when the victory has been accomplished, believers can then stand (John Chrysostom, *Ephesians* 6:13; PG 62.159-160; Schlier 1971:293; Yoder Neufeld 2002:298). Others consider it to mean that, having prepared by donning the full armor of God, believers will be able to stand or hold their ground against the attacks of the devil and his partisans (Lincoln 1990:446; Best 1998:597; O'Brien 1999:472). This latter view is preferred for the following reasons: (1) It is consistent with the defensive use of the verb "to stand" throughout the context (6:11, 13, 14); (2) subsequent verses (6:14-17) describe the various pieces of armor that believers are to put on in order to make their stand, and this would be pointless if it is subsequent to a victory stand but appropriate for a defensive stand; and (3) the imperative "stand" in 6:14 is unnecessary and inappropriate if it has reference to a victorious stand but entirely appropriate if it refers to a defensive stand. Accordingly, appropriately clad with the full armor of God, believers will be able to make a defensive stand against the devil and his strategies.

◆ ## 2. Stand with the armor (6:14-16)

[14]Stand your ground, putting on the belt of truth and the body armor of God's righteousness. [15]For shoes, put on the peace that comes from the Good News so that you will be fully prepared.* [16]In addition to all of these, hold up the shield of faith to stop the fiery arrows of the devil.*

6:15 Or *For shoes, put on the readiness to preach the Good News of peace with God.*   6:16 Greek *the evil one.*

NOTES

6:14 *putting on the belt of truth.* "Belt" is literally a "girdle." See commentary below.

the body armor of God's righteousness. The Greek text has only "breastplate of righteousness" and may well refer to righteous acts of believers that are based on God's righteousness.

COMMENTARY

After making the general command "put on every piece of God's armor" (6:10-13), Paul described the various pieces of the armor (6:14-16). The larger section (6:14-20) is the last of the eight long sentences in this epistle (cf. 1:3-14, 15-23; 2:1-7; 3:2-13, 14-19; 4:1-6, 11-16; 6:14-20) with 113 words. This section can be divided into two parts indicated by the two imperatives: (1) "Stand" by putting on the various pieces of defensive armor (6:14-16), and (2) "take" the final pieces of the armor together with prayer to be able to stand against the assaults of the spiritual forces of the devil (6:17-20).

Paul had exhorted believers to put on the armor of God in order to stand firmly against spiritual wickedness (6:10-13), and he further exhorted them to do just that, to "stand" (6:14a). This is the third time he used "stand" (6:11, 13, 14). Note again, believers are not exhorted to advance but to hold their ground and not retreat in the face of wicked spiritual leaders who belong to the devil. Our firm stand depends on the donning of the various pieces of armor. First, there was the girdle of truth (see note on 6:14), which was to be worn around the waist (6:14b). It was used to protect the thighs and to provide a place to tuck in articles of clothing in order to allow greater freedom of movement. It was a defensive piece of armor. The girding with "truth" may refer to the objective truth of Christianity or the gospel, but more probably refers to the believers' integrity and faithfulness. This piece of armor is basic to all other pieces because truth and trustworthiness are basic to all the other qualities that believers need in order to withstand diabolical attacks. As the soldier's girdle gives ease and freedom of movement, so truth gives freedom with self, others, and God.

Second, believers are to put on the breastplate of righteousness (6:14c). In Roman armor the breastplate was a metal plate worn over a leather jerkin or coat of mail to protect the chest and back, again a defensive piece of armor. The "righteousness" further describing the breastplate could refer to justifying righteousness but more likely is sanctifying or subjective righteousness (1 Cor 1:30), which, of course, still has its basis in justifying righteousness. In other words, by appropriating God's righteousness, believers are to act righteously in their dealings with God and people. As a soldier's breastplate protected his chest from enemy attacks, so sanctifying, righteous living (Rom 6:13; 14:17) guards believers' hearts against the assaults of the devil (cf. Isa 59:17; Jas 4:7).

Third, their feet are to be shod, literally, "with the preparation of the gospel of peace" (6:15). The heavy sandals worn by Roman soldiers had soles made of several layers of leather studded with hollow-headed hobnails, thus affording them stability. The preparation or readiness, which such footgear represents, affords believers a spiritual stability—or, if you will, surefootedness. The "gospel of peace"

(NLT, "peace that comes from the Good News") refers to the reconciliation of believing Jews and Gentiles united into one body, the church. In this regard, some suggest that in the midst of vicious attacks from evil powers, believers have shod their feet in their readiness to preach the gospel of peace (Caird 1976:93; Schnackenburg 1991:278; O'Brien 1999:476-477). This view is unlikely for the following reasons. First, it does not say that they have shod their feet with the *proclamation* of the gospel of peace but that they have shod their feet with the *readiness* of the gospel of peace. Second, the context is about wearing defensive, not offensive, armor. Third, the main verb in the present context (6:14) is "to stand" and not "to advance." Hence, Paul depicts this as another defensive piece of armor. In light of this, believers who are to be ready or prepared to stand against the onslaughts of the evil forces must be firmly grounded in the gospel of peace (Hendriksen 1967:277; Lincoln 1990:449; Best 1998:599-600). Their certainty or "surefootedness" results in tranquility of the mind and security of the heart and enables them to stand against the devil and his angelic hosts.

Fourth, they are to take up the shield of faith in which the fiery arrows of the evil one are stopped or extinguished (6:16). The Roman shield was two-and-a-half by four feet, made of two wood planks glued together with the outer surface covered first with canvas and then with calf skin. There was a metal strip on the top and bottom edges, which protected the wood when it hit the ground and a center iron boss, which caused most stones and heavy arrows to glance off. This shield not only covered the body but also the other parts of the armor described earlier; hence, Paul used the phrase "in addition to all of these." He further described this shield as a shield "of faith." Again, it is a defensive piece and represents the believers' subjective faith, a resolute faith that helps them stand firmly and resist the devil (cf. 1 Pet 5:8-9) and his schemes. The arrows are described as "fiery" like those of Roman soldiers who wrapped them with tow and ignited them, making them fiery or flaming. Their shields were soaked in water and hence the water-soaked skins and hides covering the shields prevented the wood from catching fire and extinguished the arrows. Accordingly, believers are shielded from spiritual harm aimed at them by the evil one. It would be a serious mistake to lay aside the shield of faith and attempt to stand in one's own strength.

◆ ### 3. Take the last pieces of armor (6:17-20)

[17] Put on salvation as your helmet, and take the sword of the Spirit, which is the word of God.

[18] Pray in the Spirit at all times and on every occasion. Stay alert and be persistent in your prayers for all believers everywhere.*

[19] And pray for me, too. Ask God to give me the right words so I can boldly explain God's mysterious plan that the Good News is for Jews and Gentiles alike.* [20] I am in chains now, still preaching this message as God's ambassador. So pray that I will keep on speaking boldly for him, as I should.

6:18 Greek *all of God's holy people.* 6:19 Greek *explain the mystery of the Good News;* some manuscripts read simply *explain the mystery.*

NOTES

6:17 *Put on salvation as your helmet.* Salvation here is not initial salvation, for he is addressing believers. Rather, it is an awareness of the fact of salvation, which affords confidence of deliverance from the assaults of the evil one.

6:18 *Pray in the Spirit at all times and on every occasion.* This is a good rendering of the Greek text, literally, "through every prayer and petition praying at every opportunity in the Spirit."

6:19 *so I can boldly explain God's mysterious plan that the Good News is for Jews and Gentiles alike.* The Greek text simply states "to boldly make known God's secret plan of the Good News."

6:20 *I am in chains now, still preaching this message as God's ambassador.* The NLT's rendering could imply that Paul was speaking the gospel message boldly, but in context, the object of his speaking is the secret plan—namely, that the believing Jews and Gentiles are united into one body.

COMMENTARY

This section is delineated by Paul's use of the imperative "take," which is not parallel to the preceding participles in 6:14-16 but to the imperative "stand" in 6:14a. The connective conjunction *kai* [TG2532, ZG2779] (and) indicates that this is not really a new sentence, as most translations suggest, but a continuation of the sentence begun in verse 14 (as suggested by the high point that punctuates verse 16 in most editions of the Greek text—equivalent to an English semicolon).

In physical warfare, the helmet and sword are the last two pieces a soldier takes up. During Claudius's reign (AD 37–41), the helmet was made of bronze fitted over an iron skullcap lined with leather or cloth. It covered the back of the neck, fitting slightly over the shoulder. A brow ridge fitted above the face protected the nose and eyes, and hinged cheek pieces fastened by a chin band protected the face. The helmet, hot and uncomfortable, would be put on by a soldier only when he faced impending danger. The believers having made all the preparations by putting on the other pieces of armor, Paul exhorted them now to take the helmet of salvation (6:17a). Most likely this does not refer to salvation in the objective sense but a conscious possession of it and its ability to afford safety in the midst of the onslaughts of the evil one. With the head protected, soldiers felt safe in the midst of battle. Likewise, believers' possession of salvation gives them confidence of ultimate safety during the assaults of the devil.

The last thing the soldier grabs is the sword, his only active, offensive weapon. The sword (*machaira* [TG3162, ZG3479]) used by Roman soldiers had a double-edged blade approximately two inches wide and two feet long and was very suitable as a cut-and-thrust weapon for close combat. The "sword of the Spirit," which is the word of God, is to be grabbed just before the attacks of the devil and his cohorts (6:17b). The phrase "sword of the Spirit" most likely refers to its source or origin. Thus, in accordance with the offensive nature of this weapon, it portrays the offensive empowerment of the Holy Spirit necessary in a spiritual battle (6:12). This sword of the Spirit is further described as the *rhēma* [TG4487, ZG4839] (word) of God. As mentioned in the commentary on 5:26, *rhēma* means "the spoken or proclaimed word." Briefly then, the sword of the Spirit is the offensive weapon, the spoken word of God, to be used against the spiritual wickedness of the devil. In his encounter with the devil, Christ used the written word against him (Matt 4:11; Luke 4:1-13). For instance, in reply to the devil's first temptation, Jesus quoted Deuteronomy 8:3, stating, "People do not live by bread alone, but by every word (*rhēma* [TG4487, ZG4839]) that comes from the mouth of God" (Matt 4:4). This is not preaching the gospel but speaking God's word against his foes. It should be noted, however, that God's word is not to be recited as a magic formula. On the contrary, it is speaking the words of God in Christ's name, which is being empowered by God's Spirit. Although it is the only offensive weapon listed among the pieces of the armor, in the present context it is not used to make advances by preaching the gospel but to enable believers to stand firmly so that the devil will not gain new territory in Christ's Kingdom or rob believers of their spiritual blessings in Christ. With this piece, the description of the armor comes to an end.

The entire armor is absolutely necessary in spiritual warfare against the devil and his angels. As in other parts of this book, the exhortation is directed both to the individual and the corporate body. This is in keeping with the dominant theme of the book: the unity of believing Jews and Gentiles in one body. Thus, the church, the body of believers, is in this warfare together. As Roman soldiers did not fight alone, so also believers as a body, united under their commander-in-chief, stand against spiritual wickedness in heavenly places.

With armor donned and helmets and swords in place ready for an imminent attack, the believer's state of mind must now be readied. Paul declared that believers must be in a constant state of prayer and alertness (6:18-20). Prayer is not another piece of armor, for Paul does not mention any specific piece of armor representing prayer. Rather, the two Greek participles, "praying" and "keeping alert," express the manner in which believers are to take up their helmet of salvation and sword of the Spirit. Paul states, "Pray in the Spirit at all times and on every occasion," which indicates that, in readiness for enemy attacks, believers are to pray with thoroughness and intensity at every opportunity (or critical time) in the power of the Spirit. This is spiritual warfare, so it must be fought by spiritual means. This was vividly illustrated in Christ's last hours in the garden of Gethsemane. Not only are believers to pray, they are to pray for the purpose of keeping alert individually and collectively against the devil's tricky strategies, realizing that all believers are involved with the struggle against the evil powers. Individual Christians join together to form an entire army that collectively battles against the enemy. It is noteworthy that prayer and petition are mentioned four times in this verse, suggesting the absolute urgency of prayer. The adjectives "every" and "all" are also mentioned four times with their same purpose: to emphasize the vital importance of prayer for every believer on every occasion.

Nuclear wars cannot be won with rifles. Likewise, satanic wars cannot be won by human strength or strategy. In light of this, Paul warned the saints to constantly pray and remain alert, even as they don the helmet of salvation and grasp the sword of the Spirit in order to do battle at a moment's notice.

Having instructed believers to pray for all Christians, Paul mentions two specific requests (indicated twice by the word *hina* [TG2443, ZG2671]) for prayer on his behalf. The first request is that God would give him utterance when he opens his mouth (as he did for the prophets of the OT) to make known the mystery of the gospel. This does not refer to preaching the gospel in an evangelistic sense as an offensive advance. Rather, since the context is discussing a defensive stand, rather than an offensive advance, it is better to understand that Paul was asking to be given the right words to speak boldly in order to explain the secret plan (mystery) of the Good News while under attack by the evil one. More specifically, it may well refer to his trial before Caesar in Rome (when and if the Jewish accusers would make charges against him). The Roman government viewed Christians as a sect of the Jews, whereas the Jews considered them a heretical group. In his trial before Caesar, Paul needed to make it clear that Christians are neither a Jewish sect nor a heretical group but an entirely new entity, the church, the body of Christ, composed of Jewish and Gentile believers.

In 6:20 Paul gives two further details about himself in relationship to boldly explaining the secret plan of the Good News. First, he was an ambassador in chains for the mystery. In other words, Paul was not imprisoned for the gospel per se but rather for speaking about the "mystery of the gospel"—that is, the union of believing Jews and Gentiles into one body. Paul, an ambassador in chains, was an incongruity, for normally the position of ambassador commands respect and provides immunity from imprisonment by those to whom he is sent. Instead, Paul, commissioned by the mightiest of all sovereigns, had been incarcerated. Nevertheless, diplomatic immunity or no, Paul was determined to speak boldly on behalf of the sovereign whom he represented. In light of this, the second detail in this verse is that he might speak just as boldly about the mystery. Paul was rightfully concerned about defending the mystery of the gospel against the assaults of the wicked one, who would want to confuse the issue by having the Roman tribunal dismiss the trial on the grounds of mistakenly thinking that Paul's message simply led to the formation of another sect of the Jews. As an ambassador for the Lord, Paul urgently desired to fulfill his mission by making clear the mystery of the gospel, the union of Jews and Gentiles into one body.

As discussed in the Introduction, there are some who deny Pauline authorship of Ephesians. However, if this epistle had been written in the last two decades of the first century, as some claim, then this call for prayer on behalf of the imprisoned Paul would have been rather pointless. Why would the author ask for prayer for Paul if he was already deceased? Furthermore, why would he ask for prayer for Paul when the readers would have known that Paul was already deceased and also would have known the outcome of that for which he requested prayer? It makes much more sense to see this as truly Paul asking his readers for prayer in a most difficult situation, in prison and facing a possible tribunal before Caesar.

◆   G. Conclusion (6:21-24)

21To bring you up to date, Tychicus will give you a full report about what I am doing and how I am getting along. He is a beloved brother and faithful helper in the Lord's work. 22I have sent him to you for this very purpose—to let you know how we are doing and to encourage you. 23Peace be with you, dear brothers and sisters,* and may God the Father and the Lord Jesus Christ give you love with faithfulness. 24May God's grace be eternally upon all who love our Lord Jesus Christ.

6:23 Greek brothers.

NOTES

6:21-22 It is interesting to note that a total of 32 words of these two verses in the Greek text are in verbatim agreement with Col 4:7-8, except the addition of two words (ti prassō [TG5101/4238, ZG5515/4556] "how I am getting along") in 6:21 and two Greek words kai sundoulos [TG2532/4889, ZG2779/5281] (and fellow servant) in Col 4:7. This suggests that the one document was copied from the other. Very likely Paul still had the first letter while he was penning the second, and both letters were taken by Tychicus to Asia Minor.

COMMENTARY

The major part of the letter to the Ephesians dealt with the calling and conduct of the church. The last four verses, however, contain personal matters. Paul began by informing them that Tychicus would tell them more about his circumstances. According to Colossians 4:7, Paul considered Tychicus a much-loved brother who was a faithful helper in serving the Lord with him. Tychicus and Trophimus were the two Asians who accompanied Paul immediately after the Ephesian riot (Acts 20:4). Later, in his second Roman imprisonment, Paul sent Tychicus to Ephesus to relieve Timothy in order for Timothy to come to Paul (2 Tim 4:12). He was a beloved, faithful, and trusted brother. Ephesian believers would have anxiously awaited his report concerning Paul's welfare since it was Paul's ministry to the Gentiles that caused his imprisonment. He had been arrested for proclaiming the mystery of the gospel, the unification of believing Jews and Gentiles into one body (2:11-3:13). But Tychicus was not only to inform the Ephesian believers about Paul's situation but was also to encourage them. If Paul, as some suggest, was not the author of Ephesians, then why would the congregation want to know of Paul's situation when he was already dead? Were they to pray for the dead? Also, this would have implicated Tychicus in the fraud along with the pseudonymous author. It is more logical to accept the Pauline authorship of Ephesians and to accept that it was Paul who sent Tychicus to Ephesus to give an oral report of his situation.

Paul closed this letter with a salutation (6:23) and benediction (6:24). In the Greek text, the words "peace" and "grace" introduce 6:23 and 24 respectively, and both of these words are found in the prologue of this letter (1:2) but in reverse order. The order in these concluding verses is unusual, and it is unlikely that an imitator would have deviated from the normal Pauline order. Also, "peace" is directed toward the "dear brothers and sisters," which is unique among Paul's epistles, for normally Paul addressed believers directly in the second person, "you." Again, an imitator most likely would not have deviated from the normal Pauline style. It is more likely that Paul himself diverted from his normal style since this letter was an encyclical and would include those believers with whom he had no personal acquaintance. Paul also enjoined them to love with faith. In fact, it was love combined with faith in God for which they were well known (1:15). This peace and love had their source in God the Father and the Lord Jesus Christ.

"Grace" concludes this letter, just as it introduced it in 1:2. Paul pronounced grace toward only those who unceasingly love our Lord Jesus Christ. This unusual expression is difficult to decipher in regards to its meaning and to what it is connected. The Greek term *aphtharsia* [TG861, ZG914] means "incorruptibility" or "immortality," indicating a continuous state or process not interrupted by death and hence has the sense of "unceasing, always, eternally, undying." Some suggest that this word is connected to the immediately preceding words "our Lord Jesus Christ," who is immortal (Dibelius 1953:100), while others think it is connected to "grace" mentioned in the first part of the verse, thereby signifying that the grace conferred by God on believers is immortal or indestructible (Schnackenburg 1991:291; Lincoln 1990:467-468). Most think that it is connected to "love," indicating a love that is not corrupted by death, hence referring to "those who unceasingly love our Lord Jesus Christ" (Abbott 1897:191; Robinson 1903:138, 220; Best 1998:620). Unfortunately, some Ephesian believers later left or neglected their love and were reprimanded accordingly (Rev 2:4). However, in the present context, Paul was able to give a benediction of grace to them because of their unceasing love for their Lord Jesus Christ. This is a very appropriate ending to the epistle.

The conclusion of this letter (6:21-24) illustrates to believers the kind of love and unity that Paul had been advocating throughout the book. Although imprisoned in Rome, his thoughts were for the welfare of the Ephesian believers. In light of this, he sent Tychicus to them to report on his situation. His purpose was to comfort them. This epistle began with Paul's salutation of grace and peace (1:2), and ends with a benediction that also includes grace and peace.

BIBLIOGRAPHY

Abbott, T. K. A.
1897 *A Critical and Exegetical Commentary on the Epistles to the Ephesians and to the Colossians.* International Critical Commentary. Edinburgh: T & T Clark.

Alford, Henry
1976 *The Greek Testament.* Grand Rapids: Guardian Press. (Orig. Pub. 1852)

Arnold, Clinton E.
1989 *Ephesians: Power and Magic.* Society for New Testament Studies Monograph Series, vol. 63. Editor, G. N. Stanton. Cambridge: Cambridge University Press.

1993 Ephesians, Letter to the. Pp. 238-249 in *Dictionary of Paul and His Letters.* Editors, Gerald F. Hawthorne, Ralph P. Martin, and Daniel G. Reid. Downers Grove, IL: InterVarsity Press.

Barth, Markus
1974 *Ephesians.* The Anchor Bible, vol. 34. Garden City, New York: Doubleday.

Beck, James R.
1989 Is There a Head of the House in the Home? Reflections on Ephesians 5. *Journal of Biblical Equality* 1:61-70.

Bedale, S.
1954 The meaning of κεφαλη in the Pauline Epistles. *Journal for Theological Studies* 5:211-215.

Best, Ernest
1987 Recipients and Title of the Letter to the Ephesians: Why and When the Designation 'Ephesians'? Pp. 324-379 in *In Teil II: Principat.* Editor, Wolfgang Haase. Aufstieg und Niedergang der römischen Welt: Geschichte und Kultur Roms im Spiegel der neueren Forschung, vol. 25.4. Berlin: de Gruyter.

1997 Who Used Whom? The Relationship of Ephesians and Colossians. *New Testament Studies* 43:72-96.

1998 *A Critical and Exegetical Commentary on Ephesians.* International Critical Commentary. Edinburgh: T & T Clark.

Bockmuehl, Markus N. A.
1990 *Revelation and Mystery in Ancient Judaism and Pauline Christianity.* Wissenschaftliche Untersuchungen zum Neuen Testament, vol. 36. Editors, Martin Hengel and Otfried Hofius. Tübingen: J. C. B. Mohr (Paul Siebeck).

Brown, Raymond E.
1968 *The Semitic Background of the Term "Mystery" in the New Testament.* Philadelphia: Fortress.

Bruce, F. F.
1967 St. Paul in Rome: The Epistle to the Ephesians. *Bulletin of the John Rylands University Library of Manchester* 49:303-322.

1984 *The Epistles to the Colossians, to Philemon, and to the Ephesians.* The New International Commentary on the New Testament. Grand Rapids: Eerdmans.

Caird, G. B.
1976 *Paul's Letters from Prison (Ephesians, Philippians, Colossians, Philemon) in the Revised Standard Version.* London: Oxford University Press.

Calvin, Jean
1965 *The Epistles of Paul the Apostle to the Galatians, Ephesians, Philippians and Colossians.* Translator, T. H. L. Parker. Grand Rapids: Eerdmans.

Cervin, Richard
1989 Does *kephale* Mean 'Source' or 'Authority Over' in Greek Literature? A Rebuttal. *Trinity Journal* 10:85-112.

Comfort, Philip
2005 *Encountering the Manuscripts: An Introduction to New Testament Paleography and Textual Criticism.* Nashville: Broadman & Holman.

Conzelmann, Hans
1965 Der Brief an die Epheser. Pp. 56-91 in *Die kleineren Briefe des Apostles Paulus.* 10th ed. Das Neue Testament Deutsch, vol. 8. Editors, P. Althaus and G. Friedrich. Göttingen: Vandenhoeck & Ruprecht.

Dahl, N. A.
1951 Adresse und Prosmium des Epheserbriefes. *Theologische Zeitschrift* 7:241-265.

Dibelius, Martin
1953 *An die Kolosser, Epheser, an Philemon.* 3rd ed. Tübingen: J. C. B. Mohr.

Dodd, C. H.
1929 Ephesians. Pp. 1222-1237 in *The Abingdon Bible Commentary.* Editors, Frederick Carl Eiselen, Edwin Lewis, and David G. Downey. New York: Abingdon-Cokesbury Press.

Donelson, Lewis R.
1986 *Pseudepigraphy and Ethical Argument in the Pastoral Epistles.* Hermeneutische Untersuchungen zur Theologie, vol. 22. Editors, Hans Dieter Betz, Gerhard Ebeling, and Manfred Mezger. Tübingen: J. C. B. Mohr.

Duncan, George
1929 *St. Paul's Ephesian Ministry. A Reconstruction with Special Reference to the Ephesian Origin of the Imprisonment Epistles.* London: Hodder and Stoughton.

Dunn, J. D. G.
1970 *Baptism in the Holy Spirit.* Philadelphia: Westminster.

Eadie, John
1883 *A Commentary on the Greek Text of the Epistle of Paul to the Ephesians.* Edinburgh: T & T Clark.

Ellicott, Charles
1884 *St. Paul's Epistle to the Ephesians.* London: Longmans, Green.

Evanson, Edward
1792 *The Dissonance of the Four Generally Received Evangelists and the Evidence of Their Respective Authenticity Examined.* Ipswich: George Jermym.

Gaugler, Ernst
1966 *Der Epheserbrief.* Zurich: EVZ-Verlag.

Gnilka, Joachim
1971 *Der Epheserbrief.* Freiburg: Herder.

Green, E. M. B.
1961 *2 Peter Reconsidered.* London: Tyndale Press.

Grudem, Wayne
1985 Does *kephale* Mean 'Source' or 'Authority Over' in Greek Literature? A Survey of 2,336 Examples. *Trinity Journal* 6:38-59.

Harris, W. Hall, III
1996 *The Descent of Christ: Ephesians 4:7-11 and Traditional Hebrew Imagery.* Leiden: E. J. Brill.

Harrison, P. N.
1921 *The Problem of the Pastoral Epistles.* Oxford: Oxford University Press.

Hendriksen, William
1967 *Ephesians.* Grand Rapids: Baker.

Hoehner, Harold
2002 *Ephesians: An Exegetical Commentary.* Grand Rapids: Baker Academic.

Kirby, John C.
1968 *Ephesians, Baptism and Pentecost: An Inquiry into the Structure and Purpose of the Epistle to the Ephesians.* Montreal: McGill University.

Kümmel, Werner Georg
1975 *Introduction to the New Testament.* 17th ed. Translator, Howard Clark Kee. Nashville: Abingdon.

Lincoln, Andrew T.
1990 *Ephesians.* Word Biblical Commentary. Dallas: Word.

Lincoln, Andrew T., and A. J. M. Wedderburn
1993 *The Theology of the Later Pauline Letters.* New Testament Theology. Editor, James D. G. Dunn. Cambridge: Cambridge University Press.

Lindemann, Andreas
1975 *Die Aufhebung der Zeit. Geschichtsverständnis und Eschatologie im Epheserbrief.* Studien zum Neuen Testament, vol. 12. Editors, G. Klein, W. Marxsen, and W. Schrage. Gütersloh: Gütersloher Verlagshaus.

Meade, David G.
1986 *Pseudonymity and Canon: An Investigation into the Relationship of Authorship and Authority in Jewish and Earliest Christian Tradition.* Wissenschaftliche Untersuchungen zum Neuen Testament, vol. 39. Editors, Martin Hengel and Otfried Hofius. Tübingen: J. C. B. Mohr.

Metzger, B.
1992 *The Text of the New Testament.* Oxford: Oxford University Press.

Mitton, C. Leslie
1951 *The Epistle to the Ephesians: Its Authorship, Origin and Purpose.* Oxford: Clarendon Press.

Moffatt, James
1918 *An Introduction to the Literature of the New Testament.* 3rd rev. ed. The International Theological Library. Editors, Charles A. Briggs and Stewart D. F. Salmond. Edinburgh: T. & T. Clark.

Morris, Leon
1965 *The Apostolic Preaching of the Cross.* London: Tyndale Press.

Moule, C. F. D.
1959 *An Idiom Book of New Testament Greek.* Cambridge: Cambridge University Press.

Moule, H. C. G.
1886 *The Epistle to the Ephesians.* Cambridge: Cambridge University Press.

Neumann, Kenneth J.
1990 *The Authenticity of the Pauline Epistles in the Light of Stylostatistical Analysis.* Society of Biblical Literature Dissertation Series, no. 120. Editors, David L. Petersen and Charles Talbert. Atlanta: Scholars Press.

Norden, E.
1913 *Agnostos Theos: Untersuchungen zur Formengeschichte die Religiöse die Rede.* Leipzig: Teubern.

O'Brien, Peter T.
1999 *The Letter to the Ephesians.* Grand Rapids: Eerdmans.

Patzia, Arthur G.
1984 *Colossians, Philemon, Ephesians.* Good News Commentary. San Francisco: Harper & Row.

Robertson, A. T.
1923 *A Grammar of the Greek New Testament in the Light of Historical Research.* Nashville: Broadman.

Robinson, J. Armitage
1903 *St. Paul's Epistle to the Ephesians.* London: Macmillan.

Robinson, John A. T.
1976 *Redating the New Testament.* London: SCM Press.

van Roon, A.
1974 *The Authenticity of Ephesians.* Supplements to Novum Testamentum, vol. 39. Translator, S. Prescod-Jokel. Editor, W. C. van Unnik. Leiden: Brill.

Salmond, S. D. F.
1903 The Epistle of Paul to the Ephesians. Pp. 201-295 in *The Expositor's Greek Testament,* vol. 3. Editor, W. R. Nicoll. London: Hodder and Stoughton.

Schlier, Heinrich
1971 *Der Brief an die Epheser.* 7th ed. Düsseldorf: Patmos-Verlag.

Schnackenburg, Rudolf
1991 *Ephesians: A Commentary.* Translator, Helen Heron. Edinburgh: T & T Clark.

Scholer, David M.
1987 Feminist Hermeneutics and Evangelical Biblical Interpretation. *Journal of the Evangelical Theological Society* 30:407-420.
1996 The Evangelical Debate over Biblical Headship. Pp. 28-57 in *Women, Abuse, and the Bible: How Scripture Can be Used to Hurt or to Heal.* Editors, C. Clark and J. Beck. Grand Rapids: Baker.

Turner, Nigel
1963 *Syntax.* Vol. 3 of *A Grammar of New Testament Greek.* Editor, James Hope Moulton. Edinburgh: T & T Clark.

Wall, Robert W.
1988 Wifely Submission in the Context of Ephesians. *Christian Scholar's Review* 17:272-285.

Wallace, Daniel B.
1996 *Greek Grammar Beyond the Basics: An Exegetical Syntax of the New Testament.* Grand Rapids: Zondervan.

Westcott, Brooke F.
1906 *Saint Paul's Epistle to the Ephesians: The Greek Text with Notes and Addenda.* London: Macmillan.

Yoder Neufeld, Thomas
2002 *Ephesians.* Scottsdale, PA: Herald.

Philippians

PHILIP W. COMFORT

INTRODUCTION TO
Philippians

OF ALL PAUL'S EPISTLES, Philippians is among the most autobiographical. Paul was sharing with the Philippians the desires of his spirit and heart at that time in his life. He was under house arrest awaiting trial and experiencing the anxiousness that accompanied the uncertainty of the outcome. He was prepared to die and ready to live. Both were good because both meant further relationship with Christ. Sensing that he would live, Paul expressed his aspiration to know Christ as much as possible—not just the glorious Christ but the Christ who became man and servant, forsaken and crucified—then raised and glorified. This is stated in his famous words: "I want to know Christ and experience the mighty power that raised him from the dead. I want to suffer with him, sharing in his death" (3:10-11). He urged the Philippians—and all Christians—to share the same aspirations and to pursue the goal of knowing Christ.

AUTHOR

The first verse of this epistle identifies the authors as "Paul and Timothy." Paul and Timothy are also mentioned as coauthors in 2 Corinthians, Colossians, 1 Thessalonians (with Silvanus), 2 Thessalonians (with Silvanus), and Philemon. In three of these epistles (2 Corinthians, 1 and 2 Thessalonians), the use of "we" signals joint authorship. In 2 Corinthians most of the epistle is written by Paul, who uses the personal "I." In 1 and 2 Thessalonians, the first person plural "we" is used throughout, with Paul breaking out into the personal "I" only occasionally. These two epistles were coauthored primarily by Paul and Silvanus (see Introduction to these books in this commentary). In Philippians, Colossians, and Philemon, the writers are identified as "Paul and Timothy," but the personal "I" is used throughout, signaling Paul's sole authorship. It is likely that Timothy carried the letter to Philippi and interpreted it to the Philippians, which may be why he is identified as a co-sender.

The style, manner of thought, and teachings in Philippians are those of Paul the apostle. The historical allusions throughout the epistle also establish his authorship. These can be found in the mention of Epaphroditus's journey to Paul in prison and the Philippians' contribution to Paul (4:10-18, 25), Epaphroditus's sickness (2:25-30), the reference to Timothy's care for the Philippians (2:19), and the reference to the Philippians having seen his maltreatment at Philippi (1:30). Paul's autobiographical notations also point to his genuine authorship (1:12-14; 3:4-6; 4:15-18).

Unlike Ephesians and Colossians, where historical allusions and autobiographical notations are sparse and therefore have prompted various scholars to question Pauline authorship of those two epistles, Philippians has historically been accepted as Paul's writing. Paul's authorship is noted in some of the earliest writings of the church fathers, such as Polycarp, *To the Philippians* 3.2 (a passage where Polycarp directly mentions that Paul wrote to them); Irenaeus, *Against Heresies* 4.18.4; Clement of Alexander, *Christ the Educator*; Cyprian, *Testimonies against the Jews* 3.39.

Paul's authorship of Philippians has hardly been questioned throughout the rest of church history. One notable exception is F. C. Baur (1792–1860), who founded the Tübingen school and espoused the view that Paul wrote only Romans, 1 and 2 Corinthians, and Galatians. According to Baur, all the other so-called Pauline Epistles were authored by others. Baur's theories have been challenged repeatedly, and very few scholars accept his position that Paul did not write Philippians. (For a review of the issue, see Hawthorne 1983:xxviii-xxix.)

DATE AND OCCASION OF WRITING

Assuming the tradition is accurate that states that Paul was executed during Nero's reign, this epistle must have been written before AD 68 (the date of Nero's death). Determining the particular date prior to AD 68, however, depends on the location of Paul's imprisonment. There have been three cities posited by various scholars: Rome, Ephesus, and Caesarea. (Corinth has also been proposed but dismissed by nearly every scholar.) There is a different date connected to each city, correlated with Paul's itinerary.

Rome, AD 61–63. In the letter to the Philippians, Paul indicates that he was in prison (1:13-14). Traditionally, this has been understood to be his house arrest in Rome in AD 60–62. In defense of this position is the fact that Paul mentions the Praetorian Guard (1:13), and he closed the epistle with these words: "And all the rest of God's people send you greetings, too, especially those in Caesar's household" (4:22). A few subscriptions in some Greek manuscripts also indicate that Paul wrote this letter from Rome—namely, B¹ Pᵛⁱᵈ 𝔐. These subscriptions, of course, were not part of the original work and are therefore scribe's notations about what they thought the place of origin was. The earliest (fourth century) comes from the hand of the first corrector of B.

The Roman imprisonment fits especially well with Paul's mention of the Praetorian Guard (see Tacitus *Histories* 4.46) and Caesar's household—i.e., a significant number of people employed by Caesar. The fact that Paul also spoke of an impending trial that could lead to his death (1:19-20; 2:17) also accords with the Roman imprisonment because there would be no further appeal after Paul faced Caesar's judgment, whereas any other imprisonment would have offered Paul the opportunity to appeal.

However, various scholars have figured that the amount of traveling and the time span of travel between the locations mentioned (and/or assumed) in Philippians makes another location besides Rome more likely. Deissmann (1923) was one of the first to elaborate on the travels, citing the following points: (1) Timothy was with Paul (1:1) when Paul wrote Philippians, yet Timothy was not with Paul when Paul made his journey to Rome (Acts 26–28). This would have required a journey to Rome for Timothy. (2) Someone must have taken a message from Paul to the Philippians telling them that Paul was a prisoner (4:14). (3) The Philippians collected an offering for Paul, which was brought by Epaphroditus from Philippi to Paul in prison (4:18). (4) Epaphroditus became sick, and news of this came to the Philippians (2:26). (5) Paul then received a message that the Philippians had heard of Epaphroditus's sickness, and Paul reported (in the letter known as Philippians) how this troubled him (2:26). (6) Finally, Epaphroditus, once recovered from his sickness, would have had to journey to Philippi to take Paul's epistle to them (2:25, 28). The letter to the Philippians also indicates (7) that Timothy would soon travel to the Philippians and then (8) return to Paul with news of their situation (2:19).

Deissmann thought it highly unlikely that these journeys between Rome and Philippi could have taken place within the two-year time frame mentioned in Acts 28:30. Furthermore, the adverbs "soon" (2:19, 24) and "just as soon as" (2:23) seem to indicate that the distance between the place of writing and Philippi was not great. Thus, in the end, Deissmann opted for Ephesus as the place of writing (see below).

Although Deissmann's arguments are good, they do not preclude the possibility that all these journeys could have taken place between Rome and Philippi during the two-year period. A journey from Rome to Philippi would take about seven to eight weeks (see Martin 1987:24). Thus, the eight journeys noted above could have happened within the two-year time frame (see Dodd 1953:96ff.).

Ephesus, AD 55. In order to account for the journeys mentioned above, Deissmann proposed Ephesus as the place of Paul's imprisonment. His argument was strengthened by the writings of Duncan (1929), who has been followed by many recent commentators (see, for example, Introductions to Colossians and Philemon in this volume, where Davids argues that these two Prison Epistles were very likely written from Ephesus.) Ephesus was certainly near enough to Philippi for plenty of interchange, but no imprisonment is recorded in the account of Paul's ministry there in Acts. So we would have to assume that Luke's account in Acts 19 was not complete and that Paul had been placed in protective custody at the time of the riot (Acts 19:30-31).

In order to fill in these gaps, some scholars have pointed out that Paul, in 2 Corinthians 11:23-27, noted several imprisonments prior to his Roman captivity. The first epistle of Clement of Rome (1 Clement 5:6) indicates that Paul experienced seven imprisonments. Paul's words in 2 Corinthians 1:8-10, coupled with the narrative in Acts 20:18-19, tell us that "in Asia Paul suffered extreme hardships even to the point of despairing of life" (Hawthorne 1983:xxxix). And some scholars think that Paul's cryptic remark in 1 Corinthians 15:32 about fighting with wild beasts in Ephesus is an allusion to captivity in Ephesus (see discussion by Martin 1987:28-30). These are all interesting points, but none of them prove that

Paul was ever in prison in Ephesus. In fact, Bruce (1980–1981) indicates that there is not one piece of historical evidence that points to Ephesus. Furthermore, it seems likely that at the time of the writing of Philippians, Paul was clearly facing a capital charge. Had he been imprisoned in Ephesus, could he not have exercised his right as a Roman citizen to appeal to a higher authority?

Caesarea, AD 58. Certain scholars have considered Caesarea as the place of writing. Good arguments have been offered by Robinson (1976:60-61) and Hawthorne (1983:xli-xliv), the chief of which are as follows: (1) It is certain that Paul was imprisoned in Caesarea (Acts 23:33-35); (2) the imprisonment was a long one, at least two years, allowing for the journeys back and forth from Philippi; (3) it is very possible that Paul's attack against the Jews was directed against those who were trying to kill him both in Jerusalem and Caesarea (Acts 21:37–26:32), whereas the Jews in Rome were not hostile to him (Acts 28:19); (4) the fact that the entire praetorium had heard of Paul's imprisonment for Christ (1:13) fits Caesarea well because Paul was imprisoned in the praetorium of Herod in Caesarea (Acts 23:35) and news of his imprisonment had reached the ears of many, even the procurator himself (Acts 24:24-26).

The major problem with the Caesarean location is that in Philippians Paul indicates that he was facing a life-and-death judgment (1:20; 2:17), whereas in the Caesarean imprisonment it does not appear he was facing imminent martyrdom (see Acts 23:35; 24:23). True, his life was in danger in Caesarea (Acts 21:31, 36; 23:30; 25:3, 24), but this danger came from the Jews plotting to kill him, not from an upcoming trial. Besides, Paul, as a Roman citizen, always had a "trump card"— his right to appeal to Caesar for further trial so as to avert final judgment.

In the final analysis, the traditional location, Rome, suits most elements of the scenario presented in Philippians (see Fee 1995:34-37). As such, Philippians should be dated around AD 62, the last year of Paul's house arrest.

Occasion of Writing. At the most basic level, Philippians was written as a thank-you letter for the gift that the Philippians had sent Paul (1:5; 4:18). At a deeper level, it was written to convey Paul's personal pursuit of knowing the crucified and risen Christ in his (Paul's) present crisis and to encourage the same aspiration and pursuit among the Philippians, especially as the means to promote church unity. Each of these aspects is addressed below under "Major Themes."

AUDIENCE

Philippi was a small village of Thrace until about 357 BC when the father of Alexander the Great, Philip II of Macedon, conquered the site, rebuilt it, and gave the village his name, "Philip's City." Two hundred years later in the Roman era, it became a chief city of one of the four Roman districts into which Macedonia was divided. But because it was about ten miles inland from the port of Neapolis, its growth was limited. Nearby Amphipolis (to the southwest) was the center of Roman government.

Philippi gained worldwide fame in 42 BC when the imperial armies of Antony and Octavian there defeated the Republican generals Brutus and Cassius (the assassins of Julius Caesar). The victory opened the way for the emergence of the Roman Empire under the rule of Augustus. Veterans from the war of 42 BC and other battles settled in Philippi. When Paul came to the city, it still retained its Roman military heritage. It was a stopping point on the Egnatian Way, which crossed Macedonia to connect the Adriatic Sea with the Aegean Sea.

In the book of Acts, Luke identified Philippi as "a leading city of the district of Macedonia and a Roman colony" (Acts 16:12, NRSV).[1] It possessed civic pride as a Roman colony (enjoying numerous privileges such as tax exemptions), promoted Latin as its official language, and hosted numerous Roman citizens. The city magistrates had the dignified Latin title *praetor* (given in its Greek translation, *stratēgos* [TG4755, ZG5130]—see Acts 16:20-22, 38). Philippi's government was modeled on the municipal constitution of Rome, and, as Luke records in Acts 16:21, the citizens viewed themselves as Romans. Paul invoked his rights as a Roman citizen when unlawfully imprisoned there (Acts 16:36-37), and he was released. Paul likely alluded to this citizenship in Philippians 1:27 and 3:20 when he spoke of the believers' "citizenship" in heaven (TBD 1030-1031).

Paul visited Philippi on his second missionary journey after he received the well-known Macedonian call (Acts 16:9-10). Crossing the sea toward the island of Samothrace, Paul and his companions left Asia and entered into Europe. They went to Neapolis and then to Philippi, where the Good News of Christ was proclaimed for the first time in Europe (Acts 16:14).

The account of Acts (Acts 16:11-40) gives detailed attention to Paul's visit to Philippi. There was a small Jewish community there, but it was not even large enough to have a synagogue (which required at least ten adult Jewish males). Hence, some Jewish women regularly met by the riverside for prayer. Paul and his companions approached these women and proclaimed the Good News to them (Acts 16:13). Among these women was Lydia, a Godfearer, which meant she was a Gentile who worshiped the same God as the Jews but did not fully convert to Judaism. She and her household became the first believers there (Acts 16:14-15). The church in Philippi began with her household and met in her home (Acts 16:15, 40). Other early members of this church were the jailer and his household (Acts 16:31-34), as well as some gentile converts. Several people mentioned in Paul's Epistle to the Philippians were those who had been or were residents there—namely, Epaphroditus (2:25), Euodia, Syntyche, and Clement (4:2-3); the Greek names of these people reveal that they were Gentiles. Hence, the major constituents of the church appear to have been Gentiles.

Taking the "we" sections of the book of Acts to indicate Luke's presence with Paul, it is clear that Luke spent a significant amount of time in Philippi. The first "we" section (when Luke joined Paul) begins and ends at Philippi (Acts 16:10, 40). This suggests that Luke stayed behind in the city after Paul's departure. Then on Paul's third missionary journey, Luke joined Paul again when the apostle passed through Philippi (Acts 20:6). "The presence of a Christian leader such as Luke was a powerful aid to evangelization and consolidation in the days which followed" (Martin 1987:20).

CANONICITY AND TEXTUAL HISTORY

The canonicity of Philippians is evidenced by the fact that it was included in the earliest collections of New Testament writings circulating in the early church. Paul's Major Epistles (excluding the Pastoral Epistles) and the four Gospels were two collections that the early church read widely and esteemed as Scripture. Züntz (1953:271-272) was convinced that Paul's Major Epistles were a well-known canonized collection by AD 100. Gamble (1995:53-57) also argued that the Pauline collection was assembled by the end of the first century. Manuscripts evidencing a Pauline collection are as follows: 𝔓46 (second century, all of Paul's Major Epistles), 𝔓15+𝔓16 (third century, from the same codex, preserving portions of 1 Corinthians and Philippians), 𝔓30 (third century), 𝔓49+𝔓65 (third century), and 𝔓92 (third century). Collections of Pauline letters as individual volumes (exclusive of other books of the New Testament) continued to appear in the following centuries, as evidenced in Codex I (fifth century), 0208 (sixth century), and 0209 (seventh century). (For further discussion on this, see Comfort 2005:34-37.)

Paul's Epistle to the Philippians appears in the oldest extant lists of books in the New Testament canon. It appears in the Muratorian Canon (late-second century), as well as the canon created by Marcion (c. AD 160). Thereafter, Philippians appears in all the major New Testament canons, such as those indicated by Eusebius in his *Ecclesiastical History,* Athanasius of Alexandria in his *Festal Letter* (AD 367), and the Council of Carthage (AD 397).

As for the text of Philippians, it is preserved in some early papyrus manuscripts (𝔓16 and 𝔓46), as well as in the fourth-century codices Sinaiticus (ℵ) and Vaticanus (B) and the fifth-century codices Alexandrinus (A), Ephraemi Rescriptus (C), and Washington (I). These are good Alexandrian witnesses, the earliest coming from 𝔓46, which provide some significant textual evidence to various verses in Philippians (noted throughout in the notes section of the commentary). The "Western" text of Paul's Epistles, which includes Philippians, is found in manuscripts such as the Greek-Latin diglots D F G.

LITERARY STYLE

Paul wrote a few personal letters (to Timothy, Titus, and Philemon) and several epistles. According to Deissmann (1909:227:245), a letter is a direct personal correspondence between two people not intended to be read by others; by contrast, an epistle is a stylized literary form that gives the impression of being personally directed to one or more individuals but whose real intent is to address a much wider audience. Such was the intent of many of Paul's Epistles. Two of Paul's Epistles, Romans and Ephesians, were clearly intended, from their inception, to be encyclical treatises—to be read by all the churches. Romans is Paul's masterpiece on the Christian life, and Ephesians is Paul's masterpiece on the church.

Three of Paul's other epistles—Galatians, 2 Corinthians, and Philippians—are quite autobiographical. In Galatians and 2 Corinthians, Paul was forced to make a defense of his apostleship and thereby spoke autobiographically. In his Epistle to the Philippians, most of what Paul revealed about his personal, spiritual aspirations came from a desire to share with his friends what was on his heart and to thereby encourage them (as in 1:12-26; 2:17-18; 3:7-17; 4:10-14). In this regard, Paul's correspondence to the Philippians is what is called a "letter of friendship." Many of the extant papyri display this kind of letter—a letter that was written by a friend to a friend (Stowers 1986:58-60). In these kind of letters, the writer often noted his or her yearnings for a loved one and shared his or her feelings—characteristics that are found in Philippians (1:7-8; 2:17-18).

Another major literary feature of this epistle is the well-known Christ hymn, or what I prefer to call a Christ Poem, which appears in 2:6-11. Though debate still continues as to whether this was an existing Christian hymn adapted by Paul or a poem created by Paul, all readers recognize the poetic quality of this passage. It is the literary centerpiece of the epistle, the hub around which the whole epistle revolves. Paul also penned another small poem in this epistle found in 3:20-21 (see commentary).

MAJOR THEMES

As just noted, Philippians, thematically speaking, revolves around the Christ Poem of 2:6-11. This poem traces the journey of the Son of God, Jesus Christ, as he chose not to cling to his equality with God but to empty himself, to take the form of a servant through incarnation, and to live in human form in humble obedience to God the Father—an obedience that led him to death, even death as a criminal on a cross. But the journey did not end there. The Son of God, Jesus Christ, was raised from the dead, exalted to the highest place in the universe, and given the highest name in the universe—the name that every tongue in the universe should confess, proclaiming that Jesus Christ is Lord, to the glory of God the Father.

This divine journey into humanity to experience the suffering of servanthood with a view to attaining the coming glory has become the paradigm of all spiritual aspirations and pursuits. Paul fashioned his life accordingly, the evidence of which emerges throughout this epistle (1:20-26; 2:16-18; 3:3-16; 4:11-13). The two other co-workers in this epistle, Timothy and Epaphroditus, were also models of this (2:19-22, 25-30). And Paul urged this as the preeminent pattern to be emulated by all those desiring spiritual maturity (1:9-11, 27-29; 2:1-5, 12-15; 3:15-21).

While other themes appear in this epistle, they are but spokes around the hub of the Christ Poem. Themes such as Christian unity (1:27; 2:1-4; 4:2-3), spiritual joy (1:4, 18, 25, 28; 2:2; 3:1; 4:1, 4, 10), being ready for the Lord's return (1:6, 10-11; 2:16; 3:14, 21), and giving to others in need (1:23-26; 4:10, 15-19) are the fruits of pursuing Christ and knowing him experientially. Unity comes from self-sacrifice (as Christ did in becoming man and dying on the cross), spiritual joy is the result of knowing Christ now and seeing him in his return (as Christ experienced joy when he returned to the Father), and giving to others is directly linked to Christ giving himself over to death so that all who believe in him may have eternal life.

THEOLOGICAL CONCERNS

The primary theological issues in this book are found in the Christ Poem (2:6-11). This poem contains some of the most sublime Christological expressions in the New Testament in that it speaks of Christ's preincarnate existence of being coequal with God, his willingness to become a servant, his *kenosis* (cf. *kenoō* [TG2758, ZG3033]; the "emptying-out"), his incarnation, his life of obedience, his humiliating crucifixion, his resurrection, his exaltation, and his eternal lordship. The commentary on Philippians 2:5-11 will explore each of these aspects of Christ's person and work.

The book of Philippians is not concerned with soteriological issues, such as redemption and justification—issues that are covered in Paul's other writings, especially Romans and Galatians. Rather, the focus is on spiritual maturity, as Paul's opening prayer indicates (1:9-11). He himself was occupied with his pursuit of Christlikeness (1:20-21; 3:7-14), and he urged the Philippians to pursue Christ also (3:15).

OUTLINE

  I. Opening of the Letter (1:1-2:4)
   A. Greetings from Paul and Timothy (1:1-2)
   B. Paul's Thanksgiving and Prayer (1:3-11)
   C. Paul's Report about His Situation (1:12-26)
      1. Paul's imprisonment and the proclamation of the Good News (1:12-18)
      2. Paul's desire to live in Christ and magnify him (1:19-26)
   D. Encouragement to Unity for the Sake of the Good News (1:27-2:4)
 II. The Christ Poem (2:5-11)
III. Encouragement to Emulate Christ (2:12-3:21)
   A. Shine for Christ, Be an Offering to God (2:12-18)
   B. Timothy: An Example of Selflessness (2:19-24)
   C. Epaphroditus: An Example of Servanthood (2:25-30)
   D. Encouragement to Rely on Christ (3:1-3)
   E. Paul: An Example of One Pursuing Christ (3:4-19)
      1. Paul's life before knowing Christ (3:4-6)
      2. Paul's spiritual aspirations (3:7-11)
      3. Paul's pursuit of Christ (3:12-14)
      4. Paul's admonition to follow his example (3:15-19)
   F. Another Christ Poem (3:20-21)

IV. Closing of the Letter (4:1-23)
   A. Appeal to Co-workers (4:1-3)
   B. Joy and Peace in Christ (4:4-9)
   C. Paul's Thanksgiving for the Philippians' Gift (4:10-20)
   D. Paul's Final Greetings (4:21-23)

ENDNOTES

1. The Greek text of UBS[4] and NA[27] for Acts 16:12 reads "a city of the first district of Macedonia," based on blatantly inferior manuscript support: it[c] vg[mss] slav. Not one English version follows this; only the NRSV gives it a marginal note. The superior textual variant is "a leading city of the district of Macedonia," supported by 𝔓74 ℵ A C 044 33 and followed by almost all modern versions (RSV, NRSV, NASB, NIV, NEB, REB, NAB, NLT). A variant in the TR reads, "the leading city of the district of Macedonia," supported by (B) P 049 056 0142 𝔐 and found in KJV, NKJV, and NJB. The Western text (supported by D it[d] syr[p]) reads, "capital city of the district of Macedonia." The majority of editors of UBS[4] and NA[27] adopted a reading without any Greek manuscript support because historical evidence doesn't support the fact that Philippi was the principal city of Macedonia or the capital of Macedonia. Thessalonica could make these claims (see Metzger's lengthy discussion in 1994:393-395). However, the Alexandrian manuscripts (whether in the first or second variant) are not implausible because Philippi was "a leading city of the district of Macedonia," though not *the* principal or capital city (there is no definite article in the Greek before *prōtēs* [TG4413, ZG4755]). Furthermore, Philippi could have been called "first city" as a matter of civic pride (so Ascough 1998).

COMMENTARY ON

Philippians

◆ I. Opening of the Letter (1:1–2:4)

A. Greetings from Paul and Timothy (1:1–2)

**This letter is from Paul and Timothy, slaves
of Christ Jesus.**
**I am writing to all of God's holy people
in Philippi who belong to Christ Jesus,
including the elders* and deacons.**
**2 May God our Father and the Lord Jesus
Christ give you grace and peace.**

1:1 Or *overseers;* or *bishops.*

NOTES

1:1 *Paul.* He is listed at the head of 13 epistles (Romans, 1 Corinthians, 2 Corinthians, Galatians, Ephesians, Philippians, Colossians, 1 Thessalonians, 2 Thessalonians, 1 Timothy, 2 Timothy, Titus, Philemon), sometimes alone (Romans, Galatians, Ephesians, 1 Timothy, 2 Timothy, Titus) and at other times with another co-worker or two—namely, Timothy (see below), Sosthenes (1 Corinthians), and Silas (1 and 2 Thessalonians).

Timothy. He is listed as coauthor or co-sender, as in five other epistles (2 Corinthians, Colossians, 1 Thessalonians, 2 Thessalonians, Philemon). How much Timothy actually contributed to each epistle is unknown. What we do know is that in 1 and 2 Thessalonians the authors speak in the first person plural ("we")—with Paul breaking away here and there into the first-person singular ("I, Paul" or "I"), whereas in the Prison Epistles (Philippians, Colossians, Philemon), Timothy is listed as a coauthor or co-sender in the introduction, but then the rest of the epistle is clearly written in first-person singular, signaling the authorship of Paul alone. (Timothy's status as a co-sender may originate from his role as bearer and interpreter of the letter; see commentary on 2:19-24.)

I am writing. These words are supplied to complete the formula implicit in the Greek.

all of God's holy people . . . who belong to Christ Jesus. This is a description of all the believers, one that Paul frequently used in the beginning of his epistles.

Philippi. This was a Roman colony in Macedonia, a province in northern Greece. The church in Philippi was the first one established in Greece (see Acts 16:11-40). (For further discussion, see "Audience" in the Introduction.)

including the elders and deacons. Lit., "with overseers and deacons." In the Greek, it is possible to join together the first two words (*sun* [TG4862, ZG5250] and *episkopois* [TG1985, ZG2176]) and make them one word, *sunepiskopois* [TG4901.1, ZG5297], which means "co-overseers" (or "co-bishops"). This is the reading in some later manuscripts: D^2 P^{vid} 075 33 1739. Earlier manuscripts could be interpreted either way because no spaces were left between words. However, the sense of the passage is that Paul was writing to the entire church in Philippi, which encompassed "all of God's holy people," among whom were the overseers and deacons, who had a special function in the church. It is not clear whether these church leaders were a single group or two distinct groups (as in 1 Tim 3:1-13).

1:2 *May God our Father and the Lord Jesus Christ give you.* In the beginning of Paul's Epistles, he asks for a divine blessing on the recipients of his epistle (Rom 1:7; 1 Cor 1:3; 2 Cor 1:2; Gal 1:3; Eph 1:2; Col 1:2; 1 Thess 1:1; 2 Thess 1:2; 1 Tim 1:2; 2 Tim 1:2; Titus 1:4; Phlm 1:3). God the Father is the source of grace and peace, and the Lord Jesus Christ is the giver.

grace. The Greek word *charis* [TG5485, ZG5921] denotes a gift that gives joy to the receiver. The expression "grace" reflects the traditional Hellenistic greeting (*chairein* [TG5463, ZG5897]—meaning "good wishes").

peace. The Greek word *eirēnē* [TG1515, ZG1645] denotes spiritual well-being and contentedness. The expression "peace" reflects the traditional Hebrew greeting (*shalom* [TH7965, ZH8934]—meaning "may all be well").

C O M M E N T A R Y

In a brief introduction (1:1-2), Paul followed the traditional Hellenistic pattern of letter writing. All letters opened with a prescript, which consisted of three elements: the sender, the recipient, and the salutation (see Weima 2000:642). Thus, all letters followed this pattern: (1) X (in the nominative case); (2) to Y (in the dative case); (3) greetings. An example from the first century illustrates this:

> Sarapion to our Heraclides, greeting.
> (P. Oxyrhynchus 299, AD 41).

Paul's adaptation of the formula is as follows:

1. Senders: Paul and Timothy
2. Recipients: to all of God's holy people in Philippi . . . including the elders and deacons
3. Greeting: "grace and peace."

Following these three elements, a traditional letter would often have a wish for good health (as in 3 John 1:2) or a thanksgiving formula (as in what follows in 1:3-5) or both.

The senders of the letter to the Philippians identify themselves as "Paul and Timothy, slaves of Christ Jesus" (1:1). Paul was well known to the Christian church because he contributed the greatest number of writings to what would become the New Testament canon. Timothy also was well known, especially by his association with Paul. As one of Paul's most trusted co-workers, Timothy was with Paul and Silas when they first evangelized Philippi (Acts 16:3, 11). At the time of writing, Paul was hoping to send Timothy back to Philippi in the near future (see 2:19-23).

At the beginning of most of his epistles, Paul called himself an "apostle of Christ Jesus" (see the opening verse in Romans, 1 Corinthians, 2 Corinthians, Galatians, Ephesians, Colossians, 1 Timothy, 2 Timothy). Philippians 1:1 is the only opening verse where he called himself (and Timothy) a slave of Christ Jesus. (In Titus 1:1, he called himself "a slave of God.") The reason Paul called himself a slave and not a servant is that this accords with what was on Paul's mind in this epistle—namely, that the Son of God, Christ Jesus, became a slave (2:7) as an example for others to follow.

The recipients of this epistle were "all of God's holy people in Philippi who belong to Christ Jesus" (1:1). This expression denotes three things about the recipients:

(1) They were saints—those set apart by God to be his people; (2) they belonged (lit., "were in") in Christ Jesus—that is, they were united to Christ by virtue of their faith in him; (3) they, together, constituted the church in a particular city, Philippi. Then, unique among all introductions in Paul's Epistles, he noted specifically the "elders" (*episkopoi* [TG1985, ZG2176]) and "deacons" (*diakonoi* [TG1249, ZG1356]). Who were these individuals? And why did Paul point them out?

The "elders" were church leaders whose qualifications are listed in 1 Timothy 3:2-7 and Titus 1:6-9. The word came into English versions as "bishop" or sometimes "overseer." In the New Testament, "bishop," "overseer," and "elder" refer to the same office, as shown by the apostle Paul's instructions to Titus to appoint "elders in each town" and then referring to those same individuals as "overseers" (Titus 1:5, 7; see NLT mg). While at Miletus, Paul summoned the elders from the church at Ephesus and then addressed them as "overseers" (Acts 20:17, 28; see NLT mg). In this letter to the Philippians, Paul greeted the "elders and deacons" (1:1). The fact that there were numerous overseers (bishops) at Philippi as well as in Ephesus shows that the episcopal office had not yet developed into what it later became: a single bishop governing one or more churches (TBD 224). Elders had positions of authority in the local church. One of their tasks was to combat heresy (Titus 1:9) and to teach the Scriptures (1 Tim 3:2). Paul may have singled them out because he expected them to be those mature ones who would properly pass on Paul's teachings to the church (3:15).

The word "deacon" was used by biblical writers in a general sense to describe someone engaged in various ministries or services. Not until later in the development of church leadership was the term applied to a distinct body of church officers. Among its general usages "deacon" refers to a waiter at meals (John 2:5, 9), a king's attendant (Matt 22:13), a minister of God (2 Cor 6:4), a servant of Christ (2 Cor 11:23), a servant of the church (Col 1:24-25), and even a political servant of state (Rom 13:4). By the time the church of Philippi received its instructions from Paul, the term "deacon" seems to have become a technical term referring to a specific office in the church (TBD 363-364). In 1 Timothy 3:8-13 instructions are given about qualifications for the office of deacon. First Timothy 3:11 states that the women likewise must be serious, not slanderers, but temperate and faithful in all things. This may refer not to deacons' wives but to female deacons, as several translations note (NIV, NEB; see also NLT mg). In any event, it is clear that women served as deacons. For example, Paul commended Phoebe for her service in the church at Cenchrea, using the word "deaconess" to describe her (Rom 16:1). He praised her as a helper (Rom 16:2), a word that denotes leadership qualities (cf. Rom 12:8; 1 Tim 3:4-5). We know from sources outside the New Testament that women served important positions in the church and that some were deacons. Writing in the early second century, Pliny the Younger (a governor of Bithynia), in his correspondence with Trajan verified women officeholders in the church and mentioned two deaconesses who were martyred for the cause of Christ (see *Letters* 96.1-9).

As for the Epistle to the Philippians, it seems that Paul specifically mentioned "deacons" because servanthood was on his mind when he wrote this epistle. An attitude of servanthood—like that demonstrated by Christ (2:5-11)—is the key to church unity. It is possible that Euodia and Syntyche (4:2) were deaconesses, who had influential roles in the church at Philippi. They, needing unification, could attain this by taking on the servant's mind as exhibited in Christ.

◆   ## B. Paul's Thanksgiving and Prayer (1:3-11)

[3]Every time I think of you, I give thanks to my God. [4]Whenever I pray, I make my requests for all of you with joy, [5]for you have been my partners in spreading the Good News about Christ from the time you first heard it until now. [6]And I am certain that God, who began the good work within you, will continue his work until it is finally finished on the day when Christ Jesus returns.

[7]So it is right that I should feel as I do about all of you, for you have a special place in my heart. You share with me the special favor of God, both in my imprisonment and in defending and confirming the truth of the Good News. [8]God knows how much I love you and long for you with the tender compassion of Christ Jesus.

[9]I pray that your love will overflow more and more, and that you will keep on growing in knowledge and understanding. [10]For I want you to understand what really matters, so that you may live pure and blameless lives until the day of Christ's return. [11]May you always be filled with the fruit of your salvation—the righteous character produced in your life by Jesus Christ*—for this will bring much glory and praise to God.

1:11 Greek *with the fruit of righteousness through Jesus Christ.*

NOTES

1:3 *Every time I think of you.* Lit., "at every remembrance of you." This can be rendered "every time I remember you" or "every remembrance of yours [for me]." The first is the most natural reading; the second is possible. If Paul was thanking them for remembering him, this links with 1:5, where he also thanked them for their participation in the gospel.

I give thanks to my God. As noted above, one of the elements often found in the prescript of Hellenistic letters was a word of thanksgiving offered to a god. Paul offered his thanksgiving to "my God"—the God he knew personally.

1:5 *for you have been my partners in spreading the Good News about Christ.* Lit., "for your fellowship in the gospel." The Greek word underlying "fellowship" is *koinōnia* [TG2842, ZG3126]; depending on the context, it can denote one's fellowship with Christ or one's fellowship with other believers, or it can have the notion of "sharing" and "generosity" (as in Phlm 1:6). Paul was thanking God for the Philippians' spiritual partnership, as well as their financial support (see 4:10-20).

1:6 *God, who began the good work within you, will continue his work until it is finally finished.* Although Hawthorne (1983:21) sees "the good work" as referring to the Philippians' partnership in the gospel (1:5), the words extend beyond this to encompass the entirety of God's work of grace (Martin 1987:63). This is a wonderful promise because it indicates that God takes the initiative to transform each believer into the likeness of his Son (see Rom 8:29; Eph 4:13-15).

on the day when Christ Jesus returns. When Christ returns, the believers will receive the ultimate act in the work of transformation—namely, the transfiguration of their bodies in conformity to Christ's body (3:20-21).

1:7 *for you have a special place in my heart.* The Greek here is ambiguous inasmuch as either *me* [TG1473, ZG1609] (me) or *humas* [TG4571, ZG5148] (you all) could be the subject of the infinitive, "to have." The phrase can be rendered as "because I have you in my heart" (so NLT) or "because you have me in your heart" (so NRSV). Both are contextually defensible.

defending and confirming. The language suggests a legal defense. Indeed, both Greek words suggest this. The first (*apologia* [TG627, ZG665]) is obvious, but even the second (*bebaiōsei* [TG951, ZG1012]) was typically used in first-century papyri in the technical sense of affirming truth by legal means (MM 108). Paul was ready to make a defense before the courts and in so doing defend the gospel.

1:8 *God knows.* In most manuscripts, the Greek reads, "God is my witness." The NLT seems to accord with 𝔓46 and it^a, which have the shortest reading here: "God is witness." However, since 𝔓46 is known for its accidental omissions, its testimony in such cases cannot be regarded too highly (Silva 1992:57).

long for you with the tender compassion of Christ. The Greek behind "tender compassion" (*splanchnois* [TG4698, ZG5073]) refers to the viscera. Greeks considered the deepest emotions to derive from the viscera (bowels, entrails), just as modern Americans think the deepest emotions come from the heart (BDAG 938).

1:9 *I pray that your love will overflow more and more.* The object of this love is not stated. Lightfoot (1976:86) notes that this love is "neither towards the Apostle alone nor towards one another alone, but love absolutely, the inward state of the soul."

knowledge and understanding. The first term *epignōsei* [TG1922, ZG2106] had "become almost a technical term for the decisive knowledge of God" (TDNT 1.707). The second term (*aisthēsei* [TG144, ZG151]) denotes "insight" and "perception." In short, Paul was praying that the believers would increase in their knowledge of God and spiritual insight.

1:10 *I want you to understand what really matters.* This is a functionally equivalent translation of the Greek, which reads "so that you can approve the things that are superior." The notion of approving indicates that the believers were to "put [things] to the test," and then as a result of such examination, "to accept as tested, to approve." The object of the verb here may be rendered as "the things which differ." Martin (1987:67) says the meaning here was derived from contemporary popular philosophy and is "the things which really matter."

that you may live pure and blameless lives until the day of Christ's return. The Greek word for "pure" (*eilikrineis* [TG1506, ZG1637]) probably derived etymologically from the notion of judged (cf. *krinō* [TG2920, ZG3213]) in the sunlight (*eilē*; cf. *hēlios* [TG2246, ZG2463]). The word was first used to depict a person bringing an object into the sunlight to see if it was spotless. The usage then moved from the physical realm to the moral realm and was used to denote moral purity. The Greek word behind "blameless" (*aproskopoi* [TG677, ZG718]) denotes "not causing someone else to stumble" or "avoiding anything that would cause one to stumble."

1:11 *May you always be filled with the fruit of your salvation—the righteous character produced in your life by Jesus Christ.* Lit., "may you be filled with the fruit of righteousness through Jesus Christ." Since the Philippians (as all Christians) were already made right with God by faith in Christ, this prayer must be for the Philippians to live out a life of righteousness by virtue of their union with Jesus Christ.

much glory and praise to God. This has excellent textual support: ℵ A B D² I 044 𝔐 it syr cop. There are a few interesting textual variants, however: (1) "glory and praise of Christ" in D*; (2) "my [Paul's] glory and praise" in F G; (3) "glory of God and my [Paul's] praise" in 𝔓46 (it^g). The reading followed by the NLT is common biblical terminology, found in OT passages such as 2 Sam 22:50; Pss 35:28; 41:13. Thus, it is possible that Paul drew from such sources when he concluded his prayer with the phrase, "glory and praise to God." The first variant involves a simple change from "God" to "Christ." But the next two variants are difficult to explain—either on transcriptional grounds or exegetical. Thus, it is possible that Paul originally wrote what was in the second or third variants. But the second variant, which omits "of God," looks like a scribal attempt to avoid a close juxtaposition between God and Paul (Silva 1992:64). The third variant, found in the earliest manuscript, 𝔓46, may preserve the original—not only on transcriptional grounds but also on exegetical. It was characteristic of Paul, when speaking of the Lord's return (see 1:10), to mention that the believers' transformed lives would bring glory to God and honor to Paul (see 2:16; 2 Cor 1:14; 1 Thess 2:19-20). Thus, it would not be too much for Paul to say that the Philippians would bring God glory and Paul praise (see Comfort 2008:[Phil 1:11]).

COMMENTARY

One of the usual practices of letter writing in Hellenistic times was for the writer to offer prayer and/or thanksgiving to a god or gods for the recipients of his letter. The two following examples illustrate this:

> Isias to her brother Hephaistion, [greeting]. If you are well and other things are going right, it would accord with the prayer which I make continually to the gods (*Greek Historical Documents*, 235. Translator, R. S. Bagnall; 168 BC).

> Aurelius Dius to Aurelius Horion, my sweetest father, many greetings. I make supplication for you every day before the gods of this place (P. Oxyrhynchus 1296, third century AD).

Adapting this custom in the prescript to the Philippians, Paul offered his thanksgiving and prayer to the one true God manifest in Christ Jesus, the God he personally knew, calling him "my God." Then Paul told the Philippians how often he prayed for them, why he prayed for them, and what he prayed for them.

Paul gave thanks for the Philippians every time he thought of them (1:3). They had been his partners in advancing the Good News about Christ ever since he first brought this Good News to them (1:5). Paul was confident that their good beginning would lead to a good end inasmuch as God is the originator of faith as well as its completer (1:6). This expression—completing what one has begun—is a major theme in this epistle. On one hand, God is responsible for completing in the believers what he began, for it is his goal to conform every believer to the image of his Son, Jesus Christ (Rom 8:28-30). On the other hand, it is the believer's responsibility to cooperate with God so that this work can be made complete. Paul highlights the two aspects of this symbiotic relationship in 2:12-13, where he tells the Philippians to "work hard to show the results of your salvation" and then immediately says "for God is working in you." The work of spiritual transformation is a lifelong process beginning with regeneration, continuing with the process of being made like Jesus both in his sufferings and his resurrection (3:10), and concluding with transfiguration, wherein the body is made like Jesus' glorified body (3:21).

In the next section (1:7-8), Paul elaborates on his heartfelt affection for the Philippians as well as their affection for him (see note on 1:7). He loved them so much that he was longing to see them and be with them (see 1:25; 2:24). The Philippians and Paul had shared in God's grace. As Paul suffered for the gospel and they joined with him in his suffering so they also joined with him in his enjoyment of God's grace (see 1:29, where Paul speaks of their suffering for Christ as a privilege of God's grace). Paul's suffering had extended to imprisonment, where he would continue to defend and confirm the truth of the Good News. As explained in the note above on 1:8, the language suggests that Paul was ready to make a legal defense, wherein he would verify the truth of the Good News. This defense would be made before the imperial court (see 2 Tim 4:16) or before a provincial judge (cf. Acts 25:16), depending on where one places Paul's imprisonment when he wrote Philippians (see "Date and Occasion" in the Introduction).

The content of Paul's prayer is related in 1:9-11. This opening prayer provides a window into Paul's desire for the Philippians' spiritual life, and it also provides a précis for the themes Paul will develop later in the epistle. Those who study Paul's Epistles know that his opening prayers function this way for each of his writings. In Paul's prayer for the Philippians, he focused on two aspects in which he wanted to see growth: (1) their love for Christ and/or for one another (see note on 1:9), which would promote a serving, cooperative spirit, leading to true unity; and (2) their understanding and discernment of spiritual pursuits, such that they would value the pursuit of knowing Christ as being the best aspiration. This understanding of "what really matters" would come as the result of testing spiritual things and approving what is best (see note on 1:10). Paul himself had done this, as he testified in 3:4-11, and he had come to the conclusion that all things pale in comparison to knowing Christ personally and experientially.

The pursuit of love and of knowing Christ produces pure and blameless lives (see note on 1:10). To be pure and blameless means that Christians are faultless as to their own morality and faultless as to the way they treat others. Such lives will put people in good light on the day when Christ returns. Such lives cannot be attained by human effort alone; they are the fruit—the result—of one's salvation, wherein the righteousness of Christ is lived out in daily life. Such lives, Paul teaches, are the result of human–divine cooperation, wherein God is the originator and sustainer of a living salvation and the believer is the active receiver and participant. Such lives bring much glory and praise to God, which is the ultimate purpose of human existence.

◆   C. Paul's Report about His Situation (1:12-26)
     1. Paul's imprisonment and the proclamation of the Good News
        (1:12-18)

¹²And I want you to know, my dear brothers and sisters,* that everything that has happened to me here has helped to spread the Good News. ¹³For everyone here, including the whole palace guard,* knows that I am in chains because of Christ. ¹⁴And because of my imprisonment, most of the believers* here have gained confidence and boldly speak God's message* without fear.

¹⁵It's true that some are preaching out of jealousy and rivalry. But others preach about Christ with pure motives. ¹⁶They preach because they love me, for they know I have been appointed to defend the Good News. ¹⁷Those others do not have pure motives as they preach about Christ.

They preach with selfish ambition, not sincerely, intending to make my chains more painful to me. ¹⁸But that doesn't matter. Whether their motives are false or genuine, the message about Christ is being preached either way, so I rejoice. And I will continue to rejoice.

1:12 Greek *brothers.* 1:13 Greek *including all the Praetorium.* 1:14a Greek *brothers in the Lord.* 1:14b Some manuscripts read *speak the message.*

NOTES

1:12 *brothers and sisters.* Lit., "brothers," an inclusive term commonly used to address both men and women.

everything that has happened to me here. This refers to Paul's imprisonment (see 1:13-14).

has helped to spread the Good News. The Greek word *prokopēn* [ᵀᴳ4297, ᶻᴳ4620] was used of pioneers cutting the way through tough terrain before an army so that the troops could advance (TDNT 6.703-719). The idea here is that Paul was pioneering the way for the spread of the gospel.

1:13 *the whole palace guard.* Lit., "in the whole praetorium." The Greek word *praitōrion* [ᵀᴳ4232, ᶻᴳ4550] denotes workers in the provincial governor's official residence (see 4:22). As discussed in the Introduction, this does not automatically identify Rome as the city from which Paul wrote the letter, for each province had its own praetorium. Nonetheless, Rome is the most likely place. This is all the more likely because "by the first Christian century it [*praetorium*] was frequently used also to denote the Praetorian Guard, the emperor's own elite troops, stationed in Rome" (Fee 1995:113, who cites Lightfoot 1976:99-104 as his source).

1:14 *most of the believers.* Lit., "most of the brothers in the Lord" (so NLT mg).

speak God's message. This reading is supported by diverse and early witnesses: ℵ A B (D*) P 044 33 syrᵖ·ʰ**. But other manuscripts, including the earliest (𝔓46) with D² 1739 𝔐 itʳ, read "speak the message" (so NLT mg). A few other manuscripts (F G) read "speak the message of the Lord." The two longer readings appear to be scribal attempts to make clear just what "the word" ("the message") means. Of course, this is the message about the Lord, and it is a message that came from God. But this didn't have to be said by Paul for his readers to understand (Comfort 2005:347).

1:15 *some are preaching out of jealousy and rivalry.* The Greek makes it clear that Paul was speaking of some (*tines* [ᵀᴳ5100, ᶻᴳ5516]) of the Christians mentioned in 1:14. It is difficult to understand precisely who these people were and why they were intending to make Paul's chains more painful (1:17); this is discussed in the following commentary.

1:16-17 The NLT (with all other modern versions) retains these verses in the order of verse 16 before verse 17, per the excellent testimony of 𝔓46 ℵ A B D* F G 33 1739 it cop. The KJV and NKJV have verse 17 before verse 16, following the inferior testimony of D¹ 𝔐 syrʰ. A transposition of verses was made in the majority of later manuscripts (𝔐) so that 1:16-17 would follow the order put forth in 1:15, where Paul first mentions those who preach from envy and rivalry, and second, those who preach from goodwill. But the original text displays a chiastic order:

A. preachers with envy and rivalry (1:15)
  B. preachers with goodwill
  B'. preachers [of goodwill] do so out of love, knowing that Paul is set for the
      defense of the gospel (1:16)
A'. preachers creating rivalry do so impurely, trying to increase Paul's suffering
    in prison (1:17)

Such chiasms are typically Pauline; the reversal of certain lines may promote clarity,
but it destroys the poetry.

COMMENTARY

This section is one of those portions in Paul's writing where we may wish we were
given more information. First of all, we are not told how "most of the believers"
were emboldened by Paul's imprisonment to proclaim the gospel. Second, we are
not told why some of these people did this with good motives and others with bad
motives. Third, we are not told how the preaching of the gospel by those with bad
motives could increase Paul's afflictions as a prisoner. We, the readers, are forced to
fill in the gaps here.

What we can gather from the passage is that the Philippians probably thought
that Paul's imprisonment would keep him from advancing the gospel. He wanted
to assure them that their fears were unnecessary (1:19, 28; 2:17). His situation had
not caused the hindrance of the gospel but, rather, provided an opportunity for
advancing the gospel. Paul viewed himself as a pioneer, forging the way for the gospel of Christ to spread into new territories (see note on 1:12). That new frontier was
probably Rome (see Introduction), where the whole Praetorian Guard heard that
Paul's imprisonment was for the cause of Christ. Even if it wasn't Rome, but Ephesus
or Caesarea instead, the cause of Christ was being pioneered. Indeed, by the time we
get to the end of this epistle we discover that many in Caesar's household had
become believers, no doubt through Paul's proclamation (see 4:22 and note).

This pioneering advance of the gospel emboldened several Christians to preach
the gospel. Thus, Paul's imprisonment for Christ did not bind the gospel; rather it
helped to release it. This has been the case throughout history. The suffering of
Christians increases the cause of Christ.

Among those who preached were some who did it with goodwill and pure
motives. Such a spirit of pure evangelistic zeal is not difficult for readers today to
imagine. But what is more difficult to understand is that there were some who did it
with impure motives, in that they were motivated by envy, strife, and contention to
proclaim the gospel. Could that be so? Furthermore, they were proclaiming the gospel, knowing that it would affect Paul's defense for the gospel and even somehow
add extra suffering to his imprisonment.

Who were these people? It is possible that those who were jealously trying to
attract to themselves the kind of attention that Paul was receiving were Judaizers
(2 Cor 11:14). But since Paul elsewhere expressed his disagreement with the doctrine of the Judaizers (as in the book of Galatians), and here in these verses he

expresses no such disagreement, it seems that these were not Judaizers (compare comments on 3:1-2 where Paul warns the Philippians about the Judaizers). Whoever they were, Paul didn't have a problem with the content of their preaching, only with their motives. It is quite possible that these preachers were attempting to take advantage of Paul's absence to gain a hearing for themselves. Some may have assumed that because Paul could not preach, he would be humiliated by their success (thereby intending to make Paul's chains more painful to him), not understanding that Paul's success was not staked on his own reputation.

Paul's life did not center on himself and his personal happiness but on Jesus Christ and his work (see 1:21). Thus, despite peoples' motives, Paul was happy that Christ was being proclaimed. Drawing attention to Christ, for whatever reason, was doing some good. Herein emerges one of the dominant themes in this epistle—namely, that a servant of Christ serves Christ and his message more than himself or herself. What is most important in this world is that Christ is being proclaimed. Let God be the judge of people's motives. Our duty is to proclaim Christ.

◆ ## 2. Paul's desire to live in Christ and magnify him (1:19-26)

¹⁹For I know that as you pray for me and the Spirit of Jesus Christ helps me, this will lead to my deliverance.

²⁰For I fully expect and hope that I will never be ashamed, but that I will continue to be bold for Christ, as I have been in the past. And I trust that my life will bring honor to Christ, whether I live or die. ²¹For to me, living means living for Christ, and dying is even better. ²²But if I live, I can do more fruitful work for Christ. So I really don't know which is better. ²³I'm torn between two desires: I long to go and be with Christ, which would be far better for me. ²⁴But for your sakes, it is better that I continue to live.

²⁵Knowing this, I am convinced that I will remain alive so I can continue to help all of you grow and experience the joy of your faith. ²⁶And when I come to you again, you will have even more reason to take pride in Christ Jesus because of what he is doing through me.

NOTES

1:19 *the Spirit of Jesus Christ.* This is a unique title of the Spirit in the NT. Similar titles are "the Spirit of Jesus" (Acts 16:7) and "the Spirit of Christ" (Rom 8:9; 1 Pet 1:11). Each of these titles indicates the functional union of Jesus Christ and his Spirit in terms of Christian experience. His Spirit now indwells the NT believers (see commentary for further discussion).

helps me. This is a rather bland rendering of a colorful Greek expression, *epichorēgia* [TG2024, ZG2221]. This word was originally used to describe the supply a choir manager (*chorēgos*) would provide all the members of a Greek choir (who performed in the Greek plays). In short, he took care of all their living expenses. The word then came to mean a full supply of any kind.

this will lead to my deliverance. The wording comes from Job 13:16, LXX. Paul was hereby expressing his thought that he would be released from house arrest (see 1:25-26; 2:24). This contrasts with his thought expressed in 2 Tim 4:6, written from prison at a later time, when Paul expected his imminent death.

1:20 *I fully expect.* The Greek word *apokaradokian* [TG603, ZG638] occurs only here and in Rom 8:19 in the NT. The image is one of someone eagerly expecting something very important to happen. A sixth-century papyrus speaks of peasants awaiting the coming (*parousia* [TG3952, ZG4242]) of a certain high official, assuring him that they await "as those in Hades watch eagerly (*karadokountes*) for the parousia of Christ, the everlasting God" (MM 63). This word, which is "found only in Christian writings, was returned to its earlier, better known form, *karadokia* [TG2587.1, ZG2839] in only a few manuscripts [F G]" (Hawthorne 1983:32).

my life will bring honor to Christ. Lit., "Christ will be magnified in my body." The indwelling Christ (called "the Spirit of Jesus Christ" in the previous verse) would be made visible in Paul's being and life (cf. 2 Cor 4:11; 5:14-15; Gal 2:19-20).

1:21 *living means living for Christ, and dying is even better.* This is very terse in the Greek: "to live, Christ; to die, gain." The first part of the statement cannot mean that Paul "lived Christ" as though he lived out the life of another, Jesus Christ, in his life. The reason it cannot mean this is that *Christos* [TG5547, ZG5986] (Christ) would have to be in the accusative case; instead, it is in the nominative case. The infinitive phrase *to zēn* [TG2198, ZG2409] (to live) is positioned as being equivalent to *Christos*; hence, to live = Christ. For Paul this meant his life was sustained by Christ and belonged to Christ. The second part of the statement is less ambiguous. Paul viewed death, not as a loss but as a gain because "to die" would bring him into the presence of Jesus Christ himself (1:23).

1:23 *I'm torn between two desires.* This is a functionally equivalent translation for the Greek, which when translated literally would be, "I am equally pressed by two things." The Greek sees it as pressure coming from two sides, while the English sees it as a pulling coming from two sides. Either way, the message is clear: Paul had angst over two compelling desires: to die and go with Christ or to stay alive and be with the Philippians (and other believers).

1:25 *help all of you grow.* In the Greek, this speaks of helping the believers "advance." The Greek word *prokopēn* [TG4297, ZG4620] is the same one Paul used in 1:12 to speak of the pioneering advance of the gospel (see note).

COMMENTARY

This section of Philippians is very personal. Paul related to the Philippians his inner thoughts concerning his life and death—not abstractly, but rather personally, speaking of his feelings about his life and his death. Since he was in a situation wherein he could have faced execution at any time, he had intensely evaluated his life and death. Paul struggled with the two possibilities, both of which were ultimately good.

Life, for Paul, was good because he believed that "to live = Christ." This meant that his life was involved with Christ, originated from Christ, and was for Christ. Indwelt by the Spirit of Jesus Christ, Paul chose to magnify Christ in his life, even in his body. For Paul, the only way to live the Christ life was to do so by his indwelling Spirit, which Paul named "the Spirit of Jesus Christ." In his writings, Paul often speaks of the Spirit and Christ synonymously. This is evident in Romans 8:9-10, where the titles "Spirit of God," "Spirit of Christ," and "Christ" are all used interchangeably. The Spirit of God is the Spirit of Christ and the Spirit of Christ is Christ.

The union between Christ and the Spirit transpired at the time of Christ's resurrection. This union does not mean that Christ became a bodiless spirit at the time of his resurrection but that in his new resurrected body Christ became united with the life-giving Spirit. William Milligan, author of an English classic on the subject of the resurrection, provides an insightful comment on this:

> The condition of our Lord after His Resurrection was viewed by the sacred writers as essentially a state of *pneuma*. Not indeed that our Lord had then no body, for it is the constant lesson of Scripture that a body was possessed by Him; but that the deepest, the fundamental characteristic of His state, interpenetrating even the body, and moulding it into a complete adaptation to and harmony with His spirit, was *pneuma*. In other words, it is proposed to inquire whether the word *pneuma* in the New Testament is not used as a short description of what our Lord was after His Resurrection, in contrast with what He was during the days of His humiliation upon earth. (1884:246)

Milligan goes on from there to show that several passages affirm that the resurrected Christ is spirit. He cites 1 Corinthians 6:17 to show that the believer who is joined with the risen Lord must be joined to him as spirit, because he who is joined to the Lord is said to be "one spirit" with him. He uses 2 Corinthians 3:17-18 to demonstrate that the Lord who is the Spirit is none other than the risen Christ. He also employs Romans 1:3-4; 1 Timothy 3:16; and Hebrews 9:14 to prove that the risen Lord is spirit (1884:248-256). Alford, also commenting on Hebrews 9:14, relates that "the Divine Personality in Christ in the resurrection so completely ruled and absorbed His flesh that Paul so spoke of him in 1 Corinthians 15:45 as life-giving Spirit and in 2 Corinthians 3:17 as the Spirit" (1976:4.171). And note the significant remarks of Gaffin (1978:87), who says this about Paul's view of the resurrection of Christ:

> Christ (as incarnate) experiences a spiritual qualification and transformation so thorough, and endowment with the Spirit so complete that as a result they can now be equated. This unprecedented possession of the Spirit and the accompanying change in Christ result in a unity so close that not only can it be said simply that the Spirit makes alive, but also that Christ as Spirit makes alive.

Paul identified the Spirit with Jesus Christ because in Christian experience they are absolutely identical. By the Spirit of Jesus Christ, Paul lived the Christ-life. This idea is paralleled by Galatians 2:20, where Paul says, "My old self has been crucified with Christ. It is no longer I who live, but Christ lives in me." Paul lived "by" Christ—that is, he needed Christ's empowering for every aspect of his life (4:13). Paul also lived "for" Christ—that is, he lived to serve Christ. Thus, if Jesus gave him time on earth, Paul would use it to glorify Christ by serving his church and proclaiming the gospel.

For Paul, death was gain, probably in two respects. Death releases a person from the burdens and woes of this life. Using similar language (especially the notion of "gain"), Antigone said, "Whoever has had to live in as much suffering as I have, how is it not a gain to die?" (Sophocles, *Antigone* 463-464). The other "gain" of death is that Paul would pass immediately into the presence of Christ (1:23). The divine life that Christians receive at the time of regeneration does not cease at death; it is eternal, so they never really die (cf. John 5:24; 11:25-26). Nothing, not even death, can separate them from Christ (see Rom 8:38-39). Paul saw death as giving him immediate access to Christ.

We do not know if Paul understood believers to gain a resurrection body at the point of death or some time later (at the final resurrection). According to 1 Corinthians 15:20-52 and 1 Thessalonians 4:13-17, the believers do not receive a resurrection body until after a period of "sleep" (= state of death); this new body is given at the time of Jesus' return. According to 2 Corinthians 5:1-8, a believer receives a new body after death—without any mention of an intervening period of sleep. In this passage it is very clear that the believer does not become "naked" (i.e., a bodiless spirit) at the time of death but is clothed with a heavenly body that swallows up the mortal body. The language of Paul in Philippians 1:21-23, wherein he says that he longed to depart "to be *with Christ*," parallels that of 2 Corinthians 5:8, wherein he says that he (with other Christians) would rather be away from the body and at home *with the Lord*. By putting these two passages together, a case could be made for Paul believing he would receive some kind of new body at the point of death. However, most commentators think Paul was speaking of the new body the Lord gives at the time of his coming and the great resurrection (per 1 Cor 15 and 1 Thess 4). This view is clearly affirmed by Paul's statements in Philippians 3:20-21 (see commentary). So we are left with a kind of vagueness as to what kind of existence a believer has "with the Lord" after death. Since Paul seemed to eschew any notion of becoming a bodiless spirit (Kruse 1987:114), it is not difficult to imagine that he thought of his soul somehow being embodied in a form that allowed him to be with the Lord in spirit—prior to the time he would receive a new glorified body at the time of the resurrection. Certainty about this—on this side of eternity—eludes us.

Whatever Paul's view on this matter, there is no suggestion in this text of there being a period of "soul sleep" until the final resurrection—that is, a time of waiting in death before one goes to be with the Lord. Death was "gain" to Paul because death ushered him into Christ's presence immediately. In fact, death was better than life because death would release Paul from his sufferings and usher him into that phase of his living relationship with Christ, wherein he would never have to experience death again. In other words, he would be experiencing the eternality of eternal life.

Paul was experiencing the pressure of two equally powerful forces. On one hand, he considered it "better" to die and be with Christ. On the other hand, it was more necessary to remain in the flesh for the sake of the Philippians. Paul, for the moment, was certain that the latter would take place. Consequently, the Philippians would be the direct beneficiaries of Paul's living service. For their sakes, he was glad that he would be released from prison and continue his life in the service of Christ. If the release from imprisonment was release from imprisonment in Rome, then this occurred around AD 62. We do not know of other releases from imprisonment, although it could have been from an Ephesian imprisonment in AD 55. It wasn't from the Caesarean imprisonment (AD 58) because Paul was sent from there to Rome in chains. Once reunited with the Philippian believers, Paul could continue to help them pioneer their spiritual advance (see 1:25 and note), which would give him great joy.

◆   **D. Encouragement to Unity for the Sake of the Good News (1:27–2:4)**

²⁷Above all, you must live as citizens of heaven, conducting yourselves in a manner worthy of the Good News about Christ. Then, whether I come and see you again or only hear about you, I will know that you are standing together with one spirit and one purpose, fighting together for the faith, which is the Good News. ²⁸Don't be intimidated in any way by your enemies. This will be a sign to them that they are going to be destroyed, but that you are going to be saved, even by God himself. ²⁹For you have been given not only the privilege of trusting in Christ but also the privilege of suffering for him. ³⁰We are in this struggle together. You have seen my struggle in the past, and you know that I am still in the midst of it.

CHAPTER 2

Is there any encouragement from belonging to Christ? Any comfort from his love? Any fellowship together in the Spirit? Are your hearts tender and compassionate? ²Then make me truly happy by agreeing wholeheartedly with each other, loving one another, and working together with one mind and purpose.

³Don't be selfish; don't try to impress others. Be humble, thinking of others as better than yourselves. ⁴Don't look out only for your own interests, but take an interest in others, too.

NOTES

1:27 *live as citizens of heaven.* The Philippians had civic pride because they were a Roman colony, enjoying numerous privileges. Indeed, many of them considered themselves Romans. But Paul called them to enjoy a higher citizenship.

conducting yourselves in a manner worthy of the Good News. Every citizen must be responsible to the sovereign nation or kingdom to which they belong; thus, Christians must be responsible to the citizenship of God's Kingdom. This is a repeated emphasis in Paul's writings (see Eph 4:1; Col 1:10; 1 Thess 2:12).

standing together with one spirit and one purpose. This expression is taken by most English translators to denote a unified spirit, a spiritual solidarity, a kind of *esprit de corps*. This interpretation is enhanced by the following phrase, "one soul," which is taken as an appositive. TEV collapses the two expressions into one with this translation: "with one common purpose." However, the "spirit" so mentioned could just as likely be the one divine Spirit that unites all the members of the body (as in 1 Cor 12:13; Eph 4:3). The scribe of 𝔓46 saw it that way, for he made the word *pneuma* [TG4151, ZG4460] a nomen sacrum (divine title), thereby indicating the divine Spirit.

fighting together for the faith. The Greek expression is drawn from the Greek athletic contests. The word *sunathlountes* [TG4866, ZG5254] means "competing together as athletes" (see commentary).

1:28 *a sign to them that they are going to be destroyed, but that you are going to be saved.* Lit., "which is to them a sign of destruction, but to you, of salvation." This reading has the support of ℵ A B C² P 044 33 1739. There are two variants on this: (1) "which to them, on one hand, is a sign of destruction, but to you, on the other hand, of salvation" (so 𝔐, followed by KJV and NKJV); (2) "which to them is a proof of destruction, but to us [is] salvation" (C* D* F G). The first variant is a scribal alteration that balances the two statements. The second variant makes the second statement inclusive (i.e., Paul and the Philippians). According to Hawthorne (1983:55-57), these changes were created to make the two statements parallel and thereby allow for the text to be interpreted as contrasting two perceptions: (1) the adversaries who perceived the willingness of the Philippians to fight for the faith of the gospel as an indication of their (the Philippians') destruction, and (2) the Philippians themselves who see the opposition as a sure sign of their salvation. This, of course, goes against the traditional interpretation, which emphasizes the contrast between *their* destruction and *your* salvation. The traditional exegesis says that this verse affirms that the opposition against the believers provides a twofold sign of what will be manifest when Christ returns: the destruction of those who persecute and the salvation of those who persevere (see 2 Thess 1:6-10; Comfort 2008:[Phil 1:28]).

1:29 *not only the privilege of trusting in Christ but also the privilege of suffering for him.* This is a major theme in this epistle: Believers in Christ are called to suffer for Christ. This is part of the spiritual maturation process.

1:30 *We are in this struggle together.* Both Paul and the Philippians were facing strong opposition; Paul was in prison (see 1:13-14), and the Philippians were being persecuted (see 1:27-29).

You have seen my struggle in the past. The Philippians had firsthand knowledge of Paul's sufferings in Philippi (see Acts 16:11-40; cf. 1 Thess 2:2).

2:1 *Is there . . . ?* In the Greek, there are four conditional statements, beginning with "If there is." The NLT turns these into a series of rhetorical questions, each expecting a positive answer.

fellowship together in the Spirit? Or, "fellowship with the Spirit." Lit., "fellowship of [the] S/spirit." This points to the unity of community actualized by all the members' joint participation in the Spirit.

2:2 *working together with one mind.* Lit., "thinking the one thing," which has the textual support of 𝔓46 ℵ2 B D F G 075 0278 1739 𝔐. A variant reading is "thinking the same thing," found in ℵ* A C I 044 33. The variant reading is probably the result of scribes conforming this phrase to the first phrase of the clause. No matter how subtle the difference, it is likely that Paul was making a general appeal for unity at the beginning of the verse in saying "think the same thing." Then he provided one specific focus that would unite their minds when he said "thinking the one thing."

2:3-4 *Don't be selfish.* The Greek behind "selfish" is *eritheia* [TG2052, ZG2249]. Though this could be translated as "strife" or "rivalry," it is better understood as "selfish ambition" (BDAG 392).

don't try to impress others. Lit., "don't [act] according to vain deceit." This intensifies the previous admonition, inasmuch as the Greek *kenodoxia* [TG2754, ZG3029] means excessive ambition (BDAG 538-539).

2:4 *take an interest in others, too.* The Greek here is the participle *hēgoumenoi* [TG2233, ZG2451] (esteeming), found in most manuscripts. However, a few important manuscripts (𝔓46 D I 075 0278) have the participle *proēgoumenoi* [TG4285, ZG4605], which literally means "leading the way." This word appears only one other place in the NT, Rom 12:10, which was translated in many ancient versions (it syr arm) as "trying to outdo one another in showing respect" (BDAG 869). As such, *proēgoumenoi* is an excellent word in the context of 2:1-6, where Paul is promoting willful submission among the brothers and sisters, and may be original.

COMMENTARY

This section of the epistle is key to interpreting the Philippians' condition at the time of writing. Evidently, they were experiencing opposition from opponents of the gospel (1:28-29). At the same time, they were experiencing some internal discord; if not, then Paul would not have encouraged them in so many ways to be unified. Later in the epistle we discover that there was some dissension between two female co-workers, Euodia and Syntyche (4:2). Normally, when persecution comes from outside the church, it should unify those being persecuted. The persecuted have a common bond, which is their common enemy. In Jesus' last discourse with his disciples (John 13–17), he commanded them to "love one another." The disciples were to love one another because they would take Jesus' message to a world that despised them. The external hatred should intensify, not diminish, the internal love of the Christian community. Thus, the Philippians were to love one another and stand united against their common enemy.

In typical fashion, Paul used images drawn from his culture to illustrate his points. In this section, he first drew upon the imagery of citizenship, then the imagery of athletic competition. These two images help to emphasize the main point he was trying to make: The Philippians needed to live unitedly, as a community of heavenly citizens, and they needed to compete—not against one another—but as a united team against those who opposed the gospel of Jesus Christ.

The matter of citizenship was something very well known to Paul himself, as well as to the Philippians. Paul was a Roman citizen (Acts 22:28), and Philippi was the home of numerous Roman citizens, the city itself being a Roman colony. According to the census of the emperor Augustus (cf. Luke 2:1), there were approximately 4,233,000 Roman citizens at the time of Christ's birth. By the time of Paul's ministry, the number had reached about 6,000,000 (TBD 288). Roman citizens were often required to give proof of their citizenship. That was usually accomplished by reference to the census archives, where the name of every citizen was recorded. In addition, freeborn citizens possessed a small wooden birth certificate containing information about their status at birth. Paul no doubt was alluding to this when he wrote that the citizens of heaven have proof of their citizenship in that their names are written in the Book of Life (4:3).

Roman citizens had certain privileges: the right to vote; to hold office; to purchase, possess, sell, and bequeath property; to enter into a legal contract; to have a fair trial; and to appeal to Caesar. But they also had certain responsibilities: to abide by the laws of Rome and to serve in the military (see TBD 288-289). Paul was calling upon the Philippians to not only enjoy their rights as citizens of God's Kingdom but to live in a way that befitted their citizenship. Further, he was calling them to one of their major responsibilities: to fight for the defense and advance of "the faith." Although, as we shall see, this is presented with athletic imagery, there is an overlap with military imagery. In any event, "the faith" constituted the basic tenets of Christian doctrine as proclaimed by the apostles. Any opposition to the faith was cause for action.

We are never told who the opposers were (1:28). It is possible, but not likely, that they were Judaizers who altered the message of the Christian faith (see 3:2-5 and notes). The reason I say "not likely" is that there were very few Jews in Philippi at the time the church was founded (not even enough to form a synagogue, which required ten adult males), and Paul's words about the Judaizers appear to be a warning of their coming, not of their presence among the Philippians at that time. It is more likely that the opposers were Greco-Roman Gentiles, such as the ones Paul encountered when he first came to Philippi (Acts 16), the ones who caused Paul to suffer and whom he mentions in 1:30. Either way, whether Judaizers or Gentiles, the Philippians had to stand up for the faith of the gospel, even if it caused them to suffer.

Paul mingled military imagery with athletic when he used the word *sunathlountes* [TG4866, ZG5254], which means "to struggle alongside someone" (see BDAG 964) and carries with it the idea of athletes or soldiers competing as one man for a common goal. (In Hellenistic times, the Olympic games and other athletic competitions were organized largely to promote military prowess. Thus, there may not be much of a distinction between athletic and military competition.) The verb is extremely rare in classical Greek and in the New Testament (used only here and in 4:3). Its usage in 4:3 helps our understanding, where Paul commends Euodia and Syntyche for having struggled together with him in advancing the gospel. In Hellenistic times the image might evoke thoughts of "the arena, where the gladiatorial struggle was one of life and death"; it also might evoke the thought of "the phalanx, consisting of a body of trained spearmen who fought in closed ranks" (Martin 1987:88).

In war or athletic competition, it is important that the unit be cohesive and unified. Internal wrangling degenerates the effectiveness of the unit. Thus, Paul urged the Philippians to advance the gospel against its enemies by being unified. The key to unification is the one Spirit, who unites a group of Christians into one body (2:1-2), enabling them to overcome small differences among individual members and to strive toward a common goal. Paul encouraged the Philippians to "think the same thing," to, literally, "be co-souled ones" (i.e., united souls), and even to be "thinking the one thing" (literal rendering of 2:2). Later in the epistle, Paul elaborates on this "one thing": to pursue the goal of knowing Christ Jesus. If any of the believers had a different goal, Paul prayed that they would be enlightened (see 3:12-15). Like a team of athletes, the Philippians were called by Paul to focus on one goal only—that of knowing Christ. This kind of thinking would unite their minds.

In this section (1:27–2:4) Paul piles up exhortations to unity. This is exemplified in 2:2, where he says that the Philippians will make them happy by "agreeing wholeheartedly with each other, loving one another, and working together with one mind and purpose." They were to be a unified, mutually supportive community, living with one another in harmony and love (cf. Rom 12:16; 1 Cor 1:10). They needed the communion and fellowship of the Spirit to attain this. Verses 3 and 4 are transitional verses; they close out the section begun in 1:27 (in that they provide an important key to unity—namely, humility), and they introduce the Christ Poem

(2:2-11) extolling Christ's humility. The Philippians needed humility. A humble mind is the key to cooperative unity. Humility is the realization that we are creatures who are totally dependent on God, the Creator. If we are really humble before God, we are totally relying on God. This affects our attitudes toward others, for as equally dependent creatures, we cannot take pride in ourselves.

◆ II. The Christ Poem (2:5-11)

5You must have the same attitude that Christ Jesus had.

6Though he was God,*
he did not think of equality with God
as something to cling to.
7Instead, he gave up his divine privileges*;
he took the humble position of a slave*
and was born as a human being.
When he appeared in human form,*
8 he humbled himself in obedience to God

and died a criminal's death on a cross.

9Therefore, God elevated him to the place of highest honor
and gave him the name above all other names,
10that at the name of Jesus every knee should bow,
in heaven and on earth and under the earth,
11and every tongue confess that Jesus Christ is Lord,
to the glory of God the Father.

2:6 Or *Being in the form of God.*   2:7a Greek *he emptied himself.*   2:7b Or *the form of a slave.*   2:7c Some English translations put this phrase in verse 8.

NOTES

2:5 You must have the same attitude. The Greek allows for several possibilities here: (1) "Be thinking this among you" (if the verb *phroneite* [TG5426, ZG5858] is understood as an imperative); (2) "You are thinking this among you" (if the verb is understood as an indicative); (3) "Be thinking this in you"; (4) "You are having this thinking in you." The prepositional phrase *en humin* [TG1722/4771, ZG1877/5148] can denote something taking place among the Philippians, or it can denote something taking place inwardly—in the psyche. Both are defensible from the context because Paul was asking them to have something happen *among* them corporately, as well as happen to them *in* their psyche. As for the verb, the most natural understanding is the imperative. The ambiguity was taken away by later scribes who changed *phroneite* to an imperative verb *phroneisthō* [TG5426, ZG5858]—so 𝔐 TR.

that Christ Jesus had. Lit., "that which also in Christ Jesus." The verb has to be supplied. Most translations make it past tense: "which was also in Christ Jesus." But the lack of a verb suggests a certain timeless quality to the thinking of Christ Jesus. Paul was probably thinking of the present Christ Jesus in the totality of his "history"—from the preincarnate Son of God, to incarnation, crucifixion, resurrection, ascension, and enthronement as Lord of all.

2:6 Though he was God. Lit., "who existing in God's form." The Greek doesn't say, "he was God," nor does it say he was "the form of God." Rather, it says that he was existing *in* God's form. "God's form" in Greek is *morphē theou* [cf. *theos* TG2316, ZG2536]. "*Morphē* [TG3444, ZG3671] always signifies a form which truly and fully expresses the being which underlies it" (MM 417). It is what gives expression to an essence. A man—with his body, mind, and soul—expresses the essence of humanity. A human lives in *morphē anthrōpou* [TG444, ZG476]—that is, in human expression. One who is God lives in *morphē theou*—that is, in divine expression. Another way to say this is that *morphē* denotes one's mode of being in the sense that *morphē* is that which truly characterizes a given reality—those characters and qualities that are essential to any given being (Fee 1995:204). One further point is that the NLT uses the concessive "though" to introduce the statement, but it is better to understand the phrase as "causal"—i.e., "because he was God." Because he existed as God, "his true nature is characterized not by selfish grabbing, but by an open-handed giving" (Hawthorne 1983:85).

he did not think of equality with God. Lit., "he did not consider the [his] being all things equal to God." This statement explains what it is for Christ to be "in God's form." As one existing in God's form, he is all things equal to God. Thus, we have two very profound statements asserting Christ's deity. In short, Christ is God (see commentary).

as something to cling to. In Greek this is one word: *harpagmon* [TG725, ZG772], a noun denoting "grasping." This "grasping" can be understood in three basic ways: (1) "trying to attain," "grasping so as to get"; (2) "clinging to," "retaining," "holding on to"—as in the NLT; (3) "an opportunity for grasping." The first option can be ruled out by context—namely, Christ already existed in God's form (as God), so there would be no cause for him to want to attain this. In other words, he wasn't seeking Godlikeness because he was already God. The second option does work in the context, for it denotes that Christ, being all things equal with God, could have insisted on his equality with God and not taken a servant's role. As an equal, he had this prerogative. He could have clung to his equality. Had he insisted on retaining/grasping to this equality, he would not have become the Suffering Servant, the Redeemer (see commentary). The third option denotes that Christ did not consider his equality with God as providing him with an opportunity for grasping—that is, as a matter of seizing upon this equality to his own advantage. Christ did not consider being equal with God as something to be taken selfish advantage of, something to further his own ends. Equality with God did not mean for Christ to be a grasping, seizing being as it would be for the gods and lords whom the Philippians had previously known. The normal expectation of godly/lordly power is to seize, to grasp, to take all things for themselves. Contrarily, Christ expressed his equality with God when he emptied himself (Fee 1995:207-209).

2:7 he gave up his divine privileges. The Greek term for this is *heauton ekenōsen* [TG1438/2758, ZG1571/3033] ("he emptied himself," as in NLT mg). The text does not say that he emptied himself of anything in particular; it simply says he emptied himself. We simply do not know what he emptied himself of, though scholars have written much about this. The NLT's rendering, which happens to be a prevalent interpretation of the *kenōsis*, is conjectural. It cannot be said that Christ "gave up his divine privileges." We do not know this. A better interpretation is that emptying himself is tantamount to pouring himself out—so Hawthorne (1983:86), who wrote, "it is a poetic, humanlike way of saying that Christ poured out himself, putting himself totally at the disposal of people (cf. 1 John 3:16), that Christ became poor that he might make many rich (2 Cor 8:9)."

he took the humble position of a slave. Lit., "taking the form of a slave." This parallels the expression, "the form of God" in 2:6. As such, this means that the Son of God took on a new *morphē* [TG3444, ZG3671], a new mode of being, not just a new outward visage, but an entire transformation of character from one being equal to God to one being a servant (slave) of God. This occurred in Christ's psyche prior to incarnation and was palpably realized at the Incarnation, as is expressed in the next two lines.

was born as a human. Lit., "by becoming in the likeness of humans." The Greek participle behind "becoming" is *genomenos*, from the verb *ginomai* [TG1096, ZG1181], which denotes "come to be, become, originate" (BDAG 196-198). The same verb is used in John 1:14 to describe how the Word (who was God) became flesh. The "becoming" indicates a significant origination and transformation. God became what he never was before: a human being. The Greek word behind "likeness" is *homoiōmati* [TG3667, ZG3930], a word that denotes "being similar to" or "looking like." However, this does not mean that Jesus just looked like humans but really wasn't human. "In light of what Paul says about Jesus in general it is probable that he uses our word to bring out both that Jesus in his earthly career was similar to sinful humans and yet not totally like them" (BDAG 707).

When he appeared in human form. Lit., "being found in appearance as a man." The Greek for "appearance" is *schēmati* [TG4976, ZG5386]; it indicates "outward appearance, form, shape" (BDAG 981), and it appears only twice in the NT (here and in 1 Cor 7:31). Paul used it to convey the way, the manner, in which Jesus Christ appeared. To other humans he appeared to be the same as they—simply another human being. The Greek participle for "being found" is *heuretheis*, from the verb *heuriskō* [TG2147, ZG2351], which denotes the act of discovering. In this case, it speaks of people recognizing Jesus as being nothing more than a man, not as God—which, for one who is divine, would be a cause of humiliation.

2:8 he humbled himself. This thought is parallel to "he emptied himself" in 2:7; both elucidate the meaning of the other.

in obedience to God. This expresses the Son's relationship to his Father as the subservient one (see John 10:17-18; Heb 5:8).

died. This obedience led to Jesus complying with the Father to do the unthinkable—die for the sins of humanity (see John 3:16; Rom 5:8; 8:3; 1 John 4:9-10, 14).

a criminal's death on a cross. In the Greek language, the word "cross" (*stauros* [TG4716, ZG5089]) denoted a vertical stake with a crossbeam either across the top (T) or across the middle (+). Crucifixion was a cruel, painful, and shameful execution, reserved for the worst criminals and rebels against Rome.

2:9 God elevated him to the place of highest honor. The Greek verb behind "elevated" is *huperupsōsen* [TG5251, ZG5671], literally meaning "to super-exalt," "to raise someone to the loftiest height" (BDAG 1034). Found only here in the NT, it "depicts God in one dramatic action lifting Christ from the depths to the heights" (Hawthorne 1983:91). This super-exalting incorporates the full sweep of Jesus' resurrection, ascension, and enthronement.

gave him. Lit., "graced him with" or "granted him." God the Father graced Jesus with the most glorious reputation.

the name above all other names. This is the reading according to superior manuscript evidence (𝔓46 ℵ A B C 33 1739). Inferior manuscripts (D F G 044 𝔐—so TR and KJV) read, "a name above all other names." The definite article was omitted probably because in Greek usage the article usually functions to point back to a previously mentioned subject. In this case, it points forward with a sense of anticipation—to the next verse, where the name is identified: "the name of Jesus." Thus, the name Jesus is *the* name that excels above every other person's name in human history.

2:10 every knee should bow. This verse and the following are taken from Isa 45:23, LXX, which translated into English is: "before me [the Lord] every knee will bow and every tongue will confess that in the Lord alone are righteousness and strength."

in heaven and on earth and under the earth. The entire creation—including spiritual powers and angels, humans on earth, and those who have died—will acknowledge that Jesus Christ is Lord (see Eph 1:9-10, 21; Col 1:20).

2:11 and every tongue confess. The NLT translates the Greek subjunctive, the timeless potential mood ("should confess," so 𝔓46 ℵ 044 Clement), which has a different focus than the variant, a future indicative ("will in the future confess," so A C D F G L 33 1739). It is only a difference of shortening the *ēta* to *epsilon* in Greek (*exomologēsētai* to *exomologēsetai* [^{TG}1843A, ^{ZG}2018]). Usually, a distinction in mood will not greatly impact the exegesis of a passage. But in this case it is critical. The subjunctive indicates that all people could and/or should confess that Jesus Christ is Lord—not that they necessarily will do so. But the future indicative is predictive: All people *will* confess that Jesus Christ is Lord. This prediction is categorically rejected by many Christians who think the Scriptures reveal that not all people will confess that Jesus is Lord. Those who espouse universal salvation urge that this verse looks forward to the day when all will indeed recognize Jesus as Lord. However, the future indicative could point to the fact that all people will recognize Jesus' Lordship, but not necessarily submit to him willingly.

In this light, it is not easy to say what was originally written. Certainly, one word could have been easily confused for the other, so the change might have been purely accidental. But if it was intentional, it is possible that scribes conformed the future to the subjunctive to avoid any notions of universalism or to make the verb parallel to the subjunctive verb of the previous verse, "should bend." However, it is possible that scribes changed the subjunctive to the future so as to conform Paul's wording to Isa 45:23, LXX, the OT passage he quoted here. If so, such scribes cannot be blamed for being universalists per se; rather, their intentions were to show the eschatological regency of Christ over all humanity, irrespective of identifying who is or is not saved.

that Jesus Christ is Lord. Or, more poignantly as "the Lord is Jesus Christ"—either way the verb is supplied in English. The title "Lord," a divine title representing the OT name *Yahweh*, is frequently applied to Jesus in the NT. The divine title "Lord" (see 2:11) reflects his supreme authority and power (cf. Matt 28:18; John 17:5; Acts 2:33-36; Heb 2:9; 12:2).

to the glory of God the Father. The Father is honored by the Son being hailed with the highest name in the universe.

COMMENTARY

This passage is widely regarded as an early hymn about Christ's preexistence and divine nature, incarnation and death, and exaltation and lordship. Whether the passage is to be understood as (1) a pre-Pauline hymn (i.e., a hymn Paul borrowed) or (2) a hymn composed by Paul has been debated by scholars and continues to be debated. O'Brien (1991:188-193) and Fee (1995:191-194) present excellent discussions on the issue, as does Martin (1967).

It is possible that Paul borrowed a preexisting hymn. We know that when the early Christians gathered together they sang Old Testament psalms, as well as hymns and spiritual songs (Eph 5:19; Col 3:16). The latter two—"hymns and spiritual songs"—must have been creations of the early Christians. Philippians 2:6-11 may have been such a hymn that Paul adapted for use in this letter. Even if Paul did adapt this hymn, we must consider him to be its ultimate author in that he dictated this hymn to his amanuensis (see Fee 1995:193) and thereby gave it its final written form, the words we now read in 2:6-11.

It seems more likely, however, that Philippians 2:6-11 is a poem composed by Paul. This view is supported by the fact that there are distinct lexical ties between Philippians 2:6-11 and Philippians 3:20-21 (see notes and commentary there). Since Paul was clearly the author of the verses in chapter 3, it stands to reason that he authored this passage in chapter 2. Other portions of Paul's writings exhibit his poetic ability, such as the encomium for Christ's love (Rom 8:38-39), the doxology praising Christ (Rom 16:25-27), the poetic prayer (Eph 3:14-21), the love poem (1 Cor 13:4-6), the poem to the preeminent Christ (Col 1:15-20), and two poems for Christ's epiphany (1 Tim 6:15-16; Titus 3:4-7). All of these passages display poetic language, cadence, and majesty, setting them apart even from exalted prose. In short, Paul became poetic on occasion. And Philippians 2:6-11 is one of his brilliant masterpieces.

The poem has two major strophes: 2:6-8 (the humiliation of Christ) and 2:9-11 (the exaltation of Christ). A more poetic rendering of the poem is as follows:

> Christ Jesus, God living in divine form,
> chose not to keep his divinity to himself
> but poured himself out into a servant's form
> by being born in human likeness.
> And being found among men as man
> he humbled himself in human servitude
> becoming obedient even to the point of death,
> and at that, a death by crucifixion.
> Because of this, God exalted him,
> giving him the Name above every other.
> Every knee should bend to Jesus,
> and every creature in heaven, on earth,
> and under earth—every creature with a tongue—
> should confess, "the Lord is Jesus Christ"
> to God the Father's glory.

A more filled-out rendering is as follows:

> Let us think a different way, a way beyond comprehension
> for this is the kind of thinking Christ Jesus always had.
> He was God in nature, form, and mode of being.
> He was everything God was with all divine privilege.
> Yet he did not cling to this divine equality, or use it
> for his own advantage like some god grasping for more.
> Rather, he emptied himself. He poured himself out
> into the form of a slave, a servant of divine will.
> He was born human with flesh, bone, and blood
> and looked every bit man except he was also God.
> People saw him as man, as one of them, as he humbled
> himself to the Father's mind, and became obedient,
> even when that led to humiliating death by crucifixion.
> Having abandoned himself to ultimate sacrifice,
> the Father did not abandon him. Rather, he lifted him,
> exalted him, and graced him with preeminence,
> giving him the NAME above every other in this universe,
> so that at the name of JESUS every knee should bow
> and every tongue—whether in heaven, on earth,
> or under earth—should openly confess with praise:
> "the Lord is Jesus Christ!" to the glory of his Father.

This English rendering of the poem, which includes 2:5 as an incipit to the main body of Philippians, is an attempt to elucidate the rich Greek vocabulary of the poem, as well as give the poem English cadence.

It is the nature of poetry to allow for multiple meanings, or polyvalence. The words and thoughts so expressed are intended to convey levels of connotation and denotation. As such, readers of the same poem will come away with different interpretations of various words and lines. Albeit, most readers—that is, close readers—will generally agree on what could be called a "consensus" interpretation of the poem in its entirety. Most will concur that this poem explores what it meant for the preincarnate Christ, who existed as God, to become human and a slave of the divine will, which entailed crucifixion (implicitly for the sins of humanity). This degree of humiliation was subsequently followed by the Father exalting Jesus to the highest.

Of course, the poem does not sit in empty space; it is connected to Paul's admonition for the Philippians to have true corporate unity via individual humility (see commentary on 2:1-4). Cooperative unity cannot be achieved if the individuals involved do not take on a mindset of humility. Thus, Christ is put forth as the preeminent example of someone who cooperated with the divine will of his Father by exhibiting humility to the utmost.

In order for us to appreciate what Christ's humiliation entailed, the poet first shows who the preincarnate Christ was. The reader would not appreciate the drama of the humiliation without first seeing *who* was making the sacrifice. The one who became man and became servant was not just anybody; he was God. Translating the text literally, this is said in two ways: (1) "who being in the form of God" and (2) "who being all things equal with God" (2:6). The first assertion indicates that Christ, as God, lived as God in nature, form, and mode of being. All his existence was divine. The second assertion indicates that Christ had complete equality with God. In Trinitarian terms, one could say the Son is equal to the Father; both are equally eternal and equally divine. During his ministry on earth, Jesus asserted this: "Before Abraham was even born, I AM" (John 8:58) and "The Father and I are one" (John 10:30). Those who heard these bold self-assertions made no mistake about what Jesus was claiming. They recognized he was claiming to be God (John 10:33).

In whatever way the individual words of Philippians 2:6 is interpreted (see notes on 2:6), the total meaning is clear: Christ was God and is God. Few passages in the New Testament so clearly affirm Christ's deity. But this was not unusual for Paul. Elsewhere in his writings, he ascribes deity to Jesus Christ (Rom 9:5; Col 2:9; Titus 2:13).

As for Romans 9:5, Paul names Christ as being "God, the one who rules over everything and is worthy of eternal praise!" Of this verse, F. F. Bruce wrote: "Here the Messiah is said, with regard to his human descent, to have come of a long line of Israelite ancestors; but as regards his eternal being, he is 'God over all, blessed for ever'" (1985:176). A detailed study on the issue of whether or not Paul was calling Christ "God" was done by Murray Harris, who comes to the conclusion: "Given the high Christology of the Pauline letters, according to which Jesus shares the divine name and nature . . . it should generate no surprise if on occasion Paul should refer to Jesus by the generic title *theos*" [TG2316, ZG2536] [God] (1992:171).

As for Colossians 2:9, though Christ is not called "God" directly, the attribution of full deity is bold: "in Christ lives all the fullness of God in a human body." And in Titus 2:13, the Greek syntax favors the rendering "our great God and Savior, Jesus Christ." In the Greek, there is one article governing the two titles "God" and "Savior Jesus Christ" joined by the conjunction *kai* [TG2532, ZG2779] (and). According to a Greek grammatical rule (commonly known as the "Granville Sharp Rule"), this structure indicates that the two nouns describe one person. In this case, Jesus Christ is both God and Savior. Furthermore, Paul never used the word "appearing" when speaking of God the Father (cf. John 1:18; 1 Tim 6:16). This refers only to Christ, with reference to his first coming (2 Tim 1:10) or his second coming (1 Tim 6:14; 2 Tim 4:1, 8). Several English versions affirm this interpretation by setting "Jesus Christ" in clear apposition to "our great God and Savior"—for example, see NIV, NRSV, and NLT.[1]

The two poetic assertions of Christ's deity in Philippians 2:6 then lead to a most amazing idea: Christ (as preincarnate) did not consider his equality with God as "something to cling to." This has yielded several interpretations (see notes on 2:6), the most interesting of which is that Christ chose not to cling to this equality; rather, he did not consider his equality with God as providing him with an opportunity for grasping—that is, as a matter of seizing upon this equality to his own advantage. Christ did not consider being equal with God as something to further his own ends. As God, Christ is not an acquisitional being, grasping and seizing. He is self-giving for the sake of others (Fee 1995:211).

The next verse in the Christ Poem (2:7) begins with the enigmatic expression, "he emptied himself." Readers have interpreted this differently throughout the ages. One cause for the differing interpretations is that the text does not say what he emptied himself of. Thus, various interpreters have felt compelled to discern what Jesus must have emptied himself of. The NLT text has supplied one prevalent notion: "he gave up his divine privileges." This gap filling promotes the notion that Christ gave up certain privileges (whatever those were) when he became man, but he did not give up his divine nature. Most theologians would concur: the incarnated Jesus Christ was still fully God while being fully man. But what privileges did he give up? Perhaps his omniscience. Most likely his omnipresence. But even these points can be debated.

Thus, it is best not to say that he gave anything up in emptying himself. Rather, it is best to picture the emptying as pouring himself out, the ultimate expression of divine self-denial (cf. 2 Cor 8:9). Another way to look at the "emptying of himself" is to conceive of it as the emptying out of one *morphē* [TG3444, ZG3671] (the "form"—of God) into another *morphē* (the "form"—of a servant). Thus, the next clause ("taking the form of a servant") explains the end result of the emptying. In short, the Son of God assumed a new mode of being. There is no indication that he relinquished his divinity (or divine equality) in any way. As Hawthorne put it: "In becoming human, he did not cease to be divine. At the incarnation, Christ became more than God, not less than God" (1983:88). He became the God-man.

The notion that Jesus became a slave or servant means that he became the Father's servant to carry out his will, even if that will meant death by crucifixion for the servant. Paul was most likely thinking of the Suffering Servant of Isaiah 52:13–53:12. In this Servant Song, the Servant of the Lord suffers for the sins of many, is put to death by the will of God, and then passes into glory and exaltation. Paul's poem follows the same pattern and reflects the same ideas—namely, that the Servant is debased, despised, killed by others who do not recognize him, but subsequently raised to glory by God because the Servant becomes the atoning sacrifice for sin. The Servant Song begins with an oracle in which the Lord announces the exaltation of his Servant (Isa 52:13-15), continues with a description of the Servant's sufferings, then concludes with an oracle in which the Lord vindicates the Servant's exaltation (Isa 53:10-12). So Paul's poem begins with exalted statements about Christ's deity, moves into a poetic description of his suffering, and concludes with Christ's exaltation far above all the beings in the universe.

In order to become the Father's servant, the Son participated in humanity. Paul specifically described this as, literally, "becoming in the likeness of humans" (2:7b). This "becoming" was a truly generative and transformational event (see note above). The same verb was used by John in the famous statement, "the Word became human" (John 1:14). Both Paul and John were saying that the Son of God became what he never was prior to the Incarnation: he became human. However, Paul added that the Son of God became "in the *likeness* of humans [was born as a human being]" (emphasis added). Does this mean that he was only human-like but not truly human? The language could permit this interpretation—after all, what human being ever had a divine origin and had no sin? Thus, Jesus was unlike all other human beings. Paul's language, more than anything, suggests that Jesus Christ was similar to humans in that he was fully human yet not totally like humans in that he did not have fallen humanity (see Rom 8:3).

Paul immediately followed the poetic statement "becoming in the likeness of humans" with another line that says, literally, "and being discovered in appearance as human." It could be argued that this second statement simply reiterates the first as nothing more than poetic enhancement or Hebraistic parallelism. However, the second line functions to emphasize that Jesus was considered human by the humans that came in contact with him. To them he appeared as they were—fully human. For one who was and is divine, this was an act of humiliation. This was the consequence of the Incarnation and another manifestation of the Son of God being willing to empty himself. Thus, as Paul used two expressions in 2:6 to describe Christ's nature and mode of being as deity, so in 2:7 Paul used two expressions to describe Christ's nature and mode of being as human. In short, he lived like a man because he was a man. Of course, this was an act of humility for one who by nature also was God and had lived as God.

This position of humility is explicitly stated in the Greek in the very next line, literally rendered "he humbled himself." This statement is parallel to the statement "he emptied himself" in 2:7 (cf. "gave up his divine privileges," NLT). The "empty-ing" was the "humbling" and vice versa. The pithy statement, "he humbled him-self," does not point to a specific event per se, such as the Incarnation (although that is included); rather, it embraces all that Christ did beginning with his incarnation leading up to his humiliating crucifixion—and all that is in between, from his birth to his death. Christ constantly expressed humility throughout his ministry, telling his disciples that he came not to be served but to serve and to give his life as a ran-som for many (Mark 10:45—a clear reference to the Servant's Song in Isa 52:13–53:12). Jesus constantly proclaimed that he was carrying out his Father's will in what he did and in what he said (see John 5:19-24).

Jesus' humble servanthood was constantly displayed in acts of obedience to the will of another, namely his Father. Eventually, Jesus' constant submission would bring him to do the unthinkable: experience death, even death by crucifixion. It was one thing for Jesus to experience human birth and human life; now he would expe-rience human death. The immortal would experience mortality. Jesus' anguish in the garden of Gethsemane on the evening before his death testifies to the fact that Jesus struggled with this before fully submitting to the Father's will by saying, "If it is possible, let this cup of suffering be taken away from me. Yet I want your will to be done, not mine" (Matt 26:39-42). The ultimate act of obedience was Jesus' crucifix-ion, an excruciating form of execution.

Crucifixion was practiced first by the Medes and Persians and later by Alexander the Great (356–323 BC) and the Romans. Both Greeks and Romans restricted its use to slaves, considering it too barbaric for their citizens. This is best illustrated in the famous story of the slave uprising led by Spartacus in the first century BC. Captured in war and made a Roman gladiator, Spartacus eventually escaped with 70 other men. While in hiding on Mount Vesuvius, he gathered a large army of rebel slaves from Italy's farms. His army made some significant victories, gaining most of south-ern Italy. They would have been able to escape to freedom over the Alps had not Spartacus's troops urged him to attack Rome. They were defeated in this attempt, and Spartacus himself died in battle. All the other captured rebel slaves—and there were hundreds if not thousands of them—were crucified all along the Appian Way, as a warning to other slaves in Italy.

The Romans extended the use of crucifixion to foreign criminals, but even so, it was used mainly for crimes against the government. This is why Barabbas, a revolu-tionary (Gr. lēstēs [TG3027, ZG3334]) against Rome, was supposed to be crucified (John 18:40). In his place, Jesus was crucified. Jesus was also considered a revolutionary (lēstēs) by the authorities who arrested him (Matt 26:55; Mark 14:48). Of course, the political charges against him were trumped up by the Jewish leaders. Even Pilate knew that Jesus had no aspirations to overthrow Rome. Nonetheless, he was cruci-fied on the grounds that he claimed to be a king.

Crucifixion was universally recognized as the worst type of execution. The con-demned criminal was brutally beaten and forced to carry the crossbeam to the spot where a stake had already been erected. A tablet stating the crime was often placed around the offender's neck and was fastened to the cross during the execution. The victim was tied or nailed to the crossbeam (with the nails through the wrists, since the bones in the hand could not take the weight). The beam was then raised and fixed to the upright pole. If the executioners planned a slow, agonizing death, they could drive blocks into the stake for a seat or a step to support the feet. Death came about through loss of blood circulation, followed by coronary collapse. Since that could take days, sometimes the executioners broke the victim's legs below the knees with a club, thereby eliminating any further possibility of easing the pressure on the wrists, and the victim would soon die. Usually a body was left on the cross to rot, but in some instances the body was given to relatives or friends for burial, as was the case with Jesus.[2]

Jesus suffered the worst death, that of crucifixion. In the Christ Poem, Paul does not speak of the spiritual significance of that death, as he did in so many other epistles. He did not say that this death was the sacrifice for sins of the world or for redemption. Rather, he simply stated the bare reality: "he humbled himself in obedience to God and died a criminal's death on a cross." This bareness of expression coincides with the four Gospel writers' narrative of Jesus' crucifixion wherein they simply state "they crucified him" without giving any descriptive details (Matt 27:31; Mark 15:24; Luke 23:33; John 19:18). Since readers were very aware of crucifixion, no details were necessary.

Early Christians later came to highly honor the cross, so much so that many scribes making copies of the New Testament writings wrote the word *stauros* [TG4716, ZG5089] (cross) as a *nomen sacrum* (a sacred title), along with the other divine titles, "Lord," "Christ," "Jesus," "God," and "Spirit."[3] Specifically, the scribe of 𝔓46 (a second-century manuscript) wrote this as a *nomen sacrum* in Philippians 2:8. He and other scribes (probably earlier than him) took a despised symbol and glorified it by giving it elevated status. Christians came to realize that Jesus being lifted up on the cross was the first step of his glorification, a glorification that was consummated by his resurrection and ascension (see John 12:24).

Throughout the first strophe (2:5-8), all the action has been that of the Son. He is the one who has existed in the form of God. He is the one who chose not to grasp his equality with God. He is the one who emptied himself. He is the one who took the form of a slave. He is the one who humbled himself. He is the one who became obedient even to the point of death. Having given himself over to death, he was now dependent on the Father to take over from there.

At the beginning of the second strophe (2:9), God the Father intervenes and takes action. This section is introduced in the Greek by the inferential word *dio* [TG1352, ZG1475], meaning "wherefore" or "therefore." It signals that God the Father was about to act because of what Jesus had done. Because Jesus went to the lowest depths, the Father raised him to the highest heights. Because Jesus was willing to submit to the will of the Father, even when that meant death on a cross, God the Father elevated him to the highest place in the universe.

Paul used an unusual verb to describe this exaltation, a word he never used else-where in his writings and one that does not appear elsewhere in the New Testament. The word *huperupsōsen* [TG5251, ZG5671] means to "super-exalt." The passive voice indi-cates that this was done to Jesus by the Father. Since Jesus had abandoned himself to his Father's will and given himself over to death, he was at the mercy of his Father, if you will, with regard to what would happen to him thereafter. He had to trust that the Father would raise him from the dead. The Father did this and, in so doing, showed Jesus to be the Son of God (see Rom 1:3-4). Though Paul did not use the term "resurrect" here, it is inherent in the exaltation. It should be noted that Jesus' ascension and enthronement are also inherent in the verb *huperupsōsene* because Jesus' exaltation was consummated with his ascension and enthronement. With one powerful, innovative verb, Paul captured the full sweep of Jesus' exaltation—from the Cross through resurrection to ascension and enthronement.

Jesus' exaltation was accompanied by the Father giving his Son the name above every name. What name is this? There are two options: "Jesus" or "Lord." The name in the next verse is specified as "Jesus" (2:10). If this is the name, then the sense is that the most exalted name in the universe is now the personal name of the God-man, Jesus of Nazareth. Since the Nazarene already had this name from birth, the Father did not give him this name in ascension. Rather, the Father gave new significance to the name *Jesus* in that it is now equated with *the Lord*. The "name" given to Jesus can be found in 2:11, which says that every tongue should confess that the "Lord" is "Jesus Christ."

Philippians 2:11 contains a citation of Isaiah 45:23, which says that "every knee will bend to me" (wherein the "me" is Yahweh) "and every tongue will confess alle-giance to me." That Paul substitutes "Lord" for the "me" (= "Yahweh") is to say that Jesus was granted the name "Lord" as being equal to Yahweh. Paul's use of Isaiah 45:23 is very significant, especially when seen in context:

> Let all the world look to me for salvation! For I am God; there is no
> other. I have sworn by my own name; I have spoken the truth, and I
> will never go back on my word: Every knee will bend to me, and every
> tongue will confess allegiance to me. The people will declare, "The Lord
> [Yahweh] is the source of all my righteousness and strength." (Isaiah
> 45:22-24)

In this passage the Lord (Yahweh) himself is declaring his uniqueness and pro-claiming that all people should worship him. Thus, for Paul to incorporate this prophecy into the Christ Poem was his way of saying that Jesus is the Lord (Yahweh), worthy of worship from all creatures in the universe. In other words, the identification of Jesus as "Lord" is the same as saying that he is Yahweh. Fee writes: "This emphasis on Yahweh, 'the Lord,' as the one unto whom all shall give obei-sance, seems to certify that what Paul has in mind is none other than *the* name, Yahweh itself, but in its Greek form of 'the Lord,' which has now been 'given' to Jesus" (1995:222).

Fee's statement that "Lord" is the Greek form of "Yahweh" calls for some explana-tion. The translators of the Septuagint consistently used *kurios* [TG2962, ZG3261] (Lord) as a translation of the Hebrew tetragrammaton YHWH (*yhwh* [TH3068, ZH3378]). This probably stemmed from the Jewish tradition that the name of Yahweh should never be pronounced. Thus, when they read their scriptures orally, they substituted *adonay* [TH136, ZH151] (Lord) for YHWH. It was only logical when making a Greek translation for the translators to use *kurios* for Yahweh. The early Christians then transferred this title to Jesus, calling him *kurios* (Lord).

For the early Christians, the risen Jesus was "the Lord." In his first sermon Peter said, "God has made this Jesus, whom you crucified, to be both Lord and Messiah" (Acts 2:36). For Paul, one's confession of Jesus as "Lord" was the true mark that the one making the confession was a true believer. This is clearly stipulated in Romans 10:9: "If you confess with your mouth that Jesus is Lord and believe in your heart that God raised him from the dead, you will be saved." Paul emphasized that no one could say that "Jesus is Lord" without the empowering of the Holy Spirit (1 Cor 12:3).

In the last verses of the poem in Philippians (2:10-11), Paul extends the confession of Jesus' lordship beyond Christians to include "every knee" and "every tongue"—even more, every one "in heaven and on earth and under the earth." It appears that the poem becomes eschatological at this point, in that it shifts from Jesus Christ's exaltation (via resurrection and ascension) to some unspecified event or time in the future wherein every knee will bow to the name *Jesus* and "every tongue confess that Jesus Christ is Lord." This could be the *parousia* [TG3952, ZG4242], the time of Christ's second coming. As such, the poem begins in eternity, where Christ the Son lived as God, then moves on to Jesus' incarnation, his life on earth as a servant, his crucifixion, his exaltation, and his second coming.

As to the matter of whether the confession is predictive ("every tongue will confess") or conditional/optional ("every tongue should confess"), this depends upon which textual variant is followed (see note on 2:11). Either way, the scope is universal. It includes all intelligent beings: (1) the ones "in heaven" probably being the spiritual powers such as angels and demons; (2) the ones "on earth" probably being all those alive at the time of Christ's *parousia* [TG3952, ZG4242]; and (3) the ones under the earth being the dead. As such, is the poem *saying* or *hoping* that all creatures will be saved by recognizing that Jesus is Lord? Given Paul's statements elsewhere about all the heavens and the earth coming under Christ's headship (Eph 1:9-10), all creation awaiting full salvation (Rom 8:19-24), and God's reconciliation of all things in heaven and on earth through Christ (Col 1:19-20), it would seem that the poem is expressing divine aspirations for all creation. In short, it is the hope of God that every intelligent being in this universe might proclaim openly and gladly that Jesus Christ has the right to reign (so Lightfoot 1976:115).

The last line of the Christ Poem indicates that the Father is glorified in the end. The Father is so pleased that all creatures in this universe should confess the highest name in the universe: Jesus Christ the Lord. Because of his spiritual journey through incarnation, crucifixion, resurrection, and exaltation, Jesus the Lord has now acquired the most preeminent name. No other name is higher, not even Yahweh. Jews, Muslims, and Jehovah's Witnesses all claim to worship the one true God but refuse to recognize that the one true God has given his Son the highest name in the universe, the name by which all people can be saved.

By way of conclusion, it should be said that the citation of this poem stresses Jesus' servanthood as the preeminent example for Christians. Jesus demonstrated his servanthood to his Father throughout his earthly ministry in the presence of his disciples. Jesus depicted this servant's role during his last days with his disciples by giving them the memorable illustration of washing their feet (John 13:1-17). Three of his actions reflect the greater act of Jesus' humility: leaving his position as the glorious God, becoming God's servant as a man, and returning to his glorious state as the God-man. The first step is presented in the description, "He got up from the table, took off his robe, [and] wrapped a towel around his waist" (John 13:4). This presents Jesus' willingness to divest himself of deity's privileges and leave his state of glory for the purpose of becoming a servant to humanity. The next step is described as follows: He "poured water into a basin. Then he began to wash the disciples' feet, drying them with the towel he had around him" (John 13:5). This reveals his ministry as God's servant to humanity. And the final step is as follows: "After washing their feet, he put on his robe again and sat down" (John 13:12). This completes the symbolic act; it depicts Jesus' return to his former glory after finishing his service to humanity on earth. Once willingly divested of coequal glory with the Father in order to be a servant, he now resumes his former position. The entire scene is very close to what Paul verbalized in Philippians 2:5-11. John 13:3-12 provides the portrait, Philippians 2:5-11 the caption (see Comfort 1994:113).

After Jesus gave his disciples a vivid illustration of servanthood, he told them to follow his example by becoming servants to one another (John 13:15-16). This is the point Paul was making to the Philippians: Christ's example of servanthood is the model for Christian unity and community. Christians need to have their minds spiritually renewed so as to emulate his model in a living way.

ENDNOTES
1. The same kind of grammatical formulation appears in 2 Thess 1:12, which can be interpreted to mean that Paul was calling Jesus "our God and Lord" (see commentary on 2 Thess 1:12).
2. These three paragraphs were adapted from my work, *Encountering the Manuscripts: An Introduction to New Testament Paleography and Textual Criticism* (Nashville: Broadman & Holman, 2005), ch 4.
3. For a full discussion of the *nomina sacra*, see my work, *Encountering the Manuscripts: An Introduction to New Testament Paleography and Textual Criticism* (Nashville: Broadman & Holman, 2005), ch 4.

◆ III. Encouragement to Emulate Christ (2:12–3:21)
A. Shine for Christ, Be an Offering to God (2:12–18)

[12]Dear friends, you always followed my instructions when I was with you. And now that I am away, it is even more im- portant. Work hard to show the results of your salvation, obeying God with deep reverence and fear. [13]For God is working

in you, giving you the desire and the power to do what pleases him.

¹⁴Do everything without complaining and arguing, ¹⁵so that no one can criticize you. Live clean, innocent lives as children of God, shining like bright lights in a world full of crooked and perverse people. ¹⁶Hold firmly to the word of life; then, on the day of Christ's return, I will be proud that I did not run the race in vain and that my work was not useless. ¹⁷But I will rejoice even if I lose my life, pouring it out like a liquid offering to God,* just like your faithful service is an offering to God. And I want all of you to share that joy. ¹⁸Yes, you should rejoice, and I will share your joy.

2:17 Greek *I will rejoice even if I am to be poured out as a liquid offering.*

NOTES

2:12a *you always followed my instructions.* Lit., "as always you obeyed." It is debated whether Paul was speaking of the Philippians having obeyed him as to some particular instructions or whether he was speaking of their obedience to Christ. If the former, then we should try to ascertain what Paul instructed them when he was with them. But this is hard to do from the short history of Paul's visit to Philippi, as provided in Acts 16. Thus, it is just as likely that he was urging them to be obedient to Christ.

2:12b-13a *Work hard to show the results of your salvation . . . For God is working in you.* Lit., "work out your own salvation . . . for God is the one working in you." The combination of statements seems oxymoronic: How can a believer work out his or her own salvation when it is God, not the believer, who is the one working? The reader is left to ponder Paul's intention in writing this. Perhaps Paul wanted his readers to realize that they must live with the tension that Christians must work out the results of their salvation—yet not by their own power but rather by the power of God. The emphasis seems to be a cooperative effort. Christians must know their own human responsibility in taking advantage of God's Spirit and his work in their lives. From a theological viewpoint, 2:12-13 demonstrates the balance between the Arminian position (work out your own salvation) and the Calvinist perspective (God works our salvation).

2:14 *Do everything without complaining and arguing.* As noted before, the chief problem at Philippi was dissension (see commentary on 1:27–2:4).

2:15 *so that no one can criticize you.* Lit., "that you may become blameless" (according to some mss—א B C D¹ 044 0278 1739 𝔐), or "that you may be blameless" (according to other mss—𝔓46 A D* F G). The first variant reading suggests process; the second, state of being. It is difficult to determine which is original.

Live clean, innocent lives as children of God . . . in a world full of crooked and perverse people. Though it is not a direct quote, this phrasing comes from Deut 32:5.

2:16 *Hold firmly to the word of life.* Or, "hold out the word of life" as giving witness to others. Both meanings are inherent in the expression. The Philippians were being encouraged to hold to the word of life and thereby stand firm in their faith against the attacks of external opponents. The Philippians were also being encouraged to offer the word of life to others for their acceptance (O'Brien 1991:297).

on the day of Christ's return. Lit., "in the day of Christ," referring to Christ's parousia.

I did not run the race in vain. Paul frequently used athletic imagery, especially related to running a race (see 3:12-14; 1 Cor 9:24, 26-27; Gal 2:2; 5:7; 2 Tim 4:7).

2:17 *pouring it out like a liquid offering.* In the OT, Jews poured out a libation of wine on a sacrifice or at the base of the altar on which the sacrifice lay. The drink offering was the culmination of offerings that symbolized full dedication to God—namely, the burnt offering, together with the meal offering, and the peace offering (Exod 29:38-42; Lev 2; 6:14-18; Num 15:1-10; 28:3-8; 29:30).

service. The Greek word *leitourgia* [TG3009, ZG3311] was used in Greek literature to describe the service individuals freely gave to the state. In the NT, it was usually used of priestly service, whether of the temple priests (Luke 1:23) or of Christians (2 Cor 9:12). It was used in the early church to denote the ministry of anyone working in the church (see *1 Clement* 9:2; 44:2-6).

COMMENTARY

With a flow of seemingly disconnected images, Paul exhorted the Philippians to obey, to work out their salvation, to be the pure children of God in the midst of a crooked world, to hold onto the word of life (so that Paul would not have run his race in vain), to be faithful in their service as a sacrifice to God (over which Paul would gladly pour himself out as a libation offering), and to rejoice with Paul in their shared joy. The reader has no choice but to pause in this section and ask: What is Paul trying to say? And what do all these images have to do with one another? Is there a connection, a link from image to image?

Before we try to link together Paul's images, we need to place this section in the whole of Philippians. After reading the awesome Christ Poem in 2:6-11, the reader is immediately confronted with a series of exhortations that seem to come out of nowhere. But it must be remembered that this exhortation had begun in 1:27 and continued until 2:5, where the Christ Poem commences; then the exhortation continues again in 2:12 to 2:18. Thus, the Christ Poem is the centerpiece of a long exordium.

> Exhortation (1:27–2:5)
> Christ Poem (2:6-11)
> Exhortation (2:12-18)

The exhortation begun in 1:25–2:5 is continued and filled out in 2:12-18. When the two sections are read as a unit, it becomes clear that nearly all the language and images of 2:12-18 can be linked to previous statements in 1:25–2:5. The following chart illustrates this (translation by author). It presents the thought from 2:12-18 first (noted as "b") linking to a thought in 1:25–2:5 (noted as "a"):

PHILIPPIANS 1:25–2:5	PHILIPPIANS 2:12-18
A. Paul's statement about whether he came to see the Philippians again or just heard about them (1:27)	A′. Paul's exhortation to obedience whether he was present or not (2:12)
B. A sign of the Philippians' salvation (1:28a)	B′. "Work hard to show the results of your salvation" (2:12)
C. This salvation is from God (1:28b)	C′. "God is working in you" (2:13)
D. "Don't be selfish; don't try to impress others." (2:3)	D′. "Do everything without complaining and arguing" (2:14)
E. "Live as citizens of heaven" (1:27); "Don't be intimidated in any way by your enemies" (1:28)	E′. Blameless "children of God" in the midst of a crooked world (2:15)

PHILIPPIANS 1:25–2:5 (cont.)	PHILIPPIANS 2:12-18 (cont.)
F. "fighting together for the faith, which is the Good News" (1:27)	F! "Hold firmly to the word of life" (2:16)
G. "fighting together" (lit., "being athletes together") for the faith (1:27); "We are in this struggle together" (1:30)	G! So that Paul had not run in vain (2:16)
H. "You have seen my struggle in the past, and you know that I am still in the midst of it" (1:30)	H! Paul poured out as a drink offering (2:17)
I. "You have been given the privilege of suffering for him" (1:29)	I! The Philippians' faithful service was an offering to God (2:17)
J. The exhortation to make Paul joyful (2:2)	J! The anticipation of shared joy (2:18)

The exhortation to the Philippians that Paul began in chapter 1 is completed in 2:18. He was concerned that they continue to follow Christ with wholehearted obedience whether or not he (Paul) was there to monitor and encourage their spiritual lives (1:27; 2:12). This obedience would be the working out of their salvation—in cooperation with God who was working in them (1:28; 2:12-13). In this context, this "salvation" is not initial deliverance from sin; rather, it is the complete, eschatological salvation in the sense of the believers becoming conformed to the image of Christ through the process of suffering with Christ and knowing the power of his resurrection (a process Paul was personally undergoing and encouraging all the believers in Philippi to emulate—see 3:7-17 and comments). Suffering at the hands of enemies of the gospel was part of the process of this salvation (1:28-29). The Philippians had to remain firm, like a team of athletes or a united group of soldiers, in their resolve to experience this salvation to its completed goal. This is the "salvation" Paul was speaking of in 2:12-13. Their part was to remain faithful and reliant on the empowerment of God, who was working *in* and *among* them to accomplish his purpose—that of transforming the believers into the image of Christ. This process will be consummated at the Resurrection when the believers are bodily transfigured even as Christ was (3:21), and it is at this time that the believers will experience Jesus as the ultimate "Savior" (3:20)—a title that was rarely used by Paul and therefore held great significance. Thus, the ultimate salvation believers are looking forward to will come when the Savior Jesus returns in his parousia at the time of the Resurrection and transfiguration of the believers' bodies, consummating the process of salvation. Paul yearned to participate in that ultimate salvation (3:11), and he wanted the Philippians to participate as well.

In light of that ultimate salvation, Paul encouraged the Philippians to be (or, "become"—see note on 2:15) the blameless children of God in the midst of a crooked, perverse world (2:15). This is a further explanation of what it means to live as the citizens of heaven while still on earth (1:27). God has always wanted a corporate testimony of his holy presence in a group of people shining out to the surrounding nations (Gen 12:1-3; Deut 4:6; Josh 4:24; Pss 45:17; 126:1-3; Isa 2:2-3; 14:1; Ezek 37:22-28). He wants this from the church (Matt 5:14), and he will ultimately achieve it in the New Jerusalem (Rev 21:22-25).

The surrounding, unbelieving nations have always been at odds with this divine plan. They are enemies of the gospel. As such, the believers must hold firmly to the apostolic truths of the gospel (1:27), which is the word of life (2:16). Jesus said that his message is spirit and life (John 6:63). After his resurrection, he commissioned the apostles to proclaim the word of life (Acts 5:20). This is the message that gives spiritual life (*zoē* [TG2222, ZG2437]) to those who receive it. The Philippians became believers by receiving the message of life (1:5); they needed to hold on to that life-giving message, as well as proclaim it to others and thereby continue to be Paul's co-workers in proclaiming the gospel (1:5).

Paul also exhorted the Philippians to stand together as a team of athletes, striving to advance the gospel (1:28-30; see notes). Their achievements, their victories in this regard, would also be his. Their failures would also be his, which is why he told them that they needed to remain firm until the day of Christ's return so that he (Paul) would not have run the race in vain (2:16). They were in the contest together, on the same team. One member's loss was loss for all; one member's gain was gain for all.

Paul could shift from athletic imagery to sacrificial imagery because he viewed the athletic contest as an agonizing ordeal (1:29-30) that could possibly lead to death. Even in our own times, great athletes are often spoken of as being those who have sacrificed themselves for the sake of the team. Thus, Paul in one breath could speak of "not [running] the race in vain" (2:16) and in the next breath, "even if I lose my life, pouring it out like a liquid offering" (2:17a)—a drink offering poured out upon the sacrifice of the Philippians' service (2:17b). As such, Paul viewed his sacrifice not as a solo event but rather as a completion, a crowning of the Philippians' sacrificial service in advancing the gospel. Their shared sufferings would bring shared joys in the eschaton, even as team members share together a sweet victory after great personal sacrifice (2:18).

The model for this sacrifice is Jesus Christ, whom Paul extolled in an awesome poem, a poem that speaks of the greatest sacrifice ever displayed in human history (2:5-9). The Son of God gave up his mode of living as God and took on the form of a servant in order to live as a man who became obedient to the will of the Father, an obedience that cost him his life, even in the worst way imaginable—by death on a cross. But this sacrifice brought about the greatest joy: Jesus was exalted to the highest place in the universe, to be proclaimed as "Lord" by all the beings in this universe. As the writer of Hebrews put it so well: "Because of the joy awaiting him, he endured the cross, disregarding its shame" (Heb 12:2).

Paul viewed the Philippians' service to the Lord as a sacrifice of faith upon which he would pour out his life as a drink offering. Since they had displayed sacrificial faith and loving service, what would be more fitting than for Paul to crown that consecration with the drink offering of his life? Thus, Paul considered his suffering a libation (see 2 Tim 4:6) poured out to consummate the Philippians' faithful service (see Rom 12:1; 15:16). Paul's offering could refer to his present suffering or to the blood of his death, if he were to die as a martyr.

◆ B. Timothy: An Example of Selflessness (2:19-24)

¹⁹If the Lord Jesus is willing, I hope to send Timothy to you soon for a visit. Then he can cheer me up by telling me how you are getting along. ²⁰I have no one else like Timothy, who genuinely cares about your welfare. ²¹All the others care only for themselves and not for what matters to Jesus Christ. ²²But you know how Timothy has proved himself. Like a son with his father, he has served with me in preaching the Good News. ²³I hope to send him to you just as soon as I find out what is going to happen to me here. ²⁴And I have confidence from the Lord that I myself will come to see you soon.

NOTES

2:19 *Timothy.* The name *Timotheos* [TG5095, ZG5510] means "one who honors God." He lived his name by faithfully serving God.

2:20 *I have no one else like Timothy.* Lit., "for I have no one equal-minded." The last word in Greek is *isopsuchon* [TG2473, ZG2701], a word similar to that in 2:6, which says that Christ is all things *equal* with God (*to einai isa theō* [TG2470, ZG2698]). Among all of Paul's co-workers, Timothy was the one who most cared for the church in Philippi. In this way especially he was like Paul.

2:21 *All the others care only for themselves.* Lit., "all seek the things of themselves"—a sweeping condemnation like the ones Paul used in Rom 3:10-18, especially 3:11, which says, "no one is seeking God." These kinds of sweeping statements are obviously hyperbolic.

what matters to Jesus Christ. Lit., "the things of Jesus Christ." In the context of Philippians, this refers to people seeking Christlikeness.

2:24 *I have confidence from the Lord.* Lit., "I have confidence in the Lord." This is Paul's typical way of speaking of his union with Jesus Christ the Lord.

I myself will come to see you soon. This statement shows that this is the last of the Prison Epistles, written when Paul knew the verdict was about to be given.

COMMENTARY

This section of Philippians (2:19-24) and the next (2:25-30) are the kind of sections in several of Paul's other epistles that usually appear at the end of the letter inasmuch as they are commendations of certain individuals about to be sent to the church Paul was addressing (see Rom 16; 1 Cor 16:10-18; Eph 6:21-22; Col 4:7-17; Titus 3:12-13). The placement of these two sections, followed by 3:1 (see note), suggests that Paul was about to conclude his letter but then went on. However, it is also just as likely that these two sections were purposely placed where they are because both individuals—Timothy and Epaphroditus—serve as living examples of what it means to have the kind of mind Christ had (2:4-5) and in one fashion or another modeled Christlike attributes noted in the Christ Poem (2:5-11).

. Timothy is mentioned for the second time in this epistle (see 1:1). The first occurrence, in verse one, gives the impression that he was a cowriter with Paul of this epistle. However, it becomes immediately evident from 1:3 on that Paul was the sole author. This is nowhere clearer than in this section, where Paul is speaking about Timothy. (Timothy's identification as co-sender of the epistle may stem from his role in bearing and interpreting it to the Philippians; see commentary below.)

Timothy's first appearance in Scripture is in Acts 16:1-3, in which we discover that his mother was a Jewish believer in Jesus Christ, while his father was a gentile Greek. In other writings, we learn that he had a heritage of faith in his mother Eunice and grandmother Lois (2 Tim 1:5). Paul became Timothy's spiritual father by discipling Timothy. It is in this way that Paul refers to him as "my true son" (1 Tim 1:2). Timothy, who was well spoken of by the believers at Lystra and Iconium (Acts 16:2), became Paul's companion and assistant on his second missionary journey at Lystra. He traveled with Paul into Europe following the Macedonian vision. The Philippians personally knew Timothy because he had accompanied Paul on his initial trip to Philippi (see 1:1; Acts 16:11-12; 17:15; 18:5). After being in Philippi, Paul traveled on to Thessalonica and then to Berea with Silas and Timothy. When Paul decided to go to Athens, he left Silas and Timothy at Berea to establish the church there (Acts 17:14). Timothy and Silas eventually joined Paul in Corinth (Acts 18:5). Timothy next appears with Paul in Ephesus on his third journey (Acts 19:22), and from there Paul sent him into Macedonia (the province in which Philippi was located). Thus, the Philippians would have had at least two visits from Timothy and would have known him well.

Paul did not need to introduce Timothy to the Philippians or send his commendations concerning him. This is evident when Paul says, "You know how Timothy has proved himself" (2:22). Paul was simply informing the Philippians that he intended to send Timothy to them. Such notifications were routine for Paul. In fact, when Paul mentioned Timothy in his letters, it was often in connection with Timothy having been sent by him or beckoned by him to accomplish this or that task (see Acts 19:22; 1 Cor 4:17; 16:10; 1 Thess 3:2, 6; 2 Tim 4:9, 13). During his work with Paul, Timothy was never the commander of operations or sender. He was always Paul's emissary sent to carry out Paul's will.

In this regard, Timothy exhibited one important truth expressed in the Christ Poem (2:5-11)—namely, the Son's devotion to the Father so as to obey him and be sent by him. Timothy's attitude of serving with Paul like a son with his father reflects what Jesus did in pleasing his Father. While the Son could have retained equality with God, he chose servitude and submission. The same could be said for Timothy inasmuch as he willingly chose to serve with Paul rather than compete against him. Timothy put himself in the position of being Paul's sent one. Because Timothy was so subservient to Paul, he was exalted by Paul when he said, "I have no one else like Timothy" (2:20). This reflects what God the Father did in exalting Jesus, the ultimate servant, giving him the name above every name (2:9). As Paul's sent one, Timothy had the task of communicating to the Philippians what was on Paul's mind. If the Philippians had any questions of Paul's letter, Timothy would have been the first and chief interpreter of it—which is probably why Timothy is mentioned as a coauthor of the epistle (1:1).

In the last two verses of this section, we see again the perplexity of Paul's hopes and expectations related to his house arrest, trial, and eventual freedom. In 2:23 he says that he hoped to send Timothy to Philippi "as soon as I find out what is going to happen to me here." This statement gives the impression that Paul was somewhat uncertain of the outcome of his trial at Rome, an uncertainty he had expressed before as he tottered between thoughts of life and death (1:20-23). His next statement, however, affirms his certainty that he would be released from house-arrest: "I have confidence from the Lord that I myself will come to see you soon" (2:24). In this statement, Paul is not uncertain about the outcome of his trial, a certainty he had expressed earlier (1:19, 25-26; see notes).

◆ C. Epaphroditus, An Example of Servanthood (2:25-30)

²⁵Meanwhile, I thought I should send Epaphroditus back to you. He is a true brother, co-worker, and fellow soldier. And he was your messenger to help me in my need. ²⁶I am sending him because he has been longing to see you, and he was very distressed that you heard he was ill. ²⁷And he certainly was ill; in fact, he almost died. But God had mercy on him—and also on me, so that I would not have one sorrow after another.

²⁸So I am all the more anxious to send him back to you, for I know you will be glad to see him, and then I will not be so worried about you. ²⁹Welcome him with Christian love* and with great joy, and give him the honor that people like him deserve. ³⁰For he risked his life for the work of Christ, and he was at the point of death while doing for me what you couldn't do from far away.

2:29 Greek *in the Lord.*

NOTES

2:25 *Epaphroditus.* He is mentioned only here (2:25-30) and in 4:18. A Christian from Philippi, he had brought a gift from the church to Paul. This is not the same person known as Epaphras mentioned in Col 1:7 and Phlm 1:23.

brother, co-worker, and fellow soldier . . . your messenger to help me. In the Greek, Paul gives five ascriptions to Epaphroditus: *adelphos* [TG80, ZG81] (brother), *sunergos* [TG4904, ZG5301] (co-worker), *sustratiōtēs* [TG4961, ZG5369] (fellow soldier), *apostolos* [TG652, ZG693] (apostle), and *leitourgos* [TG3011, ZG3313] (priestly servant). The penultimate term ("apostle") does not mean that Epaphroditus was among the elite group of Jesus' twelve apostles; it indicates that Epaphroditus functioned as an emissary for the Philippians to Paul.

The last term is important to this passage (2:25-30) in that it appears in the first verse and the last. The term was often employed in classical Greek to describe public service rendered at the expense of the citizen. In biblical Greek, as Plummer has noted (1896:18), it is used "of priestly service in the worship of God" (Heb 8:6; 9:21; Num 8:22; 16:9; 18:4; 2 Chr 31:2) and also of service to the needy (2 Cor 9:12; Phil 2:30)." Paul also used this word in urging Christians to present their lives as living sacrifices to God, which is their priestly service (Rom 12:1). (For a good discussion of the word, see EDNT 2.347-349.)

2:26 *he has been longing to see you.* This reading is supported by ℵ* A C D I^vid 33 81 syr cop^bo. Other mss (ℵ² B F G 044 𝔐) read, "he has been longing for you all." 𝔓46^vid reads "he has been longing to send [word] to you." Though listed as "vid," (i.e., "apparently") the reading in 𝔓46 is quite certain (Comfort and Barrett 2001:324). The reading followed by NLT, which has good testimony, makes explicit what is already implicit in the other variant—namely, Epaphroditus wanted to see the Philippians so that they could be assured that he was no longer ill. Nonetheless, the resultant text reflects Pauline idiom (see Rom 1:11). The second variant could be the result of dittography—the scribe accidentally recopying *pempsai pros humas* [TG3992/4314, ZG4287/4639] from the previous verse. If this variant wasn't an error, it is possible that the scribe of 𝔓46 was thinking of Epaphroditus sending a message to the Philippians about his recovery. However, Paul felt there was no better way than to send Epaphroditus himself back to the Philippians.

2:27 *But God had mercy on him—and also on me.* Epaphroditus' recovery from a near-fatal illness was attributed to God's mercy, both on Epaphroditus and on Paul, who would have otherwise greatly grieved his loss.

2:29 *Welcome him with Christian love.* Lit., "welcome him in the Lord."

give him the honor that people like him deserve. Epaphroditus deserved their honor, for he risked his life for the work of Christ on their behalf as a sacrificial expression of his own devotion to Christ.

2:30 *he risked his life.* This reading has the solid support of 𝔓46 ℵ A B D F G cop^sa. A variant reading on this in the TR is "he had no regard for his life" (found in C 044 𝔐 syr). The participle in the first reading is *paraboleusamenos* [TG3851, ZG4129] (having risked); the variant is *parabouleusamenos* [TG3851A, ZG4131] (having no regard). There is only a one-letter difference in Greek between the two variants: the inclusion or omission of an *upsilon*. Both readings make good sense inasmuch as Epaphroditus risked his life for the work of Christ and in so doing showed that he didn't care about his life. However, the word behind the NLT, which has superior documentary support and appears only here in the NT, is more colorful in that it means that Epaphroditus "gambled with his life" (Lightfoot 1976:124). It is possible that Paul spoke of Epaphroditus "gambling [with] his life" because Aphrodite was the goddess of gambling, and gamblers throwing dice would yell out *epaphroditos* [TG1891, ZG2073], meaning "favorite of Aphrodite," hoping for good luck (Lees 1925:46). As such, Paul may have made a play on Epaphroditus's name.

the work of Christ. This reading has the support of 𝔓46 B F G (D 𝔐) it. Other manuscripts (ℵ A P 044 33 syr^h cop^bo) read "the work of the Lord," and one manuscript (C) reads "the work." Nowhere else does Paul use the term "the work of Christ," but he does use the phrase "the work of the Lord" in 1 Cor 15:58; 16:10. Therefore, it is quite likely that the first variant is an assimilation. Lightfoot (1976:124) prefers the second variant because it is the shortest and thereby explains the other two variants. "[The] discovery of 𝔓46, however, makes this position no longer tenable, because the three-pronged support of *tou Christou* by (proto-)Alexandrian (𝔓46 B 1739), 'Western' (D F G Old Latin Vulg), and Byzantine witnesses is overwhelming" (Silva 1992:163).

he was at the point of death. The Greek here (*mechri thanatou* [TG3360/2288, ZG3588/2505]) is the same as that in 2:8, suggesting that Paul was still thinking of Jesus' obedience "unto death" when speaking of Epaphroditus's sacrifice.

doing for me what you couldn't do from far away. Lit., "that he might fill up your lack of service to me." In saying this, Paul was not being pejorative. Rather, he was stating that Epaphroditus "had risked his life in order that he might fulfill his mission to Paul on behalf of Philippi" (Fee 1995:278). The Greek word for "service" (*leitourgias* [TG3009, ZG3311]) is the same used in 2:25 (see note).

COMMENTARY

In this section, Paul commends Epaphroditus, a messenger from the church at Philippi whom he was about to send back to them, probably with this letter. The Philippians had collected a monetary gift for Paul, which was brought by Epaphroditus from Philippi to Paul in his imprisonment (4:18). In those days, prisoners completely depended on the gifts of others for their survival. The state provided nothing. Thus, Paul was very appreciative of the Philippians' gift (probably a considerable sum of money) and the messenger, Epaphroditus, who risked his life to get that gift to Paul. Epaphroditus had become very sick in the process of delivering this gift to Paul. He continued his journey in spite of his sickness, which is why Paul said he "gambled with his life" (see note on 2:30). After he reached Paul with the gift from the Philippians, his sickness progressed to the extent that he nearly died. News of this must have come to the Philippians (2:26) because Paul received a message that the Philippians had heard of Epaphroditus's sickness. Paul reported how this news troubled Epaphroditus (2:26).

His illness caused everyone anxiety, especially since it had been precipitated by his mission on the behalf of the church in Philippi for Paul. The church would have been anxious, and Epaphroditus anxious for their anxiety, and Paul anxious for Epaphroditus's recovery. So God's mercy given to Epaphroditus was extended to Paul, and then that mercy would reach the Philippian Christians with the return of their fellow citizen and brother, Epaphroditus.

This passage shows how severe sickness—the kind that can lead to death—takes a toll on the victim as well as on the people close to that person. From my own personal experience, I know this very well. In 1990 my wife was diagnosed with terminal breast cancer that had spread to her bones. I was full of anxiety for her, our children, and myself—that I might lose my dear companion and bride. During those days, certain passages from the book of Philippians came to my mind. I thought about how Paul, when faced with death, expressed his perplexity. He was torn between two options: (1) to die and thereby go to be with Christ—which, from a personal perspective, was the better option, or (2) to live and thereby remain in the flesh—which, from the Philippians' perspective, was a better option (see 1:21-25). My wife shared the same perplexity. She would prefer death over suffering from cancer and cancer treatments—and yet she would rather stay alive for the sake of her loved ones, especially our children. Thus, what Paul chose she also chose. In her case, she went through a radical bone marrow transplant that nearly killed her but at the same time killed the cancer. By God's mercy and healing hand, she didn't die from the treatment but lived to be with her family and to tell her story in an inspiring book *Dying to Live*.

In those days I also thought about Paul's feelings for a beloved co-worker, Epaphroditus, who was so sick that he was about to die. Paul's feelings about Epaphroditus express my own about my wife—especially when Paul said, "God had mercy on him [so as to heal Epaphroditus]—and also on me, so that I would not have one sorrow after another" (2:27). His healing gave her life and me life—for if she had died, our children and I would have had sorrow upon sorrow. My constant prayer was that God would extend her life. And he did.

In the last two verses of this section (2:29-30), Paul commends Epaphroditus for his self-sacrificial service, and in so doing concludes the commendation begun in the first two verses (2:25-26). Paul had given kudos to Epaphroditus by calling him a brother, co-worker, fellow soldier, apostle, and priestly servant. This was high praise. He wasn't just Paul's Christian brother; he was also the apostle Paul's co-worker. And he wasn't just a co-worker; he was a fellow soldier—meaning he had battled next to Paul in fighting for the advancement of the gospel. Furthermore, he was an "apostle" (a sent one) from the Philippians to Paul (see note on 2:25), and he represented all the Philippians when he served as a minister to Paul's needs. He was also Paul's "sent one" (his "apostle") to the Philippians (2:28) inasmuch as he carried Paul's letter (possibly along with Timothy) back to them. It was customary for the carrier of the letter to have been present while the letter was composed so that he or she could explain it to its intended audience. In this regard, Epaphroditus would have been an interpreter of this epistle.

The first and last verses of this section speak of the "service" Epaphroditus did for Paul on behalf of the Christians at Philippi (see notes on 2:25, 30). Inherent in the word for "service" (*leitourgia* [TG3009, ZG3311]) is the idea of service to God. Thus, in serving Paul Epaphroditus was serving God. At the same time, he was rendering for the Philippians service to Paul in that he did for Paul what they could not do because they were far away.

Paul asked the Philippians to give Epaphroditus the honor that was due him because he had risked his life, literally, coming "to the point of death" (*mechri thanatou* [TG3360/2288, ZG3588/2505]) in Christian service. This again parallels the Christ Poem in that the Father greatly honored his Son, Jesus, giving him the name that is above every name, because the Son was obedient unto death (*mechri thanatou*). As such, Epaphroditus became a model of one who had the same kind of thinking Christ had (2:4-5)—namely, that of self-sacrificial service for the good of others. Those who sacrifice in service should not do it to gain glory for themselves. The glory and honor will come from God, whether in this lifetime or in the next.

◆   ## D. Encouragement to Rely on Christ (3:1-3)

Whatever happens, my dear brothers and sisters,* rejoice in the Lord. I never get tired of telling you these things, and I do it to safeguard your faith.

²Watch out for those dogs, those people who do evil, those mutilators who say you must be circumcised to be saved. ³For we who worship by the Spirit of God* are the ones who are truly circumcised. We rely on what Christ Jesus has done for us. We put no confidence in human effort,

3:1 Greek *brothers*; also in 3:13, 17.   3:3 Some manuscripts read *worship God in spirit*; one early manuscript reads *worship in spirit*.

NOTES

3:1 Whatever happens. The Greek (*to loipon* [TG3588/3063, ZG3836/3370]) can be rendered as "finally," signaling a conclusion (2 Cor 13:11), or as "furthermore" or "as to what is next," signaling transition to a new topic (as in 1 Thess 4:1; 2 Thess 3:1). Since Paul didn't bring his letter to a conclusion shortly thereafter but continued on for two more chapters, the latter interpretation is more likely. But this does not rule out the possibility that Paul may have originally intended to conclude the epistle at 3:1 (see commentary on 2:19-24) and then decided to continue on with other matters (see Bruce 1989:101). This could account for the abrupt change between 3:1 and 3:2.

rejoice in the Lord. Paul mentions joy several times in this epistle (1:18; 2:17-18, 29; 4:4). Here and in 4:4 he speaks in the imperative mood to the Philippians, telling them to rejoice in the Lord. This note of joy anticipates what Paul is going to say about his own relationship with Christ in 3:7-11.

I never get tired of telling you these things, and I do it to safeguard your faith. This is sometimes interpreted as referring to the immediately preceding encouragement to "rejoice in the Lord" because a joyful spirit is a safeguard "against the ills that plague their church—murmurings, dissensions, empty conceit" (Hawthorne 1983:124). But it is better understood with reference to what follows in 3:2 (so Martin 1987:139), wherein Paul provides three strong warnings.

3:2 Watch out for those dogs, those people who do evil, those mutilators. In the Greek, the imperative verb for "watch out" (*blepete* [TG991, ZG1063]) occurs three times, emphasizing Paul's ardency in making this warning. His insulting language refers to Judaizers who preached that Gentiles must be circumcised in order to be saved. Paul reversed the traditional Jewish practice of calling Gentiles "dogs" (cf. Mark 7:27-28) by calling Judaizers "dogs." In ancient Palestine dogs were considered unclean animals and scavengers.

mutilators. The Greek is *katatomē* [TG2699, ZG2961], meaning "those who harshly cut." A wordplay follows in the Greek of the next verse, where Paul speaks of Christians as being the *peritomē* [TG4061, ZG4364] (lit., "cut around" denoting circumcision).

who say you must be circumcised to be saved. This is not in the Greek text, but the thought of 3:2-3 allows for its inclusion for the sake of clarification.

3:3 worship by the Spirit of God. This has good textual support, both diverse and early: ℵ* A B C D² F G 33 1739 𝔐 syr^hmg cop. This reading in Greek is *hoi pneumati theou latreuontes*. Other manuscripts read *hoi pneumati theō latreuontes* (worship God in Spirit), which has the support of ℵ² D* P 044 it syr (so NLT mg). One other manuscript (𝔓46) reads *hoi pneumati latreuontes* (the ones worshiping in spirit), also noted in NLT mg.

According to Greek grammar, the first reading (NLT text) can be rendered, "the ones worshiping by God's Spirit" or "the ones worshiping God's Spirit." In Greek, the verb *latreuō* [TG3000, ZG3302] (worship) is normally followed by the dative (in this verse, *pneumati* [TG4151, ZG4460] "Spirit"); hence, the Spirit becomes the recipient of the worship (see Hawthorne 1983:122). Perhaps since this grammar allows a rendering that might be offensive to those who do not think the Spirit should be worshiped, some scribes changed *theou* from the genitive to the dative case, *theō* [TG2316, ZG2536] (God)—the first variant noted above, followed by NLT mg.

It should be noted that Lightfoot (1976:145) demonstrated that the verb *latreuō* [TG3000, ZG3302] had acquired a technical sense referring to the worship of God, and therefore one does not have to understand the phrase "God's Spirit" as the object of the worship. Thus, the text does not have to include an object to convey the message that God is being worshiped in spirit. In this light, it is not unreasonable to imagine that the original reading has been preserved in 𝔓46, for it has no object after the participle and yet it must mean "worship God in Spirit" because "God" is always the object of worship. But scribes were uncomfortable with this bare expression and therefore filled it out with either *theou* or *theō* [TG2316, ZG2536]. Thus, 𝔓46 explains the origin of the other variants, which is the reason its reading was adopted for the NEB (see Tasker 1964:439).

Finally, it should be noted that the scribe of 𝔓46 put some thought into this verse because he wrote out in full the word *pneumati* [TG4151, ZG4460] (in spirit) instead of writing it in abbreviated form as a *nomen sacrum* (divine title), which would clearly indicate the divine Spirit. The scribe's way of writing it indicates his perception that this "spirit" referred to the human spirit, not the divine Spirit. This corresponds with John 4:23-24, which reveals that worshipers should worship God (who is Spirit) in spirit and in reality (Comfort 2005:347-348).

who are truly circumcised. Lit., "we are the circumcision." As in Rom 2:28-29, Paul asserts that the true Jews are those circumcised in heart and in spirit. See note on 3:2, where Paul begins the contrast between the mutilators and the circumcised. To call Christians "circumcised" corresponds with Paul's thought in Romans where he said, "a true Jew is one whose heart is right with God" and true circumcision is not external but "a change of heart produced by God's Spirit" (Rom 2:28-29; cf. Col 2:11-13).

put no confidence in human effort. Lit., "having no confidence in the flesh." In Pauline diction, the "flesh" denotes the human being and connotes human effort, especially religious effort lacking the Spirit.

COMMENTARY

This section begins with Paul warning the Philippians about "dogs"—namely, Judaizers. The fact that he made these warnings to safeguard the Philippians' faith reveals that he believed the Judaizers could hurt or even ruin a Christian's faith. Paul's harshest criticisms were directed against such people (cf. Gal 1:6-9; 5:12) because he knew that their teachings were a dangerous threat to the faith of gentile Christians (see Gal 5:1-6). The demand that believers had to be circumcised in order to be saved undermines the most basic principle of the gospel—that people are saved by God's grace alone, through faith in Christ Jesus (see Rom 4:9-12).

Judaizers were Christian Jews who, during the early days of the church, attempted to impose the Jewish way of life on gentile Christians. The issue that concerned Paul was not simply whether or not a person followed the Jewish way of life but whether one erroneously thought that salvation was attained thereby. "Following Jewish customs and traditions and observing Jewish religious laws was a normal way of life for Jewish Christians, whether they were Jews by birth or through conversion. For them, belief in Jesus as the Messiah of Jewish expectation enhanced, but did not replace, their Judaism. Christianity was not regarded as a religion distinct from Judaism. These Jewish Christians had all been circumcised as infants, or upon conversion to Judaism, and they also practiced the kosher dietary laws and rules of ritual purity prescribed in Mosaic legislation and rabbinic tradition" (TBD 753).

The growing number of gentile converts to Christianity forced Jewish Christians to face a very difficult problem: Must a Gentile first become a Jew in order to be a Christian? Some Jewish Christians gave a positive answer to this question, and these became known as the circumcision party (Acts 11:2; Gal 2:12). Others, such as Peter and Barnabas, and especially Paul, vigorously disagreed. While these two radically different points of view could have split the early church into two major factions, that did not occur, due in large part to the decision made by the elders at the Jerusalem council (Acts 15)—namely that Gentiles who believed in Jesus did not have to become Jews through circumcision. However, the Judaizers of the circumcision party were not satisfied with this decision. They went to many churches raised up by Paul and tried to convince the gentile believers that they had to become Jews through circumcision. The reason Paul wrote the Epistle to the Galatians was to combat the Judaizers who had apparently invaded the Christian communities in Galatia after his departure. These Judaizers appear to have successfully persuaded some of the Galatian Christians that salvation was available only for those who were circumcised and who kept the Mosaic law (Gal 5:12; 6:13). Other Judaizers may have started to infect the church in Philippi (3:2-3)—or, at least, Paul had reason to believe that they would inevitably come to Philippi—hence, the strong warning Paul gave the Philippians in 3:2.

Paul saw the circumcision party as being those who boasted in the flesh—an intended double entendre. They were literally those who were proud of their cut foreskin through circumcision, and they were proud of their religious accomplishments. To Paul these accomplishments were the efforts of the "flesh" (*sarx* [TG4561, ZG4922]). To Paul, the "flesh" denotes the human being and human effort, especially religious effort lacking the Spirit. Paul's animosity toward the Judaizers was expressed in three ways when he called them dogs, evil workers, and mutilators (see note on 3:2). The last anathema is especially cutting in that Paul was telling them that they were those "cutting [things] to pieces"—that is, mutilators (*katatomē* [TG2699, ZG2961]). This corresponds with his derogatory remarks in Galatians 5:12, where he told those of the circumcision to castrate themselves. Paul's harsh language reveals his personal conflict with these evil workers who went around to the churches Paul raised up and presented a different gospel, which was not really a gospel at all (Gal 1:6-9). Paul was incensed that they insisted on circumcision as a means of salvation.

Taking the image of circumcision further, Paul argued that true spiritual Christians were now the true "circumcised." The Jews, through their unbelief in Jesus as the Messiah, had cut themselves off from God's covenant. Because "Israel lost sight of the spiritual significance of circumcision, focused on the external ritual, and failed to boast in the Lord alone (cf. Jer 9:23-25), it had forfeited its right to the title, 'The Circumcision.' The church of Jesus Christ, however, is the true Israel of God (Gal 6:16), heir of all the rights and privileges belonging to it (Rom 9:24-26; 1 Pet 2:9-10), including the right to the title *peritomē*" [TG4061, ZG4364] (circumcision) (Hawthorne 1983:126).

In comparison to the Judaizers, who performed their religion in "the flesh"—that is, by human effort—Christians worship in Spirit. The contrast between "flesh" (*sarx* [TG4561, ZG4922]) and "spirit" (*pneuma* [TG4151, ZG4460]) is one that Paul made very frequently in his writings (for example, see Rom 8:4-6; Gal 3:3; 5:16). In his thinking, the two represent two entirely different realms and modes of operation. One can either perform religious acts by the flesh, or one can experience God, who is Spirit, by living in the Spirit. The revolution came in Paul's life when he realized that the risen Christ is the life-giving Spirit (see commentary on 1:19).

According to his writings, especially 1 Corinthians 15, it can be gathered that Paul believed that when Jesus arose, he became life-giving Spirit (1 Cor 15:45). In this light, Paul often united the two—the Spirit and Jesus Christ—in his writings: "the Lord is the Spirit" (2 Cor 3:17); "the Lord—who is the Spirit" (2 Cor 3:18); "the Spirit of Christ" (Rom 8:9); "the Spirit of Jesus Christ" (1:19); and "the Spirit of his Son" (Gal 4:6). The union between the risen Christ and the Spirit was fundamental to Paul's thinking. The only way to really rely on Christ was to be a person of the Spirit. That is why in one breath he can say, "we who worship by the Spirit of God are the ones who are truly circumcised. We rely on what Christ Jesus has done for us" (3:3).

The experience of the risen Christ as the Spirit is what sets Christians apart from religious people. This experience is what liberated Paul from his bondage to Judaism and initiated his pursuit of knowing Christ. It is central to all that follows in the rest of this chapter. Christians are spirit-people—people who live in spirit and who worship God in spirit. This is the mark of the new age, one predicted by Jesus when he told the Samaritan woman at the well, "the time is coming—indeed it's here now—when true worshipers will worship the Father in spirit and in truth. . . . For God is Spirit, so those who worship him must worship in spirit and in truth" (John 4:23-24).

Formerly, God was worshiped in Jerusalem, but now the true Jerusalem would be in a person's spirit. Indeed, the church is called the habitation of God in spirit (Eph 2:22). True worship requires a people to contact God, the Spirit, in their spirit. Since God is Spirit, he must be worshiped in spirit. Human beings possess a human spirit, the nature of which corresponds to God's nature, which is Spirit. Therefore, people can have fellowship with God and worship God in the same sphere that God exists in.

◆ ## E. Paul: An Example of One Pursuing Christ (3:4-19)
1. Paul's life before knowing Christ (3:4-6)

⁴though I could have confidence in my own effort if anyone could. Indeed, if others have reason for confidence in their own efforts, I have even more! ⁵I was circumcised when I was eight days old. I am a pure-blooded citizen of Israel and a member of the tribe of Benjamin— a real Hebrew if there ever was one! I was a member of the Pharisees, who demand the strictest obedience to the Jewish law. ⁶I was so zealous that I harshly persecuted the church. And as for righteousness, I obeyed the law without fault.

NOTES
3:4 *my own effort . . . their own efforts.* Lit., "in the flesh . . . in the flesh." Paul habitually used the Greek word *sarx* [ᵀᴳ4561, ᶻᴳ4922] (flesh) to signify self-reliance and self-effort in contrast to reliance on Christ.

3:5 *I was circumcised when I was eight days old.* Every male Jew was circumcised on the eighth day according to the terms of God's covenant with Abraham (Gen 17:12) and in accordance with the letter of the law (Lev 12:3).

a pure-blooded citizen of Israel. Lit., "of the people of Israel." "Having been born into the chosen race and admitted into the covenant community by circumcision, he inherited all the privileges that belong to that community—privileges he enumerates in Romans 9:4, 5" (Bruce 1989:108).

a member of the tribe of Benjamin. This was one of the smallest of the 12 tribes of Israel, made up of descendants of Jacob's youngest son (Num 1:36). Though small, the tribe of Benjamin played an important role in Israelite history, particularly in their conduct as great warriors (Judg 20:13-16; 1 Chr 12:1-2), in accord with Jacob's prophecy: "Benjamin is a ravenous wolf, devouring his enemies in the morning and dividing his plunder in the evening" (Gen 49:27). One of the most important men of Benjamin was Saul, the first king of Israel. That Saul of Tarsus shared his name may have been a source of pride—a point of pedigree he also made in Rom 11:1.

a real Hebrew if there ever was one! Lit., "a Hebrew from Hebrews." Jews still spoke of themselves as Hebrews, though the name properly applied to an earlier period of their history (cf. 2 Cor 11:22). Hebrews were "Jews who normally spoke Aramaic with one another and attended synagogues services where the service was said in Hebrew (as distinct from Hellenists, who spoke only Greek)" (Bruce 1989:108).

a member of the Pharisees. Even though his family resided in a Greek city (Tarsus), Paul came from a family of Pharisees, the Jewish sect known for strict observance of the law of Moses (see Acts 23:6; 26:5).

3:6 *I was so zealous that I harshly persecuted the church.* This is expanded in Paul's letter to the Galatians: "You know what I was like when I followed the Jewish religion—how I violently persecuted God's church. I did my best to destroy it. I was far ahead of my fellow Jews in my zeal for the traditions of my ancestors" (Gal 1:13-14). See Acts 8:1, 3; 9:1-2, 21 for a record of his involvement in this persecution; and see Acts 22:4-5; 26:9-11; 1 Cor 15:9 for other admissions of persecution. Paul's zealous devotion to Judaism was evident in his persecution of the church. In an attempt to harmonize this verse with Gal 1:13, a few Western witnesses (F G ita) expand the expression "persecuted the church" to "persecuted the church of God."

I obeyed the law without fault. In the Greek the idea is that Paul was claiming to be blameless, not perfect. To be without blame means that he adhered to the laws as prescribed by the Pharisees (see commentary).

COMMENTARY

The previous section (3:1-3) begins with a warning against Judaizers and ends with the remark that Christians are people who rely on Christ and "put no confidence in human effort"—unlike the Judaizers. Paul then remarks that he could have many reasons for having confidence in his own heritage and efforts. He presented his pedigree and credentials to show how he not only equaled but surpassed any and all boasts of the Judaizers. If anyone could brag of his Jewish credentials, it was Paul.

Before his conversion, Paul's resumé would have impressed any Jew or Judaizer. Born around AD 10, he was a Jew in a family of Pharisees of the tribe of Benjamin in Tarsus of Cilicia. He was circumcised on the eighth day in fulfillment of the law (Lev 12:3). He was a true Israelite by birth, not by being proselytized. His family could trace their lineage to Benjamin, something anyone of the ten northern tribes would have found difficult, if not impossible, to do because of the assimilation that occurred in the Assyrian captivity. The tribes of Judah and Benjamin, however, still kept their Jewish tribal identity because they were deported to Babylon as a group and were allowed to maintain many of their cultural distinctives there. The tribe of Benjamin had a good reputation because (1) the Temple and holy city Jerusalem were within its borders (Judg 1:21); (2) it was the only tribe besides Judah that remained faithful to David during the breakup of the monarchy (1 Kgs 12:21); and (3) it was the tribe that returned with the tribe of Judah from the Babylonian captivity to restore the Temple and Jerusalem (Ezra 4:1-2). This would have been a cause of pride for Paul.

Furthermore, Paul was "a real Hebrew if there ever was one" in the sense that he was not a Hellenistic Jew who spoke Greek. He spoke Hebrew (see note on 3:5). Even though he was reared in the city of Tarsus, he learned Hebrew under a Hebrew teacher, Gamaliel (Acts 5:34). Not only was he a Hebrew among Hebrews; he was a member of the strictest Jewish sect, the Pharisees. In fact, he was a son of Pharisees (Acts 23:6). At the time, this would have been a great cause of pride for Saul of Tarsus, not shame.

Two of the most influential schools during Paul's day were the rival Pharisaic schools of Hillel and Shammai. Both of these teachers had great influence on Jewish thinking. Hillel's school emphasized tradition even above the law. Shammai's school preserved the teaching of the law over the authority of tradition. Of the two, Hillel's school was the most influential. Gamaliel, the grandson of Hillel, was a member of the Sanhedrin, the high council of Jews in Jerusalem, and served as president of the Sanhedrin during the reigns of the Roman emperors Tiberius, Caligula, and Claudius. He was a member of the council that unfairly judged Jesus and sent him to Pilate for crucifixion.

In that same eventful year, Paul, then Saul, was completing his education in Jerusalem under Gamaliel. While studying under Gamaliel in Hillel's school, Paul began to advance in Judaism beyond many Jews of his own age and became extremely zealous for the traditions of his fathers. Being in the school of Hillel meant that Saul was just as zealous for keeping Jewish traditions, if not more so, than the law itself. In this way, he would have been a Pharisee among Pharisees—a strict follower of ritual and religious ceremony.

Though we don't know when the sect of the Pharisees came into being, it is likely that prior to the Maccabean revolt some distinctive Pharisaic concerns appeared in connection with the development of the Hasidim ("the faithful ones"), who were the traditionalists that opposed Greek influence in Jewish society. The Hasidim probably became disillusioned with the Maccabean rulers, whose conduct violated Jewish sensibilities. Some of the Hasidim separated themselves from the nation and developed into nonconformist sects. Those who remained tried to exert their influence on Jewish life and developed into the sect of the Pharisees. It is possible that the very name Pharisee means "separated one" if its etymology is the Hebrew *parushim* [TH6567, ZH7300].

The Pharisees were committed to the notion of a twofold law, the written Torah (the OT, principally the Pentateuch) and the oral Torah (the traditions handed down through many generations of rabbis). The oral traditions, which sought to regulate the lives of the people before God, became more and more detailed over the course of time and were eventually brought together and written down as a single document, the Mishnah (dated c. AD 210). When Paul told his Galatian readers that he had been zealous of the traditions of his ancestors (Gal 1:14), he was referring to these oral traditions (TBD 1026-1027).

By New Testament times the Pharisees were widely recognized as religious leaders. Josephus, who tells us that he belonged to this sect, wrote in the first century that the Pharisees were "extremely influential among the townsfolk; and all prayers and sacred rites of divine worship are performed according to their exposition. This is the great tribute that the inhabitants of the cities, by practicing the highest ideal both in their way of living and in their discourse, have paid to the excellence of the Pharisees" (*Antiquities* 18.15). The praise Josephus gave the Pharisees would have been something that Saul of Tarsus would have been proud of.

During the time of Jesus' ministry, the Pharisees opposed him because he did not adhere to their rules of religious purity. In Mark 7, the Pharisees complained to Jesus, "Why do your disciples not live according to the tradition of the elders, but eat with defiled hands?" (Mark 7:5, NRSV). Jesus' reply countered their criticism with a serious indictment: "You abandon the commandment of God and hold to human tradition. . . . thus making void the word of God through your tradition that you have handed on" (Mark 7:8, 13, NRSV). The Pharisees' opposition to Jesus continued to the end, when they joined the priests in paying Judas to betray Jesus (John 18:3) and in condoning Jesus' crucifixion (implicit in Matt 27:62).

After the Gospels, there is no specific record in Acts that the Pharisees specifically persecuted the church. So Paul's inclusion in that sect did not necessarily prompt his persecution efforts. In fact, Gamaliel, who was a leading Pharisee and rabbi, tried to temper the Sanhedrin's persecution of the church (Acts 5:34-39), and Paul had been a student of Gamaliel (Acts 22:3). Paul himself does not indicate that his being a Pharisee caused him to persecute the church; rather, in his own words it was because of "zeal" (*kata zēlos* [TG2596/2205, ZG2848/2419]) that he persecuted the church. This zeal, though misdirected, is what motivated Paul to become the most fervent among all his contemporaries (see Gal 1:13-14) to follow the law strictly and to keep the covenant community pure. As such, he must have viewed the sect of the Nazarenes as being a contamination within Judaism, which had to be destroyed. Fee (1995:308) said, "His zeal for the Law was demonstrated most surely by his untiring dedication to stamping out the nascent Christian movement, probably related to his conviction that God had especially cursed Jesus by having him hanged (Gal 3:13; Deut 21:23)."

The concluding item in Paul's resumé is perplexing for readers who have read Paul's other writings: "And as for righteousness, I obeyed the law without fault" (3:6). The reason this is perplexing is that Paul repeatedly indicated in his writings that righteousness can never be obtained by doing the works of the law (for example, see Paul's arguments in Rom 3; Gal 2–3). He even says the same thing three verses later in Philippians (see 3:9). So Paul must have been speaking of his strict obedience to the laws that Pharisees followed. Each Pharisee made a deliberate effort to obey the 613 commands of the Mosaic law as interpreted and expanded in Jewish Halakha (rabbinic legal decisions). Paul considered himself blameless as to these laws. This does not mean that he thought he was perfect or sinless but that he followed all the instructions of the law, including those that told a Jew how to deal with his sins through various sacrifices.

In closing this section, it should be said that Paul knew from firsthand experience the mindset of the Pharisees who had become the chief Judaizers in the early Christian movement. They were the ones who were particularly insistent that new converts who were Gentiles be circumcised and charged to keep the law of Moses (Acts 15:5). They were really demanding that Gentiles become converted to Judaism in order to be Christians. Paul had become so liberated from this mindset that God used him to proclaim to all believers, whether Jews or Gentiles, freedom from the law (see 3:9).

◆   ## 2. Paul's spiritual aspirations (3:7-11)

⁷I once thought these things were valuable, but now I consider them worthless because of what Christ has done. ⁸Yes, everything else is worthless when compared with the infinite value of knowing Christ Jesus my Lord. For his sake I have discarded everything else, counting it all as garbage, so that I could gain Christ ⁹and become one with him. I no longer count on my own righteousness through obeying the law; rather, I become righteous through faith in Christ.* For God's way of making us right with himself depends on faith. ¹⁰I want to know Christ and experience the mighty power that raised him from the dead. I want to suffer with him, sharing in his death, ¹¹so that one way or another I will experience the resurrection from the dead!

3:9 Or *through the faithfulness of Christ.*

NOTES

3:7 *valuable . . . worthless.* In Greek, the two words are *kerdē* [TG2771, ZG3046] and *zēmian* [TG2209, ZG2422], which could also be rendered as "gain" and "loss." Paul used the noun form *zēmian* in the next verse (3:8a), followed by the verbal form of the same word in 3:8b. The noun denotes "loss, damage, forfeit" (BDAG 427-428). The verb (*zēmioomai* [TG2210A, ZG2423]) denotes suffering damage and loss, or forfeiting something.

but now I consider them worthless. The insertion of the contrastive "but" (*alla* [TG235, ZG247]) appears to be a scribal addition, intended to mark a contrast between Paul's behavior before becoming a Christian and his behavior after. This conjunction, though printed in NA²⁷, is not found in 𝔓46 𝔓61ᵛⁱᵈ ℵ* A (F) G 1739. This testimony for its omission is stronger than that for its inclusion (ℵ² B D 044 𝔐 syr cop). Silva (1992:182) argues that the corrector of ℵ worked in the same scriptorium as the original scribe of ℵ and therefore would have added the conjunction to accord with the master text. But in this case it is a second corrector (ℵ²) who made the adjustment; he was part of a group of correctors working in Caesarea in the sixth or seventh century who corrected the manuscript in general conformity with the Byzantine text.

3:8 *everything else is worthless when compared with the infinite value of knowing Christ Jesus my Lord.* In his sublime prayer, as recorded in John 17, Jesus prayed this: "And this is the way to have eternal life—to know you, the only true God, and Jesus Christ" (John 17:3). The knowledge of God in Christ is eternal life—and what can be more valuable than everlasting life! Paul's sole pursuit in life was to know experientially Christ Jesus as his personal Lord. This kind of knowledge exceeds just knowing *about* Christ; it is knowing Christ himself.

garbage. The Greek word *skubala* [TG4657, ZG5032] can mean "rubbish" or "excrement." Most likely it means "that which is thrown to the dogs"—perhaps from a combination of "dogs" (*kusi* [TG2965, ZG3264] = "to dogs") and "cast" (*ballō* [TG906, ZG965]) (see MM 579).

3:9 *become one with him.* Lit., "that I may be found in him." This is probably an eschatological expression, one in which Paul was looking to the day of judgment where he would be "found out" by God as to what he was made of. Paul did not want to be standing before God with his own merits and achievements; rather, he wanted to be so united with Christ and his merits that God the Judge would see Christ in Paul.

through faith in Christ. Or, "through the faithfulness of Christ" (NLT mg). In Greek the expression is *dia pisteōs Christou* [TG4102/5547, ZG4411/5986], which can be taken as an objective genitive ("one's faith in Christ") or as a subjective genitive ("Christ's faith[fulness]"). Though both interpretations are viable, the objective genitive is to be preferred on the grounds that Paul emphasized the action of a person putting one's faith in Christ. (See an excellent survey of the debate in Fee 1995:324-325.)

God's way of making us right with himself. A right relationship with God cannot be earned by one's own efforts but only received as a free gift by putting one's trust in Christ (see Rom 1:17; 3:21-26; 4:5-8; Gal 2:16; Eph 2:8-9).

3:10 *to know Christ.* The Greek verb *gnōnai* [TG1097, ZG1182] in this context denotes personal experience (see commentary).

experience the mighty power that raised him from the dead. The verb "experience" is a carryover from the previous verb. Paul's experience of the resurrection power was directly linked to his experience of the Spirit, for Christ became life-giving Spirit via his resurrection (see 1 Cor 15:45).

to suffer with him. Lit., "fellowship of his sufferings." The Greek for "fellowship" (*koinōnia* [TG2842, ZG3126]) denotes "that which is shared" or "that which is common" to two or more people. In this sense, Paul wanted to be a sharer in Christ's sufferings.

sharing in his death. The verb "sharing" is a carryover from the previous verb (see above). The Greek is *summorphizomenos* [TG4833, ZG5214], a present passive participle, indicating that one will be made to share the same *morphē* [TG3444, ZG3671] as another. In Paul's lexicon, this meant spiritual conformity to Christ (see commentary for further exposition).

3:11 *so that one way or another.* This is an excellent way of rendering a difficult introduction to Paul's statement, which has been rendered as "if somehow" in most versions, leading people to think Paul was unsure of his future resurrection. He was sure of his resurrection (see 1 Cor 15; 1 Thess 4), but not completely sure he would be fully like Christ when he saw him.

experience the resurrection from the dead! This is the final resurrection that Christ promised to those who believe in him (see John 5:24-29; 11:25-26). This climaxes a powerful chiasm begun in 3:10, which is presented here in a literal rendering:

    A. I want to know the power of his resurrection
      B. the fellowship of his sufferings
      B'. being conformed to his death
    A'. so that I may attain the resurrection from the dead

COMMENTARY

In this passage we see Paul's desire to emulate Christ's thinking. What Paul had previously exhorted the Philippians to do—"You must have the same attitude that Christ Jesus had" (2:5)—he himself was doing. He was practicing what he preached. He was willingly emptying himself of his reputation, his gains, his achievements, and his self-reliance, so that he could be filled with the life of another—Jesus Christ. This was Paul's *kenōsis* (cf. *kenoō* [TG2758, ZG3033]—his emptying out of himself so that he could gain Christ. Thus, this is the third living example Paul presented to the Philippians: first Timothy (2:19-24), then Epaphroditus (2:25-30), now himself (3:4-14). This passage will be followed by an injunction for all the Philippians to emulate Paul in this matter (3:15-21).

The power of this passage is inherent in its personal touch, as well as in its poetic structure. This is not to say that Paul purposely wrote this as a poem, but it came out that way in the end. The repetitive contrasts of gain versus loss, the excellency of knowing Christ versus the worthlessness of religious pursuits, God's kind of righteousness versus self-righteousness, resurrection versus suffering, weave in and out of the passage, holding it together and giving it balance. The following presentation (literally translated) shows this thematic structure. The lines that are aligned further left speak of gain, knowing Christ, God's righteousness, and resurrection; the indented lines speak of loss, worthless religious pursuits, self-righteousness, and suffering. One should not think, however, that everything in these lines is negative. Loss is good when one finds Christ; and suffering with Christ is also good.

> [7]what things were gain to me
> these I have considered loss for Christ
> [8]but even more so I consider all things to be loss
> on account of the excellency of knowing Christ Jesus my Lord
> for whom I have suffered the loss of all things
> and I consider them refuse
> that I may gain Christ [9]and be found in him
> not having my own righteousness which is of the law
> but the righteousness through faith in Christ
> the righteousness of God based on faith—
> [10]to know him and the power of his resurrection
> and the fellowship of his suffering
> by being conformed to his death
> [11]if somehow I may attain to the resurrection from the dead

The first verse (3:7) is poignant in that it says that Paul considered his previous gains to be losses. It is important to note that this was a mental activity on Paul's part, for it is in the mind that spiritual transformation begins (see Rom 12:2). Even the verbs he used in 3:7-8 show a progression in transformation. First he used the verb *ēn* [TG1510, ZG1639] (were)—what things were gains to me. Then he used the verb *hēgeomai* [TG2233, ZG2451] (to think, to consider, regard) three times in 3:7-8. The first use is in the perfect tense: "I have considered loss." Then twice he used it in the pres-

ent tense: "I consider all things to be loss" and "I consider them refuse." It is not that
the things in themselves were garbage but that by comparison to knowing Christ
Paul regarded them as garbage.

When Paul put his accomplishments and the excellency of knowing Christ on a
ledger, all his accomplishments would be listed as "losses" or liabilities, while all
that belongs to Christ would be considered "gains" or assets. This was a familiar
business expression in Paul's day, one that compared *zēmia* [TG2209, ZG2422] (loss) and
kerdos [TG2771, ZG3046] (profit) on a balance sheet (see MM 273, 341). From Paul's new
perspective, his religious pedigree (circumcised the eighth day, an Israelite, a member of the tribe of Benjamin, a Hebrew born of Hebrews, a Pharisee, a blameless
law-keeper) added up to zero or less. By comparison, knowing Christ was of "infinite value" (3:8). In Greek Paul used the expression *to huperechon* [TG5242A, ZG5660],
which means "the superiority" or "the surpassing greatness" or "the supreme
advantage" (NJB). The idea is that knowing Christ personally is far more valuable
than any religious pedigree or accomplishment. The kind of knowledge (*gnōsis*
[TG1108, ZG1194]) Paul had in mind was not merely intellectual. In the context of Philippians 3, "the knowledge of Christ is personal and intimate, as the expression 'my
Lord' shows, certainly more than an intellectual apprehension of truth about
Christ. Rather, it is a personal appropriation of and communion with Christ himself. 'The knowledge of Christ' no doubt does involve one's thoughts, but in its distinctive biblical usage it may be said to involve one's heart" (Loh and Nida
1977:103-104). Paul had not known Jesus of Nazareth as the apostles did. His first
encounter with Jesus was on the road to Damascus when he was granted an appearance of the risen Christ. From that day forward, Paul was determined to know Jesus
Christ. Paul, like all Christians since, did not know Jesus Christ according to his
human life on earth. He knew only the risen Christ (2 Cor 5:15-16). From the very
beginning Paul knew the risen Christ via his Spirit, whom he called "the Spirit of
Jesus Christ" (1:19). In this regard, Paul became the forerunner of all those Christians who have never seen Jesus in the flesh and who have come to experience him
in the Spirit. It is true that Paul had seen the risen Lord; he was the last one to do so
(1 Cor 15:8). And from that time onward he realized that Jesus was exalted far
above all. Paul wrote much concerning this, but his writings did not leave the far-
above-all Jesus far away from us all because this was not Paul's experience, nor ours.
Any experienced Christian should be able to testify that the Christ in the heavens is
also the Christ in the heart.

Paul pursued an ongoing relationship with Christ throughout his entire life. In
this sense, he said he wanted to "gain Christ." This is a strange statement because
one cannot actually "gain" Christ as if he were a commodity. So we must understand it as metaphorical language couched in the business terms Paul used in this
section. In his estimation, all that he gained before knowing Christ was rubbish to
be thrown out to the dogs. In so saying, Paul was taking a shot at the Judaizers
(whom he called "dogs" in 3:2), insinuating they would "eat up" what he considered to be rubbish (Fee 1995:319).

When Paul was a zealot for Judaism, he considered his pedigree and accomplishments to be his merit for God's acceptance. He believed that on the day of judgment God would accept him for what he had done. But his horizons were different now; he wanted God the Judge to look at him and see Christ (see note on 3:9). He wanted to appear before God, not presenting his own righteousness in having kept the law, but presenting himself as one who trusted in Christ and thereby was justified by God. From Paul's other writings, we know that this was the cornerstone of his theology. Justification—being made right with God—comes by faith in Christ and not by doing the works of the law (see Rom 3-4; Gal 2-3; Eph 2:1-6).

But Paul wanted more than just a right standing with God on the day of judgment. He wanted more from Christ than just a Savior. He wanted to know Christ personally and fully so as to be made like him. Unlike many Christians, who want to know only certain aspects of Christ, Paul wanted firsthand knowledge of Christ in his complete experience of suffering and resurrection. Paul wanted to know the power of Christ's resurrection, which means he wanted to be energized day by day with the same divine power that raised Christ from the dead and seated him in the heavenly places (see Eph 1-2). Paul also wanted to fellowship with Christ in his sufferings (addressed later in this commentary). The result of this intimate knowledge and fellowship was that Paul would be conformed to Jesus' death and would attain the resurrection from the dead.

These final two verses are so terse they call for further expounding as gathered from Paul's other writings. Paul believed that each believer was destined to be conformed to the image of God's Son. To achieve this end, God works both inwardly and outwardly on each of his children. Paul called the inward process "transformation" and the outward process "conformation."

Transformation involves an inward, metabolic-like renewal of our minds through which the inner man is changed into the likeness of Christ. Paul told the Roman believers: "Let God transform you into a new person by changing the way you think" (Rom 12:2), and he wrote to the Ephesians, "let the Spirit renew your thoughts and attitudes" (Eph 4:23)—in a context that speaks of transformation. As our Christian lives progress, we should gradually notice that our thought-lives are being changed from Christlessness to Christlikeness. Transformation does not happen overnight—regeneration is instantaneous, but transformation is not. We are transformed to Christ's image gradually as we spend time with him in spiritual fellowship. Eventually, we will begin to mirror the one we behold. Paul said, "So all of us who have had that veil removed can see and reflect the glory of the Lord. And the Lord—who is the Spirit—makes us more and more like him as we are changed into his glorious image" (2 Cor 3:18). As we behold the Lord, who is now the indwelling Spirit, we begin to reflect his image. One day we shall see him as he really is, for we shall be like him (1 John 3:2).

Concurrent with the inward process of transformation, each maturing believer must undergo conformation. There is no escape, for this was predetermined for every child of God, as Paul wrote:

And we know that God causes everything to work together for the good of those who love God and are called according to his purpose for them. For God knew his people in advance, and he chose them to become like his Son, so that his Son would be the firstborn among many brothers and sisters. And having chosen them, he called them to come to him. And having called them, he gave them right standing with himself. And having given them right standing, he gave them his glory. (Rom 8:28-30)

Since God's desire and plan were to have many sons, each one would have to be conformed to the prototype, Jesus. This is our common destiny. Our "horizon(s)" have been marked out beforehand. (The Greek word for "predestine," *proorizō* [TG4309, ZG4633], literally means "to mark out one's boundary beforehand." Our English word "horizon" is a derivative.) Note how the phrases "chose," "called," "gave them a right standing," and especially "gave them his glory" in Romans 8:29 and 30 are in the past tense. That is because God, from his eternal perspective, sees this process as having been completed already. From God's perspective, we have been glorified already because he sees us like his Son. But still, in the reality of time, we must undergo the process of being conformed to the image of God's Son. God is working together all things in the lives of those who love him and are called according to his purpose. His goal is to conform each person to the image of his beloved Son.

As we read the rest of Romans 8, it is quite evident that the "things" God uses to conform us often involve various kinds of suffering. Conformity to the image of Jesus Christ necessitates conformity to his death (see 3:10). Whereas transformation involves an inward, life-imparted change in our essential constitution, conformation entails outward pressure that works the image of Christ into us. If we are to be made like him, we must have both. To know Jesus, as far as Paul was concerned, was to know both the power of his resurrection, which came to him through the Spirit, and the fellowship of his sufferings (3:10).

Paul wanted to be completely conformed to Jesus' death. Paul's ministry caused him a great deal of suffering through persecution—so much so that Paul said he always carried about in his body the death of Jesus so that the life of Jesus would be made visible in his body (2 Cor 4:10). This sentiment fits with what he told the Philippians in the first chapter: "Christ will be exalted now as always in my body, whether by life or by death" (1:20, NRSV), which is followed later by these words: "You have been given not only the privilege of trusting in Christ but also the privilege of suffering for him" (1:29).

Suffering brings one into fellowship with Jesus' suffering and into conformity with Jesus' death. To be conformed to Christ's death means that one shares the same *morphē* [TG3444, ZG3671] with Christ (see note on 3:10). The Christ Poem in 2:6-11 begins with a statement of how Christ emptied himself of one *morphē* (that of living in divine equality with God) to take on another—the *morphē* of a servant in human form and being, a servant who was obedient to death on a cross. Thus, to share Christ's *morphē* is to share in the experience of Christ's servanthood—a servanthood that cost him his life. Paul wanted this experience. At the same time, he knew he needed Christ's resurrection power made available to him in the Spirit.

This is the power that would sustain him through life and through death; the present power of resurrection would be the same power in the future that would raise him from the grave.

◆   ### 3. Paul's pursuit of Christ (3:12-14)

[12]I don't mean to say that I have already achieved these things or that I have already reached perfection. But I press on to possess that perfection for which Christ Jesus first possessed me. [13]No, dear brothers and sisters, I have not achieved it,* but I focus on this one thing: Forgetting the past and looking forward to what lies ahead, [14]I press on to reach the end of the race and receive the heavenly prize for which God, through Christ Jesus, is calling us.

3:13 Some manuscripts read *not yet achieved it.*

NOTES

3:12 *I don't mean to say that I have already achieved these things or that I have already reached perfection.* This reading has the support of 𝔓61[vid] ℵ A B D[c] P 044 33 1739 it[c] syr cop. All English versions follow. Some other witnesses (𝔓46 D* F G it[a] Irenaeus Tertullian) have an extra, embedded clause: "or already have been justified." Given Paul's penchant for proclaiming that justification is an accomplished fact that occurs concurrent with one's faith in Christ, the variant reading is noteworthy because it declares that justification is yet to come. What scribe would have invented this addition? Kennedy (1979:456) argues that some pious scribe added it because "the Divine side of sanctification was left too much out of sight." But if this is so, then a scribe surely would and could have used a term that denotes sanctification, not justification. Others (for example, see Hawthorne 1983:148) have argued that the addition was drawn from 1 Cor 4:4 or was supplemented to compensate for the lack of a direct object. But the so-called addition doesn't supply a direct object, and one wonders if any scribe would have thought that this verse was incomplete without an addition from 1 Cor 4:4.

The variant reading has three things in its favor: (1) from a documentary perspective, it has early and somewhat diverse testimony; (2) from a transcriptional perspective, it is easy to see that the phrase could have been omitted accidentally, due to homoeoarchton (the eye of a scribe passing from *ē ēdē* [TG2228/2235, ZG2445/2453] in the previous clause to the next *ē ēdē*); and (3) it is the more difficult reading, fraught with exegetical difficulties—not the least of which is that it seems to contradict what Paul himself said a few verses earlier: "So that I could gain Christ and become one with him. I no longer count on my own righteousness through obeying the law; rather, I become righteous through faith in Christ. For God's way of making us right with himself depends on faith" (3:8-9). However, there is not really a contradiction between this statement and the statement that he has not yet been justified. In both instances, the clear implication is that neither has yet been attained. Paul wanted to have this righteousness when Christ returns, and thereby be justified for having retained this faith. Thus, it is a personal call to perseverance and maintenance: to keep the righteousness he has been given because of his faith—not because of his works (Comfort 2008:[Phil 3:12]).

Christ Jesus. This reading has early and diverse support: 𝔓46 𝔓61 ℵ A 044 𝔐. The short form, "Christ," also has early and diverse witness: B D[(2)] F G 33 Tertullian Clement. Given the scribal tendency to expand divine titles, it is possible that the short form is original. For this reason, "Jesus" (*Iēsou* [TG2424, ZG2652]) is bracketed in UBS4 and NA27.

3:13 *I have not achieved it.* Lit., "I count not myself to have laid hold." This reading has the support of 𝔓46 B D² F G 044 𝔐 syr^h. Other mss (𝔓16^vid 𝔓61^vid ℵ A D* P 33 syr^h**) read, "I count myself not yet to have laid hold" (see NLT mg). Since the papyri and other early uncials (ℵ A B) are divided on this reading, textual critics are hard pressed to pick one reading against the other. Nevertheless, the first reading is a slightly better candidate because it is likely that scribes added "yet" in view of the fact that Paul later in his life claims to have finished the race and gained the prize (see 2 Tim 4:7-8; Comfort 2005:348).

looking forward. This is more graphically rendered as "stretching forward" (*epekteinomai* [^TG1901, ^ZG2085]), a word used nowhere else in the NT.

COMMENTARY

In the previous section (3:8-11) Paul expressed his desire to know Christ fully, to be conformed to his death, to be found by God with Christ's righteousness, and to attain the resurrection of the dead. This section continues his thought with a humble admission that Paul had not achieved these things. If we follow the longer reading in 3:12 (see note), Paul said he had not yet obtained these things, not yet been justified, and not yet been perfected. From a doctrinal perspective, one would think that Paul should have been assured of these blessings automatically. But from an experiential perspective, it seems that Paul wanted to own all these experiences prior to his death so that he could be assured existentially that he fully knew Jesus, was justified, had been perfected, and would participate in the resurrection of the dead. This is what motivated him in his pursuit of Christ.

The imagery Paul used in 3:12-14 is loaded with athletic images and allusions—specifically, the athletic contest of a running race. In 3:12, he says that he had not already reached perfection. The Greek term for "reached perfection" is *teleioō* [^TG5048, ^ZG5457]; it means to "reach the end, accomplish the goal, finish" (see BDAG 996). This is what every runner sets out to accomplish before the race begins. Then Paul said, "but I press on." The Greek term for "press on" is *diōkō* [^TG1377, ^ZG1503]; it means to "chase after, run, press on" (see BDAG 201). The athletic imagery here is clear: Paul viewed his pursuit of knowing Christ and being Christlike as running a race. Paul knew this is why Christ Jesus laid hold of him on the road to Damascus and why Christ stopped Paul from pursuing and persecuting (which translates the same Greek word *diōkō*) Christians, then turned him around to commence a new pursuit—that of knowing Christ. Thus, Christ laid hold of Paul so that Paul could lay hold of Christ. As such, Christ became the prize Paul was seeking. He wanted to know Christ and live for Christ during his lifetime (1:20), and he looked forward to knowing him perfectly in the next life.

In 3:13 Paul admits that he had not yet laid hold of Christ, but he was in the race to do so. As a runner in this race, his first task was "forgetting the past," which is seen by many readers as an allusion to the runner's task of not looking back while running the race and thereby slowing down his progress. The spiritual application is clear: Christians need to forget their past, whether bad or good, so as not to be impeded in the spiritual race of knowing Christ and becoming like him. The primary aim of the runner is to move ahead by "stretching forward" (*epekteinomai*

[TG1901, ZG2085]). This is a graphic word used in the Greek language to picture a runner who strains every muscle to press forward in the race (see Pfitzner 1967:139-140). It "pictures the Christian as a runner with his body bent over, his hand outstretched, his head fixed forward never giving a backward glance, and his eye fastened on the goal" (Hawthorne 1983:153).

Continuing the athletic imagery, Paul said, "I press on to reach the end of the race" (3:14). According to the Greek, "the end [of the race]" is *skopos* [TG4649, ZG5024]. In this context, it denotes the finish line of the race on which the athlete focuses throughout the course of the race (Pfitzner 1967:139-141). As such, the next Greek word, *diōkō* [TG1377, ZG1503], must mean "I run." So, Paul was speaking of running toward the goal, the finish line. His aim in so doing was to win the prize (*brabeion* [TG1017, ZG1092]), "a term that is taken directly from the athletic imagery of the games" (O'Brien 1991:429). The prize is then defined as the "heavenly prize for which God, through Christ Jesus, is calling us." Paul may have been alluding to the practice in the Greek games of when the victor's name would be announced, along with his father's name and country; and then the athlete would come and receive a palm branch in his hands. As such, Paul was saying that his prize came from God the Father and his prize was heavenly. Aside from the athletic imagery, Paul was saying he had answered God's call to pursue Christ. The goal of that pursuit is to know Christ fully, and the prize is to come into the full reality of that knowledge—a reality that will not come into being until the eschaton.

◆   ### 4. Paul's admonition to follow his example (3:15-19)

15Let all who are spiritually mature agree on these things. If you disagree on some point, I believe God will make it plain to you. 16But we must hold on to the progress we have already made.

17Dear brothers and sisters, pattern your lives after mine, and learn from those who follow our example. 18For I have told you often before, and I say it again with tears in my eyes, that there are many whose conduct shows they are really enemies of the cross of Christ. 19They are headed for destruction. Their god is their appetite, they brag about shameful things, and they think only about this life here on earth.

NOTES

3:15 *spiritually mature.* In the Greek this is *teleioi* [TG5046, ZG5455], which in this context means spiritually mature with a focus on reaching the goal of knowing Christ.

agree on these things. If you disagree. In Greek the verb both times is *phroneō* [TG5426, ZG5858], a word that denotes thinking.

3:16 *hold on to the progress we have already made.* Lit., "to what we have attained, let us follow the same." This reading has the support of 𝔓16 𝔓46 ℵ* A B Ivid 33 1739 cop. This is expanded in the TR with additional words: *kanoni to auto phronein* [TG5426, ZG5858] (to think the same thing) with the support of ℵ2 044 𝔐. Quite literally, this expression means "to keep step with the same"—as in military marching. In context it means that Christians should keep following those things that effectively work in their lives to promote spiritual transformation. The addition of *kanoni* [TG2583, ZG2834] (rule) in the second variant comes from Gal 6:16, where Paul encouraged the believers to "live by this principle" that in Christ Jesus neither circumcision nor uncircumcision mean anything—but a new creation. The substitution of the verb *phronein* [TG5426, ZG5858] (to think) in the second variant comes from 2:2, where Paul admonished the believers to be of the same mind by appropriating Christ's humble attitude.

3:17 pattern your lives after mine. This refers to Paul's pursuit of knowing Christ, as just described in 3:7-14. He urged his churches to become his disciples in the same pursuit (see commentary below for discussion).

3:18 enemies of the cross of Christ. There have been many attempts to identify these people whom Paul and the Philippians knew (see discussion in commentary). Whoever they were, they opposed the Cross of Christ, either by verbally speaking against it or by the way they lived.

3:19 headed for destruction. This refers to ultimate eternal destruction for those who reject Christ (see 2 Thess 1:8-9; 1 Tim 6:9). Since Paul spoke in 1:28 of opposers to the Philippians who would experience destruction (*apōleia* [TG684, ZG724] is the same word used in 1:28 and 3:19), they may be the same people. However, most commentators understand the opposers in 1:28 to be non-Christians, whereas those here are more likely those who think they are Christians but do not live as such.

Their god is their appetite. Lit., "their god is their belly." This refers either to their sensuality or to their self-interest (see Rom 16:18 for a similar expression). A verbal parallel to this expression is found in Euripides' *Cyclops*, where the Cyclops says, "I offer sacrifice to no god but myself, and to this belly of mine, the greatest of divinities" (*Cyclops* 334-335).

they brag about shameful things. This is a reference to these people being proud about their immorality.

and they think only about this life here on earth. This is a good dynamic-equivalence rendering for the literal, "thinking earthly things." Their thoughts were occupied by things here on earth (cf. 1 John 2:15-17), as opposed to heavenly and spiritual things (cf. Col 3:1-2).

COMMENTARY

Throughout this epistle one can find Paul telling the Philippians to appropriate a certain kind of thinking. This began with his prayer that they have more knowledge and insight into spiritual matters (1:9) and continued with his appeal to them to have the same attitude (2:5) and to take on the same kind of thinking Christ did when he emptied himself and became a servant (2:5ff). This theme then continues in this section, where he asks the Philippians to have the same kind of thinking as he has (3:15a). That kind of thinking is focused on knowing Christ and becoming like him both in his suffering and in his resurrection. This is the course worth pursuing. If anybody had a different focus, Paul asked God to reveal this to them (3:15b). Of course, Paul knew that some of them were already on the right course, so he told them "we must hold on to the progress we have already made" (3:16).

After this appeal, Paul made yet another: "Pattern your lives after mine." In a literal rendering this is bolder: "Become my imitators." How could a mere mortal ask others to imitate him and not be extremely arrogant? But pride was not urging Paul to make this declaration; rather, it was love—like a father telling his son, "Do it the way I do." Or, to continue the athletic imagery of the previous section, it could be said that Paul was acting as their coach and team captain. Since Paul was steadfast in his pursuit of knowing Christ, he felt he could urge others to follow him. In fact, in 4:9 he says, "Keep putting into practice all you learned and received from me—everything you heard from me and saw me doing." He urged the same from the Thessalonians (1 Thess 1:6; 2 Thess 3:7-9) and the Corinthians (1 Cor 4:6, 16-17; 11:1). Paul also encouraged the Philippians to learn from those who were following Paul's example. Undoubtedly, he was referring to men like Timothy and Epaphroditus, whom he highlighted before as exemplary servants of Christ.

While keeping a close eye on the good examples, the Philippians needed to keep another eye on those who would distract them from the central focus of the Christian life. Paul calls these people "enemies of the cross of Christ." Whoever they were, Paul had already warned the Philippians about these people before (3:18). So Paul knew who they were, and the Philippians knew who they were, but we are not made aware of exactly who they were. Understandably, commentators, trying to identify them, have offered many suggestions. Some think they were Jews or Jewish Christians proud of their circumcision (the "dogs" of 3:2), whose emphasis on Jewish legalism contradicted the real significance of the Cross of Christ. But the description that follows in 3:19 doesn't seem to fit a group of legalistic Jews. Others view them as professing believers who rejected Paul's Cross-centered view of the gospel. Such people considered it scandalous that a criminal condemned to die on a Roman cross should be the Savior of the world and that faith in his sacrificial death should be the exclusive means of salvation (see 1 Cor 1:23; cf. Rom 9:33; 1 Pet 2:8). Some identify the enemies with those mentioned in 1:28, who were opposers of the gospel. Others, in view of their description in 3:19, see them as pseudo-believers living a worldly, immoral life that rejects the real significance of the Cross of Christ.

Much can be said for the view that both 1:28 and 3:18-19 refer to the same group inasmuch as they are described as being opposers to the gospel, for which they will suffer destruction (see note on 3:19). However, other scholars think these were two different groups because they see those in 1:28 as being unbelievers, while those in 3:18-19 as being Christians after a fashion. Kennedy (1979:461) argues (1) that the verb for "live" (*peripateō* [TG4043, ZG4344]) in 3:18 is used of Christians in 3:17; (2) the apostle's tears would have no meaning unless the reference is to Christians (cf. Acts 20:31); and (3) the description "enemies" is a mere platitude if the reference is to heathen. These are good arguments for saying the reference was to Christians, not heathens, but these arguments can be countered. After all, Paul used the verb *peripateō* [TG4043, ZG4344] to speak of the way heathens lived (see 1 Cor 3:3; Eph 2:2), he shed tears for his unbelieving compatriots (Rom 9:1-3; 10:1), and he spoke of the same unbelieving Jews as being enemies of God (Rom 11:28). So it is just as likely that the enemies of 3:18-19 were unbelievers.

The scholars who see these enemies as being Christians of some kind argue that Paul was warning the Philippians about those known as libertines (see Bruce 1989:131) or antinomians—those who threw off "the moral code and decent behaviour on the mistaken ground that the body was an irrelevance once the mind had been illuminated and the soul redeemed. Hence, moral restraints could be ignored, and no carnal sin could stain the pure soul" (Martin 1987:161). Paul describes them in four ways: (1) They are headed for destruction. (2) Their god is their belly. (3) Their glory is their shame. (4) They think earthly things (see notes on each of these expressions). However, it must be noted that these terms could apply to nonbelievers as much as to Christians who do not live spiritual lives.

◆ F. Another Christ Poem (3:20-21)

20But we are citizens of heaven, where the Lord Jesus Christ lives. And we are eagerly waiting for him to return as our Savior. 21He will take our weak mortal bodies and change them into glorious bodies like his own, using the same power with which he will bring everything under his control.

NOTES
3:20 *citizens of heaven.* See note and commentary on 1:27.

the Lord Jesus Christ . . . our Savior. In the Greco-Roman world, it was common for the Caesars to call themselves "Lord" (*kurios* [TG2962, ZG3261]) and "Savior" (*sōtēr* [TG4990, ZG5400]). Christians stood alone in calling a man from Nazareth their "Lord." In addition to being their Lord, Christians considered Jesus to be their Savior, their deliverer. In the Greco-Roman world, the term was "applied to personalities who [were] active in the world's affairs, in order to remove them from the ranks of ordinary humankind and place them in a significantly higher position. For example, Epicurus is called *sōtēr* by his followers. . . . Of much greater import is the designation of the (deified) ruler as *sōtēr* (Ptolemy I Soter) . . . and often in later times, of the Roman emperors as well" (BDAG 985).

3:21 *weak mortal bodies.* Lit., "bodies of our humiliation," a more descriptive term of the human body that becomes old and decrepit.

change. The Greek verb is *metaschēmatisei* [TG3345, ZG3571], which denotes the process of transformation or transfiguration.

into glorious bodies like his own. This has the superior documentary support of 𝔓46vid ℵ A B D* F G 1739 it cop (𝔓46 is not cited in NA27, but the manuscript could not have contained the extra verbiage found in the variant; see Comfort and Barrett 2001:325). The TR expands this to "so that it might become conformed to his glorious body" with the inferior support of D1 044 075 33 𝔐. The variant is clearly a late scribal addition, attempting to alleviate Paul's terse syntax.

The Greek indicates that the process of transfiguration gives Christians a body like Christ's—*summorphon* [TG4832, ZG5215] (shared form). This comes from the same root as the verb Paul used in 3:10 to speak of his desire to be conformed to Christ's death. So Paul saw it in two phases: conformity to Christ's death, followed by conformity to Christ's glorious resurrected body (see commentary for further discussion).

using the same power. This is the power of Christ's resurrection that Paul spoke of in 3:10.

COMMENTARY
Although connected to the previous section (3:15-19), these two verses are an entity to themselves because they were either an early Christian hymn quoted by Paul or they are his own poetic composition. Hawthorne (1983:168-170) makes a good case for the section being an early Christian hymn that has several lexical ties with

Philippians 2:6-11, which he considered also to be a Christian hymn. However, I think Philippians 2:6-11 was Paul's own poetic creation, and as such, so was Philippians 3:20-21, which is presented here (translated literally) in poetic form:

> Our citizenship exists in the heavens
> from where also we eagerly expect
> the Savior, the Lord Jesus Christ
> who will transfigure our humiliating bodies
> that it may be like his glorious body
> by the power that enables him
> to subject all things to himself.

The lexical similarities between 2:6-11 and 3:20-21 strongly suggest they were composed by the same author, who had to have been Paul. There are six clear parallels (*a* is for the 2:6-11 passage; *b* is for the 3:20-21 passage). A literal translation is provided for the sake of showing lexical similarities:

PHILIPPIANS 2:6-11	PHILIPPIANS 3:20-21
A. in the *form* of God (*morphē* [TG3444, ZG3671]), 2:6a; in the form of servant (*morphē*), 2:7a	A'. conformed to his body (*summorphon* [TG4832, ZG5215]), 3:21
B. being (*huparchōn* [TG5225, ZG5639]) [in the form of God], 2:6a	B'. citizenship exists (*huparchei* [TG5225, ZG5639]) in heaven, 3:20
C. likeness (*schēma* [TG4976, ZG5386]) as a human being, 2:7b	C'. change likeness (*metaschēmatisei* [TG3345, ZG3571]) [transfigure] our bodies, 3:21
D. he humbled (*etapeinōsen* [TG5013, ZG5427]), 2:8	D'. humble condition (*tapeinōseōs* [TG5014, ZG5428]) [humility], 3:21
E. Lord Jesus Christ (*kurios Iēsous Christos* [TG2962/2424/5547, ZG3261/2652/5986]), 2:11	E'. Lord Jesus Christ (*kurion Iēsoun Christon*), 3:20
F. glory (*doxan* [TG1391, ZG1518]) of God the Father, 2:11	F'. his body of glory (*doxēs*), 3:21

The lexical similarities follow through to thematic similarities. The Christ Poem of 2:6-11 begins with Christ's eternal position as one existing in the form of God, who then chooses to take on the form of a servant by becoming a human being, and as a human being humbles himself in obedience to God, an obedience that takes him to the Cross. As a result, the Father raised him from the dead, exalting him to the highest place in the heavens and giving him the name that is above every name, so that all creation would be subdued by his presence and confess that Jesus Christ is Lord to the glory of God the Father. The poem in 3:20-21 picks up where the one in 2:6-11 left off. The believers, having confessed that Jesus Christ is Lord, know that they have a citizenship in heaven because their Lord went there after his resurrection and exaltation. But they have yet to enter into the reality of that citizenship, so they are waiting for the parousia of their Savior, the Lord Jesus Christ (see note on 3:21). When he returns he will transfigure their body of humiliation, which is the same human body Jesus took in his incarnation and then brought—thoroughly changed—into glory via the transfiguration of resurrection. The believers are awaiting his return because he will transfigure their bodies in conformity to his glorious body. In this way, they will share his glorified humanity. All this can take place because Jesus has been enthroned on high above every name that is named and thereby has the power to subject all things to himself.

The parousia of Christ will bring about the final salvation for Christians (Titus 2:13). Christians will be glorified with Christ as they will receive glorified, resurrected bodies like Christ's (3:21). This is called the transfiguration of the body, the final step in one's salvation. In 1 Corinthians 15, Paul devotes several words to explaining this phenomenon when answering two questions the Corinthians posed about resurrection: (1) How are the dead raised? and (2) With what sort of body do they come? (1 Cor 15:35). To the first question Paul responds, "What a foolish question! When you put a seed into the ground, it doesn't grow into a plant unless it dies first" (1 Cor 15:36). This follows Jesus' saying in John 12:24: "Unless a kernel of wheat is planted in the soil and dies, it remains alone. But its death will produce many new kernels." The grain must die before it can be quickened. Paul devoted more explanation to the second question; and the Spirit inspired his sublime utterance to unfold this mystery. Using the same natural example of the grain of wheat, Paul revealed that the body that comes forth in resurrection is altogether different in form from that which had been sown. Through an organic process, the single bare grain is transformed into a stalk of wheat. In essence, the grain and the stalk are one and the same—the latter simply being the living growth and expressed expansion of the former. In short, the stalk is the glory of the grain or the glorified grain. This illustration shows that Jesus' resurrected body was altogether different from the one that was buried. In death, he had been sown in corruption, dishonor, and weakness; but in resurrection, he came forth in incorruption, glory, and power. The natural body that Jesus possessed as a man became a spiritual body. And at the same time Christ became "life-giving Spirit." The first man, Adam, became a living soul with a "soulical" body (a term used in *The Emphasized Bible*, Rotherham); the last Adam, Jesus, became life-giving Spirit with a spiritual body (1 Cor 15:44-45). This spiritual, glorified body suited his new spiritual life. In like manner, Christians will receive a transfigured, glorified body to suit their new spiritual life post-resurrection. Thus, Christians will then bear the image of the heavenly man (1 Cor 15:49). This, as Paul put it so eloquently, is the final phase of our salvation:

> It will happen in a moment, in the blink of an eye, when the last trumpet is blown. For when the trumpet sounds, those who have died will be raised to live forever. And we who are living will also be transformed. For our dying bodies must be transformed into bodies that will never die; our mortal bodies must be transformed into immortal bodies. (1 Cor 15:52-53)

◆ IV. Closing of the Letter (4:1-23)
A. Appeal to Co-workers (4:1-3)

Therefore, my dear brothers and sisters,* stay true to the Lord. I love you and long to see you, dear friends, for you are my joy and the crown I receive for my work.

²Now I appeal to Euodia and Syntyche. Please, because you belong to the Lord, settle your disagreement. ³And I ask you, my true partner,* to help these two women, for they worked hard with me in telling others the Good News. They worked along with Clement and the rest of my co-workers, whose names are written in the Book of Life.

4:1 Greek brothers; also in 4:8.   4:3 Or loyal Syzygus.

NOTES

4:1 This verse provides a link between chapters 3 and 4 in that (1) it completes Paul's athletic imagery of running the race to achieve the prize of knowing Christ (ch 3) and (2) it introduces the beginning of a personal appeal.

stay true to the Lord. Lit., "stand in the Lord." This was to be understood in light of his warnings in 3:2 and 3:18-19.

dear friends. Lit., "beloved ones."

you are my joy and the crown I receive for my work. The NLT fleshes out the sparse expression, "my joy and crown."

4:2 *because you belong to the Lord, settle your disagreement.* Lit., "think the same thing in the Lord." Unity among members of the church depends on unity of thinking—specifically, Christlike thinking. This is one of the central themes of this epistle (see 2:2-5).

4:3 *true partner.* Since the grammar indicates that Paul was speaking to one person, some translators (see NJB NRSV mg NIV mg NLT mg) have understood the expression *erōtō kai se gnēsie suzuge* (normally translated, "I also entreat you, true yokefellow") to refer to a particular individual named *Suzugos* [TG4805/A, ZG5187] (a singular masculine noun; Latinized as "Syzygus"). Otherwise, the text leaves "the true yokefellow" unnamed. Since all the earliest manuscripts were written with uncials (capital letters), there is no way to determine if ancient scribes designated a proper name. In any event, there is no such name known in the Greco-Roman world (Fee 1995:393).

telling others the Good News. Lit., "in the gospel." Or, "the work of the gospel." Exactly how they contributed to the work of the gospel is not clear.

Clement. This is the only reference to this person in the NT. One of the earliest extant Christian documents apart from the biblical texts themselves is a letter attributed to Clement of Rome (*1 Clement*, c. AD 97), who is traditionally identified with the Clement mentioned here (Eusebius, *Ecclesiastical History* 3.15-16).

the rest of my co-workers. This reading has the support of 𝔓46 ℵ¹ A B D Ivid. A variant reading is "and my co-workers and the rest" according to 𝔓16vid ℵ*. The two readings are significantly different. In context, the first reading yields this translation: "They [Euodia and Syntyche] have labored side by side with me in the gospel together with Clement and the rest of my co-workers, whose names are in the Book of Life." The second reading is as follows: "They [Euodia and Syntyche] have labored side by side with me in the gospel together with Clement and my co-workers and the rest, whose names are written in the Book of Life."

Some scholars (such as Metzger 1994:549) think the textual variant in 𝔓16vid and ℵ* should not be taken seriously because it is the result of scribal inadvertence. Other scholars (such as Silva 1992:223) urge that it should not be easily dismissed as scribal inadvertence because the evidence of 𝔓16 shows that "it was an early competing variant." And this variant appears to reflect "a different understanding of Paul's words (i.e., that the women and Clement are not included under the category of 'co-workers')." If so, this variant could reflect an antifeminist tendency to exclude women from among those who were considered apostles and/or co-laborers with the apostles.

In any event, it is possible to interpret both variants as indicating that all the ones mentioned have their names written in the Book of Life. To make this interpretation, one has to consider that the pronoun *hōn* [TG3739, ZG4005] is generically inclusive; it is not restrictive to *sunergōn* [TG4904, ZG5301] (co-workers) or *loipōn* [TG3062, ZG3370] (rest) but includes all those previously mentioned, including Euodia, Syntyche, Clement, the unnamed co-workers, and the rest (Comfort 2005:348-349).

whose names are written in the Book of Life. This is a symbol of the record of true believers who have received eternal life. For other references to "the Book of Life," see Rev 3:5; 13:8; 17:8; 20:12, 15; 21:27; cf. Exod 32:32; Ps 69:28; Dan 12:1; Luke 10:20.

COMMENTARY

The Philippians' continuing faithfulness to Christ was a deep source of joy to Paul and the crown for his hard work. The crown was a wreath of leaves placed on the head of a victor of an athletic contest. As such, Paul was moving the athletic imagery of 3:12-14 forward and bringing it to the Philippians in new light. Previously, Paul had spoken of his pursuit of the prize (3:12); here he tells the Philippians that they are his prize, his crown. Paul told the Thessalonians the same thing (1 Thess 2:19-20).

Because the church at Philippi was Paul's work and one day would be his crowning achievement, he made another appeal for unity (cf. 2:1-2)—this time, to two women, Euodia and Syntyche. We know that the church in Philippi was started when Paul and Timothy preached the gospel to some Jewish women who regularly met by the riverside for prayer (Acts 16:13). Among these women was Lydia; she and her household became the first believers there (Acts 16:14-15). The church in Philippi began with her and met in her home (Acts 16:15, 40). It is possible that these women, Euodia and Syntyche, were among the first believers in Philippi. At some juncture they accompanied Paul as his co-workers in proclaiming the gospel (v. 3). Presumably they were leaders who were at odds with one another. This attitude promoted discord and division—an issue Paul had addressed in 2:1-5.

Paul asked his true partner, his yokefellow, to help these women restore concord. Since this person is left unidentified, scholars have attempted to name various individuals such as Timothy (but he was with Paul at the time of writing), Luke, a person name Syzygus (see note on 3:3), the husband or brother of Euodia and Syntyche, or Epaphroditus. Lightfoot (1976:158) writes, "It seems most probable that Epaphroditus, the bearer of the letter is intended; for in his case alone there would be no risk of making the reference unintelligible by the suppression of his name." However, if Epaphroditus was present at the time of writing, which was the usual custom of the day (so that the carrier of the letter could explain any difficult parts to the hearers), then it would be odd for Paul to speak of him in this way. Hawthorne (1983:180) thought Paul might have been addressing the entire church (as a single entity) to help these two women restore their unity, but this seems unlikely because the readers would not have readily recognized this.

Fee (1995:393-39) makes a good case for the individual being Luke, who presumably had spent some time with the church in Philippi. Luke is most likely the person associated with the "we" passages of Acts, which begin in Acts 16 with Luke in Philippi and do not resume until Acts 20:1-5, some four to six years later in the narrative. Furthermore, Luke had been with Paul when he wrote his earlier Prison Epistles, Colossians (Col 4:14) and Philemon (Phlm 1:24), but he was not mentioned in Philippians. Therefore, it makes good sense that Luke was in Philippi at the time of writing.

Paul wanted the Philippians to know that Euodia and Syntyche were honorable women who had been his co-workers contending together with him (*sunathleō* [TG4866, ZG5254]) for the work of the gospel. The word again comes out of the athletic games; it is the same word Paul used in 1:27 to encourage all the Philippians to contend—not against each other—but *with* one another for the sake of advancing the gospel.

At this juncture, Paul mentions a certain person named Clement as also being one of his co-workers. As far as Paul was concerned, each of these co-workers had their names written in the Book of Life. This term may have had its origin in Exodus where Moses said to God, "Forgive their sin—but if not, erase my name from the record you have written" (Exod 32:32). To which God responded, "I will erase the name of everyone who has sinned against me" (Exod 32:33). The image continued to be used in the Jewish tradition (Pss 56:8; 69:28; 139:16) and was more fully developed in Revelation, where it is also called "the Book of Life" (Rev 3:5) and "the Book that belongs to the Lamb" (Rev 13:8). In Revelation 20:12-15, all people are judged by whether or not their names are written in the Book of Life (Rev 20:12, 15); those not found there are the spiritually dead (Rev 20:15). Those who are written in this book may enter into the joys of everlasting life in the new heavens and new earth. This is the privilege of every true believer. Paul knew that his co-workers had their names written in the Book of Life because they were faithful servants of Jesus Christ. F. F. Bruce (1989:139) suggests that it is possible that their service, along with their names, is also written in the Book of Life.

◆   B. Joy and Peace in Christ (4:4-9)

⁴Always be full of joy in the Lord. I say it again—rejoice! ⁵Let everyone see that you are considerate in all you do. Remember, the Lord is coming soon.

⁶Don't worry about anything; instead, pray about everything. Tell God what you need, and thank him for all he has done. ⁷Then you will experience God's peace, which exceeds anything we can understand. His peace will guard your hearts and minds as you live in Christ Jesus.

⁸And now, dear brothers and sisters, one final thing. Fix your thoughts on what is true, and honorable, and right, and pure, and lovely, and admirable. Think about things that are excellent and worthy of praise. ⁹Keep putting into practice all you learned and received from me—everything you heard from me and saw me doing. Then the God of peace will be with you.

NOTES

4:4 *Always be full of joy in the Lord . . . rejoice!* This is the third time Paul encouraged the believers to rejoice (2:18; 3:1). Joy is not happiness derived from good circumstances; believers may have joy in the Lord even in the midst of suffering. This joy is the spiritual presence of the Lord.

4:5 *considerate.* The Greek word (*epieikēs* [TG1933A, ZG2117]) denotes gentleness, gracious-ness, and balanced temperament. Jesus Christ is the epitome of *epieikēs* (2 Cor 10:1).

the Lord is coming soon. Lit., "the Lord is near." The Greek word *engus* [TG1451, ZG1584] means "near"—spatially, temporally, or relationally. Therefore, this could speak of the Lord's presence (as in Ps 145:18 [144:18, LXX]) or of his parousia, the Second Coming (spoken of in 1 Cor 16:22; Rev 22:20); it is likely an intended double entendre (Fee 1995:407). Knowledge of the Lord's coming should stimulate believers to live holy lives because after he comes all Christians must give an account of their lives.

4:6 *Don't worry about anything; instead, pray about everything.* The first clause is a sweeping admonition against anxiety, which is tempered by the second clause. Prayer is the antidote for anxiety. Since God loves his children, he cares about their needs, which they may express to him in prayer (see Matt 7:9-11; 1 Pet 5:7).

4:7 *God's peace.* Significantly, several of Paul's letters both begin and end with an invoca-tion of peace (1:2; 4:7, 9; Rom 1:7; 16:20; 2 Cor 1:2; 13:11; Gal 1:3; 6:16; Eph 1:2; 6:23; 2 Thess 1:2; 3:16). Here Paul says what the peace of God will do: It will guard the hearts and minds of Christians.

which exceeds anything we can understand. The idea that the peace of God transcends all our understanding means that it is so wonderful that no human mind could ever grasp its significance. It can also mean that God's peace is more effective for removing anxiety than any intellectual effort or power of reasoning.

will guard. The verb for "guard" (*phroureō* [TG5432, ZG5864]) is a military term depicting God's peace as a sentinel guarding a city to protect it from attack. In a garrison town like Philippi, this would have had special meaning.

your hearts and minds. Lit., "your hearts and thoughts." This is the reading in most manu-scripts. But this differs in some Western witnesses (D F it^a,d), which read "your hearts and your bodies." This variant must have been early because the third-century manuscript, 𝔓16, has a conflated reading: "your hearts and minds and your bodies." It is not easy to account for how *noēmata* [TG3540, ZG3784] (thoughts) became *sōmata* [TG4983, ZG5393] (bodies), unless, of course, it was miscopied by a scribe due to homoeoteleuton. But if it wasn't a scribal mistake, what would have motivated a scribe to change *noēmata* to *sōmata* or vice versa? Divine protection of heart and thoughts speaks of God's superintendence over a believer's psychological life, whereas divine protection of heart and body speaks of God's care over a believer's psychologi-cal and physical life. The context guides us to think that Paul was considering God's protection over the believers' thought-life. But in later times, especially when the church was undergoing persecution, it is easy to see how this verse could have been applied to God's complete protec-tion of the believer and subsequently been altered from "thoughts" to "bodies."

4:8 *Fix your thoughts on what is true, and honorable, and right, and pure, and lovely, and admirable. . . . things that are excellent and worthy of praise.* Each of these virtues and the sum total of them are what Greco-Romans prized as the best virtues a person could display. This sentence could easily have been found in Epictetus's *Discourses* or Sen-eca's *Moral Essays*, in the context of extolling the best of moral virtues. But the words also are found in the LXX. So it is not necessary to argue that Paul drew upon either source to the exclusion of the other. However, it should be noted that he used terms that were famil-iar to his Greek readers from the philosophical moralists (particularly the Stoics).

4:9 *Keep putting into practice all you learned and received from me.* Lit., "which things you also learned and received and heard and saw in me." In Greek the verse begins with a relative pronoun (*ha* [TG3739, ZG4005], "which") that refers back to the "things" Paul was encouraging the believers to think about in 4:8 (*tauta logizesthe* [TG3778/3049A, ZG4047/3357], "these things think"). In other words, Paul was saying that the good qualities itemized in 4:8 were embodied in him and displayed in him. At first glance, this seems to be egotistical. However, it must be noted that Paul was affirming the notion that the Christian traditions were passed down from one generation to the next. "The Greek term for 'received' (*paralabete* [TG3880, ZG4161]) is a technical term used for the receiving of a tradition (1 Cor 11:23; 15:3). Before the composition of the New Testament and its acceptance as authoritative Scripture, the tradition as a standard of Christian belief and behaviour, was embodied in the teaching and example of those persons in whose lives the authority and ethical practice of the Lord was to be found" (Martin 1987:175). Paul refers to such traditions in a number of places (1 Cor 11:2; 15:1-3; Gal 1:9; Col 2:6; 1 Thess 4:1-2; 2 Thess 2:15).

COMMENTARY

The joyful words that commence this section are connected with Paul's previous statement concerning his co-workers having their names written in the Book of Life (4:3). By implication, this registry included all the believers in Philippi, for they also would have their names written in the Book of Life. This is cause for great joy!

This joy is derived from the reality that the believers are "in the Lord"—that is, he is their life and source of contentment by virtue of their spiritual union with them. Paul says in the next verse, "the Lord is coming soon." Aside from the eschatological significance of this statement, Paul was telling the Philippians that the Lord is near via his Spirit. Those who experience him as such are those who display his virtues—the first of which is showing consideration to others (see note on 4:5), the second of which is living a life of prayer rather than a life of anxiety (4:6). Those who turn to God in prayer are those who find that God's peace, as present in Christ, acts as a guard against all evils. This peace protects the believer's heart and thoughts as the believer lives in union with Christ. This is the central theme of this epistle: A believer's union with Christ will manifest itself in transformed thinking, thinking that models Christ's mind.

Those with transformed thinking—or those who aspire to have transformed thinking—are those who acknowledge that certain virtues will be the focus of their attention and their lifestyle. Paul lists eight aspects of this virtuous life:

1. True (*alēthē* [TG227, ZG239])—This speaks of what is valid, reliable, and honest.
2. Honorable (*semna* [TG4586, ZG4948])—This speaks of what is noble. It is used only by Paul in the New Testament (1 Tim 3:8, 11; Titus 2:2) as a quality that should be exhibited in elders.
3. Right (*dikaia* [TG1342, ZG1465])—This refers to what is just and fair.
4. Pure (*hagna* [TG53, ZG54])—This denotes moral purity.
5. Lovely (*prosphilē* [TG4375, ZG4713])—This refers to what is amiable and beautiful, pleasing and agreeable. This is the only occurrence of the word in the New Testament; it appears in Esther 5:2 (LXX). In Greek writings, it is used to describe

people who are kindly affectioned, well disposed, agreeable, and friendly (LSJ 1530).

6. Admirable (*euphēma* [TG2163, ZG2368])—This connotes what is of good repute and what is winsome.

7. Excellent (*aretē* [TG703, ZG746])—This denotes virtue, excellence, goodness. This is the only time Paul used the word; the other occurrences of it in the New Testament are 1 Peter 2:9; 2 Peter 1:3, 5. As far as the Stoic philosophers were concerned, *aretē* was the greatest of all virtues.

8. Worthy of praise (*epainos* [TG1868, ZG2047])—This denotes conduct that wins the praise of others.

Though these moral qualities have been presented as a list, their presentation by Paul is poetic in design, leading some to think he borrowed this section from some philosophical writing. But since no one has found such an excerpt, it stands to reason that Paul simply took over "terms that were current coin in popular moral philosophy, especially Stoicism. He wants his Philippian friends to develop those qualities which are good in themselves and beneficial to others, and so he has pressed these terms into service" (O'Brien 1991:502-503).

Paul was encouraging the Philippians to let their minds continually dwell on the positive virtues he mentioned. In so doing, they could take an active role in renewing their minds. Paul knew that right thinking precedes right action. As a man thinks, so he is. This is an important goal laid out in this epistle—namely, that the Philippians would develop a thought life like Christ's (see 1:11; 2:2-3; 3:15).

Paul also knew that the believers needed living examples of those who were pursuing this inward transformation. In this light, Paul pointed to himself as an example to be followed. If they followed his example, they would be receiving the correct traditions of the Christian life (see note on 4:9). Before the Christian traditions were committed to writing, later forming the corpus of New Testament Scriptures, the apostles exhibited them to be learned, heard, seen, and received by the people (Martin 1987:175). Paul was a man whose mind had been renewed by Christ and whose life exhibited the virtues of one who was Christlike. As such, he was bold in telling others to follow his example and thereby live in the peace of God.

◆ C. Paul's Thanksgiving for the Philippians' Gift (4:10-20)

¹⁰How I praise the Lord that you are concerned about me again. I know you have always been concerned for me, but you didn't have the chance to help me. ¹¹Not that I was ever in need, for I have learned how to be content with whatever I have. ¹²I know how to live on almost nothing or with everything. I have learned the secret of living in every situation, whether it is with a full stomach or empty, with plenty or little. ¹³For I can do everything through Christ,* who gives me strength. ¹⁴Even so, you have done well to share with me in my present difficulty.

¹⁵As you know, you Philippians were the only ones who gave me financial help when I first brought you the Good News and then traveled on from Macedonia. No other church did this. ¹⁶Even when I was in Thessalonica you sent help more than

once. ¹⁷I don't say this because I want a gift from you. Rather, I want you to receive a reward for your kindness.

¹⁸At the moment I have all I need—and more! I am generously supplied with the gifts you sent me with Epaphroditus. They are a sweet-smelling sacrifice that is ac-

ceptable and pleasing to God. ¹⁹And this same God who takes care of me will supply all your needs from his glorious riches, which have been given to us in Christ Jesus.

²⁰Now all glory to God our Father forever and ever! Amen.

4:13 Greek *through the one.*

NOTES

4:10 *you are concerned about me.* The Greek verb is *phronein* [TG5426, ZG5858], a verb that is central to Paul's message concerning Christlike thinking (see 2:2-3; 3:15). Their good, self-sacrificial thoughts for Paul became the motivation for giving money to him.

again. This is a weak translation of a vivid Greek word (*anathallō* [TG330, ZG352]), a word used only here in the NT, which denotes plants and flowers "blooming again." Many English versions render it as "renewed" or "revived."

4:11 *content.* The Greek word is *autarkēs* [TG842, ZG895], which means "sufficient in oneself, self-supporting, self-reliant, strong enough." It appears only here in the NT. The related verb is *arkeomai* [TG714A, ZG758], which means "to be strong enough, to suffice, to be sufficient, to be content." It is used in the Lord's statement to Paul, "My grace is all you need" (2 Cor 12:9), and when John the Baptist told the Roman soldiers "Be content with your pay" (Luke 3:14). The Greek noun *autakrēs* was used by Stoics to describe the essence of all virtues. The Stoic doctrine was that "man should be sufficient unto himself for all things, and able, by the power of his own will, to resist the force of circumstances" (cited by Vincent 1922:143). Seneca said, "The happy man is content with his present lot, no matter what it is, and is reconciled to his circumstance" (*De vita beata* 6).

4:12 *to live on almost nothing or with everything.* Lit., "to be humbled and to abound."

I have learned the secret. The Greek word (*memuēmai* [TG3453, ZG3679]) was used to denote the initiation experience of those entering into one of the many mystery cults. Paul's "learning the secret" meant that he had learned self-sufficiency in Christ.

it is with a full stomach or empty. Lit., "to be filled/satisfied and to go hungry."

with plenty or little. Lit., "to abound and to suffer lack." The six verbs in the Greek, all present tense infinitives, have been rendered in easy-to-understand English in the NLT. However, the rendering leads the reader to think that Paul was speaking only of his physical needs. The verbs in Greek, while speaking of physical conditions, also point to spiritual conditions such as humility, emptiness, fullness, and abundance (see commentary).

4:13 *through Christ, who gives me strength.* Lit., "in the one who empowers me," which is a reading with outstanding textual support: ℵ* A B D* I 33 1739 it cop. Other manuscripts specify that it was "Christ" who did the empowering: ℵ² D² F G 044 𝔐 syr (so TR). This variant is clearly a scribal addition (note the late corrections in ℵ and D) intended to make it absolutely clear that it was Christ who empowered Paul (see 1 Tim 1:12), as does the NLT text. But Paul hardly had to say this. Furthermore, he may have been thinking of "the Spirit of Jesus Christ" because Paul had previously referred to him as the one who supplied all he needed (see 1:19).

4:15 *you Philippians were the only ones who gave me financial help when I first brought you the Good News.* For Luke's account of Paul's initial missionary work in Philippi and the difficulties he faced there, see Acts 16:11-40.

Macedonia. This was the Roman province of northern Greece. Paul traveled on to the province of Achaia in southern Greece, spending time at Athens and Corinth. For Luke's account on Paul's initial missionary work in these two cities, see Acts 17:15–18:18; for the Philippians' gift to Paul when he was in Achaia, see 2 Cor 11:9.

4:16 *Thessalonica.* This city is about 75 miles west-southwest of Philippi, along the Aegean coast. On his first missionary trip to Macedonia, after leaving Philippi, Paul traveled directly to Thessalonica. He encountered opposition in both cities (for Luke's account of Paul's initial missionary work in Thessalonica, see Acts 17:1-8; cf. Paul's account in 1 Thess 2:1-14).

you sent help. Lit., "you sent to my need." In the Greek, this is *eis tēn chreian moi epempsate* (cf. *chreia* [TG5532, ZG5970]) and has the support of ℵ B F G 044 𝔐. In the Greek, this reading has no direct object after "sent." A variant on this reading is *tēn chreian moi epempsate*, supported by 𝔓46 A 81. This variant reading drops the preposition *eis* [TG1519, ZG1650], thereby making *tēn chreian* a direct object, which yields the translation, "you sent me what was needed" [i.e., money].

4:18 *Epaphroditus.* He was the messenger who brought the gift from Philippi (see Paul's commendation of Epaphroditus in 2:25-30).

a sweet-smelling sacrifice that is acceptable and pleasing to God. In the OT, the smell of burning sacrifices and acceptable offerings is spoken of as a pleasant fragrance to God (see Lev 1:9, 13, 17; 2:2, 9; 3:5, 16; cf. Rom 12:1; Eph 5:2).

4:19 *this same God who takes care of me.* Lit., "and my God."

will supply all your needs. This is the reading of 𝔓46 ℵ A B D2 𝔐. Other manuscripts (D* F G 044 33 1739 1881) support the reading, "may [my God] supply all your needs." According to the text followed by the NLT, the full statement here is, "My God will supply all your needs according to his riches in glory in Christ Jesus." The variant reading expresses a wish: "May God supply all your needs according to his riches in glory in Christ Jesus." Although it could be argued that the variant is simply a scribal mistake wherein an *alpha* replaced an *epsilon,* (*plērōsei/plērōsai*) it is not likely that the same mistake would have occurred in such diverse witnesses (both Alexandrian and Western). Rather, it appears that the change was motivated by some scribe (or scribes) who took issue with a statement that promises that God will take care of all our needs. Since this doesn't always square with our perceptions of things, we can imagine why a scribe would want to change it from the future indicative (denoting promise) to the aorist optative (denoting wishfulness). Thus, according to the variant reading, Paul was not promising the Philippians that God *will* supply all their needs; rather, he was praying that God *would* hopefully supply all their needs (see Hawthorne's discussion, 1983:207-208). But the reading of the text does not have to mean that God gives every believer a carte blanche promissory note. Indeed, the context indicates Paul promised that God will take care of the Philippians' spiritual needs in response to their taking care of Paul's physical needs.

from his glorious riches, which have been given to us in Christ Jesus. Lit., "according to his riches in glory in Christ Jesus." Glory is experienced in this present life, as well as in the life beyond.

COMMENTARY

In closing this epistle, Paul thanked the Philippians for the monetary gift they sent him by the hand of Epaphroditus (see 4:18; cf. 1:5; 2:25-30). His appreciation for their contribution had already been expressed in the beginning of the letter (1:5; see note), but rather subtly. In finishing his letter, Paul expressly thanked the

Philippians for their gift. He saw their giving as a true expression of Christlike thinking (see note on 4:10), which is at the core of Paul's message to the Philippians (see 2:2-3; 3:15). Their thoughts for Paul's need became the motivation for giving money to him.

They had given to him before, when he first traveled from Philippi to Thessalonica (4:16) and then into Achaia (2 Cor 11:9). Paul noted their generosity of those days and commended them for being the only church that took care of his financial needs (4:15). Evidently, they had stayed in contact with Paul for the next few years until somehow the communication between them ceased. "For some unknown reason the Philippians were cut off from Paul and he from them. As a consequence, doubts may have arisen, as would only be natural, about the genuineness of their concern for him. Hence, it was with a great sense of relief that this silence of uncertainty was broken with the arrival of Epaphroditus from Philippi" (Hawthorne 1983:197). Paul was so thankful that their thoughts for him had blossomed again (see note on 4:10).

Almost as soon as Paul uttered his thanks, he indicated that he didn't really need the money because he had learned "to be content with whatever [he had]" (4:11). The notion of contentment (Gr. *autarkēs* [TG842, ZG895]) was important in Stoic philosophy. It described the attitude of people who accepted whatever came their way in life (see note on 4:11). One cannot change the circumstances that come one's way, so fretting is useless. This philosophy fostered a self-sufficiency in which all the resources for coping with life were located within each person. In contrast, Paul claims his sufficiency is in Christ.

Borrowing a term from the mystery cults (see note on 4:12), Paul said, "I have learned the secret (*memuēmai* [TG3453, ZG3679]) of living." Earlier in the epistle he proclaimed, "For to me, living means living for Christ" (1:21). This is the key to Paul's having learned the secret of how to live in his present situation. This is emphasized by the seven present-tense infinitives used in 4:11-12 (I have noted the voice of the infinitive as active or passive in each case):

1. To be self-reliant (*autarkēs einai* [TG842/1510, ZG895/1639]; active)
2. To be humbled (*tapeinousthai* [TG5013, ZG5427]; passive)
3. To abound (*perisseuein* [TG4052, ZG4355]; active)
4. To be filled/satisfied (*chortazesthai* [TG5526A, ZG5963]; passive)
5. To hunger (*peinan* [TG3983, ZG4277]; active)
6. To abound (*perisseuein* [TG4052, ZG4355]; active)
7. To suffer lack (*hustereisthai* [TG5302, ZG5728]; passive)

The active voice verbs suggest Paul's initiative in his life choices. He actively pursued being self-reliant and self-content, enjoying abundance, and going without food. The passive voice verbs suggest the actions that came his way in life, actions he had no choice but to receive and be subject to. These life events humbled him and caused him to suffer deficit, which were prerequisites for him to be filled. Verse 13 also has two present tense expressions: "I can do everything" and "who gives me strength." Paul was an existential Christian—that is, he lived by Christ in the present, for the present. In all situations, he had learned to live by the power of another one—namely, the Spirit of Jesus Christ indwelling him (1:19). This powerful presence enabled Paul to go through bad times and good. Paul no longer relied on his own strength but on the strength of the Spirit of Jesus Christ, who lived in him and worked through him (see Gal 2:20; Col 1:27; cf. 2 Cor 1:8-10; 4:7-12; 12:8-10).

Though Paul was self-sufficient by virtue of his power source coming from Christ, he still needed and depended on the other members of the Christian community. As such, he thanked the Philippians for their gift yet again (4:14) and commended their generosity and care. At the same time, he wanted to make it clear that he was not seeking their gift (4:17). Indeed, throughout his ministry, Paul worked to support himself by tentmaking (see Acts 18:3; 1 Cor 4:12; 9:3-18). He did this so he wouldn't face the criticism that he was doing his ministry for the sake of gaining money. Since he had faced this criticism from the Corinthians, he would not accept money from them (1 Cor 9:11-18; 2 Cor 11:7-12). Because he did not face criticism from the Philippians as he did from the Corinthians, he was more ready to accept their financial help. Paul viewed the Philippians' generosity as "fruit that would increase their account" (4:17; my translation), or as it is rendered in NJB: "What I value is the interest that is mounting up in your account." Paul used a financial metaphor to tell the Philippians that their contribution would repay them richly with accruing spiritual benefits.

In concluding his expression of thanksgiving, Paul culminates the great theme of this epistle: Sacrifice is the pathway to glory. Christ willingly took this path, as is so beautifully expressed in the Christ Poem (2:5-11). Paul was taking this path, inasmuch as he was a poured-out liquid offering (2:17), who wanted to know the fellowship of Christ's sufferings and be conformed to the image of his death so that he might attain the resurrection (3:10-11). And the Philippians were taking the path of sacrifice, as Paul noted in 2:17 (he was a liquid offering poured on the sacrifice of their faith) and here again in 4:18, where he says that the Philippians' gift was a "sweet-smelling sacrifice that is acceptable and pleasing to God" (see note on 4:18). The reward for sacrifice is that God supplies the needs of believers "from his glorious riches, which have been given to us in Christ Jesus" (4:19). As was stated in the note on 4:19, Paul was offering this as a promise to the Philippians whose faith he knew. This is not a carte blanche statement that Christians can use to insist that God give them everything they want.

The final outcome of the sacrifice and God's spiritual supply is that God the Father is glorified. This was the outcome of Christ's sacrifice and exaltation, as is stated at the end of the Christ Poem: "to the glory of God the Father" (2:11). This was the goal of Paul's life, and even his death—that he would glorify Christ (1:20). And this is the goal of all spiritual transformation: that God the Father is glorified. As it says in the Westminster Shorter Catechism: "Man's chief end is to glorify God, and to enjoy him forever."

◆   D. Paul's Final Greetings (4:21–23)

²¹Give my greetings to each of God's holy people—all who belong to Christ Jesus. The brothers who are with me send you their greetings. ²²And all the rest of God's people send you greetings, too, especially those in Caesar's household.

²³May the grace of the Lord Jesus Christ be with your spirit.

NOTES

4:22 *And all the rest of God's people.* Lit., "all the holy ones," referring to the whole Christian community in the place from where Paul was writing, which was most likely Rome.

those in Caesar's household. This expression refers to those in the imperial family, as well as to those involved in the imperial service, whether slaves or freedmen. This statement, together with that of 1:13, points to Rome as the place from which Paul wrote this epistle. Fee said, "This little phrase joins with the mention of the 'Praetorian Guard' in 1:13 as the strongest kind of evidence for the Roman origins of this letter" (1995:459).

4:23 *the grace of the Lord Jesus Christ.* This benediction both opens (1:2) and concludes the letter.

be with your spirit. The reading "with your spirit" has the excellent support of 𝔓46 ℵ* A B D F G 1739 cop. Other manuscripts (ℵ² 044 𝔐 syr) read "with you all." Either variant can be attributed to harmonization to the benedictions of other Pauline Epistles: the NLT's reading with Gal 6:18 and Phlm 1:25; the variant with 1 Cor 16:24; 2 Cor 13:14; 2 Thess 3:18; Titus 3:15. Consequently, we must look to the documentary evidence for the original reading. In this case, the reading followed by the NLT clearly has superior attestation.

COMMENTARY

In accord with his usual practice, Paul had probably dictated this letter to an amanuensis (a secretary). We know that this was Paul's habit by what we read at the conclusion of several of his other epistles. The conclusion to Romans provides the name of Paul's amanuensis: Tertius (Rom 16:22). We can discern that Paul must have dictated other epistles because he specifically noted that he provided the concluding salutation in his own handwriting: 1 Corinthians (1 Cor 16:21), Galatians (Gal 6:11), Colossians (Col 4:18), and 2 Thessalonians (2 Thess 3:17). (For more on the function of the amanuensis, see Comfort 2005:4-9.) Thus, it stands to reason that he did so at the end of Philippians. Paul probably took the stylus from the amanuensis and wrote the concluding lines in his own hand. This accords with many Hellenistic letters, where the main body of the letter is in one handwriting (usually quite neat) and another handwriting (usually quite casual or scrawled) appears at the end. The first hand is that of the amanuensis, and the concluding hand is that of the author of the letter. For examples of this, see P. Oxyrhynchus 3057, late first or early second century (considered by some to be the earliest extant letter written by a Christian), and see P. London 2078 (dated AD 81–96).

The first line of the final greeting (4:21a) is unusual in that the Greek says *aspasasthe panta hagion* [ᵀᴳ782/3956/40A, ᶻᴳ832/4246/41], which means "you [plural] give greetings to every saint." The verb is second person plural, when we would have expected first-person singular ("I greet") or plural ("we greet"). Though Fee disagrees (1995:457), the "you" plural must be the overseers and deacons whom Paul specifically addressed in the opening of the letter (1:1). Evidently, they were the ones who would first read this epistle and then read it to all the members of the church in Philippi. As they did so, they were to give greetings to every single Christian in the church—as it were, one by one.

In the second sentence of the final greeting, Paul says, "The brothers who are with me send you their greetings" (4:21b). These would have been the fellow Christians closely associated with Paul while he was under house arrest. They probably would have included those mentioned in this same context at the end of his other Prison Epistles—namely, Aristarchus, Mark (Col 4:10; Phlm 1:24), Tychicus (Eph 6:21; Col 4:7), Demas, Luke (Col 4:14; Phlm 1:24), and Timothy (1:1; 2:19-24; Col 1:1).

In the third sentence of the final greeting, Paul forwards the greetings of all God's people to the Philippians. This group would be the Christians in the locality from which Paul was writing, which seems most likely to have been Rome. This is affirmed by the next statement, where Paul specifies a group of Christians within that larger group of local believers—namely "those in Caesar's household" (4:22). When coupled with Paul's statement in 1:13 (where Paul states that the whole Praetorian Guard knew he had been imprisoned for Christ), this makes it quite clear that Paul was in Rome when he wrote this epistle. It also tells us that the gospel had not been hindered by Paul's imprisonment; rather, he had advanced it by proclaiming the gospel, which had reached members of Caesar Nero's household.

Some scholars have tried to identify a few of the Christians who may have been part of Caesar's household. If this letter was sent from Rome (which seems quite likely) and Romans 16 was sent to Rome (three or four years earlier), then it could be asked if some of the individuals noted in Romans 16:3-16 were members of Caesar's household (Bruce 1989:158). Lightfoot (1976:171-178) suggested two groups in particular: "the household of Aristobulus," and "the household of Narcissus" (Rom 16:10-11). The family of Narcissus may have comprised the slaves of Tiberius Claudius Narcissus, a wealthy freedman of the Emperor Tiberius. Lightfoot suggested that Aristobulus was identical with a grandson of Herod the Great by that name who is known to have lived in Rome and enjoyed the friendship of Claudius.

In the concluding verse of the final greeting, Paul emphasizes the need for the believers to experience the grace of the Lord Jesus Christ in the spirit. This accords with his earlier exhortation for them to be one in spirit (see 2:2) and with his proclamation that Christians are those who worship by the Spirit of God (3:3). The only way to experience the Spirit of Jesus Christ (1:19) is in spirit—the human spirit regenerated by the divine Spirit in tune with the presence of Christ. This is the key to knowing Christ in his invisible spiritual presence, and this is the key to receiving his grace.

BIBLIOGRAPHY

Alford, Henry
1976 *The Greek Testament* (5 vols.). Grand Rapids: Guardian. (Orig. Pub. 1852)

Ascough, Richard S.
1998 Civic Pride at Philippi: The Text-critical Problem of Acts 16.12. *New Testament Studies* 44:93-103.

Bengel, John Albert
1971 *New Testament Word Studies.* Translator, C. Lewis and M. Vincent. Grand Rapids: Eerdmans. (Orig. Pub. 1742.)

Bruce, F. F.
1980–1981 St. Paul in Macedonia. 3. The Philippian Correspondence. *Bulletin of the John Rylands University Library of Manchester* 63:260-284.

1985 The Letter of Paul to the Romans. 2nd ed. Grand Rapids: Eerdmans.

1989 *Philippians.* New International Biblical Commentary. Peabody, MA: Hendrickson.

Caird, G. B.
1976 *Paul's Letters from Prison (Ephesians, Philippians, Colossians, Philemon) in the Revised Standard Version.* London: Oxford University Press.

Calvin, Jean
1965 *The Epistles of Paul the Apostle to the Galatians, Ephesians, Philippians and Colossians.* Translator, T. H. L. Parker. Grand Rapids: Eerdmans.

Comfort, Georgia
1992 *Dying to Live.* Wheaton: Tyndale. (Reprinted by Wipf & Stock.)

Comfort, Philip
1994 *I Am the Way: A Spiritual Journey through the Gospel of John.* Grand Rapids: Baker. (Reprinted by Wipf & Stock.)

2005 *Encountering the Manuscripts: An Introduction to New Testament Paleography and Textual Criticism.* Nashville: Broadman & Holman.

2008 *New Testament Text and Translation Commentary.* Carol Stream: Tyndale.

Comfort, Philip and David Barrett
2001 *The Text of the Earliest New Testament Greek Manuscripts.* Wheaton: Tyndale.

Conybeare, W. J., and J. S. Howson
1877 *The Life and Epistles of St. Paul.* London: Longmans.

Deissmann, A.
1909 *Light from the Ancient East: The New Testament Illustrated by Recently Discovered Texts of the Graeco-Roman World.* Translator, L. Strachan. London: Hodder & Stoughton.

1923 Zur ephesinischen Gefangenschaft des Apostles Paulus. Pp. 121-127 in *Anatolian Studies Presented to Sir W. M. Ramsey.* Editors, W. H. Buckler and W. M. Calder. Manchester: Manchester University Press.

Dodd, C. H.
1953 *New Testament Studies.* Manchester: Manchester University Press.

Duncan, J. D. G.
1929 *St. Paul's Ephesian Ministry.* London: Hodder & Stoughton.

Fee, Gordon
1994 *God's Empowering Presence.* Peabody, MA: Hendrickson.

1995 *Paul's Letter to the Philippians.* New International Commentary on the New Testament. Grand Rapids: Eerdmans.

Gaffin, Richard
1978 *The Centrality of the Resurrection.* Grand Rapids: Baker Book House.

Gamble, Harry Y.
1995 *Books and Readers in the Early Church.* New Haven: Yale University Press.

Gorday, Peter
2000 *Colossians, 1-2 Thessalonians, 1-2 Timothy, Titus, Philemon.* Downers Grove: InterVarsity.

Harris, Murray
1992 *Jesus as God*. Grand Rapids: Baker.

Hawthorne, Gerald F.
1983 *Philippians*. Word Biblical Commentary. Waco: Word.

Houlden, J. L.
1978 *Paul's Letters from Prison*. Philadelphia: Westminster.

Kennedy, H. A. A.
1979 The Epistle to the Philippians, vol. 3 of *The Expositor's Greek Testament*. Grand Rapids: Eerdmans.
(Orig. Pub. 1903)

Kruse, Colin
1987 *2 Corinthians*. Tyndale New Testament Commentaries. Leicester, England: Inter-Varsity Press.

Lees, Harrington C.
1925 Epaphroditus, God's Gambler. *Expository Times* 37:46-48.

Lightfoot, J. B.
1879 *St. Paul's Epistles to the Colossians and Philemon*. New York: MacMillan.

1904 *Notes on the Epistles of St. Paul*. London: MacMillan.

1976 *St. Paul's Epistle to the Philippians*. Grand Rapids: Zondervan. (Orig. Pub. 1913)

Lincoln, Andrew T., and A. J. M. Wedderburn
1993 *The Theology of the Later Pauline Letters*. New Testament Theology. Editor, James D. G. Dunn.
Cambridge: Cambridge University Press.

Loh, I-Jin and Eugene Nida
1977 *A Handbook on Paul's Letter to the Philippians*. UBS Helps for Bible Translators. Stuttgart:
United Bible Societies.

Marshall, I. H.
1968 The Christ-Hymn in Philippians 2:5-11. *Tyndale Bulletin* 19:104-127.

Martin, Ralph
1967 *Carmen Christi: Philippians ii:5-11 in Recent Interpretation and in the Setting of Early Christian
Worship*. Cambridge: Cambridge University Press.

1987 *Philippians*. Tyndale New Testament Commentaries. Leicester, England: Inter-Varsity Press.

Metzger, Bruce
1992 *The Text of the New Testament* (3rd ed.). Oxford: Oxford University Press.

1994 *A Textual Commentary on the Greek New Testament*. Rev. ed. New York: United Bible Societies.

Milligan, William
1884 *The Resurrection of our Lord*. London: Macmillan.

Moberly, R. C.
1909 *Atonement and Personality*. London: John Murray.

O'Brien, Peter T.
1991 *The Epistle to the Philippians*. New International Greek Testament Commentary. Eerdmans:
Grand Rapids.

Pfitzner, V. C.
1967 *Paul and the Agon Motif: Traditional Athletic Imagery in the Pauline Literature*. Leiden: Brill.

Plummer, A.
1896 *A Critical and Exegetical Commentary of the Gospel according to St. Luke*. New York: Scribners.

Reicke, Bo
2001 *Re-examining Paul's Letters: The History of the Pauline Correspondence*. Valley Forge: Trinity.

Robinson, John A. T.
1976 *Redating the New Testament*. London: SCM. (Reprinted by Wipf and Stock, 2000.)

Silva, Moisés
1992 *Philippians*. Grand Rapids: Baker.

Stowers, Stanley
1986 *Letter Writing in Greco-Roman Antiquity*. Philadelphia: Westminster.

Tasker, R. V. G.
1964 Notes on Variant Readings. Pp. 411-445 in the *Greek New Testament*. London: Oxford University Press.

Turner, Nigel
1976 *A Grammar of New Testament Greek*. Editor, James Hope Moulton. Edinburgh: T & T Clark.

Vincent, M. R.
1922 *Critical and Exegetical Commentary on the Epistles to the Philippians and to Philemon*. Edinburgh: T & T Clark.

Weima, J. A. D.
2000 Letters, Greco-Roman. Pp. 640-644 in *Dictionary of New Testament Background*. Editors, Craig Evans, Stanley Porter. Downers Grove: InterVarsity.

Westcott, B. F. and Fenton Hort
1882 *Introduction to the New Testament in the Original Greek (with "Notes on Select Readings")*. New York: Harper & Bros.

Züntz, G.
1953 *The Text of the Epistles*. London: Oxford.

Colossians

PETER H. DAVIDS

INTRODUCTION TO
Colossians

COLOSSIANS IS A FASCINATING BOOK that is often neglected, with the exception of Colossians 1:15-20. In the English Bible it comes last in the Prison Epistles (Ephesians through Colossians) because it is the shortest of them. Pauline letters were arranged by length, not by date, theme, or geographical location as we might have done today. Ephesians is, therefore, often preferred over Colossians because it is longer—i.e., it has expanded sections on some of the very topics that Colossians discusses. Furthermore, because the Pauline Epistles are arranged from longest to shortest, Colossians is separated by the Thessalonian letters and the Pastoral Epistles from its companion letter, Philemon, which was probably written about the same time (Paul references nearly the same cast of characters in Philemon as he does in Colossians). This separation often causes the two letters to be read separately rather than together, which would give a more detailed context to both.

The comparative neglect of Colossians, however, is unjustified. There is no other letter in the Pauline corpus that exalts Christ more. Indeed, the main section about Christ (1:15-20) is often lifted from Colossians and studied separately as if it were a doctrinal treatise. However, Paul's purpose for the inclusion of this hymnic section is not to talk about Christ in the abstract. Instead, he wrote about Christ in order to draw some very practical implications for the life of the church. One's view of Christ determines the way one lives. Therefore, when Colossians is read as a whole—as Paul wrote it—it becomes a very practical guide to living a healthy Christian life.

AUTHOR

It seems clear from the very first verse of Colossians (1:1) that Paul of Tarsus, the much-traveled missionary, was the author. Furthermore, the structure of the letter, including the rhetoric, is very similar to those letters that almost everyone accepts as being written by Paul (Romans, 1 and 2 Corinthians, and Galatians, the so-called "main letters" or *Hauptbriefe*). The letter also has indications of a similar cultural and historical context as Philemon, which scholars rarely dispute as a genuine letter of Paul as well. For example, the colleagues of Paul sending greetings in Philemon closely parallel those sending greetings in Colossians. However, while the authorship of Colossians is not as disputed as that of Ephesians or the Pastoral Epistles, it is contested by a significant number of scholars (Lohse 1968:249-257; Ehrman 2000:346-350; Perkins 1988:194; Freed 1986:318-320). Such notable opposition to the letter's Pauline authorship requires that we investigate the reasons for such opposition.

First, it has been asserted against Pauline authorship (Lohse 1973; several of the essays in Francis and Meeks 1973; cf. the summary in O'Brien 1982) that Colossians differs in style, vocabulary, theology (principally Christology, ecclesiology, and eschatology), and background (in its use of Gnostic traditions) from the genuine Pauline letters. It must be admitted that in Colossians, a letter in which the underlying problem involves Jewish piety being recommended to gentile believers, it is surprising that some of the key language of Romans and Galatians (e.g., "sin," "righteousness," "salvation," "believe," "justify," and "justification") do not appear. It is also striking how much of the vocabulary of Colossians overlaps with that of Ephesians and the Pastoral Epistles rather than with that of admittedly genuine Pauline letters , although this is significant only if one has already decided on other grounds that Ephesians and the Pastorals were *not* written by Paul. It is also clear that the style, principally the grammar, of Colossians is different in some respects from Romans, Galatians, or the Corinthians literature. Yet having pointed out these problems, the issue remains as to whether these differences are significant enough to demand that we posit authorship by someone other than Paul. Let us examine this question as concisely as possible.

Admittedly there is a greater emphasis in Colossians on the cosmic aspects of Christology (i.e., Christ as creator and Lord of the universe), a more universal view of the church, and less of an emphasis on futuristic eschatology than in the Pauline works used for comparison. However, none of the themes found in Colossians is entirely missing from those earlier works, nor are the perspectives of those works entirely missing from Colossians. The difference is only a matter of emphasis. To draw a black-and-white picture of contrast between Colossians and earlier Pauline literature is misleading.

Recognizing that there are differences of language in Colossians, one needs to ask whether and, if so, how much Colossians was influenced by the terms and concepts that were current in the Colossian situation. Could it be that Paul was well informed about that situation (i.e., that Epaphras and others had given him a detailed report) and was in dialogue with the various terms and ideas that were circulating in Colosse? Likewise, one's evaluation of the traditions being addressed in Colossians—such as, whether they were Gnostic (and therefore to be dated later) or Jewish (and therefore possibly earlier)—depends on one's perspective on the issue of date and the issue of the meaning of the possible Colossian slogans that Paul uses. There is certainly no exposition of Gnostic thought or of mystery religion rites in Colossians just as there is no exposition of Jewish piety. One must take the clues from the text and construct a model and compare that model to various possible backgrounds. Needless to say, many scholars do not see a mystery religion and/or Gnostic background that is seemingly apparent to some of those who deny Pauline authorship. Could it be that these backgrounds are more a projection into the text than a convincing picture arising out of the text?

Various scholars (Bruce 1984; O'Brien 1982) have defended Pauline authorship. On the question of vocabulary, these scholars argue that if Paul was indeed responding to the issues current in Colosse, then it is to be expected that his vocabulary be shaped by the key words used in that context. Paul was quite capable of taking the terms of those he opposed and inserting them into his own arguments so as to turn them to his service. We see this phenomenon in both the Corinthian correspondence and Galatians. What we may be seeing in Colossians is Paul's creativity and flexibility in using Colossian terms, not evidence against his authorship. It might, however, be objected that there is no evidence that Paul takes his style from those with whom he corresponds. Yet are the stylistic differences from his other letters significant enough to warrant that Paul could not have written this letter? To answer that question would require a detailed discussion of the Greek text, which is beyond the scope of this commentary. A brief discussion and references to the relevant literature may be found in deSilva 2004. In any case, it seems there are better answers to the objections based on stylistic differences than there are by attributing the whole letter to another author.

Regarding the Christology of Colossians, I have already noted that the issue is one of emphasis more than absolute difference. Thus the question is more, "Could there be something in the Colossian situation that led Paul to focus more on a Christology that stresses Christ as the Lord of the universe and less on futuristic eschatology?" In none of his letters was Paul a slave to his own thought, having to compulsively reproduce his key ideas, but rather he was in dialogue with the thought of others, searching out the best strategies to correct or modify it without losing the people with whom he was in dialogue. That is why in Colossians, as virtually everywhere in his correspondence, he relied more on persuasion than on authority. If, then, Paul was cognizant of and dialoguing with the background of those to whom he wrote and was using concepts from the world in which he and they were living, what is the probable background of Colossians? While many earlier scholars and a number of more recent ones favored models involving Gnostic thought patterns that developed decades after Paul's martyrdom, much recent scholarship favors models involving thought patterns with which Paul was very much at home—that is, some form of Jewish spirituality rather than Gnostic speculation or mystery cult initiation. These Jewish models for the background of Colossians fit quite well within Paul's lifetime, which is significant for authorship since it is usually assumed that if Paul did not write Colossians, it was written well after his martyrdom.

In responding to the issues raised by those who find Pauline authorship unconvincing, a counter objection can be raised: Why would a pseudonymous author produce a letter to Colosse? While it had been large, Colosse was declining during Paul's day, having been overshadowed by Laodicea and Hierapolis, which had become, respectively, the major commercial-judicial and healing destinations in the area during the first century. Furthermore, since pseudonymous authorship demands a post-Pauline date, the apparent fact that Colosse was heavily damaged or destroyed in an earthquake in AD 60–61 (i.e., before Paul was martyred) and seems never to have been prominent after that would make it a less likely destination for a pseudonymous letter (O'Brien 1982:xxvi; Dunn 1996:20-21). Paul never visited Colosse, so it was not a city associated with his ministry. What would be the purpose of creating a

Pauline letter to this city? Finally, the list of names in the greetings, eight of which also occur in Philemon, also seems to serve no purpose if the letter were not genuine. Theories of pseudepigraphy have yet to come up with a convincing reason for why someone would create this letter ostensibly addressed to a then-unimportant city that Paul was never known to have visited rather than a letter to Antioch or Berea or Athens or some other city more directly associated with the Pauline mission.

Having raised questions about theories of pseudonymity, there is yet another position on the authorship question that needs to be explored. There are a number of scholars who argue that the stylistic and theological evidence is strong enough that one should consider the possibility that while Paul was indeed alive and associated with the letter, it was actually crafted by one of his associates (i.e., Timothy) rather than by Paul himself. This could have come about because Paul's circumstances in prison did not allow him enough freedom for dictating a letter (see Dunn 1996:38) or because the associate had the personal contact with Colosse that Paul lacked. The function of this model is to explain the differences between Colossians and the main Pauline letters, as well as the numerous similarities between Colossians and those letters. In particular, this model handles the issue of stylistic differences well, for unlike vocabulary and theology, style and thus stylistic difference are unconscious and not related to subject matter. Yet, attractive as this theory is, this remains a model, one way of putting the data together. Timothy was indeed a cowriter with Paul of Colossians, but he was also a cowriter with him of 2 Corinthians (see 2 Cor 1:1, a form of wording close to that in Colossians) and Philippians (Phil 1:1, where he is even more closely tied to Paul), and, along with Silas, a cowriter of 1 and 2 Thessalonians as well. If all of these were coauthored by Paul and Timothy, then why is the style of Colossians different from that of 2 Corinthians? Of course, it is quite possible that Timothy had more or less freedom in his composition, depending on how involved Paul could be with the writing process due to his prisoner status and how involved Timothy had been with the church in question. Yet we have no way to validate or discredit this theory in any given situation. We do not know how much freedom Paul would have given someone like Timothy by the time Colossians was written. Nor do we have independent examples of Timothy's style to compare with Colossians. Thus, this is an attractive possibility that explains some of the problems encountered by pure Pauline authorship (which the letter does not claim) and avoids the problems encountered by theories of pseudonymous authorship, but it is a possibility that cannot be proved based on current literary and historical evidence.

DATE AND OCCASION OF WRITING

The date of Colossians is dependent upon two things. First, if one has decided that Paul is not the author, then Colossians was almost certainly written after his death, with some scholars placing it in the 70s (Lohse 1968, 1973; Ehrman 2000). If one has decided that Paul was the author, then it must have been written before AD 68 (per tradition and the date of Nero's death). There is, as I noted above, one alternative that dates the letter to Paul's lifetime (or possibly shortly after) but without pure Pauline authorship. Dunn (1996:38) suggests that the best hypothesis is that the letter was written about the same time as Philemon, although by one of Paul's colleagues (perhaps Timothy) rather than by Paul himself.

Second, assuming that Colossians was composed during Paul's lifetime, one still has a range of possible dates. The clearest chronological data in the letter is that Paul was in prison (4:3, 18). Paul himself wrote that he had "been put in prison more often" than other Christian workers (2 Cor 11:23; cf. 6:5), and he wrote this *before* the only two longer imprisonments that we know about—namely, those in Caesarea and Rome, so there were obviously a lot of imprisonments about which we have no information. Traditionally, for most biblical scholars the choice of Paul's imprisonments during the writing of Colossians has been Rome because there is a preference for a known imprisonment over an unknown one. This choice has not been universal, since, for example, Reicke (2001:75-78) states categorically that it was written in Caesarea. The advantage to accepting Caesarea is that it places Paul in closer proximity (500 mi or 800 km) to his ministry in the Roman province of Asia, where Colosse was located, than locating Paul at Rome does (900 mi or 1450 km), and the trip to Caesarea could be made by land (a slave, such as Onesimus, might find it difficult to pay for a sea journey). The disadvantage to placing this imprisonment in Caesarea is in trying to explain why Trophimus, who was with Paul in Jerusalem just prior to his imprisonment in Caesarea, is not mentioned in either Colossians or Philemon, and also why Tychicus, Mark, and Epaphras are not said to have been with Paul in Jerusalem or Caesarea. In its favor is the fact that Luke (if he is the "we" voice in Acts, which is debatable) and Aristarchus, both mentioned as sending greetings in Colossians 4, were with Paul in Caesarea. However, since another "we" passage suggests they also accompanied him to Rome (Acts 27:1-2), they would have been with him there as well.

Other scholars have suggested that Paul could well have been imprisoned within Roman Asia, probably in Ephesus, and that this location, with its proximity to Colosse (100 mi or 160 km), would explain both Colossians and Philemon better than other possible locations (see Martin 1973). The proximity of an Ephesian imprisonment explains why Paul would write to Colosse, a city he had never visited. Moreover, an Ephesian setting makes the journeys required by the book of Philemon more understandable (Philemon was probably written just before or perhaps just after Colossians; see the Introduction to Philemon). Considering the journeys and the cast of characters who are with Paul (Aristarchus and Paul were arrested together in Ephesus [Acts 19:29], and in 4:10 he is described as a fellow prisoner), Ephesus makes the most sense. Considering the developed Christology, Rome would make significant sense, for why would the Christology of Colossians not also appear in Romans and perhaps 2 Corinthians if Colossians was written before Romans—unless one thinks that this Christology was not appropriate to the subject matter of Romans and 2 Corinthians?

Caesarea forms a mediating solution in that Paul's two-year-plus imprisonment there comes after the writing of Romans, and it is not impossible to envisage the travel presupposed in Philemon and Colossians if Paul were in Caesarea. Still, while not impossible, it is difficult to envision someone like Onesimus heading to Caesarea (a month-long trip by foot) unless he knew Paul was there and was purposefully looking for him. Furthermore, it is difficult to envision Paul planning to leave Caesarea and travel to the small, declining city of Colosse, when we know that his previously announced plan had been to travel to Rome and then on to Spain (Rom 15:24). Thus, the probabilities still point to Ephesus or Rome, the latter only due to tradition and the high Christology. The interpretation of the letter does not depend upon which one is chosen. However, in my view, Ephesus makes better historical sense, given the journeys of Onesimus required to explain Philemon, including the probability that Onesimus carried the letter to Philemon and the certainty that Onesimus was with Paul when Colossians was written and would help carry the letter to the Colossians (which was probably at a different time than Philemon because of differences, as noted above, in who was and was not in prison—see Introduction to Philemon).

The reason why the letter was written is much clearer than the issue of where the letter was written. Paul writes "so no one will deceive you with well-crafted arguments" (2:4). Some person or persons were trying to persuade the Colossians of ideas and practices that neither came from nor were in conformity with their commitment to be followers of Jesus Christ, but instead these ideas were "empty philosophies and high-sounding nonsense that come from human thinking" (2:8). What these empty philosophies may have been will be discussed below under "Theological Concerns."

AUDIENCE

To find the audience of Colossians we need to travel south from Ephesus over a ridge that separates it from Magnesia on the Meander River. Then we travel more or less eastward up the Meander River until we come to the point, just over 60 miles or 100 kilometers inland, where the Lycus River enters it. At this point, turn south up the Lycus River, where we would first come to Laodicea and then to Colosse. The audience of Colossians was the Christian house churches in Colosse and elsewhere (4:16) in the Lycus Valley. We know that at least Colosse and Laodicea had a believing community, but we do not know whether they were the only cities in the area with house churches, although that seems to be the case because Hierapolis, another significant city of the area (situated across from Laodicea on the north side of the Lycus), is not mentioned as receiving a letter from Paul (nor is it mentioned among the churches addressed in Revelation 1–3). Paul himself had not evangelized the Lycus Valley, and while he may have passed through it on this third missionary journey (or further north through the Cayster River valley), he certainly did not stop in Colosse (2:1). Had he come through the area, he probably would have gone to Laodicea, for while Colosse had been a large city in the centuries before Christ, by the time of Paul Laodicea was more significant and the seat of government for the whole region. Colosse was by then a smaller city and in decline. It was damaged and perhaps destroyed by one or possibly two earthquakes during the time of Paul's ministry, the one certain earthquake occurring in AD 60–61

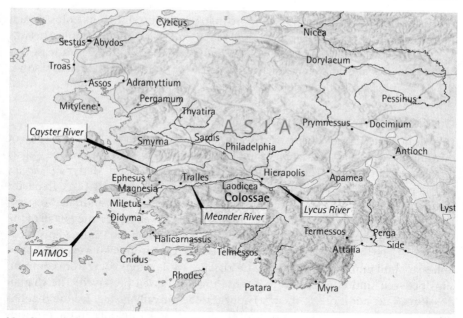

Map Showing the Seven Cities of Revelation (marked by +); note also Patmos and the Lycus River.

(i.e., about the time Paul reached Rome). Since Paul had not ministered in the Lycus Valley, it had almost certainly been evangelized by Paul's co-workers. (If someone not connected with Paul had evangelized the area, Paul would not have intervened in the church; he only felt responsible for those churches he had planted directly or indirectly.) That co-worker was probably Epaphras, possibly together with Philemon. Epaphras is prominent in the book of Colossians, since he was with Paul when the letter was being written and Philemon was not; Philemon is clearly a leader in the church and appears to have a relationship to Paul, perhaps due to visiting him in Ephesus. He may have been an early convert of Epaphras or he may have been converted during a visit to Ephesus, which would explain Philemon 1:19.

We do not know much about the composition of the church in the Lycus Valley, but certain facts suggest that it consisted of a number of Jews among a gentile majority: (1) There was a significant Jewish population in that area. The Seleucid king Antiochus III the Great had brought 2,000 Jews from Mesopotamia to settle there over 250 years earlier. (2) Paul's methodology was to reach out to the Jews before going directly to the Gentiles. (3) The church in this period did not view itself as separate from Judaism; rather, it viewed itself as a sect of Judaism, much as the Pharisees, Sadducees, Dead Sea Community, and others viewed themselves. It is thus probable that Jews were part of the church, even though it appears that the majority of the church were converted Gentiles (i.e., Greeks and Phrygians, the Phrygians being the original local population). Thus, we should envision a mixed congregation heavily weighted in the gentile direction. We do not know how large the church was, but we do know that there was more than one house church in Colosse. Paul addressed the church in Philemon's house in Philemon 1:2, but this implies his was not the whole church in Colosse; (cf. his address in 1:2; Phlm 1:2). At least two house churches appear to have met in Laodicea (cf. commentary on 4:15), so we should assume a minimum of 40 to 100 adults, and perhaps many more.

CANONICITY AND TEXTUAL HISTORY

There is no issue about Colossians' place in the canon. Colossians has been a part of the canon as long as we have had canon lists. It appears in Marcion's list, as well as the Muratorian Canon. The earliest probable citation is Justin Martyr's *Dialogue*, and it is accepted by all of the church fathers who mention it (e.g., Irenaeus, Tertullian, Clement of Alexandria). Textually it is found in Alexandrian, Western, and of course Byzantine traditions; in other words, it is well represented in all of the manuscripts—papyrus, uncial, and minuscule—containing the Pauline Epistles. A survey of 27 textual issues reveals that some issues come from taking expressions of Ephesians and introducing them into Colossians, while others come from common slips between similar words. In that sense the text is well preserved. The chapter divisions (later additions to the text) appear to be the only textual feature that has not been well served by church history. It is clear that 4:1 belongs to the previous chapter. Likewise, the break between chapters 1 and 2 splits a rhetorical unit.

LITERARY STYLE

Lightfoot (1896:123) comments, "While the hand of St. Paul is unmistakable throughout this epistle, we miss the flow and the versatility of the Apostle's earlier letters." Colossians does have a number of Pauline stylistic features, such as the use of "in Christ" and "in the Lord," as well as some grammatical peculiarities that do not come through in translation. It also has its unique features, such as 34 words that appear nowhere else in the New Testament, and some grammatical features that are far more common than in the main Pauline letters, such as pleonastic expressions ("Made strong with all the strength," 1:11, NRSV; "praying . . . and asking," 1:9, NRSV) and strings of genitives ("the word of the truth of the gospel," 1:5, KJV).

Perhaps the two most striking notes about the style of Colossians are the poetic praise of Christ in 1:15-20 and the table of household duties in 3:18–4:1. The former, possibly a quotation of an early Christian hymn, is lyrical in style, breaks in two stanzas, and forms one of the two highest praises of Christ in the Pauline canon. Philippians 2:6-11 is the other poetic passage, but, unlike the Colossian passage, Philippians focuses on the death of Christ and his subsequent exaltation rather than his action as creator of the universe and creator of the church. The latter (3:18–4:1), paralleled in Ephesians 5:22–6:1 and 1 Peter 2:13–3:7, is a section of traditional moral exhortation (found in non-Christian—such as Stoic—as well as Christian, sources) in which both sides of a relationship are paired. The appearance of this structure in 1 Peter as well as the Prison Epistles makes it probable that both authors received the traditional form from elsewhere and adapted it to their own purposes.

MAJOR THEMES

In one sense there is only one major theme of Colossians: the all-sufficiency of Christ. He who was sufficient to bring one to salvation is also sufficient to lead one through life. As a result, Colossians stresses Christ's lordship over creation as well as the church. Christ's death is mentioned (1:20; 2:14), but it is not the focus of the letter (nor is it the focus of Pauline evangelistic preaching as seen in Acts). The reign of Christ is the focus. Thus, Christ is the center of any spirituality that can claim to be truly Christian.

In another sense, there is a second major concern of Colossians: ethics. Lifestyle is to be conditioned by Christ. Thus virtues and vices, one's everyday life, and household duties are all conditioned by the present reign of Christ in heaven. Paul contrasts this Christ-centered lifestyle with the Jewish religious practices that he opposes, for such spiritual disciplines do not really deal with the ethical issues that destroy Christian community, nor are they consistent with the present reign of Christ, since they imply that other powers also need to be dealt with. Anything which detracts from Christ, including Judaism in its various forms, is part of this age.

This does not mean that the Christian is not in continuity with the redeemed of all the ages. The "saints in the kingdom of light" (1:12, NIV) surely include the Old Testament as well as the New Testament believers. Rather, Paul's perspective is much like that which he pictures in Romans 11. That is, there is one people of God throughout the ages. While the gentile Colossians were not by nature part of this people of God, they have become part of this community through their commitment to Christ. In the book of Colossians, Paul does not discuss the situation of Jews who have not committed themselves to Christ, although by referring to Jewish practices as part of this age rather than God's Kingdom he implies an answer similar to the one he gives in Romans 11. The danger to the Colossians is that they were being enticed to return to the practices of "this age" to try to obtain something that they already had in Christ. If they should do this, not only would they fail in their attempt to attain it, but they would also lose what they have in Christ.

Finally, in Colossians, as elsewhere, Paul is concerned about the relationship of the Christian to the culture around him or her. That culture is marked by the immoral lifestyle that the Christian has been delivered from, but it is still the culture in which one lives. Thus, Paul is concerned about how one lives as a Christian in the context of this culture without appearing to undermine the good order of society. This means that Colossians is marked by what has been referred to as an already/not-yet perspective: While Christ already reigns and no power is superior to him, his reign is not yet fully visible on earth. Thus one must come to terms with living in the middle of a society that does not recognize him as Lord, and forces of evil that are very real and do not appear to be under his sway. This perspective was first developed by Oscar Cullmann (1951, especially 211-213, 223-242) and later taken up by George Eldon Ladd (1993:407-411).

THEOLOGICAL CONCERNS

The theological concerns of Colossians can be broken into two parts: what Paul opposes and what he advocates.

The problem with describing what Paul is against is that we do not have a full description of the belief system that he was opposing, for the practices that he mentions are surely part of a larger belief system.

Because of the reference to philosophy and the stress on knowledge in Colossians, many scholars have argued that the teachers he opposes are Gnostic or proto-Gnostic, given that any probable date for Colossians is decades before the development of full-blown Gnosticism, teaching a salvation through knowledge or enlightenment. (For more, see essays by G. Bornkamm and M. Dibelius in Francis and Meeks 1973; Lightfoot 1896.) More likely, these people were teaching that commitment to Jesus was the first stage of salvation but that in order to go deeper one needed knowledge and/or enlightenment concerning perhaps the names of various angel guardians of the spheres of heaven and earth and the "passwords" necessary to go through their spheres of influence. This would fit with the gentile character of the church since many themes in Gnosticism, especially the stress on knowledge and the tendency to reject the body, resonate with Greco-Roman thought. While Gnostic thought was not unknown in Jewish circles, it tended to be modified there. Further candidates for the background of Colossians are the so-called mystery religions, where one was initiated in stages into deeper and deeper knowledge of the secrets of the cult and in that way learned to pass through the spheres and their angelic or demonic guardians. In practice, it would be difficult to tell an early Gnostic system from a mystery religion, at least in the context of Colossians, since we only have hints and pieces of information, although the Colossians themselves would have known very well what Paul was talking about. This type of cult was quite prevalent in Asia Minor and thus the incorporation of ideas from such a cult into the Christian belief framework was quite possible. However, our question is not whether it was possible but what in fact had happened in the church of the Colossians.

In contrast to the scholars who posit a Gnostic influence, the references in Colossians to circumcision (2:11), food regulations and holy days, including Sabbaths (2:16), and the issue of Jew versus Gentile (3:11) lead many other scholars to conclude that the individuals trying to persuade the church were Jews, perhaps Hellenistic Jews well schooled in Greek philosophy (as was Philo of Alexandria, a contemporary of Paul; so Dunn, 1996:33-35). One could easily imagine that Jews (inside or outside the church), hearing the claim of Colossian Gentiles to have been accepted by the God of Israel, might argue, "Jesus was a Jew, was he not? Then it is good that you have followed him in trusting in the one God, but you are never going to get farther in your spirituality unless you do it in God's way." Then, such a person would follow such a remark with an argument for one of the Jewish practices mentioned in chapter 2. This second scenario appears to have the most evidence in its favor, and it is the model that I will follow in this commentary. Thus, I will argue that those bothering the Colossian community were Jews. They may themselves have been influenced by Hellenistic thought or speculation about spiritual beings and angels (also found in Jewish works such as *1 Enoch* or some of the Dead Sea Scrolls), but the practices they were urging were primarily Jewish. They were not urging these as a means to salvation, for this would have brought forth from Paul arguments parallel to those in Galatians, where he is far more combative than in Colossians. But they did seem to be arguing that one must observe certain Jewish practices in order to deepen in one's spirituality. This is what Paul seems to be discussing in the letter.

What is clear, then, is that certain Jewish practices were being urged upon the largely gentile Christians in Colosse. These included observing the Sabbath and other Jewish festivals, observing dietary restrictions—probably the Jewish rules of kashrut (i.e., kosher eating) or some modification of them—and possibly practicing circumcision (2:11). Along with this came some ascetic practices, perhaps rules of fasting and/or the length of time one must spend in prayer, perhaps a call to spend whole nights in prayer, and veneration of angelic powers in some form. As noted above, this teaching does not appear to have called into question the sufficiency of their redemption but to have been taught as wisdom, mystery, or insight that would lead one to new levels of holiness and closeness to God and so help one get safely through this life, perhaps under angelic protection. Thus, unlike his concern for the Galatians, Paul was not concerned that the Colossians were in danger of not being faithful to Christ, but he was concerned that they live out the implications of their faithfulness to Christ instead of taking on alien practices, thinking the practices would be helpful. From a contemporary point of view, while the particular practices concerned were a mainly Jewish, first-century phenomena, we should be aware that these same tendencies are common in the church today. Paul's concern is first practical (it will not work in making them holy) and second theological (it shifts the focus away from Christ and his lordship), which make good guidelines for the evaluation of contemporary spiritual teachings today.

Paul's chief theological concern is to root everything in the lordship of Christ, or what we might accurately call "the Kingdom of God and his Christ." While Paul does not shout "Jesus is Lord" as he does in Romans 10:9, that is his theme. Jesus is Lord of creation, so there are no powers in the creation that are outside of his rule and must be placated separately from what Jesus has done in extending his rule over them. Jesus is also Lord of the church and thus able to rule and guide the church. This rule of Jesus is connected to the fact that the fullness of deity resides in him.

Yet Christology leads to soteriology, for Jesus is not only Lord, he is also Redeemer. Jesus redeemed people through the death of his physical body. This death is what reconciled and sanctified the Colossians. This death was their circumcision, applied to them through their identification with Christ. This death was their death, appropriated through baptism so that they became dead to this age and its powers. Yet Jesus was also resurrected, and because of their identification with Jesus in his death and their trust in the power of God that raised Jesus, the Colossians can also experience his resurrection life. Reconciliation means that guilt is gone, as are the demands of the law—thus, even Judaism and its lifestyle becomes part of this age, from which the Christian has been freed. But there are still more implications of the resurrection rule of Christ. If a person comprehends his relationship with Christ and lives out of this relationship, he will be able to overcome evil in his life. Paul's answer to sin is not more discipline (which can become man-centered) but more right. thinking about Jesus and more relationship with Jesus. In fact, because the Christian is "in Christ" and the fullness of God is also "in Christ," the fullness of God is in the Christian. Thus, no other spiritual powers have authority over them. Christ has broken their power on the Cross and shamed them in the very event that was designed to shame him. For this reason, attempts to influence spiritual powers apart from the relationship to Christ are both wrong-headed (in that Christ has already done all that needs to be done) and distracting (in that it removes the focus from Christ). For Paul, this does not mean that ethical effort is not needed. The indicative "in Christ"—Christ has transferred us into his Kingdom—implies the imperative of living out Christian community. Yet the foundational ethic guiding the Christian community is that each fellow believer is also "in Christ," thus, the only status that matters in the church. Further, it is a recognition that each person outside the Christian community is created by God in his image and has the potential of becoming "in Christ" no matter what their present state is. The recognition of Christ's rule also determines how the Christian relates to the structures of the world. The rule of Christ is, of course, a present mystery in that it is hidden from the world while revealed in the church. This revelation is the basis of the hope that fills the Christian—the "hope of glory," the hope of sharing Christ's Kingdom in its fullness, a hope that is more than just "hoping so" but also a firm conviction.

While the above is the focus of the theology of the letter, Paul's theology of the Trinity is also evident (although he would not have thought in terms of the Trinity as we speak of it). While he hardly mentions the Spirit (only in 1:8), it is not entirely absent. What is more interesting is what Paul says about the Father. The Father is behind the action of Christ. That is, he is the one who has rescued us and who has qualified us to inherit the coming Kingdom. He indwelt Christ and so also us to the extent that Christ is in us. The Father in Colossians is the seeking God, out to rescue humanity and bring them into his presence. While the focus in creation, redemption, and present reign is on Christ, the Father is viewed as behind it all. Christ is not the one rescuing humanity from the wrath of God but the expression of the seeking God, who reached out in Christ to rescue humanity, who chose to be present in Jesus in bodily form.

OUTLINE

In some ways, the structure of Colossians is quite traditionally Pauline. The book is constructed around the usual letter structure of salutation and thanksgiving at the beginning and a conclusion at the end, including, as is typical for Paul, a shift from thanksgiving to prayer within the thanksgiving section. But after the prayer we find a new element for a Pauline letter, that is, a hymnic recounting first of the greatness of the Father and then of Christ. This is the standard against which all that Paul discusses will be measured. The thanksgiving, prayer, and praise serve together as the introduction, or *exordium*, the first part of a Greco-Roman argument. The argument would continue with a narration (often a setting out of facts), a *propositio* (thesis statement), an exposition (expansion of the implications of the *propositio*) or *probatio* (argument for the truth of the *propositio*), and sometimes concluding with a *peroratio* (summation and conclusion; but not here). As is argued below, Paul had a decent basic Greek education, and his letters show his ability to use Greek rhetorical forms.

Having completed his introduction (*exordium*; 1:3-23), Paul then sets out the facts of his relationship with the Colossians (*narratio*: 1:24–2:5), culminating in his thematic statement (*propositio*; 2:6-7). But such a statement needs to be further explored and its implications worked out. In 2:8–4:6 we have more of an exposition (*expositio*) than an argument (*probatio*), but the object is clear: If one accepts the truths of the *exordium*, then the arguments and practice of the Hellenistic Jewish teachers are untenable. The implications of this argument are worked out—first in terms of practices being urged on the Colossians, and then in terms of an ethical lifestyle. These together form the body of the letter. After the closing of the body of the letter, Paul finishes Colossians with the last part of the letter structure—the conclusion, consisting of a commendation of the messenger, greetings, and a final autographed request and blessing.

I. Salutation (1:1-2)
II. Introduction (*exordium*)(1:3-23)
   A. Thanksgiving (1:3-8)
   B. Prayer for the Colossians (1:9-12)
   C. Praise to the Father and Son for Salvation (1:13-23)
III. Historical Background (*narratio*) (1:24–2:5)
IV. Thematic Statement (*propositio*): The Way In Is the Way On, and That Way Is Christ (2:6-7)
V. Exposition of the Theme (*expositio*) (2:8–4:6)
   A. Theological Implications of the Theme (2:8-23)
      1. Christ is all sufficient (2:8-15)
      2. Christ, not religious practices and rule (2:16-19)
      3. Christ, not Jewish purity (2:20-23)
   B. Ethical Implications of the Theme (3:1–4:6)
      1. General statement (3:1-4)
      2. Specific vices and virtues (3:5-17)
      3. The Christian household (3:18–4:1)
      4. Concerning prayer and concluding summary (4:2-6)
VI. Conclusion (4:7-18)

COMMENTARY ON
Colossians

◆ I. Salutation (1:1-2)

This letter is from Paul, chosen by the will of God to be an apostle of Christ Jesus, and from our brother Timothy.
²We are writing to God's holy people in the city of Colosse, who are faithful brothers and sisters* in Christ.
May God our Father give you grace and peace.

1:2 Greek *faithful brothers.*

NOTES

1:1 *chosen by the will of God to be an apostle of Christ Jesus.* Paul cited his appointment as an apostle of Jesus in all of his letters except Philippians, the two Thessalonian letters, and Philemon. 2 Cor 1:1; Eph 1:1; 1 Tim 1:1 (with a slight difference); and 2 Tim 1:1 exactly parallel the expression found here. Paul said that Jesus appointed him as his delegate following God's will.

our brother Timothy. Timothy is joined with Paul as a coauthor in the salutation here, as also in 2 Cor 1:1; Phil 1:1; 1 Thess 1:1; 2 Thess 1:1; Phlm 1:1. He is called a "brother" whenever Paul uses a title for himself that does not fit Timothy (in this case "apostle," elsewhere "prisoner").

1:2 *God's holy people.* Paul often referred to Christians as "holy people" (traditionally, "saints"). See Rom 1:7; 1 Cor 1:2; 2 Cor 1:1; Eph 1:1; Phil 1:1. In this they are the renewed Israel, picking up on the statement in Exod 19:6 that Israel would be a holy nation (so also Pss 16:3; 34:9; cf. 1 Pet 2:9). This means that they had been set apart for God, something that happens in conversion. For example, the Corinthians (1 Cor 1:2; 6:11) had been sanctified (i.e., made holy—the Greek root is the same as the expression used here) in Jesus, even though as a group they were not living what Paul considered godly lives. Their calling as the renewed Israel was nevertheless a fact of their existence. It was a stated fact, and the command to live appropriately is consequently the imperative in Paul's letter.

faithful. While Paul often speaks of people having faith, it is rare that he speaks of them as faithful. Normally, it is God who is described as faithful (e.g., 1 Cor 1:9; 10:13; 2 Cor 1:18), but at times Timothy (1 Cor 4:17), Tychicus (4:7; Eph 6:21), Epaphras (1:7), or Onesimus (4:9) are described as faithful. Only here and in Eph 1:1 is a whole church called faithful, perhaps because Paul viewed them as having remained true to Christ, needing warning and encouragement, but not correction.

COMMENTARY

Colossians opens with a very typical Pauline greeting (1:1). Paul identifies himself as an apostle or delegate of Christ Jesus, which means that he was personally appointed by Christ to represent him in a given area under certain conditions. Paul understood the area to include all lands from Jerusalem north and west through

Asia Minor to and including the Balkan Peninsula, so long as no one else had founded churches there (Rom 15:18-21). However, by the time Paul wrote Romans, he believed Christ was expanding the mandate to include Spain (Rom 15:22-24). Yet despite his personal commission from Jesus, Paul almost never worked alone. He almost always had a team of apprentices and co-workers around him, which he included in his ministry. In this case, as in five other letters, Timothy was his main co-worker, presented as the coauthor of the letter. Timothy was surely known by the Colossian church, for he had been with Paul on and off during his somewhat long ministry in Ephesus. Perhaps Timothy had even visited Colosse (he had certainly visited Corinth during this period; 1 Cor 4:17). Timothy was not an apostle in the same sense that Paul was, for Christ did not personally delegate him, but he was chosen by Paul as a colleague; he was also a brother, as were the Colossian believers. As reflected in this letter, when Paul thought of his apostleship, he stressed God's choice of him. That is, Paul did not volunteer to be Christ's delegate nor did he earn the right to be a delegate. Rather, he was fully aware that he had been a persecutor of the church and so was responsible for the death of Christians when God chose him (1 Cor 15:9; we do not know whether he ever personally killed a Christian; Acts 22:20 presents him as encouraging and assisting those who killed Stephen). Paul never lost sight of the fact that it was God's choice that made him a delegate of Christ, not his own choice or merit or training.

Paul addressed his letter to God's holy (or set apart) people in Colossians (1:2). Paul did not view the church as different from Judaism, so he freely appropriated for Christians the titles of Israel in the Old Testament. They, even the gentile converts, were those people whom God had set apart for himself. The distinctive characteristic of this group of Christians is that they are faithful, a group that is true to Christ. Therefore, this is not a group that Paul will have to call back to Christ but one that has remained firm, even if their devotion might leave them in danger of being taken in by teaching that claimed to show them a deeper or more rigorous way of following Christ. The danger will be mentioned later; at this point Paul simply pointed out their outstanding commitment. Just as Timothy was a brother, so also were they ("brothers and sisters" translating the collective plural of the term used for Timothy), and just as their leader Epaphras was faithful so also were they.

Paul closed his salutation with his typical blessing or prayer, "May God our Father give you grace and peace," which would be an appropriate way for Christians in any age to bless each other. The phrase itself is a combination of a play on the normal Greek greeting (*chairein* [TG5463, ZG5897], as in Jas 1:1, which sounds something like *charis* [TG5485, ZG5921], or "grace,") and the Hebrew greeting of *shalom*, which translates as *eirēnē* [TG1515, ZG1645] in Greek. It was a Christian greeting used not only by Paul but also by Peter and John (1 and 2 Pet, 2 John, Rev) and thus picks up God's goal through the ages of *shalom* for his people and combines it with the distinctly New Testament sense of having favor or grace from God. Its frequent use, however, could mean that it had become a stereotyped expression of the community, which was no longer conscious of its theological background.

◆ II. Introduction (*exordium*) (1:3–23)
   A. Thanksgiving (1:3–8)

³We always pray for you, and we give thanks to God, the Father of our Lord Jesus Christ. ⁴For we have heard of your faith in Christ Jesus and your love for all of God's people, ⁵which come from your confident hope of what God has reserved for you in heaven. You have had this expectation ever since you first heard the truth of the Good News.

⁶This same Good News that came to you is going out all over the world. It is bear-ing fruit everywhere by changing lives, just as it changed your lives from the day you first heard and understood the truth about God's wonderful grace.

⁷You learned about the Good News from Epaphras, our beloved co-worker. He is Christ's faithful servant, and he is helping us on your behalf.* ⁸He has told us about the love for others that the Holy Spirit has given you.

1:7 Or *he is ministering on your behalf;* some manuscripts read *he is ministering on our behalf.*

NOTES

1:3 *God, the Father of our Lord Jesus Christ.* This is the reading of 𝔓61ᵛⁱᵈ B C* 1739 (D F G add a definite article before "Father"). A number of mss have "God and Father of our Lord Jesus Christ" (ℵ A C² D¹ I 044 33 𝔐), which would conform the text to common Pauline usage (cf. NASB for Rom 15:6; 2 Cor 1:3; 11:31; Eph 1:3, 17; cf. also 1 Pet 1:3). The diversity of the manuscript evidence as well as the fact that it is the more difficult reading favors the reading behind the NLT. What is clear is that Paul, following the pattern of Jewish monotheism, normally prays to God, not to Jesus, nor does he freely refer to Jesus as God. However, for him God is not just the God of Moses but the God whom Jesus Christ revealed to his followers as Father. God is Father of Jesus in that Jesus embodies Israel (Isa 63:16; 64:8) and truly took his identity, authority, and supply from God (the functions that a father fulfilled in an ancient family). Furthermore, that means that they form a family into which followers of Jesus can be integrated.

1:4 *faith in Christ Jesus and your love for all of God's people.* The faith/love pair is seen elsewhere in Paul's writings (1 Cor 13:2, 13; Gal 5:6; Eph 1:15; 3:17; 1 Thess 1:3; 3:6; 5:8, etc.). Here, as in Ephesians, the faith is "in Christ Jesus." Most commentators argue that this indicates the sphere in which their faith operates, that is, they have faith [in God] in the context of being in Christ (Wall 1993:44-45; Bruce 1984:41; Moule 1968:49). While this is possible, it seems more likely that Paul was speaking about commitment to Christ (*pistis* [TG4102, ZG4411]) because the verb *pisteuō* [TG4100, ZG4409] indicates commitment when followed by an object rather than a "that." For Paul, too, *pistis* is always "faith in someone" since it is logical that the object of commitment would parallel the object of love (so Dunn 1996:57)—i.e., that "Christ Jesus" is the object of "faith" as "all of God's people" is the object of "love." "Love" does not indicate how they felt about "all of God's people" but how they acted toward them (i.e., lovingly), as is typical in the NT.

1:5 *confident hope of what God has reserved for you in heaven.* Hope is often linked with faith and love in Paul's writings (1 Cor 13:13; Gal 5:5-6; 1 Thess 1:3; 5:8). Here the hope is eschatological (i.e., a heavenly reward) as the "reserved for you" shows (used in a negative eschatological context in Luke 19:20, but positively in 2 Tim 4:8). What is unusual here in Paul is that faith comes from hope, although it makes sense when we understand "hope" not as something "hoped for" (being unsure of the outcome) but as something expected. The NLT translation, "confident hope," is quite fitting. It is easy to see how this expectation would birth commitment to Christ and the concomitant love for believers. Notice that in a letter without much futuristic eschatology, this is one of those few verses where such an eschatological belief shines through.

the truth of the Good News. The truth here is the revealing of the "full or real state of affairs" (see *alētheia* [TG225, ZG237]; TDNT 1.238). This is a distinctive feature of the Good News, a distinctively Christian and Pauline usage of a common Greek term (*euangelion* [TG2098, ZG2295]), rarely used in the singular outside of Christian literature. This usage stems from the use of the verb in Isa 40:9; 52:7; 60:6 ("worshiping," NLT); 61:1, which was picked up by Jesus. The Good News reveals things as they really are.

1:6 by changing lives . . . changed your lives. The verb Paul used means "to grow." The translation assumes that the participle means "causing people to grow" (cf. 1 Cor 3:6-7). Thus, it is inconsistent to translate the metaphor "bearing fruit" literally and then translate the metaphor of "growing" dynamically. In the parable of the sower (Mark 4:8), the growth is a step toward "bearing fruit," which seems to mean "multiplying." Here, with the Good News as subject, the verb most likely parallels its use in the parable (although we do not know that the author had the parable explicitly in mind) and the dual "bear fruit" + "grow" indicates the spread of the Good News among them and in the entire world, not a change within the believer. That the pair appears again in 1:10 supports this interpretation here in that, there, each term is modified to indicate that the fruit-bearing and growth is now within the believer, who is the subject of the imperative (O'Brien 1982:13).

1:7 You learned about. Although Paul says the Ephesians "learned about Christ" (Eph 4:20), this is the only place he refers to learning about the Good News. Usually he talks about believing or obeying or perhaps hearing the Good News. In fact, references to learning are relatively rare in Paul and not that common in the NT in general (see *manthanō* [TG3129, ZG3443] in TDNT 4.406-412). Here Paul may have chosen "learned" to indicate either the thoroughness with which Epaphras had instructed the Colossians or his accuracy in transmitting the truth of the Good News. Either meaning would be an affirmation of Epaphras over against the ideas that Paul will oppose later in the letter. Thus the translation "learned about" rather than simply "learned" is unfortunate, for it suggests an acquaintance with a topic rather than a thorough grounding in a subject, which is what is implied here.

Epaphras. This is a shortened form of Epaphroditus, a common name in that period. A native Colossian (4:12), Epaphras had proclaimed the Good News in Colosse and elsewhere in the Lycus Valley, including Laodicea and Hierapolis. At one point he shared Paul's imprisonment (Phlm 1:23), although at the time of the writing of Colossians he was no longer in prison. The name appears in its full form in Phil 2:25; 4:18, but the occurrence of the same name is not enough evidence to conclude that it refers to the same person, since, as indicated above, the name was common.

co-worker. Literally, "co-slave." The word appears in the NT only in Matthew, Revelation, and Colossians—the other reference in Colossians being a reference to Tychicus. Paul several times refers to himself as a slave of Christ (Rom 1:1; Gal 1:10; Phil 1:1; Titus 1:1) but rarely refers to others as slaves of Christ unless they are joined with him. The one exception to this rule is Epaphras, who in 4:12 is called a slave of Christ. While in the OT being a slave of God indicated a worshiper and/or minister of God and thus honorable, in the Greek world, which valued freedom, a slave was simply someone owned by someone else. A slave might have significant power and be treated respectfully if his or her master were a person of honor and power (e.g., Caesar), but they had no status in themselves. Thus, Paul's reference to himself as "slave" must have struck the ears of the Colossians and others as a startling expression. Here he joined Epaphras with him, meaning that Epaphras was equally Christ's slave, a full sharer in Paul's status as one totally given over to Christ. In that Paul uses this as a semi-official title for his closest co-workers, it shows how Paul honors people who have joined him in becoming slaves like Jesus (cf. Phil 2:7).

he is helping us on your behalf. The earliest mss and other witnesses (𝔓46 ℵ* A B D* F G) have "he is ministering on our behalf," as noted in NLT mg. In Greek both "our" and "your"

are words with four letters and with only one letter that differs between them. The NLT
translators (following NA[27]) assumed that the reading "our" (which occurs in the earlier
mss) was an accidental copying of the "our" from "our beloved co-worker." Yet the reading
"our" does make sense in context, for it would be a commendation of Epaphras and an
indication that Paul had indeed sent him to evangelize Colosse and therefore that his teaching there had been accurate. Thus, since "he is helping us" is a dynamic translation implied
from "on your behalf" and "Christ's faithful servant" (or "minister"), the phrase should be
dropped. Simply "ministering on our behalf" is the preferred translation (Dunn 1996:63).

1:8 Spirit. This is the only reference to the Spirit in Colossians, which is extremely surprising
given the number of times Paul normally refers to the Spirit (ten times in Ephesians, which
Colossians parallels in many ways, and three in Philippians, for example). Some take the lack
of references to the Spirit as one of the vocabulary indications that Colossians, in whole or in
part, was not written by Paul. My perspective is that it indicates that Paul so wanted to focus
on Christ that in this letter he almost failed to mention the Spirit and had relatively little to
say about the Father. That is how important it was for him to center on Christ.

COMMENTARY

The introduction to the letter includes a part of the letter structure, namely the
thanksgiving and prayer, and then bridges into praise—many would say a hymn of
praise—first to the Father and then to Christ. This forms the theological foundation
for the letter. The contents of the introduction are probably not something that the
Colossians would dispute. If the praise is indeed a hymn, it may be one that the
Colossians sang (or, more exactly, chanted) in their meetings and thus was familiar
to them. This praise and the description of their salvation are the basis of the rest of
Paul's argument. He does not have something new to reveal to them, but rather he
wants to compare the new ideas that are being foisted upon them with the foundation that they have in Christ and note the incompatibility. Thus, this introduction
serves a very important purpose in the structure of the book.

The first part of the introduction is the thanksgiving, which falls into three parts.
First we have the thanksgiving itself (1:3-10), then Paul segues into a prayer for the
Colossians (1:11-12), and finally he recites the great things that the Father and
Christ have done (1:13-22), which is the core theological insight of the letter.

It was normal in Greek letters to begin by thanking a god or gods for the recipient,
so it is not surprising that Paul begins his letter with thanks (1:3). For Paul this was
also natural, for he felt that life should be characterized by thanksgiving (1 Thess
5:18; cf. 2:7; 3:15; 4:2). In this thanksgiving, he was joined by his coauthor Timothy
and perhaps others who were sending greetings (1:4; "we"), for Paul was no lone-
wolf leader but one who served as part of a team.

In this case, the thanksgiving was based upon reports that Paul had received, perhaps through Epaphras or others, for he had never met the Colossians personally.
But what reports they were! The Colossians were firmly committed to Jesus, and they
showed this in how they loved other Christians (1:4). Interestingly enough, this
commitment was inspired and nourished by an eschatological conviction—that is, a
hope of what God had for them in heaven—for eschatology in the New Testament
serves ethics. (For more on eschatology in Colossians, see "Author" in the Introduction.) That is, our present lifestyles show what we really believe about the future.

Thus, eschatology has little to do with getting a map of the future but more with having a conviction about the future that changes life today. A disturbing aspect about eschatological or "end times" teaching today is that it does not make the lives of Christians different from those around them if various surveys are to be believed. This shows that contemporary hope is shallow at best or at worst nonexistent.

The Colossians had heard the truth of the Good News (1:5). That is, they had heard the message about Jesus and his Kingdom, and it had given them a new vision of reality. This reframing of life enabled them to view their present life from the right perspective, which had given them the depth of commitment to Christ and the basis for their active love to others. If we really believe the message of Jesus, then we will realize that this world is transitory. This releases us, for example, to share our goods with others because we know that such actions give us reward in heaven—the only reward that counts.

This Good News, this message about Jesus, is indeed exciting. It is reason enough to make reading the Gospels part of one's daily regimen. The Good News for Paul is like a plant or seed: It spreads widely. As I write I am looking out my window in the spring at dandelions. A seed dropped into the soil, and now it is growing and producing fruit. Soon the whole alley behind my office will be covered with their flowers. Such is the Good News. It had arrived in Colosse, and the Colossians had heard it. They received a new vision of reality, or, as Paul put it, they "understood the truth about God's wonderful grace" (1:6). Having already mentioned faith, love, and hope, we are not surprised that Paul moves on to grace. The fact is that God is a giving God and has given to us in many ways: in creating us, in preserving our lives, and in ministering as our living Lord. Before the Good News arrived in our lives, we experienced grace from God ignorantly, but when the Good News arrived we realized the good things came from God and learned how much more God gave us in Jesus. This truth, this new vision of reality, reorients our lives, and that is precisely what it had done for the people in Colosse.

Paul mentions all of these things in the introduction purposely. Since the Colossians already had the truth, they did not need a new truth that some were apparently teaching in Colosse. Since they had faith, love, hope, and grace, what more were they seeking? And since they had all of these in Jesus Christ, why would they seek elsewhere? Even when Paul was reporting to them his thanksgiving for them, he was at the same time laying the groundwork for issues that he would deal with later in the letter.

The Colossians, as well as the people living in Laodicea and Hierapolis, had been evangelized by Epaphras (1:7). Could it be that they were wondering whether Epaphras had given them the full message? Paul went out of his way to underscore his confidence in what Epaphras had done. They had learned the Good News, says Paul, indicating that they had received a thorough grounding in it rather than just heard about it. As for the character of Epaphras himself, he was not just a slave of Jesus (as was Paul) or even a fellow slave with Paul, but a *beloved* fellow slave. Furthermore, he was Christ's servant or minister (a different word from that meaning "slave"), which alone is certainly praise, and he was a "faithful servant" who carried out his duties fully and in whom the head of household could trust. Finally, Paul added "on our behalf" (see note on 1:7), meaning that Paul had sent him to Colosse. This was in keeping with Paul's typical methodology. He himself evangelized and planted a church in the main city in a region. During this process some of his converts developed into co-workers, or as he put it here, "fellow slave[s]" (one of the terms he appears to reserve for his closest co-workers.) It was these native apprentices of Paul whom he sent out to evangelize and plant churches in other cities of the province. In this case he had apparently sent Epaphras back to Colosse to represent him and the Good News. The Colossians had not received a second-rate imitation of the Good News but a thorough presentation by a tried, trusted, and faithful colleague of Paul's. Epaphras and his presentation were fully and unequivocally endorsed by Paul, indicating that any deviation from this presentation of the Good News would not receive Paul's stamp of approval.

Epaphras did more than carry the Good News to Colosse. He also carried news from Colosse back to Paul (1:8). In particular he reported the Good News from Colosse that the Colossians demonstrated "love in the Spirit" (NRSV), indicating either their positive regard toward Paul (perhaps expressed through a gift), whom they had never seen, or their loving deeds done to others there in Colosse. In either case, Paul viewed it as the fruit of the Spirit. To claim the Holy Spirit but not demonstrate love for others is to make a claim that is dubious at best; to claim to have learned the Good News but not be demonstrating the fruit of the Spirit is likewise to make a dubious claim. Wherever the Good News is truly received and taken to heart, the Spirit enters and transforms lives. Love for others is the evidence of this transformation. Thus, in reporting this love to Paul, Epaphras made it clear that the Colossians were truly converted. Surely such news was enough to bring great joy to Paul, whether he was in or out of prison. No wonder he was thankful.

◆　B. Prayer for the Colossians (1:9-12)

9So we have not stopped praying for you since we first heard about you. We ask God to give you complete knowledge of his will and to give you spiritual wisdom and understanding. 10Then the way you live will always honor and please the Lord, and your lives will produce every kind of good fruit. All the while, you will grow as you learn to know God better and better. 11We also pray that you will be strengthened with all his glorious power so you will have all the endurance and patience you need. May you be filled with joy,* 12always thanking the Father. He has enabled you to share in the inheritance that belongs to his people, who live in the light.

1:11 Or all the patience and endurance you need with joy.

N O T E S

1:9 complete knowledge of his will. Literally, this phrase reads, "filled with the knowledge of his will." Prayer to know God's will is found in Ps 143:10 (cf. the many cases of "seeking/inquiring of the Lord" for direction in the OT, sometimes successfully [e.g., Judg

1:1; 1 Sam 22:10; 2 Sam 2:1; the failure to do so in Zeph 1:6] and sometimes without success [e.g., 1 Sam 28:6]), but in most cases Hebrews and Christians were more concerned to *do* the will that was known (Ps 40:8; Matt 6:10; 7:21; Mark 3:35; 2 Macc 1:3) than to *discover* the will that was unknown.

spiritual wisdom and understanding. "Spiritual" modifies both "wisdom" and "understanding," so the TEV is also correct to translate, "with all the wisdom and understanding that his Spirit gives." The word pair, wisdom and understanding, occurs in the OT (e.g., Deut 4:6; 1 Chr 22:12), although it was also valued in Greek thought (Aristotle, *Nichomachean Ethics* 1.13).

1:10 *the way you live.* The metaphor underlying this translation is "walking," which is a Semitic idiom for lifestyle (e.g., Exod 18:20; Ps 86:11). Similar idioms are common in Paul's writings (e.g., Eph 4:1; Phil 1:27; 1 Thess 2:12). Christianity was a "way" and thus was expected to affect one's lifestyle.

your lives will produce every kind of good fruit. All the while, you will grow as you learn to know God better and better. The two phrases are parallel and in Greek form a chiasmus (A–B–B–A pattern: (A) nominal phrase, (B) verb, (B) verb, (A) nominal phrase); they pick up on two terms from 1:6 (see note; "causing to grow," "bearing fruit"). "As you learn to know God better and better" is literally "growing with respect to the knowledge of God," assuming that the dative is a dative of "respect" (e.g., Moule 1968:54), although other commentators (Lohse 1968:29; Martin 1973:52) read this as instrumental and would translate it "producing fruit and growing in every good work by means of the knowledge of God." The chiastic structure favors Moule's interpretation.

1:11 *strengthened with all his glorious power.* This phrase is full of Semitisms, which would sound strange in English (literally, "strengthened with all strength according to the power of his glory") and might lead to misunderstanding, so it is thus a good example of the use of a dynamic translation to bring out meaning while avoiding confusion. "Glory" itself is typically Jewish and often connected to theophanies. More importantly, the ideas of power and glory are paired in several OT passages: 1 Chr 29:11; Pss 63:2 [62:3, LXX]; 145:11; Dan 2:37; and, significantly, in Mark 13:26 and parallels, where Jesus alludes to Daniel 7, saying, "Then everyone will see the Son of Man coming on the clouds with great power and glory." The theophanic overtones and the background of Daniel for this pairing support the idea that here it is an eschatological pairing; Paul had Jesus' reign in view as he wrote here.

endurance and patience . . . joy. Patience and endurance were important virtues to early Christians; Lightfoot (1896:138) contrasts them with cowardice and revenge respectively. While they are basically synonyms, they are paired in 2 Cor 6:4-6; 2 Tim 3:10; Jas 5:10-11, which means that together they traditionally indicated a composite idea. Significantly, patience is further paired with eschatological joy (see commentary) in Jas 1:2-3 (probably dependent upon Matt 5:12, also picked up in 1 Pet 4:13; cf. Acts 5:41). This eschatological joy is picked up in Jas 5:10-11, in which "endurance" is prominent. Eschatological joy, then, is characteristic of those who express patience and endurance in life.

1:12 *has enabled you.* This is the reading of ℵ B 1739 1881. A number of later manuscripts (A C D F G 044 𝔐) read "has enabled us" rather than "has enabled you." Paul's repeated use of "you" up to this point in the letter makes it unlikely that he would have now changed to "us."

his people, who live in the light. Literally, "the holy ones in the light." A number of commentators (e.g., Martin 1973:54) think this refers to the heavenly angels and thus is a preemptive strike against the tendency of the Colossians to worship angels (see 2:18), for the Colossians are already qualified for the angelic realm. It is clear that the term "holy ones" can mean angels (Deut 33:2-3; Ps 89:6-7; and probably Wis 5:5; 1QS 11:7-8) and

that such "holy ones" stand in the light of God's presence (Jude 1:6 and 2 Pet 2:4 emphasize darkness to contrast the present fate of fallen angels with their original privilege), but
in Colossians (1:2, 4, 22, 26; 3:12), as well as elsewhere in Paul's writings, all references
to "holy ones" are to believers as those made holy by God. Furthermore, the association
of entry into light with conversion is found in a spectrum of NT literature (Acts 26:18;
Eph 5:8; 1 Pet 2:9) and some Jewish literature (e.g., *1 Enoch* 1:8: "the light of God shall
shine upon [the righteous]"). Thus, the meaning accepted by the NLT is to be preferred.
Furthermore, "his people" is less misleading than the archaic "saints" (that usually designates outstandingly holy people for contemporary speakers rather than the people of God
in general), although "holy ones" might be a clearer alternative translation.

COMMENTARY

While he was not a person given to complaining, Paul was also a man who was never
satisfied. He was not content to let things remain as they were when people
converted to Christ. He was not even content merely with signs of the Spirit's work in
the lives of his converts. Instead, Paul always wanted believers to go on and develop
more deeply as Christians. Like Aslan in C. S. Lewis's *The Chronicles of Narnia*, Paul's
cry was, "Further in and further up!" Therefore, we should not be surprised when the
news of the good state of the Colossians immediately flows over into prayer, which
Paul and Timothy shared together ("we"). Paul wanted the Colossians to know that
the positive news that he had heard about the Colossians had made him and his
companions intense in their prayers for them (1:9).

The desire expressed in the prayer is that the Colossians might know the will of
God fully. The God of the Bible is the God who has revealed himself and his will,
first in the Mosaic law, next in the priestly ministry, including the Urim and Thum-
mim, then in the prophets, and most fully in Jesus Christ, who released into the
hearts of his followers the Spirit who speaks and reveals God's will, as we see in Acts,
the Letters, and Revelation. Thus, the whole of Scripture assumes that God's will is
knowable. The knowledge desired is not just mental understanding, the type of
knowledge that might enable one to pass an examination on doctrine, but "the perception of God's will as seen in Christ and the response to it" (Moule 1968:53). This
becomes absolutely clear in the following verse. True knowledge for either Jews or
Christians was never merely theoretical but always practical. In this case the nature
of this knowledge is expanded with the Old Testament word pair "wisdom and
understanding." This is what Daniel and his friends had due to their fidelity to the
law (Dan 1:20), and it is also what the angel revealed to Daniel (Dan 9:22). But
while in the Old Testament wisdom and understanding came primarily from the
law, Paul is clear here that the Spirit is the source of this wisdom, (even in the OT,
the Spirit was sometimes the source of wisdom, e.g., Exod 31:3; Isa 11:2). In that
sense he is closer to Isaiah 11:1-2, where "the spirit of wisdom and understanding"
will rest on a "shoot" from "the stump of the line of Jesse" (NLT mg). In the context
of Pauline thought, Spirit-given wisdom and understanding is knowledge that
comes by means of the Spirit who is given by the "shoot," that is, Jesus. Thus, in
other places Paul says that the Christian is to live or "walk" as directed by the Spirit
(Rom 8:4, 13-14; Gal 5:16, 18, 25), while here he prays for Spirit-given wisdom.

"All this reflects the charismatic and eschatological character of Christian self-consciousness, not least in the transition from conviction to praxis" (Dunn 1996:71).

The transition to praxis is clear when Paul writes that this knowledge will enable them to live lives that will "honor and please" the Lord (1:10). Here "the Lord" is probably Jesus since he is the focus in this letter. The idiom that could be literally translated "to walk worthily" is rightly rendered by the NLT as living in such a way as will bring honor to Jesus, for gaining honor and avoiding shame were principal values in Paul's world. In this case, Jesus is the patron or benefactor, and one should live so as to please him (so also 1 Cor 7:32) and bring him honor, which would include living in accordance with his teaching and lifestyle. Jesus' life was as much a part of his teaching as his words were (see also 2:6). That is the reason the Gospels contain so much about his life and deeds as well as his teaching, for all of this was a model for the Christian to inform his or her actions and to be applied in their situation. Jesus is divine wisdom embodied, and thus a life that honors him will be filled with deeds like his that accord with his teaching.

The concept of living so as to honor "the Lord" is further expanded in terms of a plant bearing fruit, first mentioned in 1:6. The fruit-bearing is displayed in doing good works, such as acts of charity, which we find not only in Romans 12 but also in James 1:26-27; 2:14-26. Paul frequently urged believers to do good works as the natural expression of the Christian living in the Spirit. Indeed, if such fruit is absent, one should question whether the life of the Kingdom is really present. Likewise, believers should grow with respect to their knowledge of God. If this is the correct interpretation of this verse (see note on 1:6), then living out our faith in good works correlates with understanding God and his ways better. Jesus said that if we obeyed his teaching we would know the truth (e.g., John 8:31-32), which suggests that we must first risk and follow what little we do understand before we gain deeper insight. This may be the sense of what Paul is saying here as well. An alternative understanding of the passage is that our growth, as well as our bearing fruit, is with respect to good works and that we do all of this because of our understanding of God. That is, when we look at the world from God's (or Jesus') perspective, we will have the perspective necessary for us to recognize those good works that will honor and please God. Either understanding of the passage links our good deeds done for God to our insights into God. The Christian life does not separate heart from hands. And Paul prays for this link of heart and hand.

As people get to know God, they should experience God's power and glory (1:11)—that is, having an experience in this world that followers of Jesus will fully experience in the coming world. Such an experience strengthens believers and burns into them the reality of what is coming. Because of these experiences, believers can endure persecution patiently, not with a depressed attitude, but with deep thankful joy. This does not mean that the believer will never experience grief (cf. 2 Cor 4:8-11), but that an abiding joy will remain, grounded in thankfulness. This joy is eschatological, for it does not deny real pain and suffering but sees through to the eternal reward, a reward that the ancient followers of God have already received and which is waiting for those who presently follow Jesus. This eschatological vision bubbles up into thanks to the Father, for it is the Father who initiates these privileges and gives us this inheritance. (For the emphasis on eschatology in Colossians, see "Author" in the Introduction.) Thus the whole prayer is neatly bracketed between references to the Father—he is the one Paul thanks, he is the one Paul petitions, and he is the one whom followers of Jesus thank as they reflect on what he has granted them.

The focus of the thanks in the end of the prayer (1:12) is that the Father has enabled (or "qualified") these Colossians to enter the true Promised Land; "sharing" in an "inheritance" brings to mind narratives in the OT where Abraham was promised and Israel received an inheritance. The Colossian followers of Jesus have been qualified to share in this inheritance, which belongs to God's sanctified people in the heavenly realm. "In light" is used to refer to the full experience of God's presence. This is what Christians experience partially in worship, when they experience the presence of God, but it also points to a time when they will be among the sanctified people of God in the full light of his presence. True worship is a foretaste of heaven. If this is not our experience, then we have not yet entered into that worship that Paul and his churches experienced.

◆ C. Praise to the Father and Son for Salvation (1:13-23)

¹³For he has rescued us from the kingdom of darkness and transferred us into the Kingdom of his dear Son, ¹⁴who purchased our freedom* and forgave our sins.
¹⁵Christ is the visible image of the
    invisible God.
He existed before anything was
    created and is supreme over all
    creation,*
¹⁶for through him God created everything
    in the heavenly realms and on earth.
He made the things we can see
    and the things we can't see—
such as thrones, kingdoms, rulers, and
    authorities in the unseen world.
Everything was created through him
    and for him.
¹⁷He existed before anything else,
    and he holds all creation together.
¹⁸Christ is also the head of the church,
    which is his body.
He is the beginning,
    supreme over all who rise from
    the dead.*
So he is first in everything.

¹⁹For God in all his fullness
    was pleased to live in Christ,
²⁰and through him God reconciled
    everything to himself.
He made peace with everything in
    heaven and on earth
by means of Christ's blood on
    the cross.

²¹This includes you who were once far away from God. You were his enemies, separated from him by your evil thoughts and actions. ²²Yet now he has reconciled you to himself through the death of Christ in his physical body. As a result, he has brought you into his own presence, and you are holy and blameless as you stand before him without a single fault.

²³But you must continue to believe this truth and stand firmly in it. Don't drift away from the assurance you received when you heard the Good News. The Good News has been preached all over the world, and I, Paul, have been appointed as God's servant to proclaim it.

1:14 Some manuscripts add *with his blood.*   1:15 Or *He is the firstborn of all creation.*   1:18 Or *the firstborn from the dead.*

NOTES

1:13 For he. Literally, "he who," a construction parallel to 1:15 (there translated "Christ" to make clear to whom it refers). It is difficult to translate such constructions so that they make good sense in English and yet show the parallel structure in Greek. Furthermore, the "he who" type of construction often introduces a hymn (as in 1 Tim 3:16 and Phil 2:6-11, although some dispute that the latter is a hymn). In the case of our passage I believe at least 1:15-20 to be a hymn because of this typical hymnic introduction, the rough balance of syllables in the relatively short lines, and the parallelism between 1:15-16 and 1:17-18 (i.e., the first two strophes) with 1:19-20 forming a concluding strophe. Thus one has a three-part structure: creator, source of the church, and means of becoming that source (i.e., his death). Furthermore, the grammar is unlike Paul's normal grammar, in which he likes to develop his thoughts through long, involved sentences. The grammar in this section is that of relatively short clauses with many appositives.

rescued. This is a term commonly used in NT prayers for deliverance (e.g., "rescue us from the evil one" in the Lord's Prayer, Matt 6:13), which was perhaps borrowed from the LXX where it commonly means for deliverance from all types of danger, including deliverance from Egypt, enemies, etc. Here it is used to praise God for salvation.

kingdom of darkness. More literally "the authority of darkness" or "the power of darkness" (NRSV), here translated "kingdom" to underscore the parallel with the Kingdom of "his dear Son," a parallel that Paul surely intended in a sense, although he never used the term "kingdom" for anything other than God's rule. He may not have wanted to dignify the powers of darkness with the term "kingdom," either because they are not legitimate enough or because they are not organized enough (see commentary below).

1:14 purchased our freedom. This is the reading in several good and early manuscripts: א A B C D F G 044 075 33 1739. Some later scribes (614 630; so TR) added "with his blood" to make this verse parallel to Eph 1:7. It is theologically correct but not what Paul wrote here (see 1:20, where Paul does mention "Christ's blood on the cross").

1:15 the visible image. An image in Hellenistic Greek could mean (1) a literal image such as a statue, (2) the universe as the reflection or image of God (so Plato), (3) human beings and thus Adam (encompassing both male and female, Gen 1:27) as the image of God, or (4) Wisdom as the image of God, pointing to the way God made himself visible ("For she is a reflection of eternal light, a spotless mirror of the working of God, and an image of his goodness," Wis 7:26, NRSV). While Paul elsewhere uses an Adam Christology (Rom 5:12-21), here he seems to be using a Wisdom Christology. The focus is probably more on Jesus as the embodiment of God's Wisdom than on Jesus as essentially, ontologically being "Wisdom." In Jesus, the Wisdom of God, that revelatory reflection of God, was totally present.

He existed before anything was created and is supreme over all creation. More literally expressed this would be, "firstborn of all creation." Firstborn can mean "first created within the creation" (as the firstborn child) or "preeminent over the creation" (referring to the position of the firstborn son as future leader of the family or clan). Dunn (1996:90) may well be correct that Paul is using the image of Wisdom, which allows a certain ambiguity here given the dual role of Wisdom: Wisdom as created (Prov 8:22; Sir 1:4; 24:9) versus Wisdom as Creator (Ps 104:24; Prov 3:19; Wis 8:5; Philo *Worse* 54). Paul may be using this image to show that the Son is the bridge between the unseen Father and visible creation, although the next verse will make clear that, like Wisdom, the Son is also the agent of creation. Thus, in taking the thought of the two verses together, the NLT is correct in avoiding the English connotations of the word "firstborn" (i.e., temporal priority among created things) and choosing to put the emphasis on Christ's supremacy where Paul will put his. This phrase with its emphasis on "firstborn"/"first" may be the beginning of a meditation on Gen 1:1 (which begins with the Hebrew term "in the beginning" that is constructed from the term "first") combined with Prov 8:22 (Davies 1955:151-152 citing the work of C. F. Burney).

1:16 through him God created. The NLT expands the passive "were created in him" or "were created by him" by adding the ultimate agent, God. While this is theology with which Paul would certainly agree, and while it is implied in the passive, Paul appears to use the passive deliberately in order to avoid naming God and keep the focus on Jesus as creator.

1:17 He existed before anything else. The Greek *pro pantōn* [TG4253/3956A, ZG4574/4246] can mean existing temporally before all things, which is the interpretation of the NLT, or it can mean ranking first before all things. Thus, it is ambiguous. Paul probably intended this ambiguity, which is virtually impossible to convey in English, because for Paul temporal precedence would also mean precedence in rank.

holds all creation together. Possibly an allusion to divine Wisdom, as in Wis 1:6-7, "that which holds all things together," and Sir 43:26, "by [God's] Word (*logos* [TG3056, ZG3364], which is equivalent to Wisdom in Sirach) all things hold together." Wisdom and Sirach express the idea, but I am not sure that there is a direct allusion to them, for the idea of personified divine Wisdom is too widespread.

1:18 head. "Head" can have the sense of "leader" in the Hebrew OT and occasionally in Greek (although the LXX translates the "head = leader" references with a term for "ruler," not with the Greek term for "head") but tends to emphasize rank more than control. (The ancients did not normally think of the brain as controlling the body—Aristotle thought it cooled the blood.) In Greek it more often has the sense of "source" or "origin," which fits well with the creation references in this passage (Moule 1968:68).

body. In 1 Corinthians it was the church, especially the local church, which was thought of as a body in its entirety. Here the idea of "head" as contrasted with "body" is introduced and the "body" transcends the local gathering. In Greek thought, the physical creation was often thought of as a body, sometimes with Zeus as the head, sometimes with Logos (divine reason) as the head, and often with reason as the soul within the body. Thus "body" would first have struck the readers as a creation reference before Paul suddenly qualified it by "the church" (in the Greek, "body" is mentioned before "church"), which thus becomes the locus of new creation (Dunn 1996:94-96).

beginning. The Greek word for "beginning" is also ambiguous, for it can mean "ruler" (the plural form is so translated in 1:16) or "source" as well as temporal "beginning." While temporality could be the more prominent focus of the passage, Paul may have chosen a deliberately ambiguous word so as not to distinguish among these meanings.

supreme. As in 1:15, this is the term traditionally translated "firstborn," that is, "firstborn from the dead."

first in everything. The NLT preserves the ambiguity of the Greek, which can mean "first in every respect" or "first among all things." The latter fits well with Christ's supremacy over the various principalities and powers, but the former fits both his eschatological and his creational supremacy.

1:19 fullness. While sometimes viewed as Gnostic or proto-Gnostic, the idea of God or Wisdom filling the universe was as common in Jewish thought (see Ps 139:7-8; Jer 23:24; Wis 1:6-7; see also Philo) as in Greco-Roman thought (e.g., Seneca, *De beneficiis* 4.8.2). Furthermore, in both the OT and intertestamental literature it was also common to speak of God living in individuals (e.g., "In [the Elect One] dwells the spirit of wisdom," *1 Enoch* 49:3; "the Lord dwells in [the good person]," *Testament of Benjamin* 6:4). So what we have here is not a later Gnostic development but an insistence that it was not merely a piece of Wisdom/the Spirit/God that lived in Jesus but the totality, i.e., "all the fullness." Grammatically "all the fullness" is the subject of both parts of the couplet found in verses 19 and 20.

1:21 *far away from God.* The Greek term, *apēllotriōmenous* [TG526, ZG558] ("alienation" or "estrangement"), occurs in the NT only here and in Eph 2:12; 4:18. In Ephesians the focus is on gentile alienation from God and/or from Israel. Here it is the Colossians' alienation from God in their (largely gentile) past.

1:22 *he has brought you into his own presence.* The Greek reads "to present you before him" (similar to Eph 1:4) and implies that this is something that will happen in the future, not something that has already happened. This presentation is, in typical Pauline fashion, Jesus presenting the Christians before the Father, not their presentation before Jesus himself.

1:23 *you must.* The Greek phrase is *ei ge* [TG1487/1065, ZG1623/1145], often translated "if indeed" (NKJV), "provided that" (NRSV, NAB), or simply "if" (NIV). While the phrase does express conditionality, in its NT appearances (2 Cor 5:3; Gal 3:4; Eph 3:2; 4:21), the expression indicates conditions that are expected to be fulfilled, which is why the NLT translates it "you must," although the imperative does not exactly get at the sense of "if you X (and indeed you will X)." It is difficult to pick up this nuance of conditionality along with the confidence that is expressed here (Dunn 1996:110).

believe this truth. "Remain in this commitment" expresses the thought better, for our term "believe" is often intellectual while Paul's concern was with a commitment to Jesus as Lord (cf. Rom 10:9-10).

assurance. The Greek word here, *elpis* [TG1680, ZG1828](traditionally translated "hope"), in Paul's writings usually points to a concrete eschatological expectation. "Assurance" can indicate this sense of future hope in God's promises, but it can also indicate a particular evangelical doctrine of the conviction that one has been "saved" (note the past tense) that is not entirely congruent with Paul's meaning here.

COMMENTARY

In this commentary I have included verses 13 and 14 with the hymnic praise of Christ in 1:15-20. Thus, 1:13-14 is a hymnic praise of the Father leading to a hymnic praise of Christ. Because verse 14 (like the second half of verse 20) is more prosaic, it would be easy to join 13 and 14 to the prayer and only begin the more poetic piece in verse 15, but I see 13 and 14 as a bridge between the two sections. Praise to the Father follows logically from the prayer, and this leads to the praise of the Son. Thus we have a two-part praise, like several of the songs in Revelation.

Paul first broke into praise to the Father. He is the main actor in the drama of our deliverance. He is the one who has rescued us or saved us. This is one of the few places in the New Testament where salvation is viewed as an already completed event (versus an ongoing or future salvation). It is also a clear instance of a text in which the Father is the one rescuing. Using a term that reminds the reader of the deliverance from Egypt in the Old Testament (Exod 6:6; 12:17; Judg 6:9), Paul praised the Father for deliverance from the "Egypt" where the Colossians had been in bondage, namely the "kingdom of darkness." Paul views the world in this age as dominated by demonic or Satanic power ("the power of darkness"). While we may view it as a kingdom of sorts, Paul simply calls it "power," probably indicating that it is illegitimate and possibly indicating that they are not fully organized (as J. R. R. Tolkein portrays in his description of orcs in *The Lord of the Rings*—while a fearsome foe, they fight one another frequently and are held in order by fear of retribution;

cf. Heb 2:14-15). This belief in a "kingdom of darkness" is why, beginning around AD 200, if not before, the church practiced exorcism on all new converts, assuming that they needed deliverance from demonic powers by the power of God (see the baptismal rites described in the *Canons of Hippolytus*). Paul saw this freeing as happening directly through the power of the Father in the acceptance of the Good News. This deliverance was not simply negative (deliverance from something), but positive, in that Christians come under a new authority: "the Kingdom of his dear Son." This means that they have come under the authorized rule of his loved Son; they have submitted to his authority and have been integrated into his Kingdom, which will rule the earth in the future. This integration into the Son's Kingdom is not optional; there is no idea in the New Testament that one can be a free agent: one is either under one authority or the other.

This first part of the praise is important in that it establishes two theological foundations. First, the Father is the one who has rescued us (1:13). It was not the Son rescuing us from the wrath of the Father, as some popular forms of Christianity would have it but the Father himself rescuing us from the powers of darkness. "God loved the world" is not just the sentiment of John 3:16 but also of Paul in Colossians. Second, as noted above, salvation is communal. In being rescued the Christian is not simply released from personal sin but is transferred from a pseudo-community, the kingdom or authority of darkness, into a true community, the Kingdom of his loved Son. This means, as I have noted, that to be one who has been rescued is to be in a kingdom and subject to a king. Thus, relationship to other subjects as well as to the king is implied. Paul did not use the expression "Kingdom of God" very often, but the idea of the Kingdom underlies his whole conception of salvation and the church, as it does here.

While the Father is the primary actor, the Son is also present in the drama of our rescue from the kingdom of darkness. In our union with him we find our release from slavery to darkness. The expression "[he] purchased our freedom" (1:14) is in Greek a relative clause traditionally translated "in whom we have redemption." The transaction of "redemption" is that of buying an individual out of slavery and takes place "in him," meaning in union with Christ. It is not an arm's length transaction but something that happens as we identify with him as our Lord. This release from slavery is further defined as "the forgiveness of sins." That is, what was holding us under the power of darkness was apparently our sin, so when the sin is removed, the power of darkness has no more authority over us. And our sin is removed as we are joined to Christ.

Having transitioned from the action of the Father to that of the Son, Paul broke into a song of praise to Christ, drawing on Jewish thought about God's wisdom. The goal of this song appears to avoid any attempt to relativize the cosmic role of Christ—that is, to make him less than the supreme ruler of the whole universe, redeemed or unredeemed, physical or personal. Jesus is ruler absolutely. Scholars often argue that the thought Paul was opposing in Colosse was that while Christ accomplished redemption, there was a need beyond what Christ could offer in getting along in the present, especially in dealing with the various cosmic powers. Without attacking such thought directly, Paul spoke of Christ and his cosmic role in terms that would make anything other than Christ unnecessary.

This section (1:15-20) is probably structured as a meditation on the first words of Genesis 1:1 ("in the beginning," one word in Hebrew, which comes from a root that means "head") together with the picture in Proverbs 8:22-31 of Wisdom's creative activity ("The LORD formed me from the beginning . . . . I was the architect at his side").

Paul's meditation stresses a simple point in beautiful and memorable language. It would be wrong to try to find nuances in each phrase, for the poetic nature of the language means that it is the whole picture that Paul is intending to convey. First, Paul states that Jesus is the embodiment of divine Wisdom. Thus, Jesus makes the invisible God visible (1:15). In the Old Testament God is presented as the one who cannot be safely seen (Exod 33:20) or who dwells in darkness (Exod 20:21; Deut 5:23; Ps 18:9,11), or who, when seen, is a vague form without features (Ezek 1:26-28), all indicating that God is so exalted and different from human beings that he cannot be perceived by them. Wisdom was one way that God communicated himself to human beings in the Old Testament, but in our passage he does it in two different ways, neither of which is unconnected to Wisdom. The primary focus in this passage is on making God visible in creation (cf. Prov 8:27-31), but John 1:14 and 18 point out that Jesus was also the incarnation of the very character of the Father. He is the Word who has *become* flesh (not *taken on* or *put on* as if he clothed himself with a garment), has become what human beings are, and thus is visible and accessible to human beings. To see Jesus is to see (and experience) the Father (John 14:8-10). Thus, if you want to know what the Father is like, look at Jesus. Those descriptions of the Father in popular theology as always angry or judging or harsh are simply false images if one trusts the full New Testament picture of Jesus. The Father is just as good, just as kind, just as loving as Jesus. And the Father is only as harsh, judging, or angry as Jesus is (cf. Matt 21:12-17; John 5-8; Jas 5:9). Jesus, not the images of popular theology, is the true revelation of the Father.

Second, as the embodiment of divine Wisdom, Jesus is the creator. This implies that he existed before creation and acted as the agent of creation. In case his readers missed the point, Paul underscores that Christ made everything: visible, invisible, heavenly, earthly. Then he specifically points out that Christ made all the various spiritual authorities, no matter how exalted and no matter how good or evil any given power may be (1:16). It is in Christ and his creative rule that the Colossians are to find their security, not in finding ways to appease, control, or manipulate these spiritual powers themselves. Furthermore, while the New Testament often speaks of Jesus as the agent of creation (e.g., John 1:3; Rom 11:36; 1 Cor 8:6; Heb 1:2-3), it normally speaks of God as the ultimate cause and goal of creation (Rom 11:36; 1 Cor 8:6; Heb 2:10; Rev 4:11) (Ladd 1993:459). Here it is Jesus, as Wisdom, for whom and by whom all things were created.

In 1:17 Paul brings together his thoughts on creation: Jesus is before all things (temporally or in rank—probably both are intended) and holds all things together, as Wisdom does. (Wis 1:6-7; see note on 1:17). Thus, this summary verse serves to say, "So much for anything in creation outranking or overpowering Christ in any way."

If Jesus' preeminence is true for the original creation and all of the principalities and powers that exist in the universe, is it also true for the new creation, the redemption of the world? Just as Revelation 4:11 includes a song about creation and then moves on in 5:9 to redemption, so Paul moved on to redemption in 1:18. But unlike Revelation, Paul did not change the subject from God to the Lamb. It was Christ in the first part and also Christ in the second.

In a transitional phrase that the original readers probably understood as summing up the teaching on creation, Paul wrote of Jesus (as Wisdom) as the head of the body. Up to this point the Greek reader would have thought of the "body" as the creation and thus of Jesus as the source or leader of the creation. Now with a simple appositive, "the church," the subject is shifted. The creation becomes the church, or, as we might put it, the church is defined as the visible locus of the renewal of creation. And Jesus is the source of this new creation as well.

Structurally, the second part of the poetic unit begins with "He is the beginning" (1:18b; structurally parallel with 1:13 and 1:15), but the shift to the church has already taken place in the previous two words. Now we get further definition as to what it means for Jesus to be the beginning/source/ruler of the church.

Jesus is the beginning/source/ruler of the church, the new creation, just as he is of the original creation. That means that he is "firstborn" both in the sense that he is "supreme" over the new creation, in which death works backwards—new life is brought from the dead—and in the sense that he is the first member or product of this new creation since he has already risen from the dead to die no more.

Thus, we have two poles of a dynamic tension. If one goes to the beginning of creation, one finds him supreme over all created things, and if one goes to the end of time, one finds him supreme over all in the new creation, for the Resurrection is the start of the end, with the whole future age being an outworking of what started on the day of Christ's resurrection. Paul underlines this dynamic tension with the double use of the term often translated "firstborn."

In 1:19 the poem moves on to the most stupendous two-part claim. First, God in all his fullness was pleased to live in Christ ("the complete being of God, by God's own choice, came to dwell," NEB; "all the fullness of God was pleased to dwell," NRSV). Drawing upon Jewish conceptions of God (or Wisdom, or the Spirit of God) living in human beings, Paul took it one step further. That indwelling was true of Jesus, but in his case the indwelling was "God in all his fullness." That is, no one could have more of God. That God "was pleased" is also an Old Testament phrase that means God chose someone or something. Incarnation was not a chance act or an act of desperation but a deliberate choice on God's part. And in Jesus we meet the fullness of God, for as John said, "God gives him the Spirit without limit" (John 3:34). Here we have a repetition of what John meant in recording Jesus' words, "Anyone who has seen me has seen the Father!" (John 14:9). Again, this prohibits us from trying to shove a wedge between Jesus and the Father as if one were nice and the other not so nice. They are completely one.

Second, the act of redemption is now attributed to the Father (or, more accurately, to "all the fullness"). The Father reconciled the creation through Jesus (1:20). The term "reconcile" assumes that a state of hostility exists. Paul had already mentioned that we were part of the "kingdom of darkness" and thus controlled by a hostile power. In 1:21 he makes it clear that we were not simply deemed collectively hostile because of our submission to a dictator who is at odds with God but that we ourselves were also personally alienated from and hostile to God. We were the prodigals in a far land. However, unlike the prodigal in the parable, it is not we who came to our senses and sought reconciliation with the Father but the Father who reached out to make peace. Furthermore, the peace he made extended not to us human beings alone, but to "everything in heaven and on earth." That is, the reconciliation extends beyond humanity and has cosmic and creational effects. Exactly what this means is only hinted at in the rest of Scripture. Romans 8:19-23 points to a freeing of the creation from bondage and decay as being part of the completion of redemption. In our passage here the creation is viewed as being alien or hostile to God and his purposes. Isaiah 11:6-9 and Isaiah 65:17-25 picture a renewed creation of harmony and peace (attributed in Isa 11:1 to the reign of the "shoot" from Jesse's "old root"). But how such general or poetic descriptions work out in reality is difficult to conceptualize. Perhaps it is beyond human comprehension. A clue to our incomprehension lies in the reference to the reconciliation of things "in heaven." What could that mean? In the Old Testament and later Jewish thought, stars and planets were often conceived of as controlled by angels. Does this indicate their being brought back into heavenly order? How does one picture that in an impersonal universe—a universe that is viewed as comprehensively controlled by the forces of gravity, light, mass, and energy? The limits of our comprehension become apparent. Yet whatever the heavenly aspect may mean concretely, what is clear is that reconciliation reaches beyond saving individuals, even beyond rescuing humanity. The goal of the Father is the extension of the Kingdom of his dear Son over the whole universe, not just over humanity. He is still interested in his creation, not just in people. Creation is not disposable, to be discarded, but rather it is viewed as renewable, to be purified. And in the end we human beings will play a role, indeed apparently an important one, in a renewed creation—a role that is larger in scope than we can now imagine.

This peace was brought about through "Christ's blood on the cross" (1:20; more literally, "the blood of his cross"). This expression is unique in the Pauline writings, although both the elements of "blood" and "cross" with reference to Jesus are common enough in Paul. What we have here is a shocking juxtaposition (as well as a sudden change in subject from the Father to Jesus): Reconciliation is juxtaposed with blood, which connotes violence and death. The "supreme" one, the first to "rise from the dead" (1:18) did indeed die, and died violently. His supremacy and honor, so eloquently expressed in the previous verses, are juxtaposed with "cross," his cross, a term so degrading that in Roman society you did not mention it in polite conversation. (In fact, the cross symbol would not be used by Christians until the time of Constantine.) You could not get more shamed than to be crucified, a death reserved for those considered subhuman. Thus, the poetic flight into the heavens ends with a paradox. It was not the blood of victorious battle nor the might of a champion slashing through his foes that God used to bring peace to us; it was the blood of an inhuman form of execution, performed upon his Son. This paradox is Paul's model for the Christian life, for while our Lord lives in glorious exaltation on the other side of the Resurrection, we are still on this side of the Resurrection, and our victories, like his, are won not through might but through sacrifice and weakness.

Having written so poetically of Christ, Paul turned to his readers and addressed them. The Colossians were Gentiles, and as such had been previously alienated from God (1:20). While Ephesians makes it clear that this condition applied particularly to Gentiles because they lacked God's revelation that Israel possessed, in Colossians with its cosmic emphasis the focus is on their taking part in the alienation of the cosmos from God. At the same time, however, they were themselves hostile to God and this had worked itself out in evil deeds. It was precisely these people with whom Christ had reconciled or made peace with (1:22). The initiative to be reconciled came from him, not from the human side. He did this not by some heavenly act or divine revelation but in a concrete act in his physical body (Paul underscores the physicality of the act) by means of his death. Though the act of reconciliation is in the past, Paul maintains this past act in tension with the future, for the ultimate goal is to present the Colossians before the Father, presumably in the final judgment at the end of the age. Salvation is accomplished but not completed; it has already taken place but is not yet finished, for salvation is still in process. The ultimate goal is that the believers become "holy and blameless . . . without a single fault" (1:22).

Between God's reconciling initiative and the future consummation lies a process that would only come to completion if the Colossians continued on in their commitment to Christ (1:23). While Paul did not doubt that they would continue with respect to their commitment, he did condition the future consummation upon it. With this both Calvinists and Arminians would agree, although they would theologize it differently. It is only the relatively recent popularized mixture of the two that allows that one can be secure due to a past experience, even if there is no evidence of one's present commitment to Jesus as Lord. This would seem strange to Paul, for he, here as elsewhere (e.g., Rom 8:13; 11:22; 1 Cor 9:27; 10:11-12; Gal 5:4), insists that continuing in one's commitment to Jesus is essential if one is to have a real eschatological hope. His pictures are graphic, for "stand firmly" is a term for a building resting securely on its foundation, which naturally leads into the idea that one should not "drift away" (or "be moved away"—the verb is passive) from the eschatological hope—that is, the expectation of being presented before God in a sanctified state if one remains committed to following Jesus. Here, as elsewhere in the New Testament, eschatology is not intended to give us a map of the future but to transform our behavior in accordance with the rule of God so that we live in the present according to the values of that future toward which we are moving. (For more on eschatology in Colossians, see "Author" in the Introduction.) This confident expectation is rooted in the Good News, Paul's message, which he has been proclaiming to the whole world. He puts this in the past, apparently looking back at his ministry of proclaiming the Good News of the crucified Jesus as resurrected Lord. Paul had made this proclamation in major centers all over Syria and Cilicia, Asia Minor, and Greece. This assertion not only concludes the previous discussion but also forms Paul's transition into the following section.

It is clear that Paul has ended a major section of the letter. The references to hope, the reception of the Good News, and its universal spread echo the beginning of the thanksgiving prayer (1:3-6). Thus, this section repeats those earlier themes and focuses them on Paul's ministry, which will be the topic of the next major section.

◆ III. Historical Background (*narratio*) (1:24–2:5)

²⁴I am glad when I suffer for you in my body, for I am participating in the sufferings of Christ that continue for his body, the church. ²⁵God has given me the responsibility of serving his church by proclaiming his entire message to you. ²⁶This message was kept secret for centuries and generations past, but now it has been revealed to God's people. ²⁷For God wanted them to know that the riches and glory of Christ are for you Gentiles, too. And this is the secret: Christ lives in you. This gives you assurance of sharing his glory.

²⁸So we tell others about Christ, warning everyone and teaching everyone with all the wisdom God has given us. We want to present them to God, perfect* in their relationship to Christ. ²⁹That's why I work and struggle so hard, depend-

ing on Christ's mighty power that works within me.

CHAPTER 2

I want you to know how much I have agonized for you and for the church at Laodicea, and for many other believers who have never met me personally. ²I want them to be encouraged and knit together by strong ties of love. I want them to have complete confidence that they understand God's mysterious plan, which is Christ himself. ³In him lie hidden all the treasures of wisdom and knowledge.

⁴I am telling you this so no one will deceive you with well-crafted arguments. ⁵For though I am far away from you, my heart is with you. And I rejoice that you are living as you should and that your faith in Christ is strong.

1:28 Or *mature.*

NOTES

1:24 *my body . . . his body.* While the two terms are more or less synonyms, the first term, *sarx* [TG4561, ZG4922], is not used metaphorically and refers particularly to the physical nature of Paul's suffering, while the second, *sōma* [TG4983, ZG5393], is the normal term used when "body" is used in a metaphorical sense.

I am participating in the sufferings of Christ that continue for his body. More literally this would read, "I am filling up what is lacking of the sufferings of Christ on behalf of his body." This is indeed participation, but it also implies that there is a certain amount of suffering that needs to be completed and that Paul is filling it up. The word for "sufferings" (*thlipsis* [TG2347, ZG2568]) never refers elsewhere to what Jesus suffered on the cross, but it is used to refer to the sufferings of the end of the age (Matt 24:21, 29; Mark 13:19, 24; Rev 2:22; 7:14), which, in Jewish thought, would precede the appearance of the Messiah (the so-called "messianic woes") and which had a definite measure (Rev 6:9-11; *4 Ezra* 4:33-43: "When the number of those like yourselves is completed"; cf. *Greek Apocalypse of Ezra* 2.26–3.7). Paul wanted to "fill up" that which was "lacking," which meant he hoped that this suffering would complete what was needed before Christ appeared to consummate the age. (On the meaning of suffering in the NT, see Davids 1990:30-44.)

1:26 *message . . . secret*. Lit., "mystery . . . hidden." While the Greek term originally meant a "secret rite" and/or "the meaning of a secret rite" and would later mean "something secret or mysterious," in Judaism and the NT it generally means "a secret of God that he has now revealed" (first used in this sense in Dan 2:28-29, 47). This is clearly its meaning here in Colossians; Paul explicitly says that it is something now revealed (Moule 1968:80-82).

1:28 *we tell others*. The Greek term *katangellomen* [TG2605, ZG2859] indicates not just any type of telling but more a solemn proclamation (BDAG 515). The mystery was so great a revelation that Paul presents the picture of a divinely authorized herald announcing it.

***perfect*.** For Paul, being perfect in Christ was fully realizable. The term *teleios* [TG5046, ZG5455] when used in the Greek OT usually translates the Hebrew *tam* [TH8535, ZH9447] or *tamim* [TH8549, ZH9459]; thus we learn, for example, that Noah was *tamim* or *teleios* (Gen 6:9; cf. Sir 44:17), as were others in the OT. In Matthew Jesus calls on believers to be *teleios* just like their Father is (Matt 5:48), which sums up the exposition of the preceding verses in which Jesus concretely instructs his apprentices how to reflect the Father's character—there is no sense that this is not realizable. James expects believers to be moving in this direction, assisted by divine wisdom (Jas 1:2-5). The term *teleios* or *tam* indicates one who is morally upright and obedient to God, not one who never makes a mistake.

2:1 *I want you to know*. This is a relatively common expression in Paul's letters (Rom 1:13; 11:25; 1 Cor 10:1; 11:3; 12:1; 2 Cor 1:8; 1 Thess 4:13) and common in secular Greek letters as well. It does not mean that the readers do not know what is being referred to, but it underscores the subject and makes the readers more conscious of it.

***I have agonized*.** The chapter break at 2:1 is unfortunate. There are several word pairs that link 2:1-5 to the end of chapter 1 and indicate that Paul does not complete his thought until 2:5: "glad" (1:24) and "rejoice" (2:5) ; "riches" (1:27) and "complete" (2:2); "secret" (1:27) and "mysterious plan" (2:2); "struggle" (1:29) and "agonized" (2:1). In each case the two words in the pair are identical in Greek, although to communicate in English, different terms have been used.

2:2 *knit together*. This term is also found in 2:19 and Eph 4:16. While the word can indicate "teaching" or "proving," in this type of context it has the sense of "reconciling, bringing together, uniting, holding together" (see *sumbibazō* [TG4822, ZG5204] in TDNT 7.763-764).

***complete confidence that they understand*.** In Greek this phrase is formed by an alliteration of words beginning with *pi*, that we could literally translate "all wealth of conviction of understanding resulting in knowledge" ("all," "wealth," and "conviction" start with *pi* in Greek: *pan* [TG3956, ZG4246] (full), *ploutos* [TG4149, ZG4458] (riches), *plērophoria* [TG4136, ZG4443] (complete)—sort of a piling up of terms for understanding and knowledge.

***God's mysterious plan, which is Christ himself*.** Literally, "the mystery of God, Christ." This reading has the support of the two earliest manuscripts, 𝔓46 and B. Other manuscripts alter the wording, many by way of expansion: (1) "the mystery of God, Father of Christ" (ℵ* A C 048); (2) "the mystery of God, even the Father of Christ" (ℵ2 L 044 0208); and (3) "the mystery of God and of the Father and of Christ" (D2 𝔐 syrh**; so TR and KJV). The best attested reading (in 𝔓46 B) explains the others, which arose in order to expand this cryptic statement.

2:4 well-crafted arguments. The Greek *pithanologia* [TG4086, ZG4391] refers to the persuasive power or plausibility of an argument but carries with it "the overtone of plausible (sounding) but actually 'specious arguments'" (Dunn 1996:133). In fact, Plato, followed by Aristotle and Epictetus, contrasts this kind of "persuasion" with "wisdom."

2:5 my heart is with you. And I rejoice that. The English may imply to some readers that Paul was simply emotionally present with the Colossians. The truth is much more radical, as comparison with 1 Cor 5:3 shows. Paul felt that he was really present "by the Spirit" in the Colossian community so that he could rejoice "seeing" the positive situation in Colosse (so Dunn 1996:134; O'Brien 1982:98; Fee 1994:645-646; see also the literature they cite).The participle "seeing" is translated by "that," but it implies that Paul felt that he could in the Spirit really observe what was going on

living as you should. The sense is "well-ordered Christian behavior" (O'Brien 1982:99).

COMMENTARY

Traditionally, in developing an argument, the Greek orator would, as Paul does here in writing, set out the historical relationships involved—in this case, between Paul and the Colossians—and the facts of the matter. This structure is most clearly seen in the New Testament in Galatians 1:11–2:14. While Paul did not strictly follow in this letter the canons of rhetoric, he did loosely follow them. Accordingly, at the end of the last section he transitioned into his historical relationship to the Colossians (1:23), and he continued his discussion of that relationship in this one. Discussing this relationship is naturally more difficult in the case of the Colossians, for he had never met them and yet wished to establish the fact of his relationship with them.

Paul was no masochist. He did not enjoy suffering. But this letter reveals him sitting in prison, a rather uncomfortable location, with the threat of punishment (either a beating or execution) hanging over his head. These privations Paul viewed as Christ's sufferings, taking place in Paul's own body on behalf of Christ's body, the church (1:24). That Jesus still suffered in his body, the church, was clear to Paul at his conversion: "Why are you persecuting me?" (Acts 9:4) Thus, "suffering" in the New Testament always indicates those negative experiences that come from outside oneself, either from physical or psychological abuse or else from one's exertions for the sake of Jesus and his Good News. That is, this language does not refer to sickness itself but rather to mistreatment, danger, and exhaustion. Paul experienced these sufferings abundantly (see 2 Cor 4:8-12; 11:23-29; 12:10). What is fascinating here is that Paul viewed the amount that Christ must suffer in his church as a determined, finite amount before the consummation of the Kingdom. This is in keeping with the Jewish concept of the "messianic woes," a time of suffering before the coming of the Messiah. This idea of "birth pangs" or "woes" before the end of the age and the coming of the Messiah was based on such Old Testament passages as Daniel 12:1; Habakkuk 3:16; Zephaniah 1:15; and developed in Second Temple Judaism. Theologians of that age reflected on the suffering of the righteous during the persecution of Antiochus IV Epiphanes) in such works as 4 Maccabees (4 Macc 6:28-29 where a righteous person is able to absorb the suffering coming to the whole people) and *1 Enoch* (see *1 Enoch* 47:1-4 where a certain number of martyrs must suffer before the end). Matthew 24:8 and Mark 13:8 refer to this time of troubles (O'Brien

1982:78-79; Dunn 1996:115; Porter 1997:1180-1181). Based on this doctrine and such sayings of Jesus, followers of Jesus realized that although the Messiah had come and had suffered for them, there was still more suffering for the whole people of God before the Messiah would return (Acts 14:22; Rom 8:17; 1 Thess 3:3). This was viewed as a fixed amount of suffering. Thus, in absorbing the abuse that he did, Paul was "soaking up," so to speak, as much as possible of that amount, which meant that there was less for others. It is in this sense that he can speak of the suffering as "for you," even though he had never visited the Colossians. There is yet another sense in which he can say, "for you": Paul knew that God had given him the responsibility to preach the Good News over a given area. That is, he had the responsibility or administrative duty of serving the church by fully proclaiming God's message within a given area (1:25), and this area of responsibility included Colosse, as one can see in reading Romans 15:18-20.

Having mentioned the Good News, Paul set it into a context. God had a secret plan from the ages past (1:26; cf. Dan 2:28-29, 47). He had worked time and history to the point when he revealed it, principally through Paul (1 Cor 2:1; 4:1). The Colossians were privileged to have received this revelation, a revelation that brings more honor to God among the Gentiles. This secret plan is literally, "Christ in you [gentile believers] the hope of glory" (1:27). Elsewhere Paul speaks of this mystery as the Gentiles being included with the Jews in the people of God (Eph 3:3-6), the Good News about Jesus being preached to the Gentiles (Rom 11:25; 16:25-26), everything being brought together under the authority of Christ (Eph 1:9-10), and the transformation of all believers at the resurrection (1 Cor 15:51). Here the focus is on the presence of Christ in gentile believers, that presence being their evidence that they will be transformed according to and share in the glory of God. The scope of this is cosmic. The picture is one of God in control of the ages making a plan, a plan that was hidden in a previous period. Then the picture changes as we move into the present and discover that God made it clear that Christ will indwell Gentiles without them having to become Jews. And then there is yet another shift, as we look on into the eschatological future and see those Gentiles transformed according to and participating in the glory of God. That is the cosmic picture, Paul says, in which the Colossians were participating. Furthermore, they knew that they were part of it, for they experienced Christ within—a concept that is unusual for Paul, who normally speaks of the Spirit within, but note the shift from "Spirit" to "Christ" and back again in Rom 8:9-11. This experience of the indwelling Christ is the evidence that a person belongs to Christ (see also Rom 8:15-16, 23, 26). The Christian hope is not an "I hope that somehow" but an "I hope because I experience the presence of Christ within me."

This inspiring revelation motivated Paul to proclaim the Good News. This proclamation consisted of two parts, warning and teaching, both requiring God's wisdom (1:28; embodied in Christ and present in his agents through the Spirit). We see this dual nature of the proclamation in Acts 17:30-31: "God overlooked people's ignorance about these things in earlier times, but now he commands everyone everywhere to repent of their sins and turn to him. For he has set a day for judging the world with justice by the man he has appointed, and he proved to everyone who this is by raising him from the dead." There is an announcement of the possibility of forgiveness and a warning that judgment is coming, along with the announcement that God's ruler is the resurrected Jesus. Those who responded to this announcement would confess Jesus as their Lord and become followers of Jesus. Both before and after they committed themselves as his followers, they needed instruction about who Jesus was and what lifestyle he called them to. Thus, the goal is to present the believers before the royal throne as mature copies of Christ, joined to Christ and like Christ. (While Paul does not tell us to whom or where the presentation will take place, it is eschatological and thus likely before the throne, or the judgment seat, which in ancient times were the same thing.) At the time of the presentation, the apprentice has learned his or her lessons well and become like the master. This is a realizable goal for those who submit to the revelation of God in Christ, for the Christ they are to become like is in them. This formation of Christ in people who commit themselves to him is what motivated Paul. But a worthy goal and good motivation do not make it any less "work and struggle," even though "Christ's mighty power" was working in him (1:29). Here is one of the most beautifully balanced statements of the Christian life in the New Testament. Paul can at one and the same time be conscious of hard work, painful struggle, successes and failures, and of the power of Christ working in him. Divine power and miracles are fully compatible with blood, sweat, and tears. Divine enabling is fully compatible with human decision and endurance. The eschatological future breaks into and enables one in the current situation (the "already") but does not erase the fact that it is still the future (the "not yet"). That is, the Kingdom or rule of God in all the earth is seen in this or that event, but it is not yet fully manifested. (For more on eschatology in Colossians, see "Author" in the Introduction.)

Since Paul was working so hard for "everyone" within his assigned area, he viewed himself as having "agonized" for Christians whom he had never met (2:1; see note). It is likely that Epaphras or Archippus had founded the church in Colosse and probably the church in Laodicea, as well. The churches were about 10 miles apart along the Lycus River. Most likely Paul had met these two men in Ephesus, that being the nearest city we know of where Paul spent a significant amount of time, although it is possible that they had met him much earlier in Pisidian Antioch. Whenever and wherever they met him, it was Paul's practice to apprentice potential leaders to himself. They worked alongside him, lived with him, traveled with him, and generally learned his lifestyle, teaching, and character. Then they were either left in a city where Paul had worked or else they returned to the city that they were from and either planted or supported the church there. This created a network of leaders that knew Paul and each other personally, even if many of their churches had never seen Paul. Paul had no formal position or control, but his charismatic influence extended along the lines of personal relationship that created a type of leadership network for the churches planted under his influence. Thus, we have in Colosse a church that Paul knew about and felt responsible for, if indirectly, and yet a church that had never seen his face. He wanted these believers to know that even though they had never seen him, he cared about them. Whether it was through his general labor to spread the Good News of the Kingdom or through his prayers for them (cf. 2 Cor 11:27), he wanted them to know that he cared as much for them as for the churches in which he had been more personally involved.

Paul stated the goal of his letter when he told them that he wanted them to be "encouraged" (2:2; cf. 4:8; Eph 6:22; 2 Thess 2:17) and "knit together by strong ties of love" (an expression of communal solidarity). The outworking of the Good News is both emotional and communal; it is not just cerebral. Indeed, communal unity is very important in the New Testament (2:19; Rom 14:15; 1 Cor 16:14; Phil 2:1-2 [where love is the critical virtue that leads to unity]; 1 Thess 3:12). Yet commitment to Christ does not bypass the intellect, as Paul indicated by piling up terms for understanding. What they were to understand is God's "mystery" (see note on 2:1), and this mystery is simply Christ. He is what was hidden and has now been revealed. He is the key to all that God is about in the world. The Kingdom of God is embodied in and revealed through Christ. Thus "all the treasures of wisdom and knowledge" lie hidden in him (2:3). They are hidden because they were a mystery until Christ was revealed, and they remain a mystery to those who are not committed to being followers of Christ. For many Jews, all the treasures of wisdom and knowledge were in the Torah. This is seen in Sirach 24:23-26, which says, "All this is the book of the covenant of the Most High God, the law that Moses commanded us as an inheritance for the congregations of Jacob. It overflows, like the Pishon, with wisdom, and like the Tigris at the time of the first fruits. It runs over, like the Euphrates, with understanding, and like the Jordan at harvest time" (NRSV). This is also evident in the hymn to Wisdom as embodied in the Torah, contained in Baruch 3:15–4:1. These passages build upon Proverbs 2:3-6, which also sees Wisdom as embodied in the divine revelation. Over against such Jewish claims, Paul asserted that Wisdom is not embodied in a book but in a person. It is the person who interprets the book. It is the Messiah who is the key to the Torah.

Paul had good reason for asserting this so strongly, for some were trying to deceive the Colossians with "well-crafted arguments" (2:4), and as we shall see later, it is probable that these people were members of the local synagogue. Paul's previous argument that Christ is the embodiment of God's Wisdom would have directly contradicted the teachings of these people, who were probably arguing that the Colossians needed to add some Jewish observances to their commitment to Christ to come into a fuller truth. For Paul, anything added to Christ subtracted from Christ.

Paul's concern for the Colossians was heightened by the fact that although he was not physically present (*sarx* [TG4561, ZG4922], "flesh") with them, he was there "in spirit" (NLT, "my heart is with you"). By this he did not mean that he was there in his thoughts, for he had other language for that idea. Paul's language here is "very close to the sense of 1 Cor 5:3 . . . where Paul considers himself as truly present by the Spirit" (Fee 1994:646). Paul considered himself present as they read his letter in the gathered community in Colosse. Therefore, he rejoiced when he "sees" that they were living as they should and that their faith in Christ was strong (2:5; see note). Faced with pressure to add other practices to Christ, the Colossians were not in a crisis, for they were standing firm. Their "faith in Christ" (or, "commitment to Christ") was firm. Since Paul could "see" this in the Spirit, he was content that he was strengthening and encouraging the Colossians, not stepping in to correct a situation that had already gone bad, as in Corinth or Galatia.

◆ IV. Thematic Statement (*propositio*): The Way In Is the Way On, and That Way Is Christ (2:6-7)

⁶And now, just as you accepted Christ Jesus as your Lord, you must continue to follow him. ⁷Let your roots grow down into him, and let your lives be built on him. Then your faith will grow strong in the truth you were taught, and you will overflow with thankfulness.

NOTES

2:6 you accepted Christ Jesus as your Lord. This verb should not be understood as portraying the current evangelical usage, "accept Jesus." Rather, the verb (*parelabete* [TG3880, ZG4161]) means to receive (accept) a tradition, a process that was very important in Judaism. This is exemplified in the following citation: "Moses received Torah at Sinai and handed it on to Joshua, Joshua to elders, and elders to prophets. And prophets handed it on to the men of the great assembly" (*m. Avot* 1:1 A-B; Neusner 1988). This also occurred in the early church—that is, they received the traditional message of the Good News with respect to "the Messiah, Jesus the Lord." O'Brien (1982:105) reminds us that this message consisted of "three main elements: (a) a summary of the gospel, particularly the death and resurrection of Christ, expressed as a confession of faith; (b) various deeds and words of Christ; and (c) ethical and procedural rules."

Jesus' title here, as translated in a more formally equivalent manner, would read, "the Christ, Jesus the Lord." The expression is unusual, for the article indicates that "Christ" is a title (usually Paul uses it as a proper name) meaning "Messiah" or "Anointed One." The titular usage does appear in Paul's writings in Gal 5:24; 6:12; Eph 3:1, 11, but the combination of this titular usage with "the Lord" only occurs here and in Eph 3:11.

2:7 Then your faith will grow strong. The verbal idea here, literally translated, "being established," is a participle parallel to the previous two in the verse: "grow" and "built." Thus a better translation than "then your faith . . ." might be "Let your faith . . ." in parallel with the previous sentence. While Dunn (1996:142) sees this as a marketplace metaphor for a guarantee in the transfer of goods, "let yourselves be confirmed/guaranteed with reference to your faith," O'Brien (1982:107) is more convincing in arguing that this and the other three usages in the NT (1 Cor 1:8; 2 Cor 1:21; Heb 13:9) are more influenced by the tradition of strengthening found in the Psalms (Pss 41:12; 119:28—40:13; 118:28 in LXX): "let yourselves be strengthened in the faith" (parallel to 1:23)—that is, strengthened in the commitment that they had made to Jesus on the basis of the Good News they had received.

and you will overflow with thankfulness. Thankfulness and thanking God are relatively frequent topics in this letter (1:3, 12; 2:7; 3:15, 16, 17; 4:2). Grammatically, the participle here is active, over against the previous three, which were passive, but it is parallel to them in that it expands the main verb "continue to follow him" or "walk in him." Thus, it is not a result of the roots going down and being built up but an accompanying activity.

COMMENTARY

As is typical in a Pauline letter, the description of his relationship to the community leads to a pithy statement of the thesis of the letter. So it is here that we come to the core teaching of Colossians. The Colossians had received a tradition about Jesus, passed on to them from Paul by Epaphras and whoever else was involved in planting the church in Colosse and the surrounding area. This tradition, this message of Good News, consisted of two main parts: (1) "Jesus of Nazareth is the Messiah" (as demonstrated through his life, deeds, and teaching), and (2) "Jesus of Nazareth is the Lord" (as demonstrated in his death, resurrection, and leadership). This is the message that we find in the various Gospels and preached in Acts. Having received this message, the Colossians were to "continue to follow him"(2:6). This is the central imperative of the whole letter. We begin the Christian life by committing ourselves to Jesus of Nazareth as the Messiah and living Lord. We live the Christian life by living our lives in relationship with him—that is, submitted to his lordship and living as a person "in Christ." On one hand, this means a rejection of all rival claimants to one's loyalty, be they national (the Caesar cult then or national loyalties now), ideological, or spiritual. On the other hand, this means an active submission to Jesus' guidance (whether by his inner guidance or his recorded teaching) and his worldview in the context of the community of others who are also following him. The Christian life begins with a commitment to submit to Jesus, and the Christian life goes on by continually living out this commitment.

Paul then used a series of metaphors (2:7): one from agriculture ("roots grow[ing] down into him"), one from building ("lives be[ing] built on him"), and one from the Old Testament ("your faith will grow strong in the truth"). In the third metaphor "in him" changes to "the faith" because (1) the faith (or, more accurately, "the commitment") is about him and our commitment to him but relieves the redundancy of the statement, and (2) this expression allows for the parenthetical statement "you were taught," which refers back to the tradition they had received from Paul through his co-workers. In that sense, there is a connection between the verb for passing on tradition that starts the passage and this phrase about the receiving of the tradition of the Good News that ends it.

Yet Paul was not finished, for he added that this focus on Jesus was not a narrowing, restricting experience but one in which the believer actively "overflow[s] with thankfulness," which when expanded in 3:15-17, means to sing songs of thanks to God, both in corporate and in private situations. Living life in the Kingdom of God under the leadership of Jesus was an exciting privilege for Paul, and he wanted his readers to go deeper into their experience and respond to it with joyful praise to God. That is the core of Colossians. The rest of the book will be working out what this means in the practical situation of the community of believers in Colosse.

◆ **V. Exposition of the Theme** (*expositio*) **(2:8–4:6)**
  A. Theological Implications of the Theme (2:8-23)
  1. Christ is all sufficient (2:8-15)

⁸Don't let anyone capture you with empty philosophies and high-sounding nonsense that come from human thinking and from the spiritual powers* of this world, rather than from Christ. ⁹For in Christ lives all the fullness of God in a human body.* ¹⁰So you also are complete through your union with Christ, who is the head over every ruler and authority.

¹¹When you came to Christ, you were "circumcised," but not by a physical procedure. Christ performed a spiritual circumcision—the cutting away of your sinful nature.* ¹²For you were buried with Christ when you were baptized. And with him you were raised to new life because you trusted the mighty power of God, who raised Christ from the dead.

¹³You were dead because of your sins and because your sinful nature was not yet cut away. Then God made you alive with Christ, for he forgave all our sins. ¹⁴He canceled the record of the charges against us and took it away by nailing it to the cross. ¹⁵In this way, he disarmed* the spiritual rulers and authorities. He shamed them publicly by his victory over them on the cross.

2:8 Or *the spiritual principles; also in 2:20.*   2:9 Or *in him dwells all the completeness of the Godhead bodily.*
2:11 Greek *the cutting away of the body of the flesh.*   2:15 Or *he stripped off.*

N O T E S

2:8 *capture.* This rare term means "to carry off as booty or as a captive in war" (L&N 37.10); it is used here in a metaphorical sense.

empty philosophies and high-sounding nonsense. The two words describe the same thing since they are governed by one article in Greek; a more word-for-word translation of the Greek would be "philosophy and empty deceit" (NRSV) or "empty deceitful philosophy" (NET). "Philosophy" in this context may indicate any school of human thought, not just what is called philosophy today. Philo and Josephus used the term for Judaism and its various sects (Pharisees, Sadducees, etc.), which means that Paul also could use the term for Jewish thought. Yet whatever it indicates, the phrase "empty deceit" indicates that Paul sees this point of view not just as nonsense but as downright misleading and deceptive.

human thinking. More carefully put, "human tradition." The term *paradosis* [TG3862, ZG4142] indicates that this is a group of ideas or teachings passed down through a chain of human teachers. Pharisaic tradition would fit this description (assuming that it is proto-rabbinic tradition, as most believe). For instance, the chain of tradition in *m. Avot* 1 is as follows (Neusner 1988):

> 1:1 Moses received Torah at Sinai and handed it on to Joshua, Joshua to elders, and elders to prophets. And prophets handed it on to the men of the great assembly" . . .
> 1:2 Simeon the Righteous was one of the last survivors of the great assembly . . .
> 1:3 Antigonos of Sokho received [the Torah] from Simeon the Righteous . . . 1:4 Yose b. Yoezer of Seredah and Yose b. Yohanan of Jerusalem received [it] from them . . .
> 1:6 Joshua b. Perahiah and Naught the Arbelite received [it] from them . . . 1:8 Judah b. Tabbai and Simeon b. Shatah received [it] from them . . . 1:10 Shemaiah and Abtalion received [it] from them . . . 1:12 Hillel and Shammai received [it] from them.

This chain of tradition runs (in theory) from Moses to the time of Jesus, although most of the chain runs from the "great assembly" (the time of Ezra) to the time of Jesus (Hillel and Shammai).

the spiritual powers of this world. The basic meaning of the term *stoicheia* [TG4747, ZG5122] is "elements," either indicating natural elements (often thought of as earth, air, fire and water, although in 2 Pet 3:10, 12; Wis 7:17 it refers to the elements of the heavens, such as the sun, moon, and stars) or linguistic elements (the ABCs, as in Heb 5:12). It is also clear that in the post-NT period this term could indicate "elemental spirits." Because of this later usage some argue for "elementary principles of the world" (Moule 1968:91-92), but others point out that the elements themselves were often viewed as spiritually controlled, as were the stars, so "elementary spirits" or, more generally, "spiritual powers" is the correct transla- tion (Dunn 1996:148-151). It is this latter meaning that fits best here, and this judgment is supported by the reference to (spiritual) rulers and authorities in verse 10. So here we have human traditions and the various spiritual forces of this age (good or bad) as the two pos- sible sources of "philosophy" other than Christ and his Father.

2:9 *in Christ lives all the fullness of God in a human body.* While expressed here in words not used elsewhere in biblical Greek, the meaning of the phrase translated "the fullness of God" is well enough known from other Greek literature. It means the fullness of "divine nature" (L&N 12.13)—that is, "the [one God] of the OT has attracted to Himself all divine power in the cosmos, and in the early Christian view He has given this fullness of power to Christ as the Bearer of the divine office" (TDNT 3.119). The meaning of the term translated "body" (*sōmatikōs* [TG4985, ZG5395]) is debated. Some think that it refers to the church, the body of Christ, since that has already been mentioned in Colossians (Robinson 1904:88; Bornkamm 1952:112-113), but in those previous references *sōma* [TG4983, ZG5393] (body) is immediately qualified by "the church." Here the term is *sōmatikōs* [TG4985, ZG5395] (bodily) and there is no explanation that indicates that it refers to the church. Moule (1968:92-94), O'Brien (1982:112-113), and Dunn (1996:152) all agree that this term refers to the incar- nation. The fullness of God was physically or corporeally present in Jesus.

2:10 *complete.* This is the verbal form of the noun "fullness" found in verse 9. The Colossians would pick up on the wordplay in Greek: The fullness of God in Christ be- comes the believers' fullness in Christ. The verbal form in 2:10 is a present perfect partici- ple, indicating a condition that has already come into being. As such, those in union with Christ share in that "fullness" or "completeness" due to their union with the one in whom this "fullness" lives.

2:11 *circumcision.* On the requirements for proselytes in rabbinic Judaism, see *m. Kerithot* 2:1, *b. Kerithot* 9a and Schürer 1986:3.173-174. For instance, *b. Keritot 9a* reads in part (Neusner 1988), "5. A. The master has said, 'Just as your forefathers entered the covenant only with circumcision and immersion and sprinkling of blood through the sacrifices, so they [proselytes] will enter the covenant only through circumcision, immersion, and sprinkling of blood on the altar.'" (The Talmudic citation is a comment on *m. Keritot* 2:1; it is followed by citations from Scripture showing that all three elements are needed.) For negative Greco-Roman attitudes towards circumcision, see Robert G. Hall, "Circumcision" (ABD 1.1027-1028).

Christ performed a spiritual circumcision—the cutting away of your sinful nature. Expressed with more formal equivalency this reads, "in the undressing of the body of flesh in the circumcision of Christ," a very difficult phrase indeed. "Cutting away" is a term for undressing, unique here in Greek but found in its verbal form in 2:15; 3:9. What is stripped off is "the body of flesh," which can be understood as (1) the sinful nature (simi- lar to 2:18; Rom 6:6; Lightfoot 1896:181), (2) Christ in his death (similar to 1:22; Rom 7:4; 1 Pet 2:24; 4:1; O'Brien 1982:116-117; Dunn 1996:153-157), or (3) the Christian in his or her death, perhaps seen as having taken place in baptism. Likewise "the circumcision of Christ" can be understood as (1) his literal circumcision (that he was born "subject to the law," Gal 4:4), (2) his death, in that his "body of flesh" was in a sense cut away from him on the cross (so O'Brien, Dunn), (3) the "circumcision" Christ performs spiritually in the heart, or (4) Christian baptism as opposed to Jewish circumcision (Lohse 1971:101-103; Lightfoot 1896:182-183). As we evaluate these options, we notice first that "body" (*sarx* [TG4561, ZG4922]; "flesh") appears nine times in this letter, and the four previous occurrences all refer to a physical body, as do 2:13 and 2:23. Only in 2:18 (and possibly here) could it refer to the "sinful nature" (in 3:22 it may mean "physical" or "pertaining to this age"). The probabilities therefore lie on the side of "body of flesh" here referring to Christ's physical body. Second, this event is in the past, so it does not refer to the Colossians' death. Thus, it is most likely that this phrase refers to Christ's death (his fleshly body being "stripped" from him, not his body, the church). Since there is no other reference in Colossians to Jesus being "under the law" nor is there a comparison anywhere else in Paul's writings between circumcision and baptism, it is probable that the "circumcision of Christ" is a reference to his death. This yields a literal meaning: "This nonphysical procedure took place in your making use of the stripping away of Christ's 'flesh' in that 'circumcision' he underwent on the cross."

2:13 sins. In both cases the term is *paraptōma* [TG3900, ZG4183], often translated "transgressions," which indicates a violation of a law or rule.

because your sinful nature was not yet cut away. This is the NLT rendering of the phrase "uncircumcision of your flesh"; it understands the text as referring to a lack of a spiritual circumcision of the sinful nature ("your flesh"). As noted above, this metaphorical understanding of circumcision is championed by O'Brien (1982:115-117). In light of the normal use of "flesh" in Colossians and the Jewish nature of the teaching Paul opposes, it is more likely that this phrase refers to the physical uncircumcision of the Colossians—i.e., normal Greco-Roman males were uncircumcised. The "because" is "and" (*kai* [TG2532, ZG2779]) in Greek and thus coordinates transgression and uncircumcision, as was normal in much Jewish teaching. That is, they were dead because they transgressed the law and because they were uncircumcised, two conditions that went together in Jewish thinking (Dunn 1996:153-157).

2:14 the record of the charges. The Greek for "the record" (*cheirographon* [TG5498, ZG5934]) occurs only here in the NT and meant an I.O.U., a promissory note written out in one's own hand (so Tob 5:3; 9:5; *Testament of Job* 11). In Colossians this promissory note is with respect to public decrees , so it is a promise with respect to the decrees of God. The alternative exegesis followed by the NLT depends on reading this "record" as the charges in the heavenly books written against human beings, and while this interpretation is attractive and can be demonstrated in other works, the evidence presented by Blanchette (1961) does not show this term being used with that meaning.

2:15 disarmed. This term is a cognate of the term for undressing found in 2:11 and means "to strip off" or "to divest oneself of." The meaning "disarm" demands that the middle voice of the verb be read with an active sense, something that is not demonstrated until much later in Greek linguistic history and that none of the Greek Fathers understood. Thus, I favor the normal sense of the middle voice, which would be "to strip off of oneself" or "to undress," meaning Christ stripped the powers off himself rather than that he stripped the armor off them.

COMMENTARY

The Colossians had not gone astray, but they were threatened in their world with rival voices to that of leaders like Paul, and these other voices could conceivably lead them astray, as Paul knew well from his experience in Galatia and elsewhere. Paul therefore warned them, not against philosophy in the technical sense that we use that term today, but against the danger found in human ways of thinking and schools of thought, especially those that were deceptively persuasive and would entrap the Colossians (2:8). At this point in the letter we have not been informed about what type of "philosophy" this could be. The Colossians surely understood Paul's meaning for the word. The problem we face with reading a letter is that it is one half of a dialogue and assumes a situation that the addressees were familiar with but we are not. This "philosophy" could be some type of Jewish thought (e.g., Paul's native Pharisaism was called a philosophy by Josephus, and Judaism as a whole was called a philosophy by the Jewish writer Philo) or any other school of thought. Perhaps Paul was deliberately general in that he knew that once the immediate danger had passed other similar ones would crop up.

Paul divided all the influences on human thought into three sources: human tradition, elemental spirits, and divine Wisdom or Christ. First, human tradition contrasts with the tradition that they had received about Christ. This human tradition could be religious, such as the law or interpretations of the law, which Paul knew so well from his background and with which he struggled in Galatians, or any other human knowledge that is passed down.

Second, the various basic or elemental spiritual powers of the universe were those thought to be behind the elements themselves (earth, air, fire, and water) or controlling the stars, planets, and other parts of the universe (the meaning of the Greek term in 2 Pet 3:10, 12). The issue was not that the traditions coming from these sources were bad or demonic or entirely false, but that they came from this age, this universe, and were not philosophy "from Christ." To be "from Christ" these powers would have had to take their point of view and foundation from the rule of Christ, including the life and teaching of Jesus. But it is to the extent that they take us away from Jesus or give us a different perspective on the world than Jesus does that these spiritual powers are deceptive and may capture our minds in a negative sense. And why do they turn into lies as they diverge from Christ? Because only "in Christ lives all the fullness of God in a human body" (2:9).

This is the third source of influence on human thought. What Paul means by this is something like, "Forget about human tradition and forget about the various spiritual powers, good or evil, and the traditions stemming from them. The Wisdom of God is not scattered all over the universe, needing to be sought out by human beings, nor is the revelation in Christ a partial revelation. Rather, in Jesus we see in human form everything that God is. There is no other nature of God to be discovered, no other Wisdom of God to be found. It is all in the human being Christ Jesus." If we want to discover the will and character of God, Jesus is the one source. The implication of this fact should be obvious. Since the Christian is by definition in union with Christ, then this fullness is also in us. We are "in him," and the fullness of deity is "in him," so we participate in that fullness. There is nothing more that we need outside of the framework of Christ and his Kingdom. We cannot object that we are mere human beings and Christ is the exalted Lord, for the fullness of God was in Jesus the human, so our humanity does not make this impossible for us.

This speaks to what was evidently the problem being faced in Colosse, where some appear to have been adding religious practices of various types that would in their minds be the keys to a fulfilled life or spiritual power or whatever other benefit was promised. "No," says Paul, "you already have it all—in Christ" (2:10). It may be a potential that you have not drawn upon or even realized, but it is all there. "Furthermore," Paul adds, driving the point home, "he is the cosmic source and leader," and here Paul cites his own language found in 1:16 to remind his readers of the picture of the cosmic authority of Christ he painted there. Thus, whatever spiritual power the Colossians were being told they could influence through their religious practices, there was no need to do so. The originator, sustainer, and ruler of all such powers, good or evil, is Christ.

Paul added a series of metaphors or models to illustrate what has happened in our Christian initiation (2:11-15). The various metaphors fly by with blinding speed in order to develop a composite picture of the completeness of what happened when the Colossians committed themselves to Christ. Because they are metaphors or models, it is a mistake to press any of them too far, to develop a doctrine from what is not said as well as from what is said. We must not forget they are metaphors and models, not absolute descriptions of reality, for the reality itself is too incomprehensible to be fully captured in any human linguistic model.

What is clear is that several of the metaphors have Jewish references. When a Gentile wanted to become a Jew, there was a particular order of initiation events that he or she was led through to become a proselyte. Several of these are reflected here in this text. Below is a comparison using the order of Hillel, which eventually won the day in rabbinic Judaism but would have still been disputed in Paul's day.

Rabbinic Judaism	Colossians	Reference/Comment
Faith	Faith	Both argued for commitment to the one God, but for Christians he was found supremely in Jesus.
Instruction/Tradition	Instruction/Tradition	Preceded and followed faith, but in this term we are thinking of what was needed to understand the step being taken. 2:6, 7
Circumcision of males	Circumcision of the heart by Christ of both males and females	2:11
Baptism	Baptism	2:12
Sacrifice (often offered via a substitute)	Sacrifice of Christ	2:14

Since Paul's polemic in Colossians is not as intense as that in Galatians or Philippians, it is unlikely that the Colossians were being asked to become full proselytes to Judaism like the Galatians were. Nor is it likely that what was being asked of them was connected to their salvation, as Paul understood the situation in Galatia to be. But it does seem likely that the Colossians were being asked to adopt some Jewish practices as additions to what they had received in Christ, perhaps as something that would protect them from various spirits or as something that would lead them to a deeper spiritual level.

The first metaphor Paul used is that of circumcision, by which a proselyte entered the Old Testament covenant (2:11). This was particularly significant in Asia Minor, Greece, and Italy, where circumcision was the characteristic mark of Jewish identity and nationality for males, separating them from Gentiles, who viewed it as mutilation of the beautiful human body. Circumcision is something the Christian already has in Christ. Like the metaphors that follow, this circumcision is a completed event, already finished. While Scripture and some sects of Judaism spoke of a spiritual circumcision, this metaphorical usage never replaced physical circumcision (cf. "he should circumcise in the Community the foreskin of his [sinful] tendency and of his stiff neck in order to lay a foundation of truth" [1QS 5.5]; cf. Deut 10:16; Jer 4:4). Here in Colossians the *only* circumcision is spiritual rather than physical, or, better put, the *only* circumcision is inner circumcision, applied to the Christian on the basis of Christ's stripping off of flesh at the Cross. That act of Christ is the basis of belonging to the covenant people.

The second metaphor is that of baptism, which Paul identifies with the death of Christ (2:12). The idea that baptism is an identification with and appropriation of the death of Christ is also found in Romans 6:3-4. The people immersed in the water should view themselves as buried with Christ as a criminal and thus be dead to the values and desires of this world. This baptism is not identified with circumcision (the idea that baptism replaces circumcision would only appear much later in church history) but rather symbolizes one aspect of the spiritual circumcision—namely, the identification with the burial of Christ.

The third metaphor is that of resurrection with Christ (2:13). Unlike his other discussions of death and resurrection where resurrection is future (e.g., Rom 6), here Paul speaks of resurrection as an event in the past, for as Christ has been raised so also those in him are already raised. This is similar to the Johannine insistence that those who commit themselves to Christ already have eternal life. This resurrection "in Christ" came about because these believers trusted in "the mighty power of God," the God "who raised Christ from the dead." While in the Johannine tradition Jesus speaks of having the power to lay down his life and to take it up again (John 10:18), the more typical confession of the church was that God had raised Christ from the dead (Rom 4:24; 8:11; 10:9; 1 Cor 6:14; Gal 1:1), thereby setting his seal of approval upon Christ and also exalting him to a place of rule over all creation. This is the teaching that Paul refers to here. The reference to resurrection brings Paul back to the reason why the Colossians had needed resurrection: they had been dead.

They had been Gentiles, outside of the covenant with Israel (see Eph 2:12), and as such had transgressed God's law (1:21). Paul viewed such foreignness to the covenant as natural because they had been—and physically still were—Gentiles. For many Jews, the Gentiles were permanently taboo[1] because they lived in a state of ritual impurity ("Gentiles," DPL 336). Furthermore, as those outside of the covenant and thus ignorant of its demands, Gentiles not only continually transgressed the covenant, they also were never purified from their resultant taboo state. Paul's point in drawing this picture so starkly is not to teach them about their former state but to contrast it and the current Jewish attitude toward them with God's cleansing work and his attitude. God is the God of resurrection. He makes the dead alive ("[he is] the God who brings the dead back to life," Rom 4:17). God made the believers alive by virtue of their union with Christ. At the same time, he forgave their sins, again, using the expression "transgression" to refer to their previous violation of his law. They are already forgiven. They are already alive. The implication is that they are already part of the people of God.

The fourth metaphor is that of the dismissal of charges (2:14). Paul pictured all people as implicitly or explicitly having promised to obey some public decree, probably meaning the law of God, which many Jews saw at least in part as binding upon Gentiles as well (e.g., the commands given to Noah). According to the metaphor, this public decree is "against us" in that human beings have not fulfilled their obligations. But rather than punishing us, God wipes out the note. Then the metaphor shifts, for instead of "cancelled," God takes the note and nails it to the cross. This would remind those in the Greco-Roman world of the charges against the condemned criminal, which were often nailed to a stick affixed to his or her cross. But in this metaphorical use Paul did not mean to refer to the historical charges against Jesus ("Jesus of Nazareth, the King of the Jews") but the charges against us, graphically showing that Christ died for us and in his death the charges ended as well.

The fifth metaphor is that of a cross and a triumphal procession, where the spiritual rulers and authorities are viewed as a tunic or cloak over Christ (2:15; perhaps as a tunic representative of the universe). On the cross he was stripped naked, but this stripping is shifted from his being stripped to *his* stripping *them* off. So Paul pictures Christ at the cross rending the spiritual rulers and authorities powerless over him. Then, using a term found elsewhere only in Matthew 1:19, Paul makes another allusion to the cross: "he shamed them publicly." On the cross the criminal was utterly and totally publicly shamed, exposed as weak and totally naked to the mockery of all who passed by, but Paul inverts the imagery and depicts the spiritual rulers and authorities publicly shamed by the cross of Christ. Then there is another shift of metaphor, where it is as if the wood of the cross becomes a chariot—for, again, using a rare verb (also found in 2 Cor 2:14), Paul pictured Christ as a general leading those he had conquered. They are led along in chains, jeered at by the throng along the way, being dragged forward to imprisonment or execution. All of this happened in Christ, says Paul, in this radical reframing of the cross.

ENDNOTE

1. The term "taboo" or "ritually impure" is more precise than "pure" or "impure" and certainly "clean" and "unclean," since the concern of the food laws is for ritual purity or the ability to approach God, not uncleanness or impurity in the sense of dirt or pollution.

◆   ## 2. Christ, not religious practices and rule (2:16-19)

¹⁶So don't let anyone condemn you for what you eat or drink, or for not celebrating certain holy days or new moon ceremonies or Sabbaths. ¹⁷For these rules are only shadows of the reality yet to come. And Christ himself is that reality. ¹⁸Don't let anyone condemn you by insisting on pious self-denial or the worship of angels,* saying they have had visions about these things. Their sinful minds have made them proud, ¹⁹and they are not connected to Christ, the head of the body. For he holds the whole body together with its joints and ligaments, and it grows as God nourishes it.

2:18 Or *worshiping with angels.*

NOTES

2:17 *the reality.* While the NLT's translation of this phrase is fine, it is helpful to remember that the Greek word underlying "reality" is *sōma* [TG4983, ZG5393], often translated "body." The shadow/reality language (also found in Hebrews) sounds Platonic. (Platonic language was "in the air" of the Greco-Roman world, so this does not mean that Paul was referring to Plato's *use* of the image, just that it was a common image.) The law was the shadow, which is now superseded since the reality, Christ, has come. But why did Paul use the Greek term for "body" for the reality? Did Paul mean something more? Moule (1968:103) suggests that at the least this verse contains overtones that Christ established "the reality yet to come" in his body and that his body, the church, is where the new reality is experienced. Dunn (1996:177) cautiously suggests that one "overtone" may be that the church *is* the new reality. But if so, it is an overtone that Paul does not develop further, as O'Brien (1982:139-141) points out. One might therefore translate the second half of the verse, "but the body of Christ *is the expression of that reality,*" which would highlight "body" as the coming reality in contrast with "shadow," but would also leave the sense of "the body *is* of Christ" ambiguous, clearly meaning at least Christ's resurrection body but possibly also alluding to the community of his followers as the body of Christ present here on earth.

2:18 *condemn.* The verb *katabrabeuō* [TG2603, ZG2857] is taken from the context of the arena and has the sense of "decide against (as umpire), and so rob of a prize, condemn" (BDAG 515). Louw and Nida (30.121) say it means "to judge as a referee that someone is not worthy to receive a prize—'to disqualify, to condemn, to judge as not worthy of a reward, to deprive of a reward.'"

insisting on. While this is the traditional translation, it is probably not correct, for the Greek term *thelōn* [TG2309, ZG2527] needs a person as object in order to mean "wanting you to . . ." Instead, here it is probably a Hebraism meaning "delighting in" (cf. NIV) or "taking pleasure in" (cf. 1 Sam 18:22, LXX; 2 Sam 15:26, LXX; Lightfoot 1896:193).

pious self-denial or the worship of angels. These two items are probably intended to be linked by one preposition and thus refer to a single action. While pious self-denial could refer to the humility of angelic worship, it more likely refers to fasting as a means of entering into the angelic worship. Thus, the worship of angels does not mean that they were honoring angels but that they were joining or trying to join the worship of angels in heaven (there is enough caution elsewhere in the NT and Jewish literature; see Francis and Meeks 1973:163-195, and the commentators following them).

saying they have had visions about these things. Even more than the other phrases in this verse, this one is extremely difficult, for the literal meaning, "which he has seen upon entering," does not have a clear referent. The verb for entering is used in legal contexts for taking possession of an inheritance (Josh 19:49, 51). So it may well be that O'Brien (1982) is correct in interpreting it as referring to worship that the teachers claim to have seen upon entering into their heavenly inheritance.

Their sinful minds have made them proud. A better translation would be, "they are emptily puffed up" or "they are vainly proud" due to their "minds directed by their natural human state." The point is that they are proud about that which is of no consequence, and what they take to be spiritual is really not spiritually helpful at all.

COMMENTARY

If the previous paragraph in this passage depicts the state of the Christian and the effects of what Christ has done for him or her, then there are consequences of this insight for the Christian 'life. In what looks like an application of Jewish halakhic rules of kashrut (i.e., kosher eating), Paul told the Colossians not to allow anyone to condemn them for what they ate or drank or which festivals they did or did not celebrate, which echoes the language of Romans 14:3-13. Naturally, people cannot control what others may think or say, but they can choose to ignore it or refuse to allow the others to make them feel guilty by their condemnation. Given that the Eucharist or Lord's Supper was a communal meal in the first two centuries, it is not surprising that what people ate or drank would become an issue for others in the church. A fine lobster or a pork steak shared with the church would have been an abomination to those who wished to follow the usual Jewish rules. Something similar might have happened over the observance or nonobservance of certain festivals such as the Sabbath. Unlike the situation in 1 Corinthians 8, there was no danger of the other person being led to violate their own conscience and thus do something that they believed Christ condemned. Here the issue is that they were condemning believers. So Paul said in effect, "Don't let them put that guilt trip on you" (2:16).

Paul admitted that at least some of these rules (the Sabbath, for instance) were indeed part of the Torah, the Old Testament law, but, using language also found in Hebrews (e.g., Heb 10:1) and in Hellenistic philosophy from Plato to Philo, he insisted that these rules were shadows of something that was coming (2:17). Now in Christ, and particularly in his resurrection, that which was coming has come and the shadows are gone (or at least unnecessary). Here we have an example of a Pauline hermeneutic of the Old Testament. He reexamined the Old Testament text in the light of Christ and his Kingdom, and that reexamination determined which parts he found still binding and which he did not. For instance, he viewed the Sabbath as fulfilled in the whole of the new age that Christ inaugurated and thus found the literal Sabbath and any other Jewish festival no longer binding. In fact, Jewish practices in general are not binding on the church, nor do they make a person more spiritual for keeping them, whether it be in matters of diet or in matters of time (e.g., observing the Festival of Trumpets or the Sabbath).

Returning to the criticisms leveled against the Colossians by the teachers Paul rejected, Paul told the Colossians to not let anyone disqualify them by their delighting in practices of fasting associated with seeing and entering into the angelic worship in heaven (2:18). This disqualification could occur either by individuals condemning them and making them feel disqualified or by individuals leading them astray and causing them to disqualify themselves. That there was intense Jewish interest in angels at this time is clear: There is plenty of literature describing the participation of angels in giving the law (e.g., Jubilees), in fighting for Israel, and in influencing not only the heavenly court but also human affairs; furthermore, angels were believed to control the stars and planets. Given the exalted status of angels, there was a desire among some Jews to participate in the angelic liturgy attested in numerous pieces of late Jewish literature, from the *Testament of Job* (48-50), where the daughters of Job are given cords or sashes that enable them to speak angelic dialects, to a number of the Dead Sea Scrolls. (For example, 4Q403 1 ii 23; 11Q17 vii 12 [=4Q405 20 ii 22], also known as ShirShabb, Song of the Sabbath, or Angelic Liturgy.) The early followers of Jesus also had an interest in angelic worship. Paul refers to the presence of angels during human worship in 1 Corinthians 11:10 and to speaking in "the languages . . . of angels" in 1 Corinthians 13:1. It is not unlikely that the people who were disrupting worship by glossolalia (who are corrected in 1 Cor 14) were asserting that they were entering into angelic worship. By exalting the superior value of understandable prophecy in 1 Corinthians 14, Paul is clearly saying that this angelic worship is not higher or better. John's Revelation witnesses to an impulse to worship angels (Rev 19:10; 22:8-9), which is rebuked (Did the author fear that undue honor would be paid to the revealing angel if this rebuke was not included?), and it also records angelic worship in heaven. In arguing that Christ is superior to the angels, Hebrews witnesses at least to the temptation to exalt angels in the communities the author knew. Given this interest in angels and their worship in heaven that was "in the air" (Noll 1998), it is easy to imagine what some might have said to the Colossians regarding angelic worship and fasting: "Why don't you enter into real worship? Why do you stick with these human forms of worship and not go deeper into the worship of heaven?" Paul's response is cutting. It is not that he rejected heavenly visions. He had some himself (2 Cor 12:1-4). But, having shown how great the status of the believers in Colosse was, he opposed the assertion that they would be disqualified unless they had such visions too or worshiped according to the pattern seen in such visions (cf. 2 Cor 12:7).

Paul argued that such pride in one's spiritual privileges and the condemnation of others for not seeking such experiences is not spiritual but comes from a mind directed by one's natural humanity, one's flesh (the Greeks held the mind to be the organ through which one received visions). Such pride indicates that one has let go of Christ, who is head of the church and holds the whole church together (2:19). Paul's physiology is inexact in that the head does not nourish the body through joints and ligaments, but Paul was not giving a lesson in physiology. Rather, he was using a metaphor to indicate that Christ, as the head, holds together and nourishes the church as if it were his body and that this care for the church is not separate from the Father but is a growth that comes from the Father through him. Thus, a person cannot claim that he or she is in contact with the Father or worshiping the Father while bypassing the Son. The fact is that while Paul in other texts encourages dreams and visions, he was strongly against anything that divides the church into "haves" and "have-nots." Paul had no problem with fasting and other spiritual disciplines, but when they divided the body of Christ, with one group feeling superior to another, they betray a merely human rather than a spiritual attitude. There is one Christ to whom every Christian submits. True worship focuses on that one. And this Christ binds us together, even though being together may be uncomfortable at times. Have plenty of spiritual experiences and disciplines, Paul says, but do not think that you are better than others because you have them. The Father is in the business of growing the body through Christ, not in growing inflated heads.

◆   ## 3. Christ, not Jewish purity (2:20-23)

²⁰You have died with Christ, and he has set you free from the spiritual powers of this world. So why do you keep on following the rules of the world, such as, ²¹"Don't handle! Don't taste! Don't touch!"? ²²Such rules are mere human teachings about things that deteriorate as we use them. ²³These rules may seem wise because they require strong devotion, pious self-denial, and severe bodily discipline. But they provide no help in conquering a person's evil desires.

NOTES

2:20 *he has set you free from the spiritual powers.* This expression is expanded from, "You have died to the spiritual powers." It is a reference back to the act of baptism in 2:12. When one dies with Christ, one dies to those powers that exist in the system of this world.

2:21 *handle . . . taste . . . touch!* The first and third terms are basically synonymous. Both terms can refer to either eating or sexual contact (e.g., 1 Cor 7:1); in this context Paul does not specify exactly what sense he intends, but instead leaves them general so as to cover all types of purity concerns.

2:23 *seem wise.* This is a rare expression, which Lightfoot (1896:203-204) was the first to document, that could be translated literally as "a thing having wisdom."

strong devotion. The Greek term (*ethelothrēskia* [TG1479, ZG1615]) underlying "strong devotion" does not occur elsewhere in Greek (a search of materials from the 3rd century BC to the 3rd century AD in the Thesaurus Lingua Graece turned up only this one instance). We, therefore, have to guess at its meaning from the root words from which it is built. It could denote "chosen," "desired" (as in "delighted in"), or "wished for" worship. This could be Paul's description of the angelic worship alluded to in 2:18.

pious self-denial. The Greek term (*tapeinophrosunē* [TG5012, ZG5425]) means "humility" or "humble mindedness." However, since it is used here in connection with previous terms for worship, it seems to indicate a humility or a humbling that is connected to the worship that Paul was rejecting. Thus, it indicates either the bowing down of the person in angelic worship or the fasting that prepared one to enter into angelic worship.

and. The earliest manuscripts (𝔓46 and B) lack this conjunction, and the later manuscripts are split. The question remains whether some manuscripts rightly restored the missing "and" or whether it did not exist in the original. If it did not exist in the original, then "pious self-denial" is another name for "severe bodily discipline."

conquering a person's evil desires. This expression could be literally translated, "for the gratification of the flesh." In the term rendered "gratification" in my translation (*plēsmonēn* [TG4140, ZG4447]), we have another term used only here in the NT. In the OT this term appears in a positive sense for being filled with food (Exod 16:3, 8; Lev 25:19) and in a negative sense for overindulgence (Ezek 16:49; Hos 13:6). Here it seems to retain the positive sense since the text implies that the practices might be helpful if they had any value with respect to doing this to the flesh, but they do not have such value. However, the term "flesh" (*sarx* [TG4561, ZG4922]) can mean fallen human nature or else the physical body, and Paul would hardly speak positively of satisfying the fallen nature. Many church fathers made sense of the passage by allowing "flesh" (*sarx* [TG4561, ZG4922]) to equal "body" (*sōma* [TG4983, ZG5393]) and thus took the sentence as indicating that the body was not being properly respected and cared for under the opponents' teaching. "In Col 2:23 the [church] fathers almost unanimously equate *sarx* with *sōma* and thus take it positively, so that *plēsmonēn* is the 'satisfaction of natural (not sinful) desire.' . . . That the false teachers do not indulge the body means that they do not give it the respect accorded to it by God. . . . They deprive it rather than satisfying it" (TDNT 6.133). The disciplines encouraged by Paul's opponents were supposed to help people deal with their flesh, but these disciplines did not help. Many church fathers made sense of the passage by allowing "flesh" to equal "body" and thus take the sentence as indicating that the body was not being properly respected and cared for. While this makes sense of the words found here, it does so by assuming that Paul had confused two words. More recent scholarship has taken one of two approaches: (1) It has assumed that some term has been left out of the sentence or has been lost in transmission (such as a negative "not" as in "not gratifying the flesh") or (2) that there is a parenthesis intended. If a parenthesis were intended, the rendering would be "which is not of any value (a self-chosen devotion, pious self-denial, and severe bodily discipline), leading to the gratification of the flesh." (See the commentary below for Dunn's alternative to this interpretation.)

COMMENTARY

In this section, Paul brings this first part of his argument to a conclusion. As he already pointed out in 2:11-12, the believers in Colosse have died with Christ and therefore are "dead" to the various spiritual powers of this age (2:20). The problem was their tendency to act as though they were still living in this age and thus to follow rules that applied to this age. The rules in question appear to be basic purity rules. We find plenty of rules in the Old Testament about what one could and could not eat (see Lev 11) and what one could not touch or handle (2:21; e.g., a leper, Lev 13:45-46; a woman during her menstrual period, Lev 15:19-24; a man with a discharge, Lev 15:2-12; a corpse, Num 19:11-13). Such purity issues were very much the concern of Pharisaic Judaism and the community that produced the Dead Sea Scrolls, which had strict regulations to make sure that no one impinged upon the "purity of the many" (1QS 6-7) and was very concerned that Jerusalem become a pure city. They were also the concern of other Jewish groups that were in no way as extreme as the Pharisees, even including some parts of the Jesus movement. As one Jewish apologist said, "So to prevent our being perverted by contact with others or by mixing with bad influences, [Moses] hedged us in on all sides with strict observances connected with meat and drink and touch and hearing and sight, after the manner of the Law" (*Letter of Aristeas* 142). But these rules, argued Paul, are simply human teachings that concern things that are consumed as one uses them (2:22). In saying this, Paul was surely following the teaching of Jesus found in Mark 7:7, "Their worship is a farce, for they teach man-made ideas as commands from God" (two terms, rare in biblical Greek, occur in both Mark 7:7 and Col 2:20-23; cf. Isa 29:13). Paul was also following Jesus' further comment in Mark 7:17-19 that food cannot make one impure or taboo, since it is eaten, digested, and then expelled into the sewer. Such man-made rules are ever with the church, some groups and individuals still practicing the purity regulations of the Old Testament and others more interested in rules stemming from more recent church history (e.g., rules forbidding any consumption of alcohol). Neither Jesus nor Paul would allow any validity to even the Old Testament food laws, calling them human traditions, much less to our later interpretations and applications of them.

Paul concluded his critique of the rule-bound spirituality that was threatening the Colossians with a sentence that is so difficult in terms of both grammar and vocabulary that no scholar can be sure of its meaning (2:23). If "severe bodily discipline" was not originally preceded by "and" and is therefore an expansion of the other two terms, then Dunn (1996:194-198) is likely correct that strong devotion and pious self-denial are simply severe bodily discipline and of no value with respect to dealing with human pride, that is, trust in ethnicity or identification with the Jews (Gal 6:12-13; Phil 3:3-4). In fact these measures increase the problem. On the other hand, if the "and" is original, it is likely that O'Brien (1982:152-154) is correct that the worship, self-humbling, and severe treatment of the body (cf. 2:18 with respect to the worship of the angels), while appearing wise, is of no help whatsoever. Instead, it simply leads to the gratification of our fallen human nature. What is clear is that anything that moves Christ out of the center of one's life is not a helpful form of spirituality. One may fast in order to quiet the body and become more focused in one's communion with Jesus. One may engage in devotional exercises that enable one to submit more fully to the teaching and direction of Jesus. But the minute these things become goals in themselves or are seen as means to gaining spiritual power, they become unhelpful at best or at worst negative influences in one's life. We do not have to understand the exact meaning of the sentence to get Paul's basic point.

◆ B. Ethical Implications of the Theme (3:1–4:6)
1. General statement (3:1-4)

Since you have been raised to new life with Christ, set your sights on the realities of heaven, where Christ sits in the place of honor at God's right hand. ²Think about the things of heaven, not the things of earth. ³For you died to this life, and your real life is hidden with Christ in God. ⁴And when Christ, who is your* life, is revealed to the whole world, you will share in all his glory.

3:4 Some manuscripts read *our.*

NOTES

3:1 *set your sights on.* Traditionally the underlying Greek (*zēteite* [TG2212, ZG2426]) is translated as "seek," a term that can mean "try to obtain," not in the sense of getting into
heaven, but in the sense of trying to obtain the heavenly in this world, i.e., "keep looking
for" (Dunn 1996:205). See Matt 6:33: "Seek the Kingdom of God above all else, and live
righteously, and he will give you everything you need," or more traditionally put, "Strive
first for the Kingdom of God and his righteousness, and all these things will be given to
you as well" (NRSV).

3:2 *Think about.* This phrase can mean "hold an opinion," but also "set one's mind on,
be intent on" or "have thoughts or an attitude, be minded" (BDAG 1065-1066). The point
Paul was making is that one's attitudes are to be determined by the realities above rather
than the realities on this earth because one's thoughts are focused on those realities. Jesus
had previously pointed out that it was difficult to do this if one's treasure was on earth
rather than in heaven (Matt 6:19-21). Mark 8:33b indicates that Peter's failure was a failure
to take on this heavenly point of view.

COMMENTARY

Having concluded his discussion of the negative forms of spirituality that tempted the
Colossians, Paul moved on to a presentation of what true spirituality looks like. The
starting point of Christian spirituality is the realization that Christ's resurrection
resulted in his exaltation to sit on a throne at God's right hand (3:1). This insight led
Christians to quote Psalm 110:1 so often ("The LORD said to my Lord, 'Sit in the place
of honor at my right hand until I humble your enemies, making them a footstool
under your feet.'"). The ultimate origin of this insight, however, was not in the Old
Testament itself but in the teaching of Jesus (e.g., Matt 19:28; 25:31) and in Jesus' use
of Daniel 7:9-14: "I watched as thrones were put in place and the Ancient One sat
down to judge . . . . As my vision continued that night, I saw someone like a son of
man coming with the clouds of heaven. He approached the Ancient One and was led
into his presence. He was given authority, honor, and sovereignty over all the nations
of the world, so that people of every race and nation and language would obey him.
His rule is eternal—it will never end. His kingdom will never be destroyed." This is the
point that Paul had been making repeatedly in this letter: Not only does Christ rule
due to his creation of the world, but he also rules due to his renewal of the creation.
There is no other power or authority (other than the Father) higher than Jesus.

The next step in Christian spirituality is the realization that the Christian has been
raised with Christ (3:3-4). Identification with Christ means that one is dead to the
world, to its principalities and powers, and to the various rules of piety, since they are
all rooted in this age. But identification with Christ means that one is also resurrected
with Christ—that is, one is identified with the only life that Christ has, which is his
resurrected life (so 2:12). As in the Pauline parallel statement in Rom 6:4-6, this death
and resurrection does not mean that the one committed to follow Christ is therefore
no longer living in this world. First, there is still a significant need for instruction on
how to live in this world. The "not yet" of this life will be taken up in 3:5. Second, the
ruling Christ has not yet been revealed openly. That is, he already reigns, but his reign
is hidden from the majority of the people on earth. (Here Paul parallels the thought

of 1 Pet 1.) Thus, the Parousia of Christ (in this metaphor) is not that he will return or that he will begin to rule so much as that his present rule will become evident to the whole world. This model is eschatological and apocalyptic, rather than mystical. The point is that Christians already find their life in Christ ("your real life is hidden with Christ in God"—3:3) in that he is their hope of resurrection, he is the guide of their lives, he is the one with whom they identify, and he is the ruler to whom they submit. But it is a life hidden with Christ in God in that Christ is visibly hidden from them, and those not committed to Christ cannot understand this total identification with an unseen reality (3:2). Yet this also gives a sense of safety, for what is hidden with God cannot be attacked or destroyed by this age in the way their unhidden bodies can. The implication of their life being hidden with Christ is that they will also share that future "revelation"—that is, they will share the "glory" of Christ when his rule is revealed: "When Christ, who is your life, is revealed to the whole world, you will share in all his glory" (3:4). No matter what those around them think, these believers have a future that is as great and as sure as Christ's.

All these realizations have a significant implication, which is that one should take on the mindset of heaven, not the mindset of earth (3:2). It is not that Christians should spend their time thinking about heaven and forget about the various issues of life on earth, but, with their consciousness full of the reign of Christ, they look for how that reign is to be experienced now and view the things of earth with the values of heaven. This is what Jesus invited people to do in the Sermon on the Mount: If the Beatitudes are true and believers are already blessed, then they live this out in terms of a lifestyle modeled after the rest of the Sermon. This is a paradigm shift based on an apocalyptic perspective. Christians have a new set of values because they know that Christ reigns. This brings into sharp focus the tragedy of the statistical lack of difference in values or lifestyle between those who claim to be Christian and those who do not (Barna Group 2004a, 2004b; see further Barna 1990). To really commit oneself to following Christ is to take on a whole new perspective, one determined by the present reign of Christ and its future unveiling.

◆   ## 2. Specific vices and virtues (3:5-17)

[5]So put to death the sinful, earthly things lurking within you. Have nothing to do with sexual immorality, impurity, lust, and evil desires. Don't be greedy, for a greedy person is an idolater, worshiping the things of this world. [6]Because of these sins, the anger of God is coming.* [7]You used to do these things when your life was still part of this world. [8]But now is the time to get rid of anger, rage, malicious behavior, slander, and dirty language. [9]Don't lie to each other, for you have stripped off your old sinful nature and all its wicked deeds. [10]Put on your new nature, and be renewed as you learn to know your Creator and become like him. [11]In this new life, it doesn't matter if you are a Jew or a Gentile,* circumcised or uncircumcised, barbaric, uncivilized,* slave, or free. Christ is all that matters, and he lives in all of us.

[12]Since God chose you to be the holy people he loves, you must clothe yourselves with tenderhearted mercy, kindness, humility, gentleness, and patience. [13]Make

allowance for each other's faults, and forgive anyone who offends you. Remember,
the Lord forgave you, so you must forgive
others. ¹⁴Above all, clothe yourselves with
love, which binds us all together in perfect
harmony. ¹⁵And let the peace that comes
from Christ rule in your hearts. For as
members of one body you are called to live
in peace. And always be thankful.

¹⁶Let the message about Christ, in all its
richness, fill your lives. Teach and counsel
each other with all the wisdom he gives.
Sing psalms and hymns and spiritual
songs to God with thankful hearts. ¹⁷And
whatever you do or say, do it as a representative of the Lord Jesus, giving thanks
through him to God the Father.

3:6 Some manuscripts read *is coming on all who disobey him.*   **3:11a** Greek *a Greek.*   **3:11b** Greek *Barbarian,
Scythian.*

NOTES

3:5 *put to death the sinful, earthly things lurking within you.* This command could be
translated more woodenly as, "Put to death your members upon the earth." The language
Paul used is difficult, for, strictly speaking, "members" refers to parts of one's body, and
Paul surely does not mean that we are to put to death parts of our bodies. However, there
is a metaphorical use of the term "member" known since Plato and Aristotle (see TDNT
4.555-556), so Paul could intend some nonphysical "members." Paul's thought here
seems to develop in steps starting from "you died" (2:11-12; 3:3) to its implication "put to
death," which suggests a physical object ("members") that is further defined as belonging
to this age ("upon earth," "earthly"; cf. 3:2) and then specified in terms of behaviors rather
than body parts. Paul's ability to shift from one metaphor to another warns us not to take
most of his metaphors absolutely—they are images used to get at the truth he was trying to
inculcate, not absolute descriptions of reality.

Have nothing to do with. The NLT apparently takes the suggestion of Lightfoot (1896:209)
that one must understand a repetition of the main verb ("put to death") or similar verb as
being implied here.

3:6 *the anger of God is coming.* Several manuscripts (א A C D¹ F G H I 044 𝔐 syr copᵇᵒ)
add "on those who are disobedient," referring to the pagans, who had not obeyed the
Good News. However, the earliest manuscripts (𝔓46 B; cf. D*ᵛⁱᵈ itᵇ copˢᵃ Clement) lack
this phrase. Its addition can be explained by the fact that it appears in Eph 5:6, a parallel
passage, and subsequently was added (by the fourth century) to conform Colossians to
Ephesians.

3:8 *dirty language.* The term appears only here in biblical Greek. In its few occurrences
in nonbiblical Greek, it appears to cover both abusive and obscene speech (Lightfoot
1896:212). Since sexual vices were already denounced in verse 5 and the immediate context
of verse 8 concerns sins of the tongue, here it likely means "abusive speech" rather than
"dirty language." Paul, of course, would approve of neither. However, the problem is that
what is considered "dirty" language in particular varies from culture to culture. For example, the Romans would have considered references to a cross as dirty, not fit for polite society, and generally either avoided them or else used euphemisms such as "the extreme
penalty."

3:10 *as you learn to know your Creator and become like him.* "Becoming like him" is a
translation of the Greek for "renewed in his image." The NLT, like many other translations
(NRSV, NIV, NET), connects "into knowledge" with the Creator. But many scholars like
O'Brien (1982:191-192) and Dunn (1996:221-222) and some versions (NAB, TEV) correctly point out that the reference to knowledge is not about the knowledge of God but
rather picks up the wisdom motif of the letter and views knowledge as the result of being
formed into the image of God. The point is that wisdom is not to be found outside of

Christ but rather is the result of being reformed into the image of God. I would translate this "being renewed in knowledge and according to the image of the one who created you," or, as the NAB translates the whole of verse 10, "and have put on the new self, which is being renewed, for knowledge, in the image of its creator."

3:15 *the peace that comes from Christ.* Literally, "the peace of Christ." The phrase "God's peace" (e.g., Gal 6:16; Phil 4:7; 2 Thess 3:16; and the greetings of many of Paul's letters) is relatively common in Paul's writings, as is the phrase "the God of peace" (Rom 15:33; 16:20; 1 Cor 14:33; 2 Cor 13:11; Phil 4:9; 1 Thess 5:23); so the expression "peace of Christ" is unusual by comparison. However, Paul's sense seems to be that if the fullness of God dwells in Christ and Christ is the embodiment of the Wisdom of God, then with Christ dwelling in the believer, peace results.

be thankful. The Greek term underlying this translation appears only here in the NT, although related words for thanksgiving and thankfulness are common enough even in Colossians (1:3, 12; 2:7; 3:17; 4:2).

3:16 *message about Christ.* While some relatively early manuscripts (A C*) have "the message about God" or "the message about the Lord" (so ℵ* I), the reading "the message about Christ" is undoubtedly correct since it has early (𝔓46 and B) and diverse (ℵ² C² D F G 044 075 1739 𝔐 it cop^sa) mss on its side and it is the more unusual reading, which explains why the others arose to "correct" it (Fee 1994:648).

psalms. While this term was applied to the OT Psalms, works such as the Psalms of Solomon and the various psalms found in the Dead Sea Scrolls indicate that Jewish and Christian groups composed contemporary psalms, in addition to using the ancient ones. Thus, the term does not necessarily refer to the use of the Psalms in the church, although it may include them.

hymns. In Greek use, the term referred to songs sung to the gods and thus was virtually synonymous with "psalms."

to God. While the early manuscripts (𝔓46 ℵ A B C* D*) have "to God," the TR (following the majority of late mss) has "to the Lord," which is an attempt to conform this passage to Eph 5:19, a parallel passage. This is the reason for the translation "to the Lord" in both the KJV and NKJV.

with thankful hearts. This is a very difficult expression in Greek. Since thanks is mentioned in verses 15 and 17, it is surprising to see it here as well. Furthermore, when *charis* [TG5485, ZG5921] means "thanks," it appears without the article, so its use with the article here would normally be translated "in the grace [of God]." Thus, Fee (1994:654-655) may well be correct that they are to sing "in the grace of God" or to sing conscious of the grace of God. Dunn (1996:239) shows the difficulty of this phrase in that he is ambiguous about its meaning. What is clear is that the songs rather than the thanks/grace are what come from the heart. The focus of the sentence is not that we are thankful or that we are in the grace of God but that we sing because of this state.

COMMENTARY

Having given the general perspective that determines how a Christian lives and acts, Paul moved on to specific issues: the vices that Christians are to avoid and the virtues that they are to pursue.

What specifically characterizes life in Christ? How do we make the indicative of being dead to this age and alive to Christ into the imperative of day-to-day life and action? Part of the answer for Paul is a list of vices to be avoided and virtues to be pursued. That is, one must demolish old structures in order to make room for the new. Thus, we first have the negative side (3:5-9), and then the positive (3:10-17).

The form of argument is ancient in that such virtue and vice lists are common enough in Greek (especially Stoic) and Jewish ethical passages (starting in the intertestamental period, e.g., in the Dead Sea Scrolls as in CD 4:17-19). Our focus here is upon the fact that our deaths with Christ in baptism (as discussed above) does not eliminate the ongoing need for ethical decisions wherein we bring that death and new life into daily experience.

Based upon his previous teaching in this letter and his pastoral experience, Paul states that, even though we have died with Christ, we need to make a decision to kill certain "earthly members" (i.e., things that reflect the mindset of this age). While the metaphor demands once-for-all action, it is clear that Paul sees this as a process, not something that happened with the initial decision to turn from one's own way to follow Christ, nor does he see it as something that happens in a single burst of sanctifying enthusiasm. If it is a process, then, what are these "members" that one must kill? Paul listed them in two groups: (1) the vices that were part of the believ-ers' pagan past and had been decisively rejected at baptism, and (2) those vices that they, as Christians, may still need to get rid of.

The first group of vices includes sexual sins, meaning not just the outward acts but also the impulses underlying them (3:5; "impurity" and "lust"). In counseling terms one would say that to change a behavior a person ultimately has to deal with the inner dialogue and patterns of thought that he or she has set up for the sinful act. Without dealing with this inner dialogue, a person is likely to slip back into the pattern of sinful behavior. Then there is greed; in Greco-Roman thought this could include sexual desire and so appropriately comes next in the list, but in Jewish thought greed tended to focus more on the desire for possessions. Jesus called this desire for gaining possessions the worship of Mammon, described in terms parallel to the Baal worship of the Old Testament (Matt 6:19; Luke 16:13). Jesus was build-ing on Jewish teaching that shared this same insight, as in the *Testament of Judah*: "My children, love of money leads to idolatry, because once they are led astray by money, they designate as gods those who are not gods. It makes anyone who has it go out of his mind" (*Testament of Judah* 19:1). Paul does not go into the detail that Jesus and the *Testament of Judah* do but simply says that greed is idolatry. Naturally, few of us would admit that we are greedy, but the marks of greed are seen when the purchase or preservation of a house or car or other acquisitions become a major focus of our thoughts and actions. Perhaps the American inscription of "In God We Trust" on the dollar bill has engendered a subtle (even subconscious) redefinition of "God" that is more accurate than most would wish to admit. Is the good of Wall Street or "the American way of life" or our own lifestyles the basis on which we make decisions (including political decisions), or do we evaluate these things by the ethic of Jesus, especially that found in Matthew 6?

The combination of sexual sin with idolatry is a common association in Jewish writings and part of what Paul affirms from his heritage. Such sin is the cause of the final judgment in both Old and New Testaments, so it is not surprising to have it cited as the cause here (3:6). While Paul described these as part of the past of these believers (their life in the world, 3:7), a past renounced at baptism, he likely mentioned them not just because they were traditionally part of vice lists that described pagan behavior but also because the temptation was ever present.

The second list (3:8) consists of verbal behavior that destroys community, starting with the outburst of anger ("anger" means the outward expression, not the feeling of anger) and moving toward the less obvious expressions of inner anger, such as malicious behavior (or ill will toward another), slander, and abusive language (or "shameful language"), along with untruthful speech. Community was an important reality in the New Testament period, and such behavior makes the community unsafe and thereby destroys it since it destroys trust. This is true whether the community be a church or a marriage, although the focus here is on the house church, the basic unit of the Pauline community. Lest one think that getting rid of these vices is secondary to getting rid of sexual and material vices, we must remember that in other vice lists (e.g., Gal 5:19-21) these sins of the tongue (whether expressed verbally or only in one's inner dialogue) are included in a single list as things that disqualify a person from "the Kingdom of God." Injuring the community of Christ is a serious thing indeed (cf. 1 Cor 3:17: "God will destroy anyone who destroys this temple").

Although the preservation of community might be reason enough for getting rid of such vices, Paul gives a much more theological reason, using the metaphor of undressing and dressing (3:9). In conversion (baptism) a person has stripped off the "old man" (i.e., the sinful nature or the former life paradigm and worldview) and the behaviors that it led to, which were precisely those behaviors that Paul rejected. He or she has chosen to put on a new character, namely one that derives from Christ. But this choice in baptism must be progressively realized. That is, a person is progressively renewed according to the image of the Creator as he or she comes to know him. This renewal may come by the Spirit, although, unusual for him, Paul does not mention the Spirit here, as Fee (1994:647) points out. Further, Paul does not state who the Creator is (3:10). Since there is in this passage a clear reference to Genesis 1:26-27, that is, humanity's being created in the image of God, we would expect the Creator to be God the Father. But in 1:16 Christ is presented as the Creator so that idea could be cropping up here. However, it is more likely that what Paul was picking up here is his previous teaching about Christ (Wisdom incarnate) as the image of God. Thus, the idea is that humanity is re-created in the image of Christ, who is himself the image of God. This re-creation produces knowledge in us, according to Paul, for we are, of course, made over into the image of divine Wisdom. This fact has a major implication: Worldly distinctions do not matter. All that matters is Christ and our becoming like him, for he lives in all believers. Paul's focus is on ethnic distinctions, especially the Jew–Gentile divide, which again indicates the Jewish nature of the issues troubling the Colossians (3:11). Beyond this basic ethnic divide (Jew–Gentile; circumcised–uncircumcised) was the division of the world between "civilized" Greco-Romans and those they could not understand (the basic meaning of "barbaric"or those whose lifestyle was, in Greco-Roman eyes, sub-human. "Barbarian" was a. term originally applied to the Persians, who spoke a different language but were very much "civilized" in terms of their own culture. The Greco-Romans also had a low opinion of the Scythians, the tribes originally inhabiting northern Asia Minor, thinking them subhuman in their ways of living. A further major division of humanity was between slave and free, the latter having status and honor, and the former often having authority and derived status from their master (if their masters were powerful), but no status or honor of their own. In Galatians 3:28 Paul adds "male and female." None of these human distinctions are Kingdom distinctions nor are the prejudices that they inspire; the only thing that matters is the degree to which we have been formed into the image of God in Christ. Therefore, none of these distinctions were for Paul of practical significance in the church, where the slave might be an elder and the master a new convert or, as in the Aquila–Priscilla pair, the wife might be predominant and the husband a supportive partner (judging from Paul's unusual but consistent naming of Priscilla first).

Of practical significance for Paul, both individually and corporately, are the specifics of what it looks like to be made over into the image of Christ. First, there is a foundational theological conviction on which all the rest is based, namely that in the eyes of the Father the believers are chosen, holy, and loved (3:12). This pictures the believers as the renewed Israel, for Israel was chosen (Deut 7:6; 14:2), holy (Exod 19:6; Pss 16:3; 34:9), and loved (Jer 31:3; so also the name Jeshurun: Deut 32:15; 33:26; Isa 44:2, NASB) by God. The language here is very close to that in 1 Peter 2:9, "You are a chosen people. You are royal priests, a holy nation, God's very own possession." One reason there is no need to follow Jewish rules and celebrate Jewish festivals is that they are already God's people. It is on this foundation of acceptance and security that one is to build the virtues. The virtues are not what create acceptance before God but the means of revealing the renewed image that God has put within. These virtues can also serve to reveal their lack and thus call into question whether one has in fact ever been re-created by God, as Paul makes clear elsewhere.

Second, virtue needs to be pursued. "Clothe" is an active word (3:12). Human activity is needed in order to grow in virtue, to express outwardly what God had created inwardly. Thus, we have a list of five virtues paralleling the two lists of five vices that we had before. The central contrast of this list is the second list of vices, for these would be their opposite since mercy, kindness (goodness, generosity), humility (modesty), gentleness (courtesy, considerateness, meekness—not seeking retribution) and patience (delaying anger) would cancel out "anger, rage, malicious behavior, slander, and dirty language." Rather than trying to attack the vice, the believer need only pursue the virtue and the vice would be impossible, which encapsulates a primary strategy in Christian counseling.

It is not that within the Christian community there would be no provocation to anger. Paul was a realist. There would be those that one must "put up with," as Dunn (1996:230) put so well (3:13). More than that, there would be those who deserved a reprimand or other censure (the one who "offends you"), and the believer would be obliged to forgive these people. How can one do this? Just as Christ has. Christ has forgiven each believer. Thus, if people are to be renewed into the image of God in Christ, they will model their behavior on that of Christ. And if they have been forgiven, they will find the power to forgive as they reflect on their own forgiveness. While Paul does not refer to it, one wonders if Matthew 18:21-35 and especially the parable of the unforgiving slave starting in verse 23 might not be in the back of his mind. Whether that is the case or not, modeling one's behavior on the behavior of Jesus is a teaching that Paul has in common with other writers (e.g., Peter—see 1 Pet 2:21-23). That is, of course, the meaning of being his apprentice or "disciple." An apprentice learns to behave like the person to whom he or she is apprenticed. And believers are called to be apprentices of Jesus.

This can all be summed up in two virtues: love and peace (3:14). The love referred to is not an emotion but a decision to do good to another, a willingness to sacrifice oneself on behalf of another. Thus, love is the opposite of a self-centered attitude. For Paul, it was clear that love was a cardinal virtue, whether he spoke of it as fulfilling the law (Rom 13:9-10), as that which makes faith work (Gal 5:6), or as the virtue that makes other behaviors Christian (1 Cor 13, see esp. v. 13). Love is primary because it is an imitation of Christ. In addition to Jesus' teaching on the importance of love (Mark 12:29-31), the believer is also instructed by the behavior of Jesus— that is, his self-giving for others. Given that the example of Christ has been mentioned in the previous verse, it must lie behind Paul's thought now.

With a look back at 2:19 (specifically the word sundesmos [TG4886, ZG5278], "sinews," ["joints and ligaments," NLT] here translated "binds"), Paul referred to love uniting perfectly, but what does it unite? Does it unite the virtues, as, according to Simplicius, the Pythagoreans claimed about friendship (a word conceptually related to love)? Or does it unite the church, much as Aristeas claimed that love and affection did for a kingdom (Letter of Aristeas 265)? Perhaps Paul left this deliberately vague, only wishing to underline the binding force of love, which is necessary both personally (if our virtues are to have coherence) and communally (if our communities are to have unity). Yet here, as often elsewhere, Paul joined love with peace (2 Cor 13:11; Gal 5:22; see also Eph 4:2-3). Unlike his usual expression, "peace of God," Paul has here the "peace that comes from Christ" (3:15). This peace is surely the peace that Christ has already produced (1:20), which is to rule within the individual. That is, the believer enters into a peace that God has produced through Christ when a consciousness of this peace rules within, controlling his or her behavior. For Paul, the heart, where this peace rules, is not the seat of feelings but the core of the person, where will and choice are centered. The result is recognizing that God calls believers not to be individual holy people living in splendid isolation from others but members of a single body, in this case the house church of which they were members in Colosse. Believers can only live that out if they live at peace with one another. Inner peace founded on security in what God has done in Christ leads to outer peace with others, even though they are very different from us.

Then comes Paul's final exhortation, "Be thankful," which may seem unrelated but is most germane (3:17). When believers dwell on what they have in Christ and so become a thankful people, they cannot dwell on what their status is within the Christian community or within the world, and they cannot be concerned that others have more earthly power or goods. A thankful heart is normally a peaceful heart, for if one is filled with thanks, he or she will find it difficult to engage in conflict.

If this is how the believers are to live in community, it is fitting for Paul to close this section with comments on the activities of the Christian community (3:16). This is Paul's alternative to the attempt to enter into the angelic worship that the teachers whom he opposed were apparently urging. The basis of the Christian gathering is the Good News, the message about Christ. This message is clearly seen in 1:15-20: Christ, creator of the universe; Christ, creator of the new humanity; Christ, head of the church; Christ all and in all. This message is to "indwell" the community—that is, to enter in and live in the core of their communal lives. Since Christ is the embodiment of divine Wisdom, it is in such wisdom that they should instruct and exhort one another. Here the community carries on the ministry of the apostle (cf. 1:28) since they do this to each other.

The second aspect of the gathering of the community is communal singing. While it is likely that the early church used Old Testament Psalms, we also see numerous new songs in the New Testament (from Mary's song in Luke 1 to the songs of Revelation). Here (as in 1 Cor 14:15) Paul also includes songs composed and sung spontaneously under the direct influence of the Spirit, which one would expect, since worship is frequently attributed to the Spirit's inspiration. The meditation on Christ naturally leads to the sung praise of his Father. But worship does not end with the communal gathering; it flows out into one's life in the world. So everything believers do is to be done as Christ's representatives, as those commissioned, authorized, and sent into the world by Christ and whose identity is determined by the name of Christ. Rabbi Yose would later express a typical Jewish attitude that underlies this Pauline perspective: "And may everything you do be for the sake of Heaven" (m. Avot 2:12; "Heaven" is a circumlocution for God). In our passage, every word and deed is done for the sake and under the name of Christ. Worship thus takes place behind the doors of the house, in the workplace, and in every casual conversation, since all deeds and words are shaped by a consciousness that one is acting under the authority and presence of Christ. This attitude naturally expresses itself in thanksgiving to the Father, for it was he who rescued us from the kingdom of darkness and brought us into the Kingdom of his dear Son.

◆   ## 3. The Christian household (3:18-4:1)

[18]Wives, submit to your husbands, as is fitting for those who belong to the Lord.

[19]Husbands, love your wives and never treat them harshly.

[20]Children, always obey your parents, for this pleases the Lord. [21]Fathers, do not aggravate your children, or they will become discouraged.

²²Slaves, obey your earthly masters in everything you do. Try to please them all the time, not just when they are watching you. Serve them sincerely because of your reverent fear of the Lord. ²³Work willingly at whatever you do, as though you were working for the Lord rather than for people. ²⁴Remember that the Lord will give you an inheritance as your reward,

3:24 Or *and serve Christ as your Master.*

and that the Master you are serving is Christ.* ²⁵But if you do what is wrong, you will be paid back for the wrong you have done. For God has no favorites.

CHAPTER 4

Masters, be just and fair to your slaves. Remember that you also have a Master— in heaven.

NOTES

3:18 *submit.* The term (*hupotassō*) [TG5293, ZG5718] indicates the submission or subordination that was expected of a wife in Greco-Roman culture. Given that Colosse was in the Ionic area of Asia Minor, we can expect that Hellenistic values prevailed that required a high degree of subordination and little intimacy between husband and wife. Hellenized Jews such as Josephus and Philo were uncomfortable with the biblical Sarah, for she did not seem subordinate enough, and Abraham followed her advice. The *Testament of Abraham* (a possible basis for the Sarah of 1 Pet 3:6) made her into a "proper" Hellenistic wife. Given that Paul appears to have treated women equally and taught that there was neither male nor female in Christ (Gal 3:28), it is possible that women may have started to break free from their assigned roles after conversion, which would have brought opprobrium on the church and invited legal sanctions. Yet given that Christ subordinated himself for the good of human beings Paul had no problem with subordination and serving others *per se.* Thus Paul affirms the cultural value but reframes it by adding "in the Lord," that is, as a choice to imitate Jesus in subordination. The debate about application is whether it is appropriate to demand an attitude that was culturally appropriate in a highly hierarchal culture be followed today in a culture with far more egalitarian legal and social structures, as some teachers do, or whether such a demand might in fact be inviting analogous opprobrium and social sanctions today to those that Paul was trying to avoid and also working against intimacy, which is the major marital value of the present era (Marshall 2004:190-195).

fitting. What was or was not fitting was a topic of discussion in Greek ethics. In the Greek OT the idea of being fitting is usually thought of in a legal or political sense; in the NT, it may also have a legal force (Phlm 1:8), but it more often has a cultural or ethical sense, sometimes including a twist in that what is fitting in the culture surrounding the church is not fitting for God's holy ones (Eph 5:4; see TDNT 1.360).

3:19 *never treat them harshly.* While this is the traditional translation, Dunn (1996:249) points out that it fits the active voice of the verb better. In our passage, the verb is passive. It could be that he is right in his conclusion from this observation: "What is in view, therefore, is probably the feeling of the dominant partner who can legally enforce his will on his wife but who will not thereby win her love and respect and can thus feel cheated and embittered at not receiving what he regards as his due. . . . This is the likely outcome for anyone who stands on his rights alone and who knows and exercises little of the love called for in the first half of the verse."

3:20 *pleases.* This term (*euareston* [TG2101, ZG2298]) in the NT always means "pleasing to God," with the single exception of Titus 2:9, where it is used for a slave pleasing a master (BDAG 403).

3:21 *aggravate.* This term (*erethizō* [TG2042, ZG2241]) means "to cause someone to feel resentment" (L&N 88.168), which threatens to make them "be discouraged, feel like giving up, lack motivation" (*athumeō* [TG120, ZG126]; Analytical Lexicon of the Greek New Testament 36).

3:22 *Try to please them all the time, not just when they are watching you.* Literally, "not with eye-service as those who try to curry influence with human beings." The term for "eye-service" (*ophthalmodoulia* [TG3787, ZG4056]) is found for the first time in Greek literature in Paul's writings, so it may have been coined by him. Its meaning is explained by the second term (also found in Ps 53:5 [52:6, LXX]; *Psalms of Solomon* 4:7, 8, 19), which means "one whose final norm, born of fear and quite natural in slaves, is striving to please those who are in superior authority" (TDNT 1.456). In Ps 53:5 it contrasts with a person who fears or serves God. Here it designates a person whose goal is to please his or her earthly master.

3:24 *an inheritance as your reward.* Paul was referring to a particular inheritance that he expected his readers to know about. The idea of an inheritance is common in the NT. Jesus speaks of inheriting "the whole earth" (Matt 5:5) or "eternal life" (Matt 19:29). Paul spoke of inheriting "the Kingdom of God" (1 Cor 6:9, 10; 15:50; Gal 5:21; cf. Eph 5:5). In many other passages, the nature of the inheritance is not specified. This term, then, stands for having a place in the coming rule of God and his Christ as opposed to being rejected and cast out.

3:25 *God has no favorites.* Lit., "there is no acceptance of face." This is a passive expression with no specified subject. Although the idea that God has no favorites is a truth repeated in many places in Scripture, in this passage the phrase should probably be read as "Christ has no favorites," for throughout the passage the reference has been to Christ.

4:1 *just and fair.* Neither "just" nor "fair" is specifically defined. The idea of justice, however, is extremely common in both the OT and NT. "Fair" in Greek (*isotēta* [TG2471, ZG2699]) is a word derived from the term for "equality" and thus means what is equitable. This idea is clearly a flexible concept, determined in part by cultural values, although in Paul's view it is Christ who is the ultimate arbitrator of whether some action is just and fair. (For further information, see TDNT 3.354-355.)

COMMENTARY

Having just written about doing everything in the name of the Lord Jesus Christ (3:17), Paul inserted a section on the ordering of the household, which shows how the Christian household was to fit into the world at that time. That this is an insertion of traditional material is clear from the abrupt transition and the difference in style between this section and what precedes and follows.

All that is said about the household in the early church must be understood in light of the fact that the early churches met in homes. In the New Testament period, the local church was a house church. The church was the household of God in which the individuals experienced a familial-like relationship and treated one another as fictive brothers and sisters. However, this was "fictional" (meaning "non-blood," not "unreal") only from the point of view of legal and blood relationships, which is a perspective that belongs to this age, not the Kingdom's.

From the Kingdom perspective, these relationships in Christ are real and lasting, while legal and blood relationships are transitory, limited to this age. However, having mentioned relationships in the household of God, Paul now inserts material about relationships in the households in which the believers in Colosse lived out much of their life. Two perspectives govern this section. The first is the preceding instruction, "Whatever you do or say, do it as a representative of the Lord Jesus" (3:17), which means that one needs to represent Jesus well within the culture. The second perspective is the "Live wisely among those who are not believers" (4:5), which follows. This section is about how the Colossians can wisely represent Jesus within the Colossians' culture. In order to apply it to contemporary cultures, then, it requires not only verbal translation but cultural translation so that the resultant behavior represents Jesus as Lord and shows wisdom in living according to the new cultural norms and among those who are not believers within the new cultural situation.

With his announced goals in mind, Paul picks up three pairs of relationships that were the common topics of ethical instruction on household management in Greek literature, going back as far as Aristotle: "The investigation of everything should begin with its smallest parts, and the primary and smallest parts of the household are master and slave, husband and wife, father and children" (*Politics* 1.1253b, 1-14, cited in Balch 1981:33). The importance of these household relationships was clear to the ancients: the household or extended family was the foundation for the city or state, and if the household fell apart, the city would not be far behind. Christians viewed themselves and were in turn viewed by their society as a segment of Judaism, which meant a foreign people with a different culture (e.g., Acts 16:20-21). Varieties of Judaism, including the Christian one, could be tolerated. What set Christians apart from other Jews, however, is that they actively reached out to the local population and invited them to join their movement, adopting their way of life, and they did this without insisting on bodily mutilation (which is how Greco-Romans viewed circumcision). Thus, rather than simply living within the "host" culture (which for many members of the church was their native culture), followers of Jesus actively recruited from the host culture. Furthermore, they did this without demanding that slaves ask permission of their masters or wives ask of their husbands before joining the Christian community, adopting its customs, and thus separating themselves from their former culture and that of their masters and husbands. This recruitment appeared to undermine the authority of the household, especially since the new apprentices of Jesus started refusing to worship the household gods. This rejection flew in the face of the patriarch of the family who exercised his authority to determine the religion of the household and who seriously believed in the gods. Thus, this recruitment was undermining the security of the household, and, in the view of pagan masters and husbands, the gods might take revenge for the neglect they were receiving from the household members who had attached themselves to the Christian movement.

The first relationship that Paul discusses is the husband–wife relationship, the primary bond of the ancient household (3:18-19). However, the husband–wife relationship in antiquity was not necessarily expected to be one of intimacy but rather a practical arrangement, usually set up by the respective parents of the husband and wife who had little or no input. In this arrangement, the patriarchal authority of the husband was not questioned (or, in many cases, the husband's father, who, if he was alive, was the head of the household consisting of all of his sons and their wives). Frequently, the husband was significantly older than the wife—the Roman ideal was a man of 30 marrying a woman of 15. We do not know whether this ideal was part of the culture in Colosse, although for practical reasons the husband in most cultures of that period was usually significantly older, having had to at least learn a trade, and the wife was usually just beyond puberty.

In this passage, wives are told to submit to their husbands, for this was the culturally appropriate relationship, which Paul views as also appropriate for those who belong to the Lord (3:18). Certainly, this value would be acceptable within the church, for submitting to one another is a Christian value (Eph 5:21; 1 Pet 5:5); furthermore, Christ came to serve and so left the example of serving others. For Paul to ask women to fulfill this culturally demanded role was simply to ask them to live out a virtue asked of all Christians. Paul conditioned this virtue, however, by the phrase "in the Lord" or, as in the NLT, "for those who belong to the Lord." This is the primary relationship in the life of the Christian, and no submission to any human being can be allowed to trespass upon this relationship. Thus, submission to another person should not require something that would be incompatible with what Jesus requires. Furthermore, Paul made no attempt to justify this one-sided submission theologically. The justification comes at the end of the section in terms of living wisely in this world (4:5). What was wise in that culture and could commend the faith was a Christian wife avoiding what the world would consider insubordination, whether to a believing or unbelieving husband. Paul could teach this because he knew after all that the marriage relationship was temporary, limited to this age, and not part of the age to come (as he indicates in 1 Cor 7). Within this relationship the husband had all of the power; thus, Paul instructed him not to abuse his power (an idea also found in the best of pagan moralists) and to love his wife (3:19). In that culture, of course, the wife had little or no legal redress if her husband should happen to be harsh and abusive. The love command is at best unusual in Paul's world, so this is the fundamentally Christian part of the command. The command to love is not a command to emotional warmth, as in Western culture, but, as we saw previously in 3:14, a command to seek the good of the other. In Ephesians 5:25 this is described in terms of following the example of Christ who gave himself for the good of his "bride"; such a metaphor, while unexpressed, is surely not far from Paul's mind here in Colossians. "Love," then, means self-sacrifice and servanthood, however dimly this may have been perceived by the Colossian readers. This attitude stands in contrast to that of the patriarchal culture in which the wife existed to serve her husband.

The second part of the household structure was children and fathers (3:20-21). While we in the Western world often read this passage as applying to minors and not applying to grown children, within the cultures represented in Scripture such an idea would seem strange, for prepubescent children were controlled by slaves, if not by the parents, and there was never a time when an older child was emancipated and left the authority of the father. A male was a child as long as his father lived, and then he either became the patriarch of the family or else he was subject to an elder brother. A female child was under the authority of her father until he gave her in marriage to another family, after which she was under the authority of her father-in-law. Furthermore, there was no adolescence in that a girl often passed from child directly to wife at or shortly after puberty (Roman law allowed marriage at age 12) and a boy entered his career at the same point (often working alongside his father), marrying when he was sufficiently trained to be ready to support a family. Paul here cited cultural standards and also alluded to the fifth commandment, which is explicitly cited in the parallel passage in Ephesians 6:1-3. Obedience to parents, especially fathers, was a cultural standard, not just an idea that he found in the Old Testament. This obedience to parents was "always," or more literally translated, "in all things," including such things as marriage and vocational choice and how one raised one's own children. The reason given is that this pleases the Lord. So again, there is the unstated caveat that if behavior was asked that did not please the Lord, one's submission to the Lord was primary.

Having addressed children in the traditional way, Paul turned to the other side of the power relationship and spoke specifically to fathers (3:21). Mothers are not addressed since mothers did not have ultimate authority over any children and no formal authority over male children after age seven. The fathers are not to behave so that they aggravate or cause resentment in their children. Because the father had almost total control over the life of his grown children and was often their boss in the family workshop or farm, Paul's command had genuine import. A father's bad behavior could discourage his child, and since the father is a believer, the child's resulting resentment or discouragement might be directed toward Jesus and the church. Fathers are not to discourage virtue but to encourage it; but the son who is struggling with anger, resentment, or discouragement does not have energy or perspective to grow in more positive virtues. In this regard, the positive side of the command is found in Ephesians 6:4: "Bring them up with the discipline and instruction that comes from the Lord." Paul charges fathers to provide positive guidance, direction, and reward according to the teaching of and about Jesus rather than criticism, much less exploitation for the father's selfish benefit. (One should note that discipline does not merely mean punishment, although in some contexts it can mean that. Its primary meaning is leadership in such disciplines as will bring children to the spiritual, physical, or intellectual goals desired, much as a coach directs a team through disciplines to improve them.) For Paul, a father's authority was no longer absolute, as it was in the world around them; it was and is to be governed by higher goals than his own honor or the family's profit. It is to be governed by what will lead their family forward "in the Lord." In our culture, of course, we would have to apply this to mothers as well since many contemporary families are headed by women, and in many families women and men share the leadership.

The third part of the household structure was slaves and masters (3:22–4:1). The length of his exhortation may indicate that there were many slaves in the Colossian church. While this passage is commonly applied to employees and employers, we have to remember that there were several significant differences between first century Greco-Roman slavery and modern employment relationships. First, the slave could not quit. While it is true that at least in Rome a slave could probably expect to be freed after 15 or fewer years of service, during these years his or her service was involuntary. To desert one's master would mean whipping or worse. Furthermore, Colosse was not Rome, and there is evidence that the prospects of release were dimmer in Asia Minor. Second, there were few restrictions on how a master could treat his slaves since they were considered his property rather than persons in their own right. Sexual or physical abuse was not uncommon. Third, the slaves had few, if any, available avenues of protest or protection. (Onesimus may have taken one of the few avenues available if he purposely fled to Paul—see the commentary on Philemon.) There were no unions or grievance committees; there was no ability to strike. An employee today has options in dealing with an unjust situation that simply were not within the worldview of a slave in the first century.

Paul told slaves to obey their masters in everything (3:22), which is precisely how any first-century writer would have advised slaves. All areas of their life (including, for example, whom they married) were under the power of their master, so they were to obey in everything. However, they were not to do this as if their masters were the final authority, trying to gain influence with them, for their masters are "earthly masters," who, like spouses and parents, belong to this age. Paul had already pointed out to others that a believing slave is already free before the Lord (1 Cor 7:22), so slaves should not view slavery as something that touches the true status of the person. But for Paul this reality did not mean that the slave should rebel. If it had, the wrath of Rome would have quickly been unleashed upon the church. Instead, he or she should follow the example of their Lord, who came to serve, and thus slaves should serve their earthly masters sincerely. Sincerity, as opposed to hypocrisy, is an important Christian value. A Christian should be a what-you-see-is-what-you-get type of person. Slaves should be obedient, not out of fear of their master, but because they realize that they will answer to "the Lord" (i.e., Jesus) for all their words and deeds.

Then Paul shifted from this partial reframing of their situation to a complete reframing: Whatever they do, they are doing for Christ (3:24), and he will pay them back with "the inheritance"—that is, a place in his Kingdom, his reign in the coming age. This is a statement full of radical contrast since under Roman law a slave could not inherit anything. Here, as is usually the case, eschatology is the driving force behind ethics. (For more on eschatology in Colossians, see "Author" in the Introduction.) But if this is what one is working for, rather than keeping an earthly master happy, then one should work "willingly" or, better expressed, "put yourselves into it" (3:23, NRSV). This truth, however, cuts both ways, for the same Lord who will pay them richly for service well done will also pay back any wrong they do (3:25). The last judgment—when the Lord brings true justice to earth—can bring believers punishment rather than reward if they have not been truly serving Christ. He does indeed have no favorites, which means that he cannot be bribed nor will he tip the scales in one's favor because one has had an important position in the church or elsewhere. We need to remember that several of the Pauline passages on inheriting the Kingdom are about those who will *not* inherit the Kingdom. Paul warned the Corinthians and Galatians because some apparently thought their inclusion in the church meant that they could inherit the Kingdom despite living a lifestyle of disobedience to Christ (see 1 Cor 6:9-10; Gal 5:19-21).

Paul's instruction is based on an eschatological viewpoint, seeing life from the perspective of the return of Jesus to rule. In some applications of this passage, there is an insistence on forcing now what will be then (e.g., some forms of liberation theology). That can be appropriate if one is the master in the society and realizes in the light of Jesus' coming that it is presently inappropriate to treat someone as a slave and not as an equal (see below). The efforts of William Wilberforce were of this nature. But it is inappropriate if one is the slave and is rising up to bring about the situation of the last judgment now. That forgets the Cross. Rather Paul is talking about the slaves viewing themselves in the light of the value that Jesus has given them but like their Lord, being willing to serve and even suffer injustice, knowing that Jesus would set things right when he returned.

Paul ended this traditional section on the household with a brief comment to the masters, either because there were few of them in the church or because in one sense he had already said most of what needed to be said. He had just said that Christ has no favorites, so the masters' position in Greco-Roman society will count for nothing when Christ returns. He previously said (3:11) that in Christ there is no slave or free. So here he adds that the masters (lords) themselves are slaves since they have a master (lord), Christ, in heaven (4:1). This is consistent with what Paul had already said about free people in 1 Corinthians 7:22: namely, that to become a Christian is to become a slave of Christ. Therefore, the masters should realize that Christ will be expecting them to do what is just and fair toward their slaves, whether or not the slave is a believer. Most slaves of Christian masters would also become Christians, since the patriarch of a Greco-Roman family determined the religion of the family.

But what does it mean for the masters to do what is just and fair? That is never defined, although the Stoic Seneca and the Hellenistic Jew Philo both addressed the topic. Paul may have expected the master to take some of his cues from the surrounding culture, but the first implication of this statement is that he must treat his slaves like people, not like the property that the law said they were. When it comes to treating them as people, most likely Paul expected the master to take his primary cues from the behavior of Jesus. How did Jesus treat people? After all, it is Jesus who is their master in heaven and Jesus who will return to render judgment without favoritism. It might be advisable, then, for the masters to ask Jesus to show them the just and fair ways to treat slaves so that they could live according to his standard. This idea is expanded upon to some degree in Philemon, but there Paul is vague about what the actual standards are, for he seems to want conviction to arise from the heart rather than from some legal definitions that he lays down.

The final issue in this passage, one which I have touched upon above, is that of its practical theological use today. It is clear that the goal of the passage is (1) to preserve household values as they were understood in a first-century Greco-Roman culture, and (2) to reframe those values in terms of an overarching commitment to follow Jesus as Lord. The problem that we face is (1) that some of these relationships (e.g., master–slave), so basic to that culture, do not exist in Western culture today, and (2) that some of these relationships have changed significantly. Spouses expect emotional intimacy and companionship from marriage rather than simply procreation of legitimate children; children are expected to mature, leave home, and form a separate nuclear family rather than remain for life as a part of their extended family of origin. These cultural shifts mean that we need to translate these directions in ways that will create Paul's desired effect within our cultural setting.

Certainly, all of the relationships in life still come under the rule of Christ and are thus transformed, but in our culture being a responsible employee may mean working to make the union an effective voice for the workers, and there may be situations where resignation from a job is the godly course of action. Children as they grow to adulthood may be called on to develop mature relationships with their parents rather than simply to obey them; on the other hand, they may have to be exhorted to support their parents in their old age, while even pagan extended families would have automatically done this in the first century (cf. 1 Tim 5:8). Likewise, since neither the husband nor his father any longer has the patriarchal role in marriage assigned to him by most Western cultures, love and the type of mutual submission that it involves are the duty of both spouses in support of companionship marriage. This is more likely to contribute to a stabilized marriage with a deep adult–adult relationship than conformity to a husband's wishes would. In these ways the church would continue to be seen as supporting the foundations of culture, while at the same time applying its directives to a culture that marches to "a different drummer" than the ancient world marched to in Plato, Aristotle, Roman organization, and Greco-Roman traditions—a "drummer" that is, in part, influenced by Christian values in the Western world eroding the hierarchal values of ancient culture (see further, Marshall 2004).

4. Concerning prayer and concluding summary (4:2-6)

[2]Devote yourselves to prayer with an alert mind and a thankful heart. [3]Pray for us, too, that God will give us many opportunities to speak about his mysterious plan concerning Christ. That is why I am here in chains. [4]Pray that I will proclaim this message as clearly as I should.

[5]Live wisely among those who are not believers, and make the most of every opportunity. [6]Let your conversation be gracious and attractive* so that you will have the right response for everyone.

4:6 Greek *and seasoned with salt.*

NOTES

4:2 *with an alert mind.* In Greek this phrase is a participle (*proskartereite* [TG4342, ZG4674]), "watching" or "keeping awake" or "being on the alert." It normally refers to guard duty. The metaphorical use for moral or spiritual alertness is a Christian innovation (Dunn 1996:262).

4:3 *many opportunities to speak.* Paul used a metaphor, "open a door for the word," in which "the word" is the Good News. If 2 Cor 2:12 ("the Lord opened a door of opportunity"), another occurrence of the metaphor (also 1 Cor 16:9), is our guide, then what Paul means is not so much opportunities to speak as a receptiveness to the Good News on the part of the population that he would speak to.

his mysterious plan. A mystery in the NT is not so much something that is mysterious as something that was hidden in the past and is now revealed (as in Dan 2:18-19, 27-30, 47). In some methods of Jewish exegesis, this sort of secret is called the *raz* [TA7328/10661, ZA10661], (mystery), the true meaning of which is considered, by these methods, to have been in the OT text all along, but not yet realized(*raz* is attested in the DSS, e.g., 4Q299 Frag 3 ii.11; 1QH xvi.6). Then someone gives a *pesher* [TH6592, ZH7323] ("interpretation"; or *peshar* [TA6591/10600, ZA10600]) and the meaning of, or even the existence of, the *raz* is revealed. This means that a divinely inspired agent is necessary to reveal the *pesher* and perhaps that the text was not as clear as thought, but a *raz*. For the people of the Dead Sea this agent was the Teacher of Righteousness (and the classic example of it is 1QpHab, where one repeatedly reads "its interpretation [is]" = *peshro*), for the Christian community as a whole this was Jesus, and for several of the mysteries to which Paul refers, this was Paul.

4:4 *I will proclaim this message as clearly as I should.* The main verb is "reveal" (*phaneroō* [TG5319, ZG5746]) rather than one of the verbs for preaching (e.g., *euangelizō* [TG2097/A, ZG2294], *kērussō* [TG2784, ZG3062]), for the activity has to do with revealing a secret (mystery), not just preaching. The primary issue for Paul is not clarity (i.e., that he would communicate well), but rather duty (i.e., "as I should").

4:5 *make the most of every opportunity.* While this is a common translation (NIV, NRSV), the Greek verb (*exagorazomai* [TG1805/A, ZG1973]) means to "buy" or "buy back." It is combined with a term for time that is the word for a significant time (*kairos* [TG2540, ZG2789]), an eschatological time (in the context of the NT). Thus "gaining" or "reclaiming the time" is a better translation (Dunn 1996:265-266).

COMMENTARY

Paul had come to the point that he could sum up the whole section that began at 3:5. He signaled that he was at the conclusion of his exhortation by urging them to pray (cf. Rom 15:30-32; Eph 6:18-20; Phil 4:6; 1 Thess 5:17, 25; 2 Thess 3:1-2; Phlm 1:22). In the beginning of Colossians he prayed for them, now he called them to pray and especially to pray for him, adding some summary concerns that show the focus of the ethical section.

Prayer was extremely important to Paul, which is why he urged it on those in his various churches. Here the idea is that of diligence or persistent attention being focused on prayer. Prayer is not something that is just a religious activity but something important enough that one should "persevere" (NEB) or be tenacious. Paul combined this concern with the picture of a guard on duty, forcing himself to stay awake and alert (4:2). This may well be an allusion to the words of Jesus that we have in Mark 13:35-37 ("Keep watch! . . . Watch for him!") and in Mark 14:38 ("Keep watch and pray"), which is a story that Paul certainly knew. This vivid metaphor underscores the importance of prayer for the Pauline mission. The content of the prayer is not specified, although "alertness" is used elsewhere in the context of the Parousia and so could have overtones of prayer for the coming of Christ and the full revelation of the Kingdom that his arrival would bring (O'Brien 1982:237-238). Yet prayer, whether for the coming of Christ or for daily needs, is not founded on anxiety, but on thanksgiving. This is the sixth reference to thanks or thanksgiving in the letter. Paul demonstrated thanks in the beginning of the letter and then prayed that the Colossians would be a thankful people. He urged it in chapter 2 and twice in chapter 3. Now, as he exhorts them to pray, he instructs them to pray in the same thankful spirit in which he prayed at the beginning of the letter. If a person really believes that the Father has given him or her a new status in Christ, that person will inherit the Kingdom that Christ rules. This truth, combined with all the other tremendously exciting affirmations that Paul has made earlier in this letter, can only make a person thankful. Lack of thankfulness is an indication that "belief" is still in the head and has yet to penetrate the heart and become real conviction.

While Paul started off urging prayer in general, he felt no shame in exposing his own need and requesting their prayers for himself. In fact, he did this at the end of many of his letters, showing that he saw the churches he had planted as participating with him in his ministry. It is precisely this participation in ministry that he requested prayer for here, rather than prayer for his personal well-being (as in Rom 15:30-31), release from prison (as in Phil 1:19), or strength for travel. He asked them to pray that there would be receptiveness to the Good News, which is indeed God's secret plan concerning Christ (4:3). But what was it about Christ that was a secret needing revelation? In Colossians Paul has mentioned two aspects. First, it is "Christ lives in you. This gives you assurance of sharing his glory" (1:27). Then a few verses later it is "Christ himself" about whom Paul says, "In him lie hidden all the treasures of wisdom and knowledge" (2:3). That is, one could read the Old Testament by itself for thousands of years and, without divine revelation, fail to grasp the nature of Christ or the fact that he would indwell the believer and give them the assurance that they will share in his glory. This revelation had been given to Paul. So his desire was that he would clearly communicate this revelation in places where there would be openness to the Good News (4:4). Because the Good News needed revelation, Paul requested that he would indeed reveal it since that was what God had commissioned him to do. And why might he fail or not do this with his full strength? Because his revelation of this secret was the very reason he was in jail (that is, in prison and not simply under house arrest, for he was in chains). His message was acceptable to many strands of Judaism until he differentiated himself by revealing that the living Christ was the core of God's plan. It is this revelation in Acts 26:23 that led the procurator to call him "crazy," perhaps one of the nicer things said about Paul by people for whom his revelation did not make sense. Certainly he felt intense pressure to "pull his punches," to be silent, to keep out of trouble, for had he not suffered enough? Yet he knew that God had commissioned him to reveal Christ to the nations, so he knew where his duty lay. The fact is that Christianity is about serving the resurrected Christ. The core of the message is that Jesus is alive, that he, through the Spirit, can live within the individual and incorporate him or her into the community of faith, and that he is indeed the embodiment of wisdom and knowledge. When the Christian belief focuses anywhere else, it has become eccentric, for it has missed its own center.

Having requested prayer for his own life and speech in the world, Paul turned to the life and speech of the Colossians. The theme of living "wisely" brackets this letter, for it is introduced in 1:9-10 and then repeated in 2:6-7 (since Jesus is God's wisdom) before appearing here in the conclusion of the letter's teaching (4:5). Here the focus is on wise conduct with respect to those who are outside the Christian community, a dichotomy that is the mark of eschatological passages. The contrast is not made in order to separate the Christian community from the world in terms of withdrawing from it, but in order to highlight where the Colossians should direct their concern. This wisdom is to be marked by gaining or reclaiming the time. This, implies Paul, is the eschatological moment. Christ has come; the Kingdom has been announced; the new age has begun; the new age will soon come to its consummation in the revelation of Christ from heaven. This is a critical time of unknown length. This is the time that is to be gained or redeemed through wise conduct. By redeeming time, I mean it is to be reclaimed or gained—this time at the end of the age is not to be given over to evil forces or abandoned but used well for the purposes of the rule of Jesus and our own future with him. It is this that is accomplished through wise conduct. Wise conduct has two aspects. First, conversation is to be "gracious and attractive," literally, "in grace, seasoned with salt" (4:6). Every Greek speaker would have understood this idiom. It meant speech that was attractive, not insipid, probably implying that it included wit as well as sober declarations (Eccl 10:12; Sir 21:16; Demosthenes *Orations* 51, 9; Demetrius *Style* §127; 133; 135; Josephus *Antiquities* 18, 208; Plutarch *Moralia* 514-515; Epictetus *Dissertationes* 3.22.90). The Pauline Christian is neither one who can only speak about religious things nor one with whom it is boring to speak but one who is a good, interesting conversationalist. Interesting conversation leads to relationship, and within that relationship questions of lifestyle come up. The Christian will know (perhaps due to Christ's wisdom in them) how he or she ought (there is a sense of duty or even divine obligation in Paul's use of "ought") to answer each person. This response will be gracious, witty, and interesting, but it will also clearly point to the hope that a person has in Christ. Yet this "answer" is in response to questions asked by the non-Christian due to the Christian's wise lifestyle, not due to the Christian's aggressive invasion of the "space" of the unbeliever. Here is Paul's picture of a church engaged in the world (and thus probably not a church that has been forced underground due to persecution), but also one that is confident that if they really live as Christians should live, God will produce the opportunities for them to share about the Christ who motivates them.

◆ VI. Conclusion (4:7-18)

7Tychicus will give you a full report about how I am getting along. He is a beloved brother and faithful helper who serves with me in the Lord's work. 8I have sent him to you for this very purpose—to let you know how we are doing and to encourage you. ⁹I am also sending Onesi- mus, a faithful and beloved brother, one of your own people. He and Tychicus will tell you everything that's happening here.

¹⁰Aristarchus, who is in prison with me, sends you his greetings, and so does Mark, Barnabas's cousin. As you were in- structed before, make Mark welcome if he comes your way. ¹¹Jesus (the one we call Justus) also sends his greetings. These are the only Jewish believers among my co- workers; they are working with me here for the Kingdom of God. And what a com- fort they have been!

¹²Epaphras, a member of your own fellowship and a servant of Christ Jesus, sends you his greetings. He always prays earnestly for you, asking God to make you strong and perfect, fully confident that you are following the whole will of God. ¹³I can assure you that he prays hard for you and also for the believers in Laodicea and Hierapolis.

¹⁴Luke, the beloved doctor, sends his greetings, and so does Demas. ¹⁵Please give my greetings to our brothers and sis- ters* at Laodicea, and to Nympha and the church that meets in her house.

¹⁶After you have read this letter, pass it on to the church at Laodicea so they can read it, too. And you should read the letter I wrote to them.

¹⁷And say to Archippus, "Be sure to carry out the ministry the Lord gave you."

¹⁸HERE IS MY GREETING IN MY OWN HAND- WRITING—PAUL.

Remember my chains.

May God's grace be with you.

4:15 Greek brothers.

NOTES

4:7 Tychicus. While the name is rare, it is found most frequently in Magnesia, down the Meander from the Lycus Valley and Colosse (Lightfoot 1896:232).

4:10 Mark, Barnabas's cousin. The reference to Barnabas is surprising, for it indicates that the Colossians knew of Barnabas and perhaps knew him personally. Paul mentioned Barna- bas in Gal 2:1, 9, 13 because Paul was describing a trip that he took with Barnabas and also because Barnabas was Paul's partner as they evangelized southern Galatia. In 1 Cor 9:6 Paul mentioned Barnabas as one who, like himself, worked to support his ministry, although we do not know how the Corinthians knew this fact. It could be that the reference in Corinthi- ans and this one in Colossians indicate a ministry of Barnabas in provincial Asia and Greece about which Acts is silent.

4:11 Jesus (the one we call Justus). "Jesus" was simply the Greek form of "Joshua" and so a very common name among Jews. Justus was also a common name for Jews and prose- lytes. Titius Justus (Acts 18:7) was probably one such proselyte, while Joseph Barsabbas Justus (Acts 1:23) was more likely a Jew by birth (Lightfoot 1896:236).

comfort. While this term for comfort (*paregoria* [TG3931, ZG4219]) appears only here in the NT, the theme of comfort is a major one in both the NT and Greek literature in general (see *parakaleo* [TG3870, ZG4151] in TDNT 5.773-779). Louw and Nida list the term under two headings, 25.155 and 35.14, because it could mean "help" rather than "comfort."

4:12 Epaphras. While Epaphras is a shortened form of Epaphroditus, he is probably not the same Epaphroditus that we encounter in Phil 2:25; 4:18. That one was a messenger from Philippi and so probably himself a Philippian, while this one in Colossians is clearly identified as a member of the church in Colosse (Lightfoot 1896:237).

4:14 Luke. Luke has, of course, been traditionally identified as the author of Luke–Acts on the basis of the "we" passages in Acts and church tradition (mainly that found in Eusebius's *Ecclesiastical History*). Since the Gospel itself makes no reference to its author, we have no independent way of judging the accuracy of this tradition, which comes over two centuries after the events. As for Acts, any number of Paul's companions, named or unnamed, could fit the implied personage in the "we" passages. Thus, from a scholarly point of view, "Luke" is a convenient traditional name to apply to the author of Luke and Acts without implying that it was either the real name of the author or that this person was the same as the Luke we read about here in Colossians. What we do know for sure about this Luke (Luke would only be one of his names—he probably had two or three) is that he was a companion of Paul when Paul wrote Colossians and Philemon, that he was a physician (assuming that this is intended to indicate his literal profession and not a honorific designation due to his abilities in healing prayer), and that he remained true to Paul at the end of Paul's life (2 Tim 4:11).

4:16 *you should read the letter I wrote to them.* The Greek reads "the letter out of Laodicea," which could mean (1) a letter that the Laodiceans wrote; (2) Paul's letter to the Laodiceans, viewed from the position of the Colossians (it would come to them "out of Laodicea"); (3) a circular letter (an encyclical) traveling out from Laodicea to Colosse—this encyclical could be Ephesians (Bruce 1984:310-311). If it were a letter from Laodicea, it is surprising that an author is not named and also surprising that a copy would exist for the Colossians to read, despite its being addressed to someone else (presumably Paul, since he knew about it). The proposal that it was an encyclical has merit because both Ephesians and Colossians were carried by Tychicus and therefore could be viewed as coming "out of Laodicea," and both could be equally viewed as coming from Paul. However, it seems just as likely that what Paul was referring to was a letter from him to the Laodicean church, which has not been preserved.

4:17 *ministry.* The term *diakonia* [TG1248, ZG1355] can mean an act of specific ministry (e.g., Rom 12:7; 15:31; 1 Cor 12:5; 16:15; 2 Cor 8:4; 9:1) or a longer-term ministry (e.g., Rom 11:13; 2 Cor 4:1; 5:18; 6:3). In this latter sense, it would eventually become a technical term for the diaconate. Since Paul indicates in the case of Archippus that this was a ministry that could be fulfilled (apparently without his life being over), it is likely that the former sense is meant, not the more general latter sense.

4:18 *Remember my chains.* For conditions in Roman prisons see Rapske (1994). In ancient prisons there was often the possibility for friends and relatives to bring food, clothing, and other supplies to the prisoners; in fact, often the prison itself did not supply any of these things, so outside support was an absolute necessity for the survival of the prisoner. To prevent escape under these conditions, prisoners were often manacled.

COMMENTARY

The conclusion of the letter falls into three parts, the commendation of the messengers, the greetings, and Paul's final requests and blessing.

Paul has ended the body of his letter. He has come to the conclusion, where he will finish as one appropriately ends a Greco-Roman letter. First, he will attest to the trustworthiness of the letter bearers (4:7-9). Then he will send greetings from various leaders around him (4:10-15). Next he will give a couple of final instructions (4:16-17). Finally, he will take up the stylus himself and write his personal greeting and blessing (4:18). I will look at each of these in turn.

Tychicus was the primary letter carrier (4:7). The job of a letter carrier was not simply that of a postman. The job included reading the letter to the congregation, explaining and expanding anything that needed it, and answering the questions that arose, whether about the content of the letter or about the writer and his situation (Richards 2000). This is the reason why the commendation of the letter carrier was so important and why the authors sometimes say that the person was "faithful" or would explain how things went with the author, for that let the hearers know that the explanations and expansions of the letter carrier were authorized. The letter carrier was authorized to be the first exegete and to expand and fill in as needed. In the New Testament letters, mention is often made regarding such letter carriers, both men (e.g., Titus, some of the Corinthian correspondence; Silvanus, 1 Pet 5:12) and women (Phoebe, Rom 16:1-2). They were the first interpreters of Peter and Paul.

Furthermore, the Pauline churches were bound together not by organizational structure but by personal relationships. Men and women who had worked with Paul as co-workers for periods of time remained behind in this or that city to assist churches in the area, carried letters from Paul to churches or from churches to Paul, or returned to their home communities, bringing with them a web of relationship that bound the various Christian communities together. In the case of Colossians, the letter carrier was Tychicus, whom Acts identifies as an Asian (Acts 20:4), perhaps from the same river system on which Colosse was situated. Since he first appears with Paul at the end of his final visit to Corinth and then as an Asian delegate on Paul's trip to Jerusalem, it is possible that Tychicus became Paul's co-worker while Paul was in Ephesus. At the least, he was an Asian and so native to Asian culture and dialect.

Tychicus was identified as the letter carrier not only for Colossians but also for Ephesians (Eph 6:21) and possibly the Epistle to Titus (Titus 3:12). Paul's point, however, is that he was not only more or less local but also part of the Christian family. The Christian family was viewed as more significant than one's natural family and was treated as a real family. Tychicus is also recognized as a co-worker ("faithful helper" or, better, "faithful minister" and "fellow slave" or co-worker "in the Lord"). The expression "in the Lord" was added by Paul to make it clear that his status in this world was not that of a slave, which was important to state especially since Onesimus, a slave, was part of the group coming to the Colossians (4:9). This is how he described the Colossians themselves in 1:2 and how he described Epaphras in 1:7, which puts Tychicus on a par with Epaphras as a full member of Paul's closest group of companions.

Along with Tychicus went Onesimus, who was commended in similar terms, although not called a co-worker (4:9). Onesimus was certainly the same Onesimus about whom Philemon was written since he is "one of your own people," so presumably he returned from carrying that letter to Philemon. I do not think Colossians and Philemon were carried at the same time because there are some significant changes in the situation of those around Paul in the two greetings. Perhaps Paul omitted the "fellow slave" or co-worker term because Onesimus was new on his team and thus still an apprentice. Or perhaps Paul did not add this term because, given Onesimus's legal status as a slave, it would have been insensitive and perhaps confusing to use this designation for him. Or perhaps Paul did not add it because Onesimus was Philemon's slave and thus Paul did not feel at liberty to call him his fellow slave without a release from Philemon. Whatever the case, these two men, Tychicus and Onesimus, had the same duty: They were to report to the Colossians in detail about Paul's situation, certainly including the situation of the church in the city where he was imprisoned. Since this is repeated three times, it is clearly very important to Paul, even though he had never personally met the members of the believing community in Colosse. Personal relationships rather than church structure bound the early church together. The other job that the letter-carriers had was to encourage the Colossians (4:8; literally to "comfort your hearts"), which probably was intended to come from their personal reports about Paul, as well as from the letter and its interpretation by these two Christian workers.

Having said what he could to make sure that his messengers would be well received, Paul then turned to relaying the greetings from those known to the Colossians. Here again is an indication of the importance of personal relationships in uniting the church. Furthermore, this is another indication that the various Christian communities saw themselves as parts of an extended family and took their family relationships seriously.

The first person to send greetings is Aristarchus, a co-worker of Paul's (4:10; Phlm 1:24). He had come from Thessalonica (Acts 20:4) and had been with Paul during his Ephesian ministry (Acts 19:29). It is probably during this period of ministry that Aristarchus came in contact with some of the Colossians, either because of a trip to Colosse or because some Colossians had visited Ephesus. When Paul wrote Philemon, Aristarchus was not in prison, but at this time he too was a prisoner like Paul.

The second greeting is from "Mark, Barnabas's cousin" (4:10). Barnabas is mentioned because John Mark was closely identified with his cousin throughout the New Testament. According to Acts 13:5, John Mark went with Paul and Barnabas on the first missionary journey, probably due to Barnabas's influence (they were also going to Barnabas's home territory first). Later (Acts 13:13), however, Mark abandoned the mission party—we are not told why. When Paul and Barnabas started to set out again from Jerusalem, Barnabas wanted to take Mark again, perhaps giving him a second chance. Paul was so opposed to this and Barnabas so strongly for it that the missionary pair split, and Barnabas took Mark with him to Cyprus (Acts 15:36-39). Perhaps Barnabas was right and Mark redeemed himself on that trip. Whatever the case on that missions trip, in the years since Mark (and most likely Barnabas also; see 1 Cor 9:6) reconciled with Paul and became and would remain a trusted co-worker. He was also with Paul when Paul wrote Philemon and was there referred to as Paul's co-worker (Phlm 1:24). However, it is likely that Mark had not yet visited Colosse, for Paul had to instruct them to "receive" or "welcome" him, which they might have been reluctant to do if they had only known his early history with Paul and the conflict that this had caused (Acts 15:36-39). Paul was not certain at this time whether Mark would travel to Asia, but apparently they were discussing the idea, for Paul viewed it as expedient to mention the possible trip. At what point he had previously instructed the church to welcome Mark, we do not know. Perhaps there was a previous letter to the Colossians that we know nothing about. What we do know is that 2 Timothy 4:11 pictures Mark as being in or close to Asia and also as being very valued by Paul.

The third greeting is from Jesus Justus (4:11). He, along with Mark and Aristarchus, was identified as a Jew. If we are correct in viewing the false teaching that was threatening the Colossians as essentially Jewish, this indication that three of Paul's co-workers were Jews would demonstrate to the Colossians that some Jews held Paul's point of view. That they alone were with Paul indicates that Timothy, Silvanus (Silas), Aquila, and Priscilla were not then present in Paul's company. This would be surprising if Colossians were written in Rome, for Aquila and Priscilla were last heard of as leading a house church there (see Rom 16:3-5). However, this "only" along with the fact that these three were a comfort to Paul may also indicate Paul's sadness that large numbers of Jews had not joined the Jesus movement, a sadness that he expressed in Romans 9–11. These three, however, were his co-workers, to which title he added the unusual expression "for the Kingdom of God." When Paul speaks of the Kingdom (14 times in the Pauline corpus, half of them in the main Pauline letters), as he has already done once in Colossians (1:13), he normally speaks of inheriting the Kingdom or of the characteristics of the Kingdom, rather than working for the Kingdom. What this indicates is that Acts is correct in characterizing Paul's mission and ministry as revolving around the announcement of the Kingdom of God (Acts 14:22; 19:8; 28:23). In fact, the last we hear about Paul in Acts is that he is "boldly proclaiming the Kingdom of God and teaching about the Lord Jesus Christ" (Acts 28:31). The announcement of the reign of God and Jesus as the agent of that reign was central to Paul's gospel.

The fourth greeting comes from Epaphras (4:12). When Colossians was written Epaphras was not in jail, but when Philemon was written he was (Phlm 1:23). We learned earlier (1:7) that he had brought news about the Colossian believers to Paul and that he had previously ministered in Colosse, from which many hypothesize that he had planted the church there. Here he is identified as a Colossian, which would explain his previous work to see the church established in his city and his present concern for that church. What Paul makes clear is that Epaphras's prayers echo Paul's own. As Paul struggled for them (1:29; 2:1), so does Epaphras; Paul's term refers to wrestling in prayer, a vivid metaphor. As Paul wanted them to be mature and confident, so did Epaphras (1:28; "mature" is better translated "perfect"; cf. "confident," 2:2). And as Paul viewed confidence and maturity as measured by the will of God (cf. 1:9), which, of course, for Paul was found supremely expounded in the life, teaching, and present leadership of Jesus, so also did Epaphras. Here we have a true Pauline co-worker, a Colossian in origin, but of one heart with Paul, presumably having learned how to pray from Paul. Since he was from the Lycus Valley, the focus of his prayers was specifically directed there (4:13). Paul said that he bears witness to the fact that this "slave of Christ Jesus" did not just say that he prayed for his fellow believers at home but did in fact do so. In fact, he labored intensely in prayer, not just for those in Colosse, but also for the two nearby cities Laodicea and Hierapolis. There was certainly a church in Laodicea; however, this is the only mention of Hierapolis in the New Testament. Epaphras might be a long way from Colosse, but his heart was true, and he was doing everything he could for the good of the Colossians, a good that coincided with what Paul wished for these people.

The final greetings come from Luke and Demas (4:14), who also sent greetings in Philemon 1:24. Virtually all we know about Luke comes from this brief passage, except for 2 Timothy 4:11 ("only Luke is with me"), where Paul's love for him was mirrored in Luke's love for Paul. Luke's designation as a physician indicates that he had some learning, although given the unsystematic state of medicine at that time it would be hard to say how much education he had. Nor can we say anything about his status in that slaves were often highly educated by their masters if a particular expertise were needed in the household. Luke could have obtained what training he had as a free man or been trained as a slave and later received his freedom, perhaps as a reward for healing received through his hands. Whatever his previous history, Paul thought highly of him, which contrasts with the negative cast given to physicians in other biblical texts.

Paul's reference to Demas is the shortest of all. Did Paul already suspect that Demas would abandon him (2 Tim 4:10) and so omitted the friendly comments he had for the others, or was Demas hardly known by the Colossians so that Paul just mentioned him as a companion? The answer is unclear from the text.

Paul then instructed the Colossians to greet their neighboring church, that in Laodicea, a three-hour walk across and down the river valley (4:15). The Laodiceans were also part of the family of God (and thus Paul used brother–sister language), and perhaps the Christians in Laodicea were closer parts of the "family" in more than proximity if that church were also started by Epaphras. What we know about Laodicea (besides the references in Rev 3:14-22) is that the church was large enough to consist of more than one house church and that one of the house churches was led by a person whom Paul knew. It would be surprising for Paul to greet the church in general and then specifically greet the only house church in Laodicea, but it would be quite understandable if he greeted the whole church generally and then the one house church specifically whose leader he knew personally. Nympha was apparently a woman of some means since it was usually the wealthier members of the church who hosted the gatherings. She was either single or had a particularly tolerant husband who was not a Christian since her husband was not named. Given that she had met Paul, the former seems more likely since that would have given her the freedom to travel on business, which would be the most likely way that she came across Paul. As host of the church and its common meal, the Lord's Supper, she was also its leader. Paul knew three other leaders in Colosse: Apphia, Archippus, and Philemon (perhaps wife/mother, son, and father/husband respectively). That limited personal knowledge fits with what he said earlier about having never visited the churches in the Lycus Valley. No church or individual believers were greeted in Hierapolis, which probably means that there was as yet no church there, even if the people there were regularly prayed for by Epaphras. Whatever believers were in that city probably worshiped in one of the house churches in Laodicea.

Paul directed the Colossians to send their greetings, and the letter we know as Colossians, to the church in Laodicea; in turn the Colossians were to ask for the letter Paul had written to Laodicea, and both letters were to be read aloud in the sister churches (4:16). In antiquity it was normal for letters to be read aloud to their recipients. Here we see the beginnings of the formation of the Pauline corpus—that is, the recognition that something written to one church with its particular problems could be helpful to another church. This recognition must have driven the later collection of the Pauline letters. But here we also see the problems involved in such a collection since the letter to Laodicea has apparently not survived (unless it was a circular letter and comes to us via the Ephesian copy). Paul apparently thought that this letter was helpful enough that it should be read in a second church, yet we do not have the letter. Either the later church did not share that perspective and so did not preserve the letter or else some accident destroyed it. Either way, it means that neither apostolic authorship nor widespread usefulness were enough to get documents into the canon. The Holy Spirit selected the documents that he wished to be preserved in the canon of Scripture, whether or not they were written by apostles, and allowed others that we might wish to see for ourselves pass into oblivion.

Having made clear that the letters were to be exchanged, Paul turned to Archippus, who was clearly a leader in Colosse, having previously been a companion of Paul (4:17; cf. Phlm 1:2). He was possibly part of Philemon's household, perhaps his son. Whatever the case, Paul knew that Archippus had received some specific commission from the Lord. While some have speculated that it had to do with Onesimus, that seems unlikely in that Onesimus was with Paul when Colossians was being written, and he did not need some ministry in Colosse at that time. It was surely not some general ministry such as preaching or teaching. The fact is we will never know what it was nor how Archippus received the commission from the Lord, although apparently it came during the time he was around Paul since Paul knew about it. What is clear is that he needed some authority or encouragement to carry this ministry out. We must remember that Colossians would be read out loud before the whole church, so everyone would know that Archippus had received some commission from the Lord and had Paul's full backing in carrying it out. It does not matter the reason for Paul's words: whether Archippus was personally reluctant to carry it out or whether Paul was concerned that the church might resist him and so wanted the church to know that Archippus was fully authorized to do what he was doing. In either case the letter would serve to give Archippus the communal encouragement and backing that he might need. Ministry is not simply an individual activity but an activity carried out with the support and encouragement of a community since believers are members of a single family.

Paul had finished his letter. As the custom was, he reached out his hand to take the stylus from the scribe so that he could pen his signature and a few words in his own handwriting at the end of the letter (4:18). While the use of the scribe made the letter more readable, the personal greeting at the end made it more personable, and the author's penning of the final greeting was the custom for papyrus letters in Paul's day—a custom he pointed out on three other occasions (1 Cor 16:21-24; Gal 6:11-18; 2 Thess 3:17-18). After writing "Paul," he then wrote with his own hand: "Remember my chains." This request added to the persuasive force of the letter both because of its pathos and because it pointed to Paul as one who was suffering due to his commitment to Christ and his Kingdom. Yet it was also a genuine request that they could fulfill through prayer, through physical support, and through sending assistants like Epaphras, Onesimus, and Archippus back to Paul. In Paul's world, "remember" did not mean simply to think about something but to take appropriate action because one had thought about something.

Paul ended the letter in a typically Pauline way: "Grace be with you." Philemon 1:25 has a longer version of this short benediction, but some form of the longer version is found in other concluding verses (1 Cor 16:23; 2 Cor 13:14; Gal 6:18; Eph 6:24; 1 Thess 5:28; 2 Thess 3:18). The identical short form is found in 1 Timothy 6:21; 2 Timothy 4:22; Titus 3:15. Grace was what Paul had experienced from God. Grace was how he began the letter (1:2). Grace was how he ended it: "May God's grace be with you."

BIBLIOGRAPHY

Balch, David L.
1981 *Let Wives Be Submissive: The Domestic Code in 1 Peter.* Society of Biblical Literature Monograph Series 26. Chico, CA: Scholars Press.

Barna, George
1990 *The Frog in the Kettle.* Ventura, CA: Regal Books.

Barna Group
2004a "Faith Has a Limited Effect on Most People's Behavior." *The Barna Update.* http://www.barna.org/FlexPage.aspx?Page=BarnaUpdate&BarnaUpdateID=164.

2004b "Born Again Christians Just As Likely to Divorce As are Non-Christians." *The Barna Update.* http://www.barna.org/FlexPage.aspx?Page=BarnaUpdate&BarnaUpdateID=170.

Blanchette, Oliva A.
1961 Does the cheirographon of Col 2:14 represent Christ himself? *Catholic Biblical Quarterly* 23:306–312.

Bornkamm, Gunther
1952 *Das Ende des Gesetzes.* Munich: C. Kaiser.

Bruce, F. F.
1984 *The Epistles to the Colossians, to Philemon, and to the Ephesians.* NICNT. Grand Rapids: Eerdmans.

Cullmann, Oscar
1951 *Christ and Time.* London: SCM Press.

Davids, Peter H.
1990 *The First Epistle of Peter.* New International Commentary on the New Testament. Grand Rapids: Eerdmans.

Davies, W. D.
1955 *Paul and Rabbinic Judaism.* London: Society for the Promotion of Christian Knowledge.

DeLacey, Douglas R.
1993 Gentiles Pp. 335–339 in *Dictionary of Paul and His Letters.* Editors, Gerald F. Hawthorne and Ralph P. Martin. Downers Grove: InterVarsity.

deSilva, David A.
2004 *An Introduction to the New Testament: Contexts, Methods, and Ministry Formation.* Downers Grove: InterVarsity.

Dunn, James D. G.
1996 *The Epistles to the Colossians and to Philemon.* New International Greek Testament Commentary. Grand Rapids: Eerdmans.

Ehrman, Bart D.
2000 *The New Testament: A Historical Introduction to the Early Christian Writings.* New York: Oxford University Press.

Fee, Gordon D.
1994 *God's Empowering Presence.* Peabody, MA: Hendrickson.

Francis, F. O., and Meeks, W. A.
1973 *Conflict in Colossae.* Missoula, MT: Scholars Press.

Freed, Edwin D.
1986 *The New Testament: A Critical Introduction.* Belmont, CA: Wadsworth.

Gorday, Peter
2000 *Colossians, 1-2 Thessalonians, 1-2 Timothy, Titus, Philemon.* Downers Grove: InterVarsity.

Ladd, George Eldon
1993 *A Theology of the New Testament.* Grand Rapids: Eerdmans.

Lightfoot, J. B.
1896 *The Epistles of St. Paul: Colossians and Philemon.* New York: Macmillan.

Lohse, E.
1968 *Die Briefe an die Kolosser und an Philemon.* MeyerK. Göttingen: Vandenhoeck & Ruprecht.

1971 *Colossians and Philemon: a commentary on the Epistles to the Colossians and to Philemon.* Hermeneia. Philadelphia: Fortress Press.

1973 *Die Einheit des Neuen Testaments. Exegetische Studien zur Theologie des Neuen Testaments.* Göttingen: Vandenhoeck & Ruprecht.

Marshall, I. Howard
2004 Marriage, Mutual Love and Submission (Col 3; Eph 5). Pp. 186-204 in *Discovering Biblical Equality.* Editors, Ronald Pierce and Rebecca Groothuis. Downers Grove: InterVarsity.

Martin, Ralph P.
1973 *Colossians and Philemon.* London: Marshall, Morgan, and Scott.

Moule, C. F. D.
1968 *The Epistles to the Colossians and to Philemon.* Cambridge: Cambridge University Press.

Neusner, Jacob
1988 *The Mishnah: a New Translation.* New Haven: Yale University Press.

Noll, Stephen F.
1998 *Angels of Light, Powers of Darkness: Thinking Biblically About Angels, Satan and Principalities.* Downers Grove: InterVarsity Press.

O'Brien, Peter T.
1982 *Colossians, Philemon.* Word Biblical Commentary. Dallas: Word.

Patzia, Arthur G.
1990 *Ephesians, Colossians, Philemon.* NIBC. Peabody, MA: Hendrickson.

Perkins, Pheme
1988 *Reading the New Testament.* New York: Paulist.

Porter, Stanley E.
1997 Tribulation, Messianic Woes Pp. 1179-1182 in *Dictionary of the Latter New Testament and Its Developments.* Editors, Ralph P. Martin and Peter H. Davids. Downers Grove: InterVarsity Press.

Rapske, Brian
1994 *The Book of Acts and Paul in Roman Custody.* Vol. 3 of *The Book of Acts in Its First Century Setting.* Editor, Bruce Winter. Grand Rapids: Eerdmans.

Reicke, Bo
2001 *Re-examining Paul's Letters: The History of the Pauline Correspondence.* Valley Forge: Trinity.

Richards, E. Randolph
2000 Silvanus was not Peter's Secretary: Theological Bias in Interpreting *dia Silouanou . . . egrapsa. Journal of the Evangelical Theological Society* 43:417-432.

Robinson, J. Armitage
1904 *St. Paul's Epistle to the Ephesians.* London: Macmillan.

Schürer, Emil
1986 *The History of the Jewish People in the Age of Jesus Christ.* Edinburgh: T & T Clark.

Wall, Robert W.
1993 *Colossians and Philemon.* Downers Grove: InterVarsity.

1 & 2 Thessalonians

PHILIP W. COMFORT

INTRODUCTION TO
1 & 2 Thessalonians

WRITTEN IN AD 51, these two epistles reflect a time period in the early church that was only 20 years after the time of Jesus Christ's ministry, death, resurrection, and ascension. Among the earliest of the New Testament writings, they capture the excitement and anticipation the earliest Christians had for what they expected to be the imminent return of Christ. At the same time, the two epistles present the earliest and most basic proclamations of the apostles' teachings. As such, 1 and 2 Thessalonians should be read not only for what they teach about Christ's return (known as his Parousia) but also for what they teach about the most fundamental Christian truths—truths that will help us have the kind of spiritual lives that please Christ now and will honor him when he comes again to be glorified in and among his holy people.

AUTHORS

Although most writers ascribe the authorship of 1 and 2 Thessalonians to Paul alone, the evidence of the text itself, corroborated by the historical facts of Acts 15–18, points to multiple authorship. The names of Paul, Silvanus, and Timothy appear at the beginning of 1 and 2 Thessalonians. Plural authorship of 1 Thessalonians is signaled by the first person plural pronouns "we" and "us" appearing throughout the epistle. On three occasions in 1 Thessalonians, Paul speaks his own opinion as distinct from the other authors. In 2:18, we see the statement "I, Paul." Although some could argue that this reveals Paul's sole authorship of 1 Thessalonians, the more likely scenario is that Paul had to personally identify himself as distinct from the other authors. In other words, he had to interrupt the plural authorship to interject a personal note. In 2:18, the authors first say "we wanted very much to come to you," and then Paul interrupts by saying "and I, Paul, tried again and again." Paul had to distinguish himself from Silvanus and Timothy because they had gone back to Thessalonica after the initial visit (see Acts 18:5; 1 Thess 3:1), whereas he had never made it back.

In 1 Thessalonians 3:5, the singular "I" is found, assumed by most readers to be Paul because the speaker indicates that he had sent Timothy to the Thessalonians (an action typical of Paul with respect to his younger co-worker—see 1 Cor 4:17; Phil 2:19). In 5:27, we again see the singular "I," who is assumed to be Paul, but this is not made explicit in the text. In many ancient letters, multiple authors signed off at the end with their own distinct handwriting. Similarly, Paul probably wrote these closing comments in his own handwriting (see note on 1 Thess 5:27). Paul's hand-writing would have been his personal imprimatur of the epistle as expressed in a final exhortation: "I command you in the name of the Lord to read this letter to all the brothers and sisters." In 2 Thessalonians, also, first person plurals ("we" and "us") appear throughout—with only two exceptions where the singular "I" appears twice (2 Thess 2:5; 3:17). In 2:5 we read, "Don't you remember that I told you about all this when I was with you?" Although most commentators assume this to be Paul speaking, we cannot be certain (see note on 2 Thess 2:5). At the end of 2 Thessalonians, Paul clearly states in the penultimate verse: "I write this greeting with my own hand—Paul—which is my signature in every letter" (my translation of 2 Thess 3:17; see note). Paul's personal signature at the end of the letter does not mean he was the sole author of 2 Thessalonians. To the contrary, 2 Thessalonians 3:14 explicitly affirms plural authorship: "Take note of those who refuse to obey what *we* say in this letter." And the last verse of each epistle ends with a plural desig-nation signaling plural writers: "May the grace of *our* Lord Jesus Christ be with you [all]" (1 Thess 5:25; 2 Thess 3:18; my emphasis in both quotations).

We are not certain what part Timothy had in authoring 1 and 2 Thessalonians. He was certainly not the main author, since the first letter says "we sent Timothy . . . our brother and God's co-worker" (1 Thess 3:2) and "Timothy has just returned, bringing us good news" (1 Thess 3:6). These statements indicate that Paul and Silvanus were the senders and receivers of Timothy, thereby distinguishing Timothy's role. As is typ-ical in other epistles where Paul names Timothy as one of the senders at the beginning (2 Corinthians, Colossians, Philemon), it becomes evident in the body of the letter that Timothy was not a coauthor as we would understand the term today. It is likely that since Timothy had provided Paul and Silvanus information about the condition of the church in Thessalonica, he was thereby listed as one of the contributors to 1 and 2 Thessalonians, even though he may not have had a hand in the composition.

This means that 1 and 2 Thessalonians were essentially coauthored by Paul and Silvanus. This is affirmed by 1 Thessalonians 2:2, which says, "You know how badly we had been treated at Philippi." The "we" here is none other than Paul and Silva-nus. (Silvanus could have said this just as easily as Paul, so we need not think that Paul was speaking on their behalf when it could have been the other way around.) As already noted, Paul spoke out individually on occasion and he signed off with his personal signature at the end. This, in fact, shows that he did not pen the main body of the letter, but rather that when the letter was completed, Paul took pen (stylus) in hand to give his personal greeting in his own handwriting. Very likely, the body of the letter was in Silvanus's handwriting, so Paul's final greeting in his own handwriting would be distinct (see 2 Thess 3:17; cf. 1 Cor 16:21; Col 4:18). As noted before, it was customary for multiple-author letters to have one or more signatures with personal greetings at the end.

Silvanus (called Silas in Acts) was a leading Christian in the church at Jerusalem; he was a prophet and a Roman citizen. Silas was one of the two men (along with

Judas Barsabbas) chosen by the church to write the letter of the Jerusalem Council and deliver it to the gentile churches in Antioch, Syria, and Cilicia (Acts 15:22-23). The Greek text of Acts 15:23, *grapsantes* [TG1125, ZG1211] *dia cheiros autōn* (having written it with their hands), refers to "two of the church leaders—Judas (also called Barsabbas) and Silas" in the previous verse (Acts 15:22). It was customary in ancient times for the composer or composers of an epistle to also read the epistle publicly. Thus, Silas and Judas Barsabbas were the two who wrote the letter and read the letter to the church in Antioch (Acts 15:30-31).

When Paul went on his second missionary journey, he took Silas along with him (as a replacement for Mark). Thereafter in the record of Acts, Paul and Silas are seen together raising up the church in Philippi (Acts 16:11-40) and then the church in Thessalonica (Acts 17:1). Though Timothy had joined them prior to both of these events (Acts 16:1-3), he is not specified as having a hand in founding these two churches (although it can be assumed that he was present). Since both Paul and Silas functioned as cofounders of the church at Thessalonica, it stands to reason that they were also the coauthors of the two epistles to the Thessalonians. The entire narrative of Acts 15–18 reveals that these two were a team. Paul would not have written a letter to this church apart from Silas, nor would he merely have used his services as an amanuensis.

First Thessalonians 2:7 indicates that both Paul and Silas were "apostles of Christ." This is "an idiom that identifies both men [as being] personally commissioned by Christ" (DPL 186). Church tradition places Silas among the 70 [or, 72] apostles (see Luke 10:1; Pseudo-Hippolytus, *On the Seventy Apostles* 50; Ante-Nicene Fathers 5.256). As one of this larger group of apostles, he would have been commissioned by Jesus Christ to preach the gospel and heal people in his name (Luke 10:1ff). As one of Jesus' apostles, Silas was among those who saw the risen Christ—probably one of the 500 (1 Cor 15:3-9), who were among the larger group of "apostles." "Although the term *apostles* can be used in the NT more narrowly to refer to the Twelve, the limitation of the apostles to the Twelve plus Paul is a creation of the later church" (DPL 185).

The name Silvanus also appears at the end of 1 Peter (1 Pet 5:12), where the text explicitly states that Peter wrote the epistle "with the help of Silvanus." This means that Silvanus either functioned as an amanuensis for Peter, translated Peter's letter (from Aramaic to Greek) as Peter dictated it, or composed a letter based on Peter's thoughts. The last-mentioned function was not an unusual practice in ancient times nor in modern. Certain people, not gifted with writing, give that task to another, who expresses in words the thoughts of the author. (In modern times, this person is often called a "ghostwriter.")

However we interpret 1 Peter 5:12, it is clear that Silvanus could write Greek well and served Peter in that capacity. This also strongly suggests that he had a hand in the composition of 1 and 2 Thessalonians and was not just named at the beginning of the epistles because he was one of the cofounders of the church at Thessalonica. Of Silvanus's joint authorship of 1 and 2 Thessalonians, F. F. Bruce says, "The *a priori* likelihood that such a man would be a joint-author of letters in which he is named as one of the senders, in a substantial and not a merely nominal sense, is borne out by the internal evidence" (1982:xxxii).

The internal evidence shows that the two epistles are not peculiarly Pauline. Those who study Paul's writings will recognize that the style of 1 and 2 Thessalonians is syntactically, grammatically, and lexically simpler than what one typically finds elsewhere under Paul's name. Furthermore, the substance of the teachings in 1 and 2 Thessalonians is not uniquely Pauline. There is no discussion (or even mention) of justification by faith, the unity of Jews and Gentiles in the one body, and the war between flesh and spirit—to name a few favorite Pauline themes. This is not to say that Paul would disagree with anything in 1 and 2 Thessalonians—after all, he was a cowriter—but it is to say that had Paul himself expressed the same truths they likely would have been more complex and textured.

What we have in 1 and 2 Thessalonians are the basic tenets of the Christian kerygma circulating in the early church. These were the truths of the faith imparted by the apostles, among whom were Paul and Silvanus, as well as by other teachers such as Timothy. Thus, the letters are not distinctively Pauline. No doubt, this is what has caused some scholars to doubt Pauline authorship altogether. F. C. Burkitt thought both the epistles were the work of Silvanus (1924:130-133). Baur (1875–1876:2.85-92) was one of the first to doubt that Paul wrote either 1 or 2 Thessalonians. In Baur's view, 1 Thessalonians was based on the book of Acts, which he believed was written in the second century; and he thought 2 Thessalonians must have been influenced by the Johannine Apocalypse, with the "man of lawlessness" (2 Thess 2:3-10) patterned after the Beast of Revelation 13. However, the notion of the Antichrist preceding the coming of the Christ was discussed even prior to the first century (see Dan 9:24-27; 11:36-45). Other scholars have questioned Paul's authorship because of the difference between the teaching about significant future events in the two letters (see discussion below under "The Order of the Two Epistles"). Some have contested that both are non-Pauline; others argue that 1 Thessalonians is genuine but not 2 Thessalonians (for a good summary, see Green 2002:59-64). But 2 Thessalonians 3:17 (which has Paul's signature) makes it more than clear that Paul was one of its authors. It stands to reason then that the first letter (which is in many ways strikingly similar) was also composed by Paul (with others).

First and Second Thessalonians are the work of three individuals, with Paul and Silvanus functioning more as authors than Timothy did. Among the two, Silvanus probably took the lead in actually writing the epistles in collaboration with Paul, who signed off on both of them. In this commentary, therefore, I will use "the authors" or "the apostles" when speaking of the writers and not "Paul" (as in most commentaries).

OCCASION AND DATE OF WRITINGS

Occasion for Writing 1 Thessalonians According to Acts 17:1-14, Paul, Silas (Silvanus), and Timothy, in the course of their work in the Roman province of Macedonia, came from Philippi to Thessalonica. According to his custom, Paul first went to the synagogue, and for three Sabbaths explained and proved from the Scriptures that the Messiah had to suffer and rise from the dead and that Jesus was that Messiah (Acts 17:1-3; cf. Luke 24:45-46). A small number of Jews responded positively, while a greater contingent of Godfearers and important women of the city accepted the gospel (Acts 17:4). Godfearers were those who had adopted certain aspects of Jewish theology and conduct but had not become full converts to Judaism. Luke did not recount the entire evangelistic effort in the city since the greatest number of Christians converted from paganism (1:9). Thus, the actual time Paul, Silas, and Timothy spent in Thessalonica was certainly more than three weeks (i.e., three Sabbaths) because the authors of 1 Thessalonians spoke of working for their own support so as not to financially burden the Thessalonians (2:9). Furthermore, Philippians 4:16 speaks of the Philippian Christians twice sending help to Paul in Thessalonica.

The positive response to the gospel—especially by Gentiles—stirred up the jealousy of the Jews, who gathered some rabble from the marketplace and started a riot. They rushed the house of Jason where Paul was staying, but when they were unable to find Paul, they dragged his host and some other new believers before the city officials. They accused Paul and Silas of causing civil disturbances elsewhere and faulted Jason for extending hospitality to them (Acts 17:5-7a). The accusation was calculated to generate opposition to the gospel. They also accused the Christian workers of violating the decrees of Caesar ("They are all guilty of treason against Caesar," 17:7b). These decrees had been issued during the reigns of Augustus and Tiberius and were still in effect when Claudius ruled. They prohibited predicting anyone's death, especially that of the emperor. Paul and Silvanus had come to the city proclaiming Jesus Christ's supreme kingship; from their perspective, this appeared to predict an end to the emperor's reign (1:10; 4:16; 2 Thess 2:3-8; see Green 2002:49-51). The Thessalonian officials, anxious to preserve Roman favor, took immediate action. Jason had to post bond as a promise that there would be no further trouble (Acts 17:8-9), and in the end, Paul and his companions left town under cover of night and made their way to Berea (Acts 17:10).

The hostility of the Thessalonian Jews toward Paul is seen in the fact that when they learned he was preaching at Berea, they followed him there and stirred up the crowds against him (Acts 17:13). Paul left that city and was escorted by some Christian brothers to Athens, while Silas and Timothy stayed in Berea. Paul sent word back to Silas and Timothy that they should join him as soon as possible (Acts 17:14-15). Evidently, Silas and Timothy rejoined Paul in Athens, and then Paul and Silas sent Timothy back to Thessalonica to see how the church was faring in the midst of persecution (3:2). Paul left Athens and went to Corinth (Acts 18:1), while Silas possibly stayed in Athens for a while before going on to cities in Macedonia other than Thessalonica—because Timothy seems to have been the sole emissary to the church there. After some time, Silas joined Timothy (perhaps in Thessalonica) and returned with him to Paul in Corinth (Acts 18:5). Timothy reported to both Paul and Silvanus the situation of the church in Thessalonica (3:6-8). Subsequently, Paul, Silvanus, and Timothy wrote an epistle to them, the one known as 1 Thessalonians.

First Thessalonians is an epistle which exudes the joy that Paul, Silvanus, and Timothy felt for the new church at Thessalonica because the believers had continued in faith and love and were standing firm in hope despite the opposition they were facing (3:6-8; Acts 17:5). First Thessalonians is, above all, a letter of thanksgiving to God for the faith, love, and hope of this neophyte church (1:2-3; 2:13; 3:9). Indeed, the whole first section of the letter (1:2-10) is an extended thanksgiving. Paul and Silvanus realized the persecution they had faced in Thessalonica had continued for those they left behind, and they wanted to encourage them to stand fast (2:13-16). They had feared for them but were delighted by the news of their steadfastness (3:1-10).

The letter also deals with the issue (brought to the attention of Paul and Silvanus by Timothy) that there were those who had been maligning the apostles who had raised up the church in Thessalonica. These maligners were most likely the Jews who had initiated opposition to Paul and Silvanus when they were there (Acts 17:5). They probably said that Paul and Silvanus were religious charlatans who had turned them away from their Judaism to a new faith and then departed never to be seen again. So the apostles reminded them of their methods and attitudes among them (2:1-12) and told of their desires and plans to see them again (2:17-18).

Timothy not only conveyed news about the faith, love, and hope of the church (1:3; 3:6-8), he also informed Paul and Silvanus that some in the congregation had ignored their teaching about sexual morality (4:1-8). Sexual immorality was common in pagan life; even prostitution was publicly sanctioned. Some Thessalonian believers had considered the apostles' teaching on the matter to be nothing more than human words, so the apostles needed to affirm that their message came from the Lord.

Timothy must have also told Paul and Silvanus that new leaders had begun to surface in the church. So the apostles needed to remind the believers in Thessalonica to honor such people (5:12-13). Timothy must have also reported that some had rejected prophetic utterances in church meetings. Paul and Silvanus (himself a prophet) told the Thessalonians that they should not reject prophecies but evaluate them (5:19-22). In addition, certain persons within the church were refusing to work, ignoring the apostolic teaching and example in this matter (4:11-12; 5:14). This issue was not resolved by the instructions in 1 Thessalonians, so the writers returned to the problem in the second epistle (2 Thess 3:6-15).

When Timothy reported to Paul and Silvanus, he conveyed some questions the Thessalonians had posed. First, they wanted to know about love among the brothers and sisters of the church (4:9-10). Although we do not know why they voiced this question, Paul assured them that God wanted them to love one another and that, in fact, they were demonstrating true love. Second, the Thessalonians asked what would happen to Christians who died before Christ's return. Paul and Silvanus told them that such people would be the first to be raised from the dead and then snatched away (with the living Christians) to meet the Lord at the time of his parousia (4:13-18). Third, the Thessalonians had questions about when the Day of the Lord would come, the time of Christ's return, and the final consummation. Paul and Silvanus told them that the day would come at an unexpected moment, like a thief comes in the night (5:1-11). This explanation would lead to other questions that would be answered in the second chapter of 2 Thessalonians.

Place and Date of Writing 1 Thessalonians Several ancient scribes must have thought Silas (Silvanus) and Timothy rejoined Paul in Athens and there wrote the first epistle to the Thessalonians because the subscription in several ancient manuscripts (A B[1] 1739* 0278) indicates that Athens was the place of writing. But this epistle was most likely written from Corinth (so Codex 81). We gather this because Acts 18:5 speaks of Timothy and Silas coming back from Macedonia to join Paul in Corinth.

The writer of Acts notes that Paul spent a year and a half in that city, during which time Gallio was the proconsul of the Roman province of Achaia (Acts 18:11-12). Paul had to appear before Gallio to answer charges against him. This historical situation pertaining to these verses helps us reconstruct the date in which 1 Thessalonians was written.

The proconsul Gallio, while in Corinth, had referred a question to the Emperor Claudius (who reigned AD 41–54), and "the Emperor's reply to him is found in an inscription in Delphi from Emperor Claudius (*Sylloge Inscriptionum Graecarum* ii[3], 801). The inscription is dated in the period of Claudius's twenty-sixth acclamation as *imperator*—a period known from other inscriptions (*Corpus Inscriptionum Latinarum* iii.476, vi.1256) to have covered the first seven months of A.D. 52" (Bruce 1982:xxxv). According to Morris (1991:13), "the date given in the inscription is the 12th year of Claudius's power as a tribune, and after his 26th acclamation as Emperor. His 12th year was from January 25, 52 to January 24, 53. The date of the 26th acclamation is not exactly known, but the 27th acclamation took place before August 1, 52. That means that the Emperor's decision [about Gallio's request] would have been given in the months preceding this. Thus, it must have been during the earlier rather than the later part of the year 52. It was the custom of proconsuls to assume their office in early summer, which makes it unlikely that Gallio began his term in 52. It does not seem possible for him to assume office, come across the difficulty, refer the question to Claudius, and receive his answer in time. He must have been in office a year earlier, that is, in 51."

Paul had to appear before Gallio some time while Gallio was in office in Corinth, which was only for two years. Due to illness, Gallio returned to Rome after just beginning a one-year or, at most, hardly finishing a two-year tenure (Pliny the Elder, *Natural History* 31.62). This means that Gallio was serving as proconsul in Corinth in the year 51 or 52 (at the latest). Paul had come to Corinth in the first half of the preceding year, 50. As soon as Timothy and Silas joined him in Corinth and Paul heard the news from Timothy about the situation in Thessalonica, it is likely that the letter was penned and sent to them. Thus, 1 Thessalonians must have been written in 51.

Occasion for Writing 2 Thessalonians The first verse of the epistle indicates that Paul, Silvanus, and Timothy were still together at the time of writing (1:1). Probably a short time after writing 1 Thessalonians (see discussion below on "Place and Date of Writing"), they heard of the ongoing situation with the Christians in Thessalonica, and, in their concern for them, wrote a second epistle. Second Thessalonians 3:11 says, "we hear that some of you are living idle lives." Who did they hear this from? Holmes suggests that "in view of Thessalonica's location between Philippi and Corinth, one possibility is that someone from the church in Philippi, delegated to deliver a financial gift to Paul in Corinth (see Phil 4:15-16), shared with Paul information acquired while passing through Thessalonica" (1998:23).

Whoever brought word about the situation in Thessalonica, the most disturbing news was that the Thessalonians had been told that the Day of the Lord (i.e., Christ's *parousia* [TG3952, ZG4242]) had already happened or had already begun. Second Thessalonians 2:2 says, "Don't be so easily shaken or alarmed by those who say that the day of the Lord has already begun. Don't believe them, even if they claim to have had a spiritual vision, a revelation, or a letter supposedly from us." Though it is possible that this statement served only as a warning, it seems more likely that it speaks of something that had already occurred (which is the opinion of every commentator I have read). Therefore, it was false prophecy, more than anything, which prompted the writing of 2 Thessalonians.

In addition to this, the Thessalonians were still undergoing severe persecution, as can be gathered from the writers' words in chapter 1. As was noted above in the discussion (see "Occasion for Writing 1 Thessalonians"), the Thessalonians were still being persecuted by their own countrymen. This elicited some powerful promises about the Lord eventually rescuing them at the time of his parousia, as well as some severe pronouncements about the vengeance that the Lord would exercise against those who persecuted the Thessalonian believers.

Place and Date of Writing 2 Thessalonians Whenever 2 Thessalonians was written, it had to have been during a time when Paul, Silvanus, and Timothy were still together (2 Thess 1:1). As far as we know from the record in Acts, this occurred during Paul's stay in Corinth, which lasted 18 months (Acts 18:11-17)—from "the late summer of A.D. 50 to the spring of A.D. 52" (Bruce 1982:xxxv). There is no further mention of Silas in the book of Acts after 18:5. He is mentioned again in the New Testament in 2 Corinthians 1:19 in connection with the trio's ministry in Corinth. Thus, it stands to reason that the second epistle to the Thessalonians was written by the three of them while they were in Corinth. Because only a few months had passed since the composition of the first letter, we may date 2 Thessalonians in AD 51, making it the third oldest of the surviving Pauline Epistles (if Galatians is dated AD 49).

The Order of the Two Epistles In extant ancient manuscripts, 1 Thessalonians (labeled as "To the Thessalonians A [= 1]") always precedes the epistle we know as 2 Thessalonians (labeled as "To the Thessalonians B [= 2]"). This can be seen in such manuscripts as 𝔓30 𝔓46^vid ℵ A B Ψ and 1739. Greek editions and English translations have followed the same order. However, books were arranged in the New Testament canon according to length (the longer book before the shorter), not according to chronology. So the order that has come down to us does not necessarily represent the chronological order of the two epistles to the Thessalonians. In fact, various scholars think the order should be reversed. Their reasons for doing so are explained cogently by Bruce (1982:xl-xlvi) and Morris (1991:26-30), who both aptly defend the traditional order.

In short, those who have argued for the priority of 2 Thessalonians have noted that Paul's personal signature at the end of the epistle (2 Thess 3:17), with the attached note that this signature authenticated the letter, would seem to be needed for a first letter to a church, not a second. But this argument can be countered when we recognize that Paul did this in 2 Thessalonians to guard against any potential forgeries, as noted in the previous chapter (2:2). Furthermore, the Thessalonians could compare the two handwritings—that of Paul's final greeting in 1 Thessalonians 5:27-28 (which would have been in his own hand regardless of who actually penned the main body of the epistle), and that of the signature in 2 Thessalonians 3:17.

Another argument for the priority of 2 Thessalonians is that it seems odd that the authors of 1 Thessalonians would say that the Thessalonians did not need to be taught about the timing of the Lord's second coming (1 Thess 5:1) without having first read 2 Thessalonians 2:1-12. But this previous teaching did not have to come to them via the written word; it could have been communicated orally. In fact, in the middle of 2 Thessalonians 2:1-12 Paul or Silvanus personally noted, "Don't you remember that I told you about all this when I was with you?" (2 Thess 2:5).

Yet another argument for the priority of 2 Thessalonians is that the believers' persecution is ongoing according to 2 Thessalonians 1:4-7, whereas in 1 Thessalonians it appears to be over. Though this impression seems fair enough, 1 Thessalonians never says that their persecution was over; rather, the authors were commending them for how they had endured the persecutions up to the present moment.

In the end, the best argument for the traditional order comes straight from the text of 2 Thessalonians. In 2:15, the authors write, "dear brothers and sisters, stand firm and keep a strong grip on the teaching we passed on to you both in person and by letter." These teachings had been given to the Thessalonians when Paul, Silvanus, and Timothy had been with them (Acts 17) and when Paul, Silvanus, and Timothy had written them an epistle—which has no reference to a previous letter. Thus, 1 Thessalonians likely came before 2 Thessalonians.

AUDIENCE

According to Strabo, the famous Greek geographer, Thessalonica was founded in 315 BC by the Macedonian general Cassander, who named it after his wife, the daughter of Philip and half-sister of Alexander the Great. It was settled by refugees from a large number of towns in the same region that had been ravaged by war.

When Macedonia was divided into four districts (167 BC), Thessalonica was made the capital of the second district. Its influence continued to expand when the area became a Roman province. In the second civil war between Octavian (Augustus Caesar) and Pompey (42 BC), Thessalonica remained loyal to Antony and Octavian. Consequently, it was rewarded with the status of being a free city. This gift of autonomy allowed the city to appoint its own magistrates, who were given the unusual title of politarchs.[1] Cicero, a Roman statesman who lived shortly before the time of Christ, spent seven months in exile at Thessalonica, giving further testament to the city's prominence in the region.

In addition to having an excellent harbor, Thessalonica was located on the major route from Italy to the East. This famous highway, called the Egnatian Way, went by the northwest corner of the city. Two Roman arches, the Vardar Gate and the Arch of Galerius, marked the western and eastern boundaries. The population of Thessalonica included Macedonians, Romans, Jews, and other peoples who settled in the city. Many of the Romans who settled there became wealthy benefactors in the town. The city integrated these Romans, some of them becoming chief city officials (*politarchs*, see Acts 17:6, 8 and endnote 1). A number of inscriptions in the city were written both in Latin (the Roman language) and in Greek (the language spoken by the Macedonians). The Jewish population was large enough to have a synagogue (Acts 17:1), though we do not know the exact size of this community. While some Thessalonian Jews converted to Christ when Paul preached in the synagogue, the majority of the converts were Roman or Macedonian Gentiles who abandoned idolatry to follow Christ (1 Thess 1:9). Thus, Acts 17 does not give us the complete record of the evangelistic efforts there inasmuch as we are told by Luke that it was Jews and Godfearers who received the gospel.

The fact that there is not one direct quotation from the Old Testament in 1 and 2 Thessalonians shows that both Paul and Silvanus must have made a conscious effort to communicate with a gentile audience unfamiliar with the Jewish Scriptures. This also seems to demonstrate that their writing was planned and collaborative.

CANONICITY AND TEXTUAL HISTORY

The canonicity of 1 and 2 Thessalonians is evidenced by the fact that they were included in the earliest collections of New Testament writings circulating in the early church. Specifically, 1 and 2 Thessalonians were included in the earliest codices containing Paul's Epistles. The practice of compiling works in a codex was first adopted by Christians for the sake of placing all of Paul's Major Epistles (Romans— 2 Thessalonians) into one volume—inasmuch as this was a sought-after and recognized collection in the life of the early church. (This doesn't completely discount the possibility that the codex format was first used for the fourfold Gospel,[2] but Paul's Epistles were likely first because they were written earlier than the Gospels and because they circulated among the churches as a group before the four Gospels did.) Of particular note is the indication in 2 Peter 3:15-16 that Paul's writings (as a collection) were considered "Scripture" early in the life of the church. Züntz (1953:271-272) was convinced that Paul's Major Epistles were a well-known canonized collection by AD 100. Gamble (1995:53-57) also argued that the Pauline collection was assembled by the end of the first century. Manuscripts evidencing a Pauline collection are as follows: 𝔓46 (second century, all of Paul's Major Epistles), 𝔓15+𝔓16 (third century, from the same codex, preserving portions of 1 Corinthians and Philippians), 𝔓30 (third century, containing portions of 1 and 2 Thessalonians), 𝔓49+𝔓65 (third century, containing portions of Ephesians and 1 Thessalonians), and 𝔓92 (third century, containing portions of Ephesians and 2 Thessalonians). Collections of Pauline Letters as individual volumes (exclusive of other books of the New Testament) continue to appear in the following centuries, as evidenced in Codex I (fifth century), 0208 (sixth century), and 0209 (seventh century). (For further discussion, see Comfort 2005:34-37.)

The manuscript evidence indicates that 1 and 2 Thessalonians have been part of the Pauline collection of Epistles as early as the second century and probably earlier. This is most evident in Chester Beatty II, also known as 𝔓46, a codex of Paul's Epistles dated to the middle to late second century (for a detailed discussion of this dating, see Comfort 2005:136-144). The extant portion of 𝔓46 preserves Romans 5:17 through 1 Thessalonians 5:28 (with Hebrews following Romans). The lost leaves on the front end of the codex (seven leaves = fourteen pages) would have been filled by Romans 1:1–5:16. The seven leaves on the back end would have easily been filled by 2 Thessalonians and Philemon, with about nine pages left blank.[3]

There are three third-century papyri that were part of a Pauline collection that contained either 1 or 2 Thessalonians or both. 𝔓30 (also known as P. Oxyrhynchus 1598) contains 1 Thessalonians 4:12-13, 16-17; 5:3, 8-10, 12-18, 25-28; 2 Thessalonians 1:1-2; 2:1, 9-11.[4] Two papyri that were originally part of one codex, 𝔓49 and 𝔓65, contain 1 Thessalonians 1:3-10; 2:1, 6-13.[5] The papyrus 𝔓92 (P. Narmuthis 69.39a + 69.229a), dated c. 300, contains portions of Ephesians (1:11-13, 19-21) and of 2 Thessalonians (1:4-5, 11-12).[6] The three papyri (𝔓30, 𝔓49+65, 𝔓92), together with the testimony of 𝔓46, indicate that the Thessalonian epistles were part of a Pauline canon in the second, third, and fourth centuries.

The epistles of 1 and 2 Thessalonians appear in the oldest extant lists of books in the New Testament canon. They appear in the Muratorian Canon (late second century), as well as the canon created by Marcion (c. 160). Thereafter, 1 and 2 Thessalonians appear in all the major New Testament canons, such as those indicated by Eusebius in his *Ecclesiastical History*, Athanasius of Alexandria in his *Festal Letter* (AD 367), and the Council of Carthage (AD 397). Several of the early church fathers cited portions of 1 and 2 Thessalonians, including Polycarp (*To the Philippians* §11); Irenaeus (*Against Heresies* 5.6.1); Clement of Alexandria (*Christ the Educator* 1.17, 88); and Tertullian (*The Resurrection of the Body* §24).

As for textual fidelity, the best witnesses to the original wording of 1 and 2 Thessalonians are the papyri 𝔓30 𝔓46 𝔓49+𝔓65 𝔓92 (Comfort 2005:318-319), as well as א B A C H𝗉 I Ψ 33 81 104 326 1739 (Metzger 1992:216). Züntz

(1953:212-213) makes it clear that 𝔓46, B, and 1739 are primary manuscripts for Paul's Major Epistles and Hebrews (which was considered part of the Pauline corpus by the early church). The so-called "Western" manuscripts of 1 and 2 Thessalonians are the Greek-Latin diglots Dᵖ Eᵖ Fᵖ Gᵖ; Greek fathers to the end of the third century; the Old Latin and early Latin fathers; and Syrian fathers to about 450. The Byzantine manuscripts are L, 049, and most minuscules.

LITERARY STYLE

Both 1 and 2 Thessalonians are among the earliest and most pristine examples of what has come to be known as the New Testament epistles. The epistle was a well-known literary form in Hellenistic times. It was used for both simple friendly letters and formal treatises. The New Testament writers used it in both ways, such that their epistles conveyed messages between friends as well as comprehensive Christian teachings. Indeed, much of New Testament doctrine comes from what the apostles wrote in their epistles.

A year before composing 1 and 2 Thessalonians, Silas had participated in writing an encyclical epistle appearing in Acts 15:23b-29. In fact, he was one of the two men (along with Judas Barsabbas) chosen by the church to write and deliver the letter of the Jerusalem Council (assembled in AD 50) to the gentile churches in Antioch, Syria, and Cilicia (Acts 15:22-23). (See discussion of Silas in "Authors," above.) Paul, also present at that first church council, realized the authority behind the letter that emerged from it. It was authoritative because it was apostolic, and it was received as God's Word. If an epistle came from an apostle (or apostles), it was to be received as having the imprimatur of the Lord. Building on this precedent, Paul and Silvanus wanted the churches to receive their words as being the word of the Lord. This is made explicit in 1 Thessalonians (1 Thess 2:13), an epistle they insisted had to be read to all the believers in the church (1 Thess 5:27). In their second epistle, Paul and Silvanus indicated that their epistles carry the same authority as their preaching (see 2 Thess 2:15).

Those who have studied Paul's Epistles cannot help but recognize that 1 and 2 Thessalonians are the easiest to read and understand. There are few long sentences like there are in Ephesians. There are no complicated arguments drawn from Old Testament Scriptures as readers encounter in Galatians. In fact, there are no direct quotations of the Old Testament at all in 1 and 2 Thessalonians. There are no arguments against Gnosticism as one finds in Colossians. There are few church problems to address, contrary to what readers face in 1 Corinthians. Though there is a little biography presented in these two epistles, it is far easier to grasp than what one must deal with in 2 Corinthians or Philippians. And, finally, the theology of 1 and 2 Thessalonians is far more basic and pristine than what readers encounter in a book like Romans. As will be discussed in the next section, this simplicity accords with the fact that Paul and Silvanus together were presenting the kerygma (the proclamation) of the early apostles. Had these two epistles come from Paul alone, we would probably see more elaboration. (After all, many scholars think Galatians was written prior to 1 and 2 Thessalonians, and one need not read too far in that epistle to see Paul's elaborate argumentation.) The collaborative nature of 1 and 2 Thessalonians put a check on Pauline individualism. The message is direct and easy to follow because the style is poignant and felicitous. Most likely, Silvanus (as the actual writer) should get the credit for this (see discussion under "Authors" above).

MAJOR THEMES

Before we look at some of the major themes, it is necessary to recognize that 1 and 2 Thessalonians are among the earliest New Testament books—if not *the* earliest (depending if one dates Galatians to AD 49 or to 56/57—see discussion on date in Borchert 2007). The Thessalonian writings present the Christian truths as assimilated and propagated by the apostles and other leaders during the 30s and 40s. Thus, they contain the basic, primitive aspects of the gospel. Many of the themes found in these two books come to us in seed form; in later writings they grow into fuller form.

Eschatology First and Second Thessalonians are most noteworthy for their passages about the end times and Jesus Christ's *parousia* [TG3952, ZG4242], in our parlance, the "coming again" of Jesus Christ. His parousia is highlighted four times in 1 Thessalonians (1 Thess 2:19; 3:13; 4:15; 5:23) and twice in 2 Thessalonians (2 Thess 2:1, 8) in the midst of important eschatological passages.
1 Thessalonians:
2:19 "What will be our proud reward and crown as we stand before our Lord Jesus when he *returns?*"
3:13 "May he [the Lord], as a result, make your hearts strong, blameless, and holy as you stand before God our Father when our Lord Jesus *comes again.*"
4:15 "We who are still living when the Lord *returns* will not meet him ahead of those who have died."
5:23 "May the God of peace make you holy in every way, and may your whole spirit and soul and body be kept blameless until our Lord Jesus Christ *comes again.*"
2 Thessalonians:
2:1 "Let us clarify some things about *the coming* of our Lord Jesus Christ and how we will be gathered to meet him."
2:8 "The Lord Jesus will kill him [the man of lawlessness] with the breath of his mouth and destroy him by the splendor of his *coming.*"
As these are the earliest statements in the New Testament concerning the Parousia, they are significant. First of all, it must be noted that the term was used in the earliest decades of the church as a common expression for Jesus Christ's return. It was not unique to Paul, who used the term only once with respect to Jesus' coming outside the Thessalonian epistles (1 Cor 15:23). (This, again, shows that 1 and 2 Thessalonians are the embodiment and expression of the early church's kerygma and not uniquely Pauline.) It is very likely that Jesus himself was responsible for inaugurating this term to describe his second coming. In Matthew 24, a chapter that

focuses entirely on Jesus' presentation of eschatology, the term is found four times. Though Matthew was written later than 1 and 2 Thessalonians, it may very well preserve terminology used by Jesus and the apostles (see Matt 24:3, where the disciples ask Jesus a question about his parousia; and see Matt 24:27, 37, 39 where Jesus three times speaks about the Parousia of the Son of Man).

The main teaching on the Parousia in 1 Thessalonians is found in chapter 4, which pertains to the matter of who will meet Jesus at his coming—namely, those Christians who have died and those who are alive at the time. Following this teaching, the authors indicate that this coming will be sudden and unexpected like a thief in the night (1 Thess 5:2). The main teaching on the Parousia in 2 Thessalonians is found in chapter 2, which presents certain events that must precede the coming of Jesus.

Some scholars have seen these as contradictory teachings and thereby claimed that either 1 or 2 Thessalonians was a fraud (see discussion above). But it must be remembered that Jesus' teachings on the Parousia also have this tension. For example, in Mark 13, Jesus' discourse on the end times focuses on the prominent signs (Mark 13:1-31) and then concludes with statements telling his disciples that they will not know when the time will come and therefore must be vigilant (Mark 13:32-37). This accords with Jewish eschatology where we see the same juxtaposition of the prophecy that the end will come at an unexpected moment and also that there will be certain signs before the end comes (Marshall 1983:37; Morris 1991:20). Another perspective is that the image of the Parousia as sudden and unexpected like a thief in the night pertains only to the unwatchful masses, whereas for watchful Christians, the coming is preceded by certain events. First Thessalonians contains statements that reveal both positions (cf. 1 Thess 5:2 with 5:4).

The Theology of 1 and 2 Thessalonians First and Second Thessalonians are very forward-looking as to the work of Jesus Christ, especially in comparison to many other epistles that look back on Christ's death and resurrection and then attribute spiritual significance to these events. The authors of 1 and 2 Thessalonians present Jesus Christ as one who suffered and died without any reference to what that death accomplished in terms of redemption or salvation. The authors simply indicate that Jesus Christ rose from the dead without giving any interpretation to the event. Most of their Christology is presented with the view that Jesus Christ, who recently went to heaven (i.e., just 20 years earlier) would soon return from heaven to carry out many significant events: (1) the resurrection of dead Christians (1 Thess 4:15-16); (2) salvation of the believers from their persecutors (2 Thess 1:5-9); (3) the Rapture of the Christians living at the time of Jesus' parousia (1 Thess 4:17); (4) the gathering together of all the believers in the presence of the Lord (1 Thess 4:17; 2 Thess 2:1); (5) the destruction of the lawless one, whom the Lord Jesus will slay with the spirit of his mouth (2 Thess 2:8); and (6) the complete sanctification of Christians—body, soul, and spirit (1 Thess 5:23).

What is most evident to me as I study these epistles is that the authors were presenting the gospel of God that was current in their thinking and preaching, a gospel that was focused preeminently on the imminent return of Jesus Christ. As the church grew older, its theology became more mature, especially with respect to the signifi-cance of Christ's death and resurrection, as well as his incarnation and ascension. Furthermore, later writings provide greater understanding about the deity of Jesus Christ. Nonetheless, both 1 and 2 Thessalonians contain language that ascribes deity to Jesus (see notes and commentary on 1 Thess 3:11-13; 2 Thess 1:12).

In 1 and 2 Thessalonians the authors present a very clear view of God's role in the believers' salvation and life. Believers are those who have experienced the calling of God (1 Thess 2:13; 4:7; 5:24; 2 Thess 1:11) because they are the chosen ones of God (1 Thess 1:4; 5:9; 2 Thess 2:13). Their salvation comes when they hear and believe the gospel of God, which is none other than the Word of God (1 Thess 1:8; 2:2, 8, 13). The goal of their salvation is holiness, a necessary condition for being ready for the parousia of Jesus (1 Thess 3:13; 4:3, 7; 5:23-24).

The Holy Spirit is instrumental in the entire process of the Christian life—from salvation to complete sanctification. When the Thessalonians first heard the gospel, it was the Spirit that empowered it (1 Thess 1:5). When they encountered persecu-tion, they were inspired by the Spirit to face it with joy (1 Thess 1:6). All throughout their Christian lives, whether in suffering or in joy, God gives believers the Holy Spirit (1 Thess 4:8) to be the presence of God in their lives and in their meetings (1 Thess 5:19). It is the Holy Spirit who makes the believers holy and thereby pre-pared to meet the Lord Jesus with confidence (1 Thess 5:23).

OUTLINE OF 1 THESSALONIANS

OUTLINE OF 2 THESSALONIANS (COMMENTARY BEGINS ON P. 381)

ENDNOTES

1. The historical accuracy of Acts is seen in the fact that while the term *politarch* does not appear in earlier Greek literature, it is used in Acts 17:6-8 and has been found on an inscription on the Vardar Gate and in other inscriptions from the area. At the beginning of the first century, Thessalonica had a council of five politarchs.

2. Scholars such as T. C. Skeat and Graham Stanton have provided convincing arguments that the Christians' adoption of the codex was motivated by a desire to establish the fourfold Gospel as the authoritative norm for the church. See T. C. Skeat, "Irenaeus and the Four-Gospel Canon" in *Novum Testamentum* 34 (1992):194-199; "The Earliest Gospel Codex?" in *New Testament Studies* 43 (1997):1-34; and see Graham Stanton, "The Fourfold Gospel" in *New Testament Studies* 43 (1997):317-346.

3. The missing leaves could not have accommodated all the Pastoral Epistles (1 and 2 Timothy, Titus), even if the scribe attempted to fit more letters per page. Of course, the scribe could have added another two leaves (= 4 pages) at the end of the codex to accommodate all three Pastoral Epistles. Such a practice was not unheard of, but was rare. The more usual practice was to add one leaf, not two, if and when the scribe realized he was running out of room. The long and short of this is that we cannot be certain whether or not 𝔓46 contained the Pastoral Epistles. For a full discussion of this matter, see Jeremy Duff, "𝔓46 and the Pastorals: A Misleading Consensus?" *New Testament Studies* 44 (1998):578-590.

4. A few new portions of 𝔓30 in 2 Thess 2 were identified by Comfort and Barrett (2001:128-133)—namely, 2:1, 10-11; the authors also offer a different reading for this manuscript on 2 Thess 1:1 (see note).

5. 𝔓49 is in New Haven, Connecticut: Yale University Library (inv. 415 + 531); 𝔓65 is in Florence, Italy: Istituto di Papirologia G. Vitelli. 𝔓49 contains Eph 4:16-29; 4:31–5:13; 𝔓65 contains 1 Thess 1:3-10; 2:1, 6-13. 𝔓49 was first published in 1948 by Hatch and Welles. 𝔓65 was published by Bartoletti in 1957, who indicated that he thought 𝔓49 and 𝔓65 were produced by the same scribe. 𝔓49 (which is Yale Papyrus 415 + 531) was republished in a superior transcription by Oates and Welles in the Yale Papyri series. These editors then affirmed that the two manuscripts (𝔓49 and 𝔓65) came from the same hand. Both manifest a very idiosyncratic formation of certain letters, such as the tilted *lambda*, tilted *sigma*, doubled curved and extended *iōta*, and long-tailed *upsilon*. Welles remarked that "there is not a single case of difference in the letter shapes in the two papyri." And in both manuscripts the nomina sacra are written with a crossbar extending to the right, the width of one letter. Furthermore, in both manuscripts there are marginal bounding marks that served to help the scribe keep the left margin fairly straight and vertical. I have presented further details for the position that the two manuscripts are part of the same codex in Comfort and Barrett 2001:355-358; Comfort 2005:177-180.

6. For photograph and transcription, see Comfort and Barrett 2001:624-626.

COMMENTARY ON
1 Thessalonians

◆ I. Opening of the Letter (1:1–10)
A. Greetings from Paul, Silvanus, and Timothy (1:1)

This letter is from Paul, Silas,* and Timothy.

We are writing to the church in Thessalonica, to you who belong to God the Father and the Lord Jesus Christ.

May God give you grace and peace.

1:1 Greek *Silvanus*, the Greek form of the name.

NOTES

1:1 *Paul*. He is listed at the beginning of 13 epistles, sometimes alone (Romans, Galatians, Ephesians, 1 and 2 Timothy, Titus), and at other times with another co-worker or two—namely, Timothy (2 Corinthians, Philippians, Colossians, 1 and 2 Thessalonians, Philemon), Sosthenes (1 Corinthans), or Silvanus (1 and 2 Thessalonians).

***Silas*.** Lit., "Silvanus." Silas was probably a Semitic name, possibly seila, the Aramaic form of Saul. There is little doubt that he is to be identified with "Silvanus" (1:1; 2 Cor 1:19; 2 Thess 1:1; 1 Pet 5:12), which is probably the Latinized form of "Silas" (NBD 1112). Silvanus was a coauthor of this epistle (see "Authors" in the Introduction and commentary).

***Timothy*.** He is here listed with Paul, as in four other epistles (2 Corinthians, Colossians, 2 Thessalonians, Philemon). See Introduction under "Authors" and commentary for a discussion of Timothy's participation in writing this epistle.

***the church*.** The word *ekklēsia* [TG1577, ZG1711] was used in common parlance to denote the assembly of free citizens in a Greek city (Acts 19:32, 39, 41). This familiar, nonreligious term among the Greeks was picked up by the NT writers in its most basic meaning of "gathering" to describe the assembly of believers. The term was also used in the LXX to refer to the assembly of God's people and may have been carried over into the NT from there.

***in Thessalonica*.** Lit., "of the Thessalonians."

***you who belong to God the Father and the Lord Jesus Christ*.** There is no uniformity in Paul's Epistles as to how each of the local churches are described: (1) all God's beloved in Rome (Rom 1:7); (2) the church of God in Corinth (1 Cor 1:2; 2 Cor 1:1); (3) the churches of Galatia (Gal 1:2); the holy ones [in Ephesus] (Eph 1:1); (4) the holy ones in Christ Jesus in Philippi (Phil 1:1); (5) the holy ones and faithful in Christ in Colosse (Col 1:2); and (6) the church of the Thessalonians in God the Father and Lord Jesus Christ (1:1; 2 Thess 1:1). It is worthy of note that the epistles addressed to the same localities get the same designations twice in a row, perhaps suggesting that Paul or his amanuensis kept and used the exemplar when writing the next epistle. Other than that, the common element of the Pauline Epistles is that the locality is always listed.

***grace and peace*.** This reading has the support of B F G 044 0278 1739 it cop^sa. Other manuscripts (ℵ A D I 33 𝔐 syr^h** cop^bo) add "from God our Father and the Lord Jesus

Christ." Had this phrase originally been in the text, there is no good reason to explain why it was deleted. Rather, it is easier to understand why it was added. In the introduction to nearly all of his epistles, Paul gave the blessing of grace and peace as coming from God the Father and Lord Jesus Christ (see Rom 1:7; 1 Cor 1:3; 2 Cor 1:2; Gal 1:3; Eph 1:2; Phil 1:2; 2 Thess 1:2; 1 Tim 1:2; 2 Tim 1:2; Phlm 1:3). Thus, it would seem very unusual to some scribes for it not to be the same here; consequently, the verse was conformed to Pauline style. But the authors of 1 Thessalonians chose not to use the expression "God the Father and Lord Jesus Christ" twice in a row (the first part of the verse reads, "to the church in Thessalonica, to you who belong to God the Father and the Lord Jesus Christ"), so they wrote a short blessing: "May God give you grace and peace." Indeed, "grace and peace" was the most primitive expression, which then became elongated in subsequent epistles. The simple expression (without attaching divine names) may have come from the hand of Silvanus, the writer of 1 Pet (cf. 1 Pet 1:2). "Grace" (*charis*) is the usual Greek greeting, and "peace" (*eirēnē*) is derived from the usual Jewish greeting (*shalom*).

COMMENTARY

Ancient letters opened with a prescript, which consisted of three elements: the sender(s), the recipient, and the salutation (cf. Weima 2000b:642). Thus, all letters followed this pattern: (1) X (in the nominative case); (2) to Y (in the dative case); (3) greetings. An example from the first century illustrates this:

> Seneca to his own Lucilius, greeting.
> (Seneca, *Moral Essays* Letter 6, c. AD 62–64)

The adaptation in 1 Thessalonians is as follows:
  1. Senders: Paul, Silvanus, and Timothy.
  2. Recipients: to the church of the Thessalonians.
  3. Greeting: Grace to you and peace.

Following these three elements, a traditional letter would often have a wish for good health (as in 3 John 1:2) or a thanksgiving formula (as in what follows in 1:2).

The three senders of 1 Thessalonians are listed as Paul, Silvanus (otherwise known as Silas), and Timothy. Paul and Silvanus were the founders of the church at Thessalonica (Acts 17:1-14) and the main coauthors of this epistle (see the full discussion on this in the Introduction under "Authors")—with Timothy functioning as a contributor to its content. First and Second Thessalonians are unique among all the New Testament books in that they were the products of multiple authorship. Even in the other epistles where more than one person's name appears at the head (Paul and Sosthenes in 1 Corinthians; Paul and Timothy in 2 Corinthians, Philippians, and Colossians), the author is clearly Paul, who uses the singular "I" throughout the body of each epistle. Joint composition of letters was known in the ancient world. For example, in Cicero's letter *To Atticus* he says, "For my part I have gathered from your letters—both that which you wrote in conjunction with others and the one you wrote in your own name . . ." (11.5.1). We are not certain what part Timothy had in authoring 1 Thessalonians. He was probably not the actual writer, and he was very likely not one of the main authors, since the letter says, "We sent Timothy to visit you. He is our brother and God's co-worker" (3:2) and "But now Timothy has just returned" (3:6). These statements indicate that Paul and Silvanus sent and received Timothy, thereby excluding Timothy from the authorial "we." Nonetheless, Timothy supplied information concerning the situation at Thessalonica and thereby became an important contributor to the content of the epistle.

This epistle is addressed to "the church in Thessalonica, to you who belong to God the Father and the Lord Jesus Christ." This nomenclature indicates that the church was identified by specific locality and consisted of the local believers. This was the ecclesiastical situation of the early church. All churches were local churches designated by the name of their locality—in this case, Thessalonica. There was no hierarchy greater than the local church governing a region or a state or a country. The New Testament speaks of the church in Rome, Corinth, Ephesus, Philippi, Thessalonica, etc. All the believers in a particular locality comprised the church in that locality, whether they met in one house or several houses.

In the New Testament, the Greek word *ekklēsia* [TG1577, ZG1711] (usually translated "church") is used primarily in two ways: (1) to describe a meeting or an assembly, and (2) to designate the people who participate in such assembling together—whether they are actually assembled or not. The New Testament contains a few passages that speak of a secular assembly (Acts 19:32, 39, 41); every other passage speaks of a Christian assembly. Sometimes the word *ekklēsia* is used to designate the actual meeting together of Christians. This is certainly what Paul intended in 1 Corinthians 14:19, 28, and 35, in which the expression *en* [TG1722, ZG1877] *ekklēsia* must mean "in a meeting" and not "in the church." Aside from the few instances where the word clearly means the actual meeting together of believers, *ekklēsia* most often is used as a designation for the believers who constitute a local church (such as the church in Corinth, the church in Philippi, and the church in Colosse) or all the believers (past, present, and future) who constitute the universal church, the complete body of Christ (Comfort 1993:153-158). In 1 Thessalonians 1:1 it refers to all the Christians who lived in Thessalonica.

The blessing of "grace and peace" is the earliest form of blessing exchanged among believers; it is found at the beginning of nearly all the New Testament epistles. (See all of the Pauline Epistles, including 1 and 2 Timothy, which add "mercy" to "grace and peace"; see 1 and 2 Peter; Revelation 1:4.) The Greek word for "grace" (*charis* [TG5485, ZG5921]) denotes a gift that gives joy to the receiver. The Greek word for "peace" *eirēnē* [TG1515, ZG1645]) denotes spiritual well-being and contentedness. The expression "grace" reflects the traditional Hellenistic greeting (*chairein* [TG5463, ZG5897], "good wishes"), and the expression "peace" reflects the traditional Hebrew greeting (*shalom* [TH7965, ZH8934], "may all be well"). The fact that the blessing of "grace and peace" is short and sweet in 1 Thessalonians probably speaks to the fact that this epistle is one of the earliest writings (see note on 1:2). In due course, the blessing was often expanded with the prepositional phrase, "from God the Father and our Lord Jesus Christ."

◆   B. Opening Prayer (1:2-10)

²We always thank God for all of you and pray for you constantly. ³As we pray to our God and Father about you, we think of your faithful work, your loving deeds, and the enduring hope you have because of our Lord Jesus Christ.

⁴We know, dear brothers and sisters,* that God loves you and has chosen you to be his own people. ⁵For when we brought you the Good News, it was not only with words but also with power, for the Holy Spirit gave you full assurance* that what we said was true. And you know of our concern for you from the way we lived when we were with you. ⁶So you received the message with joy from the Holy Spirit in spite of the severe suffering it brought you. In this way, you imitated both us and the Lord. ⁷As a result, you have become an example to all the believers in Greece—throughout both Macedonia and Achaia.*

⁸And now the word of the Lord is ringing out from you to people everywhere, even beyond Macedonia and Achaia, for wherever we go we find people telling us about your faith in God. We don't need to tell them about it, ⁹for they keep talking about the wonderful welcome you gave us and how you turned away from idols to serve the living and true God. ¹⁰And they speak of how you are looking forward to the coming of God's Son from heaven—Jesus, whom God raised from the dead. He is the one who has rescued us from the terrors of the coming judgment.

1:4 Greek *brothers.*   1:5 Or *with the power of the Holy Spirit, so you can have full assurance.*   1:7 *Macedonia and Achaia* were the northern and southern regions of Greece.

NOTES

1:2 *We always thank God for all of you.* This is the first of three thanksgivings for the church the authors express (cf. 2:13; 3:9).

1:3 *faithful work . . . loving deeds . . . enduring hope.* This is an excellent dynamic-equivalence rendering of three expressions that are literally, "work of faith, labor of love, endurance of hope." The three genitives indicate that work comes out of faith, labor comes out of love, and endurance comes out of hope. In the context of 1 Thessalonians, the hope is in the coming of the Lord Jesus, a hope that helped the Thessalonians endure persecution.

because of our Lord Jesus Christ. Or, "in our Lord Jesus Christ," as an objective genitive, connecting it with "hope." The believers' hope is in the hope of Jesus Christ's return (1:10).

1:4 *God loves you and has chosen you.* A similar thought is expressed in 2 Thess 2:13 (see note). Ephesians 1:4 also indicates that divine love was the motivation of God's election: "God loved us and chose us in Christ." The believers are called the "elect" two times in 1 Peter (1 Pet 1:1; 2:9), an epistle cowritten by Silvanus (1 Pet 5:12).

1:5 *we brought you the Good News.* This is a good functional equivalent of "our gospel." Since this expression appears only one other place in the Pauline Epistles (2 Thess 2:14), it adds evidence for the multiple authorship of 1 and 2 Thessalonians. Paul had a habit of calling the gospel "my gospel" or "the gospel I preach" in an effort to affirm the apostolic authority of his gospel message (Rom 2:16; Gal 1:11). One scribe (C) changed it to "the gospel of God," and another scribe (ℵ*) changed it to "the gospel of our God."

but also with power, for the Holy Spirit gave you full assurance. The NLT mg provides an alternative rendering: "with the power of the Holy Spirit, so you can have full assurance." A similar expression appears in 1 Pet 1:12, which speaks of the Good News being brought to people through the Holy Spirit. The Greek word for "full assurance" (*plērophoria* [TG4136, ZG4443]) can also mean "complete fullness," in this case the fullness of the divine work.

Green (2002:96) says, "in this context the focus is on the divine operation in the apostolic preaching . . . and not on the conviction of the missionaries nor on the way the Thessalonians received the message. The proclamation of the gospel came 'with miraculous power, with the Holy Spirit and with great fullness.'"

1:6 you received the message. The Greek word for "received" (*dechomai* [TG1209, ZG1312]) connotes a warm welcome. The Thessalonians welcomed the word with joy even in the midst of persecution.

joy from the Holy Spirit. Despite their sufferings, they had joy from the Holy Spirit—a thought expressed elsewhere in 1 Pet 4:12-14.

1:7 an example to all the believers. The Greek word for "example" (*tupos* [TG5179, ZG5596]) was used in several ways in Hellenistic Greek; it could denote a model from which clay pots were made—like a prototype (MM 645). It was used of a relief carving or painting that represented not only the one depicted but also the person's character; the word was also used to denote the seal that leaves an impression (TDNT 8.247). Metaphorically speaking, it denoted a "model" of conduct (TDNT 8.246-259; BDAG 1020). The Thessalonians' faith and life had become a model for other churches to emulate.

in Greece—throughout both Macedonia and Achaia. The Greek text does not mention "Greece"; rather it speaks of the two regions, Macedonia and Achaia, that comprise the modern country known as Greece. Strabo, the ancient geographer, called Thessalonica the metropolis (or "mother city") of Macedonia.

1:8 is ringing out. Literally, "has sounded out." This term, which appears only here in the NT (*exēcheomai* [TG1837, ZG2010]), could refer to the clap of thunder (Sir 40:13), the loud cry of a multitude (Philo, *Against Flaccus* 39), or the roar of ocean waves. In this context, it signifies that the Thessalonians' faith was heard loudly throughout the region.

wherever we go we find people telling us about your faith in God. We don't need to tell them about it. There are two ways to interpret these statements: (1) The authors could have been commending the Thessalonians for their vibrant faith, which had become a solid testimony to people in the surrounding area—so much so that the writers (Paul, Silvanus, and Timothy) did not need to boast on behalf of the Thessalonians (Bruce 1982:17). Affirming this interpretation is the fact that a few years later, Paul did boast of the churches in Macedonia, which would include Thessalonica, with respect to their generous giving (2 Cor 8:1-5). (2) Alternatively, the authors could have been commending the Thessalonians for proclaiming the gospel to the surrounding peoples to such an extent that the writers (Paul, Silvanus, and Timothy) did not need to proclaim the gospel in that same area (so Green 2002:103-104). The interpretation hinges on whether the text is saying that the Thessalonians' reputation had been "ringing out" or that their gospel preaching had been ringing out. Most commentators and the NLT affirm that it was their reputation. However, it is possible that both happened: Their good reputation opened the doors for them to proclaim the gospel throughout Macedonia and Achaia.

1:9 you turned away from idols to serve the living and true God. The word order in the Greek is significant: "you turned to God from idols to serve a living and true God." The first action is to turn to God; the second, subsequent action is to turn away from idols. Those who hear the gospel need to be attracted to God first and then they will turn away from their idols. The positive precedes the negative. Conversion is described in the Bible as turning to God (Hos 14:2; Joel 2:12-13; Amos 4:8; Acts 14:15; 15:19; 2 Cor 3:16) and turning away from idols (Acts 14:15). Idolatry is the worship of false gods, usually by paying homage to images—called idols. God's people in the Old Testament were constantly tempted to participate in idolatry and often gave in. By the time of Jesus, however, the Jews had basically been cured of idolatry. Thus, there is no mention in the Gospels of Jesus ever speaking about idolatry—except in a specialized sense concerning the worship of Mammon—that is, money (Matt 6:24). Outside of Palestine, however, idolatry was pervasive.

1:10 *you are looking forward to.* The term (*anamenein* [TG362, ZG388]) means "to wait for, to expect someone or something" (BDAG 68).

the coming. The Greek text does not have the word *parousia* [TG3952, ZG4242] (coming) here, although that is certainly the event which the Thessalonians are expecting; the word's first occurrence is in 2:19.

whom God raised from the dead. This is the centerpiece of the early Christian gospel (see commentary).

the one who has rescued us from the terrors of the coming judgment. In the Greek it is stated in the present tense: "the one rescuing us from the coming wrath." This "wrath" (*orgē* [TG3709, ZG3973]) of God bringing judgment is more fully described in 2 Thess 1:6-10.

C O M M E N T A R Y

Paul, Silvanus, and Timothy opened the letter to the Thessalonians with an extended thanksgiving. They first thanked God for the Thessalonians' faith, love, and hope (1:2-3). The Christian virtues of faith, love, and hope, along with their fruit in work, deeds, and continual anticipation of Christ's return characterized these believers (3:6, 8; 5:8; 2 Thess 1:3-4). The authors then recalled how the gospel was proclaimed to the Thessalonians (1:4-5) and how they received the divine message (1:6-10). The authors would return to these themes in the following chapters, highlighting the apostolic proclamation of the gospel in 2:1-12 and the Thessalonians' reception of the message in 2:13-16.

First Thessalonians 1 gives us more detail of what happened spiritually among the Thessalonian believers than what is described in Acts 17:1-11. The authors' recollections of the Thessalonians' spiritual conversion tells us that the proclamation of the gospel came with miraculous power, with the Holy Spirit, and with great fullness (see note on 1:5). The awesome power and living presence of the Holy Spirit, which is none other than the spiritual presence of Christ (cf. John 14:16-18), is what really convinced the pagans in Thessalonica to turn to the living God and abandon idols.

These were signs that the Thessalonian believers were chosen by God. God's elect are a privileged people. They constitute a royal priesthood, and they, collectively, are God's habitation (1 Pet 2:5, 9). Membership among God's people, the church, is due to God's initiative, prior to all human response, made before time began (Eph 1:4; cf. John 15:16, 19). It is God who has called men and women to be his people, and those who respond are elect. God's call does not depend on any virtues or merits of humankind. Indeed, he chooses the foolish things by worldly standards to shame the wise, the weak to confound the strong, and the low and insignificant to bring to nothing those who think that they are something (1 Cor 1:27-28). Because of election there are no grounds whatever for human boasting in achievement or position. Whatever the elect are, they owe it entirely to God, and they cannot boast or compare themselves with other people.

Although God calls many through the gospel, only some of those respond to the call and become his elect people. The New Testament does not fully explain why only some become God's people. Certainly, when a person does respond to God's call, it is because the gospel comes to him or her in the power of the Holy Spirit and with full conviction (1:4-5). When men and women refuse the gospel, it is because they have become hardened as a result of sin and their trust in their own works. Scripture does not go beyond that point in explanation, and neither should Christians.

One of the obvious signs of the Thessalonians' election was that they abandoned idolatry. Throughout the entire Greco-Roman world "idols were venerated in temples dedicated to the traditional Gentile gods, in popular magic and superstition, as well as in mystery religions and mystery worship" (ISBE 2.799). Thus, when Paul went out on his missionary journeys into the gentile world he encountered idols of every sort and those who participated in idolatry. For example, when Paul went to Athens, he was "greatly distressed to see that the city was full of idols" (Acts 17:16, NIV). Athens was typical of other Hellenistic cities that were committed to many forms of idolatry. In Thessalonica, the people "worshiped a variety of gods, some being traditional and others being imports from Samothrace, Egypt, and Rome" (Green 2002:107).

In the early days of the church, the apostles proclaimed a gospel to the Gentiles wherein they pointed to the reality of the one true living God, Creator of all life. Conversely, they proclaimed the falsehood of idols (see Acts 14:11-18; 17:22-31). What convinces pagans and idolaters to turn to God and away from idols is the living spiritual presence of God. As for myself, I can say that it was the empowering presence of Christ's Spirit vivifying the words of the gospel that persuaded me to pursue Christ and abandon my old way of life. The apostles' words, no matter how true, do not have the power to convict and regenerate without the life-giving Spirit active and present in the words (cf. John 6:63).

Belief in dogma alone would not have sustained the Thessalonians through the immediate onslaught of persecution against them. They "received the message with joy from the Holy Spirit in spite of the severe suffering it brought" them (1:6). The writers of 1 Thessalonians, relieved to hear that the spiritual joy was still sustaining them, wanted to remind them that suffering was part and parcel of following Jesus (cf. Acts 14:22). The Lord Jesus suffered, the apostles of Jesus suffered, and believers in Jesus would suffer.

The Lord Jesus left Christians a pattern of suffering that cannot be avoided. This is the path that he, the pioneer of our salvation, took. The Father perfected him through sufferings (Heb 2:10)—that is, he, as a man, was made fully qualified to be our leader and even our merciful high priest because of what he suffered on our behalf. Christians should expect to suffer, at least in part, some of the things Jesus suffered. Of course, this does not mean that any of us can repeat his unique act of suffering on the cross for redemption. The annual reenactment of the crucifixion, as is practiced in some countries like the Philippines and Spain, is a travesty when it is done to achieve some sort of further atonement or complement the crucifixion of Jesus Christ. His passion was complete once and for all. We do, however, partake of other things that Jesus suffered. Peter tells us that Jesus "is your example, and you must follow in his steps" (1 Pet 2:21). The Greek word underlying "example" (*hupogrammos* [TG5261, ZG5681]) in common Greek usage designates a tracing tablet that contained the entire Greek alphabet. Students would use this to trace the alphabet. They would have to learn each letter, from *alpha* to *ōmega*. The life of Jesus, a life of suffering, is just such a tracing tablet. We, the learners of Jesus, have to trace this life, beginning from *alpha* and going on to *ōmega*.

As the Thessalonians followed the pattern and example set by Jesus and the apostles, they became an example to others. As those empowered by the Spirit, they endured persecution with joy, and maintained their faith in God; consequently, they became an exemplary church in the surrounding regions of Macedonia (northern Greece) and Achaia (middle and southern Greece). This is the only place in the entire New Testament where a church is called an exemplary model (see note on 1:7) for all other believers. The Thessalonians modeled a living faith in the face of persecution. Not only were their lives exemplary and influential to those around them, the Thessalonians may have also proclaimed the gospel to the surrounding region (see note on 1:8).

Either way, it became known to many people that the Thessalonians had a dramatic conversion, which is described as turning from idols to serve the true and living God (1:9). The earliest apostles exhorted gentile pagans to abandon idolatry and turn to the true, living God who created all things (Acts 14:11-18; 17:22-31). In a pluralistic religious culture, this call to forsake ancestral gods and to worship one true and living God was extremely unique (1 Cor 8:4-6). Since Jews abhorred idolatry, it stands to reason that most of the believers in Thessalonica had been pagan Greeks. Acts 17:4 tells us that whereas only "some" of the Jews in the synagogue at Thessalonica believed Paul's message, "many God-fearing Greek men" (*tōn te sebomenōn* [TG4576, ZG4936] *Hellēnōn plēthos polu*) "and quite a few prominent women" were persuaded by his message and became believers. These devout Greeks were the same as the "Godfearers" mentioned elsewhere in Acts (Acts 10:2, 22; 13:16, 26; 17:17; see Bruce 1990:252). Godfearers had abandoned polytheism and become adherents to the belief in the one true God of the Jews—but without becoming proselytes to Judaism. The devout Greeks in Thessalonica could have been the same group described in 1 Thessalonians 1:9. However, it is likely that Acts 17 does not give us the complete record of the evangelistic efforts in Thessalonica and that, in fact, the missionary efforts extended beyond those in the synagogue to include polytheistic Gentiles.

The Thessalonians had heard the gospel message empowered by the Spirit and had believed that Jesus was the Son of God raised from the dead. Belief in the risen Christ is the core of the Christian faith (Rom 10:9-10; 1 Cor 15:3-4, 12-19). As the risen one, Jesus is invisibly present in the Spirit. For the Thessalonians to have experienced the power and joy of the Holy Spirit (1:5-6) was for them to have experienced their living link with Jesus (see John 14:16-20). However, they had not yet seen Jesus and were therefore looking forward to his coming, which from their perspective was imminent. This coming (Gr. *parousia* [TG3952, ZG4242], see note on 2:19) is the sudden return of Jesus Christ to gather together his believers and to execute God's judgment. At this point, they would experience their ultimate salvation—salvation from God's wrath.

For the most part, salvation was seen as an imminent, future event, one that would happen when Jesus returned from heaven to deliver the believers from their enemies. The early Christians hoped the Lord's return would occur at any moment. The infinitive "to wait for" (*anamenein* [TG362, ZG388]; see note on 1:10) pictures an eager and expectant looking forward to the coming of the Lord Jesus whose arrival was anticipated at any time. When he came, Jesus would rescue them from the terrors of the coming judgment.

We who live in the twenty-first century must shift our horizons of interpretation when we read 1 Thessalonians 1. We look backwards to the cross of Christ as the means by which we are saved from our sins, whereas the earliest believers (living only 20 years after Christ's death and resurrection), were looking forward to the salvation Jesus would bring in his imminent return. This salvation would be a deliverance from the enemies and persecutors of God's people. We in the twenty-first century (and I speak primarily for Christians in the U.S.) are not as excited about the Lord's parousia as were the Christians at Thessalonica. Of course, there are many reasons for this, the chief of which is that a lot of time has passed since AD 50, and Jesus has not yet come. In any event, modern Christians—at least those in the United States—are far more interested in studying and debating eschatology than in waiting with rapt attention for Jesus' parousia. The modern focus is radically different from the horizon of expectations of the Thessalonians and many other early Christians. They were not so much looking for certain events to precede the Parousia as much as they were looking for their Savior to come. Of course, 2 Thessalonians was written to address the issue of the prominent events, and we are not told whether this letter had a tempering effect on these early believers' excitement. Nevertheless, it is clear that the early Christians were far more fervent in their desire to see Jesus Christ return than many Christians are today.

The Kerygma of the Early Apostles. In the first chapter of 1 Thessalonians we see elements of the kerygma—the basic proclamation—of the apostles in the early church. It is what Paul and Silvanus and Timothy called "the Good News" (see note on 1:5). In 1 Thessalonians 1:1 we do not see a well-developed theology per se, as one would read in later epistles, whether Paul's or Peter's (1 Peter being cowritten by Silvanus). Nor do we see anything particularly Pauline in this section. This not only points to the collaborative authorship of this epistle (see "Authors" in the Introduction), but it also suggests that Paul and Silvanus were using language that was common to the early apostolic message.

Some examples from this first chapter illustrate this. First, the authors tell the Thessalonians that God loves them and chose them (1:4). The doctrine of election is thereby stated in very simple terms. When Paul himself had opportunity to express the doctrine of election, he would elaborate further. He would write of how election was the result of divine predestination for God's purpose of regenerating children (Rom 8:28-30; Eph 1:3-5). Peter, in collaboration with Silvanus, also expressed the believers' election in more expressive terms (1 Pet 1:2; 2:9).

Second, the authors of 1 Thessalonians described the conversion of the Thessalonians as those who had "turned to God from idols" (1:9, NIV). Had Paul alone written about the conversion experience, it is likely he would have spoken of regeneration (Gal 4:6) or justification (Rom 3:21-24) or salvation (Rom 10:9-10). Peter, writing in collaboration with Silvanus, would have also spoken of their conversion in terms of regeneration (1 Pet 1:23) and salvation (1 Pet 1:5, 9-10; 2:2). The terminology in 1 Thessalonians 1:9, according to Bruce (1982:18), "suggests that we are dealing with a pre-Pauline formula, which has left its mark also on Acts 14:15." Offering similar observations on 1 Thessalonians 1:9, Morris says, "It seems very probable that we have here an example of the common terminology among the early Christians for the success of a mission, for there is very little that is Pauline in the expression. It is difficult, for example, to imagine that Paul would give an account in his own words of people entering into a genuine Christian experience with no mention of their being justified by faith and without any reference to the cross" (1991:52).

Third, the final verse of this section (1:10) includes other fundamental features of the early apostolic kerygma. The authors extolled the Thessalonians for how they were patiently waiting (see note on 1:10) for the parousia of God's Son from heaven. This categorically expresses the fervent expectation of the early Christians who believed that Jesus, who only recently ascended to heaven (20 years prior), would soon return (1:3; 2:19; 3:13; 4:14; 5:10, 23; 2 Thess 1:7-10; 2:1, 8).

Fourth, the early apostles made a point of proclaiming that Jesus was the Son of God among Gentiles, while among Jews they proclaimed he was the Christ (the Messiah). Gentiles would not have understood what it meant for a person to be "the Christ" (= the Messiah) because this was a title used exclusively among Jews to denote the "Anointed One" of God. Gentile confusion at the title "Christ" is evident in that it was apparently mistaken for the word "Chrestus." A Roman historian, writing about the disturbances among the Jews in Rome around AD 49 (disturbances that led to them being expelled by Claudius), said these riots were instigated by one called "Chrestus." Chrestus (meaning "useful one") was a common Greek name, especially for slaves, who were "useful" to their owners (see, for example, Suetonius *Claudius* 25.4). Chrestus also meant "kind one." It could be that this is what the Roman historian Tacitus thought when he called Jesus "Chrestus" in his record of how Nero blamed the Christians for the great fire of Rome in AD 64 and how he persecuted them.

"Son of God" was a title that was accessible to Gentiles, but confronted them with a decision of faith as much as the title "Christ" did among the Jews. During Jesus' earthly life, the Roman authorities were disturbed by his claim to be the Son of God. The first glimpse we get of this is in Jesus' trial before Pilate, who became extremely agitated when he heard from the Jewish leaders that Jesus claimed to be "the Son of God" (John 19:7-9). Why was he agitated? Because Romans believed that gods could visit the human race in human form. Pilate did not want to be responsible for convicting and crucifying a god! Yet Jesus' claim to divinity and kingship set him up as a rival to the emperor—a fact which Jesus' enemies exploited to push the reluctant Pilate to that action (John 19:12). After Jesus' resurrection, his followers had all the reason in the world to proclaim that he was God—who else but God could conquer death? In a Greco-Roman world that depicted the emperor as the incarnate Zeus and called him "worship-worthy Son of God," such proclamations continued to force decisions of faith. Some, like Pilate, feared the emperor, while others, like the centurion in charge of Jesus' crucifixion, recognized that "this man truly was the Son of God" (Mark 15:39).

Fifth, the final verse of the section (1:10) says that God had raised Jesus from the dead. This was the primary proclamation of the early apostles. In their earliest messages, the apostles did not proclaim salvation through Jesus' death on the cross; rather, they proclaimed Jesus' resurrection from the dead. That is not to say that they did not speak of Jesus' suffering—they did; but they did not speak of his suffering in terms of atonement. In each of the earliest recorded proclamations, as written in the book of Acts, the apostles speak of Jesus' suffering (without regard to atonement) and subsequent resurrection. In Peter's earliest gospel proclamations, he cited Old Testament prophecies pertaining to Jesus' resurrection from the dead, but he did not cite any prophecies pertaining to Jesus' crucifixion as an act of atonement for sin. In Peter's first proclamation (Acts 2:14-36), he declared that Jesus' resurrection from the dead fulfilled Psalms 16:8-11 and 110:1—all verses about the resurrection from the dead. In his second message, Peter spoke of the lame man having faith in the risen Jesus (Acts 3:14-16). In Peter's message to Cornelius, Peter proclaims that belief in Jesus brings forgiveness of sins, but he did not tie this exclusively to Jesus' death (Acts 10:38-43).

Paul's first message as recorded in Acts was to the Jews in the synagogue in Antioch of Pisidia (Acts 13:16-41). His message paralleled Peter's in pointing to the Scriptures that spoke of the Messiah's resurrection (Pss 2:7; 16:10, LXX; Isa 55:3, LXX; cf. Acts 2:31-32). Then Paul stated that forgiveness of sins is available to those who believe in the risen Jesus (Acts 13:36-39). Paul did not explicitly state that Jesus' death produced the means by which believers are redeemed. When we come to Acts 17, Paul preaches in the Thessalonica synagogue that, according to the Scriptures, the Messiah had to suffer and then rise again from the dead. This was not the messianic expectation in the synagogue where Paul was speaking. Jews were not looking for a suffering savior but a conquering king. We can imagine that Paul used the same verses just noted. After convincing some of his audience that this was an accurate interpretation of messianic prophecy, he then told them that Jesus, who had suffered death and then risen from the grave, was that Messiah (Acts 17:3-4). In this argument, however, Paul did not mention that the suffering was for the sake of redemption.

A year later (AD 50 or 51), Paul and Silvanus wrote to the Thessalonians the first letter. In this epistle we see that the primary focus, again, is on Jesus' sufferings and his resurrection from the dead (1:6, 10; 2:15; 4:14; 5:9-10). When Jesus' suffering is noted, there is no attached significance that the suffering was for redemption from sin. Rather, the apostolic proclamation focused on Jesus' resurrection (and subsequent appearances to the disciples) and ascension. There is only one mention of Jesus' suffering as a salvific act—namely 5:9b-10a, which literally says "obtaining salvation through our Lord Jesus Christ, who died for us that we might live." Even in this verse, there is no mention that Jesus' death accomplished redemption. Rather, it views Jesus' death and resurrection as being the means that saves the believers from death by bringing them into life.

◆ II. The Apostles' Concern for the Thessalonians (2:1-16)

You yourselves know, dear brothers and sisters,* that our visit to you was not a failure. ²You know how badly we had been treated at Philippi just before we came to you and how much we suffered there. Yet our God gave us the courage to declare his Good News to you boldly, in spite of great opposition. ³So you can see we were not preaching with any deceit or impure motives or trickery.

⁴For we speak as messengers approved by God to be entrusted with the Good News. Our purpose is to please God, not people. He alone examines the motives of our hearts. ⁵Never once did we try to win you with flattery, as you well know. And God is our witness that we were not pretending to be your friends just to get your money! ⁶As for human praise, we have never sought it from you or anyone else.

⁷As apostles of Christ we certainly had a right to make some demands of you, but instead we were like children* among you. Or we were like a mother feeding and caring for her own children. ⁸We loved you so much that we shared with you not only God's Good News but our own lives, too.

⁹Don't you remember, dear brothers and sisters, how hard we worked among you? Night and day we toiled to earn a living so that we would not be a burden to any of you as we preached God's Good News to

you. ¹⁰You yourselves are our witnesses—and so is God—that we were devout and honest and faultless toward all of you believers. ¹¹And you know that we treated each of you as a father treats his own children. ¹²We pleaded with you, encouraged you, and urged you to live your lives in a way that God would consider worthy. For he called you to share in his Kingdom and glory.

¹³Therefore, we never stop thanking God that when you received his message from us, you didn't think of our words as mere human ideas. You accepted what we said as the very word of God—which, of course, it is. And this word continues to work in you who believe.

¹⁴And then, dear brothers and sisters, you suffered persecution from your own countrymen. In this way, you imitated the believers in God's churches in Judea who, because of their belief in Christ Jesus, suffered from their own people, the Jews. ¹⁵For some of the Jews killed the prophets, and some even killed the Lord Jesus. Now they have persecuted us, too. They fail to please God and work against all humanity ¹⁶as they try to keep us from preaching the Good News of salvation to the Gentiles. By doing this, they continue to pile up their sins. But the anger of God has caught up with them at last.

2:1 Greek brothers; also in 2:9, 14, 17.   2:7 Some manuscripts read we were gentle.

NOTES

2:1 our visit. Lit., "our entrance." This refers to their entry into Thessalonica (the same term appears in 1:9, eisodon [TG1529, ZG1658]). The kind of entrance they had could be judged by its credible results.

was not a failure. The Greek word behind "failure" (*kenē* [TG2756, ZG3031]) speaks of fruit-lessness (of accomplishment) and emptiness (of content). *Kenos* signifies that which is empty and hollow—hence, pointless and futile. In Paul's writings *kenos* expresses the emptiness of all that is not filled with spiritual substance; it speaks of the "zero-ness" of human words and human endeavors that lack divine content. Nothing comes from this nothing-ness; it is futility. Paul used *kenos* to describe the hollow utterances (see 1 Tim 6:20; 2 Tim 2:16 where *kenophōnia* [TG2757, ZG3032] appears) spoken by Judaizers and/or Gnostics trying to entice the believers with philosophy and empty deceit (see Col 2:8; cf. Eph 5:6). In contrast, Paul claimed that his preaching was not "futile" but purposeful and effective (see 1 Cor 15:14). He and Silvanus made the same claim for their labor among the believers (2:1). They were eager to know that their labor had not been for nothing (3:5).

2:2 how badly we had been treated at Philippi. The Greek verb is *hubristhentes* [TG5195, ZG5614]. It means, in the passive voice, to be abused, to be insulted, to be mistreated out-rageously (BDAG 1022). The abuse to Paul and Silvanus occurred when they were proclaim-ing the gospel in Philippi (Acts 16:19-24). This affirms their coauthorship of 1 Thessalonians in that Paul and Silvanus are both speaking here of their common suffering (see "Authors" in Introduction).

courage to declare. Or, "we spoke out freely" (Bruce 1982:25).

opposition. The Greek word *agōn* [TG73, ZG74], borrowed from its use in describing fierce athletic competition, was used often by Paul to describe the struggles he underwent in proclaiming the gospel.

2:3 preaching. The Greek word is *paraklēsis* [TG3874, ZG4155], which in this context means "appeal" (cf. 2 Cor 5:20).

deceit. This word (*planēs* [TG4106, ZG4415]) connotes error, delusion, deceit; in this context it speaks of teaching that leads people astray (BDAG 822).

impure motives. The Greek is *akatharsias* [TG167, ZG174], a word normally used to denote moral impurity. Here it speaks of immoral intent and motive (BDAG 34).

trickery. Gr. *dolos* [TG1388, ZG1515], which could also be rendered as "cunning."

2:5 pretending to be your friends just to get your money. This is an excellent functional equivalent of the Gr. *prophasei pleonexias*, [TG4392/4124, ZG4733/4432] which more tersely trans-lated is "a pretext for [satisfying] greed" (BDAG 889).

2:6 human praise. In a similar vein, decades after Paul's writing, the ancient author Plu-tarch (*Moralia* 78A) criticized orators who were not only motivated by hope of financial gain but also by desire for glory and fame. Similarly, Dio Chrysostom (*Ad Alexandrinos* 32.11) spoke of a Sophist who was "being destroyed by popular opinion; for his liver swelled and grew whenever he was praised and shriveled again when he was censured."

2:7 apostles of Christ. This statement indicates that both Paul and Silvanus were apostles (see Introduction under "Authors"). Timothy, their trusted co-worker, could also be consid-ered an apostle (see note on 3:2).

demands. Paul and his associates did not wield their apostolic authority in an oppressive way.

we were like children among you. The NLT follows the mss that have the word *nēpioi* [TG3516A, ZG3758] (children/infants), instead of other mss that have the word *ēpioi* [TG2261, ZG2473] (gentle). The ms support for the text followed by NLT is impressive: 𝔓65 ℵ* B C* D* F G I 044*it cop^bo. The NLT was among the first English versions to follow this reading, along with the NET Bible and the CEV. (TNIV followed thereafter.) The variant is noted in other versions such as RSV NRSV NASB NJB NAB, but these and all other versions (includ-ing KJV NKJV NIV NEB REB) adhere to the reading *ēpioi* [TG2261, ZG2473] (gentle). The ms support for this is inferior: ℵ^c A C² D² 044^c 0278 33 1739 𝔐.

There is a one-letter difference (*nu*) between the variants: *nēpioi* (infants) and *ēpioi* (gentle). Concerning transcriptional errors, it is difficult to know which reading may have produced the other. The first word (*nēpioi*) could have been created by dittography—the preceding word (*egenēthēmen* [TG1096, ZG1181] = "we became") ends in *nu*; or the second word *ēpioi* could have been created by haplography—also influenced by the preceding word.

The reading *ēpioi* (gentle) seems to be the most natural in context—especially in connection with the following metaphor: "we were gentle in your midst, like a nursing mother caring for her children." This is why so many English translators have adopted this reading. However, it is highly suspect, in part because it is the more natural reading. First, several manuscripts (א C D 044) originally had the reading *nēpioi* [TG3516A, ZG3758], but were later corrected to *ēpioi* [TG2261, ZG2473]. This strongly suggests that scribes and correctors had a problem with the meaning of the wording *nēpioi* and made an emendation. Second, the reading *nēpioi* has early and diverse attestation, including 𝔓65 (third century). Third, Westcott and Hort (1882:128) argue that the adjective *ēpioi* (gentle) is not compatible with the expression *in mesō* [TG3319, ZG3545] *humōn* (in your midst). The appropriate word should be a noun, not an adjective (for a full discussion of this textual issue, see Comfort 2005:349-350).

As was just noted, translators have been hesitant to accept the word "infants" because of the following metaphor in the same verse: "we were infants in your midst, like a nursing mother caring for her children." The NLT alleviates this problem with this rendering: "we were like children among you. Or we were like a mother feeding and caring for her own children." Fowl (1990:469-473) notes that such mixing of metaphors is consistent with Pauline style (see also Weima 2000a). Jesus told his disciples that they needed to become like children (Mark 10:15); here is an example of some disciples doing just that.

a mother feeding and caring. The Greek word, a hapax legomenon in the NT, is *trophos* [TG5162, ZG5577], which was used in Greek writings of a wet nurse and of a mother.

2:9 *we toiled to earn a living.* Paul, Silvanus, and Timothy did manual labor to support themselves (cf. Acts 18:1-3), not only to be an example to the Thessalonians (2 Thess 3:8-9), but also to avoid being an economic burden to them.

2:10 *You yourselves are our witnesses—and so is God.* The apostles invoked two witnesses, the Thessalonian believers and God himself (cf. Deut 19:15; 1 Tim 5:19).

devout. The Greek word, an adverb, is *hosiōs* [TG3743, ZG4010] meaning "devoutly, piously, holy."

honest. The Greek word is *amemptōs* [TG274, ZG290], an adverb meaning "blamelessly."

faultless. The Greek word is *dikaiōs* [TG1346, ZG1469], an adverb meaning "justly."

believers. Most manuscripts read "the ones believing"—the present tense denoting their ongoing faith in Christ. But the earliest extant manuscript for this verse, namely 𝔓65, and most Old Latin manuscripts designate them as "the ones having believed"—the aorist tense denoting the point of conversion.

2:12 *live your lives in a way that God would consider worthy.* This is a good functional equivalent of the terse expression "walk worthily of God."

he called you to share in his Kingdom. This reading, reflecting an aorist participle in the Greek, has the support of א A and several ancient versions (it syr cop); it emphasizes God's initial call to salvation. Other manuscripts (B D F G 33 1739) have a present participle and thereby convey the ongoing nature of God's call to the believers, for God is identified as "the one calling you into his own kingdom."

2:13 *we never stop thanking God.* This is the second of three thanksgivings for the church (1:2; 3:9).

2:14 churches in Judea. Paul himself knew of the persecutions against these churches because he was "formerly a perpetrator of the attacks (Acts 8:3; Gal 1:22-23; 1 Tim 1:13). Beginning with the martyrdom of Stephen, the churches in Judea suffered greatly (Acts 8:1-3; 9:1). . . Herod [Agrippa I] renewed the persecutions (Acts 12:1-5) and saw how these attacks brought him favor among the populace" (Green 2002:143).

the Jews. Grammatically, four participles (in the next two verses) are attached to the action of the persecuting Jews: (1) They are the ones having killed Jesus and the prophets; (2) they are the ones persecuting "us" (the apostles); (3) they are not pleasing to God and contrary to all people; and (4) they are forbidding "us" (the apostles) from preaching the gospel to the Gentiles. The result is expressed in an infinitive form: "to fill up their sins always."

2:15 the prophets. This reading has the excellent documentary support of ℵ A B D* F G I 0278 33 1739 it cop Origen. Other manuscripts and witnesses (D¹ 044 𝔐 syr Marcion; so TR) read, "their own prophets." According to Tertullian (*Against Marcion* 5.15.1), Marcion altered the reading "the prophets" to "their own prophets" probably in an attempt to make the Jews even more culpable: "They [the Jews] killed the Lord Jesus and their very own prophets." Marcion's interpolation had its effect on the textual tradition, as is evidenced by the same interpolation being in several later witnesses and by finding its way into the TR (and so the KJV and NKJV).

have persecuted us. The Greek comes from the verb *ekdiōkō* [TG1559, ZG1691], which can be rendered "drove us out" (NRSV) or "severely persecuted us."

2:16 they try to keep us from preaching the Good News of salvation to the Gentiles. This is a good functional equivalent for "forbidding us to speak to the Gentiles that they might be saved."

to pile up their sins. This is a good idiomatic rendering of the literal, "to fill up their sins." Once sins reach their full measure, God's judgment will come (Gen 15:16; Dan 8:23). Second Maccabees 6:14 says, "the Lord waits patiently to punish [the other nations] until they have reached the full measure of their sins" (NRSV). Paul and Silvanus applied this teaching to their own people, the Jews. Jesus did the same (Matt 23:31-36).

COMMENTARY

Chapter 2 begins the body of the letter. This chapter has a lengthy discussion of the apostles' character (2:1-12) and of the way the Thessalonians received the gospel (2:13-16). Both topics were introduced in the opening thanksgiving (1:2-10). The writers' primary concern was to explain their heartfelt concern for the believers in Thessalonica. So Paul (especially) and Silvanus related their attempts to return to the church (2:17-20) and how, when they were unsuccessful, they sent Timothy back to the church (3:1-5). They recounted their joyful reaction to Timothy's report about his visit (3:6-10) and then offered prayers for God to open the way for their return (3:11-13).

Several scholars think the lengthy defense in chapters 2 and 3 is most likely a response to criticisms about Paul's and Silvanus's abrupt and prolonged absence (see Bruce 1982:23-24; Green 2002:111-112; Morris 1991:57-58). Although this view has merit, this section is not exclusively a defense of Paul's and Silvanus's apostleship against certain opposers or critics. Instead, it appears that this section has a threefold purpose—as stated in the opening three verses (2:1-3), which is then elaborated throughout the rest of the chapter. The main three points are covered chiastically (A 2:1; B 2:2; C 2:3; C' 2:4-12; B' 2:14-16; A' 2:13) as follows:

1. The apostles' proclamation to Thessalonica was not a failure (2:1); in fact, it was a great success (2:13).
2. The apostles suffered for the sake of proclaiming the gospel (2:2); in truth, suffering is the portion of all who follow Jesus, including the Thessalonians (2:14-16).
3. The apostles' preaching was not motivated by any kind of desire to take advantage of the Thessalonians (2:3); in reality, they loved the Thessalonians and demonstrated this with their lives (2:4-12).

The Success of the Apostles' Proclamation in Thessalonica (2:1, 13). This section begins with Paul and Silvanus rehearsing the beginning of their relationship with the Thessalonians. The thought of 2:1 is carried over from 1:9; this is quite clear in the Greek where the same word (*eisodon* [TG1529, ZG1658], "entrance") appears, translated in NLT as "welcome" in 1:9 and "visit" in 2:1. The apostles recalled what a good entrée they were given. The Lord had opened the door for them to proclaim the gospel to the Jews, to the Godfearers, and then to pagan Gentiles, who turned to the living God and abandoned their idols. In 2:1 the apostles affirm that their mission was not a failure and that their message was not empty (see note on 2:1).

Returning to this theme in 2:13, we see that the apostles' reminiscences about their time with the Thessalonians were cause for great thanksgiving. Their supreme joy was that the Thessalonians did not receive the message as the word of humans but as it really is—the word of God. This is bold and beautiful—bold to say that their words were divine, beautiful to say that the Thessalonians received the message as coming from God. Since 1 Thessalonians is one of the earliest writings of the New Testament, this is one of the earliest records we have of the apostles attributing divine authority to their words.

Their boldness in saying their words came from the Lord was justified in that (1) Paul received his commission directly from the risen Lord (Gal 1) and (2) Silvanus is traditionally believed to have been one of Jesus' 72 disciples and thereby also received his commission from the Lord Jesus (Luke 10:1ff). Silvanus had the experience of entering various towns as one of the 70 (or 72 in other mss) disciples sent out by Jesus Christ (see Luke 10:1; Pseudo-Hippolytus, *On the Seventy Apostles* 50; ANF 5.256). In fact, he would have been just as experienced as Paul, who had entered several cities at this point in his ministry. By reading Luke 10, the passage that records the sending-out of the 72, we discover that the disciples were instructed to go out two-by-two and enter the home of anyone who offered them the exchange of peace. In Thessalonica, it was Jason who received the apostles into his home (Acts 17:5). Jesus instructed the disciples to eat whatever food they were given because "those who work deserve their pay" (Luke 10:7)—this point factors in our interpretation of 2:7 discussed below. While living in the town, it was the task of apostles to heal people and proclaim the gospel so that people could come into the Kingdom of God (Luke 10:9-11; cf. comments below on 2:12).

The Suffering of the Apostles and the Believers (2:2, 14–16). As the apostles recalled their visit with the Thessalonians, they also vividly remembered how they had come to them just after being severely punished at Philippi. Paul and Silvanus (Silas) were stripped and severely beaten with wooden rods in public, then thrown into a dungeon (Acts 16:22-24). This was not only unlawful—Paul and Silvanus were Roman citizens (Acts 16:37), which gave them the right to a trial—it was extremely humiliating. But this shameful suffering did not keep Paul and Silvanus from continuing their mission of preaching the gospel in the very next city they came to after Philippi—namely, Thessalonica. And even though they faced great opposition in Thessalonica from certain Jews and civil authorities, they took courage in God to speak the message of the gospel.

When the apostles returned to the theme of suffering later in this section (2:14-16), they congratulated the Thessalonians for having joined the sacred throng of those who have suffered for God at the hands of their own people. Among those who suffered in this way were some prophets who were killed by their own people; Christ Jesus, who was killed by his own people; and the apostles of Jesus who were persecuted by Jews trying to keep them from taking the gospel of salvation to the Gentiles. As is noted in 2:14, Paul and Silvanus blamed the Jews for four things: (1) killing Jesus and the prophets, (2) persecuting the apostles, (3) being displeasing to God and contrary to all men, and (4) forbidding the apostles from preaching the gospel to the Gentiles. In so doing, the Jews were piling up their sins.

Jesus also noted the persecution of the prophets when he bewailed Jerusalem as the city that killed the messengers God sent to her (Matt 23:29-37). The Old Testament tells us of these persecutions (1 Kgs 19:9-18; 2 Chr 36:15-16; Jer 2:30), as do some other Jewish writings, such as the *Martyrdom of Isaiah* 5:1-14, which says that Isaiah was sawed in two (cf. Heb 11:37). The Jewish leaders in Judea were also responsible for killing Jesus (see Acts 2:23, 36; 3:13-15; 4:10; 7:52; 10:39; 13:28), even though the execution was carried out by Roman soldiers under the command of Pontius Pilate. Caiaphas, the high priest, was the most culpable (John 11:45-53), even as Jesus himself intimated when being judged by Pilate (John 19:10-11).

When we examine the early history of the church as recorded in the book of Acts side by side with these statements, it seems that the words in 2:14-15 were more likely those of Silvanus than of Paul. This does not exclude Paul from having coauthored these words, but he may have taken a backseat at this point in the composition. As to 2:14, it was far more natural and right for Silvanus to speak of what the Jewish Christians in Judea suffered from the Jews than for Paul to speak of this, because, in fact, Paul (as Saul of Tarsus) was one of the worst persecutors against the Christians in Judea. Paul would have had to put himself among those "Jews" who had persecuted the churches in Judea (Acts 9:1-4). He wouldn't have denied this; in fact, he admitted this in other writings (Gal 1:13; Phil 3:6), but in the context of 1 Thessalonians 2, it is clear that there is no self-condemnation going on. As to 2:15, the idea of being "driven out" (see note), in the context of the verse (which speaks of Jews killing Jesus and the prophets—events that occurred in Jerusalem), very likely refers to the expulsion of Jewish Christians from Jerusalem, an event in which Saul of Tarsus himself (as a former persecutor) had a violent hand. As such, these words would likely have come from Silvanus, who was there to see many Jewish Christians expelled from Jerusalem for their faith in Jesus Christ. Of course, if these words refer to Silvanus and Paul being expelled from Thessalonica by persecuting Jews, then this statement could have legitimately come from both of them. But the scope of the persecution described is much greater than that which they experienced in Thessalonica.

Paul and Silvanus, themselves Jews, were not anti-Jewish. In fact, Paul expressed his deep love for his own people; he longed and prayed for their salvation (Rom 9:1-5; 10:1). Yet Paul and Silvanus recognized that the Jews were the persecutors of God's messengers, including Jesus, and it was Jews who had driven them, the apostolic messengers, out of Thessalonica (Acts 17:5-10).

The main point of the passage is that suffering for the faith, as evidenced in Jesus, his apostles, and the churches in Judea, was now replicated in the Thessalonian church. According to Acts 17:5, the persecution against the church had come from certain Jews. The text of 1 Thessalonians 2:14 indicates that the Thessalonian Christians, who were primarily Gentiles, were suffering at the hands of their own countrymen, who were also primarily Gentiles. Thus, the picture presented from both sides here is that both Jews and Gentiles were persecuting the Thessalonian church, comprised mainly of Gentiles but also of Jews. The point is this: To suffer from one's enemies is one thing, to suffer from one's compatriots is another. Their own countrymen were causing them to suffer, although precisely in what way is not stated in the text. We can suppose that the suffering involved "social rejection, including verbal abuse and accusations (cf. Acts 17:5-9), and possibly came to the point of physical attacks" (Green 2002:143).

Jesus indicated that there would be many trials and sorrows for his followers (John 16:33). Paul taught that entrance into the Kingdom of God comes with many tribulations (Acts 14:22), which must not shake a Christian's faith (3:3). The biblical picture is that affliction will grow more intense as "the end" approaches (Matt 24:9-14; 2 Tim 3:13). The forces of Satan will attack in an effort to deceive and destroy the elect (Matt 24:24; 2 Thess 2:9-12; Rev 20:7-9). But when Jesus Christ is revealed from heaven in flaming fire, God will afflict those who have afflicted believers and will bring vengeance upon those who have not submitted to the gospel of Jesus Christ (2 Thess 1:5-10; 2:7-8).

The Character and Motives of the Apostles (2:3-12). We are not sure why Paul and Silvanus thought it was necessary for them to affirm, even defend, their motives and character to the Thessalonians. Some commentators think that the apostles' motives in going to Thessalonica had apparently been attacked both by pagan Gentiles and by Jews clinging to their Old Testament faith. From this chapter and the next, I find it to be more likely that the apostles felt they needed to explain to the Thessalonians that the suffering and persecution they had experienced (ever since they received the gospel from them) was not an accident nor a result of the

Thessalonians' poor character. The true apostles of Jesus accepted and even expected suffering as part of their commitment to Jesus (Acts 9:15-16; 2 Cor 11–12)—it was a mark of their authenticity. And those who follow Jesus—specifically the Thessalonians—would also suffer persecution. This was just as Paul and Silvanus had taught them when they were with them (3:3-4). The persecution that broke out against Paul and Silvanus had spilled over to the church (Acts 17:5-9).

The Thessalonians could take heart in the fact that they had received the gospel from authentic apostles. Paul and Silvanus asserted that they were messengers shown by testing to be genuine and entrusted with the gospel (see note on 2:4). Years of preparation had preceded their presentation. God had purified their hearts to the extent that their motive in proclaiming the gospel was not for self-gain but to please God.

When Paul and Silas proclaimed the gospel, they did not trick the Thessalonians into thinking that becoming a Christian would give them an easygoing, persecution-free life. Their gospel was a straightforward presentation, free of deception, impurity, and guile. Their message was not motivated by impure motives; their message was not deceitful; and their message would not lead anyone astray (see notes on 2:3). In preaching about Jesus Christ the apostles had plainly told the Thessalonians that suffering would be their lot (3:3-4).

Furthermore, the apostles Paul and Silvanus wanted to make it clear they had not proclaimed the message for self-gain. They denied they used flattery, which, in ancient times and now, has been used as a means to get financial gain from others. Their preaching did not have a "pretext for greed" (2:5, NRSV; see note). Since their motives could only be known by God, the apostles appealed to God as their witness. They also appealed to the Thessalonians, who had seen the way the apostles labored to make their own money. Thus, it should have been obvious to the Thessalonians that the apostles were not out to get their money.

Moreover, the apostles were not desiring human praise or seeking position, especially one from which they could make demands as apostles of Christ (see note on 2:7). Instead of being demanding on the Thessalonians, the apostles became "like children among [them]" (see note on 2:7). As to this metaphor, we should take note that in this very same chapter the authors liken themselves to an orphan (2:17; see note)—as a child who had been separated from his loved ones. Their brief time with the Thessalonians, cut short by persecution and subsequent forced departure, caused them to acutely sense their separation. Thus, they used an emotive image in which they pictured themselves as a child who had been orphaned from his parents. In like manner, in 2:7-8 they picture themselves as an infant in their midst to show that they were guileless, innocent, and unpretentious (see 2:3-6). In other words, they had no intention to take advantage of them. As such, the image of a child is fitting.

It is possible that the image of a child came from Silvanus, who had been one of the 72 disciples sent out by Jesus, as recorded in Luke 10. When these disciples returned from their successful mission ebullient and enthused, Jesus thanked the Father for their mission and said, "thank you . . . for revealing [these things] to the childlike (*nēpioi* [TG3516A, ZG3758])." It is possible that Silvanus had remembered this and therefore spoke of how their behavior among the Thessalonians was as "children."

Switching metaphors, Paul and Silvanus indicated that they were like mothers to the Thessalonians, feeding and caring for them (see note on 2:7). The apostles' love for the Thessalonians was to the extent that they would have sacrificed their lives for them if necessary. They would have given them not just the gospel but their very own lives (2 Cor 12:15; Phil 2:17).

The apostles pointed out that their affection for the Thessalonians was demonstrated in labor (*kopos* [TG2873, ZG3160]; the same word as 1:3, which indicates weariness and fatigue from strenuous activity). Paul apparently made tents to provide for his financial needs, performing hard labor (*mochthon* [TG3449, ZG3677]) so that he might not be a burden to the Thessalonians. In Thessalonica, as in Corinth, Paul paid for his own living by the works of his own hands (2:9; cf. 1 Cor 9:3-15; 2 Cor 11:7-11). Silvanus also worked with own hands (2:9), as did Timothy.

This expression of care is in keeping with that of parents who take the responsibility for providing for their households. Indeed, the entire exhortation was one of comfort and challenge, the kind of exhortation a loving father would give to his own children.

◆ III. Timothy's Report about the Church (2:17–3:8)

¹⁷Dear brothers and sisters, after we were separated from you for a little while (though our hearts never left you), we tried very hard to come back because of our intense longing to see you again. ¹⁸We wanted very much to come to you, and I, Paul, tried again and again, but Satan prevented us. ¹⁹After all, what gives us hope and joy, and what will be our proud reward and crown as we stand before our Lord Jesus when he returns? It is you! ²⁰Yes, you are our pride and joy.

CHAPTER 3

Finally, when we could stand it no longer, we decided to stay alone in Athens, ²and we sent Timothy to visit you. He is our brother and God's co-worker* in proclaiming the Good News of Christ. We sent him to strengthen you, to encourage you in your faith, ³and to keep you from being shaken by the troubles you were going through. But you know that we are destined for such troubles. ⁴Even while we were with you, we warned you that troubles would soon come—and they did, as you well know. ⁵That is why, when I could bear it no longer, I sent Timothy to find out whether your faith was still strong. I was afraid that the tempter had gotten the best of you and that our work had been useless.

⁶But now Timothy has just returned, bringing us good news about your faith and love. He reports that you always remember our visit with joy and that you want to see us as much as we want to see you. ⁷So we have been greatly encouraged in the midst of our troubles and suffering, dear brothers and sisters,* because you have remained strong in your faith. ⁸It gives us new life to know that you are standing firm in the Lord.

3:2 Other manuscripts read *and God's servant;* still others read *and a co-worker,* or *and a servant and co-worker for God,* or *and God's servant and our co-worker.* 3:7 Greek *brothers.*

NOTES

2:17 we were separated. The Greek (*aporphanisthentes* [TG642, ZG682]) means "having been orphaned." The writers described their experience of separation from the Thessalonians (Acts 17:10) as "being made orphans." Although this Greek word could refer to parents who lost children, the word was not used that way in Hellenistic Greek. Rather, it was used of children bereft of parents (Weima 2000a).

2:18 I, Paul, tried again and again. At this juncture in the composition of the epistle, Paul interrupted the corporate "we" with a personal expression. Timothy had returned to the Thessalonians (3:2, 6). And, presumably, Silvanus had also visited them—although we cannot be certain (Acts 18:1-6). Paul had not been able to get back to them.

Satan. The Greek term means "the adversary."

prevented us. The Greek verb (*enkoptō* [TG1465, ZG1601]) was used in military contexts to denote how armies "prevented" the advance of their enemies: Soldiers would tear up and destroy roads to prevent their passage (NIDNTT 2.222-223; TDNT 3.855; G. Milligan 1908:34). Thus, "warfare imagery is embedded in the metaphor, Satan himself being their adversary" (Green 2002:152).

2:19 our proud reward and crown. Despite present fears (3:5) and frustrations (2:15, 18), the apostle anticipates Christ's royal return when he will receive the honor described, literally, as a "crown of boasting." An honorific crown would have been made of laurel, pine needles, or oak leaves and would be given to those who received great civic honor or who were victorious in the games.

when he returns? Lit., "in his coming." The word is *parousia* [TG3952, ZG4242].

2:20 pride and joy. This is a good modern idiomatic rendering for the Greek, which says, "our glory and joy."

3:1 we decided to stay alone in Athens. The chronology of Acts 17 does not mention that Silas (= Silvanus) and Timothy joined Paul in Athens. So this verse fills in some history for us.

3:2 our brother and God's co-worker. This is the reading in NA[27] and UBS[4], supported slimly by D* 33 it[b]. Other variant readings (some noted in NLT mg) are as follows: (1) "our brother and co-worker" (B); (2) "our brother and servant of God" (ℵ A P 044 0278 1739 cop); (3) "our brother and servant of God and our co-worker" (D[2] 𝔐 syr); (4) "our brother and servant and co-worker of God" (F G). The third and fourth variants are obviously conflated readings. The true reading must be preserved in the reading of the text or in one of the first two variants. After Paul called Timothy "our brother," he called him either (1) a co-worker of God, (2) a co-worker, or (3) a servant of God. The third option has the best attestation, but it is suspect as a scribal adjustment because it avoids the presentation of Timothy being called "God's co-worker"—which is quite an acclamation. The second option has the testimony of B as the shorter reading; as such, it could be considered the reading from which all the others deviated. However, scholars (see Metzger 1992:240-242) argue that *sunergon* [TG4904, ZG5301] (co-worker) would not have been purposely expanded to *sunergon tou theou* [TG2316, ZG2536] (co-worker of God) because the latter is the more difficult reading. But we know that the Bezaean reviser (the scribe of D) had a propensity for expansion, and he may have understood *sunergon tou theou* to be an objective genitive, not subjective—hence, the rendering "a co-worker for God," which is not at all offensive. Yet—and finally—it must be said that Paul could have been saying that Timothy was a worker with God. After all, Paul made similar assertions in 1 Cor 3:9 and 2 Cor 6:1.

3:3 troubles. The Greek word *thlipsis* [TG2347, ZG2568] denotes "distress that is brought about by outward circumstances" (BDAG 457). These troubles were the persecutions the Thessalonians were suffering (1:6; 2:14; 2 Thess 1:4-6).

you know that we are destined for such troubles. The Greek word behind "destined" is *keimai* [TG2749, ZG3023]; it means that one is appointed for something. It is not the same word usually translated "predestined" (*proorizō* [TG4309, ZG4633]), but close in meaning. The early Christians were taught that suffering for the faith is part of the Christian life (1:6; 2:14; Acts 14:22; Phil 1:29). This theme is prominent in 1 Pet (1 Pet 1:6; 2:21; 3:17; 4:13-19), an epistle cowritten by Silvanus. Paul believed he was called to participate in the sufferings of Christ for the sake of really knowing Jesus (Phil 3:10; cf. Col 1:24).

3:5 the tempter. Satan is called the tempter in Matt 4:3 (see NIV), and identified as a source of temptation in 1 Cor 7:5. The apostles were concerned that Satan might have undermined the Thessalonians' stability in the faith (3:2, 7-8) and thereby ruined their apostolic labors among them (cf. Gal 2:2; Phil 2:16).

3:6 your faith and love. These virtues are the hallmark of true Christians (5:8; 1 Cor 13:13; Gal 5:5-6; Col 1:4-5; 2 Thess 1:3-4). Faith is expressed as trust in Jesus Christ; love is manifested as care for other Christians and other human beings.

3:8 It gives us new life to know that you are standing firm in the Lord. Lit., "now we live if you stand firm in the Lord." The idea is that the apostles' lives are so connected with the believers at Thessalonica (as common branches in the same vine) that the Thessalonians' spiritual prosperity gives the apostles life.

COMMENTARY

This section pertains to the apostles' separation from the Thessalonians and their desire to return to them. Paul, Silas (Silvanus), and Timothy had quickly left the Thessalonians due to persecution and gone down to Berea (Acts 17:10). After this, Paul was escorted by some Christian brothers to Athens, while Silas and Timothy stayed in Berea. Paul sent word back to Silas and Timothy that they should join him as soon as possible (Acts 17:14-15). Evidently, Silas and Timothy rejoined Paul in Athens (implied by 3:1), and then Paul and Silas sent Timothy back to Thessalonica to see how the church was faring in the midst of persecution (3:2-3). Paul left Athens and went to Corinth (Acts 18:1), while Silas stayed in Athens and/ or went on to some other cities in Macedonia—but most likely not Thessalonica because Timothy was the sole emissary to that church. In due course, both Timothy and Silas left Macedonia and rejoined Paul in Corinth (Acts 18:5). Timothy reported to Paul and Silas the situation of the church in Thessalonica (3:6-8).

Paul personally stated he had made two attempts to return to the church, but he was roadblocked by Satan (2:18; see note). In Romans 15:22, Paul used the same Greek verb (*enkoptō* [TG1465, ZG1601]) in telling the Roman Christians that he had been hindered from making a visit to them. The hindrance in that situation was that Paul was occupied with proclaiming the gospel to other regions and localities. In the case of the Thessalonians, by contrast, Paul and Silvanus said it was Satan (lit., "the adversary") who was hindering them from coming. We are not told how Satan had done this. Perhaps they considered the legal situation against them in Thessalonica as being the work of Satan. Acts 17:9 tells us that Jason and others in Thessalonica were required to have posted a bond, and this bond most likely "served as a guarantee to the officials that Paul and company would not return" (Green 2002:153). Apparently, the bond had nothing to do with Timothy because he was able to visit the church again (3:1, 5). The bond must have pertained specifically to Paul and Silas (Silvanus).

Whatever way Satan was blocking Paul and Silvanus from going to Thessalonica, their letters sent there were not blocked. These two letters, 1 and 2 Thessalonians, gave the Thessalonians spiritual comfort and illumination. And the two letters have reached a greater church audience for nearly 2,000 years, providing Christians with significant insights about how to handle persecution and about the most basic events of Christ's parousia. So, in the end, God triumphed over Satan. Eventually, Paul himself returned to the region of Macedonia (Acts 20:1-3), where he undoubtedly enjoyed sweet fellowship with the Thessalonian believers. But this did not happen until six years later, in AD 56 (see Bruce 1990:422-423).

In the meantime, Paul and Silvanus sent Timothy to the Thessalonians to find out whether their faith was still strong and stable in the midst of their sufferings (3:5). The apostles were fearful that the Thessalonians had been tempted by Satan to give up or compromise their faith so as to lessen the sufferings of persecution. So Timothy's primary mission was to strengthen the faith of the Thessalonians (3:2). He could do this by reminding them that the followers of Jesus are called to a life of suffering. The apostles had always taught that suffering for the faith is part of the disciples' life. In fact, Paul and Silvanus had reminded the believers at Thessalonica that they told them beforehand that they would suffer. And it happened as they predicted.

Herein is a conundrum: Christians are destined for suffering—and this by the directive hand of God. At the same time, Satan, the tempter, will use the suffering of tribulations to tempt Christians to compromise their faith or even abandon their faith. Beale says, "The tension can be resolved as an antinomy, an apparent contradiction from the human perspective but not from God's. [Herein] a causal chain may be perceived: (1) God as the ultimate cause, (2) Satan as the intermediate cause, and (3) human persecutors . . . as the most immediate cause" (2003:101). Mature Christians will have gone through this experience so many times in their lives that they will recognize this chain when they are undergoing persecution or any kind of suffering for that matter. While Paul and Silvanus were still with the Thessalonians, they had exhorted them to see the bigger picture (from the divine perspective), and later Timothy encouraged them to remain faithful to Christ during persecution.

When Timothy reported to Paul and Silas the situation of the church in Thessalonica (3:6-8), he brought good news of the church's faith and love, as well as of their steadfastness (3:8), a sign of their endurance motivated by hope (1:3). Paul and Silvanus were also told that the Thessalonians had good remembrances of their time together and that the Thessalonians also longed to see them again. In short, the feelings were reciprocated (2:17-20; 3:1, 5, 7-10).

◆ IV. Thanksgiving and Prayer (3:9-13)

9How we thank God for you! Because of you we have great joy as we enter God's presence. 10Night and day we pray earnestly for you, asking God to let us see you again to fill the gaps in your faith.

11May God our Father and our Lord

Jesus bring us to you very soon. ¹²And may the Lord make your love for one another and for all people grow and overflow, just as our love for you overflows. ¹³May he, as a result, make your hearts strong, blameless, and holy as you stand before God our Father when our Lord Jesus comes again with all his holy people. Amen.

NOTES

3:9 *we thank God for you!* The Greek verb is *antapodidōmi* [TG467, ZG500], which means "to pay back"—often in the sense of revenge (see 2 Thess 1:6). Here it means to pay back God with thanks.

as we enter God's presence. This is an excellent functional equivalent for the Greek expression literally translated as "before our God."

3:10 *to fill the gaps in your faith.* This is an excellent functional equivalent for the Greek expression literally translated as "to supply the shortcomings of your faith."

3:11 *God our Father and our Lord Jesus.* In the Greek, *autos de ho theos* [TG2316, ZG2536] (God himself) is followed by *kai . . . kai* [TG2532, ZG2779], which is normally translated as "both . . . and." Therefore, the rendering should be "may God himself—both our Father and our Lord Jesus—direct you." This rendering is substantiated by the fact that a singular verb, *kateuthunai* [TG2720, ZG2985] (may he direct), follows. If two agents were being thought of, the verb would be plural. But one agent, God (who is both the Father and Lord Jesus), is the subject. The singular verb highlights the apostles' belief in the unity of God and Jesus (Morris 1991:106-108) and thereby affirms that, in the apostles' thinking, entering the presence of God was entering the presence of Jesus.

bring us to you very soon. Lit., "direct our way to you." This imagery connects with that found in 2:18, which speaks of Satan hindering the apostles from coming to the Thessalonians.

3:13 *when our Lord Jesus comes again.* The coming of the Lord Jesus is known as his *parousia* [TG3952, ZG4242].

with all his holy people. This rendering indicates that holy people will accompany Jesus in his parousia. Although the Greek allows for this, the more likely interpretation is that "all the holy ones" are angels (see commentary). This language closely follows Zech 14:5 and *1 Enoch* 1:9. In a parallel verse, Jude 1:14, Jude cited *1 Enoch* 1:9 to exhibit a prophetic parousia of Christ, who is accompanied by "thousands of his holy ones." This is the reading in Jude in several manuscripts (A B C 33 1739 𝔐 syr^h cop^bo). However, other manuscripts read "holy angels" (ℵ 044 𝔓72) instead of "holy ones." Osburn (1976:334-341) makes the case that 𝔓72's wording closely follows the manuscript 4QEnoch (first century BC) and may therefore be original—especially for a writer such as Jude, who was used to thinking in Aramaic and was consciously following *1 Enoch* as he wrote his epistle. Whether 𝔓72 is original or not, it seems very likely that Paul and Silvanus, as well as Jude, were thinking of angels (see commentary).

Amen. This word is included in some manuscripts (ℵ* A D* cop^bo) and omitted in several others (ℵ² B D² F G 044 0278 1739 𝔐 syr cop^sa). If "amen" had originally been in the text, there is no good reason to account for its omission on transcriptional grounds. Furthermore, the same manuscripts that have an additional "amen" here also have one at the end of 5:28 (see note). In fact, the scribes of ℵ, A, and D had a marked propensity for appending an "amen" to the end of prayers (e.g., at 1 Cor 16:24; 2 Cor 13:14; Eph 6:24; Phil 4:23; Col 4:18). This is a strong sign that this is a scribal enhancement intended to mark the end of a prayer prior to further discourse (4:1ff).

COMMENTARY

Paul and Silvanus had attempted to return to Thessalonica on numerous occasions, but they were hindered by Satan from going to them (see 2:17-18 and commentary). They responded to this spiritual warfare by entering God's presence through prayer (3:9). Paul and Silvanus prayed constantly, intensely, and earnestly that they would be able to see the Thessalonians. They wanted to spend some time with them so they could fill up whatever was lacking in their faith (3:10). The apostles viewed their function as being those who explained to believers all facets of the Christian faith so as to fortify them with the truth.

In their times of prayer, Paul and Silvanus asked God to direct their way to the Thessalonians. Satan had set up a roadblock against them (see note on 2:18), and they needed a way through; they asked God himself, who is both the Father and the Lord Jesus (see notes on 3:11), to provide that access. Their prayer was finally answered six years later (AD 56), when Paul returned to the region of Macedonia (Acts 20:1-3).

Paul and Silvanus also prayed that the Thessalonians would increase in their love for one another (1:3; 4:9; 2 Thess 1:3-4) as well as for those outside the community of believers (cf. 5:15; Gal 6:10; 2 Tim 2:24; Titus 3:2). The final part of the prayer is that in their conduct and moral resolve (the seat of which is their hearts; Matt 5:8; Heb 10:22) they might be established (see 3:2), and therefore be found "blameless, and holy" (3:13) when the Lord returns. The first word (*amemptous* [TG273, ZG289]; cf. 2:10) indicates "a condition of blamelessness in which an individual is found to have done nothing deserving condemnation by God" (Wanamaker 1990:144). The second word (*hagiōsunē* [TG42, ZG43]) indicates "moral conformity to the very character of God" (Wanamaker 1990:144). To be blameless means to be in good standing with God; it does not mean sinless perfection. To be holy means to be set apart for God, so as to be a person who can live with him and serve him. The final evaluation of Christians' motives and conduct will come when they stand before God, who will return with his holy ones, at the time of the Lord's parousia.

The final image of the chapter (3:13) is taken from Zechariah 14:5, which reads, "the LORD my God will come, and all his holy ones with him." That Paul and Silvanus substituted "the Lord Jesus" for "the LORD my God" shows they identified him with Yahweh, the subject of this prophecy. But who are "the holy ones" that accompany him? Elsewhere in the Old Testament, these "holy ones" are angels (Deut 33:3; Ps 89:4-7; Dan 4:13; 8:13). And when Jesus himself spoke of the end time and his parousia, he said that angels would come with the Son of Man (Matt 13:41; Mark 8:38; 13:26-27). Second Thessalonians 1:7 affirms the same: "When the Lord Jesus appears from heaven[, h]e will come with his mighty angels." The angels come to fight alongside Jesus against God's enemies and then to gather together God's chosen people.

However, we cannot completely exclude the idea that "holy ones" may be referring to people, because 2 Thessalonians 1:10 speaks of the Lord Jesus coming to be glorified in his "holy people" (cf. Rom 8:19). As such, we cannot dismiss the rendering found in the NLT. This rendering interprets the holy ones as people who have gone to be with the Lord who will return with him at the time of the Parousia. This presumes that they went to be with the Lord Jesus (1) either at the time of their deaths or (2) in some kind of secret Rapture prior to the manifest parousia of Jesus Christ. The first option is possible but does not readily fit this passage nor 4:13-17, which indicates that the dead believers will rise again to meet Jesus at the time of his parousia.

◆ V. The Apostles' Advice on Life in the Community (4:1-12)

Finally, dear brothers and sisters,* we urge you in the name of the Lord Jesus to live in a way that pleases God, as we have taught you. You live this way already, and we encourage you to do so even more. ²For you remember what we taught you by the authority of the Lord Jesus.

³God's will is for you to be holy, so stay away from all sexual sin. ⁴Then each of you will control his own body* and live in holiness and honor—⁵not in lustful passion like the pagans who do not know God and his ways. ⁶Never harm or cheat a Christian brother in this matter by violating his wife,* for the Lord avenges all such sins, as we have solemnly warned you before. ⁷God has called us to live holy lives, not impure lives. ⁸Therefore, anyone who refuses to live by these rules is not disobeying human teaching but is rejecting God, who gives his Holy Spirit to you.

⁹But we don't need to write to you about the importance of loving each other,* for God himself has taught you to love one another. ¹⁰Indeed, you already show your love for all the believers* throughout Macedonia. Even so, dear brothers and sisters, we urge you to love them even more.

¹¹Make it your goal to live a quiet life, minding your own business and working with your hands, just as we instructed you before. ¹²Then people who are not Christians will respect the way you live, and you will not need to depend on others.

4:1 Greek *brothers;* also in 4:10, 13.   4:4 Or *will know how to take a wife for himself;* or *will learn to live with his own wife;* Greek reads *will know how to possess his own vessel.*   4:6 Greek *Never harm or cheat a brother in this matter.*   4:9 Greek *about brotherly love.*   4:10 Greek *the brothers.*

NOTES

4:1 *to live in a way that pleases God.* In formal equivalence translations, the Greek verb (*peripateō* [TG4043, ZG4344]) behind "live" is usually rendered as "walk," but this is a Greek idiom for "conducting one's life."

4:2 *what we taught you.* The Greek is stronger: "what orders we gave you" (cf. 4:11; 2 Thess 3:4, 6, 10, 12).

by the authority of the Lord Jesus. Lit., "through the Lord Jesus," but the NLT expansion is justified on the basis of context (4:2a, 8).

4:3 *God's will is for you to be holy.* Holiness is the most important aspect of Christian disposition and nature, as emphasized in 1 Thessalonians (see 3:13; 4:4, 7; 5:23).

sexual sin. The Greek is *porneias* [TG4202, ZG4518], which pertains to any sexual union outside marriage.

4:4 *will control his own body.* The Greek reads, "to know how to possess his own vessel"— the idea of *possess* can mean "acquire" or perhaps "control." The Greek verb *ktasthai* [TG2932, ZG3227] usually means "to acquire" (BDAG 472). In classical Greek the word ranged in meaning from being proficient in something, such as music or poetry, to exercising mastery over slaves (LSJ 1001). Since mastery over something is conveyed by this word, it could mean "control." However, it must be noted that there are no known examples in Greek literature of one exercising mastery (*ktaomai*) over one's sexual passions (cf. BDAG MM). The more natural meaning has to do with acquiring or procuring a wife, when the context speaks of marriage (Ruth 4:10, LXX; Sir 36:24; Xenophon, *Symposium* 2.10).

The Greek noun in this phrase is *skeuos* [TG4632, ZG5007], which literally means "vessel," but in this context must be read metaphorically—as either a person's body, or male organ, or wife. If the verb *ktasthai* [TG2932, ZG3227] means "to control," then the most natural corresponding noun would be "body" (or, "male organ"). If the verb *ktasthai* means "acquire," then the most natural corresponding noun would be "wife." The NLT renders the verb as denoting "control" and the metaphor of the "vessel" as signifying one's "body" (as in 2 Cor 4:7; cf. Rom 9:21-23). Several scholars favor this interpretation: "will control his own body" (Marshall 1983:107-109; Wanamaker 1990:152-153; Morris 1991:119-121). In the OT, this Greek word was also used as a euphemism for the genitals (1 Sam 21:5, LXX); this is also the usage in *Epistle of Barnabas* 21:8. Thus, it stands to reason that the writers were exhorting male Christians to control their own bodies as to sexual desire.

However, *skeuos* is used as a metaphor for "wife" in 1 Pet 3:7 and rabbinic writings, which points toward the two other renderings provided in the NLT margin: (1) "will know how to take a wife for himself"; (2) "will learn to live with his own wife." The first alternative concurs with the NAB and is supported by some (TDNT 7.365-367; Best 1972:160-163). It speaks of taking a wife so as to avoid sexual immorality (as in 1 Cor 7:1ff). In the second alternative, the sense is "keep on acquiring" or "live with" in the sense of cultivating the wife's favor (R. Thomas 1978:271).

live in holiness and honor. Holiness is central to the Christian life; honor (*timē* [TG5092, ZG5507]) is the benefit of living a holy life. First Peter 3:7 also speaks of honor as marking a good Christian marriage.

4:5 lustful passion. The Greek is *pathei epithumias* [TG3806/1939, ZG4079/2123]; the second term usually denotes erotic passion, as in Rom 1:24; Col 3:5; and throughout Greek literature (BAGD 603; BDAG 372; MM 473; TDNT 5.926-930).

pagans who do not know God. Ignorance of God characterizes people who worship multiple gods (Rom 1:21-23; Eph 4:17-18).

4:6 Never harm or cheat a Christian brother in this matter by violating his wife. Lit., "not to overstep and to defraud your brother in this matter." The verb "harm" is a translation of *huperbainein* [TG5233, ZG5648], a word that literally means "to overstep" or "to trespass." The verb "cheat" is a translation of *pleonektein* [TG4122, ZG4430], which means "to defraud" or "to exploit." In this context the verbs indicate that a person who commits adultery has "overstepped the boundary set by the divine command and [has] transgressed against fellow Christians. This transgression is also condemned as an exploitation of another member of the church" (Green 2002:196). The expression "by violating his wife" is not in the Greek, but its presence in the NLT is justified as a helpful explanatory gloss.

the Lord avenges all such sins. Though this sounds like an OT quotation, it is not. In fact, there are no OT quotations in 1 or 2 Thessalonians. But the statement parallels Deut 32:35 and Ps 94:1.

4:7 God has called us to live holy lives. God's election leads to moral purity, a theme that appears often in 1 and 2 Thessalonians (1:4; 2:12; 5:23-24; 2 Thess 2:13-14), as well as in 1 Pet 1:15-16.

4:8 refuses to live by these rules . . . not disobeying human teaching. The Greek verb in both instances is *atheteō* [TG114, ZG119], which means "reject"—with the object of the first rejecting unspecified: "the one rejecting is not rejecting a human, but God." The apostolic rules are correctly implied.

who gives his Holy Spirit to you. In Greek the word order is "his Spirit, the holy one,"— with an emphasis on the holiness of God's Spirit.

4:9 *we don't need to write to you.* Green (2002:202) believes the wording in the Greek (*peri* [TG4012, ZG4309] *de* = "now concerning") comes in response to questions the Thessalonians asked (cf. 1 Cor 7:1) concerning love in the Christian family (4:9-12), the destiny of deceased believers (4:13-18), and when the Day of the Lord would come (5:1-11). F. F. Bruce disagrees, saying "it is unlikely that *peri de* ["now concerning"] refers to a question sent to the missionaries by the Thessalonian Christians; it is not the kind of specific subject on which ruling would be sought, and the writers indicate that it is not something on which the Thessalonians require instruction" (1982:89). R. Thomas (1978:273) says that the writer or writers were responding to different elements of Timothy's oral report.

loving each other. Gr., *philadelphias* [TG5360, ZG5789], which denotes fraternal love or love among family members.

God himself has taught. Gr., *theodidaktoi* [TG2312, ZG2531], which could also be rendered "you are divinely taught." This is the only occurrence of this word in the NT and its earliest occurrence in Greek literature (Bruce 1982:90).

to love one another. The Greek shifts here from "brotherly love" to "agape love": *eis to agapan allēlous* [TG25/240, ZG26/253] (to love one another). In this instance, the variation of vocabulary points to the fact that the words could be used interchangeably.

4:11 *Make it your goal.* This is a rendering of *philotimeomai* [TG5389, ZG5818], which could also be rendered "aspire" or "consider it an honor" (BDAG 1059).

to live a quiet life. This is a good rendering of the Greek expression *hēsuchazein* [TG2270, ZG2483]. In the Greek, the full clause is something of an oxymoron—"Be ambitious to be quiet."

minding your own business. This was often an exhortation to avoid meddling in the affairs of others.

working with your hands. They should earn their own living (2 Thess 3:6-15), as Paul previously commanded them through both his teaching (2 Thess 3:10) and personal example (2 Thess 3:7-9).

4:12 *people who are not Christians.* Lit., "the outsiders." The same expression appears in 1 Cor 5:12-13 and Col 4:5; it defines those who are not part of the Christian community.

COMMENTARY

First Thessalonians 4:1-12 introduces the next section of the letter. It seems that Paul and Silvanus composed the second part of the letter in response to news that Timothy brought about the church and questions that they put to Paul and Silvanus. They addressed the problem of sexual immorality (4:3-8) before responding to the issues of fraternal love (4:9-12), the destiny of Christians who have died before the coming of the Lord (4:13-18), and the timing of the Day of the Lord (5:1-11).

Paul and Silvanus begin this section by urging the Thessalonians in "the name of the Lord Jesus" to live a life pleasing to God. The apostles' claim to the authority of the Lord Jesus comes from their union with the risen Lord. For the early Christians, "the Lord" referred particularly to the risen Jesus. In his first sermon, Peter said, "God has made this Jesus, whom you crucified, to be both Lord and Messiah" (Acts 2:36). For Paul, one's confession of Jesus as being "Lord" was the mark of a true believer. This is clearly stipulated in Romans 10:9: "If you confess with your mouth that Jesus is Lord and believe in your heart that God raised him from the dead, you will be saved." Paul emphasized that no one could say that "Jesus is Lord" without the empowering of the Holy Spirit (1 Cor 12:3). To be under the lordship of Jesus was to be united with the Spirit of the risen Jesus, as were the apostles, and thereby given the boldness to proclaim that their message had come "by the authority of the Lord Jesus" (4:2) and by God who gives the Holy Spirit (4:8). Since the apostles considered their teachings to have come from the Lord, their instructions were commands that had to be obeyed (4:2, 8).

The apostles' primary instructions in this section had to do with holiness or what some call sanctification. To be holy means to be set apart for God, who is different from all. Holiness was and is the Christian's calling, especially for those who were formerly pagan idolaters. As such, Christian standards had to be different from the prevailing standards among the heathen, who didn't know God. And what was true then is true today: Sexual relationships must not be determined by lust but expressed in holiness and honor within the bonds of marriage.

Sexual immorality was rampant and generally tolerated in the Mediterranean world. Prostitution was allowed, and Roman marriage contracts allowed men to have extramarital affairs. But adultery—specifically sexual relations with another's wife—was prohibited. In AD 18 Augustus established the Julian Law, which prohibited adultery, even though the law's effectiveness in restraining it was questionable (Treggiari 1991:277-298).

Since the Thessalonians were pagans steeped in a world of sexual liberties, Paul and Silvanus gave them instructions on living holy lives in the midst of their pagan contemporaries. First, they urged them to abstain from "all sexual sin" (lit., "fornication"), which was a censure against all illicit sexual activity (4:3). In order to not be taken over by lustful passions that lead to fornication, Paul and Silvanus urged each brother to "know how to take a wife for himself" (NLT mg) and thereby avoid sexual immorality (as in 1 Cor 7:1ff). A second alternative, as noted in the NLT mg, is that a brother should "learn to live with his own wife." This idea is paralleled in 1 Peter 3:7, where both the husband and wife are called "vessels" in the Greek, and where the writer urges husbands to live with their wives in an understanding way so as to promote holiness and honor (a thought remarkably similar to that of 1 Thess 4:4 and likely showing Silvanus's participation in cowriting both epistles). A third understanding of the instruction in 4:4, as printed in the NLT ("each of you will control his own body"), pertains to one's ability to control his own sexual desires (see note on 4:4 for an extensive discussion of the alternative interpretations). No matter what the interpretation, the apostles were urging the Thessalonians to keep all their sexual activity within the bounds of marriage—an exhortation that sorely needs to be heeded in the twenty-first century, with sexual sin rampant among Christians. Above all, the Thessalonians were exhorted to refrain from engaging in sexual activity with a wife of another Christian (see note on 4:6), which is a very grave sin that will be severely punished by the Lord.

Holiness involves separation from the world and devotion to God. According to this passage, the way to achieve holiness is twofold: (1) Live in a way that differs from pagan unbelievers, especially in regard to sexual behavior; and (2) live by the Holy Spirit of God, who sanctifies believers by his indwelling presence and transforming power. The writers of 1 Thessalonians spoke frequently of the divine Spirit because their experience of the Spirit was key to the Thessalonians' first encounter with the gospel (1:5), their joy in the midst of persecutions (1:6), and revelation from God in their gatherings (5:19). This Spirit was living and working in the believers' spirits, souls, and bodies so as to make them ready for the Lord's parousia (5:23).

The Spirit of God was also working in the Thessalonians to instill a love in them for one another, a love that is called *philadelphia* [TG5360, ZG5789] (brotherly love). The members of God's family love one another because they share the same Father and the same divine life. This love was divinely taught by the same Spirit who indwells all Christians. It was also taught by Jesus to his disciples (John 13:34-35). Paul and Silvanus were not commanding the Thessalonians to love one another anew but to keep on loving one another and to do so with abundance. They told the Thessalonians: "you already show your love for all the believers throughout Macedonia" (4:10). Their love for believers in Macedonia (including the cities of Philippi and Berea; see also 1:7-8), was perhaps demonstrated through economic aid (cf. 2 Cor 8:1-5). This exemplary behavior was cause for kudos and encouragement to abound even more.

At the same time, Paul and Silvanus encouraged the Thessalonians to aspire to quiet living. As was noted, this is a paradox (see note on 4:11). Most people aspire to achieve honor from others by thrusting themselves into public view. Aspiring to live a quiet life is defined as Christians minding their own business and working with their own hands for their own living. This exhortation was important for the community of believers who needed to become ever more self-sufficient within their own ranks, especially in light of the persecution coming against them, a persecution that could cut them off from societal support. They needed to become sufficient among themselves so as not to be dependent on outsiders (non-Christians) for financial support.

◆ VI. The Parousia of the Lord Jesus (4:13–5:11)

¹³And now, dear brothers and sisters, we want you to know what will happen to the believers who have died* so you will not grieve like people who have no hope. ¹⁴For since we believe that Jesus died and was raised to life again, we also believe that when Jesus returns, God will bring back with him the believers who have died.

¹⁵We tell you this directly from the Lord: We who are still living when the Lord returns will not meet him ahead of those who have died.* ¹⁶For the Lord himself will come down from heaven with a commanding shout, with the voice of the archangel, and with the trumpet call of God. First, the Christians who have died* will rise from their graves. ¹⁷Then, together with them, we who are still alive and remain on the earth will be caught up in the clouds to meet the Lord in the air. Then we will be with the Lord forever. ¹⁸So encourage each other with these words.

CHAPTER 5

Now concerning how and when all this will happen, dear brothers and sisters,* we don't really need to write you. ²For you know quite well that the day of the Lord's return will come unexpectedly, like a thief in the night. ³When people are saying, "Everything is peaceful and secure," then disaster will fall on them as suddenly as a pregnant woman's labor pains begin. And there will be no escape.

⁴But you aren't in the dark about these things, dear brothers and sisters, and you won't be surprised when the day of the Lord comes like a thief.* ⁵For you are all children of the light and of the day; we don't belong to darkness and night. ⁶So be on your guard, not asleep like the others. Stay alert and be clearheaded. ⁷Night is the time when people sleep and drinkers get drunk. ⁸But let us who live in the light be clearheaded, protected by the armor of faith and love, and wearing as our helmet the confidence of our salvation.

⁹For God chose to save us through our Lord Jesus Christ, not to pour out his anger on us. ¹⁰Christ died for us so that, whether we are dead or alive when he returns, we can live with him forever. ¹¹So encourage each other and build each other up, just as you are already doing.

4:13 Greek *those who have fallen asleep;* also in 4:14.   4:15 Greek *those who have fallen asleep.*   4:16 Greek *the dead in Christ.*   5:1 Greek *brothers;* also in 5:4, 12, 14, 25, 26, 27.   5:4 Some manuscripts read *comes upon you as if you were thieves.*

NOTES

4:13 *And now.* This expression introduces the response to the second question the Thessalonians addressed to Paul (4:9; 5:1).

the believers who have died. NA²⁷ and UBS⁴ read *peri tōn koimōmenōn* [ᵀᴳ2837, ᶻᴳ3121] (concerning the ones sleeping) with the excellent manuscript support of ℵ A B 0278 33 1739. The TR reads *peri tōn kekoimēmenōn* [ᵀᴳ2837, ᶻᴳ3121] (concerning the ones having slept) with the support of D (F G) 044 𝔐. The variant reading in the TR is a scribal alteration intended to conform this idiom to the more familiar form, which usually appears in the perfect tense (see Matt 27:52; 1 Cor 15:20). But the writers' emphasis here is not on those who experienced death (which is conveyed by the euphemistic idiom "sleeping") but on those who are presently dead, for which the present tense is appropriate. These are the Christians who sleep (in death) until the parousia of Christ and their subsequent resurrection. Although death is spoken of as "sleep," it seems that conscious existence continues after death (Luke 23:40-43; Acts 7:55-60; 2 Cor 5:6-10; Phil 1:20-24; Rev 6:9-11).

grieve like people who have no hope. For the pagan neighbors of the Thessalonians, "living hope as a fundamental religious attitude was unknown in Greek culture. . . . In the final analysis men had to stand without hope before the hostile forces of guilt and death" (NIDNTT 2.239).

4:14 *For since we believe that Jesus died and was raised to life again.* The Greek here for "raised to life" (*anestē* from *anistēmi* [ᵀᴳ450, ᶻᴳ482]) is not the word Paul characteristically used when speaking of Jesus being raised from the dead. Paul normally used the word *egeirō* [ᵀᴳ1453, ᶻᴳ1586]; in fact, he used it 37 times. Green writes, "These characteristics suggest that the apostle appeals to a pre-Pauline creed that had been handed over to the church and that both the apostolic company and the Thessalonians confessed" (2002:220). I would add that this points to the fact that Paul was not the solo or lead writer of this epistle; rather, it seems that Silvanus used a term that was common to the early kerygma.

when Jesus returns, God will bring back with him the believers who have died. This is more precisely, "God will take [in resurrection] with him [Jesus] the believers who have died in Jesus [i.e., in union with him]" (see commentary for full discussion).

4:15 *We tell you this directly from the Lord.* Lit., "for this we say to you by a word from the Lord." There are two critical issues here: (1) What does "this" refer to—just the following statement in 4:15 or all of 4:15-17? (2) What is "a word from the Lord" the writers had received—was it a supernatural prophecy they received directly from the Lord Jesus or was it some word spoken by Jesus when he was on earth?

As to the first issue, Greek grammar allows for *touto* [TG3778A, ZG4047] (this) to point to the following complete sentence, which runs until the end of 4:17 (see punctuation in NA²⁷ and UBS⁴). This means that 4:15-17 is "a word from the Lord." But several scholars think it points to only the statement in 4:15 ("We who are still living when the Lord returns will not meet him ahead of those who have died"). It is apparent that our present Gospels do not record Jesus saying such a thing. So this is either an unrecorded statement or it is a Spirit-inspired word that came to Paul and/or Silvanus. On the other hand, if the "word from the Lord" includes all of 4:15-17, then much of what is said in 4:16-17 can be found in Matthew 24 (see commentary for detailed discussion).

We who are still living . . . will not meet him ahead of those who have died. Paul wants the Thessalonians to know that the dead will not be disadvantaged when Jesus returns; they will occupy the place of honor.

when the Lord returns. The Greek is *parousian tou kuriou* [TG3952/2962, ZG4242/361] (parousia of the Lord). In modern Christian jargon, this is often spoken of as the Lord's "return," but the term "parousia" is richer than this. In Hellenistic usage, it had two primary definitions: (1) "The word served as a sacred expression for the coming of a hidden divinity, who makes his presence felt by a revelation of his power, or whose presence is celebrated in the cult" (BDAG 780). This was used, for example, of Dionysius's *parousia* on earth—*he tou theou parousia* (Diodorus Siculus 3.65.1). (2) The word "became the official term for a visit of a person of high rank, especially of kings and emperors visiting a province" (BDAG 781). Citations in MM (497) show that the word was used "from Ptolemaic times onwards to denote the 'visit' of a king, emperor, or other person in authority, the official character of the 'visit' being further emphasized by the taxes or payments that were extracted to make preparations for it." This is seen, for example, in Petrie Papyri II 39, l. 19 (3rd century BC), which speaks of a crown being offered to a king on his arrival (*parousia*) and in P. Tebtunis 48, l. 14 (113 BC), where a sum of wheat is to be laid aside for the coming (*parousia*) of a king. But the word doesn't always have to be associated with payments; P. Paris 26, l. 1, 18, for example, speaks of the visitation (*parousia*) of King Ptolemy Philometor and Cleopatra to Memphis (163/162 BC).

In the NT, the term *parousia* [TG3952, ZG4242] was used to denote the presence of a certain person at a certain place (1 Cor 16:17; Phil 2:12), as well as a normal visitation of a person to a certain place (2 Cor 7:6; Phil 1:26). Both these ideas mingle when it is used of Jesus Christ's coming to be present with his people (2:19; 3:13; 4:15; 5:23; Matt 24:3, 27, 37-39; 1 Cor 15:23; 2 Thess 2:1, 8).

4:16 *will come down from heaven.* The early Christians expected Jesus to descend from heaven (see 1:10; Acts 1:11; 2 Thess 1:7); see commentary for the possible meanings of this.

with a commanding shout. Although it is not said who makes this shout, it could very well be Christ because he said the dead would hear his voice at the time of the resurrection (John 5:28-29).

with the voice of the archangel. According to Jesus' discourse on the end times, angels will come with Jesus to gather together the chosen ones (Matt 24:31). Here we have reference to an archangel; the only other use of the word in the NT is Jude's mention of Michael (Jude 1:9).

with the trumpet call of God. According to Jesus' discourse on the end times, a trumpet blast will announce the Parousia (Matt 24:31; see also 1 Cor 15:52).

4:17 we who are still alive and remain on the earth. This statement indicates that the writers, Paul, Silvanus, and Timothy, expected to be alive at the time of Christ's parousia.

will be caught up. The Greek comes from the word *harpazō* [TG726, ZG773], which means "snatch," "seize," "take away suddenly." This term in Latin, *raptus,* "is the source of the popular designation of this event as the 'rapture'" (R. Thomas 1978:279). In its NT usage, the word often speaks of a violent or sudden snatching away, as when a wolf snatches a sheep (John 10:12), or when the crowds wanted to snatch Jesus and force him to be their king (John 6:15), or when the soldiers rescued Paul by snatching him away from a violent mob (Acts 23:10). It is also used of the activity of a thief (Matt 12:29). On occasion, it is used of a person being snatched away by the Spirit (Acts 8:39) and snatched away into heaven (2 Cor 12:2, 4; Rev 12:5). Morris says that in this verb there is "often the notion of a sudden swoop, and usually that of a force that cannot be resisted. The applicability of such a verb to the snatching away (the 'rapture') of the saints is obvious" (1991:145).

in the clouds. The image of the Son of Man coming on the clouds originated in the OT with Isa 19:1 and Dan 7:13. Jesus himself affirmed the image (Matt 24:30; 26:64), which John saw in his apocalyptic vision (Rev 14:14-16).

to meet the Lord. The Greek expression for the verb is *eis apantēsin* [TG529, ZG561]; this refers to the custom of sending an official delegation out of the city to meet a visiting dignitary (Matt 25:6; Acts 28:15-16). They would go out to accompany the dignitary and return with him to the city. The implication is that the risen and raptured Christians will leave earth and go to meet Jesus in the air and then return with him to earth.

in the air. The Greek word for "air" (*aēr* [TG109, ZG113]) denotes the atmosphere above earth, not heaven.

4:18 encourage each other with these words. Paul and Silvanus presented these teachings so that believers can comfort and encourage each other in the face of death. The purpose is not to promote speculation about the end times.

5:1 Now concerning. Gr. *peri de.* The same expression appears at the beginning of 4:9 to signal a new section. As such, some readers might think 4:13-18 and 5:1-10 are addressing two different events. Ryrie (1974) thought the two sections are so different as to be in contrast. However, many commentators see 5:1-10 as continuing the general theme of the preceding paragraph (Beale 2003:143). It is probably best to recognize that *peri de* marks "the transition from relating the Parousia to the dead to pointing to its importance to the living" (Morris 1991:148).

when all this will happen. Lit., "the times and the seasons."

we don't really need to write you. Some scholars think this wording suggests that the Thessalonians had written a letter to Paul and Silvanus with various questions. Paul and Silvanus responded to some of these questions (see note on 4:9).

5:2 For you know quite well. The apostles appealed to the teaching the Thessalonians had already received (3:3-4; 2 Thess 2:5).

the day of the Lord's return. Lit., "the day of the Lord." This is the time when God will come to judge humanity (Isa 13:6, 9; Ezek 30:3) and save his people (Joel 2:21-32; 3:18; Zech 14:1-21). See commentary for further discussion.

like a thief in the night. This image of Christ coming as a thief, which appears throughout the NT in association with the *parousia* [TG3952, ZG4242], communicates the unexpected nature of Christ's second coming (see 5:2, 4; Matt 24:36, 42-43; Luke 12:39-40; 2 Pet 3:10; Rev 3:3; 16:15).

5:3 *"Everything is peaceful and secure."* The expression "peace and safety" (*pax et securitas*) was common during the era of the *pax Romana* (Roman peace). During this time period, people in the Roman Empire felt protected against barbarian attacks.

suddenly. The word *aiphnidios* [TG160, ZG167] occurs only one other time in the NT—namely Luke 21:34, a word from Jesus about the suddenness of the Parousia.

a pregnant woman's labor pains. Jesus used the same image in speaking of the suddenness of the Parousia (Matt 24:8; Mark 13:8).

5:4 *the day . . . comes like a thief.* This reading has the support of $\aleph$ D F G 0278 33 1739 $\mathfrak{M}$. A variant reading is "the day comes upon you as if you were thieves," as in A B cop^bo (so NLT mg). There is great diversity of opinion about the variant reading. For example, Metzger (1994:565) considers it "near nonsense," whereas Lightfoot (1904:73-74) considers it the more probable reading because it is more difficult and because it is far more likely that a scribe would change *kleptas* (plural) to *kleptēs* [TG2812, ZG3095] in order to make it conform to 5:2. Indeed, it is not unlike Paul to shift his metaphor—from "the day of the Lord's return will come unexpectedly, like a thief in the night" (5:2) to "you won't be surprised like thieves when the day of the Lord comes" (5:4). The idea is that the Thessalonians were being warned not to be caught in the act of living in darkness, as if they were thieves caught in the act of stealing. The natural antithesis follows: "For you are all children of the light and of the day" (5:5). Thus, the variant reading, supported by A and B, is likely original, and one that is worthy of acceptance into the text (as in WH).

5:5 *children of the light and of the day.* Lit., "sons of light, sons of day." In the writings at Qumran (1QS 1:9-10; 3:13; 3:24-25; 1QM 1:1), the "sons of light" are the elect of God, while "the sons of darkness" are those excluded from God's community. This expression, found also in John 12:36 and Eph 5:8, means that the people who follow Christ are those who live in his light.

5:6 *be on your guard.* This follows Jesus' call to preparedness at all times since his believers will not know the day of his return. In fact, the same verb (*grēgoreō* [TG1127, ZG1213]) appears here as in Mark 13:35, 37 (cf. Matt 24:42, 44; 25:13; 1 Pet 1:13).

5:7 *sleep . . . get drunk.* Sleep refers to moral indifference (5:6). Drunkenness is a similar metaphor referring to those who do not exercise moral self-control and who will therefore be surprised by the Day of the Lord (5:4; Matt 24:48-51).

5:8 *clearheaded.* Gr. *nēphōmen* [TG3525, ZG3768], which has traditionally been rendered as "sober."

the armor of faith and love. The image of spiritual armor perhaps comes from Isa 59:17. Paul's most complete depiction of the Christian's spiritual panoply is found in Eph 6:11-17. Faith and love are the most noble virtues of the Christian; living in these protects the believer from the attacks of doubt.

our helmet the confidence of our salvation. The believers' helmet is the hope of Christ's parousia (see 1:3; 3:6, 8; 2 Thess 1:3-4).

5:9 *chose to save us.* God destined believers for salvation and not wrath (2 Thess 2:13-14). Believers will escape the terrors of the Day of the Lord (5:1-3; 1 Cor 1:8; 2 Pet 2:9).

our Lord Jesus Christ. 𝔓30 B and a few other mss read "our Lord Jesus," versus all other mss, which have the divine title as in NLT. But since we know that scribes tended to add names to divine titles and that the two earliest mss do not contain the word "Christ," it is possible that 𝔓30 and B contain the original reading and that the other mss exhibit an expansion influenced by 1:1 and 5:28.

his anger. This is God's wrath (1:10; 2:16; Rom 5:9), described in 2 Thess 1:6-10; 2:8; it is the execution of God's judgment against evil.

5:10 *Christ died for us so that . . . we can live with him.* This is the only reference in 1 and 2 Thessalonians to the substitutionary aspect of Jesus' death on the cross. "The form of this sentence, where the statement of the death or self-giving of Christ is followed by a clause expressing its purpose, is a recurring one in the letters of Paul" (Bruce 1982:113; see Rom 14:9; 2 Cor 5:15, 21; Gal 1:4). As in 2 Cor 5:15, 21, the message is that there is an interchange: Christ died so that his people may live.

whether we are dead or alive. Lit., "whether are awake or sleeping." This is a reference to living and deceased believers (4:13-15).

5:11 *encourage each other and build each other up.* This nearly repeats 4:18, thereby emphasizing that the writers wanted most of all to encourage the Thessalonian believers who were grieving for those among them who had died.

COMMENTARY

This section of 1 Thessalonians (4:13–5:11) is one of the portions of Scripture most consulted and studied by Christians seeking to understand the Lord's parousia (commonly known as the Second Coming) and the events associated with it—especially the resurrection from the dead. Two other events are also very important: the Rapture and the meeting of believers with Jesus. All of these critical components of the Parousia are discussed below.

The Source of the Message on the Parousia. One of the key verses in this section is the statement: "We tell you this directly from the Lord" (4:15). This also could be rendered as "we tell you this by the Lord's message." The significance of this proclamation is that Paul and Silvanus were claiming that their words were the Lord's message—and it is likely that this "message" extends from 4:15 to 4:17 (see note on 4:15). As to the words recorded in 4:15 that those "who are still living when the Lord returns will not meet him ahead of those who have died," it is possible that we have here the words of Jesus unrecorded in any of the four Gospels. But it seems hard to imagine that this remarkable statement would have been passed over by the Gospel writers (so G. Milligan 1908:58). Thus, it is far more likely that this statement came as direct revelation from the Lord Jesus to certain leaders of the church. Robert Thomas argues that this message was "probably a direct revelation to the church through one of her prophets, Paul himself or possibly some other" (1978:277). Following this, Thomas elaborates on the function of the New Testament prophets but never once mentions Silvanus—though he was among the most prominently known prophets of the early church (Acts 15:22, 32). Silvanus is habitually skipped in the commentaries because most commentators are thinking of Paul's sole authorship of 1 and 2 Thessalonians. As such, most speak of Paul alone as being the receptor of this word from the Lord. For example, Beale said that Paul was "recollecting the words of the earthly Jesus and paraphrasing him" (2003:136). But how could Paul recollect the words of Jesus when he had never been with the earthly (pre-resurrected) Jesus?

As to the words that are written in 4:16-17, it is very likely that Silvanus was saying that he had received (and was passing on) a message from the Lord Jesus that he spoke while on earth. It is likely that Silvanus had heard these teachings directly from Jesus as one of the 72 disciples (see discussion of "Authors" in Introduction). Nearly every single detail of the Parousia presented in 1 Thessalonians 4:16-17, as well as in 1 Thessalonians 5:1-10, is found in the Lord Jesus' teachings in the Gospels, especially in the chapters including Jesus' eschatological discourses (see chart below). Significantly, 1 and 2 Thessalonians are the earliest attestation of these teachings (AD 50–51), at least 10 to 15 years earlier than the Synoptic Gospels. Thus, source criticism should look to 1 and 2 Thessalonians before looking to the Gospels (specifically Matthew 24, Mark 13, and Luke 21). The earliest written sources concerning the Parousia are 1 Thessalonians 4:13–5:10 and 2 Thessalonians 2.

1 THESSALONIANS 4:13–5:10 AND THE GOSPEL SAYINGS OF JESUS

Christ returns	1 Thess 4:16	Matt 24:30; Mark 13:26; Luke 21:27
descends from heaven	1 Thess 4:16	Matt 24:30; Mark 13:26; Luke 21:27
a commanding shout	1 Thess 4:16	John 5:28-29
accompanied by angels	1 Thess 4:16 (an archangel)	Matt 24:31; Mark 13:27
with a trumpet call	1 Thess 4:16	Matt 24:31
the Christians who have died will rise	1 Thess 4:16	John 11:25-26
believers gathered to Christ	1 Thess 4:17	Matt 24:31; Mark 13:27
caught up in the clouds	1 Thess 4:17	Mark 13:26 (= Matt 24:40-41; Luke 21:34-35—one taken, another left)
to meet the Lord	1 Thess 4:17	Matt 25:6
be with the Lord forever	1 Thess 4:17; 5:10	John 17:24 (cf. Phil 1:23)
time unknown	1 Thess 5:1-2	Matt 24:36; Mark 13:32
coming like a thief	1 Thess 5:1-2	Matt 24:43
the Parousia will be sudden	1 Thess 5:3	Matt 24:37-39; Luke 21:34
judgment comes as labor pains	1 Thess 5:3	Matt 24:8; Mark 13:8
believers should be watchful and on guard	1 Thess 5:4-6	Matt 24:42-44; Mark 13:35-37; Luke 21:34-36
warning against drunkenness	1 Thess 5:7	Matt 24:48-50; Luke 21:34
live in the light	1 Thess 5:8	John 8:12; 12:35-36
chosen for salvation, not for God's wrath	1 Thess 5:9	Matt 24:13; Mark 13:13

The Parousia. As was explained in the note on 4:15, the word "parousia" had two usages in Hellenistic times: (1) as a term to describe the coming of a hidden divinity who made his presence felt by a revelation of his power; (2) as an official or technical term denoting the visit of a person of high rank. "These two technical expressions can approach each other closely in meaning, can shade off into one another, or even coincide" (BDAG 781). When the New Testament writers used the word "parousia," they must have known these two definitions, as did their readers. Thus, the notion of Jesus Christ's parousia speaks of his coming out of hiding to reveal his presence, and it speaks of his royal visitation. We must keep both of these ideas in mind when we study the parousia of Jesus Christ.

It is very likely that Jesus himself was responsible for inaugurating the term *parousia* [TG3952, ZG4242] to describe his second coming. In Matthew 24, a chapter that focuses entirely on Jesus' presentation of eschatology, the term is found four times. Though Matthew was written later than 1 and 2 Thessalonians, it may very well recapture terminology used by Jesus and the apostles (see Matt 24:3, where the disciples ask Jesus a question about his *parousia*, and see Matt 24:27, 37, 39 where Jesus three times speaks about "the parousia of the Son of Man").

Speaking of himself as the Son of Man, Jesus said he would come in clouds with great power and glory (Matt 24:30). This language is derived from the Old Testament, especially from Daniel's vision in which "someone like a son of man" comes with the clouds of heaven to receive everlasting dominion from the Ancient of Days (Dan 7:13-14). Jesus' last reference to his second coming was made at his trial before the Jewish authorities. When asked by the high priest to say whether or not he was the Christ, the Son of the Blessed, he replied, "I AM. And you will see the Son of Man seated in the place of power at God's right hand and coming on the clouds of heaven" (Mark 14:62).

Among all the New Testament writings, 1 and 2 Thessalonians have the most to say about the Parousia (see Introduction). In these two letters, Silvanus (especially) and Paul followed Jesus' teachings quite closely in speaking of Christ descending from heaven, accompanied by angels, a commanding shout, and a trumpet call, and resurrecting believers who are gathered to Christ in the clouds to be with him forever. They also concur with Jesus' teachings that the time of the Parousia is unknown, for it will come like a thief, catching unbelievers unaware, as when labor pains come to a woman. Therefore, believers should be watchful, not living in drunkenness but in the light; for the believers are chosen for salvation, not for wrath.

The Parousia, in this light, is presented as the glorious coming of the Lord Jesus (2:19; 3:13; 4:15-17). This mainly accords with the second definition of *parousia*—namely, it is the visitation of royalty. But we need to add to this the first definition of *parousia*—namely, that it is the manifestation of a hidden deity. The terminology of 2 Thessalonians 2:8 underscores this aspect of parousia, wherein Paul and Silvanus speak of "the splendor of [Christ's parousia]" (see note on 2 Thess 2:8 and commentary on 2 Thess 2:1-12).

The Parousia and the Resurrection. In the Gospels we cannot find a particular continuous passage where Jesus mentions both the Parousia and the resurrection. It is possible that the gathering together of the elect referred to in Jesus' eschatological discourse (Matt 24:31; Mark 13:27) implies resurrection, but it could refer to Rapture just as easily, if the two events are distinguished. A closer link is found in John 5:26-29 where we hear Jesus talking about the Son of Man being given the authority to execute judgment in "the time [that] is coming"; at that time he will call forth the resurrection of all people in two aspects: the resurrection that leads to eternal life and the resurrection that leads to judgment. It is possible, however, as was noted above, that this word "from the Lord" about the resurrection occurring simultaneous with the Parousia came directly to Paul and Silvanus.

The concept of the resurrection of the dead is found in some Old Testament passages, most clearly in Isaiah 25:8 ("He will swallow up death forever") and Daniel 12:2 ("Many of those whose bodies lie dead and buried will rise up, some to everlasting life and some to shame and everlasting disgrace"). The concept becomes more pronounced in intertestamental writings. According to 2 Maccabees 7, the seven brothers and their mother were suffering for the sins of the Jewish people (2 Macc 7:18, 32, 38), which would hasten the day when God would act against their enemies (2 Macc 7:17, 19, 31, 34-36) and restore them to life (2 Macc 7:9, 14, 23, 29). Josephus reported how the two famous and revered scribes, Judas and Matthias, urged their youthful adherents to tear down the eagle Herod had placed over the Temple gate with the assurance that even if they were killed for their action, it was noble to die for the Torah, and their souls would be deathless and attain eternal felicity (*War* 1.648-650)—that is, they would live in the restored Kingdom forever. The idea of resurrection to life in the restored Kingdom continued in Judaism as evidenced in the Mishnah: "All Israelites have a share in the world to come . . . And these are they that have no share in the world to come: he that says that there is no resurrection of the dead" (*Sanhedrin* 10:1). *Second Baruch* 30:1-2 says that when the Messiah comes, "all who have fallen asleep in hope of Him shall rise again." Many Jews, particularly the Pharisees, believed one's individual resurrection was the inaugural event for participation in the messianic kingdom of the age to come was one's individual resurrection (Dan 12:2; 2 Macc 7:14; *1 Enoch* 51:1-5; *Psalms of Solomon* 3:11-12). The Sadducees and Pharisees differed on what happens to human beings after death (cf. Acts 23:8). The Pharisees affirmed both an intermediate state and a final resurrection (Josephus, *War* 2.163; *Antiquities* 18:14; see *2 Baruch* 51:5, 10 for evidence of Jewish belief in an intermediate state like the angels; *1 Enoch* 22:3, 7; 103:3-4 for post-death existence as spirits). The Sadducees affirmed neither (Josephus, *War* 2.165; *Antiquities* 18:16; cf. Luke 20:36).

First Thessalonians, written not more than 20 years after the death and resurrection of Christ, is one of the earliest New Testament writings. In this letter, Jesus' parousia is presented by way of comfort and encouragement to those whose Christian friends and relatives had died. Paul and Silvanus had been forced to leave Thessalonica before they had time to give the new believers as much teaching as they required, and when some of their number died shortly after their departure, their friends wondered if they would suffer some serious disadvantage at the Parousia—especially in contrast to those who would still be alive to meet the returning Lord. Paul and Silvanus assured them that those who had died would suffer no disadvantage; on the contrary, the first thing to happen when the Lord himself descends from heaven is that the dead in Christ will rise. Only after that will those who survive be caught away to join them and be forever with the Lord (4:15-17).

Jesus Christ's death and resurrection serve as the prototype for all Christians. As he died and then rose again, so all who believe in him will experience the same. This is the message of 1 Thessalonians 4:14, which says, "since we believe that Jesus died and was raised to life again, we also believe that when Jesus returns, God will bring back with him the believers who have died." The final clause of this verse literally reads "God will bring [or, take] with him the ones having fallen asleep [i.e., died] through Jesus." This is a difficult sentence to interpret and translate, especially since the Greek verb *axei* [TG71, ZG72] can mean "bring" or "take." The statement could mean that God will bring from heaven, with Jesus, the souls of those Christians who have died. Or it could mean that God will take, with Jesus, the Christians who have died. "This second interpretation understands the verb as a reference to the resurrection or even the ascension, which presupposes the resurrection. This second interpretation is preferable since the concern of this verse and of vv. 15-16 is to show that the death and resurrection of Christ becomes the paradigm and foundation for the destiny of believers" (Green 2002:220). The expression "having died through Jesus" is a way of saying that these Christians died in union with Jesus (Moule 1971:57). Death does not separate Christians from Jesus. "This phrase then becomes an implicit affirmation that those who die as Christians do not cease to exist between the time of their death and the resurrection" (Green 2002:221).

Five years after writing his first letter to the Thessalonians, Paul provided further insights about the resurrection in the epistle known as 1 Corinthians. First Corinthians 15 is the most complete discussion on this subject in the Bible. In this chapter, the resurrection of believers is said to be the full harvest that was inaugurated by the resurrection of Christ: Christ the firstfruits of the harvest, then at his parousia those who belong to Christ (1 Cor 15:23). An additional revelation is imparted: Not only will each believer who has died be raised with a spiritual body (1 Cor 15:44), but those who are still alive will be changed so as to have bodies suitable for life in resurrection. For dead and living believers alike, Paul proclaimed that as we have borne the image of the man of dust (Adam; cf. Gen 2:7), we shall also bear the image of the man of heaven (the risen Christ; 1 Cor 15:49). To the same effect Paul writes in Philippians 3:20-21, a few years later, that from heaven "we await a Savior, the Lord Jesus Christ, who will change our lowly body to be like his glorious body" (RSV).

The Parousia and the Rapture. One of the events of the Parousia is known as the Rapture. As was noted (see note on 4:17), our English word "rapture" is loaned from Latin; it translates a Greek word *harpazō* [TG726, ZG773], which conveys an immediate, forceful snatching away. The word bears the triple connotation of (1) a snatching away as in a rescue from evil or danger (John 10:28-29; Jude 1:23), (2) a snatching away as in thievery (Matt 12:29; 13:19), and (3) a snatching away as in being caught away (Acts 8:39; 2 Cor 12:2, 4). Revelation 12:5 carries two of these connotations: The newly born child is snatched away from the jaws of the dragon and carried away to the throne of God.

In the context of 1 Thessalonians, the Rapture is seen as a snatching away of the living believers at the time of Christ's parousia. This Rapture is the activity of Jesus coming as a thief in the night (5:2) to snatch away his people from their tribulations (5:9) and their mortality (4:17; 5:10) by taking his living saints from earth to the air. The divine disappearance of Enoch (Wis 4:10-11) as well as divine kidnappings in classical mythology (*Apollodorus* 1.5.1; *Quintus Smyrnaeus* 11.289-290) were spoken of with the same verb *harpazō* [TG726, ZG773]. Green notes that "in all of these cases, . . . only some people were caught away. So the striking revelation for the Thessalonians would have been to hear how all the resurrected dead along with the living believers would be snatched away. Never had such a glorious event been contemplated" (2002:226).

There are three main views about the timing of the Rapture with respect to the Great Tribulation (Rev 7:14): (1) "pre-Tribulation Rapture"—Christians are taken away before the Great Tribulation; (2) "mid-Tribulation Rapture"—Christians are taken away at various times during the Great Tribulation; (3) "post-Tribulation Rapture"—Christians are taken away after going through the Great Tribulation.

Various writers have promoted the idea of a pre-Tribulation Rapture as an event that will suddenly and secretly remove the Christians from this world prior to the Great Tribulation. But Jesus makes it more than clear that his second coming will not be secret; rather, it will be an open manifestation for all to see (Matt 24:26-27; Luke 17:23-24; Rev 1:7). Jesus' eschatological discourses (in Matt 24; Mark 13; Luke 21) also make it clear that the believers will pass through tribulation before being rescued by the Lord Jesus at his coming (e.g., Matt 24:21-22). Any notion of a pre-Tribulation Rapture certainly cannot be found in Jesus' discourses in the Synoptic Gospels nor in 1 and 2 Thessalonians. Thus, I would personally rule out a pre-Tribulation Rapture. Mid-Tribulation Rapture is possible, but is not easy to substantiate. Post-Tribulation Rapture can be defended on the basis of Jesus' eschatological discourses, but it must be said that Jesus did not speak specifically of a Rapture in these discourses. The truth of the matter is 1 Thessalonians 4:13-18 "is the only place in the New Testament that speaks unambiguously of the rapture (there are other places that may justly be held to refer to it when it is established by this passage, but none that is sufficient to establish it). [Therefore], we must not be unduly dogmatic about it. Had we an abundance of detail recorded we could say a great deal, but as it is we have no more than a few simple facts. We must not read our pet theories into them" (Morris 1991:145).

The Parousia and Meeting with the Lord. The last event of the Parousia according to 1 Thessalonians 4:17 is a meeting between the Christians and the Lord Jesus Christ. Hellenistic customs help us visualize this meeting. The first example is drawn from the New Testament in the book of Acts (Acts 28:15), where Luke uses the same Greek expression as in 1 Thessalonians 4:17 (*eis apantēsin* [TG529, ZG561]) to describe a delegation of Christians going out from Rome to meet Paul as he was approaching the city. "The customary procedure was for the delegation to return to the city with the visiting dignitaries" (Green 2002:226).

When the dignitary was an important person, his visitation to the city was called a *parousia* [TG3952, ZG4242]. F. F. Bruce explains, "when a dignitary paid an official visit (*parousia*) to a city in Hellenistic times, the action of the leading citizens in going out to meet him and escort him back on the final stage of his journey was called the *apantēsis*" (1982:102). Cicero described Julius Caesar's travels throughout Italy in 49 BC wherein the people are enthusiastically greeting him; Cicero said, "Just imagine what *apantēsis* he is receiving from the towns, what honors are being paid to him" (*To Atticus* 8.16.2). Five years later Cicero said nearly the same about Caesar's adopted son, Octavian: "the municipalities are showing the boy remarkable favor . . . wonderful *apantēsis* and encouragement" (*To Atticus* 16.11.6).

In this custom, those who went out to meet the dignitary then accompanied him to his destination. Apparently, Jesus Christ's destination will be the new earth inasmuch as the text says he will "come down from heaven" (4:16). The resurrected and "raptured" believers will go to meet him "in the air" (i.e., the atmosphere above earth, see note on 4:16) and then return with him on his journey to earth. Though this is not stated explicitly, it is the implicit message first-century readers would have understood. Holmes said, "the implication of Paul's use of the word here is that the resurrected dead and raptured living together will meet the descending Lord 'in the air' and accompany him in glory and honor the rest of his way to earth" (1998:151; so also Bruce 1982:103; Marshall 1983:131).

This scenario is further established by Jesus' parable of the ten bridesmaids (Matt 25:1-13), a parable that definitely illustrates aspects of the Parousia he discussed in the previous chapter (Matt 24). In that parable, all the bridesmaids are called to go out "to meet [*eis hupantēsin*] the bridegroom"—which is virtually the same Greek expression used in 1 Thessalonians 4:17. (Both words are compounds of the classical verb *antaō* and a preposition, with no difference in meaning.) Five of the bridesmaids met the bridegroom and then accompanied him to the wedding feast.

The Parousia and the Day of the Lord. Questions about when the end will come have occupied Jews (Dan 12:6) and Christians (Matt 24:3; Luke 17:20; Acts 1:6) for centuries. Biblical writers call this event "the day," sometimes absolutely, more often with a qualification, such as "the day of Christ" (Phil 1:10; 2:16), "the day of the Lord Jesus" (2 Cor 1:14), "the day of Christ Jesus" (Phil 1:6), and "the day of our Lord Jesus Christ" (1 Cor 1:8). (In most of these verses, the NLT adds the explanation that it is the day of Christ's return.) In 1 and 2 Thessalonians it is called "the day of the Lord" (5:2; 2 Thess 2:2). When such expressions are used, there is often some reference to judgment to be executed at the coming of Christ: his day is "the day of judgment" (1 John 4:17) or "the day of anger" (Rom 2:5).

Judgment is associated with the Second Coming in Jesus' teaching in the Gospels (see Matt 25), which builds on the Old Testament teaching about the day of Yahweh (Isa 13; Jer 46; Joel 2; Amos 5:18-20). The association is equally plain in the New Testament epistles. Paul, in particular, put the subject on a personal level. Paul knew that his own apostolic work would be assessed "when [our Lord Jesus] returns" (2:19). Elsewhere, Paul urged other Christians to bear in mind that they, with himself, must appear before the divine tribunal, variously called "the judgment seat of God" (where each of us must give a personal account to God, Rom 14:10-12) or the judgment seat of Christ (where each will receive good or evil, according to what he or she has done on earth, 2 Cor 5:10). This judgment will take place at the second coming of Christ, who will then "judge the living and the dead" (2 Tim 4:1). Because Paul was writing to Christians, he tended to concentrate on the judgment or assessment that the believers would experience at the Lord's return. But he (with Silvanus) also made it plain that the same coming would bring judgment to those who opposed the Christian faith (2 Thess 1:6-10).

Unbelievers will be unaware of Christ's coming and unprepared for it. Just as thieves never announce their arrival, so also, for those who live in darkness and are asleep to spiritual reality, the Lord's coming will not be known until it is too late (5:2-4). The image of Jesus coming as a thief (which is also found in Matt 24:43-44; Luke 12:39-40; 2 Pet 3:10; Rev 3:3; 16:15) seems to militate against all attempts to compute the time of his return. This further substantiates Jesus' response to the disciples' inquiry as to the time of the end: "No one knows the day or hour when these things will happen, not even the angels in heaven or the Son himself. Only the Father knows" (Mark 13:32).

Another reason unbelievers will be unprepared for the Parousia is that they will feel secure in the protections provided for them by their government. This is inherent in the statement, "When people are saying, 'Everything is peaceful and secure,' then disaster will fall on them" (5:3). "Peace and security" (*pax et securitas*) was a "popular slogan of the imperial Roman propaganda machine. The promise of peace and security was what Rome offered to those people who submitted (willingly or unwillingly) to Roman rule and military power; it was seen as Rome's gift to those it conquered, virtually equivalent to an offer of deliverance or 'salvation' from turmoil and danger" (Holmes 1998:167). Christians should not trust in this false sense of security. One day Christ will come, and with him, sudden destruction. Christians should be looking for that day no matter what their political situation is.

The reason the "day of the Lord" should not surprise believers is not because they know the date of its coming, but because they live in the light. Living in the light is the result of union with Christ, who is light and who said that his followers will live in the light (John 8:12; 12:36). Jesus' divine life penetrates people's inner lives—illumining them to the divine truth and exposing their sin. So it is for the Christian who is indwelt by the Spirit of Christ. They will be prepared when the Lord comes; they will be those who have the daystar arise in their hearts (2 Pet 1:19).

Those who live in the light are those who live a watchful life, making themselves ready day by day for Christ's return: "be on your guard, not asleep like the others"

(5:6). This accords with Jesus' concluding words in his eschatological discourses, where he tells his listeners to be on guard and be alert so as not to be found sleeping (Matt 24:42-44; Mark 13:33, 36). Those who live in the light and want to have a guarded life realize they need spiritual protection, which is here pictured as the "armor of faith and love" and "our helmet the confidence of our salvation" (5:8). The Christians' armor provides a defense against being surprised by the Lord's parousia.

The ultimate message concerning the Parousia is that it is just the beginning, the entrée into eternal life with Jesus Christ. The Parousia is not the end of all things. The Parousia will be the means by which Jesus Christ comes to live with his people forever. None of his people will be excluded—neither the Christians who have died nor the Christians who will be alive on that day. This is affirmed in 4:17, "Then we will be with the Lord forever," and in 5:10, "When he returns, we can live with him forever." This is the hope of his coming, the hope of resurrection; this is the hope of the Rapture, and the hope of that final meeting with Christ. All these events lead to the blessed reality of living with Jesus Christ forever.

◆ VII. Final Exhortations (5:12-22)

12Dear brothers and sisters, honor those who are your leaders in the Lord's work. They work hard among you and give you spiritual guidance. 13Show them great respect and wholehearted love because of their work. And live peacefully with each other.

14Brothers and sisters, we urge you to warn those who are lazy. Encourage those who are timid. Take tender care of those who are weak. Be patient with everyone.

15See that no one pays back evil for evil, but always try to do good to each other and to all people.

16Always be joyful. 17Never stop praying. 18Be thankful in all circumstances, for this is God's will for you who belong to Christ Jesus.

19Do not stifle the Holy Spirit. 20Do not scoff at prophecies, 21but test everything that is said. Hold on to what is good. 22Stay away from every kind of evil.

NOTES
5:12 honor. Lit., "know," which can be taken in two ways: (1) an exhortation to honor church leaders, or (2) a recognition of the emerging leaders in the church (cf. 1 Cor 16:15-16).

those who are your leaders. This is a participle in the Greek (*proistamenous* [TG4291A, ZG4613]) which means "the ones protecting" or "helping."

work hard among you. The same Greek root (*kopiaō* [TG2872, ZG3159]) is used in 2:9; 2 Thess 3:8 to describe Paul and Silvanus's hard labor.

give you spiritual guidance. Lit., "admonish" (Gr. *nouthetountas* [TG3560, ZG3805]), the same verb translated in 5:14 as "warn."

5:13 Show them great respect. The believers' responsibility toward the leaders (5:12) is to honor them highly.

and wholehearted love. Lit., "most exceedingly in love."

live peacefully. This is literally "be at peace among yourselves," Gr. *eirēneuete en heautois* [TG1514/1438, ZG1644/1571], a reading found in A B D2 L 33 1739. However, some other manuscripts (𝔓30 ℵ D* F G P 044) read *eirēneuete en autois* [TG846, ZG899], which should be rendered as "be at peace with them." Since the textual evidence is evenly divided between the two readings, it is difficult to determine which is original. The first reading presents a general call to corporate peace and unity among all the members of the church in Thessalonica. Though the second reading could mean the same thing, it also allows for the interpretation that Paul and Silvanus were calling the Thessalonians to be at peace with the leaders in their church (see 5:12, where *proistamenous* [TG4291A, ZG4613] is the most natural referent for *autois* [TG846, ZG899]).

5:14 *warn*. Lit., "admonish" (Gr. *noutheteite* [TG3560, ZG3805]), the same verb used in 5:12.

***those who are lazy*.** Lit., "disorderly" (*ataktous* [TG813A, ZG864]), a word describing those who do not live by the rules (see 2 Thess 3:6-15).

***timid*.** Lit, "small-souled" (*oligopsuchous* [TG3642A, ZG3901]), signifying dispirited and discouraged people.

***Take tender care*.** Lit., "uphold."

5:18 *this is God's will*. This refers to the joy (5:16), prayers (5:17), and thanksgiving (5:18).

5:19 *Do not stifle the Holy Spirit*. Lit., "do not quench the Spirit."

5:20 *Do not scoff at prophecies*. Lit., "do not reject prophecies."

5:21 *test everything that is said*. Lit., "test all things," but the context calls for testing of the uttered prophecies.

***Hold on to what is good*.** In context this speaks of the prophecies that have been tested and found to be genuine.

5:22 *Stay away from every kind of evil*. In context this means the Thessalonians should reject false prophecies (5:19-21).

COMMENTARY

The final section of 1 Thessalonians presents a series of staccato exhortations, a typical feature of New Testament epistles. This is a hefty list of exhortations, 17 in all, which can be arranged in the following groups:

Attitudes and actions toward church leaders (5:12-13):
1. Honor those who are your leaders.
2. Show them great respect and wholehearted love.
3. Live peacefully with the leaders.

Attitudes and actions toward others (5:14-15):
4. Warn those who are lazy.
5. Encourage those who are timid.
6. Take tender care of those who are weak.
7. Be patient with everyone.
8. See that no one pays back evil for evil.
9. Always try to do good to one another and to all.

Self-attitudes and actions (5:16-18):
10. Always be joyful.
11. Never stop praying.
12. Be thankful in all circumstances.

Attitudes and actions about prophecy (5:19-22):
>   13. Do not stifle the Spirit.
>   14. Do not scoff at prophecies.
>   15. Test everything that is said.
>   16. Hold on to what is good.
>   17. Stay away from every kind of evil.

As organized above, this section of 1 Thessalonians (5:12-19) displays four categories of attitudes and actions. The first category pertains to the church members'
relationship with their leaders. As a new church, both the leaders and the members
were neophytes. As such, it would be difficult for the members to show respect for
the elders who had been Christians only as long as they had been. Since we are not
told in Acts 17 of the apostles selecting elders and since it appears that Timothy
brought back word to Paul and Silvanus about the leaders, the leaders may have
risen up from among them without any apostolic appointments. Stott (1991:199)
thinks Aristarchus and Secundus were leaders in the Thessalonian church. Although
this is possible, the New Testament record presents them as being Paul's traveling
co-workers and not as local elders (see Acts 19:29; 20:4; 27:2; Col 4:10; Phlm 1:24).

The marks of local leadership were distinguished by three functions: (1) The
leaders were laboring among the believers; (2) they were presiding over the church;
(3) they were admonishing the believers. (In the Greek, one definite article governs
three participles, thereby indicating these were three functions of the same person.)
As to the leaders "presiding" (*proistamenous*) over the church, the same Greek word
appears in Romans 12:8, which describes the function of one who leads. A noun
derived from this verb is used of Phoebe, who was a deacon in the church at Cenchrea, to denote her as a helper of many people (Rom 16:1-2). The term should not
be regarded as an official designation (Bruce 1982:118) as much as it is a description of what leaders do. Primarily, leaders "admonish" others, which means they
impart spiritual understanding designed to correct others while not provoking or
embittering them (TDNT 4.1019, 1021).

The leaders in the church should be held in high regard and esteemed in love
because of their labor for the church. The members of the church should also strive
to have a good relationship with the leaders. According to the variant reading of
5:13, which I prefer (see note), Paul and Silvanus were exhorting the members to be
at peace with the leaders. Community harmony between the believers and the leaders was especially important because the church was young and was suffering persecution (2:14).

The exhortations then turned to relationships among the church members themselves, as well as to other people living in their community. The first exhortation
was for the Thessalonians to admonish the disorderly or idle (which the NLT renders as "those who are lazy"). The term was used in Hellenistic Greek for idleness in
the sense of loafing. Some of the Thessalonians had stopped working and thereby
imposed themselves on the generosity of others (Morris 1991:168-169). The

Thessalonians were to "warn" (the same Greek word used in 5:12; see note) these people about such behavior because this was a discredit and shame to the church.

The Thessalonians were called upon to encourage the faint-hearted and dispirited among them, as well as to uphold the weak, those with little or no economic or social power. These attitudes and actions balance that of the admonishment to the idle in that some members of the church were not able to work due to various weaknesses, whether physical or mental. Above all, the Thessalonians had to be "long-suffering," (NLT, "patient") one of the most important attributes in maintaining long-term healthy relationships. Believers should display this fruit of the Spirit in their relationships with others (Gal 5:23; Eph 4:2).

One manifestation of long-suffering is that a person will not seek vengeance or retribution. Jesus warned against retaliation (Matt 5:38-48; Luke 6:27-36), as did Paul (Rom 12:17-21) and Peter (1 Pet 3:9). Instead of retaliating against people, Christians should pursue goodness. Doing good to others includes extending kindness to members of the church (i.e., "each other") as well as those outside the Christian community ("to all people"; cf. 3:12).

As for their own personal attitudes and actions, the Thessalonians were exhorted by Paul and Silvanus to "always be joyful" (5:16). To have joy in the midst of suffering is a common Christian phenomenon (1:6; Matt 5:11-12; 1 Pet 1:6; 4:13). Such joy comes independently of one's circumstances; it is given to those who live in the Spirit (1:6; Rom 14:17; Gal 5:22). Of course, such people will likely be those who maintain an attitude and practice of regular prayer (5:17; cf. 1:2; Rom 12:12; Eph 6:18), and typically give thanks to God, no matter what their circumstances.

The last verses of this section (5:19-22) are not an assortment of random exhortations. Rather, they all have to do with the matter of prophecy in church gatherings. The first two verses (5:19-20) are connected by language that was well known to first-century Christians inasmuch as "the Spirit" was often associated with prophetic utterance (2 Thess 2:2, see note; 1 John 4:1-2; Rev 1:10; 19:10). The next two verses (5:21-22) address the issue of how various prophecies should be received or rejected.

Prophets, along with apostles and teachers, did not hold offices in local churches like elders and deacons. Rather, they were chosen, not by individual congregations, but by divine commission, and so were honored and accepted in all local churches. Both Silvanus and Paul were prophets. Silvanus (also known as Silas) was among the most prominent prophets of the early church (Acts 15:22, 32). He may have personally encouraged the Thessalonians to practice prophesying. Of course, Paul was also known as a prophet, and he had much to say about its practice in church gatherings (1 Cor 14).

It is possible that the church at Thessalonica had stopped the practice of prophesying in church gatherings or had minimized it. Thus, both Paul and Silvanus encouraged the believers to not quench the Spirit's fire (Matt 3:11; Acts 2:3-4; 2 Tim 1:6) by restricting prophetic speech. Since the Spirit of Christ was active in Christian worship, prophecy was a major means whereby Christ communicated with his people. According to Paul, the primary purpose of prophecy is to edify the church. According to 1 Corinthians 14:3, "one who prophesies strengthens others, encourages them, and comforts them." Again, in 1 Corinthians 14:4, Paul states that the "one who speaks a word of prophecy strengthens the entire church." When he wrote to the Corinthians, Paul discussed the subject of spiritual gifts, particularly tongues-speaking and prophecy. Paul did not object to speaking in tongues (1 Cor 14:18, 39), but the church could be edified only to the extent that it was comprehensible. Prophecy, which consisted of comprehensible speech inspired by the Spirit, contributed to the mutual edification, encouragement, and consolation of everyone gathered (1 Cor 14:20-25, 39; see TBD 1084).

Paul and Silvanus instructed the Thessalonians not to reject prophecies but rather to test them (1 Cor 12:10; 14:29). Those who are indwelt by the Spirit have the ability to discern the Spirit of truth from the spirit of error because the anointing of the Spirit teaches them about these things (see 1 John 2:20, 27). In those days, many may have claimed to have Spirit-inspired messages. Those messages had to be tested. Early Christian teaching was expressed in the *Didache*: "But not everyone who speaks in a spirit is a prophet, except he have the behavior of the Lord" (11.8). The church has had to test prophecies as well as the prophets, so as to evaluate the doctrinal teaching (1 John 4:1-3; 2 Thess 2:2) and the character of those who made the utterances (Matt 7:15-20). As for the Thessalonians, it appears that they had received false prophecies concerning the Lord's parousia—that it had already happened—an issue Paul and Silvanus address in 2 Thessalonians 2:1-3 (see commentary there).

◆ VIII. Concluding Prayer (5:23-24)

23Now may the God of peace make you holy in every way, and may your whole spirit and soul and body be kept blameless until our Lord Jesus Christ comes again. 24God will make this happen, for he who calls you is faithful.

NOTES

5:23 the God of peace. This title also appears in Rom 15:33; 2 Cor 13:11; Phil 4:9. It is emphatic in the Greek: "may the God of peace himself."

may [he] make you holy in every way. The mood of the verb (*hagiasai* [TG37, ZG39]) is optative; it is often used in prayers expressing a wish or desire for something to happen. The Greek behind "in every way" is one word: *holoteleis* [TG3651, ZG3911], a word found only here in the NT. Nero used the word in a proclamation of "complete [*holotelē*] exemption of taxation" to all Greeks attending the Isthmian Games of AD 67 (Bruce 1982:129).

may your whole spirit and soul and body. This is an expression for one's entire being: spiritual, mental/personal, and physical.

be kept blameless. The same word for "blameless" appears in 3:13; this word (*amemptōs* [TG274, ZG290]) indicates "a condition of blamelessness in which an individual is found to have done nothing deserving condemnation by God" (Wanamaker 1990:144).

until our Lord Jesus Christ comes again. The parousia of Jesus is the motivation for holiness.

COMMENTARY

First Thessalonians contains two prayers that are very similar in thought: the one found in 3:11-13 and the prayer here in 5:23-24. "As the first prayer summarized major themes of the first section of the letter, so this one touches on the major themes of the second section: Note the emphasis on holiness (5:23) and on the coming of Jesus" (Holmes 1998:199). In both prayers, Paul and Silvanus were asking God to make the Thessalonian Christians so completely holy (sanctified) that they would be ready for the Lord Jesus at his coming. In 3:13, they prayed that the Thessalonians' hearts would be "strong, blameless, and holy as you stand before God our Father when our Lord Jesus comes again." This is echoed in 5:23: "may the God of peace make you holy in every way, and may your whole spirit and soul and body be kept blameless until our Lord Jesus Christ comes again." The God of peace is the source of peace, "which for Paul is not merely the absence of conflict but, more positively, a state of wholeness and well-being characterized by reconciled relationships (cf. Rom 5:1-11); as such it is virtually a synonym for salvation" (Holmes 1998:200).

Paul and Silvanus were asking the God of peace to keep the Thessalonians "blameless" until they experienced the parousia of Jesus. The final evaluation of Christians' motives and conduct will come when they stand before God at the time of the Lord's parousia (3:13). Our desire should be that we would be found to be without blame. To be blameless means to be in good stead with God; it does not mean sinless perfection. It means that we have been sanctified. We cannot attain such blamelessness on our own. It is impossible. That is why we need the empowering presence of the God who called us to this holiness; that is why Paul and Silvanus said, "God will make this happen" (5:24). The God who calls us (1:4; 2:12; 4:7; 2 Thess 2:13-14) is the one who will complete the work he began in us (Phil 1:6). This sentiment is echoed in the words of Paul in Romans 8:28-29, where he affirms that the God who called us will sanctify us and glorify us so that we all will be conformed to the image of his Son. The foundation of our confidence in this sanctifying work of God is the very character of God, who is faithful (1 Cor 1:9; 2 Thess 3:3; 2 Tim 2:13).

Paul and Silvanus believed that God's sanctifying work would extend to the whole being of the Christian—"spirit and soul and body." Greeks would have had problems thinking about the need for sanctification of the body because they believed the body was merely a prison to the spirit, which would be released at the time of death. By contrast, the apostles taught a bodily resurrection and a bodily existence in the life to come. Believers will not just be spirit beings, but human–spiritual beings with transformed souls and glorified bodies (see Paul's full discourse on this in 1 Cor 15).

◆ IX. Closing of the Letter (5:25-28)

[25]Dear brothers and sisters, pray for us.

[26]Greet all the brothers and sisters with Christian love.*

[27]I command you in the name of the Lord to read this letter to all the brothers and sisters.

[28]May the grace of our Lord Jesus Christ be with you.

5:26 Greek *with a holy kiss.*

NOTES

5:25 *pray for us.* Paul often solicited prayer from the churches he prayed for (Rom 15:30-32; 2 Cor 1:11; Col 4:3-4; 2 Thess 3:1-2).

5:26 *with Christian love.* Lit., "with a holy kiss," an expression that also occurs in Rom 16:16; 1 Cor 16:20; 2 Cor 13:12; 1 Pet 5:14. Kissing on the cheek or forehead was a common form of greeting exhibiting sentiments such as honor, friendship, or love (Mark 14:44-45; Luke 7:36-47; 15:20; Acts 20:37).

5:27 *I command you in the name of the Lord.* As discussed in the Introduction and in the commentary below, Paul interjects his own voice here. And his words are quite strong. The Greek verb (*enorkizō* [TG1774.1, ZG1941]) means "to put someone under oath." As such, he was demanding that they swear by or before the Lord that would read this letter to the entire church.

read this letter. This means, "read this letter out loud," which was the practice of those days (see commentary).

to all the brothers. This reading is found in א* B D F G 0278 it cop^{sa}. A variant reading is "to all the holy brothers" (א² A 044 33 1739 𝔐 it^a syr cop^{bo}). It is difficult to determine which reading is original. On one hand, it can be argued that *hagiois* [TG40, ZG41] (holy) accidentally dropped out due to homoeoteleuton, the eye of the scribe confusing the ending of *hagiois* for *adelphois* [TG80, ZG81]. On the other hand, it can be argued that *hagiois* was added by scribes who had taken notice that holiness was a key theme in this epistle and was therefore an appropriate descriptor of the believers. Since the textual evidence slightly favors the first reading and since later scribes had a propensity for interpolation, the reading of the NLT text is more likely original.

5:28 *May the grace of our Lord Jesus Christ be with you.* Many manuscripts add "amen" at the end of this verse (א A D¹ 044 1739^c 𝔐 syr cop^{bo}), but the testimony for its omission is impressive: B D* F G 0278 33 1739* cop^{sa}. Furthermore, it is more likely than not that the final word "amen" was added by scribes for liturgical purposes. Only three epistles (Romans, Galatians, Jude) appear to have a genuine "amen" for the last word.

COMMENTARY

Interpreting these closing words is informed by some practices of letter writing and reading in the first century AD. In those days, several people may have signed off a letter, and most writing was read aloud to its recipients. Both of these play a part in interpreting the closing to 1 Thessalonians.

The first thing we encounter in this closing section is a personal command by one of the writers (5:27). We can assume that the person was Paul because he was the one who spoke out individually in 2:18 (see note), and the only other occurrence of "I" is found in 5:27. In some extant ancient letters multiple authors signed off at the end of the document with their own distinct handwriting. One noteworthy example is a letter about sending books between Alexandria and Oxyrhynchus. This original letter, known as P. Oxyrhynchus 2192, shows the main body of the letter in one handwriting, followed by three short notes in three different hands.

In 1 Thessalonians 5:27 Paul's handwriting would have been his personal imprimatur of the epistle as expressed in a final exhortation: "I command you in the name of the Lord to read this letter to all the brothers and sisters." But we cannot rule out the possibility that the person who wrote 5:27 could have been Silvanus, who concluded the epistle with his own adjuration, which was then followed by a final benediction from Paul in 5:28.

However, it seems best to reconstruct the scenario as Paul writing the last two verses in his own hand. Very likely, the body of the letter was in Silvanus's handwriting, so Paul's final greeting in his own handwriting would have been distinct. This practice is explicitly mentioned in 2 Thessalonians 3:17 (see note), as well as in 1 Corinthians 16:21, Galatians 6:11, and Colossians 4:18. In all these verses, Paul identifies himself (as distinct from the amanuensis) and then shortly thereafter writes "grace be with you," or "the Lord's grace be with you," or some such expression with the word "grace" (see 1 Cor 16:23; Gal 6:18; Col 4:18; 2 Thess 3:18). This customary habit of concluding a verse with a blessing of grace would tell us that other verses at the end of Pauline Epistles would have most likely been written in Paul's hand (Rom 16:20; 2 Cor 13:13; Eph 6:24; Phil 4:23; 1 Tim 6:16; 2 Tim 4:22; Titus 3:15; Phlm 1:25). Indeed, the concluding blessing of grace became his trademark. This is the case with 5:27-28, which would have been Paul's signatory conclusion.

According to the custom of the day, the amanuensis or secretary of official documents was often the same person who carried the document to its destination and read it out loud to its intended audience. Since this person had been present at the time of writing, he could explain to the hearers anything that needed explaining. It could be assumed, then, that Silvanus was the one who carried this letter to the Thessalonians, read it to them, and then returned with further news of the situation in Thessalonica, which then prompted the writing of 2 Thessalonians.

Since most people in Paul's day were not literate (on average, only 10 percent of the population in Hellenistic times could read), they depended on oral reading for communication. The entire church was urged to come together to hear the entire epistle read to them. We know from church history that this was the usual practice. Gamble reasoned that the practice of the liturgical reading of Scripture began in the first century and was an established custom of the churches by the early second century (1995:151-152).

Other passages clearly point to the one who read the Scriptures out loud to an assembly of believers. In 1 Timothy 4:13, Paul urged Timothy to "give attention to the reading." Significantly, Paul didn't even need to provide a direct object to the expression, for the expression seems to have become an idiom for the public oral reading of Scripture. Revelation 1:3 promises a blessing to "the one who reads the words of this prophecy"—speaking specifically of each of the readers who would read aloud the book of Revelation to each of the seven churches addressed in the book.

BIBLIOGRAPHY
See page 412, the bibliography for the Thessalonian epistles.

COMMENTARY ON
2 Thessalonians

◆ **I. Opening of the Letter (1:1–2)**

This letter is from Paul, Silas,* and Timothy. We are writing to the church in Thessalonica, to you who belong to God our Father and the Lord Jesus Christ.

²May God our Father* and the Lord Jesus Christ give you grace and peace.

1:1 Greek *Silvanus*, the Greek form of the name. 1:2 Some manuscripts read *God the Father.*

NOTES

1:1 Paul, Silas, and Timothy. This epistle is the work of three authors, not just Paul (see discussion on "Authors" in the Introduction).

the church in Thessalonica. Lit., "church of the Thessalonians."

Lord Jesus Christ. All manuscripts read this, including 𝔓30vid, according to Grenfell and Hunt's reconstruction (see *editio princeps* of P.Oxyrhynchus 1598). According to Comfort and Barrett (2001:131), however, it seems more likely that 𝔓30 reads "grace of the Lord Jesus."

1:2 God our Father. This is the reading found in ℵ A F G I 0278 𝔐 it syr copsa. Other manuscripts read, "God [the] Father": B D 0111vid 33 1739. Since the manuscript evidence for the two readings is evenly distributed, it is difficult to make a decision on external grounds. Internal considerations are no less divided. On one hand, it could be argued that "our" was added to conform this verse to other Pauline introductions where the formulaic expression nearly always is "God our Father." On the other hand, it could be argued that "our" was dropped to avoid repeating the wording of the first verse ("God our Father").

1:2 grace and peace. These two words appear as a pair at the beginning of all Paul's Major Epistles (Rom 1:7; 1 Cor 1:3; 2 Cor 1:2; Gal 1:3; Eph 1:2; Phil 1:2; Col 1:2; 1 Thess 1:1).

COMMENTARY

Ancient letters opened with a prescript, which consists of three elements: the sender(s), the recipient, and the salutation (cf. Weima 2000b:642). Thus, all letters followed this pattern: (1) X (in the nominative case); (2) to Y (in the dative case); (3) greetings (see commentary on 1 Thess 1:1 for an example). The adaptation in 2 Thessalonians is as follows:

1. Senders: Paul, Silvanus, and Timothy.
2. Recipients: to the church of the Thessalonians.
3. Greeting: Grace to you and peace.

The three senders of 1 Thessalonians are listed as Paul, Silvanus (otherwise known as Silas), and Timothy. Paul and Silvanus were the founders of the church at Thessalonica (Acts 17:1-14) and the main coauthors of this epistle (see the full discussion in the Introduction under "Authors"). Timothy was their co-worker and had been an emissary between them and the Thessalonians.

First and Second Thessalonians are unique among all the New Testament books in that they were the products of multiple authorship. Even in other epistles where more than one person's name appears at the head (Paul and Sosthenes in 1 Corinthians; Paul and Timothy in 2 Corinthians, Philippians, and Colossians), the author is clearly Paul, who uses the personal "I" throughout the body of each epistle. Joint composition of letters was known in the ancient world. For example, in Cicero's letter *To Atticus* he says, "For my part I have gathered from your letters—both that which you wrote in conjunction with others and the one you wrote in your own name" (11.5.1).

The recipients of the letter are the same as those who received 1 Thessalonians: "the church in Thessalonica . . . who belong to God our Father and the Lord Jesus Christ" (1:1).

◆ II. Praise for Enduring Persecution until the Lord's Parousia (1:3-12)

[3]Dear brothers and sisters,* we can't help but thank God for you, because your faith is flourishing and your love for one another is growing. [4]We proudly tell God's other churches about your endurance and faithfulness in all the persecutions and hardships you are suffering. [5]And God will use this persecution to show his justice and to make you worthy of his Kingdom, for which you are suffering. [6]In his justice he will pay back those who persecute you.

[7]And God will provide rest for you who are being persecuted and also for us when the Lord Jesus appears from heaven. He will come with his mighty angels, [8]in flaming fire, bringing judgment on those who don't know God and on those who refuse to obey the Good News of our Lord Jesus. [9]They will be punished with eternal destruction, forever separated from the Lord and from his glorious power. [10]When he comes on that day, he will receive glory from his holy people—praise from all who believe. And this includes you, for you believed what we told you about him.

[11]So we keep on praying for you, asking our God to enable you to live a life worthy of his call. May he give you the power to accomplish all the good things your faith prompts you to do. [12]Then the name of our Lord Jesus will be honored because of the way you live, and you will be honored along with him. This is all made possible because of the grace of our God and Lord, Jesus Christ.*

1:3 Greek *Brothers.* 1:12 Or *of our God and our Lord Jesus Christ.*

NOTES

1:3 *your faith is flourishing.* The testing of the Thessalonians' faith was foremost on the minds of the apostles. They were very glad to hear that their faith was not diminishing under persecution. Rather, it was flourishing.

your love for one another is growing. In the first epistle the writers commended them for their love to other believers (1 Thess 3:6) and prayed that it would increase (1 Thess 3:12).

1:4 *your endurance and faithfulness in all the persecutions and hardships you are suffering.* This statement lies at the heart of this epistle. Since the Thessalonians were suffering persecution, the writers felt inspired to encourage them and to reveal to them the outcome of this ordeal—all of which is described in the following verses (1:5–2:12).

1:5 *to show his justice.* This is a dynamic rendering of "an evident indication of righteous judgment," which stands in apposition to 1:4. As such, it is saying (quite contrary to our ways of thinking) that suffering persecution is evidence of God's righteous judgment (see commentary for further discussion).

make you worthy of his Kingdom. Lit., "counted worthy of the Kingdom." The same Greek verb (*kataxioō* [TG2661, ZG2921]) in a similar context appears in Acts 5:41, where the apostles were counted worthy to suffer for the name of Jesus. Those whom God calls to participate in his Kingdom will suffer for the Kingdom (Acts 14:22; 1 Thess 2:12).

1:6 *justice.* God's justice will become evident when he punishes the Thessalonians' persecutors (1:8-9).

he will pay back. This quite literal translation of the Greek is an excellent, easily understood rendering for modern readers who know and use the idiom "payback" as an expression for "exacting revenge."

1:7 *rest.* The Greek is *anesin* [TG425, ZG457]; in this context it refers to relief from sufferings, an experience to be shared by both the apostles and the Thessalonians ("for you . . . and also for us").

when the Lord Jesus appears. Elsewhere, the writers speak of Christ's coming as a *parousia* (2:1; 1 Thess 2:19; 3:13; 4:15; 5:23), but here it is said to be an unveiling (*apokalupsei* [TG602, ZG637]). The Lord's parousia will be an epiphany (see note on 2:8), whereby the invisible Jesus will become visible to the persecuted Christians, as well as to their persecutors (Matt 24:30; 1 Pet 4:13).

from heaven. This points to Jesus' present dwelling place, as well as to his authority (1 Thess 1:10; 4:16).

1:8 *in flaming fire, bringing judgment.* God's judgment is often said to be accompanied by fire (Isa 66:15-16; 2 Pet 3:7, 10). But fire is also used to depict God's glory (Exod 3:2; 19:18; Deut 33:2; Ps 18:8; Ezek 1:13, 27). So the expression also depicts the glory accompanying the Lord's parousia.

bringing judgment on those who don't know God and on those who refuse to obey the Good News. This combines allusions to Isa 66:15 and 66:4 in the LXX: "he will bring punishment with the fury of his anger" and "for when I called, they did not answer." Some commentators (see Marshall 1983:177-178) think two groups of people are designated here: Gentiles who don't know God (1 Thess 4:5), and Jews who disobeyed the gospel (Rom 10:16). Other commentators (see Green 2002:290-291; Morris 1991:202-203) see this as two descriptions of the same kind of people—those who are culpably ignorant of God (that is, they willfully chose not to know him; cf. Rom 1:18) and therefore rejected the gospel when it was presented to them (Rom 2:8).

1:9 *will be punished.* Lit., "will pay a penalty."

eternal destruction. The combination of words in Greek, *olethron aiōnion* [TG3639/166, ZG3897/173], conveys the idea of "eternal death" (BDAG 702). The word *olethron* was also used in 1 Thess 5:3 to speak of the utter ruin and destruction that would come upon unbelievers at the time of Jesus' parousia.

separated from the Lord. The Greek preposition *apo* [TG575, ZG608] (from) signals separation. The result of the punishment of eternal destruction is to be separated from the Lord eternally. Such separation means absolute destruction (*olethron*) because the Lord is the source of life; to be cut off from the Lord Jesus is to be cut off from life (1 John 5:12).

and from his glorious power. This language harkens back to Isa 2:10, 19, 21, which speak of the dreadful day of Yahweh's judgment, a day when people will try to hide from the splendor of his majesty.

1:10 *When he comes on that day.* This alludes to Ps 96:13, which speaks of the Lord coming to judge the earth. This is the Day of the Lord (2:2; 1 Thess 5:2, 4), a day wherein the Lord Jesus will execute judgment on those who reject the gospel.

glory from his holy people. Lit., "to be glorified in his holy people" or "to be glorified among his holy people." This parallels the language of Ps 89:7 [88:8, LXX]: "God is glorified in the council of his holy ones."

praise from all who believe. The verb translated *praise* is *thaumazō* [TG2296, ZG2513] (marvel). This is an allusion to Ps 68:35 [67:36] as it appears in the LXX: "God will be marveled at in/among his holy ones."

for you believed what we told you about him. How people respond to Jesus Christ will determine their eternal destiny (see 1:8).

1:11 *to live a life worthy of his call.* The Greek verb (*axioō* [TG515, ZG546]) means "count worthy"; it shares the same root as the verb used in 1:5 (see note).

1:12 *Then . . . Jesus will be honored because of the way you live.* Lit., "So that . . . Jesus may be glorified in you."

the name of our Lord Jesus. This reading has the support of ℵ B D L 044 0111 it[b] cop[sa]. The title is expanded to "the name of our Lord Jesus Christ" in other mss (A F G P 0278 33 1739 syr—so TR). The documentary evidence for the text is superior to that of the variant, not to mention that the variant is probably the result of scribal assimilation to the next clause of this verse, which reads "Lord Jesus Christ."

and you will be honored along with him. This is spoken of again in 2:14, as well as in 1 Thess 2:12. This glorification is linked to Jesus' coming (Rom 8:17-18; Col 3:4).

the grace of our God and Lord, Jesus Christ. The marginal rendering ("the grace of our God and our Lord Jesus Christ") is favored by several commentators who think God and Jesus are mentioned separately here (see Harris 1992:265-266). However, others (including myself) think the NLT rendering is preferable because in the Greek, there is one article governing the two titles "God" and "Lord Jesus Christ" joined by the conjunction *kai* [TG2532, ZG2779] (and). According to a Greek grammatical rule called the "Granville Sharp Rule" (see Dana and Mantey 1927:146-153), this structure indicates that the two nouns describe one person. In this case, Jesus Christ is both God and Lord. This rendering is affirmed by Turner (1965:16), Porter (1992:110-111), and Green (2002:299-300), to name a few. The same kind of structure appears in Titus 2:13 and 2 Pet 1:1, where there is one article governing two nouns joined by *kai*, yielding the rendering "our God and Savior, Jesus Christ" (so NLT). Jesus Christ is called God elsewhere in the NT (John 1:1, 18; 20:18; Rom 9:5; Phil 2:6).

COMMENTARY

This section is the mirror image of 1 Thessalonians 1:4-10 in that both passages emphasize the Thessalonians' endurance in suffering (1:4; 1 Thess 1:3, 6) as a model for other churches (1:3-4; 1 Thess 1:7-10). Second Thessalonians 1:3-10 adds to 1 Thessalonians 1:4-10 extra emphasis concerning the eschatological judgment of their oppressors (1:5-10).

Immediately after thanking God for the Thessalonian church (1:3-4a), the writers addressed the issue of their persecution (1:4b). The persecution against the church appears to have intensified since their first letter to them (1 Thess 1:6; 2:14; 3:3-4). As was noted in the Introduction, we are not told how Paul, Silvanus, and Timothy found out about the situation, except that they had heard (3:11) from some unnamed person about the affairs in Thessalonica. And we are not told the exact nature of the persecution they were suffering. Nonetheless, it is known that the Thessalonian Christians were being persecuted by their own people (see commentary on 1 Thess 2:14-16)—that is, fellow Hellenists.

According to the record of Acts 17:1-9, Jews in Thessalonica instigated the persecution against Paul, Silvanus, and Timothy. They prompted the civil authorities to take action against the apostles by accusing them of being "guilty of treason against Caesar, for they profess allegiance to another king, named Jesus" (Acts 17:7). This is the same kind of strategy the Jews in Jerusalem used when they convinced Pontius Pilate to condemn and crucify Jesus. In any event, the civil authorities in Thessalonica took this accusation as truth and arrested several Christian believers (including Jason, who had housed the apostles). Later, they were released from jail on bond. In the meantime, the apostles had escaped and gone on to Berea. Evidently, the persecution continued against the Thessalonian Christians—primarily from their fellow Hellenists because 1 Thessalonians 2:12-14 makes it clear that their suffering came at the hands of their own countrymen. Although this doesn't exclude Jewish Thessalonians, it most likely means Hellenistic Thessalonians. This is further suggested by the wording in 2 Thessalonians 1:8, which names the enemies of God's people as being "those who don't know God"—an expression used of pagans. However, the very next phrase, "those who refuse to obey the Good News of our Lord Jesus" could be applied to unbelieving Jews as well as to pagans (see note on 1:8). Whoever was persecuting the Thessalonians, it must have been severe to have evinced such a strong response from the apostles in 1:7-9. In short, the writers promised the Thessalonians that the Lord Jesus would enact his wrathful vengeance on those who had persecuted them. This promise would have influenced the Thessalonians in two ways: (1) It would give them hope during their trials, and (2) it would prevent them from seeking their own ways to get revenge. Vengeance is the Lord's.

Though we are not told exactly what kind of suffering the Thessalonians were experiencing, we can gather from the record in Acts and other early writings what the Christians had to deal with. Christians were hated by Jews because they accepted a Messiah whom the Jews rejected. This is made more than clear throughout the book of Acts. And Christians were hated by fellow Hellenists because they rejected the gods and festivals the Hellenists revered. In this regard, they were considered "atheists" (those not believing in the traditional Roman gods) and disloyal rebels (for they would not recognize Caesar as lord and god). The pagan perception of Christians during the first two centuries is shocking to modern readers. This perception can be gathered from the writings of Roman historians and governors. When Tacitus and Suetonius described Nero's persecution against the Christians (AD 62–65), they termed Christianity as "a pernicious superstition . . . a disease . . . horrible and shameful"; "a new and mischievous superstition" (see Tacitus, *Annals* 15.44; Suetonius, *Nero* 16.2). Tacitus indicated that Christians were "hated for their vices" and that they "were convicted, not so much on the count of arson [Caesar had blamed them for the fire in Rome] as for hatred of the human race" (*Annals* 15.44).

According to Pliny (who was writing to the Emperor Trajan in AD 112), their worship of Jesus threatened to exterminate the traditional forms of Roman worship. And the Christians' refusal to invoke the Roman gods and make offerings to the emperor's statue was a treasonous act, which undermined the empire's security (see Pliny's *Letters* 10.96). When Pliny asked Trajan on what grounds Christians should be punished, three criteria emerged:

1. Was age a factor?
2. Are apostates (those who renounce Christ) to be pardoned?
3. Is it the name (*nomen*) or the crimes (*flagitia*) associated with the name that are to be punished?

Trajan left it up to Pliny's discretion as to whether or not he should execute the young or old. But the other two matters called for an answer, which was not easy for Trajan to give because the two are intertwined: Being a member of the group—i.e., to bear the name of Christ—was considered a crime in itself. Christians thought they should be judged for actual, specific crimes, but they were punished for being members of the group—for owning and confessing the Name.

Pagans, misunderstanding Christian terminology, had spread many false rumors about what went on in the meetings of Christians. Misunderstanding "the partaking of the body and blood of Jesus," they accused Christians of infant sacrifice and cannibalism. Misunderstanding the notion of a Christian love feast (which was simply the sharing of a meal on the Lord's Day), pagans accused Christians of having sexual orgies (see Minucius Felix, *Octavius* 9, 31). This is reflected in Peter's words in which he says that unbelievers considered the Christians to be wrongdoers: "Be careful to live properly among your unbelieving neighbors. Then even if they accuse you of doing wrong, they will see your honorable behavior, and they will give honor to God when he judges the world" (1 Pet 2:12).

Above all the charges, the most potent was that Christians were "haters of the human race" (*odio humani generis*). They had acquired this stigma because of their refusal to participate in the Roman religions and because the Christian community was secluded, secretive, and self-contained. Outsiders perceived this community to be aloof and mysterious. The early Christians shouldn't be blamed for this. Their secretive solidarity was caused by the outside persecutions, first from the Jews and then from the Romans—even as Jesus had predicted (see John 16:1-4).

The claims that early Christians made about Christ—the very names they called him ("Lord," "Christ," "Savior," "God," "King")—were being attributed to many of the Roman leaders of their times. Roman generals and emperors assumed divine status as soon as they penetrated Asia Minor, especially after Augustus Caesar came to full power (27 BC). Augustus saw his reign as the inauguration of a new age of peace for Rome and the world. The Romans acclaimed him as "savior." In Antioch, coins depicted Augustus as the incarnate Zeus or "worship-worthy Son of God," and altars were erected in his honor. Augustus encouraged the cult as a unifying element in his diverse empire and as a type of patriotism. After his death, temples were built in his honor, and the symbols of divinity were transferred to succeeding emperors. For decades, all new temples were made for the imperial cult.

Gaius Caesar, nicknamed Caligula (AD 37-41), was the first emperor to be worshiped in Rome during his own lifetime. On hearing of a dispute between Jews and Gentiles over worshiping him in Jamnia, he ordered a statue of himself placed in the temple in Jerusalem. His plan, which would have caused a major revolt among the Jews, was averted only by the intercession of Herod Agrippa I. Under the succeeding emperors Claudius (AD 41-54) and Nero (AD 54-68), the cult reached ridiculous extremes. Domitian (AD 81-96) also decreed that he should be worshiped as "God the Lord." Later emperors varied in how seriously they took the imperial cult, but it remained a test of loyalty to the Empire. For the sake of the Empire's unity, other religions had to accommodate emperor worship one way or another.

Emperor worship understandably caused problems for Christians, since the titles given to the emperor ("Lord," "Prince of Peace," "Son of God," "Savior") were the same as those used for Christ. The confession "Jesus is Lord" (Rom 10:9) was bound to conflict with the claim "Caesar is Lord." Christians who would not sacrifice to the emperor were charged with treason. The accusation against the Christians in Thessalonica started when they accused Paul and Silas of having "caused trouble all over the world . . . and now they are here disturbing our city" (Acts 17:6). They also accused the Christian workers of violating the decrees of Caesar ("They are all guilty of treason against Caesar," Acts 17:7). These decrees had been issued during the reigns of Augustus and Tiberius and were still in effect when Claudius ruled. They prohibited predicting anyone's death, especially that of the emperor. Paul and Silvanus had come to the city proclaiming Jesus Christ's supreme kingship; from their perspective, this appeared to predict an end to the emperor's reign (2:3-8; 1 Thess 1:10; 4:16).

The Thessalonian believers had experienced hostility from the time of their conversion (1 Thess 1:6; 2:14), which was something Paul and Silvanus had repeatedly warned them would happen (1 Thess 3:3-4). The apostles had anxiety about whether the Thessalonians would be able to keep the faith despite Satan's temptation to give it up (1 Thess 3:5). To their credit, the Thessalonians had stood firm in faith, love, and persevering hope. This was noticed and commended by the apostles in the first epistle (1 Thess 3:6-8) and again in the second (1:3). Paul and Silvanus were so pleased with their faithful endurance that they held up the Thessalonians as an example to other churches (1:3-4).

In 2 Thessalonians 1:5, the writers make the startling statement that the Thessalonians' suffering persecution was a manifestation of the righteous judgment of God. To our way of thinking, "the fact of suffering seems to deny, rather than to prove, that God is working out his righteous purpose" (Morris 1991:196). The thought in 2 Thessalonians 1:5 is quite similar to that in Philippians 1:27-28, where Paul indicates that the perseverance of the believers undergoing suffering is a sign of their salvation. Suffering tries believers and transforms them into the image of Christ, which is the goal of salvation. Therefore, when trials come to the Christian, they come from the hand of God as the means of making believers what they ought to be. These sufferings make the believers worthy members of God's Kingdom (see note on 1:5).

The teaching of enduring persecution completely accords with Jesus' eschatological messages in Matthew 24, Mark 13, and Luke 21, wherein he made it plain that the believers need to remain faithful during great days of tribulation—with the promise that those who endure to the end will be saved (Matt 24:13; Mark 13:13). The same message runs through the book of Revelation: Those who remain faithful to Christ during tribulation, even if it means suffering martyrdom, will receive a great reward (see Rev 20:4-6). Modern Christians who teach that believers will escape by being raptured prior to the Tribulation are wishful dreamers. There is no such teaching in the New Testament. Nowhere can I find a verse that indicates that believers will be raptured prior to the Tribulation and that the coming of the Lord will then follow. (For more on this, see commentary below on 2 Thess 2.) The teaching of the New Testament consistently presents the view that the believers will undergo persecution until the coming of the Lord. This, in fact, is what Paul and Silvanus were telling the Thessalonians.

After commending the Thessalonians for enduring persecution, the writers assured them that their persecutors would experience terrible judgment at the coming of the Lord and that the Lord would give them relief from their suffering (1:6-10). Christ would come to destroy the enemies of the gospel and to deliver the persecuted believers, who would receive rest from their trials and the reward of being honored by Christ, as well as glorifying him. The apostles believed that Jesus would return soon (within their own lifetimes) to judge the persecutors of Christ's people and rescue the believers. After this dramatic separation of unbelievers from believers, the Lord would establish his Kingdom on earth wherein he would be glorified in and among his holy people.

Paul and Silvanus spoke of a horrible end to those who do not know God and who do not obey the gospel of Jesus Christ. They would experience eternal destruction and separation from the Lord. The language is left vague as to what this entails: Is it speaking of complete annihilation or eternal torment? In Paul's writings we do not find any notion of eternal punishment per se; rather, Paul speaks of death as being the ultimate end for those who reject the gospel. It is true and dreadful that other portions of the New Testament speak of eternal torment and punishment (Matt 25:46; Mark 9:43-48; Luke 16:24-25; 2 Pet 2:9; Rev 14:10; 20:10), but Paul's theology views rejection of the gospel as spelling one's destruction, without saying what form this takes.

In stark contrast to those who will suffer separation from the Lord's presence, the holy ones of God will be indwelt by Christ's glorious presence and express him to the world. This glorification of Christ through his people will happen at the time of Jesus' coming (Rom 8:17-18). For now, Christ is hidden, and his glory is hidden inside his people. But on the day of the Parousia he will be fully glorified through his people (Col 3:4). While the glory of his might will overwhelm unbelievers, the glory of his splendor expressed through his people will incite awe.

The final and very significant point to make about the end of this section (1:8-12) is that the writers attributed to Jesus the status of deity. The Lord Jesus (who is clearly the subject of 1:8ff) is presented as the one who will come to execute eternal destruction upon people who will be forever separated from the Lord and his glorious power (1:9). Such actions were attributed to Yahweh by the prophet Isaiah (Isa 2:10, 19, 21). Furthermore, 1:10 speaks of the day when he will come to be glorified in his holy people. The day is none other than the Day of the Lord, which also echoes Isaiah 2:11, 17, LXX. And the idea of God being glorified in his holy ones may come from the Septuagint rendering of Psalm 89:7 (88:8 in LXX), which reads "God will be glorified in the council of his holy ones." These actions attributed to Jesus are theophanic (Bruce 1982:152).

When the writers offered a prayer to God at the end of this chapter (1:11-12), they asked for a blessing of grace that comes from "our God and Lord, Jesus Christ" (see extensive note on 1:12). In saying this, they were attributing deity to Jesus. He is both God and Lord. It is his name—the Lord Jesus—that will be glorified in his holy ones in the coming Kingdom. Jesus has the Name that is above every name—the name that every tongue should confess (Phil 2:9-11) because he is God incarnate (John 1:1, 14; Phil 2:6). The early Christians proclaimed Jesus' name, preached his name, and healed the sick by the power of his name (see Acts 4:7-18; 8:12; 9:28). They were willing to suffer for his name (see Acts 5:28, 40; 15:26), and even die for his name (see Acts 21:13). In an era when the Caesars were being deified and hailed as God, Christians, at great risk, were proclaiming that Jesus is God. They were scoffed at and persecuted for doing so. But at the end of this age, the vindication will come. Christ will be so manifest in his many children (Rom 8:17-21) that Christ's divine name will be glorified thereby.

◆ III. The Parousia of Jesus and the Parousia of the Lawless One (2:1-12)

Now, dear brothers and sisters,* let us clarify some things about the coming of our Lord Jesus Christ and how we will be gathered to meet him. ²Don't be so easily shaken or alarmed by those who say that the day of the Lord has already begun. Don't believe them, even if they claim to have had a spiritual vision, a revelation, or a letter supposedly from us. ³Don't be fooled by what they say. For that day will not come until there is a great rebellion against God and the man of lawlessness* is revealed—the one who brings destruction.* ⁴He will exalt himself and defy everything that people call god and every object of worship. He will even sit in the temple of God, claiming that he himself is God.

⁵Don't you remember that I told you about all this when I was with you? ⁶And you know what is holding him back, for he can be revealed only when his time comes. ⁷For this lawlessness is already at work

secretly, and it will remain secret until the one who is holding it back steps out of the way. [8]Then the man of lawlessness will be revealed, but the Lord Jesus will kill him with the breath of his mouth and destroy him by the splendor of his coming.

[9]This man will come to do the work of Satan with counterfeit power and signs and miracles. [10]He will use every kind of evil deception to fool those on their way to destruction, because they refuse to love and accept the truth that would save them. [11]So God will cause them to be greatly deceived, and they will believe these lies. [12]Then they will be condemned for enjoying evil rather than believing the truth.

2:1 Greek brothers; also in 2:13, 15.   2:3a Some manuscripts read the man of sin.   2:3b Greek the son of destruction.

NOTES

2:1 *the coming of our Lord Jesus Christ.* The Greek behind "coming" is *parousia* [TG3952, ZG4242], the paramount event spoken about in 1 Thess (1 Thess 2:19; 3:13; 4:15; 5:23) and 2 Thess (1:7-12; 2:8).

we will be gathered to meet him. This gathering together occurs at the time of the resurrection and rapture of the church (see notes and commentary on 1 Thess 4:13-18).

2:2 *the day of the Lord.* This reading has excellent documentation behind it: $\aleph$ A B D* F G L P 044 0278 (33) 1739 it syr cop. An inferior reading is, "the day of Christ" (D² $\mathfrak{M}$—so TR). The variant is likely the result of scribal conformity to other Pauline texts that designate the eschaton as "the day of Christ" (see 1 Cor 1:8; Phil 1:10; 2:16). In the end, however, there is no difference in meaning—both terms denote the Parousia.

has already begun. The Greek verb is *enestēken,* a perfect active verb of *enistēmi* [TG1764, ZG1931], which means "is present"—"the regular force of the perfect tense of *enistēnai* in NT usage" (Bruce 1982:165). The idea is not imminence (see Morris 1991:216), for what cause of alarm would have there been for some to say that the day of the Lord's coming was imminent? This was standard apostolic teaching at that time.

a spiritual vision. Lit., "by spirit." This is a metonymy for revelation given by Spirit-inspired prophecy (see note on 1 Thess 5:19).

a revelation. Lit., "a word" or "a message"—whether orally delivered or written.

or a letter supposedly from us. It is hard to imagine that someone had sent a forgery to the Thessalonians, but the writers wanted to guard against this. Thus, Paul in 2 Thess 3:17 signed the letter with his own personal signature to guarantee its authenticity.

2:3 *a great rebellion against God.* This is an expanded rendering of one Greek word, *apostasia* [TG646, ZG686]. In Hellenistic times, the word denoted either political rebellion (see Josephus, *Life* 43, who used the word concerning the Jewish revolt against Rome) or religious defection—a falling away (as in Acts 21:21, which speaks of defection from the law of Moses). The verbal form of the word appears in 1 Tim 4:1, where the context clearly points to a departure from the faith. Jesus predicted this kind of apostasy before the end (Matt 24:11-14).

the man of lawlessness. This rendering is based on a superior textual variant supported by the two earliest manuscripts, $\aleph$ B, as well as 0278 1739 cop. A well-known yet inferior variant reading is "the man of sin," found in A D F G 044 $\mathfrak{M}$ it syr (so TR and KJV). "The man of lawlessness" or "the man of rebellion" (NIV) is "the anarchist." He is opposed to all moral, religious, and civil law. Just as Christ embodied righteousness, so the "man of lawlessness" will embody lawlessness and rebellion (see Dan 11:36). This one is probably the same as "the Antichrist" (1 John 2:18; 4:3). He will perpetrate the worst crime ever: that of claiming to be God and demanding worship from all human beings (see next note). In this regard, he is the worst of sinners; therefore, it is understandable why he came to be known as "the man of sin." However, the title "the man of lawlessness" not only has superior attestation, but it aptly describes the one who incites the eschatological apostasy.

the one who brings destruction. Lit., "the son of destruction." The NLT understands this as one who brings destruction; other versions (NRSV, etc.) understand it as the one who is destined for destruction.

2:4 He will exalt himself and defy everything that people call god. This language parallels Dan 11:36, which speaks of the king of the north, who is thought by many commentators to be Antiochus IV Epiphanes, commonly mocked by Jews as Epimanes ("the Madman"). Daniel 11:36 would seem to reflect what is recorded of Antiochus IV in 2 Macc (2 Macc 9:1–10:5), where he admits he had thought himself to be equal to God (2 Macc 9:12). In terms of eschatological prophecy, the prediction pertains to the Antichrist, the man of lawlessness.

and every object of worship. This language probably alludes to the notorious "sacrilegious object that causes desecration" (Dan 9:27; lit., "an abomination of desolation"), which is also referred to by Jesus in Matt 24:15 and Mark 13:14. Some think the profaning of the temple in Jerusalem by Antiochus IV Epiphanes in 169 BC (see Dan 9:27; 11:31; 12:11) prefigures the event predicted here. Others see an allusion to the attempt of the Emperor Caligula, called "the new god manifest," to erect his own image in the temple in AD 40.

sit. This reading has the support of ℵ A B D* 044 33 1739 it cop. Other mss (D² F G 𝔐 syr) add "as God." The variant is a scribal expansion that attempts to clarify the point that the lawless one will perform an activity that only God can do—i.e., occupy a place of worship in the Temple. However, the addition is not needed inasmuch as the next expression in the verse ("claiming that he himself is God") makes it more than clear what the lawless one will attempt to do.

in the temple of God. The NT writers used two different Greek words to describe the Temple: *naos* [TG3485, ZG3724] and *hieron* [TG2411, ZG2639]. The word *naos*, used here, refers to the actual sanctuary of the Temple, the place of God's dwelling. *Hieron* refers to the temple precincts as well as to the sanctuary (TDNT 4.880-890). Generally speaking, *naos* was used to designate the inner section of the Temple known as the holy place and the Holy of Holies, whereas *hieron* would designate the outer court and the Temple proper. Fee (1987:146) said, "The distinctions between the two words do not necessarily hold in all the Greek of the NT period, but the usage in the LXX, where the distinction is common, seems to have influenced Paul."

claiming that he himself is God. Lit., "presenting himself—that he is God." The Greek word behind "claiming" is *apodeiknumi* [TG584, ZG617], which means "show forth, display, exhibit, proclaim" (cf. 1 Cor 4:9).

2:5 I told you about all this. The Greek verb *elegon* [TG3004, ZG3306] can be first person singular or third person plural. However, "they told" does not fit the context, so it must be "I told." Either Silvanus or Paul reminded the believers of what they had previously been taught and of what they already knew (3:10; 1 Thess 2:9; 3:4; 4:1; 5:1-2). This shows, again, that one of the authors interrupted the corporate voice with his personal voice. Nearly all commentators assume this was Paul. But it could just as easily have been Silvanus, who was a prophet and therefore could have been the one to tell the Thessalonians about these prophecies.

2:6 And you know what is holding him back. The use of the English word "what" accurately reflects the neuter in Greek; in 2:7 the word is masculine—hence, the rendering, "the one who is holding it back." The language suggests that the restraining force is both a power and a person, variously identified as God, the Holy Spirit, the church, the gospel, Paul, the emperor, the Roman Empire, or the government (see commentary). The Greek expression (*to katechon* [TG2722, ZG2988]) literally means "that which possesses." It is here rendered as if it were a positive force (against lawlessness) that restrains (see MM 337, which notes its use in connection with the notion of detaining someone), but the force could also be an evil one that possesses (see MM 336, which notes that the word was used to describe possession of a god).

2:7 *this lawlessness is already at work.* This is similar in thought to the notion of the many antichrists whom John said were already present in the world as prefiguring the Antichrist (1 John 2:18).

at work. The Greek word *energeitai* [TG1754, ZG1919]) implies supernatural intervention, whether good (1 Thess 2:13) or, as here, evil (2:9; Eph 2:2).

secretly. This word, *mustērion* [TG3466, ZG3696], was a descriptor commonly used of rituals in the mystery religions (see 2:6).

the one who is holding it back. Compared to the wording in 2:6, which speaks of a force or power (neuter in Greek) that restrains or possesses, the wording here speaks of a person (masculine in Greek).

steps out of the way. The Greek is *ek mesou* [TG3319, ZG3545] *genētai* (lit., "comes out of the midst"), which is here rendered in an active voice. But the verb can also have a passive sense: "is removed" (the rendering of this verse according to BDAG 199). Bruce (1982:170) argues that *ek mesou genētai* could have an active sense or a passive; he cites examples from the literature that have an active sense ("he decided to live by himself, having moved away out of public view," Plutarch, *Timoleon* 5.3) and a passive sense ("when Clio has been removed," Achilles Tatius, *Leucippe and Clitophon* 2.27). The "restraining one" or "possessing one" will either step out of the way or be taken out of the way, giving way for the unveiling of the lawless one (2:8).

2:8 *Then the man of lawlessness will be revealed.* This is the third mention of the revealing (*apokaluptō* [TG601, ZG636]) of the man of lawlessness (2:3, 6). This revealing will come at the time of his parousia.

the Lord Jesus. This is the reading in א A D* F G L^c P 044 0278 33 it syr cop. A variant reading of this is "the Lord" (B D^2 1739 𝔐—so TR).

will kill. This has the support of A B P 0278 it, which read *anelei* [TG337, ZG359] ("he will destroy" or "he will kill"). Other mss read *aneloi*, an optative verb meaning "may he destroy" (א D^{*vid} F G 33 1739). The documentary evidence is nearly evenly divided between these two readings. Lightfoot (1904:115) considered the wording *aneloi* to be original because it explained the other variant (plus and additional variant). If so, the verse reads, "may the Lord Jesus destroy him with the breath of his mouth—even as he will destroy him by the radiance of his coming." One point can be added to Lightfoot's argument: *anelei* might be the result of scribal conformity to the LXX of Isa 11:4, the verse alluded to here.

with the breath of his mouth. This is based on Isa 11:4, LXX, which says that at the coming of the prince of the house of David "the earth will shake at the force of his word, and one breath from his mouth will destroy the wicked."

destroy him. In the Greek there is a wordplay here. Jesus will "destroy" (= "will render inoperative"; *katargēsei [TG2673, ZG2934]) the operating/working (energeian [TG1753, ZG1918]) of Satan in the man of lawlessness (2:9).*

the splendor of his coming. The first Greek noun is *epiphaneia* [TG2015, ZG2211]. The second Greek noun is *parousia* [TG3952, ZG4242]. This is the only place in the NT where the two terms appear together. In ancient literature, an epiphany was the revelation of a deity or a demonstration of his power that evoked worship. In 1 and 2 Thess, the term *parousia* is used to denote Christ's coming—his personal visitation (2:1; 1 Thess 2:19; 3:13; 4:15; 5:23).

2:9 *will come.* In Greek this is a noun, *parousia* [TG3952, ZG4242]. Even as Jesus Christ will come in royal and divine power (his *parousia*; 2:1, 8; 1 Thess 2:19; 3:13; 4:15; 5:23), so this figure will have his royal entrance and visitation.

to do the work. The word here, *energeian* [TG1753, ZG1918], implies supernatural action (cf. 2:7-8; 1 Thess 2:13).

Satan. The power and force motivating or even indwelling the man of lawlessness is Satan (see 1 Thess 2:18; 3:5), who will display wonders.

2:10 *destruction.* The Greek word comes from *apollumi* [TG622A, ZG660], a verb denoting ruin and destruction. It is used in the NT in connection with the destruction of those who do not believe in Jesus as the Son of God (John 3:16; 1 Cor 1:18; 2 Cor 2:15; 4:3).

they refuse to love and accept the truth that would save them. This will happen because of the deception of the man of lawlessness and because they will reject the truth of the gospel (cf. Eph 1:13; Col 1:5; 2 Tim 2:15).

2:11 *God will cause them to be greatly deceived.* Lit., "God sends them a powerful delusion."

believe these lies. These are the satanic deceptions of the man of lawlessness (2:9-10).

2:12 *Then they will be condemned.* This condemnation is described in 1:6-9.

enjoying. The Greek word *eudokēsantes* [TG2106, ZG2305] means "to consent to" or "to accept."

evil. The Greek word is *adikia* [TG93, ZG94], often translated as "unrighteousness."

COMMENTARY

The Day of the Lord. The term "day of the Lord" refers to the parousia of Jesus Christ, as used in 1 Thessalonians 5:2 and 2 Thessalonians 2:2. According to 1 Thessalonians 5:2, Paul and Silvanus said the Day of the Lord would come unexpectedly, like a thief in the night. Someone or several people had told the Thessalonians that the Day of the Lord had already happened, which would mean that the events of 1 Thessalonians 4:15–5:2 (the Parousia, Resurrection, and Rapture) must have already transpired. So Paul and Silvanus wrote to tell the Thessalonians that two events must precede that day: a great apostasy will occur and the man of lawlessness will be unveiled (2:3-12). Then the Day of the Lord will come, and he will gather together his people via their resurrection and rapture.

The gathering together of the believers on the Day of the Lord, spoken of in 2:1-2, must be concurrent with the parousia of Jesus Christ (with the subsequent Resurrection and Rapture) spoken of in 1 Thessalonians 4:15–5:2. And the text of 2:1-3 makes it more than clear that the Day of the Lord is *preceded* by the great apostasy and unveiling of the man of lawlessness. As such, Christians will be around to witness this apostasy, as well as the man of lawlessness and the subsequent Tribulation. And then the Lord Jesus will come to destroy the man of lawlessness, as well as to gather together his believers.

There are some commentators, however, who think Christians will be raptured before the Day of the Lord comes. As far as I know, this interpretation began with the father of dispensational teaching, J. N. Darby (who may have gotten some of his ideas from Manuel Lacunza and Edward Irving). Darby recorded that it was 2 Thessalonians 2:1-2 which (in about 1830) made him "understand the rapture of the saints to occur before—perhaps a considerable time before—the day of the Lord (that is, before the judgment of the living)" (cited in Kelly 1903:5-8 and in Bruce 1982:163). Darby's dispensationalism became the mainstay of eschatological doctrine for certain Bible teachers throughout the last 100 years. This is evident, for example, in the teachings of two scholars who hold a dispensational view—namely T. L. Constable and R. Thomas. In his commentary on 2 Thessalonians, Constable wrote, "The day of the Lord is the period of history mentioned repeatedly in the Old Testament during which God will bring judgment and blessing on the people of the earth in a more direct, dramatic, and drastic way than ever before (cf. Isa 13:6, 9; Zeph 1:14-16). From other New Testament revelation concerning this period of time it is believed that this [the day of the Lord] will begin after the Rapture of the church" (1983:717). R. Thomas argues that there must be a "removal of Christians (including the Thessalonian believers) from earth before this persecution. It is another group of God's people, following the church's translation, who must face the terror of this archenemy" (1978:318). Inexplicably, Thomas doesn't say who this other group is, and so we are left to ponder.

The strangeness of the teaching known as the pre-Tribulation Rapture is that it means Christ will be coming back twice—once before the Tribulation and once after the Tribulation. Holmes (1998:239) put it well:

> The view that Jesus could come at any moment to take up believers [and] carry them to heaven prior to the Tribulation, and will then come again in judgment at the end of the Tribulation, is widely publicized and wildly popular. But apart from the embarrassment this creates by having *two* "second comings" (or, if you will, both a second and a third coming), Paul in both 1 Thessalonians and 2 Thessalonians links the "catching up" (1 Thess 4:17) and the "gathering" (2 Thess 2:1)—terms that to Paul are synonyms—as closely as possible to the coming of the Lord on the Day of the Lord (1 Thess 4:16; 5:2; 2 Thess 2:1-3). And since Paul explicitly says that the Day of the Lord will not occur until after the revealing of the Antichrist, it follows that the "catching up" or "Rapture" will not occur until after the revealing of the Antichrist.

Another strong argument against a pre-Tribulation Rapture is that if Christians are raptured before the Tribulation, what is the point in telling them to look for events that will happen during the Tribulation? How could this in any way prepare them? To the contrary, the purpose of 2 Thessalonians 2 is to inform the Thessalonians that the day of the Lord's parousia will be preceded by a great apostasy and the unveiling of the man of lawlessness. This will be a time of trial and tribulation, after which the Lord will come to slay the evil one and rescue his people.

This accords with Jesus' eschatological teachings in Matthew 24, Mark 13, and Luke 21, where Jesus makes it clear that believers will suffer intense persecution and then be rescued by the Lord's intervention. Indeed, he indicates that those will be terrible days, even for the elect, so terrible that he will shorten them for the sake of the elect. The following chart shows the parallelism between 2 Thessalonians 2 and Jesus' discourses on the eschaton:

2 THESSALONIANS 2:1-12 AND THE ESCHATOLOGICAL TEACHINGS OF JESUS IN MATTHEW 24, MARK 13, LUKE 21

the coming (parousia) of the Lord Jesus	2 Thess 2:1	Matt 24:3, 27, 37, 39; Mark 13:26; Luke 21:27
being gathered together to him	2 Thess 2:1	Matt 24:31; Mark 13:27
don't be easily shaken or alarmed	2 Thess 2:2	Matt 24:6; Mark 13:5; Luke 21:9
the Day of the Lord preceded by apostasy	2 Thess 2:3	Matt 24:10
the desolating sacrilege in the holy place	2 Thess 2:4	Matt 24:15; Mark 13:14 (spoken by the prophet Daniel)
the man of lawlessness deceiving many with his power, signs, and miracles	2 Thess 2:9	Matt 24:5, 23-24; Mark 13:5, 21-22 (= the false Christ(s))
Jesus coming with open boldness and great power	2 Thess 2:8	Matt 24:27, 30; Mark 13:26
a call for endurance	2 Thess 2:15	Matt 24:13; Mark 13:13; Luke 21:19

The overall tenor of Jesus' eschatological discourses in Matthew 24, Mark 13, and Luke 21 concurs with that found in 2 Thessalonians 2. There will be an apostasy, a time of great tribulation, the desolating sacrilege, and the manifestation of many false christs deceiving people. The call to the believers is for endurance to remain faithful to the end during the Tribulation, for eventually the Son of Man will be revealed in his parousia with great power and glory to terminate evil and to gather together his believers.

One of the major differences between the two scenarios is that Jesus' discourses do not focus on one Antichrist (= the lawless one) who is then annihilated by Jesus Christ at the time of his coming. There is no showdown between these two in Jesus' discourses. Jesus' teaching points to several false christs and false prophets in the spirit of the "ongoingness" of the mystery of lawlessness (see commentary below for more on this).

Both accounts, however, do agree that an apostasy or rebellion will occur before the Parousia. Some scholars see the apostasy as a large-scale revolt against public order (so Bruce 1982:166-167). Morris sees it as people setting themselves in active opposition to God; this could happen with Jews, Christians, and humanity as a whole—the creatures rebelling against their Creator (1991:218-219). Others see it as a great falling away from the faith in the worldwide church (so Beale 2003:203-204; Green 2002:307). The sense one gets from reading Jesus' eschatological discourses is that he was speaking of a great falling away from the faith. As to the context of 2 Thessalonians, either connotation works. If the sense is that of massive rebellion against God, this perfectly accords with the notion of calling the Antichrist "the lawless one." If the sense is that of religious defection, then one could see how the lawless one will either take advantage of this defection to deceive people or create such extraordinary deception that people will be led astray. (See discussion below on how the apostasy/rebellion figures into the prophecy of the defilement taking place in the temple of God.)

The Parousia of Jesus and the Parousia of the Man of Lawlessness. Jesus' parousia is described in 2 Thessalonians 2:8 as an epiphany (see note on 2:8). When we tie this together with 2 Thessalonians 1:7, which speaks of the revelation (*apokalupsis* [TG602, ZG637]) of the Lord Jesus from heaven, we understand that Jesus' parousia will be an epiphanic unveiling. The one now invisible to us will become visible. As Beale says, "this fits admirably with an apocalyptic notion of Christ's final coming as a sudden appearing from a formerly invisible dimension to all instead of some kind of directional return from a literal sky to the earth" (2003:138-139). Beale presents an illuminating quote from Josephus to illustrate that a parousia is an epiphany—the sudden manifestation of divinity to human beings:

> Josephus paraphrases the episode of 2 Kings 6:17, where Elijah [sic., Elisha] prays that his servant would see the divine armies hidden in an invisible heavenly dimension, as follows: "reveal . . . his power and presence [*parousia*] to his servant" (*Antiquities* 9.55). A few lines later, Josephus refers to this "power and presence" as the "manifestation [*epiphaneia*] . . . and the power" (*Antiquities* 9.60). This appears to be just the way Paul is using *parousia* [TG3952, ZG4242] here with reference to Christ's final appearance. (2003:139)

The significance of this is that we must not think of Christ's parousia as only a directional, geographical event—Christ coming down from heaven to earth. We should also think of the Parousia as a transformational event—Christ coming out of hiding so as to be visibly present among his people. At this time in history, he is invisibly present with his people by means of his Spirit. The parousia will mean that the invisible one will become visible. The way Christ will become visible is by a transformation of this present universe as we know it. "The present physical reality will in some way disappear and the formerly hidden heavenly dimension, where Christ and God dwell, will be revealed" (Beale 2003:138). As such, the hidden Christ will be unveiled and his presence manifested in such a way that all people throughout the earth can see him (Matt 24:27). According to our notion of three-dimensional geography, this would be impossible. But a new dimension will break into our universe, one in which Christ will be able to reveal his presence with all his people at one time.

Second Thessalonians 2 presents the parousia of Jesus as the manifestation of a great warrior coming to destroy the man of lawlessness soon after his own parousia.

The unveiling of the man of lawlessness, who is empowered by Satan, will come when he presents himself to the world as God and deceives the world with his many miracles. The unveiling of Jesus, the Son of Man, will come with an epiphany so powerful that he will destroy the man of lawlessness with one breath of his mouth.

The contrasting lexical elements found in this passage are well worth noting because the language shows that the writers were pairing up Jesus and the man of lawlessness as the prominent opponents in the eschaton. First, there is the element of their divinity. Jesus, who is both Lord and God (see note on 1:12; cf. 3:12), is presented as being God by virtue of the passage speaking of "the parousia of his epiphany." Only those who are divine make epiphanic appearances. And this very epiphany will be so powerful that it will destroy the lawless one instantly. The man of lawlessness, by contrast, will claim divinity and feign divinity by doing miracles. But his destruction will show that he is no God at all.

Second, both Jesus and the man of lawlessness are said to have a parousia—a royal entrance into the world. When Jesus makes his parousia (2:1), it will be a time for gathering together his people as well as destroying the man of lawlessness, who will have just had his parousia to do the work of Satan. Third, the man of lawlessness will be revealed (mentioned three times—2:3, 6, 8) at an appointed time. So will Jesus (1:7), the Son of Man, who will come suddenly and then swiftly annihilate the man of lawlessness, the son of destruction.

The Identity of the Man of Lawlessness. We are told a few other things about this rebellious man, each of which could help us identify him. These are found primarily in 2:4, which has three participial phrases in the present tense (not the future), and thereby denotes the timeless activity of the lawless one, as well as his abiding character (see note on 2:4). In other words, 2:4 is a timeless definition of what the lawless one is and does:

1. He is one who opposes.

The first identification of the man of lawlessness is that he is called *ho antikeimenos* [TG480, ZG512], which means he is "the one who stands against"—i.e., the opposer, the adversary. This term is used in the Septuagint (1 Kgs 11:25) as a rendering for the Hebrew term for adversary, and the verb is used in Zechariah 3:1 to describe the one who opposes. In 1 Timothy 5:14 the same expression (*ho antikeimenos*) is used to describe Satan, the supreme adversary (Bruce 1982:167-168). It is evident, then, that this one bears the satanic disposition of being the opposer and adversary.

2a. He is one who exalts himself above everything called God.

This language parallels Daniel 11:36, which says, "Then the king will do as he pleases, and he will exalt and magnify himself above every god" (NASB). As noted above (see note on 2:4), this language speaks of the prophesied king of the north, recognized by most scholars as referring to the Antichrist, the man of lawlessness.

2b. He exalts himself above every object of worship.

The lawless one's exaltation above every object of worship is an allusion to what is otherwise known in Scripture as "a sacrilegious object that causes desecration"

(Dan 9:27; 11:31), which is also referred to by Jesus in Matthew 24:15 and Mark 13:14 in his predictions of events in the end times.

3. He even sits in the temple of God, presenting himself as God.

This language harkens back to Ezekiel 28:2, where God reiterates the boast of the prince of Tyre, "I am a god; I sit in the seat of gods," and then confronts him: "Yet you are a man and not God, Although you make your heart like the heart of God" (Ezek 28:2, NASB).

This description of the man of lawlessness also harkens back to Isaiah 14:12-14, which is a poem about the king of Babylon with these lines: "How you have fallen from heaven, O star of the morning, son of the dawn! You have been cut down to the earth, You who have weakened the nations. But you said in your heart, 'I will ascend to heaven; I will raise my throne above the stars of God. . . . I will ascend above the heights of the clouds; I will make myself like the Most High'" (NASB). Some of the church fathers, linking this passage to Luke 10:18 and Revelation 12:8-9, took it to refer to the fall of Satan. "However, the great expositors of the Reformation were unanimous in arguing that the context here does not support such an interpretation. This passage is discussing human pride, which, while monumental to be sure, is still human and not angelic" (Oswalt 1986:320).

Undoubtedly, many wish the writers of 2 Thessalonians would have given us more information about the lawless one so that we could make a more positive identification. What we are given are fragments. Putting the pieces together is somewhat similar to what a papyrologist does in the process of reconstructing a text, adjoining several fragments together and hypothesizing about the text that existed in the missing portions. Many commentators have attempted to take the fragments in 2 Thessalonians 2 and reconstruct a picture of the man of lawlessness. As would be expected, there are different results.

It appears to me that the man of lawlessness is the ultimate incarnation of apotheosis; he is one who aspires to be God by replacing God—or I could say—by replacing Christ (hence, the term "antichrist"). This picture emerges from the fact that both Ezekiel and Isaiah spoke of individuals (the king of Tyre and the king of Babylon, respectively) who displayed such pride that they aspired to usurp the throne of God. Daniel also spoke of one called "the king of the north" who will attempt to usurp the throne of God.

Since the participles of 2 Thessalonians 2:4 are in the present tense (see note), it suggests that the lawless one is characteristically one who attempts to usurp the position of God. There does not necessarily have to be only one particular "lawless one," even though the passage eventually gets to this. The "ongoingness" of lawlessness is inherent in the idea of the mystery of lawlessness being presently at work (note the present tense, *energeitai* [TG1754, ZG1919] = "is working"). This idea is also present in John's discussion of the Antichrist in which he says, "You have heard that the Antichrist is coming, and already many such antichrists have appeared" (1 John 2:18). In his discourses about the end times, Jesus also spoke about the coming of many false messiahs (Matt 24:5, 23-24; Mark 13:6, 21-23; Luke 21:8). Of course, there will be one figure at the end of this age who is none other than *the* lawless one claiming to be God and demanding worship. In the interim, however, there have been and will continue to be those who do the same.

Since the text tells us that this lawless one will operate according to the power of Satan, it stands to reason that this figure has the same aspirations as Satan—namely, to usurp the throne of God. As noted before, some of the church fathers thought this was an attitude and activity carried out by Satan at some point before the creation of man and that he will do so again in the future. This thinking was strongly influenced by interpreters identifying both the king of Babylon in Isaiah 14 and the prince of Tyre in Ezekiel 28 as Lucifer (= Satan). The language of self-promotion to deity status, especially with the translation of "Lucifer" (meaning "son of the morning") from the Latin in Isaiah 14:12, prompted various commentators in the past to see in this passage a reference to Satan. (The translation "Lucifer" is untenable and no longer found in new translations.) The notion that Satan was called Lucifer before his fall is a very widespread idea, which shows up in literature affected by the Latin Bible and the KJV (see Youngblood 1997:22-31); this is nowhere more prominent than in John Milton's epic poem, *Paradise Lost*. Most commentators today, however, believe that Isaiah 14 and Ezekiel 28 are directed at two humans who were guilty of exceeding hubris, such that they thought they were gods. They are not passages about Satan per se, and therefore do not tell us about the origin of Satan and his fall.[1]

However, the fact that Satan is behind the man of lawlessness in all that he does gives us a good idea of what Satan's aspirations have been—namely, he has wanted to usurp the throne of God. The writers of 2 Thessalonians used language that alludes to Isaiah 14 and Ezekiel 28 because these are passages that speak of mortals attempting to claim divine status—so also the man of lawlessness. The presentation of the same figure in Daniel concurs; this one will claim to be God, desecrate the temple by setting up an image of himself, and then demand people to worship him as God. This is what is otherwise known in Scripture as the sacrilegious object that causes desecration (see Dan 9:26-27; 11:31; 12:11; Matt 24:15; Mark 13:14).

Historical Identifications of the Man of Lawlessness. The man of lawlessness has taken on different faces throughout history. The first figure, who appeared before the time of Christ, was predicted by Daniel (see Dan 9:27; 11:31; 12:11); he was the Seleucid king, Antiochus IV Epiphanes (meaning "manifest"), who claimed to be the earthly manifestation of his patron deity, Olympian Zeus. He set up a pagan altar in the holy place in 167 BC (1 Macc 1:54, 59; 6:7; 2 Macc 6:1-5). Antiochus Epiphanes' outrageous sacrilege prompted the Hasmonean revolt.

The next figure appeared shortly after the time of Christ's prediction concerning the desolating sacrilege. This was Gaius Caesar, nicknamed Caligula (AD 37–41); he was the first emperor to be worshiped in Rome during his own lifetime. On hearing of a dispute between Jews and Gentiles over worshiping him in Jamnia, he ordered a statue of himself placed in the Temple in Jerusalem. His plan, which would have caused a major revolt among the Jews, was averted only by the intercession of Herod Agrippa I. Thus, Caligula never carried out desolating sacrilege in the Temple.

The next figure was Caesar Nero, who is the "beast" depicted in John's Apocalypse (Rev 13). We know that Nero is the Beast because the number of the Beast in Revelation 13:18 is said to be 666 (in some manuscripts: 𝔓46 ℵ A) or 616 (in other manuscripts: 𝔓115 C), both of which designate "Nero Ceasar" by way of gematria (an ancient Jewish practice of assigning numerical values to words and, thus, names by adding together the values of their letters). The number "666" comes from a transliteration of "Nero Caesar" from Greek into Hebrew; the number 616 is either the Latin equivalent of the name *Nero Caesar* by way of gematria (Aune 1998a:770-771; NET mg) or a different spelling of *Neron Caesar* which drops the final *n* (Metzger 2003:308). Nero (who reigned AD 54-68) claimed to be God and demanded that he should be worshiped as "God the Lord." But there is no record that he ever entered the Temple in Jerusalem and desecrated it. Thus, if Nero was the personage in mind, then the temple of God must be understood as God's church. And, in fact, Nero did enter the church and wreaked havoc with his persecutions against thousands of Christians. Almost the same could be said for Domitian (who reigned AD 81-96), who also decreed that he should be worshiped as "God the Lord" and who also persecuted Christians.

Others have seen this figure as being Titus, who entered into Jerusalem and then destroyed the Temple (Josephus *War* 6.4.7). While the sanctuary was going up in flames at the end of August, AD 70, Roman legionnaries set up their standards in the Temple court and offered sacrifices to them opposite the east gate (Josephus *War* 6.316). But Bruce comments, "while Josephus may have seen a fulfillment of Daniel's prophecy in this event, . . . the Evangelists probably did not; the temple court was not 'the holy place,' and there was no demand that the Jews should join in the worship of the Roman standards" (1982:181). That having been said, many commentators think the prophecies of Jesus spoken in Matthew 24, Mark 13, and Luke 21 (especially Luke 21:20-24) did find partial fulfillment in the events that took place in Jerusalem in AD 68-70.

After the death of Nero and the destruction of the Temple in Jerusalem, various interpreters looked for a different person to be the fulfillment of the Antichrist or man of lawlessness. It was then that some spoke of him as "Nero *redivivus*"—the "head" in Revelation 13:3, whose mortal wound was healed. Some saw him as Genseric the Vandal (of the fifth century), others as Muhammad (of the seventh century), or certain powerful popes, who were regarded as unworthy occupants of a sacred office, usurpers who took a seat in the sanctuary of God (cf. 2:4). During the Reformation, this view about the pope became official. Indeed, the Westminster Confession of Faith (1646) says, "the Pope of Rome . . . is that Antichrist, that man of sin, and son of perdition, that exalteth himself, in the Church, against Christ and all that is called God" (25.6).

None of the above mentioned individuals completely fulfilled all the predicted aspects of the man of lawlessness. Therefore, such a one is still expected to come.

This fits the scenario depicted in 1 John where the apostle indicates that there were, are, and will be many antichrists on earth who precede the advent of the one Antichrist (1 John 2:18).

Identifications of the Temple. The "temple" that the lawless man inhabits has taken on different identifications throughout history: the Second Temple, if we are talking about Antiochus IV, Caligula, or Titus; perhaps some imperial temple erected in honor of this figure, if we are talking about Nero or Diocletian; the church, if we are taking about the present entity which is known throughout the New Testament as the temple of God; a newly rebuilt temple in Jerusalem, if we are looking for a future literal fulfillment on earth.

According to normal Pauline usage of *naos* [TG3485, ZG3724], the sanctuary of God would most likely be the church. In Paul's Epistles the word *naos* appears six times (2:4; 1 Cor 3:16, 17; 6:19; 2 Cor 6:16; Eph 2:21). In four of these verses, *naos* is a symbol for the church as the habitation for God's Spirit (1 Cor 3:16, 17; 2 Cor 6:16; Eph 2:21). In 1 Corinthians 6:19, Paul used the word *naos* with respect to the local church body being a sanctuary for the Holy Spirit. So that leaves 2 Thessalonians 2:4. On one hand, we can imagine Paul using the word to designate the inner sanctuary of an actual temple. This is affirmed by the wording, "he will sit." On the other hand, it is possible that—in conjunction with his normal usage—Paul (and Silvanus) were speaking of the church as the sanctuary of God. (See my article, "Temple," in DPL 923-925, for a full discussion of Paul's use of the word.)

When we couple together the prophecy of an apostasy/rebellion with the desolating sacrilege taking place in the Temple of God, there seem to be two scenarios. (1) Paul and Silvanus were speaking of an apostasy that would happen in the future in the land of Israel during which the Antichrist would come to defile a rebuilt temple in Jerusalem. Or (2) they were speaking of a future apostasy throughout the church accompanied by the Antichrist's defiling influence in the church, which is the temple of God. In accord with the first scenario, many Christians are looking for a rebuilt temple in Jerusalem as being *the* significant event that precedes the coming of the Antichrist before the coming of Jesus Christ. However, is it not possible that the present Islamic mosque, known as the Dome of the Rock, standing where the Temple once stood, is the sacrilegious object that causes desecration in some sense? If so, the abominable act has already occurred. In accord with the second scenario, Christians should be wary of those who enter the church to deceive and to destroy. This has been a constant problem in the church, as predicted by Jesus (Matt 24:22-26; John 10:10); it will one day be fully manifested in the presence of the man of lawlessness.

The Mystery of Lawlessness and the Restraining/Possessing Power. Prior to the final manifestation of the lawless one, the mystery of lawlessness is at work. This is a power or force unidentified by the writers of 2 Thessalonians because they assumed that the Thessalonians already knew the identification through prior teachings. So readers today are left to guess. Most likely, this power is linked with the continual manifestations of antichrists, false messiahs, and other apparently divine figures who have appeared throughout history and who will continue to appear (see Matt 24:24; Mark 13:22; 1 John 2:18). Nonetheless, the fact that this power is called a "mystery" ultimately leaves it an enigma.

The writers indicated that there is a mysterious power that is either restraining lawlessness or is in itself an evil possessing force. Most commentators have understood the power to be a restraining force (see notes on 2:6-7) that will let go of its restraint prior to the manifestation of the lawless one. However, a few commentators have understood this power to be a precursor to the lawless one. For example, Green (2002:314-317; essentially following Giblin 1990:459-469) thinks the Greek expression in 2:6, *to katechon* [TG2722, ZG2988], may not refer to some restraining power at all but to something that seizes or possesses—and is therefore a power that prefigures the man of lawlessness, an agent of the lawlessness active at that time (2:7-8). It has nothing to do with holding back but with "possessing"—that is, there is a possessing power that holds on until the man of lawlessness is revealed. So this power precedes the coming of the lawless one. Green argues that in Greek literature the word could describe demonic possession ("the one who seizes" or "possesses") like that associated with the pagan cults of Serapis or Dionysus. Thus, this figure would pave the way for the man of lawlessness to be revealed (2:3, 8).

Most commentators view the power as a restraining force for good, not a possessing evil force. Among the various identifications of this power are the following:

1. The Roman Empire or emperor
2. The principle of law and order (personified in 2:7)
3. The Jewish state
4. God and his power
5. The Holy Spirit
6. The proclamation of the gospel (the neuter participle in 2:6) by Christian missionaries, especially Paul himself (the masculine participle in 2:7)
7. An angelic figure restraining evil until the gospel has been preached to all nations
8. The church[2]

It doesn't seem likely that the restraining power is any kind of human government (options 1-3), even though God does operate through human institutions. The restraining power could certainly be the power of God, the Holy Spirit, the church, or all three. However, I think it is very unlikely that the removal of this restraining power implies the Rapture of the church. Some angel (such as Michael) could be holding back the evil powers until the gospel is fully proclaimed to the whole world (Mark 13:10; cf. Dan 10:13). Or it is possible the gospel itself is the restraining power. In my opinion, it is most likely the proclamation of the apostolic truths that restrains false teachings and lawlessness. However, ultimately we don't know what or who (see notes on 2:6-7) this restraining power is. Paul, Silvanus, and Timothy knew, and they passed that knowledge on to the Thessalonians when they were with them. From our perspective, it is best to confess our inability to discern the identity of the restraining power. This is what Augustine was confessing when he said:

> [Paul] was unwilling to make an explicit statement, because he said that they [the Thessalonians] knew [what he was referring to]. And thus we, who don't know what they knew, desire to understand what the apostle referred to, but even with hard work are not able, especially as his meaning is made still more obscure by what he adds [in 2:7-8a]. (*City of God* 20.19)

As soon as Paul and Silvanus describe the unveiling of the man of lawlessness (2:8), they announce his doom (as in 2:3). In 2:8, the writers were paraphrasing Isaiah 11:4, which says that the coming prince of the house of David will "shake [the earth] at the force of his word, and one breath from his mouth will destroy the wicked." Jesus is that prince of David who will destroy the lawless one by the "splendor of his coming." As noted, the first Greek noun is *epiphaneia* [TG2015, ZG2211] and the second is *parousia* [TG3952, ZG4242]. In 1 and 2 Thessalonians, the term *parousia* is used to denote Christ's coming—his personal visitation (2:1; 1 Thess 2:19; 3:13; 4:15; 5:23). In the Pastoral Epistles the term "epiphany" is used (1 Tim 6:14; 2 Tim 1:10; 4:1, 8; Titus 2:13) to denote the same event. But this word provides a different nuance in that it means "manifestation" or "appearance." Thus, the epiphany of the Parousia signifies that Christ's coming will be a manifestation of his divinity to human beings (1:7).

At the same time, the very epiphanic nature of Jesus' parousia will destroy the lawless one who has just made his own parousia. Prior to this, the lawless one will have been operating according to the empowering of Satan to perform miracles, signs, and wonders so as to deceive people (2:9). Those who will be deceived are those who refuse to accept the truth of the gospel, the gospel that could bring them salvation if they loved and believed the truth. But they will reject the truth of the gospel (2:10) and believe the lie of the man of lawlessness (2:9-10). "It is not just any lie that these people will accept, but Satan's last and greatest piece of deception, the lie that the Man of Lawlessness is God" (Morris 1991:234).

The point of this passage is that Paul and Silvanus did not want the Thessalonians to be deceived by false teachers (2:3). Deceptive teachers, false prophets, and false teachers are those who have and will continue to lead many people astray from the truth and thereby damage the church. At the end of time, the man of lawlessness will be the preeminent deceiver. Until then, the mystery of lawlessness is at work through various deceptions that have entered into Christendom. The restraint against these falsehoods is the proclamation of the truth.

ENDNOTES

1. D. Thomas (1991:126) says, "Despite the fact that Satan is not referred to specifically in [Isa] 14:12, his shadow lies behind this passage." About the Ezekiel passage, it may be said, "The prince of Tyre in several instances in this passage is identified by terminology which reminds the reader of Satan, especially in light of Isaiah 14:12-15. But it

is by no means clear that the Isaiah reference has anything directly to do with Satan" (Douglas and Hoffmeier 1990:1144). Some commentators, however, have read Jesus' statement in Luke 10:18 ("I saw Satan fall from heaven") back into Isaiah 14 and Ezekiel 28 and have come out saying that Jesus was referring to the same downfall. The more likely scenario is that Jesus was commenting on Satan's downfall because his disciples had exorcised many demons and thereby diminished Satan's kingdom. The truth of the matter is the Bible doesn't clearly tell us how Satan "fell" from heaven.

2. This list comes from Holmes (1998:233-234), who provides a thorough bibliography for each suggestion.

◆ IV. Thanksgiving for Salvation (2:13-17)

¹³As for us, we can't help but thank God for you, dear brothers and sisters loved by the Lord. We are always thankful that God chose you to be among the first* to experience salvation—a salvation that came through the Spirit who makes you holy and through your belief in the truth. ¹⁴He called you to salvation when we told you the Good News; now you can share in the glory of our Lord Jesus Christ.

¹⁵With all these things in mind, dear brothers and sisters, stand firm and keep a strong grip on the teaching we passed on to you both in person and by letter. ¹⁶Now may our Lord Jesus Christ himself and God our Father, who loved us and by his grace gave us eternal comfort and a wonderful hope, ¹⁷comfort you and strengthen you in every good thing you do and say.

2:13 Some manuscripts read *chose you from the very beginning.*

NOTES

2:13 *God chose you to be among the first.* Lit., "God chose you as firstfruits" (Rom 16:5; 1 Cor 16:15). This reading has the manuscript support of B F G P 0278 33 1739 syr^h cop^bo. Other mss (𝕏 D 044 𝔐 it syr^p cop^sa) read, "God chose you from [the] beginning." The textual attestation for these two variants is divided, as is the internal evidence. In an ancient Greek manuscript (written in continuous letters with no space between words), the word for "firstfruits" (*aparchēn* [^TG536, ^ZG569]) could have easily been confused for the expression "from [the] beginning" (*ap archēs* [^TG575/746, ^ZG608/794]), or vice versa. The reading of the text could be original because Paul had the habit of calling the first converts in certain geographical regions the "firstfruits" (see Rom 16:5; 1 Cor 16:15), and the Thessalonians were among Paul's first converts in Europe. But the variant reading also has legitimacy because it was customary for Paul to speak of God's selection of his elect before the foundation of the world (see Eph 1:4; 2 Tim 1:9).

belief in the truth. Whereas the unbelievers were those who rejected the truth (2:10, 12), believers are those who respond positively to the truth and thereby experience salvation.

2:14 *He called you to salvation when we told you the Good News.* God calls his chosen ones to himself through the preaching of the gospel (1:11; 1 Thess 2:12; 4:7; 5:24). The message is from God but is proclaimed by humans. The Thessalonians heard God's word proclaimed through the apostles (1 Thess 2:13).

2:15 *stand firm.* Ever since Paul and Silvanus left the church after its founding, they had been concerned for the stability of the Thessalonians' faith (1 Thess 3:2, 5, 8; 4:1-2). Their concern was increased due to the false teaching about the Day of the Lord, which had destabilized the church (2:1-2).

the teaching we passed on to you. Lit., "the traditions (*paradoseis* [TG3862, ZG4142]) you were taught." The traditions are the apostolic truths proclaimed to the believers in oral teaching and in written word.

2:16 *may our Lord Jesus Christ himself and God our Father.* These two names are followed by two nominative singular participles (*agapēsas* [TG25, ZG26] and *dous* [TG1325, ZG1443] = "having loved" and "having given") and one third person singular verb (*parakelesai* [TG3870, ZG4151] = "may he encourage"), thereby indicating the two were addressed in prayer as one.

2:17 *comfort . . . strengthen.* The first Greek verb *parakalesai* could mean "console" (as in 1 Thess 4:18), but here it probably means to "encourage." The second Greek verb (*stērixai* [TG4741, ZG5114]) means to strengthen so as to establish. Both verbs are in the optative mood, a mood that expresses hope.

COMMENTARY

While many people will be deceived by the man of lawlessness (2:10-12), Paul, Silvanus, and Timothy were thankful that God had elected, called, and saved the Thessalonian believers by the Spirit with a salvation that would lead to their sanctification and glorification (2:13-14). Verses 13-14 contain the essence of the gospel in a nutshell: God's election prompts God's calling, which is enacted by the proclamation of the gospel and the reception of the Spirit by those who believe the truth. This leads to salvation—"salvation that came through the Spirit who makes you holy" (2:13). The Thessalonians were saved by experiencing the Spirit (1 Thess 1:5; 4:8). The reception of the Spirit set them apart positionally from other people—i.e., made them holy. The ongoing work of the Spirit is to make the believers dispositionally holy. The ongoing work of the Spirit is also to transform the believers into the image of Christ so that they can "share in the glory of our Lord Jesus Christ" (2:14). Thus, we have election, calling, belief in the truth of the gospel, reception of the Spirit, sanctification, and glorification.

The apostles encouraged the Thessalonians to hold firm to the truths and promises of their salvation; these truths were the traditions the apostles had taught (see note on 2:15) both orally when they were with the Thessalonians and in writing—specifically with the two letters they wrote the Thessalonians. Paul and Silvanus knew the importance of authorized apostolic letters, for they saw the authority behind the letter that came from the first Jerusalem church council. The first epistle from the church leaders who had assembled at Jerusalem was the prototype for subsequent epistles (see Acts 15). It was authoritative because it was apostolic, and it was received as God's word. If an epistle came from an apostle (or apostles), it was to be received as having the imprimatur of the Lord. This is why Paul and Silvanus wanted the churches to receive their word as being the word of the Lord. This is made explicit in 1 Thessalonians (1 Thess 2:13), an epistle they insisted had to be read to all the believers in the church (1 Thess 5:27). In their second epistle to the Thessalonians, Paul and Silvanus indicated that their epistles carry the same authority as their preaching (2:15).

The writers concluded this section with a prayer to God, who is both the Lord Jesus Christ and God the Father (see note on 2:16). The prayer recalls the purpose of

Timothy's visit to the church: to strengthen and encourage the Thessalonians in their faith, as was noted in 1 Thessalonians 3:2. In this prayer, they invoked God to comfort the Thessalonians and strengthen them. Both these verbs are in the optative mood, a mood often used in prayers to express hopefulness and wishfulness. Knowing the Thessalonians were suffering persecution, the apostles hoped the very best for them and prayed so. Above all, the Thessalonians needed encouragement and strengthening. The source for both is God, who lives in the believer by the presence of the Spirit.

◆ V. Prayer for the Proclamation of the Gospel (3:1-5)

Finally, dear brothers and sisters,* we ask you to pray for us. Pray that the Lord's message will spread rapidly and be honored wherever it goes, just as when it came to you. [2]Pray, too, that we will be rescued from wicked and evil people, for not everyone is a believer. [3]But the Lord is faithful; he will strengthen you and guard you from the evil one.* [4]And we are confident in the Lord that you are doing and will continue to do the things we commanded you. [5]May the Lord lead your hearts into a full understanding and expression of the love of God and the patient endurance that comes from Christ.

3:1 Greek *brothers;* also in 3:6, 13.   3:3 Or *from evil.*

NOTES
3:1 *Finally.* Paul, like other Greek authors, sometimes used this expression to introduce a new theme (Phil 3:1, NASB), and not necessarily to signal the end of the discourse (2 Cor 13:11, NASB).

spread rapidly and be honored. Lit., "may run and be glorified." This image alludes to Ps 147:15, which speaks of God's message running swiftly. This image also pertains to the athletic games in which a victor was honored (1 Cor 9:24-26).

3:2 *that we will be rescued from wicked and evil people.* This request for prayer parallels Isa 25:4, LXX, which says that God delivers his people from the wicked. Paul and Silvanus had suffered greatly for preaching the gospel (Acts 16:19-23; 1 Thess 2:2). The opposition against them was founded in people's rejection of the gospel.

3:3 *guard you from the evil one.* In the Greek, there is a definite article before *ponērou* [TG4190A, ZG4505] (evil), strongly suggesting the rendering "the evil one," instead of just "evil" (see NLT mg). The same lexical feature appears at the ending of the Lord's Prayer, where many versions render it as "evil one" (Matt 6:13).

3:5 *the love of God and the patient endurance that comes from Christ.* This is a prayer for them to experience God's love and to endure sufferings as Christ endured.

COMMENTARY
This section begins with a request from the apostles that the Thessalonians would pray for them as they carried out their mission of spreading the gospel (3:1-2). Like the Thessalonian church, the apostles were meeting great opposition because of the gospel. At that time, Paul and Silvanus and Timothy were engaged in preaching the gospel in Corinth. They had been opposed and reviled by Jews when they preached that Jesus was the Messiah (Acts 18:5-7). Evidently, Paul was discouraged, so the

Lord came to him in a vision and encouraged him with these words: "Don't be afraid! Speak out! Don't be silent! For I am with you, and no one will attack and harm you, for many people in this city belong to me" (Acts 18:9-10). Paul stayed in Corinth for another year and a half proclaiming the gospel. As he wrote the Thessalonians, he felt he needed their prayers. On two other occasions, Paul asked certain believers to pray for him. When he wrote to the Romans, he asked them to pray that he would be rescued from the hand of unbelievers and that his ministry would be acceptable to the believers in Jerusalem (Rom 15:30-32). The unbelievers were Jews who had resisted the gospel of Jesus Christ and become persecutors of Paul. In the same way, the Thessalonians had been persecuted by Jewish unbeliev- ers, as well as by unbelieving pagans. At the end of Ephesians (Eph 6:19-20), Paul requested prayer for boldness in proclaiming the gospel.

Though the apostles requested prayer for their situation, they did not dwell on their own troubles. No sooner did they alert the Thessalonians to their situation than they assured the Thessalonians of God's power to make *them* strong in faith and guard *them* from the evil one (a clear need, cf. 2:9; 1 Thess 3:5). The apostles recognized the sufferings the Thessalonians faced (1:4-6; 1 Thess 1:6; 2:14; 3:3-4) and assured them of the Lord's faithful care in the midst of their troubles (3:3-5). Despite the sufferings the church had endured (1:4-7) and the false teaching they had encountered (2:2), the apostles were persuaded that the Thessalonians were doing what they had been commanded to do.

◆ VI. Final Exhortations (3:6-15)

⁶And now, dear brothers and sisters, we give you this command in the name of our Lord Jesus Christ: Stay away from all believers* who live idle lives and don't follow the tradition they received* from us. ⁷For you know that you ought to imi- tate us. We were not idle when we were with you. ⁸We never accepted food from anyone without paying for it. We worked hard day and night so we would not be a burden to any of you. ⁹We certainly had the right to ask you to feed us, but we wanted to give you an example to follow. ¹⁰Even while we were with you, we gave you this command: "Those unwilling to work will not get to eat."

¹¹Yet we hear that some of you are liv- ing idle lives, refusing to work and med- dling in other people's business. ¹²We command such people and urge them in the name of the Lord Jesus Christ to settle down and work to earn their own living. ¹³As for the rest of you, dear brothers and sisters, never get tired of doing good.

¹⁴Take note of those who refuse to obey what we say in this letter. Stay away from them so they will be ashamed. ¹⁵Don't think of them as enemies, but warn them as you would a brother or sister.*

3:6a Greek *from every brother.* 3:6b Some manuscripts read *you received.* 3:15 Greek *as a brother.*

NOTES

3:6 *idle lives.* The Greek is *ataktōs peripatountos* [ᵀᴳ814/4043, ᶻᴳ865/4344], which can be rendered "living idly" or "living disorderly." The second rendering is to be preferred because the context of the passage points to disruptive behavior as opposed to idleness (see commentary).

the tradition they received. This has the support of ℵ* A 044 0278 33 1739 𝔐. Other manuscripts read, "the tradition which you received" (B F G syr^h cop^sa). The TR reads, "the tradition which he received," with very slim support (1962 syr), followed by KJV NKJV. The first variant (accepted in WH and followed by many English versions) could be original, given its documentary support; if not, it is the result of scribal conformity to the immediate context in which the second person plural is predominant. The second variant (in the TR), with virtually no manuscript support, specifies the recipient of the apostolic traditions as a brother who lived a disorderly life.

3:7 *We were not idle.* The verb here, *atakteō* [^TG812, ^ZG863], shares the same root as *ataktōs* [^TG814, ^ZG865] in 3:6. The apostles did not live disorderly, idle lives. They worked for their own food and thereby set an example for the Thessalonians (see 1 Thess 2:9). There was harmony between the apostles' words ("tradition" in 3:6) and their actions.

3:8 *without paying for it.* Lit., "not as a gift." In Greco-Roman times, it was common practice for clients to be supported by the free gifts of patrons. The apostles did not have this kind of economic relationship with the Thessalonians.

3:10 *"Those unwilling to work will not get to eat."* While the apostles were in Thessalonica, they gave the Thessalonians the command quoted here. The Thessalonians were not ignorant of their obligation to work, but some had become disobedient and disorderly.

3:11 *we hear.* We do not know how the apostles heard that some in the church were living disorderly lives. Whoever brought them the report also told them of the false teachings that had spread among the Thessalonians.

living idle lives. In Greek this reads *peripatountas . . . ataktōs* [^TG4043/814, ^ZG4344/865], which can be rendered "living idly" or "living disorderly." This is the same wording as that found in 3:6 (see note).

3:12 *settle down and work.* Lit., "working with quietness" (*hēsuchias* [^TG2270, ^ZG2484]). The same wording occurs in 1 Thess 4:11, where the apostles command the believers to lead a quiet life instead of meddling in the affairs of others. Philo of Alexandria used nearly the same language as here, speaking about worthless people who caused public unrest because they had not "been trained to that quietness [*hēsuchian*] which in season is most excellent" (*Abraham* 20-22).

3:14 *Stay away from them.* The congregation should take special note of the disobedient and disassociate themselves from such people. This was a common form of church discipline (Matt 18:17; Rom 16:17-19; 1 Cor 5:9-11; Titus 3:10-11).

so they will be ashamed. In a culture where honor and shame were extremely important, the norms of the community were maintained by praise or blame. The loss of public honor would bring shame, thus motivating people to adjust their behavior within the norm of the community.

3:15 *warn them as you would a brother.* The apostles warned the Thessalonians that the prescribed discipline (3:14) should not result in animosity. Rather, the church should warn them as family members.

COMMENTARY

In 1 Thessalonians, Paul and Silvanus addressed the problem of disorderly Christians who refused to work (1 Thess 4:11-12; 5:14). From a report that came back to them, it was apparent that some had not heeded their message nor followed their example they set when they lived with the Thessalonians. Consequently, the apostles gave explicit instructions as to how the church community should treat these individuals.

Some commentators have supposed that some of the Christians in Thessalonica refused to work because they expected that Christ's coming would occur soon (see Best 1972:331). However, the apostles' teachings never connected the end times with instruction about work (3:6, 10). A more recent suggestion is that those who refused to work were clients of prominent patrons (Russell 1988:105-107; Wanamaker 1990:282; Green 2002:341-342). Patronage was a feature of the Roman economic world wherein wealthy patrons often had numerous clients whom they supported in various ways, such as by giving them food or money and representing them in public assembly. Having numerous clients increased the honor of a patron.

A third possibility is that Paul and Silvanus were addressing individuals who refused to work for a living and became dependent upon the church. This situation had nothing to do with fervency about the Lord's coming because the problem was already there before 1 Thessalonians was written—in fact, the problem had been addressed while Paul and Silvanus were among the Thessalonians (1 Thess 4:11-12, note the wording "just as we instructed you before"). And the situation may have had nothing to do with patron–client relationships. Quite simply, certain Christians may have become sycophants, draining the community and giving it a bad testimony.

Paul and Silvanus had provided the Thessalonians with living examples of those who worked to provide for their own living (3:7-8; 1 Thess 2:9). In other writings, Paul taught that Christian workers could receive pay for their labor (1 Cor 9:7-14; 1 Tim 5:17-18), but Paul did not take advantage of that privilege (3:8-9; 1 Thess 2:9). He had not taken any support from the Thessalonians while he ministered to them, although he received some offerings from the Philippians (Phil 4:15-16). The Thessalonians should have followed this example and the teaching of 1 Thessalonians 4:10-11. However, some continued on with their ways.

Consequently, the apostles called upon the church to exercise disciplinary measures toward those who lived disorderly lives. First, they told the church to stay away from these disobedient people (3:6). Second, they commanded the church to not support such people, who should be working with their own hands to earn their daily bread (3:10). Then they addressed these disorderly members directly, telling them to get to work (3:11-12). At the same time, they encouraged the church to continue being generous to those in genuine need (3:13). They concluded the exhortation by again asking believers to stay away from the disorderly so that they might be ashamed and behave differently. But they admonished the church community not to treat them as hostile enemies, rather as improper members of God's family.

As was the custom, this letter would have been read aloud to the entire church (1 Thess 5:27). So everyone would have heard the apostles' direct exhortation to the disorderly. If the exhortation was effective, the disorderly would have been shamed and then sought to rectify their behavior so as to receive the approval from the rest of the church community (see note on 3:14).

◆ VII. Closing of the Letter (3:16-18)

16Now may the Lord of peace himself give you his peace at all times and in every situation. The Lord be with you all.

17HERE IS MY GREETING IN MY OWN HANDWRITING—PAUL. I DO THIS IN ALL MY LETTERS TO PROVE THEY ARE FROM ME.

18May the grace of our Lord Jesus Christ be with you all.

NOTES

3:16 *may the Lord of peace himself give you his peace.* In 1 Thess 5:23, the title is "the God of peace." This language echoes Num 6:26, as well as Jesus' blessing of peace (John 14:27; 20:19).

at all times. Lit., "through everything."

in every situation. Lit., "in every way." The Greek is *en panti tropō* [TG5158, ZG5573], an expression that is supported by good mss (ℵ A^c B D^2 044 0278 1739 𝔐 syr cop) and is followed by all English versions. A variant reading on this is *en panti topō* [TG5117, ZG5536] (in every place): "May the Lord of peace himself always give you peace in every place." This is the reading in A* D* F G 33 it. The two words in these two readings could have been easily mistaken for the other in the transcriptional process inasmuch as there is only a one-letter difference (*rho*) between them: *topō* and *tropō*. Furthermore, both make good idiomatic sense—the blessing of peace should accompany the believers in every manner or wherever they are. But the text has superior attestation, and the variant is probably the result of scribal conformation to the wording in verses such as 1 Cor 1:2; 2 Cor 2:14; 1 Thess 1:8; 1 Tim 2:8.

3:17 *HERE IS MY GREETING IN MY OWN HANDWRITING—PAUL. I DO THIS IN ALL MY LETTERS TO PROVE THEY ARE FROM ME.* According to custom, Paul had used a secretary to compose the letter (cf. Rom 16:22; 1 Pet 5:12), but then took the pen to add a final greeting in his own hand (1 Cor 16:21; Gal 6:11; Col 4:18; Phlm 1:19). The change in hand (displayed in the NLT by the small capitals) indicated another writer besides the one who composed the main body of the letter. In this case, Silvanus had probably composed the main body of 2 Thessalonians, to which Paul appended his personal signature (see commentary).

3:18 *May the grace of our Lord Jesus Christ be with you all.* As per Paul's custom, he ended the letter with a blessing. Ancient letters often ended with a wish for health or prosperity for the reader(s), but Paul's blessing was much grander as he called upon the Lord Jesus Christ to grant them grace.

COMMENTARY

This final section exhibits the writers' final blessings and greetings. First, they asked that the Lord of peace himself would give the Thessalonians his peace. They needed this blessing because of the hostile and chaotic situation these believers faced in Thessalonica (1:4-10). The ultimate control of their situation was in the Lord's hands. His peace would come to them through his presence with them: "The Lord be with you all" (3:16). The writers were aware that the Lord Jesus' presence with his people is the best blessing, a blessing that issues peace (see Matt 28:20).

The blessing in 3:16 came from all three authors—Paul, Silvanus, and Timothy (see 1:1). At this point, Silvanus (who was probably the writer of the main body of the letter) handed over the stylus to Paul, who signed off in his own hand in 3:17-18. It was customary in Hellenistic times for the author of a letter to dictate the letter or official document to his or her amanuensis and then sign off in his own handwriting—usually in cursive, so as to distinguish one's personal identity. There are countless examples of this phenomenon in the extant papyri preserving letters and documents. For good examples, I refer the reader to P. Fayum 110 (AD 110; for photo, see Comfort 2005:145); P. London II, 308 (AD 146; for photo, see Montevecchi, plate 52); P. Oxyrhynchus 246 (AD 66); P. Oxyrhynchus 286 (AD 82); P. Oxyrhynchus 3057 (c. AD 100, perhaps the earliest extant Christian letter).

In three of Paul's letters, we see explicit references to the practice of the writer signing off in his own hand—here in 3:17, as well as in 1 Corinthians 16:21 and Colossians 4:18. In 3:17-18, Paul said, "I, Paul, write this greeting with my own hand, which is my signature in every letter—this is the way I write it" (my translation). At this point, Paul concluded the epistle with his own signature, probably in cursive (so as to give it his personal distinctiveness). In two other letters (Gal 6:11-18; Phlm 1:19-25), Paul took up the stylus and signed in his own hand—and then probably continued writing until the end of the letter. In Galatians 6:11, he noted how he wrote in large script—i.e., larger than the script of his amanuensis. In Philemon, he took the pen from the amanuensis and wrote in his own hand, "I, Paul . . . will repay." These are the only explicit references to Paul writing in his own hand. It can be inferred, however, that all of Paul's final greetings of grace would have been written in his own hand. (Ancient letters often had a change in penmanship at the end of the letter, even when the author of the main body of the text did not acknowledge the change.) Paul's handwriting would have been seen in Romans 15:33 (assuming chapter 16 to be a separate attachment; see 𝔓46) or Romans 16:20; 1 Corinthians 16:21-24; 2 Corinthians 13:13; Galatians 6:11-18; Ephesians 6:23-24; Philippians 4:21-23; Colossians 4:18; 1 Thessalonians 5:26-28; 2 Thessalonians 3:17-18; 1 Timothy 6:21b; 2 Timothy 6:22; Titus 3:15; and Philemon 1:19-25. It is noteworthy that in every conclusion to all of the extant Pauline Epistles there is a mention of grace. This, Paul's personal hallmark, not only identified himself to his readers but also authorized the letter as coming from him.

Any letter that lacked this signature would not be authorized. Since Paul suspected that a letter he had not written was circulating under his name (2:2), he specifically pointed out that it was his habit to personally sign his letters with his own handwriting. The most obvious way to write this signature was to include his actual name—"Paul"—penned in a way that was his own handwriting (as here in 3:17). However, the concluding statements at the end of his epistles would be in his unique hand and thereby serve to authenticate the letter. All the Thessalonians had to do was compare his handwriting in 1 Thessalonians 5:27-28 with that in 2 Thessalonians 3:17-18 and they could tell that it was the same hand and same person. The Thessalonians could be assured that the teachings in 2 Thessalonians, especially those concerning eschatology (in ch 2), were the truth because these teachings were apostolic.

BIBLIOGRAPHY

Alford, Henry
1976 *The Greek Testament* (5 vols.). Grand Rapids: Guardian Press. (Orig. Pub. 1852)

Aune, David
1997 *Revelation 1-5*. Word Biblical Commentary. Dallas: Word.

1998a *Revelation 6-16*. Word Biblical Commentary. Dallas: Word.

1998b *Revelation 17-22*. Word Biblical Commentary. Dallas: Word.

Baur, F. C.
1875-1876 *Paul: His Life and Works*. Translator, A. Menzies. London: Williams and Norgate.

Beale, G. K.
2003 *1-2 Thessalonians*. IVP New Testament Commentary. Downers Grove: InterVarsity.

Bengel, John Albert
1971 *New Testament Word Studies*. Translators, C. Lewis and M. Vincent. Grand Rapids: Eerdmans.
    (Orig. Pub. 1742)

Best, Ernst
1972 *The First and Second Epistles to the Thessalonians*. Harper's New Testament Commentaries.
    New York: Harper & Row.

Borchert, Gerald L.
2007 Galatians in *Cornerstone Biblical Commentary: Romans, Galatians*. Carol Stream, IL: Tyndale House.

Bruce, F. F.
1982 *1 & 2 Thessalonians*. Word Biblical Commentary. Waco: Word.

1989 *The Canon of Scripture*. Grand Rapids: Eerdmans.

1990 *The Acts of the Apostles*. Grand Rapids: Eerdmans.

Burkitt, F. C.
1924 *Christian Beginnings*. London: University of London Press.

Comfort, Philip
1993 The New Testament Ecclesia: The House Church and the Local Church. Pp. 153-158 in *The Topical
    Encyclopedia of Christian Worship*, vol. 1. Editor, Robert Webber. Nashville: Abbott-Martyn Press.

1999 New Reconstructions and Identifications of New Testament Papyri. *Novum Testamentum*
    XLI.3:214-230.

2005 *Encountering the Manuscripts: An Introduction to New Testament Paleography and Textual Criticism*.
    Nashville: Broadman & Holman.

2008 *New Testament Text and Translation Commentary*. Carol Stream: Tyndale.

Comfort, Philip and David Barrett
2001 *The Text of the Earliest New Testament Greek Manuscripts*. Wheaton: Tyndale.

Constable, T. L.
1983 1, 2 Thessalonians. Pp. 687-725 in *The Bible Knowledge Commentary*. Editors, J. F. Walvoord, Roy Zuck.
    Wheaton: Victor Books.

Conybeare, W. J., and J. S. Howson
1877 *The Life and Epistles of St. Paul*. London: Longmans.

Dana, D. E., and Julius R. Mantey
1927 *A Manual Grammar of the Greek New Testament*. New York: Macmillan.

Dodd, C. H.
1953 *New Testament Studies*. Manchester: Manchester University Press.

Douglas, J. D., and James Hoffmeier
1990 *New Commentary on the Whole Bible: Old Testament*. Wheaton: Tyndale.

Fee, Gordon
1987 *The First Epistle to the Corinthians*. Grand Rapids: Eerdmans.

1994 *God's Empowering Presence*. Peabody, MA: Hendrickson.

Fowl, S.
1990 A Metaphor in Distress: A Reading of *nēpioi* in 1 Thessalonians 2:7. *New Testament Studies* 36:469–473.

Gaffin, Richard
1978 *The Centrality of the Resurrection.* Grand Rapids: Baker.

Gamble, Harry Y.
1995 *Books and Readers in the Early Church.* New Haven: Yale University Press.

Giblin, Charles H.
1990 2 Thessalonians 2 Re-Read as Pseudepigraphal: A Revised Reaffirmation of *Threat to the Faith.* Pp. 459–469 in *The Thessalonian Correspondence.* Editor, R. Collins. Leuven: Leuven University Press.

Gorday, Peter
2000 *Colossians, 1–2 Thessalonians, 1–2 Timothy, Titus, Philemon.* Downers Grove: InterVarsity.

Green, Gene L.
2002 *The Letters to the Thessalonians.* Grand Rapids: Eerdmans.

Gundry, Robert
1973 *The Church and the Tribulation.* Grand Rapids: Zondervan.

Harris, Murray J.
1992 *Jesus as God.* Grand Rapids: Baker.

Holmes, Michael
1998 *The NIV Application Commentary: 1 and 2 Thessalonians.* Grand Rapids: Zondervan.

Kelly, William
1903 *The Rapture of the Saints.* London: T. Weston.

Kim, Young–Kyu
1988 Paleographic Dating of $\mathfrak{P}$46 to the Later First Century. *Biblica* 69:248–257.

Lightfoot, J. B.
1904 *Notes on the Epistles of St. Paul.* London: Macmillan.

Malherbe, A. J.
1987 *Paul and the Thessalonians.* Philadelphia: Fortress.

Marshall, I. Howard
1983 *1 and 2 Thessalonians.* Century Bible Commentary. Grand Rapids: Eerdmans.

Metzger, Bruce
1992 *The Text of the New Testament.* 3rd ed. Oxford: Oxford University Press.

1994 *A Textual Commentary on the Greek New Testament.* Rev. ed. New York: United Bible Societies.

2003 *The New Testament: Its Background, Growth & Content.* 3rd ed. Nashville: Abingdon Press.

Michaels, J. Ramsey
1988 *1 Peter.* Word Biblical Commentary. Dallas: Word.

Milligan, George
1908 *St. Paul's Epistle to the Thessalonians.* Old Tappan, NJ: Revell.

Milligan, William
1884 *The Resurrection of our Lord.* London: Macmillan.

Montevecchi, Orsolina
1953 *Papyri Bononienses.* Milan: Vita e pensiero.

Morris, Leon
1991 *The First and Second Epistles to the Thessalonians.* New International Commentary on the New Testament. Grand Rapids: Eerdmans.

Moule, Charles F. D.
1971 *An Idiom Book of New Testament Greek.* Cambridge: Cambridge University Press.

Osborne, Grant
1992 Resurrection. Pp. 673–688 in *Dictionary of Jesus and the Gospels.* Editors, Joel B. Green, Scot McKnight, I. Howard Marshall. Downers Grove: Intervarsity.

Osburn, Carroll D.
1976 The Christological Use of 1 Enoch 1.14 in Jude 14, 15. *New Testament Studies* 23:334–341.

Oswalt, John
1986 *The Book of Isaiah: 1–39*. Grand Rapids: Eerdmans.

1998 *The Book of Isaiah: 40–66*. Grand Rapids: Eerdmans.

Pfitzner, V. C.
1967 Paul and the Agon Motif: Traditional Athletic Imagery in the Pauline Literature. Leiden: Brill.

Porter, Stanley
1992 *Idioms of the Greek New Testament*. Sheffield: Journal for the Study of the Old Testament Press.

Reicke, Bo
2001 *Re-examining Paul's Letters: The History of the Pauline Correspondence*. Valley Forge, PA: Trinity.

Richards, E. Randolph
1991 *The Secretary in the Letters of Paul*. Tubingen: J. C. B. Mohr.

Roberts, Alexander, and James Donaldson, editors
1994 *The Ante-Nicene Fathers*. Peabody, MA: Hendrickson. (Orig. Pub. 1885–1887)

Robinson, John A. T.
2000 *Redating the New Testament*. Eugene, OR: Wipf and Stock. (Orig. Pub. 1976)

Russell, R.
1988 The Idle in 2 Thess. 3:6-12: An Eschatological or Social Problem. *New Testament Studies* 34:105-107.

Ryrie, Charles
1974 The Church and the Tribulation: A Review. *Bibliotheca Sacra*. April–June.

Sailors, Timothy B.
2000 Wedding Textual and Rhetorical Criticism to Understand the Text of 1 Thess. 2:7. *Journal of the Study of the New Testament* 80:81-98.

Skeat, T. C.
1997 The Oldest Manuscript of the Four Gospels? *New Testament Studies* 43:1-34.

Stott, John
1991 *The Gospel and the End of Time. The Message of 1 & 2 Thessalonians*. Downers Grove: InterVarsity.

Stowers, Stanley
1986 *Letter Writing in Greco-Roman Antiquity*. Philadelphia: Westminster.

Thomas, Derek
1991 *God Delivers*. Durham: Evangelical Press.

Thomas, Robert L.
1978 1, 2 Thessalonians. Pp. 229-337 in *The Expositor's Bible Commentary*, vol. 11. General Editor, F. E. Gaebelein. Grand Rapids: Zondervan.

Treggiari, Susan
1991 *Roman Marriage*. Oxford: Clarendon.

Turner, Nigel
1965 *A Grammar of New Testament Greek*. Editor, James Hope Moulton. Edinburgh: T & T Clark.

Wanamaker, Charles
1990 *The Epistles to the Thessalonians*. New International Greek Testament Commentary. Grand Rapids: Eerdmans.

Weima, J. A. D.
2000a But We Became Infants Among You: The Case for NHPIOI in 1 Thess. 2:7. *New Testament Studies* 46:547-564.

2000b Letters, Greco-Roman. Pp. 640-644 in *Dictionary of New Testament Background*. Editors, Craig Evans, Stanley Porter. Downers Grove: InterVarsity.

Westcott, B. F. and Fenton Hort
1881 *The New Testament in the Original Greek*. Cambridge: Macmillan.

1882 *Introduction to the New Testament in the Original Greek: with Notes on Selected Readings*. New York: Harper and Brothers.

Youngblood, R. F.
1997 Fallen Star: The Evolution of Lucifer. *Bible Review* 14:22-31.

Züntz, G.
1953 *The Text of the Epistles*. London: Oxford.

Philemon

PETER H. DAVIDS

INTRODUCTION TO
Philemon

PAUL'S SHORT LETTER to Philemon is normally placed at the end of the Pauline canon because it is the shortest of his works. In fact, it is about the same length as Jude, each having 25 verses; only 2 and 3 John are shorter. Because of its length, one rarely finds a commentary devoted entirely to Philemon (Stuhlmacher 1975, Barth and Blanke 2000 are happy exceptions). Despite its brevity, the letter is a fascinating glimpse into the world of the early church in the Roman province of Asia.

AUTHOR
Few scholars have doubted the genuineness of Philemon as one of the letters of the apostle Paul (Barth and Blanke 2000:103). The only major exception has been the Tübingen school (second half of the 19th century). While Philemon is too short to apply any stylistic tests, its straightforward theme, lack of specific theological issues, and inclusion of many personal details make it unlikely that anyone other than a person with the authentic concern it addresses would have invented such a letter. The issue for most scholars is not whether Paul wrote the letter, but when he and Timothy wrote it.

DATE AND OCCASION OF WRITING
The date and place of writing make virtually no difference to the interpretation of the letter. However, it is of some import in placing it within the Pauline corpus, which in turn impacts the dates and occasions of other Pauline writings, which then impacts their interpretations, most notably among them being Colossians. The letter to Philemon was clearly written by Paul when he was in prison (v. 1) and Timothy was not. But Paul was "often" in prison (2 Cor 11:23), and we know nothing more about most of these imprisonments other than that. In the case of Philemon, we know that the imprisonment and the writing of the letter must have occured during or after Paul's ministry in the Roman province of Asia (i.e., when Paul's base was in Ephesus), for Philemon lived in the eastern part of that province and Paul was unlikely to have known him until he had worked there. The two known imprisonments that fit that time frame are those in Caesarea and Rome. Although supported by some scholars (Reicke 2001:73-75), the Caesarean imprisonment is unlikely, for (1) Paul appears to have had less freedom there and (2) Palestine is both far from Colosse and not the natural direction to go for a fugitive slave (if that

is what Onesimus was) fleeing from Asia. That leaves Rome as the other known imprisonment, but that also has the issue of its being a long and difficult trip from Colosse, including at least one and probably two journeys by ship. Therefore, other scholars suggest that Paul may have been imprisoned in Ephesus at the end of his time there. While hypothetical, such an imprisonment would not be surprising given Paul's frequency of ending up in jail (cf. 2 Cor 1:8-9; Paul's references to life-threatening circumstances in Asia might or might not include imprisonment). It would also be far closer to where Philemon lived than Rome was and so easier for a fugitive slave to reach (Stuhlmacher 1975:21). How shall we decide between these two options?

Two other pieces of information that Paul provides may help us: (1) He was an "old man" (v. 9), and "Mark, Aristarchus, Demas, and Luke" were with him (v. 24). If we accept the information found in 2 Timothy as genuine, at some time during Paul's Roman imprisonment Demas left (2 Tim 4:10) and Mark had not yet arrived (2 Tim 4:11), although Luke was already there. There is no mention of Aristarchus in 2 Timothy. Mark had apparently worked with Paul earlier, for 2 Timothy 4:11 mentions that he was helpful to Paul, something that Paul did not think initially (see Acts 15:37-39). Aristarchus appears to have traveled with Paul on his third missionary journey and also on his trip to Rome (Acts 19:29; 20:4; 27:2). Furthermore, at some point he was "in prison with [Paul]" (cf. Col 4:10; possibly in Rome, but likely in the same place where Philemon was written); and Mark, Demas, and Luke were also, at some point, in the city where Paul was in prison (Col 4:14). Since all of these men sent greetings to Philemon, it is likely that they had been part of Paul's team for at least part of the time he was ministering in Ephesus. The result of this survey of the data is that if we assume that 2 Timothy gives us accurate data on Paul's companions, it is difficult to fit Philemon into a Roman setting. However, if we hypothesize that Mark came to Rome, left, and then later returned, then the earlier part of Paul's time in Rome is the likely time of Philemon's writing (i.e., c. AD 62). However, given that this traditional Roman setting requires that Mark and probably Aristarchus left and then returned and, further, given that Paul expected to visit Philemon in the near future (v. 22), I suggest a date around AD 56 and an imprisonment in Asia (Ephesus) as the more likely setting. Still, I recognize that any determination of the place of imprisonment is no more than an educated guess.

AUDIENCE

It has been argued by Knox (1959) and more recently by Winter (1987) that Philemon was not written to Colosse but is the "lost" letter to Laodicea (Col 4:16). They go on to argue that even though it is addressed to the whole church and Philemon and Apphia are leaders in that church, Archippus is the main addressee of the letter instead of Philemon. Thus, the letter is to be read in Colosse as well as Laodicea to put more pressure on Archippus to accede to Paul's request (v. 2; cf. Col 4:17). The thesis has not garnered significant support among other scholars (O'Brien 1982:266). While the argument is fascinating and reminds us that there is a lot that we do not know about Paul's letters, it is ultimately unconvincing for two reasons. First, even though Paul is being persuasive, to have the letter read in two different churches would surely be to put the type of pressure upon the recipient that Paul denies that he is doing. Second, "the church that meets in your house" of verse 2 would not normally be read as referring just to Archippus's house since there is nothing to set off Archippus from Philemon and Apphia. Instead, it reads as if Philemon is the *paterfamilias* and the other two are indeed church leaders but also part of his household, with the "your" being singular and referring to Philemon.

The letter ostensibly has a primary audience of one person, Philemon. We know nothing about Philemon except what we can glean from this letter. He was a resident of Colosse, a man of enough means to own at least one slave. Apphia and Archippus were also greeted in the letter (probably Philemon's wife and son, respectively). We do not know a lot about Philemon's social position in Colosse, but we know more about his status in the church. Paul greeted Philemon as a co-worker and Archippus as a fellow soldier (cf. Col 4:12; Phil 2:25). Such titles were not used lightly by Paul. They designate people who had worked together with him, that is, whom he had apprenticed to himself and who had proved themselves as Christian leaders. Since Paul had probably not yet visited Colosse (Col 2:1), Philemon and Archippus must have spent time with Paul elsewhere, perhaps in Ephesus, roughly 120 miles to the west. Philemon had since returned to Colosse and was now the host and leader of a house church (v. 2) and had a significant influence in the larger group of house churches (v. 7), probably in part because he was generous with his means—that is, he functioned in the cultural role of benefactor or patron.

Yet the picture is not as simple as the portrait above suggests. While in Colossians Epaphras is Paul's connection to Colosse (Col 1:7; 4:12), in Philemon only Onesimus is mentioned as linking Paul to Colosse. Epaphras is mentioned (v. 23) but only as one of several sending greetings. Was Epaphras not involved with Philemon's particular house church prior to this time, or are these differences due to the ostensibly private nature of the letter? Possibly so, but the letter is certainly not just a private correspondence between Paul and Philemon concerning Onesimus. Even if Philemon's family and the church in his house had not been addressed, given that most people could not read and that even a person like Philemon may well have had the letter read to him, and given that letters were not that common, the arrival of a letter would have been a significant semipublic event. The whole church would have wanted to hear the letter, especially when they learned that part of this church was addressed. Furthermore, the letter carrier would have been expected to expand upon what was written in the letter and to comment on the situation of Paul and his co-workers. The letter to Philemon primarily addressed one man, but it did so before at least his house church and probably before the whole church in Colosse. We do not know how many house churches there were in Colosse, but there were at least two and quite possibly several more. The Christians did not live separately from the community of believers to which they belonged.

Some go farther than this and argue that Philemon was not a private letter that would have been publicly known or even read in public; they argue that it was intended as a public letter. Patzia (1993:705-706) and Winter (1987:1-2) argue that the inclusion of the church in the address and the large number of commercial and legal terms in the letter, among other items, suggest that it was intended as a public letter, although Llewelyn (2005:263) cautions that comparing the legal terminology with papyri that are primarily legal or commercial may skew our reading. What is clear is that the letter was not intended to be kept private, for at a minimum the greeting to the church would raise inquiries about the content of the letter. It is longer than most private letters of the time, but, on the other hand, while the drama may be played out before the church, the church is not specifically addressed. In my view it is better to read it as a private letter but to realize that private did not mean that Philemon was to keep it to himself. His private affairs affected the church, and his reputation before the church was at stake, so the private–public line is very much blurred.

CANONICITY AND TEXTUAL HISTORY
It is possible that the Epistle to Philemon is referred to multiple times in Ignatius's epistle *To the Ephesians* 2–6, although none of the references are so clear as to be undisputable. Likewise, it is not certain that Onesimus, bishop of Ephesus, to whom Ignatius repeatedly refers, is the Onesimus our letter mentions. The name was relatively common. If Ignatius does refer to the letter, then it was known and used by AD 100. What is clear is that Philemon was part of the Pauline corpus that Marcion used (about AD 140; Tertullian, *Against Marcion* 5.21). It was also part of the Muratorian Canon (AD 200). Thus, it is probable that this work was part of the earliest collection of Paul's works, and we can be certain that it had a secure place in the Pauline corpus by the mid-second century. Its presence in the canon was never disputed. It is found in papyri from the late second century on (specifically, 𝔓46 and 𝔓87), as well as in Codices Sinaiticus and Alexandrinus. (Codex Vaticanus lacks several books at the end of the NT, including Philemon.) There are relatively few textual issues in the letter.

LITERARY STYLE
Philemon was a carefully written letter in proper epistolary form. Thus, we have an opening, including a salutation and thanksgiving, then the body of the letter, and finally the closing of the letter, including greetings and a blessing. These reflect the principal parts of a typical Greek letter. However, Philemon belongs to a particular type of Greek letters that we may term "letters of intercession." While no other early Christian examples are known, 40 to 50 years later, the younger Pliny would write a similar letter to his friend Sabinianus on behalf of a freed slave (Pliny, *Letters* 9.21, 24; see text in Stowers 1986:160). We also have two similar letters from the fourth and fifth centuries, both from Christians (see Deissmann 1927:184-185; Barth and Blanke 2000:87). In other words, this type of letter was not unknown in the ancient

world. We have here a letter written to a friend aiming to persuade him to take an honorable course of action, even if it might not be the most natural course. The style is typically Pauline, which is decent formal Greek—that is, neither vulgar Greek (as in Mark) nor an elevated style (as in parts of 1 Peter). While the Greek is formal rather than colloquial, it is not so formal as to mask Paul's friendship with Philemon. Since he was a friend, only one of Philemon's names was given, and so we will never know if he was the Marcus Sebastius Philemon whose tomb a freed slave erected in Colosse (Barth and Blanke 2000:149).

MAJOR THEMES

Philemon has one major theme, which is the reception of a slave who has been absent from his master, either having run away as an attempt to escape slavery or having fled to a patron for assistance in his relationship with his master. We are not informed why Onesimus chose to absent himself nor in what ways he had wronged Philemon in doing so. We do know that he was not a Christian when he left but then became a believer. What we have here is a plea for clemency on Paul's part. This plea brings up two subthemes: (1) All Christians are family, which means Onesimus is now a brother to both Paul and Philemon. (2) Paul is Philemon's benefactor by virtue of his bringing Philemon to faith (v. 19).

An underlying issue about which Paul may not be conscious, but which likely played a role in the preservation of the letter, is the relationship of the church to Roman society. Christians were often viewed as subversive of the good order of society in that they allowed and even encouraged wives and slaves to commit themselves to Christ without the approval of their husbands or masters. Since it was the right of the *paterfamilias* to set the religion of the household (the husband perhaps allowing his wife to have a private devotional practice so long as she fulfilled her duties associated with his chosen gods), this direct appeal by Christians to family members against the will of the family head was viewed as subversive of the good order of the family, which was seen as the foundation for the state. Furthermore, the acceptance of slaves as equals within the Christian community raised suspicions that Christians might assist slaves in escaping, which would indeed be an attack on the order of the state. Thus, we have in Philemon a very difficult pastoral situation (Friedrich 2000:189). That Paul sent Onesimus back and that he used persuasion rather than command demonstrated that, while Christians might choose a different lifestyle than their pagan neighbors, they were careful not to appear to be undermining the social order.

THEOLOGICAL AND ETHICAL CONCERNS

There are no theological issues under dispute in this letter, although it is clear that Paul assumed that he and Philemon shared certain theological perspectives. Paul assumed the value of salvation in Christ and the honorable status of one who works to spread that Good News. He also assumed that all Christians are brothers and sisters (i.e., family) and that this relationship rather than social status and role designations from the surrounding culture should determine their treatment of one another. Furthermore, he assumed the relevance of Jesus' substitutionary life and death as a model for the Christian life, since he identified with Onesimus and offered to become a substitute for him in similar manner (although in less depth or scale) as Jesus had done for Paul.

The core concern of Philemon is ethical. Onesimus was a slave. Slavery in itself was not an issue for Paul, who wrote, "And remember, if you were a slave when the Lord called you, you are now free in the Lord. And if you were free when the Lord called you, you are now a slave of Christ" (1 Cor 7:22). Thus, his counsel was, "You should remain as you were when God called you" (1 Cor 7:20). Therefore, the Pauline *Haustafeln* ("tables of household duties") in Ephesians (Eph 5:21–6:9) and Colossians (Col 3:18–4:1) are concerned with how one treats slaves, but they do not breathe a word about the ethics of having slaves. For Paul, one's eschatological status, which was lived out in the church, was far more important than one's societal status, which was passing away, so Paul expended no effort on changing the latter.

The modern reader needs to read Paul's position in light of several factors: (1) Ancient Roman and Greek cultures were built on slavery, and thus the continuation of the culture without slavery was unthinkable; (2) slavery in these cultures was not linked to race or occupational level, which means that there was no slave class and that many whom we would now call professionals (e.g., physicians) were slaves; (3) manumission of slaves was possible, although it appears to have been more frequent in Rome than in Greece; and (4) life expectancy in the ancient world was relatively short (about 40 years compared with over 70 years today), with poor freedmen finding it more difficult to survive than many slaves (slaves working in mines or galleys were the exception, for their life expectancy was short). Furthermore, there was no tradition in ancient philosophers and moralists of speaking out against slavery (Bartchy 1997:71; Harrill 2000; Barth and Blanke 2000:1-102). While these facts do not diminish the fact that slaves were property (sometimes with limited rights) and in effect "socially dead to the free population" (Harrill 2000), they do mean that there was nothing in Paul's background, including his Jewish background, that he could draw upon to criticize slavery as such. Such criticism would also have been socially inflammatory, undermining the economic security and social stability of the society. Furthermore, Paul had every reason to stress eschatological life, for it was eternal while societal life was temporary at best.

Yet Paul had ample precedent to appeal to Philemon to be gracious toward Onesimus. Some argue that Onesimus was not a fugitive, but had come to Paul as someone Philemon respected, hoping Paul would intercede for him in some conflict with his master (so Dunn 1996:305; Patzia 1993:705; Llewelyn 2005:265 suggests he may have been a slacker, not a runaway). But from the societal point of view, Onesimus had robbed Philemon of his services, if not his property, and Philemon had the right to be angry (as Pliny's letter shows). In order to discourage other slaves in the household or in the community from following Onesimus's behavior, most in that society would have felt it appropriate to make an example of him. In Roman society, such punishment could range from putting off or canceling the hope of manumission to whipping, branding, or, in some cases, crucifixion. The Greek world did not manumit as frequently, so corporal punishment was even more likely. Since Onesimus's return was voluntary and Philemon would lose his investment in Onesimus if he killed him, corporal punishment might well be limited. Yet it still could be severe and disfiguring. Both Philemon's own social background and the expectations of his peers would pressure him to carry out some type of punishment. Paul's goal in the letter was to reframe the situation so that Philemon felt he had a better reason to forgive than to punish. With this in mind, Paul's letter is a long argument for forgiving one who has wronged us, and as such it applies to us today even in our very different social milieu.

OUTLINE
The outline of Philemon is easy to discern. It fits into the pattern of a typical Christian letter of the period.
  I. Opening of the Letter (vv. 1-7)
     A. Salutation (vv. 1-3)
     B. Paul's Thanksgiving and Prayer (vv. 4-7)
  II. Paul's Appeal for Onesimus (vv. 8-22)
  III. Paul's Final Greetings (vv. 23-25)

COMMENTARY ON
Philemon

◆ **I. Opening of the Letter (vv. 1–7)**
  A. Salutation (vv. 1–3)

This letter is from Paul, a prisoner for preaching the Good News about Christ Jesus, and from our brother Timothy.

I am writing to Philemon, our beloved co-worker, ²and to our sister Apphia, and to our fellow soldier Archippus, and to the church that meets in your* house.

³May God our Father and the Lord Jesus Christ give you grace and peace.

2 Throughout this letter, *you* and *your* are singular except in verses 3, 22, and 25.

NOTES

1 *Paul, a prisoner for preaching the Good News about Christ Jesus.* Instead of referring to himself as an "apostle" or some other more exalted title, Paul referred to himself as a prisoner, a title he used three other times: Eph 3:1; 4:1; 2 Tim 1:8. Paul referred to himself as Christ Jesus' prisoner, however, not a prisoner of Rome (his legal status). The expression "for preaching the Good News about" is an explanatory expansion that describes why Paul had been imprisoned, but one should not let it distract from the main point: Paul's status as a prisoner. A more rigidly literal translation would be "prisoner of Jesus Christ," which can mean "a prisoner because of Jesus Christ" as in the NLT or "Jesus Christ's prisoner." That is to say, it is not the government that has Paul there, but Jesus Christ

co-worker. The same title is also used for Priscilla and Aquila (Rom 16:3), Urbanus (Rom 16:9), Timothy (Rom 16:21; 1 Thess 3:2), and others (Phil 2:25; 4:3; Col 4:11), as well as the colleagues mentioned in v. 24. It denotes an associate or apprentice of Paul and thus indicates the rank of Philemon in Paul's eyes.

2 *our sister Apphia.* The earliest and best mss (א A D* F G I P 048 0278 33 1739) read "sister." A later tradition found in the manuscripts behind the KJV (D² 044 𝔐) read "beloved." "Sister," adopted by the NLT, is the far better reading.

our fellow soldier Archippus. While Archippus is mentioned in Col 4:17, this title is only found here and in Phil 2:25, where it is paired with "co-worker" as a title for Epaphroditus. Thus, it indicates that Archippus was at some point Paul's co-worker.

the church that meets in your house. The early church met in the homes of various members. Since the meetings were centered on a common meal, which recalls the last meal Jesus ate with his disciples, the groups could not be larger than the home could accommodate for eating, between 9 and 18 people, depending on the size of the house, perhaps up to 30 adults when necessary (Banks 1988:41-42; Stuhlmacher 1975:70-75; Smith 2003:22-27). Several such house churches together made up a city church (such as that addressed in Colossians). The Pauline city churches were led by a team of elders. It is likely that Philemon was part of this team, and it is clear that he was at least the patron of the church meeting in his home.

3 *grace and peace.* The normal Greek salutation was "greetings" (*chairein* [TG5463, ZG5897]), which sounds similar to the Greek word for "grace" (*charis* [TG5485, ZG5921]). The normal Jewish greeting was *shalom* [TH7965, ZH8934] (peace). Paul's letters combine the two as a matter of form. While Christianized, they probably do not mean more than the initial "Dear" in an English letter, since they might have become standard usage for a Christian letter in Paul's day.

COMMENTARY

When Paul opened the letter, he avoided the term "apostle" with its overtones of authority and chose the title "prisoner" because that would incite pity, or "pathos," would show his need, and would give him a status parallel to that of Onesimus (v. 1). In this letter Paul was not only interceding for Onesimus but also identifying with him and, as we shall see later, substituting for him. As Paul does for another person what Christ has done for him (admittedly on a much larger and deeper scale) we see Christ's identification with humanity being lived out by Paul, one of Christ's best apprentices.

The letter addresses Philemon, who himself was a co-worker of Paul. We do not know when and where this took place, but it is quite possible that it was during Paul's long stay in Ephesus, since that city was relatively near to Colosse. Despite the personal nature of the issue at hand, Paul did not address Philemon in isolation, but included Timothy on his end and two others, Apphia and Archippus (perhaps Philemon's wife and son respectively), along with the whole house church on Philemon's end (v. 2). Paul did not view Christianity as a matter of individual choice and relationship with God but as a transfer of citizenship from one kingdom or community into another. Thus, Paul always surrounded himself with apprentices who became his co-workers, and he always addressed individuals within the context of their church community. Issues and relationships are not to be worked out individually but within the context of the community that gives insight, support, and context to the process.

Finally, we are reminded that the church context in the New Testament was not that of a gathering of 50 to 100 individuals sitting in rows and staring at what is happening "up front," but that of a house church, a small group of up to 20 or so individuals who would have come to know one another intimately. There was no back row that one could sit in but rather a circle around a table from which they shared a full meal. The struggle we sometimes have today in applying the New Testament letters may come in part from the fact that our context differs from that of the early Pauline churches. We either withdraw into our individualism or else are submerged into a group so large that we may never be in intimate relationships with one another. Some churches reclaim the Pauline sense of church through small groups, which are effective so long as they function as safe places where one can develop intimate relationships. Thus, the term "church" needs to be defined within Paul's theological and experiential understanding if we are to grasp its meaning in his letters.

◆   ## B. Paul's Thanksgiving and Prayer (vv. 4–7)

⁴I always thank my God when I pray for you, Philemon, ⁵because I keep hearing about your faith in the Lord Jesus and your love for all of God's people. ⁶And I am praying that you will put into action the generosity that comes from your faith as you understand and experience all the good things we have in Christ. ⁷Your love has given me much joy and comfort, my brother, for your kindness has often refreshed the hearts of God's people.

NOTES

5 *faith in the Lord Jesus and your love for all of God's people.* While it is quite possible to read *pistis* [TG4102, ZG4411] as referring to trust/faithfulness/loyalty toward both Jesus and God's people (Bruce 1984:208), most likely the NLT is correct translating it as "faith" (in Jesus), that is, commitment to Jesus. What we have in the Greek is a literary form called a chiasmus: love is mentioned first, then faith, then Jesus, then God's people in an A B B' A' pattern. That love is placed first is an unusual order for Paul (cf. Col 1:4); he did it here because love will be Paul's emphasis in the letter (Stuhlmacher 1975:32-33; Patzia 1990:108-109).

6 *generosity.* There are a number of interpretations of the Greek term *koinōnia* [TG2842, ZG3126], from "fellowship," either with Christ (Stuhlmacher 1975:33) or other believers (Lohmeyer 1956:178; Wall 1993:198-199; Dunn 1996:318-219), to the notion of "sharing," "almsgiving," and "generosity." It is difficult to decide which meaning is intended; Barth and Blanke (2000:282-283) argue that the ambiguity is deliberate and each of these meanings is included. Most likely, however, Lightfoot (1896:333) and Bruce (1984:208-209) are correct that Philemon's generosity is intended. This is the meaning of a parallel expression in Phil 1:5, "because of your sharing in the gospel from the first day until now" (NRSV), with Phil 4:18-20 making it clear that this means financial support, and this meaning fits best with the theme of the letter.

I am praying that you will put into action the generosity that comes from your faith as you understand and experience all the good things we have in Christ. Paul prays that Philemon will have or increase in the generosity that flows from trust in Christ. Then he also prays that this will take place in the context of experience or understanding. In order to make sense of Paul's clause we have to add "I am praying," which is implied from a previous part of the complex sentence. But the stress is on the idea of "generosity that comes from your faith."

all the good things we have in Christ. There is a textual problem here in that a significant selection of mss read "you" (𝔓61 ℵ P 33 1739 itᵃ·ᵇ syr cop) rather than "we." The NLT correctly chooses the more difficult "we" that is supported by a widespread group of mss: A C D 044 048ᵛⁱᵈ 𝔐 syrʰᵐᵍ. However, the real issue is how to understand this phrase. The "good things" Philemon is to understand are at the least the good things that we have as a result of our trust in Christ and specifically the good things that we receive due to our generosity (so 2 Cor 9:8-10; see note on "generosity" above). The NLT correctly conveys that they are the good things that come to us either as a result of our faith in Christ (taking the Greek *eis* [TG1519, ZG1650] as *en* [TG1722, ZG1877]) or as a means of drawing us closer to Christ (accepting the *eis* as having a telic force).

7 *refreshed the hearts of God's people.* This is a good idiomatic English translation of the Greek phrase, which speaks of refreshing the guts or entrails of God's people. In the ancient world it was thought that the entrails were the seat of emotions, probably because we tend to experience the effects of strong emotions in our gastrointestinal tracts.

COMMENTARY

It was customary in a Greek letter to thank one or more gods for the well-being of the person addressed. Paul normally expanded this customary section in his letters, as he did here (vv. 4-5). In this letter the thanksgiving itself is quite short, but Paul transitioned into a prayer that is part prayer and part affirmation of those very qualities in Philemon that will be required for meeting Paul's request (vv. 6-7).

Unfortunately for us, Paul's expression of this thanksgiving is very complicated. In fact, verse 6 is so complicated that commentators differ significantly, and many are not at all certain of their interpretations. It is truly one of the more obscure verses in the New Testament. Having admitted this, I will nevertheless dare to give my view of what Paul was expressing.

While the thanksgiving section was a formal part of the letter, Paul's life was normally characterized by thankfulness, especially thankfulness for those in the churches he influenced who were doing well. This thankfulness was appropriate for Paul, since he could not conceive of a person really understanding what Christ had done, was doing, and would do in the future for him or her without that resulting in a deep, heartfelt thankfulness, a thankfulness that was multiplied as one looked on what Christ was doing in others in the churches, as well. It was out of thankfulness that Paul continually prayed for his friends in the faith. Paul's thankfulness was triggered by the reports he repeatedly received (perhaps through Epaphras or others) of Philemon's trust in Christ and love toward others, a love that was expressed in generosity (v. 6). Those who trust in Christ should indeed be generous, for they should be inspired by Christ's generosity and feel secure in him and thus able to share generously with others. A lack of generosity is, in fact, indicative of a lack of true trust in Christ. This is a theme that Paul expands upon in 2 Corinthians 8–9.

Paul's response to what he heard about Philemon was, "More, Lord." He wanted this generosity (flowing from Philemon's faith) to increase and to work itself out in an understanding flowing from experience, an understanding of the good things we have from Christ that draw us closer to him. In our rationalistic Western world we often want to know and understand before we will risk and act. Our motto is "Understanding before action." Paul and Jesus thought differently. First, one needs to do the right thing (in this case allow trust in Christ to work itself out in generosity) and then that will produce its effects, one of which will be new insights into all the good things we have from Christ (such as a new level of intimacy with him, a new revelation of his nature, or a new experience of his provision). This, in turn, will increase our commitments and draw us closer to Christ. The cycle of knowledge–risk–deeper knowledge is something that Paul would pray for us as well as for Philemon. Thus, his and Jesus' motto was "Obedience brings understanding."

At this point, the prayer ended, and Paul made a comment. The reports he had heard and his own contact with Philemon had given him joy and comfort (v. 7). We can picture him sitting in prison and smiling as he thought about what he had heard about Philemon. For the moment, the problems of imprisonment were forgotten, as he savored deep satisfaction. And what did Paul hear? He heard about Philemon's loving deeds (the NT is rarely if ever concerned with our feelings toward one another, but it is very concerned that we act lovingly toward one another). And Paul also heard how the hearts of God's people were encouraged through these loving deeds. It is because he was so aware of Philemon's character that Paul could move on to make a request that would stretch Philemon to new levels of loving action.

◆ II. Paul's Appeal for Onesimus (vv. 8-22)

⁸That is why I am boldly asking a favor of you. I could demand it in the name of Christ because it is the right thing for you to do. ⁹But because of our love, I prefer simply to ask you. Consider this as a request from me—Paul, an old man and now also a prisoner for the sake of Christ Jesus.*

¹⁰I appeal to you to show kindness to my child, Onesimus. I became his father in the faith while here in prison. ¹¹Onesimus* hasn't been of much use to you in the past, but now he is very useful to both of us. ¹²I am sending him back to you, and with him comes my own heart.

¹³I wanted to keep him here with me while I am in these chains for preaching the Good News, and he would have helped me on your behalf. ¹⁴But I didn't want to do anything without your consent. I wanted you to help because you were willing, not because you were forced. ¹⁵It seems you lost Onesimus for a little while so that you could have him back forever. ¹⁶He is no longer like a slave to you. He is more than a slave, for he is a beloved brother, especially to me. Now he will mean much more to you, both as a man and as a brother in the Lord.

¹⁷So if you consider me your partner, welcome him as you would welcome me. ¹⁸If he has wronged you in any way or owes you anything, charge it to me. ¹⁹I, PAUL, WRITE THIS WITH MY OWN HAND: I WILL REPAY IT. AND I WON'T MENTION THAT YOU OWE ME YOUR VERY SOUL!

²⁰Yes, my brother, please do me this favor* for the Lord's sake. Give me this encouragement in Christ.

²¹I am confident as I write this letter that you will do what I ask and even more! ²²One more thing—please prepare a guest room for me, for I am hoping that God will answer your prayers and let me return to you soon.

9 Or *a prisoner of Christ Jesus.*   11 *Onesimus* means "useful."   20 Greek *onaimen,* a play on the name Onesimus.

NOTES

8 *boldly asking a favor.* In the NLT, the term "boldly" is attached to the wrong part of the sentence. In Greek the boldness or authority that Paul has is a boldness to *command* Philemon to do "the right thing," not a boldness to ask a favor, which comes in the next verse and is not connected to the term for boldness. Paul said that instead of boldly commanding, he was instead appealing (a stronger term than asking a favor). He was taking a "one-down" position, that of a slave, rather than a superior (i.e., a "one-up" position). So we might translate this, "although I am bold enough in Christ to command you to do your duty . . ." or "although I have enough boldness in Christ to command you to do your duty, instead I would rather appeal to you (or 'beg you to do me a favor') on the basis of love. "

9 *old man.* The Greek term is *presbutēs* [TG4246, ZG4566]. Lightfoot (1896:336-337), followed by Bruce (1984:211-212) and O'Brien (1982:290), argue that this should be translated "ambassador," which differs by only one letter in Greek (*presbeutēs* [TG4242.1, ZG4562]). The latter was sometimes interchanged with the word *presbutēs* [TG4246, ZG4566] (old man), which denotes either someone in their midfifties or older than sixty, depending on which of two schemes of age designation was in mind. Wall (1993:204) and Dunn (1996:327) are more likely correct in supporting the normal translation of "old man," although it is culturally inaccurate, as Dunn points out, to the extent that it connotes in English one who is pitied for the disabilities of old age. There is a more negative Greek term for what modern English speakers typically mean by "old man," and that is not the term used. The term used here is for an older man who is respected for his age and wisdom, not one who is feeble or declining.

10 my child. Paul used the term to denote not just affection but one converted through his ministry (see 1 Cor 4:14, 17; Gal 4:19; cf. also Phil 2:22; 1 Tim 1:2, 18; 2 Tim 1:2; Titus 1:4). Thus, he had established a special bond with Onesimus, a bond that he would later indicate he also had with Philemon (v. 19).

11 Onesimus. As the NLT mg indicates, the name "Onesimus" means "useful." This was a common name in the Roman province of Asia, especially for slaves but also for other people. The name itself did not indicate that one was a slave, even if it was for obvious reasons very common as a slave name. Slaves were either named at birth by their masters or renamed when they sold themselves or were reduced to slavery by a court or capture in war. The name is derived from the verb *oninamai* [TG3685, ZG3949] meaning "profit," "benefit," or "help," yet Onesimus was a Phrygian (i.e., from Colosse), and both slaves and Phrygians were stereotyped as being useless (Lightfoot 1896:310n1-2, who cites Ovid *Amores* 1.15.17, and Cicero *Pro Flacco* 27 [65], among other references).

hasn't been of much use to you in the past, but now he is very useful to both of us. In "use" and "useful" Paul plays on another Greek root (*chrēstos* [TG5543, ZG5982]) with a similar meaning to Onesimus's name, but the form and sound of this root are far closer to *Christos* [TG5547, ZG5986] (Christ), which may intend to suggest, via a pun, Onesimus's present state as a Christian, although some (e.g., Llewelyn 2005:262) dispute that such a pun is intended.

12 my own heart. This is the same strong word used in verse 7 (see note). Philemon refreshed the "guts" or emotions of the believers. The KJV has "receive him," a phrase that is not in the earliest manuscripts (𝔑* A F G), although whoever added it did express Paul's implied intent.

13 I wanted to keep him here. The Greek implies some struggle on Paul's part in giving up Onesimus, but also implies Onesimus himself was ready to return to Philemon, despite whatever risks he perceived in doing so (Dunn 1996:330-331).

15 lost. The Greek simply says "was separated from you." It is clear that the separation was without Philemon's permission, but we do not know whether Onesimus was running away or fleeing to Paul to get him to intercede with Philemon over some issue between slave and master. The latter would not have been considered running away in the ancient world. This separation is expressed very diplomatically in that (1) Paul used a passive ("he was separated from you"), suggesting divine initiative, and (2) Paul implied it was never intended to be permanent, since it was only for "a little while."

have him back forever. The language echoes Exod 21:6 and Deut 15:17, in which a Hebrew slave could become a permanent slave of a master, but it is only a linguistic echo, perhaps due to Paul's being steeped in the Hebrew Scriptures. In this passage Paul does not imply that any such ceremony would be necessary for Onesimus, since Paul knew all too well that in Greek or Roman law the slave was automatically a slave forever, unless the master manumitted him or her. Even if slaves saved enough money to purchase their freedom (which was not at all impossible in those cultures), their master was not obligated to allow them to do so.

16 *as a man and as a brother in the Lord.* The Greek reads literally, "more than a slave, a beloved brother . . . both in the flesh and in the Lord." The relationship of slave was a relationship of this age, or "in the flesh," while the relationship of beloved brother was an eternal relationship, or "in the Lord."

17 *partner.* "Partner" is found in the commercial sense in Luke 5:10, but in 2 Cor 8:23 Paul used it for Titus and pairs it with "co-worker," which he has already used for Philemon. Thus, he was thinking of Philemon as a partner in the gospel enterprise, as a person like Titus or Timothy.

18 *owes.* The verb Paul used (*opheilei* [TG3784, ZG4053]) implies debt, not necessarily that a theft was involved.

19 *I, PAUL, WRITE THIS WITH MY OWN HAND.* This expression, which in the original would be accompanied by a visible change in the handwriting, indicates that at this point Paul took the stylus from the scribe and penned the end of the letter himself. See 2 Cor 10:1; Gal 5:2; 1 Thess 2:18 for his use of "I, Paul," and see 2 Thess 3:17 for a parallel example of Paul taking the stylus. Galatians 6:11 provides another reference to his personally writing the end of a letter.

20 *do me this favor.* Literally, "let me have [this] benefit from you." The verb in Greek is *onaimēn* [TG3685, ZG3949]. This is a wordplay on Onesimus's name.

Give me this encouragement. Here is the third time that Paul refers to the emotions, that is, "heart" (in many English translations) or "guts" (the more literal gloss). It is the second time that he refers to "refreshing the heart" or "encouraging"; v. 7 uses the same vocabulary, translated "refreshed the hearts," (cf. NRSV, "refresh my heart"). Thus, Paul was asking Philemon to do to him exactly what he praised Philemon for in verse 7; the idea of "refreshing the heart" brackets the body of the letter (vv. 7, 20).

21 *you will do what I ask.* This phrase represents a Greek word (*hupakoē* [TG5218, ZG5633], "obedience") that was mostly used in Christian circles. It indicates Christians being open to others. Conversion comes by one's obedience to Christ (Rom 15:18; 16:26; 2 Cor 10:5, 6), and the Romans' obedience was well known (Rom 16:19). The Corinthians were obedient to Titus (2 Cor 7:15). Obedience is a Christian virtue that marks even Christ himself (Heb 5:8).

22 *prepare a guest room for me.* In a world where inns were places for Christians to avoid, since they were of ill repute, hospitality was an important service that Christians rendered to one another.

God will answer your prayers. As Dunn (1996:346) points out, the main verb (*charisthēsomai* [TG5483/A, ZG5919]) does not mean that Paul expected a normal release from prison, but that God would grant it as an act of his "gracious giving." Humanly speaking, Paul would not expect release, but he knew that they were praying for him, so he hoped God would intervene with his gracious favor and grant him release so he could visit them.

COMMENTARY

Paul's appeal comes in three parts, carefully crafted rhetorically and divided according to Greek custom. In the first two verses (vv. 8-9), he created the proper atmosphere. In the second part (vv. 10-16), Paul argues that his request is in Philemon's best interest. In the third section (vv. 17-22), he restates the request on a personal basis.

Paul here, as always, preferred persuasion and appeal to command, for these treat others as mature individuals in Christ rather than children. He did indeed have the authority to tell Philemon to do the "right thing" (v. 8)—a thing that was in stark contrast with what Philemon's fellow citizens would think was right. But instead Paul appealed to him on the basis of love and Philemon's respect for him as an old man (see note on v. 9) and a prisoner (which might call forth respect for him as one suffering for Christ or might call forth sympathy). Similarly, 1 Peter 5:1-4 appeals to elders to lead by example, not by command. A command may seem to get things done more efficiently, but it builds resentment and keeps people immature. Furthermore, it implies a theology of hierarchy in the body of Christ, rather than seeing Christ as the only leader (so also Matt 23:8-12). Paul took the higher road by treating Philemon as a mature equal in Christ. Indeed, one sure mark of insecurity in a church is when the leadership turns to command rather than leading by example.

The content of Paul's appeal focuses on Onesimus. We are never told what it is that Onesimus had done, whether he had wronged Philemon in some way and had then fled to Paul to get Paul to intercede for him, or whether he had simply fled slavery and somehow had bumped into Paul. Whatever the case, Onesimus had come into contact with Paul, who was already in prison, and thereby had come to faith in Christ (v. 10). This conversion puts Onesimus on the same level as Philemon: Both were converted through Paul, and so they were brothers in a dual sense (i.e., both in Christ and in having the same person lead them to faith in Christ), with Paul being their mutual father and patron.

Whatever Onesimus had done in the past, Paul admits that he had not been useful to Philemon. But that was the past; that was before Onesimus had submitted his life to Christ. As a Christian, Onesimus had become useful to both Paul and Philemon (v. 11). Paul took very seriously the transformation that takes place when a person truly comes under the leadership of Jesus, confessing him to be their Lord (clearly seen in Col 3, a text written to the same church about the same time). The chief expression of this transformation from useless to useful was Onesimus's care for Paul. A prisoner in the ancient world was dependent upon visitors for many of the necessities of life, often starting with food. Onesimus had taken care of these needs for Paul, perhaps by bringing food, clothing, means of heating, and perhaps books into the prison from the Christian community in the surrounding area, as well as carrying out messages from Paul—and likely Paul's bodily waste as well. But this care, Paul suggested, was to Philemon's credit, for as Paul was Philemon's father-in-Christ, teacher, and patron, Philemon should have cared for Paul. Instead, unknown to Philemon, his slave was doing all that would have been appropriate for him to do, which was nonetheless a benefit for Philemon. Of course, given Onesimus's faithful service to Paul, there was every reason to expect that he would also provide faithful and useful service to Philemon upon his return. Christian character is not something that can be put on and taken off, but something that becomes a part of the individual and is expressed in every situation once Christ has transformed the person who has submitted to his rule.

In sending Onesimus back, Paul had to struggle with two principles (v. 13). The first was his own need and his knowledge that Philemon would surely want to meet it if he could. The second was the need for reconciliation between Onesimus and

Philemon. Both needs were respected in Paul's response. Onesimus had to return to Philemon, for only then could Philemon willingly release him to Paul. Onesimus was present with Paul without Philemon's consent. Onesimus had apparently separated from Philemon without permission (although some scholars, e.g., Winter 1987:3, argue the less likely hypothesis that Onesimus had been sent and Paul was asking Philemon to make the temporary situation permanent). There was a need for him to be received back, for some form of reconciliation to take place, if Philemon's benefit to Paul were to be freely given (v. 14). Paul ignored the legal implications of his having someone else's slave without their permission, for that was not what was motivating him. What was motivating him was the need for Christian brothers to be reconciled.

The critical issue for Paul was that Onesimus had a changed status. He was a brother in Christ as well as a slave (v. 16), and the "beloved brother" side of the relationship was the enduring aspect. In one sense, Philemon would have him back "forever" because as brothers in the same family they would eternally have that relationship (v. 15; Lightfoot 1896:340; Lohse 1971:202; O'Brien 1982:296). In another sense, Philemon, at best, would only have him back for life since he had come back as a permanent slave, if Paul intended the reference to the Pentateuch to be actual and not just a linguistic echo (Moule 1968:146; Sasse 1963:1.209; but see note on v. 15). The ambiguity here may well be deliberate, for Paul appears to wish only to suggest ideas rather than state them explicitly. Thus the "forever" language fits better with Onesimus being a brother while the more commercial "receiving him back" language fits better with his continuing slavery. This apparently deliberate ambiguity allows Philemon to take the meaning that he can accept, although at the least, he must realize that Onesimus is now a brother as well as a slave (Dunn 1996:334).

So how was Philemon to deal with Onesimus's new dual status? Surely Paul at least intended that Philemon would not punish Onesimus (since to do so would clearly be to wound Paul). But was he asking more than this? Was he simply stating that Onesimus be received back as a useful slave, one more valued because he was also a Christian brother, or was he suggesting that the tension between the eternal relationship and the temporal one be resolved by manumission? The answer is that we do not know. I would like to think that Paul was suggesting manumission and there are some hints in church tradition that might give substance to this desire (namely that an Onesimus became bishop of Ephesus). But my hope is probably born of my modern Western sensibilities—as far as we can tell, Paul leaves the question ambiguously open. Perhaps Philemon would pick up subtleties in the language that we cannot. Perhaps Paul did not know how far he could push Philemon. Certainly the issue of slavery did not mean much to Paul. Would he have been delighted had Philemon sent Onesimus back to him with orders to serve Paul, or would he have wanted Philemon to send him back as a free man? Paul may not have cared about the difference. The difference that he cared about was how Philemon treated Onesimus, not whether Onesimus was called a slave or a free man. He was to be treated as family, not estranged family, but beloved family. This treatment is not something that starts when we pass through the pearly gates but something that affects our relationships with believers now. We are brothers and sisters, children of the same Father, with the same older brother, Jesus. We recognize this fact by behaving accordingly.

In verse 17 Paul moves into a personal appeal, which contains two aspects. The first aspect we notice is the personal language Paul used, calling Philemon "partner" and "brother." The second aspect pertains to the commercial issues that this section discusses. Philemon had suffered economic loss through the loss of Onesimus. Thus, Paul thought it appropriate to bring up the issue and deal with it.

Philemon had been and was still Paul's partner (v. 17), a relationship Titus and Timothy also enjoyed. Paul, of course, was the senior member of the partnership. Leaning on the strength of this relationship, Paul urged Philemon to "welcome [Onesimus] as you would welcome me," which is surely more than even a good, obedient slave would receive when coming home.

But what about Philemon's loss? Paul has avoided this topic until the end of the letter, but then he delicately brought it up with an "if," which is a polite way of admitting that this was the case (v. 18). We do not know the nature of Onesimus's debt to Philemon. Had he damaged or misappropriated Philemon's property and because of that had run to Paul to intercede for him? Or was Paul referring to the fact that his leaving had robbed Philemon of Onesimus's services? Whatever the economic loss, Paul assumed that he and Philemon (and Onesimus) agreed on its nature. Paul could have used an appeal similar to the one he used in 1 Corinthians 6:7: "Why not just accept the injustice and leave it at that? Why not let yourselves be cheated?" After all, it was only money, and no one (according to the NT) should let that disturb relationships and so control the church. But this time, using very commercial language, Paul agreed to take the wrong upon himself: "Charge it to me." How like Jesus, who paid the charges for our wrongdoing against his Father and himself! The offer was surely grounded in Paul's Christology.

Paul then took the pen, which he usually did at the end of a dictated letter, but here he did it before the closing and did so to write an IOU with his own hand: "I, PAUL, WRITE THIS WITH MY OWN HAND: I WILL REPAY IT" (v. 19). Since we do not know whether Philemon could read and since we realize that the letter was read to the church, by writing this Paul allowed everyone to understand the change in handwriting that the reader could clearly see. Having written the IOU, the commercial language was almost done, but Paul added one last comment, which seems almost an afterthought yet was surely intended to settle the issue: "I WON'T MENTION THAT YOU OWE ME YOUR VERY SOUL." While Paul did not refer to Philemon as his "son," as he did with Onesimus, Timothy, and others whom he personally led to the Lord, it is clear that Philemon came to Christ directly or indirectly through Paul. Paul had agreed to pay Onesimus's debt and surely meant this, but if Philemon reflected a little he would realize that he was himself far more in Paul's debt than Paul could be in his. Paul did not linger on the point, for it was too delicate. It just hangs there at the end of the commercial transaction.

Paul quickly left the financial language and returned to personal language (v. 20). Using a play on Onesimus's name, Paul asked a favor on the basis of their common standing "in the Lord" ("for the Lord's sake," NLT). Paul was not asking Philemon to do what would feel natural to him, nor was he asking him to do what his culture would demand that he do; he was asking Philemon to set himself apart as a Christian by acting "in the Lord" and refreshing or giving encouragement to Paul "in Christ." Christian behavior takes an entirely different reference point than our natural inclinations.

Paul moved on from the request to express his personal trust in Philemon, a trust that developed during their time of serving together (v. 21). He was confident that Philemon would listen to or respond positively to his request. This does not mean that responding positively to Paul's request would be easy for Philemon. Paul's careful expression of his request shows that he knew that he was putting a lot of weight on the bridge of their relationship. But in the end he believed that Philemon had been transformed by Christ and so would come through with not only what Paul requested—warmly welcoming Onesimus and not holding his debt against him—but more. As a further encouragement not to let his trust down, Paul mentioned that he hoped to come to them (v. 22).

At this point, he shifted to the plural "you," for here the whole church was in view. While Paul did not express any certainty about his release, the language sounds like he was not too far away and he hoped God would act relatively soon. Perhaps he knew that some judicial decision would be made in the near future and hoped that God would graciously and unexpectedly turn it in his favor. Whatever the case, the announcement of a visit was both good news and bad news for Philemon. Of course, it would be delightful to see his Christian leader and mentor. Yet if Paul came and discovered that Philemon had punished Onesimus or was holding him at arm's length, Paul would discover that his leadership had meant little and his mentoring had not taken root. Christian character is not a matter of what we agree to or what we do when everyone else is doing it but what we do when we have to make difficult, even painful, decisions. Paul had placed before Philemon one such decision, and if Paul came, he would discover the answer in the presence of the whole church.

◆ III. Paul's Final Greetings (vv. 23–25)

23Epaphras, my fellow prisoner in Christ Jesus, sends you his greetings. 24So do Mark, Aristarchus, Demas, and Luke, my co-workers.

25May the grace of the Lord Jesus Christ be with your spirit.

NOTES

23 *Epaphras.* He is also mentioned in Col 1:7; 4:12. He was from Colosse and had apparently been a leader there.

24 *Mark, Aristarchus, Demas, and Luke.* These also sent greetings in Col 4:10, 14. Mark and Aristarchus were Jews, while the other two were Gentiles.

COMMENTARY

It was proper to end a letter with greetings from people who knew the recipients and then to add a prayer to a god or gods for well-being. Paul, as usual, followed the Greek letter form but added his own twists.

Pride of place is given to Epaphras, a Christian leader whom the Colossians had sent to assist Paul (Col 1:7). Now we discover that at some time he had been effective enough to have ended up in prison with Paul (v. 23). When Colossians was written, it was Aristarchus, not Epaphras, who was in prison. Paul apparently had to face a fluid situation among his co-workers. Sometimes they were with him, able to help him. Sometimes they ended up in prison with him. Sometimes they were off on journeys, going where he wanted to go. Yet they were always his companions and co-workers. He did not work alone. What is more, he elevated "prisoner" to a title of praise when it became "fellow prisoner."

Mark, whom Paul at one time had not wanted to take with him (see Acts 15:37-39), had clearly been reconciled to Paul (v. 24). He was presently with Paul wherever Paul was in prison. According to Colossians, he was also with Paul but was about to set off on a journey that might bring him to Colosse (see Col 4:10). Demas and Luke are the two that we know least about. The last word we hear about Demas was that he had deserted Paul, while the last word about Luke is "only Luke is with me" (see 2 Tim 4:10-11). It is important not only to start the Christian life well but also to end it well. All of the faithful service that Demas rendered (he is called a co-worker here) is forgotten in the face of his failure to end well, while Mark's failure in Acts 13:13 is forgotten because he proved faithful in the end.

When we come to the place in a Greek letter for the normal prayer to the gods, Paul, of course, blessed Philemon and his companions by the one God (v. 25; he shifted back to the plural "you" for this final verse). Jesus showed grace to us, and Paul prayed that Philemon would experience the grace of Jesus with his spirit.

Does this not sum up all the hopes of Paul for Philemon? Philemon was being asked to go against societal expectation by showing grace to Onesimus. He could and would do this if, in fact, his spirit was filled with the grace of "the Lord Jesus Christ." That is the power that would enable him to overcome his cultural conditioning, and it is the model that he should follow. Both reason and tradition indicate that Philemon did indeed follow this model of grace, for it is logical to suppose that had he rejected Paul's appeal he would not have preserved this letter for others to read.

Furthermore, tradition tells us that a certain Onesimus, likely this very Onesimus, was the bishop of Ephesus toward the end of the century (Ignatius, *To the Ephesians* 1.1; Eusebius, *Ecclesiastical History* 4.26). Does this mean that Philemon had freed Onesimus and sent him back to Paul, or that Onesimus had served Philemon until Philemon died and had then been freed, migrating back to the city where he had found faith? We can never know the answers to these questions—but we can apply to ourselves Christ's model of grace that Paul both commended to Philemon and practiced himself.

BIBLIOGRAPHY

Banks, Robert J.
1988 *Paul's Idea of Community: The Early House Churches in Their Historical Setting.* Grand Rapids: Eerdmans.

Bartchy, S. Scott
1997 Slavery: New Testament. Pp. 6.65-73 in *Anchor Bible Dictionary.*

Barth, Markus, and Helmut Blanke
2000 *The Letter to Philemon.* Eerdmans Critical Commentary. Grand Rapids: Eerdmans.

Bruce, F. F.
1984 *The Epistles to the Colossians, to Philemon, and to the Ephesians.* New International Commentary on the New Testament. Grand Rapids: Eerdmans.

Deissmann, A.
1927 *Light from the Ancient East: The New Testament Illustrated by Recently Discovered Texts of the Graeco-Roman World.* 2nd ed. Translator, Lionel R. M. Strachan. London: Hodder & Stoughton.

Dunn, J. D. G.
1996 *The Epistles to the Colossians and to Philemon.* Grand Rapids: Eerdmans.

Friedrich, Gerhard
2000 *Der Brief an Philemon.* Göttingen: Vandenhoeck & Ruprecht.

Harrill, J. A.
2000 Slavery. Pp. 1124-1127 in *Dictionary of New Testament Background.* Editors, Craig Evans, Stanley Porter. Downers Grove: InterVarsity.

Knox, John
1959 *Philemon among the Letters of Paul.* Nashville: Abingdon.

Lightfoot, J. B.
1896 *The Epistles of St. Paul: Colossians and Philemon.* New York: Macmillan.

Llewelyn, Stephen
2005 Paul's Letter to Philemon in the Light of the Documentary Papyri. *Biblische Zeitschrift* 49(2):262-263.

Lohmeyer, Ernst
1956 *Die Briefe an die Philipper, an die Kolosser und an Philemon.* MeyerKomm. Göttingen: Vandenhoeck & Ruprecht.

Lohse, Eduard
1968 *Die Briefe an die Kolosser und an Philemon.* MeyerKomm; Göttingen: Vandenhoeck & Ruprecht.

1971 *Colossians and Philemon: a commentary on the Epistles to the Colossians and to Philemon.* Hermeneia. Philadelphia: Fortress Press.

Moule, C. F. D.
1968 *The Epistles to the Colossians and to Philemon.* Cambridge: Cambridge University Press.

O'Brien, Peter T.
1982 *Colossians, Philemon.* Word Biblical Commentaries. Dallas: Word.

Patzia, Arthur G.
1990 *Ephesians, Colossians, Philemon.* Peabody, MA: Hendrickson.

1993 Philemon, Letter to. Pp. 702-706 in *Dictionary of Paul and His Letters.* Editors, Gerald Hawthorne, Ralph P. Martin, and Daniel Reid. Downers Grove: InterVarsity.

Reicke, Bo
2001 *Re-examining Paul's Letters: The History of the Pauline Correspondence.* Harrisburg, PA: Trinity Press International.

Sasse, Hermann
1963 Aionios. Pp. 1.208-209 in *Theological Dictionary of the New Testament.*

Smith, Dennis E.
2003 *From Symposium to Eucharist: the Banquet in the Early Christian World.* Minneapolis: Fortress.

Stowers, Stanley K.
1986 *Letter Writing in Greco-Roman Antiquity.* Philadelphia: Westminster.

Stuhlmacher, Peter
1975 *Der Brief an Philemon.* Evangelisch-Katholischer Kommentar. Neukirchen: Neukirchener Verlag.

Wall, Robert W.
1993 *Colossians and Philemon.* Downers Grove: InterVarsity.

White, John L.
1999 *The Apostle of God.* Peabody, MA: Hendrickson.

Winter, Sara C.
1987 Paul's Letter to Philemon. *New Testament Studies* 33(1):1-15.